W9-BWE-154

QUALITIES
OF COMMUNITY
LIFE

Roger G. Barker
Phil Schoggen

Louise Shedd Barker, Fred R. S. Binding,
Paul Gump, and Maxine Schoggen
Principal Field Workers

Dan D. M. Ragle
Principal Data Analyst

Margaret Brown, Dorothy Dempster, Natalie Gump,
Steven Heeren, Celia Barker Lottridge, Maxine Mize,
Margaret Ashton Reti, Leida Schoggen Slater, Marsha Cole Tosh,
Olive Turner, Edwin Willems, and Gwendolyn Willems
Assistants in Field Work and Data Analysis

Isla Herbert, Marjorie Reed, Kathlyn Dempster Scott,
and Dorothy Streator
Technical and Editorial Assistants

RECEIVED

JUL 2 0 1976

MANKATO STATE UNIVERSITY
MEMORIAL LIBRARY
MANKATO, MINN.

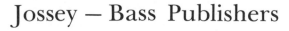

Jossey — Bass Publishers

San Francisco . Washington . London . 1973

HT
153
.B34

QUALITIES OF COMMUNITY LIFE
Methods of Measuring Environment and Behavior Applied to an American and an English Town
by Roger G. Barker and Phil Schoggen

Copyright © 1973 by: Jossey-Bass, Inc., Publishers
615 Montgomery Street
San Francisco, California   94111

and

Jossey-Bass Limited
3 Henrietta Street
London WC2E 8LU

Copyright under International, Pan American, and
Universal Copyright Conventions. All rights
reserved. No part of this book may be reproduced
in any form—except for brief quotation (not to
exceed 1,000 words) in a review or professional
work—without permission in writing from the publisher.

Library of Congress Catalogue Card Number LC 72-13601

International Standard Book Number ISBN 0-87589-172-1

Manufactured in the United States of America

JACKET DESIGN BY WILLI BAUM

FIRST EDITION

Code 7315

The Jossey-Bass
Behavioral Science Series

General Editors

WILLIAM E. HENRY, *University of Chicago*

NEVITT SANFORD, *Wright Institute*

388550

Preface

T he research reported
here describes differences and changes over a decade in the living conditions an American town and an English town provide their inhabitants, and it describes some of the behavior consequences of the differences. The study was initiated as an investigation of the links between
the habitat and the behavior and development of the children of the
towns. However, the conceptual and methodological problems of describing and measuring the human habitat became so dominant that the
focus of the study shifted to these issues. The completed study is
therefore both a presentation of concepts and methods for assessing
quality of life in terms of the environments which communities provide
their inhabitants and the behavior these environments engender, and
an elucidation of American and English cultural differences in these
respects in the 1950s and 1960s.

 Qualities of Community Life is the latest product of many years of
effort to develop an ecological psychology of human action. Concepts
and methods of special importance for intercultural comparisons and
studies of change are thoroughly set forth in this report; they are
grounded upon research first presented in *Midwest and Its Children*
(Barker and Wright, 1955) and further developed in *Ecological Psychology* (Barker, 1968). Our early research uncovered one quality of life that
derives from population pressure on habitat—namely, the involvement
of the inhabitants in the maintenance and operation of the town—and
care has been taken to secure data bearing on this quality. Otherwise the
study is widely exploratory.

Differences and similarities in American and English society and culture and in the personality and character of Americans and Englishmen have fascinated observers from the earliest days. Published statements are innumerable, and systematic studies are numerous. This investigation follows along an old, honorable, and well-worked vein of interest, and it is appropriate to begin the report with observations by Frances Trollope and Nathaniel Hawthorne. It may well be asked: What more can be added? A frequency distribution of previous studies would have two nodes: studies of the nature of the societies and studies of the characteristics of the peoples. *Qualities of Community Life: Measurements of Environment and Behavior in an American and an English Town* involves both. It relates differences in social and cultural habitat and differences in behavior. Furthermore, it attempts to move beyond impressions and verbal description to quantitative measures of habitat and behavior differences.

We have probed many facets of the two towns with the hope of discovering conditions significant for an understanding of culture differences and for the solution of practical and theoretical problems. Therefore the data reported in the tables pertain to many topics. For the guidance of those with special interests, we identify in the index the locations of many classes of data, and we provide guides for persons with a variety of concerns in the section below on how to read this book.

In order to keep the study within practical limits, only the public (nonfamily) habitats of the towns are investigated. Private, family settings that occur within homes (and home surrogates, such as hotel rooms) inhabited only by family members and their guests are not included. This is, then, a study of the public habitats of the towns. The major research was done simultaneously in Midwest and Yoredale on two year-long occasions: September through August 1954–55 and September through August 1963–64; changes are charted over the ten-year period.

The descriptions and measures of habitat and behavior and their interrelations are reported in terms of particular concepts and operations, with a minimum of wider interpretation. The most detailed descriptions of the towns as human habitats are in Appendices A and B, which include catalogs of all behavior settings occurring in the 1963–64 survey.

Midwest is the name we use in the report for Oskaloosa, Jefferson County, Kansas; it is identified in the text in some cases by the symbol *MW*, and the residents of the town are called *Midwesterners*. *Yoredale* of the report is Leyburn, North Yorkshire, England; it is identified by the symbol *YD*, and its residents are called *Dalesmen*.

How to Read this Book

The student who wishes a systematic and thorough understanding of the research will wish to peruse the parts and chapters of

Qualities of Community Life in the order in which they are given, proceeding from the problems and methods of the study (Part One) to the data on the habitat characteristics of the towns (Part Two), then to the data on their behavior outputs (Part Three), and finally to the general and selective perspectives of the towns (Part Four). However, for those with limited concerns and as a preliminary survey for the systematic student, another order may be preferred after Chapters 1 and 2, which are essential for all readers.

Those concerned with the total towns as undifferentiated units will wish to turn to Chapters 3 and 4 for the overall habitat measures, to Chapter 7 for the theory of habitat-behavior interrelations, to Chapter 8 for the total output measures, and to Chapters 13 and 14 for a general overview of the findings.

Readers interested in special features of the towns—such as their aesthetic, gross motor, high local autonomy, or church-connected qualities, for example—will find the habitat measures in Chapters 5 and 6 and the output measures in Chapters 9 and 10.

Data on the behavior of inhabitants of different ages, sexes, and social classes are reported in Chapters 11 and 12.

For those wanting a rapid review, the index items under "Salient Findings" and "Summary" provide the necessary guides; and, for readers with special interests, the items referring to particular qualities and particular inhabitant subgroups cite the locations of the requisite definitions, procedures, and habitat and output measures. In general we have provided few cross-references within the text, relying instead upon the index to guide readers to relevant textual locations.

Acknowledgments

Our obligations to the citizens of Midwest and Yoredale are inestimable. All community studies depend for their success upon acceptance by the citizens, but few studies have asked so much of so many for so long a time. It is sometimes said that detailed, continuing community research of the kind reported here is not feasible because it makes too great demands upon the townspeople. We are pleased to offer this study as evidence that this contention is not always true. Midwesterners and Dalesmen did not find the research too burdensome; they were more than merely accepting, they were understanding and helpful. And we are sincerely appreciative.

The study was initiated in 1954 with the support of a grant from the Carnegie Corporation of New York. Over the years other grants have been received from the U.S. Public Health Service (MH-1513, MH-11211) and the University of Kansas and its Endowment Association (Child Psychology Fund); the final field work in 1963–64 was undertaken with the help of a grant from the National Science Foundation (GS-116). Data processing at the University of Kansas Computation Center has been done as a part of the Center's service to research.

Work on this research was greatly facilitated by a Public Health Service Research Career Award (K6-16682) to Roger Barker and by support from the Center for Advanced Study in the Behavioral Sciences (Stanford) during his tenure there as a fellow in 1957–58.

Preparation of this report was supported in part by Biomedical Sciences Support Grant FR-5 S05 RR07087-05 from the General Research Support Branch, Division of Research Resources, Bureau of Health Professions, Education and Manpower Training, National Institutes of Health. This grant was awarded to George Peabody College, Nashville, Tennessee, and was administered by the College's John F. Kennedy Center for Research on Education and Human Development. Peabody College also provided sabbatical leave to Phil Schoggen in 1971–72 to speed completion of this report.

Oskaloosa, Kansas   ROGER G. BARKER
January 1973   PHIL SCHOGGEN

Contents

xi

QUALITIES OF COMMUNITY LIFE

Methods of Measuring Environment and Behavior Applied to an American and an English Town

PART I

This research describes Midwest and Yoredale in terms of behavior settings. *These are community units that frequently enter the ordinary communications of laymen; the statement "The Red Cross held a successful coffee morning in the Methodist Hall, Yoredale, on Friday last week" identifies such a unit. (Coffee mornings are common phenomena in Yoredale, and their near relative, food sales, are common in Midwest.) Nevertheless, our approach differs sharply from that of the laymen of the towns in two ways. First, our descriptions and measurements of the towns are solely in terms of behavior settings, whereas laymen, and some systematic disciplines too, make use of many descriptive units—for example, buildings and institutions (which usually circumscribe a number of behavior settings) and persons and equipment (which are always circumscribed by behavior settings). Thus this research, in contrast to other approaches, is concerned with the towns in terms of phenomena of a particular, limited order of magnitude. Second, our approach differs from others by describing and measuring the phenomena with which we are concerned in terms of concepts and operations that do not occur in everyday experiences or in the intellectual armories of other disciplines. The special nature of behavior settings has required special concepts and procedures. For these reasons, we thoroughly explain in Part One the phenomena with which we deal and the concepts and operations we apply to them.*

Some of the concepts and methods we use have been described elsewhere

PHENOMENA
AND METHODS

ᛜᛜᛜᛜᛜᛜᛜᛜᛜᛜᛜᛜᛜᛜᛜᛜᛜᛜᛜᛜᛜᛜᛜᛜ

(Barker, 1968) and are presented briefly here; others have issued from this research and are described in detail in Chapter 2. The latter (with their technical identification in parentheses) concern measurement of habitat extent (urbs *and* centiurbs), *changes in habitat variety* (genotype sites of substantial change), *similarities in the habitats of different cultures* (common *and* distinctive genotypes), *positions of responsibility* (habitat-claims for human components), *potential inhabitants* (penetration zone 0), *and habitat continuity* (accretion *and* erosion). *We follow Binding (1969) in the analyses of leadership* (leader acts *and* leaders).

CHAPTER 1

Prelude to Method

ᛝᛝᛝᛝᛝᛝᛝᛝᛝᛝᛝᛝᛝᛝᛝᛝᛝᛝᛝᛝᛝᛝᛝᛝᛝᛝᛝᛝ

Differences have often been reported in the circumstances of American and English children and in their behavior and development. Frances Trollope (1832, p. 70) described an incident in a Cincinnati academy as follows:

> He [a new French teacher] soon found that the "sage called Deci-pline" was not one of the assistants, and he remonstrated against the constant talking and running from one part of the room to another, but in vain; finding, however, that he could do nothing 'till this was discontinued, he wrote some rules, enforcing order, for the purpose of placing them at the door of the academy. When he showed them to his colleague [a German-American who conducted the school], he shook his head, and said, "Very goot, very goot in Europe, but America boys and gals vill not bear it; dey vill do just vat dey please; Suur, dey vould all go avay next day." "And you will not enforce these regulations *si nécessaires, Monsieur?*" "O lar! not for de vorld." "*Eh bien, Monsieur,* I must leave the young republicans to your management."

From this and other instances which she observed, Trollope concluded (p. 173) there was a "total want of discipline and subjection . . . among [American] children of all ages."

Nathaniel Hawthorne (1855, pp. 191–192 in 1887 edition) reported some observations of English children, and he proposed a theory to account for the differences he noted between them and American children.

> August 17th. – Yesterday afternoon J＿＿＿ and I went to Birkenhead Park. . . . It so happened that yesterday there was a large school

spending its holiday there, a school of girls of the lower classes, . . . who disported themselves on the green under the direction of the schoolmistresses and of an old gentleman. . . . In America there would be a good deal of grace and beauty among 150 children and budding girls, belonging to whatever rank of life; but here they had universally a most plebeian look—stubbed and sturdy figures; round, coarse faces; snubnoses—the most evident specimens of the brown bread of human nature. They looked wholesome and good enough, and fit to sustain their rough share of life; but it would have been impossible to make a lady out of any of them. Climate no doubt has most to do with diffusing a slender elegance over American young womanhood; but something, perhaps, is also due to the circumstance that classes are not kept apart there, as they are here; they cross-breed together, amid the continual ups and downs of our social life; and so, in the lowest stratum of life, you may see the refining influence of gentle blood. . . . To be sure I have seen no similar evidence, in England or elsewhere, that old gentility refines and elevates the race.

Many travelers have made and reported similar observations. Our research in America and England is a modern, systematic version of this old, observational method: We have collected, analyzed, and compared samples of American and English behavior and circumstances in these places themselves, as one might sample and compare the countries' native grasses and grass environments.

Although the methods we have used are old, our rationale is new and deeply based. Our aim from the beginning of the research has been to explore the relations between the environments and the behavior and psychological development of American and English children. This aim required a thorough reconsideration of a number of methodological issues, and this reconsideration led, in turn, to the rediscovery and reevaluation of old methods. A recapitulation of the main problems and their solution elucidates the research tasks as we finally formulated them and presents the research methods we finally adopted.

An experience we had at the very beginning of the English field work may clarify for the reader, as it did for us, one problem that we faced. Everyone familiar with America and England knows that national differences exist in methods of moving persons and materials within and between communities. English locomotion and transportation, in contrast to these processes in the United States, are characterized by more walking, more vigorous walking, heavier shoes, more carrying of things in baskets and fabric bags, greater use of walking sticks, more bicycling, less use of automobiles, smaller automobiles, slower auto speeds, shorter trips, narrower roads, more winding paths and roads, better bus service, cheaper bus fares, both finer and poorer vehicles. Many of these English conditions and ways of traveling were well-known to us before we arrived, and we had decided to unobtrusively but obdurately continue our American ways of behaving in this one respect, whereas in most others we were ready and eager to be as English as possible. But we underestimated the strength of the system we were entering and, in fact, were defeated almost before we could begin.

The first minutes after we landed went well. There was little traffic as we drove from the dock to the hotel. And what a pleasure it was to find plenty of parking space right in front of the hotel. But not so. "No night parking on the streets without parking lights!" the police constable told us, five minutes after lighting-up time. There was no parking lot at the hotel, and the garage was five blocks away. So within fifteen minutes of arriving, we were walking through the half-mist, half-snow, and vigorously, too—resolved to get some heavy shoes the first thing in the morning to ward off chilblains and also a walking stick to help cope with the cobbles. The English transportation system had won a small but complete victory.

The conditions that defeated us in the beginning, and which thereafter shaped all our travel to the English mold, were not periodic learning situations; they were omnipresent environmental conditions which coerced our locomotions in spite of our intentions and our active efforts to behave in an American way in this respect. Some sources of the power of the English system and some modes of its application could be seen directly: the physical arrangements (such as winding roads, which prevent fast driving), rules and enforcing authorities (lighting-up time, ubiquitous police constables), ongoing patterns of behavior (the inexorable line of traffic bearing down as one happily starts out on the right—that is, the wrong—side of the road). We did not come to a scientific, conceptualized understanding of the English transportation system. This was not our business. But we did experience it, and we struggled ineffectually against it.

After considerable trial and error exploration of the behavior and situations of English children, our experience with English locomotion and transportation came to mind and suggested that child behavior might be as ubiquitously controlled by environmental conditions as transportation behavior is. This possibility confronted us with a problem: how does one search for, explore, and scientifically describe the environment of a culture as it relates to the behavior and development of children? We were sure only that it was necessary to begin with concrete, denotable manifestations, with particular units of the relevant phenomena. But what units?

Children as Units

We first considered a sample of children in both countries, including different ages, social classes, sexes, schools, communities, economic levels, and parental vocations, but there were insuperable problems along this path. Some were technical problems. Because the sampling requirements of this approach apply to situations as well as to subjects, it would have been necessary to obtain data—that is, to observe and record behavior and its immediate circumstances—within the separate communities, schools, Sunday schools, Scout troops, friendship groups, and so forth, of each child in the sample. One therefore has to multiply the number of subjects by a factor of 10, 20, maybe 50, to obtain an estimate of the number of data sources. Even 50 subjects grow into a formidable number of sources: 500, 1000, 2000. This was, for us, an impossible task.

But a more fundamental difficulty for our purpose was the fact that the behavior and situations of a sample of children do not focus upon the phenomenon with which we were concerned, namely, the child behavior system that constitutes the environment of the children. The limitation of a sample of children is dramatically revealed by the fact that what children do *not* do (but which others in the culture do do) can be as revealing of the child behavior system as what children *do* do. It may be as significant for understanding the behavior of the children of an English town to know that they do not attend the plays of the Dramatic Society as to know that they do go to the cinema, and the former fact is missed if one studies only the behavior and interactions of the children. A game model may be clarifying. One would not simplify the game of cricket for a novice and make the position of bowler intelligible to him by having him watch this player exclusively—for example, through field glasses focused exclusively on him—thus isolating the bowler from the rest of the game. This would in fact greatly interfere with comprehending the overall structural and dynamic characteristics of intact cricket and the place of the bowler within the cricket "system." Similarly, if one uses children as units and records segments of their behavior and proximal situations, one isolates them from the rest of the community system and obscures the place of children within it.

Finally, concepts which are adequate for describing the behavior of individual children within cultures are not relevant to child behavior systems. A game analogy is appropriate here too. Explanations of individual behavior in terms of personality theory can hope to explain the behavior of a pitcher in a baseball game who blows up in a tight place, and the different behavior of one who calmly pitches his way out of a difficulty; but personality theory cannot explain why Joe Smith is inactive, even listless, most of the time when he plays center field in a game of baseball, and is a ceaseless dynamo of energy as quarterback in a football game. If some of the differences in the behavior of American and English children are due to the kinds of factors that are behind Joe Smith's behavior transformation between baseball and football, and if data concerning the total "game" of which children are a part are not included, these possibly important factors are eliminated by methodological fiat.

Perhaps prolonged exposure to the forces which bear upon a center fielder or a quarterback, an American child or a British child, bring about irreversible changes, so that the person no longer behaves "appropriately" when exposed to the forces of the different position or culture. In this case personality changes have occurred, and the concepts of personality theory apply. However, the first step in this permanent transformation is, in all known cases, a reversible accommodation of an individual's behavior to the demands of the system. Only the final, irreversible resultant, which we call a personality change, requires personality concepts. To use an example from physical systems, a broken (severed) beam has a permanent property (twoness) which is entirely different from the forces which cause it, and different too from its initial reversible accommodation to these forces—namely, resistance and change of shape. In this study, as it developed, we became interested primarily in the forces within the American and English child behavior systems and in the original accommodation of children's behavior to these forces, rather than in the irreversible personality resultants of the forces.

For these practical, methodological, and conceptual reasons we found individual children as they enter a usual sampling design to be inadequate units for the study, although individual children are adequate subjects for some purposes in cross-cultural studies. If the personality which a culture produces, rather than its precise cultural sources, is being studied, or if one is interested in the frequency of occurrence and the resultants of particular, circumscribed person-environment interactions, such as may be relevant to a particular theory, a sample of independent subjects is usually adequate.

Tesserae as Units

We considered sampling the general situations and behavior of children by means of grids with time and space axes. We could determine what happens and the place of children therein, on street corner G7 at 4:23–4:28 P.M. on July 16, 1955, and in schoolroom 9 at 9:29–9:34 A.M. on May 6, 1955. Would not a detailed schedule of this sort provide a sufficiently complete picture of the American and English child behavior systems?

Countries can be divided into arbitrary parts, and such scientific tesserae are common, well-tested ways of sampling not individuals, but aggregations of related phenomena. A beaker of pond water, a quadrat of the earth's surface, a ten-minute moving picture of a beehive, and a five-minute observation on a playground provide larger pieces of functioning systems than do individual amoebae, plants, bees, or children. They provide some of the larger contexts within which the individuals live. But unfortunately such tesserae are destructive of the encompassing systems. An individual has a basic integrity; a person is a self-limited unit. On one level, a person is an intact functioning part of the context in which he lives; he creates and is created by it; he is a subsystem of the system. His boundaries, shape, size, and internal arrangements provide some indication of his place within the system and hence of the nature of the system. One knows that the system provides a fitting place for a person. But the beaker, the quadrat, the ten-minute film, and the five-minute observation are true fragments with a randomly imposed relation to the intact system; they cannot inform an investigator of the system because he, not the system, establishes the boundaries of the tessera without reference to the system.

Here we obtained help from the older sciences. We noted that all of them are concerned with the experimenter-free structure, with the self-bounded particles of their material on all levels of inclusiveness. Many sciences have special, tender-minded, nondestructive techniques for revealing structure: X-ray analysis and electrical, magnetic, and resonance techniques. A primary concern of the physical and biological sciences is, precisely, with the unrearranged structures of atoms, genes, pollen grains, crystals, estuaries, the planet earth and beyond. The problem of determining the units of material, uninfluenced by the investigator, is fundamental for every science. This was precisely the problem we faced; we wished to describe the child behavior systems of the United States and England without alteration by our methods and without bias by our assumption of the primacy of entities on one level—for example, of the individual person. We wished, indeed, to do as other sciences have done: to look at the units of our material at different levels of inclusiveness and to study the interrelations of these levels. For this purpose, space-time tesserae were inadequate.

Towns as Units

Towns did not have the disadvantages for our purposes which attach to individual subjects or to tesserae. The children within a town do not confront an investigator with an ever-expanding number of data sources, because subjects' paths cross, and the same schools, Sunday schools, friendship groups, and Scout troops appear and reappear. The investigator can choose towns with the number of persons and environments appropriate to his problem and to his resources. With proper selection in this respect, he is able to see the children in their environment, with virtually all of each child's interpersonal and community connections intact and functioning—that is, with the total child behavior system of the town undisturbed, ready to be observed, analyzed, and understood. Furthermore, towns in contrast to tesserae are self-limited parts of the larger system. They have integrity within the system; they are intact functioning parts of it.

A disadvantage of towns as units is obvious too. What do one or a few towns in the United States and England represent? Do they represent anything but themselves? Are they the United States and England? How does one sample the towns of a country? We think that all intact, thriving American and English towns that are integrated into the larger society do display the American and English systems of rearing children; however, only data can prove whether this is true (Barker and Barker, 1963). But if the towns chosen do represent only themselves and have no larger significance for the United States and England, and if they differ with respect to the environments of their children, they still provide the opportunity to study the operation and effects of these differing environments. If, in addition, the towns exhibit important aspects of the whole American and British systems, the significance of the study is enhanced. We thus concluded that towns are adequate parts of the American and English systems and the largest units necessary for our purpose. We selected as our study material two whole towns: an American town, Midwest, Kansas, a county seat, and an English town, Yoredale, Yorkshire, a market town.

Behavior Settings as Units

But towns cannot be studied whole and undivided. So the issue with which we started was raised in a new framework: What parts of Midwest and Yoredale are significant and scientifically adequate for our study of the relations between their environments and the behavior of their children? When we turned our attention from the behavior of individual children to the goings-on around them, we found that their molar actions are environed by *behavior settings* in the way that cells are environed by organs, atoms by molecules, keystones by arches, and spark plugs by engines: in all cases, the environing entity stands between the environed entity and still larger circumjacent systemic units (organisms, molecular aggregates, buildings, automobiles). The intermediate entity (the behavior setting, in our case) sifts and alters the influences from the larger environment (the town and other inclusive units) and channels, dampers, and augments the actions of the smaller entity (the inhabitant). (In this connection see Barker, 1968, pp. 145–159.)

In our search for the community units that constitute the environment of molar actions, we looked beyond individual children and discovered *behavior settings*. This influenced the design of the re-

Table 1.1
Most Heavily Inhabited Behavior Settings;
Percentage of Public Time Spent in Them

Midwest		Yoredale	
Behavior Setting	%	Behavior Setting	%
Trafficways	7.8	Trafficways	20.1
Weylens Grocery	3.7	Moorside Nursing Home	1.9
Gwyns Cafe	3.0	Kings Arm Pub	1.7
Ellsons Drugstore	2.7	Market Day	1.7
Midwest State Bank	2.3	British Railways Freight Office & Delivery	1.7
Reids Grocery	2.2	Marat Milk Bar & Shop	1.5
Hookers Tavern & Pool Hall	1.9	County Primary School, Infants Acad. Class	1.5
Pearl Cafe	1.5	County Primary School, Upper Juniors Acad. Class	1.4
Wayside Restaurant	1.5	Harbough & Lawens Gen' Draper	1.3
High School & Upper Elem. School Hallways	1.4	Hay Garage	1.3

search—for, according to this theory, it is prerequisite to an understanding of the habitat and behavior of the children of Midwest and Yoredale to understand the behavior settings, the systemic units of the habitat, within which the children are incorporated. So the research became a two-step undertaking: to describe Midwest and Yoredale as habitats in terms of behavior settings and then to determine the place of children within the settings. However, the first step was so large an undertaking (requiring new methods, new analytical tools, and new concepts) that the second step, the place of children in Midwest and Yoredale, inevitably assumed a less central place in the research than we originally intended. This report is, therefore, a general description of Midwest and Yoredale as human habitats and of the behavior occurring in the two habitats, with only occasional special reference to children.

Behavior settings were first described in Barker and Wright (1955); they were presented in more detail, and with later methodological and theoretical developments, in Barker (1968), and are further elaborated here.

GENERAL CHARACTERISTICS

The quotations from Trollope and Hawthorne do not describe the behavior and circumstances of any particular child. Rather, characteristics of the behavior patterns of children in general in a particular school and in a particular park are briefly reported ("constant talking and running from one part of the room to another"; the girls "disported themselves on the green"), together with very meager overall aspects of the school situation (remonstration by the teacher) and the park situation (direction by the schoolmistresses). Nonetheless, the narratives refer to concrete phenomena which at the times they occurred could have been verified by other observers. The narratives describe extra-individual behavior-and-situation phenomena; in fact, they describe aspects of two behavior settings: French Class at the Cincinnati Academy and School Outing at Birkenhead Park.

The 10 behavior settings of Midwest and of Yoredale in which the inhabitants of the towns spent the greatest amount of time during the year from September 1, 1963, to August 31, 1964, are listed in Table 1.1. The hours spent in each setting are reported as percentages of the total number of hours town inhabitants spent in all public behavior settings. Each of the behavior settings listed exhibits the defining attributes of all behavior settings. Take, for example, the restaurants Gwyns Cafe, Pearl Cafe, Wayside Restaurant, and Marat Milk Bar and Shop; they have the following attributes which are common to all other settings:

They are not created by experimenters for scientific purposes; they are experimenter-free units; they are natural parts of a town.

Restaurants are objective in the sense that they exist independent of anyone's perception of them, as restaurants; they are pre-perceptual entities; they are ecological phenomena.

Restaurants have univocal space-time loci; Marat Milk Bar and Shop occurs at the northeast corner of Commercial Square in Yoredale between 9 A.M. and 6 P.M. daily except Sunday, and at no other time or place.

Restaurants have two sets of components: human components (cooks cooking, waitresses serving, customers paying) and nonhuman components (air conditioners cooling, chairs supporting diners, adding machines adding, thermostats regulating). Restaurants are ecobehavioral, people-milieu phenomena.

A boundary surrounds each restaurant.

The behavior and milieu of a restaurant are internally organized via a program of component events into a characteristic spatial-temporal pattern; a restaurant has a unique standing pattern of behavior and milieu.

The pattern of behavior occurring within a restaurant and the pattern of its nonbehavioral milieu have a synomorphic relation; they fit. The diners conform to the chairs as they sit and eat; the waitresses move around the tables as they serve.

The pattern of a restaurant, including the boundary, is self-generated.

The bounded entity which is a restaurant is circumjacent to its components; the customers and equipment are within the restaurant.

The unity of a restaurant does not derive from the similarity of its parts; its parts are in fact dissimilar: cooking occurs in one part of a restaurant, dining in another, paying in another. The unity of a restaurant is based, rather, upon the interdependence of its parts and upon their independence of outside phenomena. Events in different parts of a restaurant (the kitchen and the dining room) have a greater effect upon each other than do equivalent events beyond the boundary of the restaurant.

The degree of interdependence of the parts of a restaurant and their degree of separation from outside phenomena fall within limits which can be operationally determined with precision.

The people who inhabit a restaurant are to a considerable degree interchangeable and replaceable. Customers change; even the proprietor may be replaced and yet the restaurant continues as serenely as an old car with new rings and new tires.

The pattern of events within the restaurant cannot be greatly altered without destroying it: there must be cooking, there must be serving, there must be eating.

The inhabitants of a restaurant have two positions within it: they are essential, functioning parts of an extraindividual entity (without cooks or customers a restaurant ceases); and they are also individuals with unique experiences and behavior (one customer likes his meal, another does not).

Within a restaurant there is a hierarchy of positions with respect to influence upon the setting and responsibility for its functioning. A waitress has power over a greater extent of a restaurant and she is more essential to its operation than a single customer; the proprietor has greater power and responsibility than either a customer or a waitress.

Every restaurant requires a definite minimum number of inhabitants to remain viable. The Pearl Cafe in Midwest must have one cook, two waitresses, and an average of 75 customer meals a day to keep going.

Restaurants generate forces that impose the programed temporal-spatial pattern upon their component parts, impel the necessary people and materials into them, and repel and expel disrupting people and materials from them.

Undergirding a restaurant is a control system that maintains the restaurant intact and functioning when the properties of its components and the characteristics of its larger context vary widely. A restaurant has greater stability as a whole entity than its parts have separately; it has means of adjusting to the absence of its cook, to the breakdown of its lighting system, to deviant behavior by its customers, to a period with a few customers. The self-maintaining processes of behavior settings, which consist of mechanisms for countering the deviances of its components and of eliminating inadequate components, give them stability in spite of internal and external instability.

Restaurants, which we have here used as prototypes of all behavior settings, are, in summary, bounded, spatially-temporally anchored, and spatially-temporally extended phenomena with polymorphic but stable behavior-and-milieu patterns; behavior settings are extraindividual ecobehavioral entities. On the structure side, a behavior setting consists of a standing pattern of behavior and milieu, with the milieu circumjacent and synomorphic to the behavior; on the dynamic side, the behavior-milieu parts of a behavior setting have a specified degree of interdependence that is greater than their interdependence with similar parts of other behavior settings.

WIDE PERSPECTIVE

Behavior settings are by no means unique to Hawthorne, Trollope, and the present authors; we end this chapter with three examples which reveal the varied contexts in which they occur. However, in no other case that we have discovered are behavior settings so much the focus of concern as in the present report. We hope that these examples aid in establishing for the reader the reality of behavior settings as unitary phenomena.

Sensitive observers of the human scene sometimes describe in remarkably true and rich detail particular behavior-habitat entities we have identified as behavior settings. This excerpt from Priestley (1934, pp. 79–82) describes a whist drive, a behavior setting that occurs in Yoredale, though on a somewhat reduced scale.

The whist drive I attended was not a private social function, the equivalent of a bridge party, but a public affair, a combined entertainment and gamble. . . . You paid two shillings to compete, but there were money prizes amounting to 23 pounds. . . . The whist drive . . . was held in a certain public hall and began at 8:15. . . .

The hall was large, austere in coloring and decoration, and lighted in the most uncompromising fashion by unshaded bulbs of high voltage.

It had about as much intimate charm as the average big railway station. . . . Suspended from the ceiling, about a third of the way down the room, was a large indicator, showing the four suits. The remaining two-thirds of the hall, beyond this indicator, were filled with very small chairs ranged round very small tables. . . . When you paid your two shillings, you were given a scoring card, either black or red. (Mine was black.) On this card were the rules, the number of your first table, and then spaces for the numbers of your succeeding tables, the tricks you made, and your totals. There were several hundred people there, and most of them seemed to be regular patrons and to know one another. They were mostly middle-aged, decent working folk, with only a sprinkling of younger men and women. Nearly all the men smoked, and a fair proportion of the women; but there were no ashtrays. I knocked my pipe out on my heel. What the cigarette smokers did, I do not know. After about ten minutes, a man shouted at us through a megaphone and we all went to our tables. The indicator told us what were trumps by lighting up a gigantic ace of clubs. We started. There followed what seemed to me one of the most strenuous hours I have ever spent. To begin with, the games were played at a tremendous speed, aces being banged on kings without a moment's hesitation. Then there was so much to do. You had to fill in your card and to initial the card on each table. If you were the losing man arriving at a new table—and I nearly always was—you had to shuffle the cards before the cut for deal. And three times out of four it seemed to be my fate to deal. . . . So what with shuffling, cutting, dealing, playing, gathering tricks, . . . clerkly work with the table card and your own card, changing tables, pushing past enormous fat women, I was kept so busy that after about half an hour of it I was fairly perspiring. And there was never a minute to lose. The whistle blew, as a signal to change tables, the indicator lit up its new suit of trumps, and if you had not finished your game, there were people waiting and looking very cross about it. There was practically no time for conversation, hardly time to smile. . . . When the whistle blew after the twelfth game, everybody made a rush for the top end of the hall and reappeared a few minutes afterward, eating fruits, tarts, and slabs of cake.

This was the interval, and by this time I had had quite enough whist-driving, but it seemed to me that if one player disappeared the whole elaborate organization would be flung into disorder. So I stayed on and played another twelve games, nearly always losing and so going from table to table; . . . and I found myself in a far corner where the tables were almost touching one another, . . . and it was sweatier and hotter and smokier than ever. My total score was 155, which was some 30 or 40 below the best. But there was still a chance that I might win a prize for a "mystery number," which was drawn by the promoter, after he had given the prizes for the winning scores. There was no excitement at the end, no cheering, no applause. It was all as brisk and businesslike as the whole evening had been. When the last prize had been awarded, everybody cleared off, rather as if they were leaving a factory than making an end of a night's pleasure. I suppose they enjoyed it—which was more than I did—otherwise they would not regularly attend these functions, as they undoubtedly do, but anything superficially less like a night's pleasure I never did see. . . . The purely social side of the whist drive was neg-

ligible; or at least so it seemed to me, though of course I was a stranger
and may have missed some quiet fun. . . . These people . . . were surprisingly good-mannered and good-humored. I never saw one exhibition
of bad temper all the evening. Some were obviously much better players
than others and there was money at stake, but nevertheless there was
never an embarrassing moment. Even the witchlike, iron-spectacled little
women were never actually rude to anybody.

Political science characteristically deals with large units of human
behavior and situation. In the following excerpt (J. S. Barker, personal
communication, 1969), a political scientist finds behavior settings to be
the smallest of a series of large-scale units that interest him as having
"enduring importance in human affairs."

Human life is patterned in time and space. When we observe
behavior as historians, sociologists, psychologists, novelists, or untitled
laymen we see regularities coordinated with places and periods. When we
recall our experiences we often find that our thoughts and feelings are
organized in spatial-temporal terms. . . . It makes sense to look at
human affairs in terms of a series of spatial-temporal units of differing
scales which we shall refer to as "situations." . . .

To begin to grasp the ordering of situations in an included-
inclusive series, imagine a camera which records the physical activity of
men, where necessary penetrating objects, but also recording their presence in outline. The camera produces a film showing human behavior in
its milieu. It is employed to make a set of films each designed to record
activity on a different spatial-temporal scale. The first film records human
behavior over the whole of man's existence. A frame is exposed every
year, compressing 35,000 years into about six hours of viewing. The film
is like an animated scatter diagram; it shows the expansion and contraction of population centers and the accelerating rhythm of population
increase and migration. Large-scale environmental changes such as the
shrinking of the polar ice caps and the contraction of forests would be
apparent, but they would be difficult to interpret.

The second film is shot from somewhat closer to the earth and
records patterns of behavior and milieu of the scale of a major region of
the globe such as South Asia or North America. Appropriate regions
could be identified by patterns revealed in the first film. The time scale is
shortened; instead of exposing one frame a year for 35,000 years as in the
case of the first film, this film is made by exposing one frame a day for a
few hundred years. It is impossible to perceive the continuity of behavior
of individuals, but the changing outlines of even small settlements show
up and so do seasonal rhythms in behavior and the growth and decay of
transportation links.

The third film focuses upon one of the settlements which can be
identified on the second film, say a small city of around 100,000 inhabitants. A frame is exposed every minute, and the film spans a few years. It
is almost possible to follow individual actions, and the broad pattern of
behavior in parks, factories, streets, markets, theaters, sports arenas, and
the like can be followed. The different diurnal rhythms of schools and

night clubs, factories and residential neighborhoods are apparent. Changes in patterns of residence, hours of work, daily transportation, size of work groups, use of mechanical equipment, and size of buildings can be observed. In the third film it would be possible to identify ongoing or repetitive patterns of behavior such as the behavior represented by a factory, a school, a store, or a thoroughfare, which have considerable stability in time. Persons could be seen moving toward these places by quite direct routes, and a major break in patterns of movement could be seen at the edges of the place. On the inside, movement would be restricted to specific limited modes.

The fourth film takes one of these establishments as its subject and records behavior within it by exposing a frame every second. In this film it is possible to follow individual behavior in cases where gross physical movement is slow or small. Major differences in personal appearance such as size and style of dress begin to be discriminated. The film records many of the details of the relatively fixed objects and surroundings which comprise the milieu of behavior. In some cases discrete tasks can be identified, and the interrelationships of tasks can be inferred. Within the fourth film it is possible to distinguish smaller-scale behavioral patterns which cluster in time and space within the establishment filmed. A single classroom in the school or a particular production line in the factory would stand out.

The fifth film records behavior in a particular setting of this scale. The camera in this case differs but little from the human eye. It exposes the standard sixteen frames per second from a slightly greater distance than a participant in the setting in order to show the boundaries of the behavior pattern, but it records the movement and facial expressions of individuals, the details of objects, and the intricacies of interpersonal interactions. This film shows the world from the point of view of a standoffish observer. . . .

The device of the films gives some feeling for the different scales of situation in which human behavior is structured in time and space. The films correspond roughly to a series of situational units which have an enduring importance in human affairs. The first corresponds to world history. The second corresponds to countries or groups of countries. The third corresponds to local communities, the fourth to enterprises under one roof, and the fifth to ordinary social occasions or "behavior settings." . . .

Many behavior settings contain face-to-face interactions and it is tempting to see them as persons interacting; yet to grasp the idea of the behavior setting as a unit it is necessary to shift the focus of attention away from the persons involved to the pattern of behavior-cum-physical milieu to which their actions contribute. . . . The behavior setting is a flow of activity in which persons, objects, machines, furniture, walls, and floors interact through the media of verbal communication, perception, touch, and direct manipulation. The ongoing or repetitive behavior-milieu pattern is independent of the presence or absence of particular persons. In a sense the persons themselves are among the media for the behavior setting pattern. . . .

If you think of a community with which you are familiar you can locate almost all behavior in behavior settings. . . . Trafficways, church services, stores, parks, kitchens, city council meetings, bars, doctor's offices, polling booths are examples of kinds of behavior settings. Examples of behavior setting clusters are schools, factories, police headquarters, and rooming houses. Or consider your own movements during a day in your life or the movements of a Yugoslav peasant. In day-to-day experience we move from one behavior setting to another. The outward pattern of our behavior is highly constrained by the behavior settings we enter, and our subjective experience is much affected by them. Each small-scale situation "requires a more or less radical transformation of the persons who comprise it. Consider the metamorphoses that one man may go through in one day as he moves from one form of sociality to another—family man, speck of crowd dust, functionary in the organization, friend. These are not simply different roles; each is a whole past and present and future, offering different options and constraints, different degrees of change or inertia, different kinds of closeness and distance, different sets of rights and obligations, different pledges and promises" (Laing, 1967, p. 82).

Small-scale situations have a multifaceted, dense, and profound relationship with individuals which we can only begin to analyze. Small-scale situations form the immediate environments of individuals. All the external stimuli which reach the receptors of persons originate in or traverse small-scale situations more or less independently of the will or action of the person who receives them. This means that situations limit and create opportunities for experience for individuals (Laing, 1967, p. 28). In a slightly more limited perspective, situations structure patterns of personal causation in the environment; they have a causal structure which comes into play when action is attempted as a means to an end. They are the contexts of choice. The close relationship between the structure of situations and opportunity for experience and for consequential action means that the common identification of well-being with discrete satisfactions and particular objects is misleading. Well-being may be better defined in terms of access to particular kinds of situations conceived in their totality.

From another standpoint, small-scale situations are parts of larger situations. A city, for example, exists through the existence of the behavior-milieu units identified with homes, schools, offices, factories, and so forth. The character of the city is given in the kinds and numbers of small-scale situations, their level of functioning, and their interrelations.

Dictionary definitions of behavior settings treat them as unitary entities. The definitions are spare, including only the most essential attributes of settings; always explicitly stated or clearly implied are (*a*) a space-time locus, (*b*) a characteristic standing pattern of behavior and milieu, (*c*) human components, and (*d*) nonhuman components. Here are examples (from *Webster's Seventh New Collegiate Dictionary*), with analyses into the four attributes; implied attributes are in parentheses.

Bank: "An establishment for the custody, loan, exchange, or issue of money, for the extension of credit, and for facilitating the transmission of funds." (*a*) Space-time locus: an establishment (place of business with furnishings and staff); (*b*) standing pattern: custody, loan, exchange, issue of money; extension of credit; transmission of funds; (*c*) human components: (staff and clients); (*d*) nonhuman components: money, (furnishings).

Football game: "A game played with a football on a rectangular field having two goalposts at each end by two teams whose object is to get the ball over a goal line or between goal posts." (*a*) Space-time locus: a rectangular field; (*b*) standing pattern: game to get the ball over goal line or between goal posts; (*c*) human components: teams; (*d*) nonhuman components: football, goal posts.

Hotel: "A house that provides lodging and usually meals, entertainment, and various personal services for the public." (*a*) Space-time locus: a house; (*b*) standing pattern: providing lodging, meals, entertainment, personal services; (*c*) human components: the public (staff); (*d*) nonhuman components: (food, beds, and so forth).

Market: "A public place where people meet for the purpose of trade." (*a*) Space-time locus: a public place; (*b*) standing pattern: trade; (*c*) human components: people; (*d*) nonhuman components: (articles traded).

These illustrations from literature, another social science, and lexicography demonstrate that concern for environmental units at the level of behavior settings is found in a variety of contexts. We turn next to a detailed consideration of the concepts and methods used in the present investigation of the behavior settings of Midwest and Yoredale and the behavior of their inhabitants.

CHAPTER 2

Variables of Habitat and Behavior Output

The phenomena, concepts, and methods of this research are not common currency of the behavioral sciences, so we are unable to refer to general reference sources for their elucidation. Herewith, therefore, are explications of the ideas and operations we have used; further elaboration of many of them are presented in previous studies, especially in Barker (1968).

The Towns

We chose Midwest and Yoredale (see Figures 2.1 and 2.2) for the research in order to eliminate insofar as possible community differences with which we did not wish to be concerned; the towns were selected for their similarity in the following respects:

Both towns are naturally bounded regions differentiated from surrounding farming areas by greater population density, and by dissimilar prevailing patterns of behavior.

Both towns have open channels of communication with the larger culture via roads, telephones, radio, television, newspapers, and mail; neither town is isolated in a cultural backwater; both are vigorous, thriving communities.

The people of both Midwest and Yoredale are overwhelmingly from

FIGURE 2.1.   Aerial View of Yoredale.

family lines whose historical roots are in northern Europe. However, there are 26 Negroes in Midwest.

Both towns are nonindustrial, rural, retail trade and local government
centers. Midwest is a county seat; Yoredale is the seat of a rural
district council and of a judicial district.

The economic bases of both towns are dairying and the raising of
grain and livestock.

The towns are within similar population ranges: on January 1, 1964,
Midwest had a population of 830 people, including 159 children
under 12 years of age, and Yoredale had 1310 citizens, with 210
children under 12 years of age.

The geographical areas of the towns are within a similar size range:
Midwest covers approximately 400 acres and Yoredale approximately 260 acres.

The towns are similarly situated with respect to cities. Midwest is 20,
35, and 45 miles, respectively, from cities of 30,000, 100,000, and
800,000 population, and Yoredale is 17, 30, and 45 miles from
cities of 25,000, 100,000, and 700,000 population.

Each town is an inland town located almost equidistant from its
country's borders.

The local regions surrounding both towns are conservative politically;

FIGURE 2.2. Aerial View of Midwest.

though not the most depressed regions, both are economically backward in comparison with the national economies; and both are growing in population at a slower rate than the countries as wholes.

But the towns differ, too:

The ages of the towns are markedly different. Midwest's one historical building, the courthouse, was built in 1867; it was damaged by a tornado in 1960 and has now been replaced by a modern building. Yoredale's neighboring castles were built before 1400 and wrecked during the Civil War of 1647; their ruins still dominate the countryside. The people of the towns live within very different historical perspectives.

Weather and water pose different problems to the towns. Midwest's winter is colder than Yoredale's, and its summer is hotter. The similar annual rainfalls of the towns are distributed quite differently: Yoredale has almost three times as many rainy days as Midwest, and often has to cope with long periods of too much precipitation (at hay harvest, particularly); Midwest is sporadically troubled by brief floods followed by periods of drought.

Midwest and Yoredale differ dramatically in the geometry and the boundaries of their interior spaces. The inhabitants of Midwest, and their forebears, have imposed upon the town's rolling landscape a rigid, right-angled grid of land boundaries and trafficways, while the people of Yoredale have accommodated the shape of their living areas and the courses of their streets to the town's irregular hillside terrain. Within Midwest, fences are few and fragile, and there are no walls; gates are almost unknown. There is an openness to Midwest; the land rolls freely across unclear land boundaries. But within Yoredale, the irregular shapes are bounded by high, strong walls and iron fences; the boundaries are barriers, breached only by gates — 362 of them. Yoredale is a system of enclosures.

In the area around Midwest there are many isolated farms; the nearest town is six miles away. The area about Yoredale contains few isolated farms, but there are six villages, most having one or more small general stores, one or more pubs, an elementary school, a post office, and a church. The population of Midwest's surrounding area is smaller than Yoredale's (see Table 3.5 for details). The economic and social levels of the residents of Midwest's hinterland approximate those of the town's inhabitants, but in Yoredale's tributary area there are a number of country houses and estates occupied by members of the gentry and of the business elite, classes represented only slightly in Yoredale itself.

The persisting and fundamental difference with which we are primarily concerned is this: Midwest is a component and expression of the American human behavior system, and Yoredale is a component and expression of the English human behavior system. In this study we have explored differences in the American and English systems as represented in Midwest and Yoredale, including the embedded differences in the towns' ages, climates, geography, geometry, and hinterlands.

Identifying Behavior Settings

Behavior settings stand out with great clarity within Midwest and Yoredale. An analysis of all reports of behavior phenomena in a single issue of Midwest's newspaper reveals that half of the reports are in terms of behavior settings: "Ellsons Drugstore will hold a sale on Friday and Saturday," "The annual meeting of the Lake Club executive committee was held on January 13; routine business was transacted and all officers were reelected." To laymen, behavior settings are as visible and objective as rivers and tornadoes; they can be defined by denotation.

But the identification of behavior settings for scientific purposes requires precise, technical procedures. The problem is to identify as behavior settings only those setting-like entities with a *defined degree of internal interdependence*. Practical problems of identifying behavior settings take the following form: Are the Chaco Garage and the adjoining Service Station one behavior setting (Chaco Garage and Service Station) or two settings (Chaco Garage, Chaco Service Station)? To determine this, it is necessary to rate the degree of interdependence of the garage and the service station. If the ratings are below the established, critical value, the two are parts of a single setting; if the ratings are above this value, they are separate behavior settings. The rating of degree of interdependence is based upon the observed degree to which a putative behavior setting (Chaco Service Station) shares leaders, members (customers), action patterns, behavior mechanisms, and behavior objects with another putative setting (Chaco Garage), and upon their closeness in space and time. It turns out that Chaco Garage and Service Station are a single behavior setting.

This raises the question whether behavior settings are, in fact, experimenter-free units, or if they are space-time tesserae selected and arranged by the investigator. How can the former be when behavior setting size is influenced by a criterion chosen by the investigator? Here we shall only suggest the answer in terms of an analogy. How many rooms has a house? Are walled areas joined by doorways without doors, by double doors, by archways, one room or two? What about areas separated by different floor levels, by railings, by counters, by curtains? An investigator is free to define as he wishes the degree of separation an area must have to be identified as a room. But when this degree is established, the number of rooms in different houses is determined by the houses, not by the investigator. The situation is similar in the case of behavior settings.

It is important to note that all behavior settings have the same defining attributes, and that in terms of these attributes they are equivalent entities. It is this that makes it legitimate to enumerate them and perform arithmetical manipulations with respect to measures of their common attributes. Two Yoredale behavior settings, Magistrates Court Sessions and Mather's Dairy Barn, differ in many ways, but in behavior-settingness they are identical. One attribute of behavior-settingness is spatial extent, measured by the same operations on the court and the barn; it is, therefore, legitimate to report that Mather's Dairy Barn is greater in extent than Magistrates Court by a factor of 6.1. The relationship of behavior settings to spatial extent is discussed later in this chapter in the section "Physical Milieu and Habitat Extent."

The interested student should study carefully the basis of identifying behavior settings as set forth in *Ecological Psychology* (Barker, 1968, pp. 35–46). Because the list of settings reads, for the most part, like a commonsense directory of a town's business establishments, organization meetings, school classes, and so forth, it is sometimes overlooked that their identification involves highly technical operations.

Every behavior setting has, in addition to its defining attributes, relatively stable idiosyncratic characteristics that are defined by its program and maintained by its homeostatic control mechanisms. These enduring, whole-entity characteristics of the behavior settings of a town make it possible to describe the habitat the town provides its inhabitants. We turn next to methods of measuring and describing the relatively stable, distinctive attributes of a town's behavior settings.

Theory of Habitat Extent

The primary whole-entity attribute of a behavior setting is *existence* (occurring, happening). A list of the behavior settings occurring during a year in a town, or part of a town, is a roster of its habitat regions. Three direct enumerations of the extent of this habitat are: the number of behavior settings in the roster, the sum of the daily occurrences of the behavior settings in the roster, and the total hours of duration of the behavior settings in the roster. From these direct enumerations of behavior settings we have derived a single measure of habitat extent which we shall now explicate. The measure is called an *urb;* 0.01 of an urb of habitat is a *centiurb* of habitat.

RELATIONS AMONG NUMBER, OCCURRENCE, AND DURATION
OF BEHAVIOR SETTINGS

On Tuesday, October 22, 1963, between 10 and 11 A.M., there were 148 behavior settings in Yoredale and 126 settings in Midwest. In Yoredale there were 2 places for banking behavior (compared with 1 in Midwest); there were 7 places for "hallwaying" (4 in Midwest), 4 places to engage in beauty-shop behavior (1 in Midwest), and 3 places to place bets (none in Midwest). This ratio, in general, holds true; the mean number of behavior settings occurring in Midwest in an average hour in 1963–64 was 88 percent of the number occurring in Yoredale.

But the story is different for a year-long period. During 1963–64, 884 behavior settings occurred in Midwest and 758 settings in Yoredale; that is, by the year, in 1963–64 the number of behavior settings in Midwest was 117 percent of the number in Yoredale.

These data are surprising and confusing; they raise some fundamental questions: Is there a basic temporal interval for enumerating behavior settings? Are years more basic for this purpose than hours? When is a behavior setting a region of the habitat? When is it *at hand* for inhabiting? Finally, is there, in fact, a univocal measure of the extent of the environment? Some examples reveal the generality of the situation from which these questions arise.

First, an institutional example. A philanthropist endows a number of display galleries in four museums and fills them with art treasures. These permanent exhibits amount to 13, 15, 18, and 22 percent of the exhibit galleries in the fortunate museums. The museum directors, for administrative reasons, place restrictions on the days the galleries are open to the public. Counting each day a gallery is open to the public as one gallery-day, it turns out that the philanthropist's galleries are open for 4.5, 5.0, 3.6, and 7.0 percent, respectively, of the museums' total gallery-days. But the galleries, when open, are not always open for full days, so that the philanthropist's galleries account for 0.7, 0.9, 0.8, and 1.7 percent of the museum's total gallery-hours. The question is: What is the extent of the philanthropist's contributions to these museums?

To the museum directors, who see themselves as conservators of art treasures, he contributed 13 to 22 percent of their collections. But to museum visitors, the philanthropist contributed 3.6 to 7 percent of the exhibits; for, wandering freely through the open galleries on their occasional visits, they would find these proportions of the galleries acknowledging his gift. And to museum guards, the philanthropist's gifts account for 0.7 to 1.7 percent of their work hours.

So there are three answers to the question: The philanthropist contributed 13 to 22 percent of the museums' resources, he contributed 3.6 to 7 percent of the museums' daily accessible exhibits, and he contributed 0.7 to 1.7 percent of the gallery-hours of operation. Is one of them truer than the others? Are there ways to combine them into a single measure of extent of museum environment?

Here is a biological example. Tidepools are important ecological features of the shore environment. Like behavior settings, some tidepools are year-round, continuous fixtures, while others have limited durations. Tidepools that are not continuous may be reconstituted each day by the tides, or they may be reconstituted only occasionally, during periods of conjunction of high tides and winds; they then last for varying times. A tidepool, like a behavior setting, has an identity that can be specified by spatial-temporal coordinates; it can be denoted by pointing; it can be examined and reexamined. One can enumerate precisely those present during any period of time: 45 minutes, 7 hours, 13 days, 9.5 months, and so forth. But what period? One might find the following numbers of tidepools on two shore areas: (a) total number of pools during a year—884 in area 1 and 758 in area 2; (b) mean number of pools during random days—146 in area 1 and 178 in area 2; (c) mean number of pools during random hours—33 in area 1 and 37 in area 2. In this conjectural example, the 1963–64 data for the behavior settings of Midwest and Yoredale have been used (Table 3.1); they are in fact data that might be duplicated on a shore region. It is obvious that the different measures of tidepool extent would have different consequences for different animal species. Measure (c) indicates that both areas are meager habitats for rapidly migrating birds; neither area is rich in pools for short-time visitors, but area 2 is more favorable for them than area 1. Measure (b) shows that both areas have more extensive tidepool environments for slower migrants, or for long-time residents that are day-long feeders, and that area 2 is more extensive than area 1. But for the staff of a permanent marine laboratory, size measurement (a) is salient; over the seasons, area 1 is richer in tidepool collection sites than area 2.

Finally, another institutional example. One college offers 450 different classes in a particular semester; there are 418 meetings of these classes during an average week, 260 during an average school day, and 35 during an average hour. Another college offers 500 classes, with 400 meetings during an average week, 200 during an average day, and 50 during an average hour. Which college is larger in terms of classes that are "at hand" for attending? The second school is 111 percent as large as the first in terms of classes per semester, 96 percent as large by the week (it has more less-than-weekly classes), 80 percent as large by the day (it has more classes that meet only once or twice a week, and fewer that meet four or five times a week), and 143 percent as large by the hour (it has more multihour classes).

These examples show that our discovery that Midwest and Yoredale are of different relative extents when their behavior settings are enumerated by the hour, day, and year is not peculiar to them. This equivocal relation occurs in all cases where the rate of recurrence of the entities enumerated is not the same in the localities compared. We conclude, therefore, that the same enumerating-time interval must be used when comparisons are made, and it must be chosen for its relevance to the problem under consideration. So the question arises: What is the relevant interval for determining the extents of Midwest and Yoredale as habitats? Some fundamental facts about human action are relevant to this question.

TEMPORAL RELATIONS BETWEEN BEHAVIOR AND BEHAVIOR SETTINGS

Our concern is primarily with molar behavior. In the present connection it is of great importance that molar actions extend over varying lengths of time. "Doing the family shopping" may continue for an hour, while "getting married next June" extends for months. Intentions (Lewin, 1951), plans (Miller, Galanter, and Pribram, 1960), and cognitive maps (Tolman, 1932) are stable states that have been postulated to account on the organism side for the elementary fact that behavior occurs in units that persist over time. A molar action takes place within behavior settings that are at hand during its time span, and our investigations show that the number of settings at hand varies with the duration of the span. "Doing the family shopping" occurs within a smaller time span and smaller habitat (number of behavior settings) than "getting married next June." If we knew the durations of the molar actions which occur in Midwest and Yoredale, these would provide the needed temporal frames for determining the extents of the towns' habitats.

We have some bases for estimating the durations of molar actions, for they are governed by the segments into which time is divided by clocks and calendars, by sunrise and sunset, by noon whistles and the six-o'clock news. Time in Midwest and Yoredale is marked off by hours, days, weeks, months, and years as clearly as space is marked off by inches, feet, and miles. Engagement books, diaries, programs of organizations and institutions, schedules of events are ubiquitous in both towns, and they are almost all segmented by hours, days, months, and years. In consequence, the actions of the inhabitants of Midwest and Yoredale, their plans and intentions, are arranged in terms of hourly, daily, monthly, and yearly periods as inevitably as they are arranged in accordance with the towns' spaces and their temperatures, precipitations, and terrains.

However, another elementary attribute of molar behavior attenuates for individual actions the coerciveness of these imposed time intervals: molar behavior is goal-directed. When environmental circumstances change, alterations occur in the molar actions underway so that they usually maintain their goal directions until they are completed. An important environmental change is the periodic termination and initiation of the behavior settings of a community. Molar actions have a special property that maintains their directions under these circumstances — namely, flexible duration. If the behavior setting Grocery Store shows signs of terminating its daily occurrence at 5:30 instead of the expected 6 P.M., the action of "doing the family shopping," which usually continues for an hour, is either telescoped and completed before 5:30 or extended into the next day, when Grocery Store again occurs. In either case "doing the family shopping" continues and is completed; the absence of Grocery Store between 5:30 P.M. and 8 A.M. the next day is not crucial. Most molar actions have this flexibility, and it makes their completion independent, to some degree, of the temporal schedules of the behavior settings they require for their completion. This means that a behavior setting is almost equally at hand for many molar actions if it occurs this hour, this day, tomorrow, or on following days.

Although the relative frequencies of molar actions of different durations are not known with precision, it seems probable on the basis of general observation, that the behavioral present, the time interval within which intentions are carried out, is distributed with about equal frequency around the modal intervals *during this hour, during this day,* and *during this year*. On this basis, the most general single measure of relative habitat extent is one that weights equally the number of behavior settings that occur within these three periods. When we do this for Midwest and Yoredale in 1963–64, we find that Midwest has 1.17 as many behavior settings per year as Yoredale, it has 0.82 as many settings per day, and it has 0.87 as many settings per hour (Table 3.1, Rows 1, 2, 3, Columns 3a/4a; for the conventions used in citing tabular data see section Formats and Conventions in the latter part of this chapter). The mean of these ratios, which weights them equally, is 0.95. For a sample of molar actions centering with equal frequency on completion *during this hour, during this day,* and *during this year*, there are 95 percent as many behavior settings at hand in Midwest as in Yoredale.

STANDARD TOWN

In order to make general comparisons of habitat extent across towns and years, we require a common base. For this purpose we have created a hypothetical standard town whose dimensions in terms of number of behavior settings per year, mean number per day, and mean number per hour are measured by obtaining in each of these three dimensions the mean of four values: Midwest in 1954–55 and in 1963–64 and Yoredale in 1954–55 and in 1963–64. From the data of Table 3.1 we calculate that the dimensional values of the standard town are: (*a*) behavior settings per year, 680.5; (*b*) mean behavior settings per day, 151.0; (*c*) mean behavior settings per hour, 34.1. We have called the standard town with these dimensional values an *urb*. The dimensional values of the towns, of parts of the towns, and of individual behavior settings are reported in terms of percentages of the urb values. Here, as an example, are the dimensional values and extent in *centiurbs* of Midwest's habitat in 1963–64: (*a*) behavior settings per year as percentage of urb, 100(884/680.5) equals 130.0; (*b*) mean behavior settings per day as percentage of urb, 100(146/151) equals 96.7; (*c*) mean behavior settings per hour as percentage of urb, 100(32.6/34.1) equals 95.6; extent in centiurbs (mean of *a, b,* and *c*) equals 107.4. By the same process, we find that the extent of Yoredale's habitat in 1963–64 was 112.8 centiurbs (cu).

Many combinations of the dimensional values sum to the same habitat extent. Relatively few behavior settings per year may be compensated as far as habitat extent is concerned by relatively many per day or per hour, and vice versa. This is an aspect of behavior-habitat reality; it is in accord with the fundamental nature of molar action (flexible means and stable goal direction); and it is in accord with the fundamental nature of the human habitat (particular parts present and absent on regular or irregular schedules). This feature of habitat extent is shown by the data of Table 2.1 respecting Midwest's 1963–64 habitat within its different authority systems (classes of behavior settings, under the aegis of the town's churches, government agencies, private enterprises, schools, and voluntary associations).

Churches and Voluntary Associations have authority over almost the same extent of Midwest's habitat, 12.2 and 12.3 cu respectively, even though the authority of the Churches extends to fewer settings in the

Table 2.1
Measures of Midwest's Habitat Within Its Authority Systems, 1963–64:
Number of Behavior Settings per Year, per Day, and per Hour as
Percentages of Urb Values; Extent in Centiurbs

Measure	Churches	Government Agencies	Private Enterprises	Schools	Voluntary Associations
Behavior Settings per Year	28.4%	16.8%	19.4%	34.2%	31.2%
BS per Day	6.6%	14.9%	43.5%	27.7%	3.8%
BS per Hour	1.8%	20.8%	58.9%	12.3%	1.8%
Extent (Mean of Rows 1, 2, 3)	12.2 cu	17.5 cu	40.6 cu	24.8 cu	12.3 cu

Table 2.2

Standard Behavior Setting: Dimensional Values and Extent in Centiurbs

Dimensions	No. of Settings	Dimensional Values
Behavior Settings per Year	1	$100(1/680.5) = 0.147\%$
Mean BS per Day	1	$100(1/151.0) = 0.662\%$
Mean BS per Hour	1	$100(1/34.1) = 2.932\%$
Extent		1.25 cu

Note: A standard behavior setting is one that occurs continuously throughout a survey year.

year. However, Church settings occur on more days than settings of Voluntary Associations, and this compensates almost precisely for the Churches' fewer settings per year. Midwest's Private Enterprises have authority over fewer behavior settings per year than do its Schools, but their much greater daily and hourly occurrence results in 164 percent as much Private Enterprise habitat as School habitat.

STANDARD BEHAVIOR SETTING

The dimensional values of a behavior setting that occurs every hour of each day in a survey year provide convenient weights for determining the measurement in centiurbs of any town, part of a town, or single behavior setting. The dimensional values of this *standard setting* in terms of percentages of the values for *standard town* (urbs) are reported in Table 2.2, and an example of the use of the values as weights is given in Table 2.3.

REGULAR AND OCCASIONAL HABITATS

A distinction of importance for some analyses is that between *regular* and *occasional* behavior settings. Regular settings recur on many days in a year for many hours per occurrence. Vista Cafe in Yoredale and Skelly Service Station in Midwest are regular behavior settings; they recur day in and day out. Such settings constitute a town's regular habi-

Table 2.3

Dimensional Values of Standard Behavior Setting (SBS)
Used as Weights for Determining Extent of Midwest's
Primary Aesthetic Habitat (PAH) in 1963–64

Dimensions	Number of Settings in PAH[a]	Dimensional Values of SBS as Weights[b]	Dimensional Values of PAH (Col. 1 × Col. 2)
Behavior Settings per Year	75	0.147%	11.025%
Mean BS per Day	5.8	0.662%	3.845%
Mean BS per Hour	0.4	2.932%	1.173%
Extent			5.35 cu

Note: Primary Aesthetic Habitat consists of behavior settings where the action pattern Aesthetics is prominent.

[a] Data from Table 5.1.

[b] Data from Table 2.2.

tat; they are routinely at hand. Occasional settings recur on one or a few days in a year for one or a few hours per occurrence; Church of England Garden Fete in Yoredale and Parent-Teacher Association Carnival in Midwest are occasional behavior settings. Such settings constitute a town's occasional habitat; plans and advance arrangements must be made to inhabit them, for if missed, they are not at hand again for a long time.

In measurement by centiurbs (Tables 2.2 and 2.3), the first dimension, "behavior settings per year," contributes equally to all behavior settings, whether regular or occasional; if a behavior setting occurs 365 days for 24 hours per day or once a year for one hour, it is one setting with a weight of 0.147, and the first dimension contributes 0.147/3 to the centiurb measure of extent. But the second dimension, "mean number of behavior settings per day," contributes more to the extent of a regular setting than to that of an occasional setting; to a regular setting that occurs every day it contributes 0.662/3 to the centiurb measure, whereas to an occasional behavior setting that occurs once a year for one hour it contributed, in 1963–64, 1/366 of this amount. The third dimension of the centiurb measure, "mean number of behavior settings per hour," contributes still more to the centiurb measure of the extent of regular settings than of occasional settings; to a regular setting that occurs continuously throughout the year, the third dimension contributes 2.932, whereas to an occasional setting occurring once a year for one hour it contributed 1/8784 as much in 1963–64.

For these reasons, the relative contributions of behavior settings per year, per day, and per hour to the centiurb measure is an indication of the relative presence of regular and occasional behavior settings in the habitat. It will be noted, for example, in Table 2.1, that Private Enterprises and Government Agencies receive greater proportions of their centiurb measure from behavior settings per hour than from behavior settings per year, whereas the reverse is true for Churches, Schools, and Voluntary Associations. These data show that the habitats controlled by Private Enterprise and Government Agencies have relatively more regular and fewer occasional behavior settings than the habitats controlled by Churches, Schools, and Voluntary Associations.

HABITAT EXTENT AS A MEASURE OF RESOURCES FOR MOLAR ACTIONS

Many kinds of molar actions occur only within particular kinds of settings: sentencing a man to jail takes place only in settings of the District or County Courts (not in Grocery Stores or Worship Services); getting a haircut occurs only in Barbershops (not in Business Meetings or Basketball Games); filling a tooth is carried out only in Dentists' Offices (not in Garages or Dances). Where this relation holds, molar actions for which there are no appropriate settings do not occur: cricket is not played in Midwest, there is no behavior setting Cricket Game; Latin is not taught in Yoredale, there is no setting Latin Class.

Because of this relation between behavior settings and molar actions, number of behavior settings is a more important component of the extent of the habitat of molar actions than number of behavior-setting occurrences or number of hours' duration. This is obvious when one considers the more limited behavior resources of the 12 monthly occurrences of the single Midwest recreational setting Bridge Club II in comparison with 12 occurrences of a wider sample of recreational settings: three meetings of Bridge Club II, High School Home Economics Club Christmas Party, Old Settlers Pet Parade, Garland Lanes Bowling Exhibition, American Legion Auxiliary Card Party for March of Dimes, Married Couples Bridge Club Meeting in March, Elementary School Operetta, Tractor Pulling Contest, Women's Bridge Club III May Meeting, Women's Bridge Club IV September Meeting. In terms of centiurbs, the 12 monthly occurrences of Bridge Club II have a habitat extent of 0.06 cu, and the 12 settings (including three Bridge Club II Meetings) have a habitat extent of 0.50 cu. According to the centiurb measurement, the opportunities to set goals and attempt to achieve satisfactions (molar behavior resources) are 12 percent as great in the former case as in the latter. Measurement of habitat extent by centiurbs weights an additional behavior setting 365 (or 366) times greater than an additional occurrence of an existing behavior setting, and it weights an additional behavior setting 8760 (8784) times greater than an additional hour of an existing setting.

Measurement of habitat extent in terms of centiurbs is a measure of the at-handness of habitat supports and coercions for molar actions; it is a temporal-spatial proximity measure. The larger the centiurb measure of habitat extent, the greater the number of molar behavior opportunities and requirements within the normal time perspective—that is, the greater the number of goal possibilities and obligations immediately at hand.

The term *territorial range* (TR) is used to indicate the extent of a designated part of a town's habitat; for example, the TR of Aesthetics is the extent in centiurbs of the behavior settings where the action pattern Aesthetics occurs, and the TR of Infants is the extent of the behavior settings which generate behavior via one or more infants.

PHYSICAL MILIEU AND HABITAT EXTENT

It will be noted that amount of space is not included in determinations of habitat extent; it is based entirely on the number, occurrence, and duration of behavior settings. This does not imply that extent of physical space is not a factor of importance in the programs of behavior settings, including the behavior of their human components. It means only that habitat extent as we have defined it and measured it in centiurbs is independent of geographical area. In fact, many habitat regions of the same extent in centiurbs are geographically larger in Midwest than in Yoredale. They usually differ in some other physical properties, too; they are usually warmer in Midwest, and have boundary

MANKATO STATE UNIVERSITY
MEMORIAL LIBRARY
MANKATO, MINNESOTA

walls that are less solid and less well insulated against sound transmission. All of these differences in the physical properties of the towns' settings are undoubtedly causally interrelated with their standing patterns of behavior, and deserve investigation, but we judge them to have no systematic relation to the extent—the temporal-geographical proximity, the at-handness—of the towns' habitats. When the area of Ellson Drugstore was doubled, it did not appreciably change its temporal-geographical proximity to the inhabitants of Midwest; it was still a single 7:30 A.M.-to-6 P.M.-Monday-through-Saturday locus, no more and no less at hand within the time perspective of Midwesterners for planning and engaging in drugstore behavior. However, when the Midwest behavior setting Dentons Drugstore ceased in the period between 1954–55 and 1963–64, leaving only Ellsons Drugstore, the extent of the genotype Drugstores decreased in Midwest from two loci to one locus, from 365 to 300 days, and from 5110 to 2400 hours of occurrence. After this happened, travelers stopping for an hour in Midwest and day-long visitors to the town were more likely to find no resources for drugstore behavior, and the plans of the town's inhabitants for drugstore behavior had to be plotted within a future with drugstore settings less immediately accessible in time and space. According to the measurement by centiurbs, the extent of the genotype Drugstores decreased from 2.5 cu before the demise of Dentons Drugstore to 1.4 cu after its demise, a decrease of 44 percent.

Ellsons Drugstore program was immediately changed by the loss of its genotype mate in complex ways, one being the production of more person-hours of behavior. And this, in fact, was an important factor behind the spatial expansion of the setting. Reduction in the extent of the genotype Drugstores caused an expansion of the spatial dimension of the remaining drugstore, but it did not increase its extent as measured in centiurbs—its at-handness, its geo-temporal proximity.

Measuring Habitat Variety

Similarity of parts has no place in the identification of a behavior setting; interdependence is the sole criterion. However, settings identified on the basis of degree of internal interdependence may have greater or less similarity. Weylen's Grocery and Reid's Grocery are more similar in standing pattern than Weylen's Grocery and Hooker's Tavern. Similarity of standing patterns provides a basis for the meaningful classification of settings into similar categories or genotypes.

BEHAVIOR SETTING GENOTYPES

The degree of behavior setting similarity that we have adopted for establishing a genotype is, essentially, the lowest degree of pattern similarity compatible with the exchange of major components between settings. The standing patterns of Pearl Cafe and Gwyn Cafe in Midwest are sufficiently similar that major components (staff, equipment, kitchens) could be transposed without appreciably disturbing the functioning of either setting; these behavior settings, therefore, belong to the same genotype. Exchange of major standing behavior pattern components would not be possible between Gwyn Cafe and the Midwest State Bank; they therefore belong to different behavior setting genotypes.

Within every behavior setting there are operating instructions, there is a *program*. Sometimes the program is coded via written language, as in a baseball rule book. In such cases, the programs of different settings can be compared, item by item, to determine their degree of equivalence. However, written programs are not usually available. The program of most behavior settings is incorporated in the person or persons within the central zones of the settings—their human operatives (functionaries and leaders as defined under Penetration Zones, Table 2.4). An important problem of behavior-setting operation is to get the proper program incorporated within central zone inhabitants. This is accomplished by formal training or experience in the setting, and it requires time. But when the program of a setting is incorporated within a person, it is one of his relatively permanent attributes and he is often identified by the code name of the program: Attorney, Postmaster, Grocer, etc. This provides a practical basis for judging whether different behavior settings are of the same or different genotypes, even when details of their programs are not known. If settings A and B continue to function without change when the inhabitants of their most central zones are interchanged, then A and B have the same program and are identical in genotype.

A description of the genotypes of a town portrays the varieties of standing patterns within its environment, and the number of genotypes in a town is a measure of its habitat variety—the diversity of molar behavior resources and the range of molar behavior opportunities.

MAJOR GENOTYPES AND GENOTYPE SITES OF SUBSTANTIAL CHANGE

A major genotype is one whose behavior settings make up 3 percent or more of the habitat under consideration. For example, in 1954–55, 5.0 percent of Midwest's primary educational habitat (the part of Midwest's habitat where education is prominent) was made up of behavior settings of the genotype Business Meetings (Table 5.10; R20; C1); this is therefore a major genotype within this particular habitat. A minor genotype is one that constitutes less than 3 percent of a habitat.

A genotype is the locus of a marked increase in habitat variety if its behavior settings were new to a habitat in 1963–64 or if it was a continuing genotype that increased in extent between 1955 and 1964 by 0.25 cu or more. A genotype is the locus of substantial decrease in habitat variety if it ceased to occur in a habitat between 1955 and 1964 or if it was a continuing genotype whose settings decreased in extent between 1955 and 1964 by 0.25 cu or more. To be identified as new, a genotype *must not* occur in the habitat in 1954–55 or in any of the eight following

years, and it *must* occur in the habitat in 1963–64; to be identified as
ceasing, a genotype *must* occur in 1954–55, and it *must not* occur during
any of the eight intervening years or in 1963–64. A change of 0.25 cu in
the extent of a genotype is greater than the change that occurs in the
total extent of 81 percent of Midwest's genotypes and of 79 percent of
Yoredale's genotypes between 1954–55 and 1963–64. These criteria of
substantial accretion and erosion and of new and extinct genotypes in-
sure that only relatively important and permanent increments and
decrements in habitat variety are identified (Chapter 4).

COMMON AND DISTINCTIVE GENOTYPES

Crucial questions in comparative studies are: How similar are the
habitats? What do they have in common? We have identified seven
degree-of-commonality genotype categories, ranging from genotypes
fully common to both towns to those unique to one town.

Category 1. Common genotypes. The behavior setting genotypes of
category 1 occur in both towns in both years. The criteria of "occur in
both towns" are the same as the criteria of "belong to the same genotype" within towns. *Example:* The genotype Barbershops is common to
both Midwest and Yoredale, because the program of a barbershop in
Midwest is so similar to the program of a barbershop in Yoredale that
an efficient barber in one town could transfer to a barbershop in the
other town and become efficient in less than a quarter of the time
required by a complete novice.

Category 2. Intermittently common genotypes. The genotypes of category 2 occur in both Midwest and Yoredale, but they do so intermittently. There are two subcategories: (*a*) genotypes with programs that
are interchangeable between the towns in one but not both survey years;
(*b*) genotypes that do not occur in both towns during the same survey
year, but occur in one town in a survey year and in the other town
within the intervening eight-year period. These genotypes usually do
not occur during the same survey years for adventitious reasons; for example, Blood Collection Laboratories occur in both towns, but they happened not to occur in Midwest during either survey year.

Category 3. Genotypes with common but rearranged programs. The
genotypes of category 3 have programs that occur in both years in both
towns, but in dismantled form. This happens in two ways: (*a*) The parts
of an intact program in one town are distributed among settings of a
number of genotypes of the other town. For example, the program of a
behavior setting of the genotype Drugstores in Midwest is distributed
among settings of the genotypes Chemists, Confectioners and Stationers
Shops, and Restaurants in Yoredale. (*b*) The program as it occurs in one
town is incorporated within a more inclusive genotype of the other
town. For example, the program of Yoredale's genotype Baptismal Services is incorporated as part of Midwest's genotype Religious Worship
Services.

The essential feature of this similarity category is that its programs are present in both towns, but they are distributed among different genotypes of the towns.

Category 4. Partly common genotypes. Some elements of the programs of genotypes of category 4 regularly occur in both towns. There are three subcategories: (*a*) Genotypes whose programs could be transferred to settings of the other town in one-quarter to one-half the time a novice requires to master the program. For example, the fundamental theories of Midwest's genotype Banks are the same as those of Yoredale's Banks, but the details of operation vary widely; it is judged that a Midwest banker could become a Yoredale banker in one-quarter to one-half the time it would take an untrained Yoredale inhabitant to become a banker. (*b*) *Parts* of the programs of these genotypes occur within genotypes of the other town. For example, one subprogram of Midwest's genotype Newspaper and Printing Plants (the job-printing department) occurs in Yoredale's genotype Printing Shops. (*c*) This subcategory is similar to category 4(a), except that interchange of programs between the towns would require one-half to three-quarters as much time as is required to program a novice. For example, although Midwest lawyers perform most of the functions performed by Yoredale solicitors, it is judged that the laws and procedures are so different in the towns that it would require a Midwest lawyer one-half to three-quarters as much time to master the Yoredale solicitor's program as it would a Yoredale citizen without legal training.

Category 5. Genotypes common to rural district. The genotypes of category 5 occur in only one town, but they occur in the rural district surrounding the other town. It is often due to adventitious circumstances that these genotypes are not common to the towns. For example, the Midwest genotype Timber Sales and Removal Services occurs in villages neighboring to Yoredale; Yoredale's Livestock Exhibits and Competitions occurs in a town within Midwest County.

Category 6. Genotypes common to regional cities. These genotypes occur only in one town, but they occur in cities within the region of the other town. For example, the program of Midwest's Animal Feed Mill does not occur in Yoredale or in the district around Yoredale, but it does occur in neighboring cities; the program of Yoredale's Bookbinding Classes does not occur in Midwest or in Midwest County, but it does occur in cities neighboring to Midwest.

Category 7. Unique genotypes. The genotypes of category 7 occur in only one of the towns; they are absent from the other town and from its surrounding rural district and neighboring cities. For example, skilled players in Midwest's genotype Baseball Games would have almost no advantage in becoming programmed for any behavior setting of Yoredale, or of its rural district or neighboring cities; the proprietor of a setting in Yoredale's genotype Commission Agents' Offices (Betting Shops) would find that his knowhow had no congruence with any genotypes of Midwest or neighboring areas.

Behavior setting genotypes of commonality categories 3 to 7 identify habitat parts that are not common to the towns at any time between 1954–55 and 1963–64; they identify parts of the towns that are in some way distinctive. It is the settings within these genotypes that give the towns their individuality, ranging from different mixes of programs within behavior settings (category 3) to behavior setting programs that are unique to one town (category 7).

HABITAT EXTENT AND HABITAT VARIETY

The centiurb measure of habitat extent assumes that habitat extent is positively related to number of behavior settings, number of behavior setting occurrences, and hours of behavior setting duration. Undoubtedly it is also, positively related to variety of behavior settings (number of genotypes). The addition to a habitat of a behavior setting of a new genotype would appear to increase goal-setting opportunities more than would adding a setting of an already present genotype. However, we have chosen to deal with variety separately, in the first place, and to combine it later with other habitat measures, including habitat extent as measured by centiurbs, to obtain a measure of habitat salience.

Describing the Habitat

We have presented methods of discriminating habitat units (behavior settings), of measuring habitat extent (centiurbs), and of measuring habitat variety (genotypes and commonality categories). We have not, however, presented methods of describing habitat units and of measuring the degree to which they possess various *qualities* (also termed *attributes*). What we have done is analogous to presenting ways of measuring the extent of a forest, counting the varieties of trees which compose it, and comparing the commonality of forests with respect to their trees, but without presenting methods of describing the trees. So we turn next to the attributes in terms of which we have described habitat units.

ACTION PATTERN QUALITIES

We have identified and investigated the degree of occurrence of 11 habitat qualities which we have named action patterns: *Aesthetics* (making the environment more beautiful), *Business* (exchanging goods, services, or privileges for money), *Education* (formal education of any kind), *Government* (making, implementing, and evaluating government regulations), *Nutrition* (eating and drinking), *Personal Appearance* (improving appearance via clothing, grooming, adornments), *Physical Health* (promoting health), *Professional Involvement* (paid rather than voluntary performance in setting), *Recreation* (play, sports, games), *Religion* (behavior concerned with worship), *Social Contact* (interpersonal interaction). These action patterns are defined in more detail in Chapter 5.

The degree to which each action pattern occurs in a behavior setting is rated and reported as prominent, secondary, or absent. A prominent action pattern is one which occurs in connection with 80 percent or more of the standing pattern of a behavior setting; it is a major component, a definitive attribute of a setting. For example, the action pattern attribute Recreation (play, sport, games) is present in almost the entire standing pattern of Midwest's behavior setting High School Boys Basketball Game; it is present in the jumping players, in the bouncing ball, in the performing band, in the cheering spectators. Recreation is, therefore, prominent in High School Boys Basketball Game. On the other hand, the action pattern Business (exchanging goods, services, or privileges for money) is present in only a small part of the standing pattern of High School Boys Basketball Game, in buying and selling tickets and refreshments; Business is, therefore, a secondary action pattern of this setting; it is present, but not prominent.

The reverse situation occurs with respect to these action patterns in the Midwest behavior setting Household Auction Sales. Here Recreation occurs to only a minor degree; it is a secondary attribute, but Business is present in almost all the standing pattern: it is present in the patter of the auctioneer, in the display of household goods, in the bidding of the buyers, in the conditions of sale. Business is, therefore, prominent in Household Auction Sales. Basketball Games are *for* recreation; Auction Sales are *for* buying and selling.

More than one action pattern can be prominent in a behavior setting. Social Contact is prominent in High School Boys Basketball Game in addition to Recreation, and it is prominent in Household Auction Sales in addition to Business.

The behavior settings of a town where an action pattern is prominent are the primary environmental loci of the action pattern; they make up its *primary habitat,* and *their extent is a measure of a town's major habitat resources for generating behavior possessing the action pattern.* For example, the behavior settings of a town where Education is prominent make up its primary educational habitat (PEH); in Yoredale in 1963–64 PEH is 14.2 cu in extent and constitutes 12.6 percent of the town's total habitat. This means that 12.6 percent of Yoredale's habitat consists of behavior settings made up of classrooms, lesson plans, enrolled students, textbooks, certified teachers, and so forth, that produce educational actions (formal teaching and learning) when they function in accordance with their prescribed programs of events. The behavior generated by a town's primary educational habitat is the town's major output of educational behavior. When we speak of a town's output of educational behavior, aesthetic behavior, or religious behavior, we refer to the outputs of the towns' primary educational, aesthetic, or religious habitats.

A quality is secondary within a setting if it occurs in some but less than 80 percent of the standing pattern of the setting. An attribute is absent if it does not occur with sufficient regularity to qualify as secondary.

The *territorial range* (TR) of an attribute is the sum of its prominent and secondary extents.

BEHAVIOR MECHANISM QUALITIES

The standing pattern of a setting involves different effector systems to various degrees. The following mechanisms have been systematically studied: *Affective Behavior* (overt emotionality), *Gross Motor Activity* (use of large muscles), *Manipulation* (use of hands), and *Talking* (all forms of verbalizing). As with action pattern attributes, a number of behavior mechanism attributes may be prominent in a single behavior setting. Behavior mechanisms are defined in more detail in Chapter 5. The degree to which mechanisms occur in a behavior setting is rated in the same way as action patterns.

PENETRATION QUALITIES

Behavior settings have internal structural and dynamic arrangements. One important feature of these arrangements is the power different parts of a setting exercise over it. This ranges from parts with virtually no power over the setting (such as the parts "sidewalk superintendents" occupy in the setting High School Construction Project) to those with control over the entire behavior setting (such as the part occupied by the single teacher of the setting Fourth Grade Music Class). We have called this dimension of behavior settings the penetration dimension, and we have identified seven zones of penetration from zone 0, the most peripheral zone and the one with least power, to zone 6, the central and most powerful zone of penetration. Attributes and the nomenclature of the penetration zones are described in Table 2.4. Three terms of the table require definition.

Habitat-claims for human components. The behavior settings that comprise the towns' habitats specify human components for certain loci (slots, positions) within them. These are habitat-claims for human components. The honorary secretaryship of Yoredale's Agricultural and Horticultural Society Meeting is such a habitat-claim; this position requires an appropriate human component, one with the necessary knowledge and skills, in order to become operational. Habitat-claims are stable structural and dynamic features of a town's habitat. The number of habitat-claims of a behavior setting for operatives is the number of positions of responsibility that must be filled (operatives that must be present) for the normal occurrence of the setting. For example, Presbyterian Church Worship Service in Midwest requires 20 operatives (1 minister, 1 organist, 12 choir members, 2 ushers, 2 candlelighters, 2 greeters). In 1963–64, Yoredale had 7764 habitat-claims for human components within its operating zones—that is, habitat-claims for operatives. If all of Yoredale's behavior settings were to occur simultaneously, it would require 7764 human components to operate the town's habitat. The *operational* range of a class of inhabitants is the extent in centiurbs of the behavior settings in which members of the class are opera-

Table 2.4

Penetration Zones of Behavior Settings: Their Functions, Power, Habitat-Claims, and Human Components; examples of implemented habitat-claims

Penetration Zone	Functions	Power	Habitat-Claims	Human Components	Implemented Habitat-Claims
6	Control and implementation of program and maintenance circuits	Direct control of entire setting	Single leaderships	Single leaders	Claim-leader actions: club president presiding at meeting
5	Control and implementation of program and maintenance circuits	Direct, but shared, control of entire setting	Multiple leaderships	Multiple leaders	Claim-leader actions: team captain conferring with coach
4	Joint control (with zone 5 or 6) and implementation of subsystems of program and maintenance circuits	Direct, shared control of part of setting	Factorships	Factors (functionaries, assistants, etc.)	Claim-factor actions: church organist playing for worship service
6–4	Control and operation of program and maintenance circuits	Direct control of entire setting	Habitat-claims for operatives; positions of responsibility	Operatives	Claim-operations or claim-operator actions (responsible actions): lawyer or his secretary answering query of client
3	Implementation of major goal and emergency maintenance circuits	Indirect control of most of setting	Memberships	Members (customers, clients, etc.)	Claim-member actions: store customer making purchase
2	Implementation of minor goal and emergency maintenance circuits	Some influence on part of setting	Spectatorships	Spectators (audience, invited guests, etc.)	Claim-spectator actions: parade viewer watching parade
1	No functions	Almost no power	None; neutral places	Onlookers (loafers, etc.)	Claim-onlooker actions: infant accompanying mother in grocery store
0	Recruiting and dissuading potential inhabitants	Region of influence external to setting	None; potential places	Potential inhabitants	Potential guest reading invitation

tives—for example, in 1963–64 aged persons in Yoredale were operatives in 18.3 cu, or 16 percent of the town's total habitat.

Human components. Single leaders (zone 6), multiple leaders (zone 5), factors (zone 4—those who act or transact business for another, *Webster's Seventh New Collegiate Dictionary*), operatives (zones 6–4), members (zone 3), spectators (zone 2), onlookers (zone 1), and potential inhabitants (zone 0) identify the human components of the indicated penetration zones of behavior settings.

Implemented habitat-claims. These are habitat-claims in operation—that is, habitat-claims *and* their human components. The Yoredale behavior setting Women's Luncheon Club Meeting has a habitat-claim in its program called vote-of-thanks (to the speaker), and the setting is incomplete without a particular human component to fill this slot. When Mrs. Shields moves the vote-of-thanks at the March meeting, at the request of the president, this is one claim-factor action. The vote-of-thanks is analogous to the motor-compressor assembly of a refrigerator: without the compressor and without the motor, the assembly is nonfunctional and the refrigerator is incomplete; without the vote-of-thanks in the program and without the mover, the Women's Luncheon Club Meeting is incomplete.

Habitat-claims, human components, and implemented habitat-claims (claim-operations) are all attributes of a town's habitat; they are whole-entity properties, created by the component behavior settings of the habitat. The Women's Luncheon Club Meeting determines if a vote-of-thanks shall be an event in its program, and it determines who shall implement the event; Mrs. Shields is a factor (she transacts business) of the setting.

Penetration zone 0 requires special comment. It is the region surrounding a behavior setting within which the forces of the setting operate to impel people and materials into it or to repel them from it. Zone 0 is the zone of *potential* inhabitants. It is the region where advertisements urging attendance circulate, and where warnings such as "No Minors Allowed" are posted; it overlaps with zones 1 to 6 of other behavior settings. For example, if a client in the Yoredale behavior setting Blacketts Ladies Hairdresser reads a notice on the counter stating that the annual Church of England Jumble Sale is being held, and soliciting attendance, the client is simultaneously in zone 3 of Blacketts Ladies Hairdresser and in zone 0 of Church of England Jumble Sale. The zero penetration zones of a number of behavior settings overlap: the client of Blacketts Ladies Hairdresser may not only be invited by the notice to become an inhabitant of Church of England Jumble Sale, she may in addition be urged by a fellow client to take advantage of the good values in the setting Harbough and Laverne, General Draper. In towns the size of Midwest and Yoredale, almost all town inhabitants are, over a survey year, occupants of zone 0 of most of the town's behavior settings—that is, the population of zone 0 of most settings is the population of the town.

Penetration zones 4, 5, and 6, the operating zones, are particularly important. Their human components, the operatives, are the most immediately essential inhabitants of a behavior setting; they man its program and maintenance circuits, where they are responsible for maintaining the setting as a structural unit and operating its program. This responsibility entails power over the setting, but it also involves coercion by the setting, for along with the greater power of the more central penetration zones over a behavior setting there is greater power over the inhabitants. Behavior-setting operatives are more strongly constrained by the homeostatic controls of the settings they implement than are members, spectators, or onlookers (inhabitants of zones 1–3). The strength of the forces acting upon the chairman of a meeting, the proprietor of a store, or the preacher in a worship service to enter the setting and behave in accordance with its program are greater than those upon the typical member, customer, or parishioner. The more central the penetration zone, the more essential is each inhabitant to the occurrence of the setting. In behavior settings of the genotypes Baseball Games, Business Meetings, and Attorneys' Offices, for example, larger proportions of their claims for operatives than of their normal complements of members and spectators must be filled for adequate functioning on any occasion.

Operatives fill *positions of responsibility* within behavior settings; they are the human components of the habitat-claims that are most crucial for the normal operation of settings, and these habitat-claims are located within stronger force fields than other habitat-claims. In psychological language, the inhabitants of the operating zones of behavior settings carry out important and difficult actions; they are important, hard-working people; they control the setting and are controlled by it. They are the setting's most responsible inhabitants.

This does not mean that the inhabitants of penetration zones 0–3 are not important components of a town's habitat. In the long run, they are the *sine qua non* of behavior settings; without them, a setting is like a kindled fire without a supply of fuel. Furthermore they, along with operatives, man the maintenance circuits in emergencies; when behavior settings of a town's habitat are less than optimally habitable, the homeostatic controls of these settings pressure the inhabitants of all the penetration zones into the maintenance circuits. A town with relatively few inhabitants per centiurb falls below its optimally habitable state relatively frequently, and when it does so, pressures per available component toward maintenance circuits are relatively great. On the average, therefore, the inhabitants of such towns are more important to its survival as a human habitat than are the inhabitants of towns with high inhabitant/centiurb ratios. These issues are considered in more detail in Chapter 7.

ATTENDANCE ATTRIBUTES

Behavior settings differ in the degree to which they bring to bear upon different population subgroups pressure to inhabit or avoid them. In Midwest six-year-old children are required by law to inhabit the behavior setting First Grade Academic Subjects (positive pressure) and they are prevented from inhabiting the behavior setting Boy Scout Troop Meeting. Measures of the positive and negative pressure of behavior settings upon population subgroups indicate the degrees of freedom and restriction of the subgroups. We have investigated five degrees of pressure upon members of two inhabitant subgroups, children and adolescents, to inhabit behavior settings: attendance required, attendance encouraged, neutral to attendance by subgroup members, attendance discouraged, attendance prohibited. These forces are independent of those discussed in Chapter 7 in connection with the manning of behavior settings.

BENEFICENCE ATTRIBUTES

Behavior settings differ in the degree to which they promote the welfare of different classes of inhabitants. The *raison d'etre* of Kindergarten Classes is to benefit preschool children; the milieu and its standing behavior pattern are congenial to preschool inhabitants. On the other hand, Methodist and Presbyterian Youth Hayrack Ride is *for* adolescents; it is harmonious with them. The extent of the behavior settings that promote the welfare of a particular population subgroup indicates the degree to which the town's environment is uniquely favorable to the subgroup. We have investigated four beneficence relations of behavior settings toward members of two inhabitant subgroups, children and adolescents: benefits directly, benefits indirectly, unconcerned with welfare of these subgroup members, setting receives benefit from subgroup members.

LOCAL AUTONOMY QUALITIES

Behavior settings differ in the extent to which their functioning is influenced by occurrences originating within the community and at different geographical distances from it. For example, crucial features of the program of the Yoredale behavior setting British Railways Freight Office and Delivery are subject to control from the national level by executive settings located outside of Yoredale, outside of the surrounding rural district, and outside of the surrounding dale region; its performers are appointed and its program is determined at a great distance from Yoredale. British Railways Freight Office and Delivery has, therefore, a low degree of local autonomy. On the other hand, the performers and program of the Yoredale behavior setting Dramatic Society Reception are determined almost entirely by the executive setting Dramatic Society Committee Meeting, which is located in Yoredale; therefore the setting Dramatic Society Reception has a high degree of local autonomy. The extent of a town's behavior settings that are locally autonomous is a measure of the degree to which its inhabitants control the environment in which they live.

We report three degrees of local autonomy: high, medium, and low. A behavior setting with *high* local autonomy is predominantly controlled from sources within the town or the circumjacent district within approximately a four-mile radius of the town; this embraces a governmental district in each case: Midwest's School District and Yoredale's Rural District. A behavior setting of *medium* local autonomy is predominantly controlled from sources outside the town and district, but within the surrounding rural region approximately four to ten miles from the town, embracing Midwest County, of which the town of Midwest is the county seat, and the Yoredale valley, of which the town of Yoredale is the trading and transportation center. A setting of *low* local autonomy is predominantly controlled from sources beyond the town, beyond the district, and beyond the region, at the state and national levels in the case of Midwest, and at the county and national levels in the case of Yoredale.

AUTHORITY SYSTEM QUALITIES

A behavior setting may have power over a number of other settings or over no other setting. In Midwest the behavior setting Elementary and High School Board Meeting has authority over 227 other behavior settings ranging from Elementary School Principal's Office to Sixth Grade Hike; this constitutes one authority system, a multi-setting authority system. At the other extreme, Burgess Beauty Shop has authority over no other setting. This also constitutes one authority system, a single-setting authority system.

Authority systems are grouped into five classes on the basis of the following characteristics of the *controlling* or *executive* setting: *Private Enterprises* include all settings under the control of behavior settings operated by private citizens in order to earn a living; *Churches* comprise those settings that are controlled by central administrative settings of churches; *Government agencies* embrace all behavior settings managed by executive settings of town, county, state, or federal governments, excluding school-controlled settings; the authority system *Schools* covers the settings under the aegis of executive settings operated by private or public educational agencies (town, district, county, state, or national school boards or committees); *Voluntary Associations* comprise all settings other than those in the first four classes. Each behavior setting of a town occurs in only one authority system; the five classes of authority systems control all public behavior settings of a town.

The authority system to which a behavior setting belongs identifies one category of influence upon its program. For example, many aspects of the Midwest behavior setting Methodist Church Worship Service are controlled by the setting Methodist Church Official Board Meeting, the local executive setting of the Midwest Methodist Church. The Official Board can determine the aesthetic attributes of Methodist Church Worship Service, and it has this power over the action patterns of all settings under its aegis. The latter settings constitute the Methodist Church Authority System of Midwest. The executive settings of all churches of a town, and all the behavior settings they control, constitute the Church Authority Systems of the town. On a similar basis, each town has Government Authority Systems, School Authority Systems, Private Enterprise Authority Systems, and Voluntary Association Authority Systems.

INHABITANT ATTRIBUTES

A behavior setting has a determinate number of inhabitants during a specified period of time. This is an important habitat attribute. The inhabitants can be identified with respect to whatever inhabitant characteristics are relevant to any particular problem. Inhabitant subgroups with the following characteristics have been discriminated in our studies:

Age Subgroups	*Identification*
Infants (Inf)	Under 2 years of age
Preschool children (PS)	2 to 5:11 years of age
Younger School ages (YS)	6 to 8:11 years of age
Older School ages (OS)	9 to 11:11 years of age
Adolescents (Adol)	12 to 17:11 years of age
Adults (Adu)	18 to 64:11 years of age
Aged (Aged)	65 years and over

Sex Subgroups
    Male (M)
    Female (F)

Social Class Subgroups

Social Class I	Social Classes I, II, III correspond
Social Class II	fairly well to Warner's Upper Middle,
Social Class III	Lower Middle, and Upper Lower
Social Class G (Gentry)	Classes, and G to Warner's Upper Upper Class (Warner and others, 1949).

Race Subgroups
    White (W)
    Negro (N)

VIABILITY QUALITIES

Within periods of time covering months and years, some behavior settings of a town continue to occur, some settings cease, and some settings are initiated. These processes are sources of both quantitative and qualitative changes in the habitat characteristics of a town; valid evidences of the continuity, erosion, and accretion of behavior settings are, therefore, important.

When the Midwest behavior setting Kanes Grocery Store was sold to a new owner and became Weylens Grocery Store, did this mark the end of the former setting and the beginning of a new setting? When Midwest State Bank moved across the central square and enlarged its space and modernized its equipment, did the same setting continue? The doors of Dr. Must's Chiropractic Office were closed when the doctor moved from Midwest; the setting ceased to function. When, later, Dr. Harbough came to town and established the behavior setting Dr. Harbough's Chiropractic Office, was this a new setting or a continuation, after a lapse, of Dr. Must's Chiropractic Office? When the Mens Sunday School Class and the Womens Sunday School Class of the Presbyterian Church merged, was the resulting Adult Sunday School Class a continuation of the two previous settings? Or were the former settings ended by the merger and a new setting initiated? These are the kinds of issues with which the study of behavior setting change has to deal.

Solutions to these issues are provided by the principles involved in behavior setting identification presented earlier; according to them, the same behavior setting continues from an earlier to a later period if the later occurrences are interdependent to a defined degree with the earlier occurrences. However, the evidences of interdependence are different for long periods of time; the overlap of leaders and members is always, finally, reduced to zero, and connections via temporal contiguity are inevitably attenuated. It appears that long-time connections are mediated via enduring written or oral programs of behavior setting operation (charters, constitutions, traditions, bylaws, rules of procedure) that are passed between successive behavior settings; it is by creating or altering such enduring programs that an early behavior setting influences the standing pattern of a setting years later.

We judge that a single program, a relatively permanent standing pattern template, is involved over long periods when earlier and later behavior setting occurrences: (*a*) belong to the same genotype, (*b*) belong to the same authority system, (*c*) have the same classes of performers, (*d*) have the same classes of members, (*e*) have the same classes of behavior objects, (*f*) involve the same behavior mechanisms. If the first two conditions hold for an earlier and a later behavior setting occurrence and if conditions *c* to *f* hold to the degree that there is at least a two-thirds overlap between the stated elements of the earlier and later occurrences, they are *two occurrences of the same behavior setting;* the setting is continuous. Otherwise the earlier and later occurrences are different behavior settings. Here are elaborations of the conditions of behavior setting continuity:

> Condition (*a*): Earlier and later occurrences of the same behavior setting belong to the same genotype; they have sufficient similarity of standing patterns that major components could be exchanged between them without interfering with their functioning. For example, 1954–55 inhabitants of penetration zones 4 to 6 of Kanes Grocery could carry on effectively as 1963–64 inhabitants of its successor, Weylens Grocery Store.
>
> Condition (*b*): Earlier and later occurrences of the same behavior setting belong to the same authority system. An authority system is the same at earlier and later periods when the controlling setting has continuously functioned in accordance with the program of the earlier period.

When zone 5 or 6 leaders change, there is continuity if the guiding template of the program (the rules, constitution, directive, franchise, license, contract, convenant, law, canon, ordinance, regulation) is accepted by the new leaders. When a new sheriff is "sworn in," the continuity of the setting Sheriff's Office is assured; when Kanes Grocery was "signed over" to Weylens Grocery, the authority system was made continuous. For behavior setting continuity, there must be an overt act of transference: a signing, an acceptance, a swearing-in, an oath of office, an investiture. When Dr. Must closed the setting Dr. Must's Chiropractice Office, there was no act of conveyance to Dr. Harbough; and when later Dr. Harbough opened the setting Dr. Harbough's Chiropractic Office, there was no act of reception from Dr. Must. So the earlier setting died and the later setting was born, even though both were of the same genotype and had the same classes of performers, members, behavior objects, and mechanisms; the authority that controlled the first setting did not pass on its program to the authority that controlled the second setting.

Conditions (c) and (d): Earlier and later occurrences of the same behavior setting have two-thirds or more of these classes of performers and members in common. The classes are common when the eligibility rules are the same. Membership in the Midwest behavior setting Eastern Star Past Matrons Club Meeting is restricted to persons who have held the position of Worthy Matron in the setting Eastern Star Lodge Meeting. If at a future time the eligibility rules of the Past Matrons Club were changed to permit membership without regard to the Eastern Star Lodge, so that some future members would not have been eligible for 1963–64 membership, the 1963–64 club and the hypothesized future club would not have the same classes of members.

Conditions (e) and (f): Earlier and later occurrences of the same behavior setting have two-thirds or more of their classes of behavior objects in common. Behavior objects are of the same class when they belong to categories of objects with the same dictionary definitions. And occurrences of the same behavior setting have two-thirds or more of these behavior mechanisms in common: gross motor actions, manipulation, verbalization, singing, writing, observing, listening, thinking, eating, reading, emoting, tactual feeling.

A 1963–64 behavior setting is continuous with one of 1954–55 — that is, it is a recurrence of the same setting — if by these criteria their programs are the same; it is a new, an accreted, behavior setting if no 1954–55 setting had the same program. A 1954–55 behavior setting is continuous with one in 1963–64 if by these criteria their programs are the same; it is an eroded setting if no 1963–64 setting had the same program. Erosion and accretion refer only to occurrence or nonoccurrence in 1954–55 and 1963–64; the intervening years are omitted from these determinations. These are, therefore, cruder measures than those involved in the commonality categories.

TOWN POPULATION

The habitat attributes we have described are stable, inherent properties of behavior settings; they are maintained by homeostatic control systems in accordance with the programs of the settings. A general, town-wide habitat attribute that is not inherent in the behavior settings of a town, but is nonetheless relatively stable over long periods, is the population of the town. Whatever the programs of a town's behavior settings may be, they are constrained by the town's population, for it is from this population that the settings draw their human components. The total population of a town (and of its tributary district and region) is, therefore, of special importance, for it is a measure of the human components available for the town's behavior settings.

Inhabitants per centiurb of habitat (population/centiurbs) is a fundamental town-wide habitat property; it is an inverse measure of each inhabitant's share of the resources of the town. Inhabitants per habitat-claim for operatives is an inverse measure of each inhabitant's share of the operational and maintenance tasks.

DIFFERENTIAL HABITATS

The behavior settings of a town with any stated attribute (such as action pattern Aesthetics prominent, Local Autonomy high, authority system Private Enterprises) can be selected for analysis, and this is done in many cases. The selected settings are called *differential habitats* with an appropriate identification: primary aesthetic habitat, high autonomy habitat, private enterprise habitat, etc. A genotype is present within a differential habitat if the habitat includes one or more settings with the genotype program; the extent and output of the genotypes within the habitat are determined solely by the extent and output of these particular behavior settings. Thus, the towns' primary educational habitats embrace the genotype Business Meetings, but only very few of the business-meeting settings of the towns are concerned primarily with education.

Behavior Output of Habitats

DESCRIBING BEHAVIOR OUTPUT

We have pointed out earlier in this chapter that particular kinds of molar actions occur only in particular behavior settings, and that this fact provides a basis for determining the habitat resources of a town for stated molar actions. Contrariwise, behavior settings with particular habitat resources inevitably produce behavior appropriate to the resources; this is the case because the inhabitants of a behavior setting have two positions within it. On the one hand, they are habitat components: they are parts of the machinery of the setting, functioning according to its programs of operation. On the other hand, they are persons, each with his unique perceptions and intentions. This dichotomous, incommensurate condition is discussed in some detail in Chapter 7. But we can state here that it provides the basis for the fact that the habitat attributes of a behavior setting describe its behavior output, too. If District Court Sessions, Barbershops, Dentists' Offices, Cricket Games, and Latin

Classes are present in a town, sentencing-to-jail, hair-cutting, tooth-filling, cricket-playing, and Latin-teaching inevitably occur. If the action pattern Religion is an attribute of the standing pattern of a behavior setting, religious actions are among the actions of its inhabitants (in the same way, a factory with facilities and a program for manufacturing phosphate fertilizer actually produces phosphate fertilizer when it is in operation). However, the habitat characteristics of a behavior setting where the action pattern Religion is present (and of the facilities and program of a phosphate factory) do not reveal the amount of output of religious actions (or of phosphate fertilizer); they reveal only the pro-grammed kind of output. The amount of output is a function of the amount and nature of the input—of the human components, in the case of behavior settings.

MEASURING BEHAVIOR OUTPUT

We present five measures of behavior output in the various anal-yses: person-hours (P-H), inhabitant-setting intersections (ISI), claim-operations (C-O), leader acts (LA), and leaders (L). We report such a variety of output measures because in some cases they measure the same phenomena with different degrees of precision via different operations, thereby providing checks on the findings; in other cases, they measure different output phenomena. However, not all measures are appropriate for all differential habitats, and we have not obtained all measures for all the habitats for which they are appropriate. The out-put measures reported, therefore, vary greatly among the differential habitats.

Person-hours of behavior (P-H). The inhabitants of a behavior set-ting act continuously in accordance with its standing pattern; therefore, the sum of the times all inhabitants spend in it is a measure of the amount of behavior with the attributes of its standing pattern. This sum for a survey year is the *person-hours* of behavior it produces. This is the most comprehensive measure we have used to determine the amounts of behavior generated by the total and the differential habitats of Mid-west and Yoredale. *Examples:* In Midwest in 1963–64, the 830 inhabi-tants inhabited the town's public behavior settings for 1,125,134 hours. This time can be partitioned among classes of inhabitants (children, adults, aged), among genotypes (Worship Services, Funerals), among authority systems (Private Enterprises, Schools), among action patterns (Religion, Education) for many analytical purposes. For example, 27,000 (2.4 percent) of the Midwest hours occur in behavior settings where the action pattern Religion is prominent—that is, the town's primary religious habitat. Of special importance for the analysis and presentation of the data are the person-hours of behavior generated via all inhabitants—that is, the gross behavior product of the town (GBP)—and the person-hours generated via the residents of the town, the town behavior product (TBP).

Inhabitant-setting intersections (ISI). An inhabitant-setting intersection consists of a unique combination of *a particular behavior setting* in any of its occurrences and *a specific human component* in any penetration zone of the setting during one or more of its occurrences. If Jane White attends the Midwest Presbyterian Worship Service once during 1963–64, this is one ISI; if she attends the Methodist Church Worship Service 30 times during the year, this is also one ISI. The ISI of a behavior setting is the number of different persons via which it generates behavior during all of its occurrences in a year. The ISI of Yoredale's Middle Juniors Academic Class in 1963–64 is, for example, 30 — that is, the number of persons, 3, who filled the position of teacher during the year, plus the number of children, 27, in attendance for one or more days. For a town, or part of a town, the number of inhabitant-setting intersections is the sum of the ISI of all of its behavior settings; it is equivalent, for example, to the number of class enrollments in a school. ISI is a less precise, operationally independent measure of the output phenomena measured by P-H. Whereas the ISI output measures for Midwest's Presbyterian and Methodist Worship Services via Jane White are both one, the P-H output measures are 1 for the Presbyterian Worship Service and 30 for the Methodist Worship Service.

ISI are important in this research because, although cruder measures of behavior output than P-H, they are secured independently. P-H are determined from records and observations of each occurrence of a behavior setting in the survey year, whereas ISI are determined from records, observations, and reports of informants for all occurrences of a behavior setting in a survey year.

Claim-operations (C-O). A claim-operation is a special type of ISI; it is a unique combination of *a particular behavior setting, a specific habitat-claim in penetration zones 4 to 6* of the setting, and *a particular human component* implementing the claim. Table 2.5 gives some examples from

Table 2.5
Examples of Claim-Operations in Midwest

Behavior Setting	Habitat-Claim	Human Component	Claim-Operation
English Class	Position of Teacher	Jane White	English Teacher White teaching
Saddle Club Organization Meeting	Position of Secretary	Jane White	Saddle Club Secretary White recording
Saddle Club Organization Meeting	Chairmanship	George Smith	Saddle Club Chairman Smith chairmaning
Presbyterian Church Worship Service	Pastorate	George Smith	Presbyterian Pastor Smith preaching
Presbyterian Church Worship Service	Pastorate	Walter Jones	Presbyterian Pastor Jones preaching

Midwest. Claim-operations such as these keep the towns habitable for shoppers, pupils, golfers, taxpayers, diners, etc.; they implement the programs of behavior settings and maintain their milieux; claim-operations are crucial for the continuance of the towns as human habitats. The number of claim-operations is a measure of the essential operations a town's habitat requires of its human components; it includes the actions of both leaders and functionaries. In psychological language, number of claim-operations is a measure of the responsible, important, and difficult actions a town's inhabitants perform in the process of operating and maintaining the settings of the town as a human habitat. Claim-operations implement habitat-claims in all *operating* zones of behavior settings: in zones of single leaderships (zone 6; for instance, bank presidencies), in the zones of multiple leaderships (zone 5, for instance, joint proprietorship of stores), and in the zone of factorships (zone 4, for instance, office clerkships). They occur only in the program and maintenance circuits of behavior settings.

Leader acts (*LA*). In terms of implemented habitat-claims, a town's output of leader acts consists of its claim-leader actions, its claim-factor actions in executive settings, and its claim-member actions in executive settings. Executive settings are behavior settings which control other settings; some examples are Yoredale Rural District Council Meetings and Midwest Presbyterian Church Session Meetings. The number of leader acts of a town is the sum of all the instances (*a*) of George Smith filling Presbyterian Worship Service pulpit, (*b*) of Adam White serving as City Council member, (*c*) of Jane White serving as English Class teacher, (*d*) of Walter Jones filling Presbyterian Worship Service pulpit, (*e*) of Joseph Baker acting as Bethel Service Station manager, (*f*) of George Smith officiating as Saddle Club Meeting chairman, (*g*) of Jane White carrying out duties of Bridge Club hostess, etc. These implemented habitat-claims guide at the highest levels of responsibility the operation and maintenance of the town as a human habitat.

Leaders (*L*). A leader is an inhabitant who during a year implements one or more of its behavior setting leaderships (single or multiple), executive-setting factorships, or executive setting memberships. *Examples:* Miss Broxman is proprietress of Broxman Confectioner and Stationer Shop in Yoredale; she implements one leadership and is one leader. Mr. Snaith is proprietor of Snaith Photograph Studio and Shop; he is President of the Camera Club Meetings and Chairman of the Liberal Party Society Committee Meetings; he implements three leaderships and is another leader. Mrs. Tucker is a member of the Yoredale Rural District Council; she implements one executive-setting membership and is another leader. Our data are limited to town inhabitants who are leaders—that is, to town leaders. To secure data on change in leadership, we have identified all town leaders in 1963–64 who continue to lead the same settings in 1967–68, and we have identified all behavior settings with the same town leaders in the two years.

Statistical Issues

The data of this research are not samples of the towns' components; they are complete enumerations. Our primary statistical treatment is, therefore, with indicator statistics rather than inferential statistics. When we report that 6.4 cu of Midwest habitat are located in the town's churches in 1954–55 and 12.2 cu are located in them in 1963–64, we do not *infer* that Midwest's church-connected environment is larger in 1963–64, we state that (as operationally defined, and within the limits of our measurement procedures) it *is* larger in 1963–64: 5.8 cu larger. And because the centiurb index of extent is based upon complete enumerations of the town's behavior settings (converted to percentages of a common base), it provides a ratio size scale; Midwest's church-connected habitat is 1.9 times as large in 1963–64 as in 1954–55.

Because we do not treat Midwest and Yoredale as samples of larger populations of behavior settings, we do not report probabilities that the findings hold for a larger universe of settings. The generalization of our findings to other American and English towns is an empirical problem. Even if statistical tests of significance could be legitimately made, it would leave untouched our chief concern with the eco-behavioral significance of the actual habitat differences between Midwest and Yoredale and between 1954–55 and 1963–64, whether or not they are of wider generality. Russian roulette with a single bullet in a six-chamber gun may give the player only a one-sixth chance of death on a single play, but if that chance occurs, his death is as complete as if the gun held six bullets. We are concerned, here, in the first place, with occurrences and their consequences, whether likely or unlikely, general or limited in extent.

Field Methods

The data reported have been secured by a variety of methods that are described in detail elsewhere (Barker, 1968; Barker and Wright, 1955, 1971). The following methodological notes are intended to provide the reader with a general orientation regarding methods.

The information required for the identification of behavior settings is obtained: (*a*) from maps and reports by field workers of the physical structures of the community (for example, walled, fenced, and otherwise bounded areas) that are potential loci of behavior settings; (*b*) from newspaper reports, telephone and other classified directories, school schedules, organization programs, church bulletins, placards, etc., that announce setting-like occurrences; (*c*) from informants selected for their knowledge of particular community areas; and (*d*) from observations by field workers. These sources provide the data that analysts use in making the judgments which identify a town's behavior settings in terms of their defining structural and dynamic attributes. Using such data, independent analysts identify a town's behavior settings with an acceptable degree of agreement.

Data on the frequencies and schedules of occurrence and the duration of behavior settings are readily available: posted on the doors of business establishments; announced in newspapers, bulletins, programs, etc.; reported by informants. So far as the public settings we have studied are concerned, this is public information.

The number of inhabitants of many settings, and the age and sex of the inhabitants, are recorded in precise form in school, Sunday school, and organization records. These data for less formal settings are obtained by field workers attending settings and counting the inhabitants; this is done for commercial, sport, and governmental settings, for example. Data on the penetration zones of behavior settings and on the inhabitants of the zones come from records and from observations by field workers.

The action pattern, behavior mechanism, attendance and beneficence qualities of behavior settings are ratings by field workers based upon their direct observations of the settings and on data from informants.

The local autonomy of behavior settings and the authority systems to which they belong are determined on the basis of direct observation and information provided by operatives in response to questions as to where decisions are made and who exercises authority.

Research of the kind reported here has a number of methodological advantages. Behavior settings are relatively permanent and can usually be observed and assessed repeatedly by different field workers; they are known to numbers of informants who provide independent reports. All the data reported have been independently checked and rechecked. To these advantages may be added those of a permanent field station with a number of long-time staff members well informed about the community and with archives of verified community data.

Complete behavior setting surveys were made in the 2 survey years, September through August 1954–55, and September through August 1963–64; the towns were kept under general observation in the intervening years, with two-month periods of field work in 1957 and 1960, so that we know if a behavior setting or a genotype occurs at intervals between the surveys, thus making it possible to say if the settings that occur during the survey years are stable or intermittent parts of the towns' habitats. In addition, some special studies of leaders were made in 1967–68 for comparison with 1963–64 data.

The 1963–64 data are most complete; hence the presentation focuses upon them.

The behavior setting genotype Public Toilets and Lavatories has not been included in any of the analyses.

Formats and Conventions

The great amount and variety of data available have made it necessary to report them in terms of a number of arbitrary formats and conventions.

TABULAR AND NARRATIVE PRESENTATIONS

All data relevant to an issue are reported in the tables, but the narrative exposition focuses upon the data that are of most general significance. These are often the 1963–64 data, for they are the most complete. In any case, all data mentioned in the text are clearly identified by table number (T), row number (R), and column number (C). For example, the tabular location of the data on the towns' extents in centiurbs is (T3.1, R4; C3,4). The parenthesis indicates that the data referred to can be found in Table 3.1, row 4, columns 3 and 4, respectively. Other data relevant to habitat extent in centiurbs are reported in the table.

Some data presented in the text involve manipulation of the tabular values; the values and manipulations are indicated thus: (*a*) (T5.16; R10/11; C1): the number in row 10 is divided by the number in row 11, Table 5.16, column 1. (*b*) (T3.4; R3; C4−2): the number in column 2 is subtracted from the number in column 4, Table 3.4, row 3. (*c*) (T3.4; R1/1 + 4 + 6; C4): the number in row 1 is divided by the sum of the numbers in rows 1, 4, and 6, Table 3.4, column 4. (*d*) (T3.4; R1; C3/T5.1; R8; C3): the number in Table 3.4, row 1, column 3, is divided by the number in Table 5.1, row 8, column 3. (*e*) [T3.2; 100 − (R1; C1)]: the number in row 1, column 1, is subtracted from 100, Table 3.2.

All values in the tables except the frequency counts (of behavior settings, habitat-claims, genotypes, person-hours, claim-operations, leader acts, and leaders) are rounded from the more precise values of the computer printouts. The degree of rounding varies across types of data in accordance with the magnitudes of the values involved, the analyses to be made with them, and our judgment of the legitimate degree of precision in view of the accuracy of the data. All textual comparisons involving differences and ratios between Midwest and Yoredale and between 1954–55 and 1963–64 are computed from the table values.

Separate *sections* of the chapters are devoted to specified classes of data (action patterns, behavior mechanisms, and so forth), and separate *parts* of the sections deal with particular data (for example, with the action pattern Aesthetics). In the interest of efficiency, most tables of the parts have identical formats, so that the tabular locations of most data mentioned in the text can be identified in one part only. This part is the one that deals with Aesthetics; the table citations within it provide a key to the location of the data of all other parts.

The headings of the text are self-explanatory in most cases, though explication of a few may be in order.

Salient findings. Section parts are introduced by brief paragraphs giving the general purport of the data to be reported in detail. Perusal of such paragraphs, therefore, provides a synopsis of the results of the whole research; the locations of the salient findings are given in the index.

Special features. Unique aspects of the phenomena covered by the section parts are presented under this heading; the common key to table locations does not apply to these parts.

Graphic summaries. Sections of the chapters are terminated with graphic representations of crucial data across all variables covered in the section. These provide another précis of the trends of the findings; their locations are given in the index.

Appendices. The habitat phenomena we have isolated and then described and measured in terms of the concepts and procedures presented in this chapter are identified in the appendices. In Appendix A, each of the Midwest behavior setting genotypes occurring *in either survey year* is identified by number and name, and a brief description of its program is given. The description is followed by the extent in centiurbs of the 1963–64 genotypes and by a listing of all the behavior settings which occurred *in the 1963–64 survey.* Appendix B shows comparable data for Yoredale.

In some ways, these are the most basic data presented in this report. The genotype catalogues provide the most detailed descriptions of the towns as human habitats, and the behavior setting lists specify the particular habitat entities that comprise the genotypes in 1963–64. The lists demonstrate important features of the phenomena we have investigated: that behavior settings have time-space loci, that they are particular entities; and that they are not samples of the towns' habitats, they comprise the towns' entire habitats.

PART II

*In this part we describe
the habitats the two towns provide their inhabitants by means of the concepts and
procedures presented in Part One. Detailed data are presented on the extent and
variety of the towns' total habitats (Chapters 3 and 4) and of classes of behavior
settings possessing a wide range of habitat qualities in specified degrees (Chapters
5 and 6). This part of the book is analogous to the section of an ecological study
of a prairie region that reports soil conditions, such as surface texture, permeabil-
ity, loam content, and acidity, within the entire region and within specified
subregions. Some of our "soil conditions" are local autonomy, aesthetic content,
and control by churches. We chose these qualities on the assumption that they are
important in shaping the behavior and development of inhabitants. In our analyses of the data we emphasize quantitative differences between Midwest and
Yoredale and changes between 1954–55 and 1963–64. In the final chapter of
this part, we discuss implications of differences in the towns' habitats for the
behavior and the experiences of their inhabitants in terms of behavior setting
theory.*

MIDWEST AND YOREDALE
AS HUMAN HABITATS

CHAPTER 3

Size of the Towns

We report the size of the towns as human habitats in terms of centiurbs, habitat-claims for operatives, and human components. Behavior outputs are reported in Chapter 8.

Centiurbs of Habitat

SALIENT FINDINGS

The towns were equal in size in 1954–55; Midwest's habitat was smaller than Yoredale's in 1963–64, and it was less stable in the decade between the survey years.

CENTIURB MEASURES

The towns' habitats were 95 to 113 cu in extent during the two survey years (T3.1; R4; C1b to 4b). These measures gain significance when converted into a variety of equivalencies: for example, Midwest's 107 cu of habitat in 1963–64 (T3.1; R4; C3[b]) is equivalent to 86 settings that occur every day of the year for 24 hours a day, such as Trafficways and 24-hour Restaurants (standard behavior settings); to 2140 settings that occur once a year for a single hour, such as Boy Scout Installation and Playing Fields Committee Annual Meeting (the smallest measured settings); and to 1244 settings that occur each week for one hour, such as Methodist Church Worship Services. (These conversions are made by the procedures exemplified in Table 2.3.)

Differences. Midwest and Yoredale were the same size in 1954–55;

in 1963–64 Midwest was 6 cu smaller than Yoredale (T3.1; R4; C3-4), amounting to 95 percent as much habitat (T3.1; R4; C3/4).

People familiar with both towns in 1963–64 report that on short acquaintance Midwest appears to be smaller, relative to Yoredale, than the data indicate. This impression arises because *regularly recurring* behavior settings (measured by settings per hour) contribute less to Midwest's than to Yoredale's habitat by a factor of 0.87 (T3.1; R3; C3b/4b), whereas *occasional* behavior settings (measured by settings per year) contribute more to Midwest's than to Yoredale's habitat by a factor of 1.17 (T3.1; R1; C3b/4b). On an average day in 1963–64, there were 146 behavior settings at hand in Midwest and 178 at hand in Yoredale (T3.1; R2; C3a, 4a). However, over the following weeks and months more new behavior settings were added in Midwest than in Yoredale: approximately 61 per month in Midwest, and approximately 48 per month in Yoredale. (These estimates are based upon the data of Table 3.1. They are computed for Midwest in 1963–64 as follows: Of the town's yearly total of 884 behavior settings, the daily mean occurrence is 146 settings; this leaves 738 settings to be introduced during the twelve directly ensuing months at a mean rate of sixty-one behavior settings per month.) Over a three-month period there are 329 different behavior settings in Midwest and 322 in Yoredale, and month by month Midwest's excess increases until at the end of the year it generates 884 behavior settings and Yoredale generates 758 settings. These habitat arrangements—whereby a smaller number and proportion of Midwest's than of Yoredale's behavior settings are at hand by the day and hour and a greater number and proportion take place tomorrow or later in the year for fewer occurrences—require more long-time plans and arrangements and more long-continued actions by Midwesterners than by Dalesmen. In 1963–64 the temporally most distant habitat constituted 40 percent of Midwest's and 33 percent of Yoredale's habitat [T3.1; R1/(1 + 2 + 3); C3b, 4b].

Table 3.1

Habitat Extent in Terms of Behavior Settings and Centiurbs

	1954–55				1963–64			
	Midwest		Yoredale		Midwest		Yoredale	
	No. (1a)	%[a] (1b)	No. (2a)	%[a] (2b)	No. (3a)	%[a] (3b)	No. (4a)	%[a] (4b)
(1) Behavior Settings per Year	576	85	504	74	884	130	758	111
(2) Mean BS per Day	136	90	144	95	146	97	178	118
(3) Mean BS per Hour	32.4	95	34.3	101	32.6	95	37.2	109
(4) Extent in Centiurbs (mean of rows 1, 2, 3)		90		90		107		113

[a] Percentage of standard town.

Changes. Both habitats were larger in 1963–64 than in 1954–55. Midwest was 17 cu larger in 1963–64 (T3.1; R4; C3-1), amounting to 119 percent as much habitat (T3.1; R4; C3/1); and Yoredale was 23 cu larger (T3.1; R4; C4-2), amounting to 125 percent as much habitat (T3.1; R4; C4/2).

HABITAT STABILITY

The increases in the towns' habitats are not due simply to the addition of new behavior settings. The 884 settings which constituted Midwest's habitat in 1963–64 were not the 576 settings present in 1954–55 plus 308 others added between the survey years. Some of the original 576 settings were terminated (*eroded*), some were continued (*conserved*), and some new behavior settings were initiated (*accreted*) in the interval. By these processes communities decline, grow, and change in character.

Accretion was greater than erosion in both towns, hence the towns' increments in habitat extent. Approximately one-third of Midwest's and one-quarter of Yoredale's 1954–55 habitats were eroded between the survey years (T3.2; R1; C1, 2), and roughly two-fifths of the 1963–64 habitats of both towns were accreted between the survey years (T3.2; R5; Cl, 2).

Both erosion and accretion were greater in Midwest than in Yoredale: 10 percent more of Midwest's 1954–55 habitat was eroded (T3.2; R1; C1-2), and 6 percent more of its 1963–64 habitat was accreted (T3.2; R5; C1-2). Thus, habitat turnover between 1955 and 1963 was greater in Midwest, and Midwest's stable, continuing habitat was smaller than Yoredale's; 65 percent of Midwest's 1954–55 habitat

Table 3.2
Habitat Stability: Erosion and Accretion

	Midwest (1)	Yoredale (2)
Erosion		
Percentage of 1954–55 habitat eroded before 1963–64		
(1) Centiurbs	35	25
(2) Behavior Settings per Year	39	39
(3) BS per Day (mean)	35	21
(4) BS per Hour (mean)	32	18
Accretion		
Percentage of 1963–64 habitat accreted after 1954–55		
(5) Centiurbs	45	39
(6) BS per Year	57	60
(7) BS per Day	39	33
(8) BS per Hour	33	24

was conserved [T3.2; 100 − (R1;C1)], and it formed 55 percent of the town's 1963–64 habitat [T3.2; 100 − (R5; C1)]; 75 percent of Yoredale's 1954–55 habitat was conserved [T3.2; 100 − (R1; C2)], and it formed 61 percent of the town's 1963–64 habitat [T3.2; 100 − (R5; C2)].

The occasional habitats of both towns, such as the once-a-year Tinker Brothers Circus in Yoredale and the Implement Company Auction Sale in Midwest, are most subject to both erosion and accretion; there is greater stability among the regular behavior settings that function on many days for many hours. However, there is an important difference between the towns in these respects. Equal percentages of the occasional settings were eroded (T3.2; R2; C1, 2), and almost equal percentages were accreted (T3.2; R6; C1, 2); but 32 percent of Midwest's most regular settings and 18 percent of Yoredale's regular settings were eroded (T3.2; R4; C1, 2), and 33 percent of Midwest's most regular 1963–1964 settings and 24 percent of Yoredale's behavior settings were accreted (T3.2; R8; C1, 2). Yoredale's greater overall habitat conservation occurs primarily in connection with its day-in-day-out habitat; Midwest's regular habitat is more subject to both erosion and accretion than is Yoredale's.

Habitat-Claims for Operatives

SALIENT FINDINGS

The towns' habitats are highly dependent upon human components for their operation and maintenance. An average centiurb of Midwest's habitat—for example, its 20 Cultural Meetings and its 16 Parties in 1963–64—has 96 habitat-claims for operatives (chairmen, hostesses, entertainers, cooks, speakers); and an average centiurb of Yoredale's habitat—such as its 17 Cultural Meetings and its 21 Parties in 1963–64—has 69 slots requiring human components. Midwest has more positions of responsibility than does Yoredale, and both towns had more in 1963–64 than in 1954–55.

HABITAT-CLAIM MEASURES

The towns had 4123 to 10,220 habitat-claims for operatives in 1954–55 and 1963–64. These are the number of slots that require human components to make the towns' public habitats operational in accordance with their prescribed programs. If all the behavior settings of the two towns were to occur simultaneously in 1963–64, it would require 10,220 persons to operate and maintain Midwest's habitat, and 7764 persons to operate and maintain Yoredale's habitat (T3.3; R1; C3, 4). In fact, however, the essential personnel is not so great, for the irregular stop-and-start occurrence of behavior settings and the multiple behavior setting programs of some inhabitants mean that they can implement a number of habitat-claims; for example, Midwest's Jane White is the human component of two habitat-claims for operatives: English teacher and Saddle Club recording secretary.

Table 3.3
Habitat-Claims for Operatives

	1954–55		1963–64	
	Midwest (1)	Yoredale (2)	Midwest (3)	Yoredale (4)
(1) Total Number	5360	4123	10,220	7764
(2) Number per/cu of Habitat	60	46	96	69
(3) Number per Town Inhabitant	7.5	3.2	12.3	5.9

There are 96 and 69 habitat-claims for operatives per centiurb of Midwest's and Yoredale's habitats, respectively (T3.3; R2; C3, 4). But this number varies greatly across genotypes. The genotype Barbershops has 2.6 claims for operatives per centiurb in Midwest and 5.4 in Yoredale, whereas the genotype Programs of Choral Music has 1800 and 1200 claims for operatives per centiurb in Midwest and Yoredale, respectively.

Differences. Midwest has more claims for operatives than Yoredale in 1963–64 it had 2456 more claims (T3.3; R1; C3-4), amounting to 132 percent as many in all (T3.3; R1; C3/4), to 138 percent as many per cu of habitat (T3.3; R2; C3/4), and to 208 percent as many per town inhabitant (T3.3; R3; C3/4).

Changes. Both towns had more claims for operatives in 1963–64. Midwest had 4860 more claims in 1963–64 (T3.3; R1; C3-1), amounting to 191 percent as many (T3.3; R1; C3/1), to 160 percent as many per cu (T3.3; R2; C3/1), and to 164 percent as many per town inhabitant (T3.3; R3; C3/1). Yoredale had 3641 more claims in 1963–64 (T3.3; R1; C4-2), amounting to 188 percent as many (T3.3; R1; C4/2), to 150 percent as many per cu (T3.3; R2; C4/2), and to 184 percent as many per town inhabitant (T3.3; R3; C4/2).

Human Habitat Components

SALIENT FINDINGS

Midwest has fewer human components than Yoredale does; it has fewer in all, fewer per cu of habitat, and fewer per claim for operatives.

COMPONENT MEASURES

Midwest and Yoredale are small towns; they had 715 to 1310 permanent inhabitants in the two survey years (T3.4; R1; C1 to 4). These permanent inhabitants are the most available human components for the public habitats; there are in addition visitors and commuters, an overwhelming proportion of whom are residents of the districts and regions immediately surrounding the towns.

Most permanent inhabitants are occupants of penetration zone 0 of most behavior settings – that is, almost all Midwesterners and Dalesmen are recipients of forces from all behavior settings, at least to the extent that they are aware of the settings and of their general attributes. We assume that the town residents for whom this is not true amount to essentially the same proportion of the population in both towns. We have therefore based measures of amount of interaction between behavior settings and human components upon these approximately known populations. We know less well how many residents of the districts and regions surrounding the towns are in fact aware of the town settings.

Differences. Midwest has fewer human components than Yoredale; in 1963–64 it had 480 fewer town inhabitants (T3.4; R1; C3-4), amounting to 63 percent as many (T3.4; R1; C3/4), to 67 percent as many per cu (T3.4; R2; C3/4), and to 47 percent as many per claim for operatives (T3.4; R3; C3/4). Midwest's population inferiority was still greater in the surrounding districts and regions (T3.4; R4 to 7; C3/4); and it was of the same order in 1954–55 as in 1963–64 (T3.4; R1 to 7; C1/2).

Changes. Midwest had more human components in 1963–64 than in 1954–55, whereas Yoredale's population was essentially unchanged. Midwest had 115 more town inhabitants in 1963–64 (T3.4; R1; C3-1), amounting to 116 percent as many (T3.4; R1; C3/1), to 99 percent as many per cu (T3.4; R2; C3/1), and to 61 percent as many per claim (T3.4; R3; C3/1). Yoredale had 10 more town inhabitants in 1963–64 (T3.4; R1; C4-2), amounting to 101 percent as many (T3.4; R1; C4/2), to 81 percent as many per cu (T3.4; R2; C4/2), and to 55 percent as many per claim (T3.4; R3; C4/2). Increases in the populations of both towns' surrounding districts and regions were small (T3.4; R4, 6, 7; C1-3, 2-4).

Table 3.4
Human Habitat Components

	1954–55		1963–64	
	Midwest (1)	Yoredale (2)	Midwest (3)	Yoredale (4)
Town Inhabitants				
(1) Total No.	715	1300	830	1310
Mean No.				
(2) per cu	7.9	14.4	7.8	11.6
(3) per claim for operatives	0.13	0.31	0.08	0.17
Inhabitants of Town and District[a]				
(4) Total No.	1615	3800	1680	4000
(5) Mean No. per cu	17.9	42.2	15.7	35.4
Inhabitants of Town, District, and Region[b]				
(6) Total No.	5000	15,000	6000	17,000
(7) Mean No. per cu	55.6	166.7	56.1	150.4

[a] Within a four-mile radius of the town (estimated from governmental census figures).
[b] Within a ten-mile radius of the town (estimated from governmental census figures).

SUMMARY

The data show that Midwest has fewer inhabitants than Yoredale to implement a greater number of habitat-claims for operatives. Midwest's habitat calls for more proprietors, secretaries, choir members, teachers, court reporters, chairmen, janitors, team members, bandsmen, organists, waitresses, speakers, election officials, bus drivers, bookkeepers, umpires, salesmen, mechanics, librarians, and so on, yet it has a smaller pool of inhabitants from which to draw them.

From the habitat viewpoint, Midwest is less efficient than Yoredale in its use of human components; it requires more human implementation for its operation and maintenance. Midwest's Methodist Choir has approximately 11 positions (claims for choir operatives) regularly filled at worship services, whereas Yoredale's Methodist Choir has about 4 such positions. In 1963–64 each cu of Midwest's habitat had, on the average, 138 percent as many claims for operatives as each cu of Yoredale's habitat (T3.3; R2; C3/4).

From the human component viewpoint, Midwest involves its inhabitants in more important and difficult operations than Yoredale does, and at the same time it confronts its inhabitants more frequently with the inevitable difficulties and breakdowns that occur in the course of such operations. The difference between the towns in this respect is not small; in 1963–64 the mean number of habitat-claims for operatives per Midwesterner was more than twice that per Dalesman — 12.3 and 5.9 (T3.3; R3; C3/4). It must be remembered that habitat claim is the property of a behavior setting that may occur on one or a number of days in the year. In fact, the mean numbers of occurrences of behavior settings in 1963–64 were 60.4 in Midwest and 86.0 in Yoredale; hence there were 743 *occurrences* of claims for operatives per Midwesterner and 507 per Dalesman. Town inhabitants do not implement all the claims — commuters and other visitors from nearby implement many of them — but within the total pools of potential operatives, Midwesterners constitute a greater proportion (14 percent) than do Dalesmen (8 percent). Thus there are relatively fewer other persons with whom Midwesterners share the opportunities and burdens of manning behavior settings. Consequences of these habitat differences for the inhabitants are reported in Chapters 7 and 8. Here the important findings are that Midwest's public habitat contains more claims for operatives than Yoredale's does, and that Midwest has fewer human components to implement them.

CHAPTER 4

Variety Within the Towns

The data on the extents of the towns' habitats say nothing about their variety. In this respect the habitat data are like the rainfall data for the regions; Midwest's and Yoredale's precipitation, like their habitats, are similar in amount, but the forms of the precipitation—as snow, sleet, hail, light rain, heavy rain, rain with wind—are quite different. Midwest has less snow and sleet, more hail, and many more heavy downpours with wind. We turn next to an exploration of habitat variety within the towns, which we have measured by number of behavior-setting genotypes.

Amount of Habitat Variety

SALIENT FINDINGS

The amount of habitat variety within the two towns was similar in 1954–55 but increased more in Yoredale between the survey years, so that in 1963–64 Midwest had less habitat variety than Yoredale did.

VARIETY MEASURES

There were 168 to 213 genotypes in the two towns (T4.1; R1; C1 to 4). These are the numbers of standing behavior setting patterns whose programs are not interchangeable. There are no common standards for judging the significances of these measures of habitat diversity; we shall therefore place them in contexts that impart some wider meanings to them.

64

Table 4.1
Behavior Setting Genotypes

	1954–55		1963–64	
	MW (1)	YD (2)	MW (3)	YD (4)
(1) No. of Genotypes	171	168	198	213

We shall consider them first in the context of an unlikely application. If the towns and their inhabitants were completely destroyed, the genotype data would inform those responsible for reconstituting the towns as they existed as human habitats in 1963–64 that 198 and 213 skilled experts would be required as advisors: an attorney, a band conductor, a banker, a barber, a dentist, a fire chief, a librarian, a pastor, a printer, a shorthand teacher, a speech therapist, a veterinarian, an x-ray technician, and so forth. In this respect the undertaking would be extensive and expensive; the habitats of the towns are so differentiated and specialized that it is beyond the capacity of even the most capable and versatile person to master more than a small portion of the towns' genotype programs.

The next context for the data is a fantasy of the future. If future antiquarians establish folk museums to recreate the variety of living conditions in the public parts of two small rural twentieth-century towns, our genotype data will assist them. They will learn that 198 animated dioramas are required to reconstitute the range of one town's 1963–64 environment, and that 213 are needed to represent the other town. If the exhibits are arranged alphabetically and placed wall-to-wall along one side of a corridor, the Midwest Museum will begin with an Abstract and Title Company Office; next to it will be an Agricultural Advisor's Office; an Agronomy Class will come next; and other exhibits will follow in order, as the genotypes are listed in Appendix A, until # 220 X-ray Mobile Laboratory, is reached. To produce one occurrence of the Abstract and Title Company genotype will require 10 hours of museum time; the Agricultural Advisor's Office will continue for 8 hours, and the Agronomy Class 1.5 hours; the Self-Service Laundry exhibit will operate 24 hours a day. A museum visitor who wishes to view a complete occurrence of each Midwest genotype will have to devote 1447 hours to the task. To provide the human components for a simultaneous display of all the environments of Midwest, the museum will require a staff of 5959 persons. The Yoredale Museum will have 15 more dioramas than the Midwest Museum; the time to view all its genotype occurrences will be 1536 hours, and the staff to man the displays will call for 8681 people.

By bringing together all the genotypes of the towns simultaneously, the extent of environmental variation within the towns will be even more evident to the museum visitors than to the present-day inhabitants, who cannot view all behavior-setting genotypes on a single occasion. After viewing 198, or 213, different genotype exhibits, the museum visitors will probably wish these ancient towns had not been so varied (as do the present inhabitants when their versatility is taxed by the many different behaviors the genotypes require). And if the visitors are informed that the panorama of genotypes before them occurred among a total of 884 behavior settings in Midwest and 758 in Yoredale, the impression of relatively rich diversity will undoubtedly be enhanced.

The extent of the towns' diversity on a great number of dimensions will be shown by the displays. A park and an x-ray laboratory, an organ concert and a machine shop, a worship service and a service station, will be seen to differ widely on many behavior-milieu dimensions: size, spatial and temporal patterning, materials, technologies, action patterns, behavior mechanisms. And it will be clear that the environments of the towns generated behavior differing widely in verbal and motor skills, muscular strength, visual acuity, and intelligence.

If the visitors are informed that 830 Midwest residents and 1310 Yoredale residents provided 47 percent and 36 percent, respectively, of the human components of the environments on display, environments that require museum staffs of 5959 and 8681 when all genotypes function simultaneously, the visitors will surely conclude that living conditions are varied for the inhabitants of Midwest and Yoredale and that they had to be versatile people.

Differences. Midwest and Yoredale had almost the same amount of habitat variety in 1954–55; Midwest's habitat was less varied than Yoredale's in 1963–64, when it had 15 fewer genotypes (T4.1; R1; C3–4), amounting to 93 percent as much variety (T4.1; R1; C3/4). These data indicate that Midwesterners visiting Yoredale in 1963–64 would have found a somewhat wider range of habitat variety and therefore somewhat greater variety of molar behavior opportunities than Dalesmen visiting Midwest would have found. However, compared with some other attributes of the towns, habitat variety is relatively similar within them. For example: There is much more racial variety in Midwest, where there are American Indians, Negroes, and Caucasians, than in Yoredale, where there are only Caucasians. Air temperature is more varied in Midwest—ranging in most years from −5° to 100° Fahrenheit—than in Yoredale, where 15° to 75° is usual. On the other hand, types of passenger vehicles are much more varied in Yoredale—where mini-cars, Rolls Royces, limousines, double-deck buses, three-wheel sedans, mo-ped cycles, and luxury coaches are regularly present—than in Midwest, where almost the only passenger vehicles are standard American cars and buses and Japanese motorcycles. In view of the many such differences, the similarity of the towns in number of genotypes is noteworthy.

Changes. The towns' habitats were more varied in 1963–64 than in 1954–55. Midwest had 27 more genotypes in 1963–64 (T4.1; R1; C3-1), amounting to 116 percent as much variety (T4.1; R1; C3/1); and Yoredale had 45 more genotypes (T4.1; R1; C4-2), amounting to 127 percent as much variety (T4.1; R1; C4/2). These data show that both towns provided their inhabitants with substantially wider ranges of behavior opportunities in 1963–64 than in 1954–55 and that habitat variety increased less in Midwest than in Yoredale.

Nature of Habitat Variety

SALIENT FINDINGS

The habitats of both Midwest and Yoredale consist of many small genotypes, none dominating either town, and many genotypes are fully common to the two towns.

VARIETIES OF HABITAT

A behavior setting genotype identifies a micro-range of habitat; a catalogue of the genotypes of a town defines its total range of habitat and behavior opportunities and requirements. Genotype catalogues of Midwest and Yoredale for the two survey years are presented in Appendices A and B. Each genotype is identified by name and number, a synopsis of its program for the inhabitants of its different penetration zones is given, and the behavior settings it embraces and its 1963–64 extent in cu are reported. The synopses of the genotype programs are obtained from such sources as dictionaries and handbooks of vocations and occupations, rulebooks of games, and manuals of procedures modified in accordance with observed local practices. The genotype catalogues provide an overview of the varieties of habitats within the towns. A stranger to one of the towns who had mastered its genotype programs would be "at home" in the town on arrival. Readers who are not familiar with the towns will find it essential to refer to the catalogues for descriptions of particular genotypes mentioned in the text.

A study of the extents of the towns' genotypes shows that no genotypes are dominant in the sense that their behavior settings extend over appreciable portions of the towns. Only one genotype, Business Meetings, encompasses more than 3.5 cu (3.2 percent) of Midwest's habitat in both years; and a single genotype, Grocery Stores, encompasses more than 4.5 cu (3.8 percent) of Yoredale's habitat in both years. The least extensive genotypes, involving only one occurrence of one behavior setting, cover 0.05 cu of the towns' habitats. Genotypes between 0.05 and 0.49 cu in extent make up 62 to 69 percent of the towns' genotypes, and genotypes over 2.5 cu in extent constitute 2.4 to 3.5 percent of the towns' genotypes. The environments of Midwest and Yoredale consist of many small genotypes, none covering as much as 5.5 percent of a town.

SIMILARITY OF HABITATS

It is theoretically possible that while the towns have similar amounts of habitat variety, none of Midwest's behavior setting genotypes are identical and few are similar to Yoredale's genotypes. The question is: How much of the towns' habitats is within the various geno-

Table 4.2
Behavior-Setting Genotypes of Midwest and Yoredale
of Different Degrees of Commonality
Percentage of town's genotypes (V%) and extent of town's habitat
in centiurbs (cu) in stated commonality categories

Commonality Category	1954–55				1963–64				Mean of 4 town-years[a]	
	MW		YD		MW		YD			
	(1)	(2)	(3)	(4)	(5)	(6)	(7)	(8)	(9)	(10)
	V%	cu	V%	cu	V%	cu	V%	cu	V%	cu[b]
(1) 1	38	48	39	47	33	55	31	57	35	52
(2) 2a	4	3	4	3	13	7.5	12	9		
(3) 2b	12	3	9	3	4	2.5	6	3		
(4) 2(a&b)	16	6	13	6	17	10	18	12	16	8.5
(5) 3	15	12	15	14	15	12	17	15	15.5	13
(6) 4a	5	5	2	2	4	6	3	4		
(7) 4b	6	5	8	10	6	5	7	10		
(8) 4c	5	4	2	1	4	4	1	1		
(9) 4(a,b,c)	16	14	12	13	14	15	11	15	13	14
(10) 5	4	3	5	2	5	3	5	3	5	3
(11) 6	5	5	10	5	10	9	13	6	9.5	6
(12) 7	7	2	7	3	7	4	6	4	7	3

[a] The evidence for consolidating the data of the seven main commonality categories across the towns and years as reported in Table 4.2 and Figure 4.1 is Kendall's Coefficient of Concordance, W. Both for centiurbs and for proportion of genotypes, W is .74, p < .01.

[b] The total mean habitat extent for the four town-years is 100 cu (from Table 3.1); hence the mean habitat extents, in centiurbs of the commonality categories, are also percentages of total mean habitat extent.

type commonality categories? For example, what percentage of each town occurs in genotypes common to both towns (category 1), and what percentage occurs in genotypes unique to each town (category 7)? These data are reported in detail in Table 4.2; they are summarized in Figure 4.1.

About one-third of the genotypes (T4.2; R1; C9) and one-half of the habitats (T4.2; R1; C10) are interchangeable between the towns in both years (category 1). Midwest residents visiting Yoredale, and vice versa, would find about 1 in 3 of the town's genotypes, and about 1 in 2 of the behavior settings at hand for inhabiting, so familiar that they could enter into the ongoing programs at all levels of penetration with little difficulty. Probably the greatest significance of the data on habitat similarity is their indication that half of the public environments of Midwest and Yoredale are regularly common to the towns.

The genotypes that occur in both towns *at some time* during the period 1954–55 to 1963–64 (categories 1 *and* 2) amount to approximately half of the genotypes of the towns (T4.2; R1 + 4; C9), and their settings cover over three-fifths of the towns' habitats (T4.2; R1 + 4; C10). When we add behavior settings with programs that are common to the towns, though differently distributed across genotypes in some cases (category 3), we find that two-thirds of the towns' genotypes (T4.2;

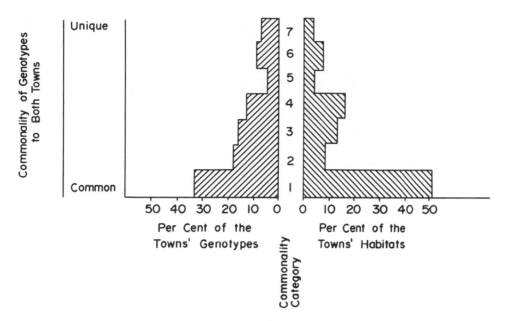

FIGURE 4.1. Percentage ot Towns' Behavior Setting Genotypes and Habitats in Genotype Commonality Categories.

R1 + 4 + 5; C9), and almost three-quarters of their habitats (T4.2; R1 + 4 + 5; C10), have programs with common elements.

At the other end of the similarity series, the fully unique genotypes of category 7—those that occur only in one town and not in the other town or its surrounding rural district or neighboring cities—comprise about 7 percent of each towns' genotypes and about 3 percent of its habitat (T4.2; R12; C9, 10). The fully common genotypes of category 1 are greater in extent than the fully unique genotypes of category 7 by a factor of 17.

It is evident that the habitats of Midwest and Yoredale have a high degree of equivalence. However, the common genotypes of the towns are not identical. In judging equivalence via the transposability of operatives, there is a 24 percent time allowance for adapting to the programs of the fully equivalent settings of category 1. This margin is allowed primarily to provide time for coping with different inputs, but also for adjusting to minor differences in programs—such as driving on the left instead of the right side of the road, in the case of Trafficways, and in the case of Grocery Stores, computing in pounds, shillings, and pence rather than in dollars and cents. Included in the minor program differences are some that are obvious and impressive to visitors, and some may be significant for behavior. We turn next, therefore, to a closer inspection of the common habitats of Midwest and Yoredale.

Common habitats. The genotypes that occur in both towns in both years (commonality category 1) are listed in Table 4.3 with their extents in centiurbs; they are described in the Appendices. These genotypes are of utmost importance; they identify the common ground of the towns. It is behavior settings of these genotypes that would make Midwesterners feel "at home" in Yoredale, and Dalesmen "at home" in Midwest; they act year after year via auction sales, dances, elementary school classes, libraries, parades, plays and programs, Scout meetings, worship services, and so forth, to form the behavior of the towns' inhabitants into whatever common patterns they display.

We have seen that the common habitat extends over about half of each town. However, there remains the possibility that the extents of particular common genotypes are different in the two towns. The data of Table 4.3 bear upon this possibility. Inspection shows that the extents of only 5 of the 65 common genotypes differ in Midwest in both years from those in Yoredale by 1.0 cu or more: Clothiers and Dry Goods Stores, Grocery Stores, and Hotels are more extensive in Yoredale; Business Meetings and Religion Classes are more extensive in Midwest. Of the 130 Midwest-Yoredale differences in extents of common genotypes, 88 percent are less than 1.0 cu; the greatest difference is 3.95 cu. These data make it clear that the common genotypes are very similar in extent in the two towns.

A rapid inspection of the common genotypes shows that they are not severely limited with respect to their attributes; there are recreational, educational, and governmental genotypes, and those under the aegis of schools, churches, and government agencies. Detailed analyses of the towns' common habitats are reported in connection with particular behavior setting attributes in Chapters 5 and 6; but even here it is clear that the common genotypes do not have restricted programs.

We conclude that about half of the public habitats of both Midwest and Yoredale are so similar that their standing patterns, programs, and operatives are fully interchangeable between the towns in both years, and that the extents of the pairs of common genotypes within the towns are very similar.

Distinctive habitats. The habitats that are not common to the towns in either survey year (categories 3 to 7) comprise those that are to some degree distinctive to the towns. They range from habitats with common behavior setting programs that are, however, differently distributed among the settings and genotypes of the two towns (category 3) to habitats completely unique to one town (category 7). These are the parts of the towns' habitats that stand out and are noted by exchange visitors between the towns. They comprise about half of the towns' genotypes and about two-fifths of their habitats.

Unique habitats. We turn to a consideration of the genotypes that are most different. Genotypes of commonality categories 6 and 7 identify, and their programs describe, behavior settings whose programs occur in one town but not in the other town or the rural district surrounding it. We have selected for inspection from these peculiarly Midwest and Yoredale genotypes those which occur in both survey years. Whereas the genotypes of category 1 constitute the *consistently*

Table 4.3
Behavior-Setting Genotypes Common to Midwest and Yoredale
in 1954–55 and 1963–64 (Category 1) and Their Extents in Centiurbs

| | Extent (cu) | | | |
| | 1954–55 | | 1963–64 | |
Genotype	MW	YD	MW	YD
Auction Sales, Household Furn., & Genl. Merch.	0.05	0.05	0.10	0.10
Award Ceremonies	0.15	0.05	0.15	0.10
Barbershops (Mens Hairdressers)	0.85	0.89	0.77	0.56
Beauty Shops (Ladies Hairdressers)	0.50	1.01	0.60	1.41
Building, Construct'n, & Repair Serv.	1.64	1.19	2.00	1.41
Bus Stops	0.18	0.77	0.43	1.19
Card Parties	0.59	0.71	0.46	0.26
Cemeteries	0.38	0.28	0.45	1.24
Classrooms, Freetime	1.34	0.88	2.53	2.64
Clothiers & Dry Goods Stores	0.60	2.40	0.57	2.69
Dances	0.34	0.09	0.20	0.16
Delivery & Collect'n Routes	1.76	1.64	1.36	1.14
Dentists Serv.	0.38	0.58	0.40	0.60
Dinners & Banquets	0.25	0.10	0.66	0.11
Dinners w/Dances	0.05	0.10	0.05	0.70
Dinners w/Recreat'n and Cult'l progs.	0.60	0.55	0.80	0.70
Elections, Polling Places	0.20	0.10	0.20	0.15
Elem. School Basic Classes	2.02	1.51	2.99	1.92
Excurs'ns & Sightsee'g Trips	0.40	0.37	0.76	1.39
Fire Alarms & Fire-fighting	0.06	0.05	0.11	0.07
Fire Stations	0.41	0.10	0.40	0.09
Food & Rummage Sales (Jumble)	0.35	0.15	0.35	0.40
Funeral Servs., Church	0.16	0.21	0.16	0.16
Garages	1.23	1.46	1.21	1.94
Grocery Stores	3.21	4.97	1.33	5.28
Hallways	1.56	1.94	1.67	1.82
Hardware Stores	0.58	0.93	1.03	0.93
Home Econ. Classes	0.32	0.07	0.42	0.06
Home Econ. Compets. & Exhibs	0.05	0.15	0.10	0.20
Hotels	1.71	2.96	0.94	2.32
Installat'n & Induct'n Ceremonies	0.20	0.05	0.15	0.05
Insur. Offices & Sales Routes	1.31	0.81	0.78	1.23
Jewelry Stores	0.30	0.46	0.47	0.48
Libraries	0.47	0.28	0.53	0.59
Lodge Meetings	0.27	0.06	0.46	0.05
Machinery Repair Shops	2.96	0.77	0.91	0.98
Meetings, Business	3.57	2.53	5.63	2.84
Meetings, Cultural	0.71	0.34	1.09	0.95
Meetings, Discussion	0.05	0.05	0.61	0.11
Meetings, Social	0.22	0.21	0.16	0.25
Moving Picture Shows	0.45	0.63	0.11	0.16
Music Classes, Instrum.	0.38	0.45	0.94	0.50
Music Classes, Vocal	0.89	0.50	1.13	1.39
Nursing Homes	0.68	0.74	0.68	0.76
Parades	0.20	0.10	0.36	0.10

Table 4.3 (*continued*)

Genotype	Extent (cu)			
	1954–55		1963–64	
	MW	YD	MW	YD
Parks & Playgrounds	1.68	2.11	1.28	1.48
Parties	0.89	0.60	0.91	1.05
Phys. Ed. Classes	0.27	0.42	1.78	1.68
Plays & Programs	0.98	0.65	1.45	0.64
Progs. of Choral Music	0.30	0.30	0.30	0.35
Receptions	0.05	0.10	0.10	0.20
Relig. Classes	1.95	0.73	3.26	0.96
Relig. Fellowship Meetings	0.77	0.52	0.56	0.11
Relig. Prayer & Medit'n Servs.	0.05	0.78	0.38	0.72
Relig. Worship Servs.	0.92	1.77	1.55	1.54
Restaurants	2.51	1.44	2.98	2.37
Scout Meetings	0.21	0.18	0.48	0.08
Sewing & Dressmak'g Classes	0.21	0.37	0.16	0.48
Sewing Club Meetings	0.07	0.14	0.16	0.05
Solicitat'ns of Funds	0.43	0.65	0.52	0.65
Street Fairs	0.05	0.11	0.10	0.10
Trafficways	1.25	1.25	1.25	1.08
Wallpaper'g & Paint'g Serv.	0.17	0.15	0.17	1.34
Weddings, Church	0.10	0.20	0.10	0.15
Weddings, Civil	0.06	0.07	0.05	0.06
Total	47.53	46.79	54.70	57.29
Percentage of Town	52.90%	52.00%	51.00%	50.77%

common genotypes of the towns, the genotypes we have selected from categories 6 and 7 constitute the *consistently unique* genotypes of the towns, the stable core of genotypes that differentiate each town from the other in both years.

Midwest's 16 consistently unique genotypes (Table 4.4) encompass 5.5 cu (6.2 percent) of Midwest's habitat in 1954–55 and 6.5 cu (6.1 percent) in 1963–64. None of the unique genotypes covers as much as 1 cu of the town in both survey years. These data indicate that varieties of habitat that occur regularly and exclusively in Midwest and its surrounding district are minor parts of the town. Detailed information about Midwest's unique genotypes is given in Chapters 5 and 6 in connection with the analyses of the behavior setting attributes; however, it is of interest to note here that 7 of the 16 regularly unique Midwest genotypes are recreational: Baseball, Basketball, and American Football Games, Charivaris, Gift Showers, Ice Cream Socials, and Sales Promotion and Patron-Attracting Openings.

Yoredale's 22 unique genotypes (Table 4.5) encompass 10.1 cu (11.2 percent) of the town's 1954–55 habitat and 11.0 cu (9.8 percent) of its 1963–64 habitat. As in Midwest, none of the unique genotypes covers as much as 1 percent of the town in both years; and as in Midwest,

Table 4.4

Unique Genotypes: Midwest
Genotypes that occur in Midwest in both survey years but not
in Yoredale or in the rural regions neighboring to Yoredale
(Categories 6 and 7)

No.	Name	Midwest	
		Centiurb Size	
	Category 7	1954–55	1963–64
17	Baseball Games	0.26	0.85
18	Basketball Games	0.94	0.79
29	Charivaris	0.05	0.05
30	Chiropractors Offices	0.25	0.25
74	Football Games (American)	0.18	0.29
79	Gift Showers	0.10	0.16
93	Ice Cream Socials	0.05	0.10
142	Piano Recitals	0.05	0.10
166	Sales Prom. Openings	0.05	0.46
	Category 6		
47	Day Care Homes & Nurseries	0.16	0.77
62	Excavat'g Contract'g Servs.	0.56	0.51
75	Funeral Directors	0.14	0.16
98	Ironing Serv.	0.76	0.72
101	Judges Chambers	0.64	0.54
107	Latin Classes	0.19	0.25
109	Laundry Serv.	1.17	0.50
	Total cu	5.55	6.50
	Total Percent	6.17%	6.07%

too, a surprising number of the consistently unique genotypes are
recreational: Lawn Bowling, Cricket, Darts, Badminton, Chess, and Soccer Games, Dancing Classes, Sports Days, Stamp Club Meetings, Public
Bonfires, Betting Offices.

It will be noted that Midwest's unique habitat is smaller than
Yoredale's, consisting of 16 instead of 22 genotypes and encompassing
in 1963–64 6.1 instead of 9.8 percent of its habitat. Visitors to Midwest
from Yoredale would find the town less "foreign" than would visitors to
Yoredale from Midwest. About 1 in 16 of the behavior settings of
Midwest would be completely new to the visitors from Yoredale; this
would be true of about 1 in 10 of Yoredale's settings for visitors from
Midwest.

CHANGES IN NATURE OF HABITAT VARIETY

A genotype is lost when all behavior settings of the genotype are
eroded; a new genotype appears when one or more behavior settings of
a previously nonexistent genotype occur. Differential rates of genotype
erosion and accretion are processes by which the nature of a town's hab-

Table 4.5
Unique Genotypes: Yoredale
Genotypes that occur in Yoredale in both survey years but not
in Midwest or in the rural regions neighboring to Midwest
(Categories 6 and 7)

No.	Name	Yoredale	
		Centiurb Size	
	Category 7	1954–55	1963–64
12	Automobile Assn. Serv.	0.30	0.38
28	Bonfires, Public	0.05	0.05
30	Bowling Games (Lawn)	0.15	0.19
52	Commiss'n (Betting) Agents	0.96	1.37
58	Cricket Games	0.26	0.48
65	Darts Games	0.06	0.30
92	Fish & Chips Shops	0.95	0.41
129	Markets, Public	0.15	0.18
182	Sales Routes, Corsets	0.33	0.07
184	Sales Routes, Fish	0.10	0.10
	Category 6		
14	Badminton Games	0.29	0.21
39	Chess Games	0.11	0.22
40	Chimney & Window Repair Servs.	0.15	0.07
50	Coal Depot & Delivs.	0.92	0.69
64	Dancing Classes	0.06	0.20
95	Football Games (Soccer)	0.27	0.43
137	Military Train'g Classes	0.08	0.39
138	Milk Collect'n Depots	0.50	0.61
149	Nurses Serv.	0.16	0.21
204	Sports Days	0.05	0.10
208	Stamp Club Meetings	0.06	0.06
213	Taxis	0.81	0.79
	Total cu	10.08	11.04
	Total Percent	11.20%	9.77%

itat changes; this may result in renewal, adaptation, and increased vigor, or it may result in deterioration.

Midwest's eroded genotypes. Of Midwest's 1954–55 genotypes, 21 were not present in 1963–64; this amounts to 12 percent of the town's 1954–55 genotypes and 6.2 percent of its habitat.

Of the lost genotypes, 10 are judged to be manifestations of fundamental and widely ramifying changes in American culture and are almost certainly not reversible. The most crucial evidence of this is absence of local demand for their return; the town has provided substitutes, or the needs of the inhabitants have changed. The permanently eroded genotypes, which constitute 5.8 percent of Midwest's genotypes and 2.9 percent of its habitat, are listed below with their extents in centiurbs.

Identification Number	Midwest's Permanently Eroded Genotypes	Centiurbs
21	Book Exch. Serv.	0.05
23	Box Socials	0.05
31	Circuses	0.05
43	Cream Collect'n Stations	0.25
45	Dairy Barns	0.40
66	Farm Practices Classes	0.07
94	Ice Depots	0.24
95	Initiations	0.06
165	Rug Weaving Serv.	0.21
198	Telephone Exchs.	1.25

Five of these permanent losses stem from technical-economic changes: the erosion of Cream Collection Stations and Dairy Barns is a reflection of a revolution in the milk industry deriving from new processing and distributing techniques; Ice Depots succumbed to electric refrigeration; Telephone Exchanges yielded to the dial telephone; and Rug Weaving Services were killed by machine-made products and greater local affluence. Two other apparently irreversible losses were due, immediately, to changes in governmental policy, but they surely evidence basic social changes: Book Exchange Services (where used school books were bought and sold) ceased when a statewide policy of renting textbooks was introduced; and Farm Practices Classes ended when a special Federal program of on-the-farm training for World War II veterans was terminated. Circuses seem to have been lost to Midwest by economic pressures, transportation difficulties, competition of television, and mobility of the local population by automobile. We cannot guess the sources of two other apparently permanent genotype losses in Midwest: Box Socials and Initiations . There appear to be no technical, economic, or governmental reasons for the disappearance of settings of these genotypes. The initiation of High School Freshmen was officially banned by the school board; but this was a local action accepted by the community, as it undoubtedly would not have been in earlier years.

The lost genotype Physicians' Offices and Services requires special discussion. There are undoubtedly strong technical and economic forces acting to destroy this genotype in Midwest and other towns of its size. Because of them, it is becoming more and more difficult to secure zone 6 operatives. However, there are strong demands and continuing efforts by the inhabitants of Midwest to establish and maintain this habitat variety. In fact, during the period under consideration there was at various times a fully equipped doctor's office in Midwest, and three different physicians operated it for brief periods. There is clearly a balance of forces for and against the retention of this genotype; it is not impossible that technical-economic resistances to its revival may be overcome in Midwest. In this respect, Physicians' Offices and Services differs from Midwest's permanently lost genotypes; there is a steady demand for its return.

Organizational changes only, and not losses of behavior-setting programs, are involved in 4 genotype losses: Court Sessions, Justice of the Peace (incorporated into Court Sessions, County), School Custodians Rooms (incorporated into Hallways), Used Car Sales Lots (incorporated into Garages), and Seed Corn Storage and Sales Routes (incorporated into Animal Feed Mills).

The 6 remaining genotype losses are judged to be absent from Midwest in 1963–64 for local, adventitious reasons, and seem likely to return in the future. They are: Agricultural Economics Classes, Horse Shows, Lotteries, Shoe Repair Shops, Upholstering Services, and Veterinary Services.

Yoredale's eroded genotypes. Of Yoredale's 1954–55 genotypes 17 were not present in 1963–64; this amounts to 10 percent of the town's 1954–55 genotypes and 4.1 percent of its habitat.

We judge that 6 of the lost genotypes are permanent erosions of Yoredale's environment; they constitute 3.6 percent of the town's genotypes and 2.2 percent of its 1954–55 habitat:

Identification Number	Yoredale's Permanently Eroded Genotypes	Centiurbs
23	Beetle Drives	0.05
24	Bicycle Runs	0.12
101	Garden Allotments	0.38
102	Gasworks	0.68
172	Railway Maintenance Shops	0.50
199	Slaughterhouses	0.25

Three of these permanent losses are clearly resultants of technical-economic changes: Gasworks (local production of gas from coal is no longer efficient), Railway Maintenance Shops (greatly reduced traffic on the Yoredale line), and Slaughter houses (central meat processing more economical than by local plants). Two other permanent losses appear to be secondary consequences of the general change in English technology and economics: Bicycle Runs succumbed to the more crowded highways and to the greater affluence of Yoredale inhabitants, who have substituted motorcycles and automobiles for bicycles; Garden Allotments lost out to a greater supply of vegetables in the market and more money to purchase them. We have no clues to the apparently permanent loss of the genotype Beetle Drives. As with Box Socials and Initiations in Midwest, the demise of Beetle Drives in Yoredale appears to express a change in recreational taste of obscure origins.

One of Yoredale's genotype losses involves an organizational change only, and not a loss of behavior-setting programs: TV and Radio Appliance Services is incorporated as part of the genotype Electrical Appliance and Service Companies.

The 10 remaining losses to the environment of Yoredale are, we judge, due to local, adventitious, temporary conditions; the inhabitants

of the town appear ready to take advantage of the opportunities these
genotypes provide when their settings are reestablished: Beauty Culture
Classes, Coach Agents' Offices, Dinners with Business Meetings, Elections–Party Headquarters, Hikes and Camps, Knitting Services, Sewing
Services, Social Science Classes, Solicitation of Goods, Trips by Organizations to Visit the Sick.

Midwest's accreted genotypes. In Midwest in 1963–64 there were 48
genotypes not present in 1954–55, amounting to 24 percent of the
town's 1963–64 genotypes and 12.1 percent of its habitat. It is not possible to divide the new genotypes into temporary and permanent additions; however, 21 of the 48 result from the reorganization of behavior
settings: They occurred in 1954–55 as subordinate, nonspecialized parts
of settings of other genotypes. The remaining 27 genotypes identify
habitat resources totally new to Midwest in 1963–64; they amount to 14
percent of the town's genotypes and 8 percent of its habitat. The new
genotypes are listed below, with their authority systems (indicated in the
parentheses), and their extents, in centiurbs:

Identification Number	Midwest's Totally New Genotypes	Centiurbs
11	Auditing & Investig. Co. Offices (PE)	0.46
22	Bowling Games, Ten Pins (PE)	2.02
34	Cleaners, Dry Cleaning Plants (PE)	0.51
64	Factory Assembly Shops (PE)	0.51
80	Golf Games (VA)	0.39
102	Kennels (PE)	0.65
103	Kindergarten Classes (VA)	0.13
108	Laundries, Self-Service (PE)	1.25
122	Motor Veh. Operators' Classes & Exams (G)	0.18
126	Music Competit'ns (S)	0.10
130	Optometrists Servs. (PE)	0.05
131	Painting Classes (VA)	0.08
150	Psychol. Serv. Offices (S)	0.31
151	Public Speaking & Drama Competit'ns (S)	0.10
163	Retarded Childrens Classes (VA)	0.08
164	Roller Skating Parties (Ch)	0.16
167	Sales Promotion Parties (PE)	0.05
169	Savings Stamp Sales Stands (S)	0.06
183	Sign-Painting Servs. (PE)	0.15
188	Speech Therapy Servs. (S)	0.15
196	Telephone Automatic Exch. Bldgs. (PE)	0.30
197	Telephone Booths (PE)	0.31
202	Tractor-Pulling Contests (VA)	0.05
211	Volleyball Games (S)	0.10
213	Water Supply Plants (G)	0.30
218	Welfare Workers Classes (G)	0.05
220	X-ray Labs. (G)	0.05

These are crucial growing points of Midwest; they identify habitat innovations. An obvious feature of the innovations is their wide scope; many broad categories of habitat variety are added. There are new habitat resources for recreation (for example, Bowling Games), for education (Kindergarten Classes), for personal services (Dry Cleaning Plants), for advanced technology (Telephone Automatic Exchanges), for mental health (Psychological Service Offices), for physical health (Optometrists' Services), for manufacturing (Factory Assembly Shops). Furthermore, the habitat innovations are under the aegis of all authority systems, with no single authority system predominant. The percentages of the new genotypes initiated by the authority systems are: Churches, 3.7 percent; Government Agencies, 14.8 percent; Private Enterprises, 40.7 percent; Schools, 22.2 percent; Voluntary Associations, 18.5 percent.

Yoredale's accreted genotypes. In Yoredale in 1963–64 there were 62 not present in 1954–55, amounting to 29 percent of the town's 1963–64 genotypes and 13.1 percent of its habitat. Of the 62 new genotypes 29 are due to reorganization of 1954–55 genotypes; the remaining 33 are entirely new molar behavior resources for Yoredale, amounting to 15.5 percent of the town's genotypes and 4.9 percent of its habitat. The new genotypes are listed below, with their authority systems (indicated in the parentheses) and their extents, in centiurbs:

Identification Number	Yoredale's Totally New Genotypes	Centiurbs
4	Agronomy Classes (S)	0.12
5	Animal Husbandry Classes (S)	0.05
20	Basket-Making Classes (S)	0.06
29	Bookbinding Classes (S)	0.14
41	China-Painting Classes (S)	0.14
60	Cross-Country Running Competit'ns (S)	0.15
72	Dog Shows (VA)	0.06
74	Educatnl. Methods Classes (Ch)	0.05
75	Egg-Packing Plants (PE)	0.50
89	Fire Drills (S)	0.05
91	First Aid Classes & Demonstrat'ns (VA)	0.23
94	Football (Rugby) Games (S)	0.25
97	French Classes (S)	0.15
104	German Classes (S)	0.07
112	Hockey Games (S)	0.15
115	Horse Races (VA)	0.05
126	Locker & Shower Rooms (S)	0.63
135	Metalwork Classes (S)	0.28
136	Military Communicat'ns Exhibs. and Demonstrat'ns (S)	0.05
140	Motor Veh. Operators Classes (GA)	0.05
148	Newspapers, School (S)	0.07
183	Sales Routes, Cosmetics & Household Suppls. (PE)	0.23
189	School Monitors' (Prefects') headqtrs. (S)	0.29
191	Science Classes (S)	0.42
198	Shorthand Classes (S)	0.15
206	Stage Makeup Classes (S)	0.06

207	Stamp Club Exhibit'ns (S)	0.05
210	Swimming Classes (S)	0.34
211	Swimming Competit'ns (S)	0.05
214	Technical Drawing Classes (S)	0.15
222	Typing Classes (S)	0.10
223	Upholster'g Classes (S)	0.14
225	Vocational Counsel'g Servs. (S)	0.25

Yoredale's habitat innovations are less broadly based than Midwest's; the percentages of the new genotypes initiated by the authority systems are: Churches, 3.0 percent; Government Agencies, 3.0 percent; Private Enterprises, 6.1 percent; Schools, 78.8 percent; Voluntary Associations, 9.1 percent. It is clear that Yoredale's Schools are the main source of its habitat innovations; in this respect Yoredale differs greatly from Midwest, where the main sources of habitat innovation are Private Enterprises. Aside from the new genotypes originating in the School authority system, there were only 7 entirely new genotypes in Yoredale, whereas in Midwest there were 20 nonschool genotype innovations.

Qualities of the Towns as Habitats I

Action Pattern and Behavior Mechanism Habitats

In this chapter we describe Midwest and Yoredale in terms of two classes of habitat qualities: action patterns (such as Aesthetics, Business) and behavior mechanisms (such as Gross Motor Activities, Manipulation). Measures of three dimensions of these qualities are reported: *extent* (centiurbs of habitat), *human component requirements* (number of habitat-claims for operatives), and *variety* (number of genotypes).

Those parts of the towns with specified qualities comprise their *differential habitats.* For example, the behavior settings of Midwest with prominent educational components (textbooks, pupils, teachers) make up its primary educational habitat—a differential habitat that comprised 15.4 percent of Midwest's total habitat in 1963–64. We present in this chapter reports on the dimensions of 15 differential habitats. Each report has these eight sections: Definition, Salient Findings, Territorial Range, Extent, Claims for Operatives, Variety, Nature of the Differential Habitat, and Control by Authority Systems. In addition, some reports include sections on the Genotype Sites of Change and Special

Features, including data on Local Autonomy. It should be clearly understood that these differential habitats are not mutually exclusive; for example, some settings with recreational qualities (for instance, Darts Games) have nutritional qualities as well (in this case, ale).

The behavior outputs of the differential habitats are reported in Chapters 9, 10, and 12; the reader who wishes to peruse the complete account of a differential habitat serially can do so by referring to these chapters.

This chapter is presented in two parts, one dealing with action patterns and one with behavior mechanisms. Each part ends with graphic and narrative summaries; some readers may wish to refer to these before reading the separate reports. The graphic summaries consist of pairs of curves representing for Midwest and Yoredale the extents and changes in extent of the differential habitats. In each case the habitats are ordered on the ordinate by their increasing extent in Midwest. The curves do not represent continuous functional relationships; they are *diagrams* representing the extents of discrete habitat qualities. They are presented in this form, and ordered by their extents in Midwest, because in these ways differences between the towns and changes between the years are more clearly revealed than by other representations, such as bar diagrams and a constant, arbitrary order.

The first report, on the action pattern Aesthetics, serves as a model for the others; in it the tabular locations of the data are identified. Data loci are not repeated in the subsequent reports with formats (including tables) that are identical with the format of the first report. The report on Aesthetics, therefore, provides a key to the tabular location of the data of subsequent reports.

ACTION PATTERN HABITATS

We have investigated 11 action pattern qualities of the towns' habitats: Aesthetics, Business, Education, Government, Nutrition, Personal Appearance, Physical Health, Professional Involvement, Recreation, Religion, and Social Contact. Our data bear upon such issues as the degree to which Midwest and Yoredale differ in habitat resources for the occurrence of actions directed toward particular classes of goals—in the case of Physical Health, for example, habitat resources for actions toward goals related to the maintenance and improvement of health. Posing this particular issue implies that towns that differ in resources (such as Physicians' Offices, Physical Education Classes, Nurses' Offices and Services) for health-directed actions are indeed different living places for humans and that they have different behavior consequences.

None of the action pattern habitats specify particular behavior mechanisms for engaging in the appropriate molar actions; aesthetic goals, for example, may be achieved via the skilled hand movements and dulled auditory awareness of a member of a knitting class, or they may be achieved via the relaxed hands and alert ears of a guest at a choral concert. Furthermore, data regarding the extents of action pattern habitats imply nothing directly as to the amount of behavior that occurs within them. Habitat extent and habitat productivity are measured independently; the relationship between them is an empirical question in the beginning, and ultimately it raises theoretical issues.

Summaries of the data for action pattern habitats are presented in Figures 5.1 to 5.5.

Aesthetics

DEFINITION

The action pattern Aesthetics is present within a behavior setting to the extent that the concrete occurrences which constitute the program of the setting make the environment more beautiful, as this is locally defined. Aesthetic occurrences may take any form: providing artistic objects and events, removing the unbeautiful, supplying materials for aesthetic behavior, evaluating and appreciating aesthetic behavior and accomplishments, teaching and learning aesthetic behavior. These are the defining attributes of the action pattern Aesthetics.

Aesthetics is *prominent* in a behavior setting if most of its standing pattern enhances beauty via occurrences with one or more of the defining attributes stated above. For example, in most behavior settings of the genotype Religious Worship Services, Aesthetics is prominent because virtually all components of the setting (the design and decoration of the sanctuary and its furnishings, the music, the ceremonies, the language) contribute to its beauty, in addition to providing a suitable space, behavior objects, and program for religious behavior (prayer, study, praise, contemplation). Aesthetics is *secondary* within a setting if some, but less than 80 percent of the standing pattern, enhances beauty; this is true, for example, of a restaurant with pictures on the wall and flowers on the tables. Aesthetics is *absent* from a setting if no components of the standing pattern *regularly* enhance beauty; this is true of most machine shops and of some business meetings.

The behavior settings where Aesthetics is prominent constitute a town's *primary aesthetic habitat* (PAH)—that is, its primary habitat resources for aesthetic behavior. Settings where Aesthetics is prominent *or* secondary comprise the *territorial range* of Aesthetics.

Basic data for Aesthetics are presented in Table 5.1.

SALIENT FINDINGS

The territorial range of Aesthetics extends over about two-thirds to three-quarters of the towns' habitats. Habitats where resources for aesthetic behavior are prominent (PAH) comprise 5 to 7 percent of the total habitats. Midwest's PAH is smaller than Yoredale's, and the PAH of both towns was larger in 1963–64 than in 1954–55. Positions of aesthetic responsibility—that is, habitat-claims for operatives within the towns' PAHs—constitute 18 to 24 percent of the towns' total claims for operatives; Midwest has more claims for aesthetic operatives than Yoredale. The towns have similar amounts of aesthetic variety, and variety increased in both towns between the survey years.

TERRITORIAL RANGE OF AESTHETICS

Aesthetic action patterns are regularly present in some degree in about two-thirds to three-quarters of the towns' habitats (T5.1; R14; C1 to 4); conversely, approximately one-quarter to one-third of the towns' habitats are without aesthetic components. The TR of Aesthetics extends over fewer centiurbs (T5.1; R13; C1–2, 3–4) and a smaller percentage (T5.1; R14; C1–2, 3–4) of Midwest's than of Yoredale's habitat; it increased in extent in both towns between 1954–55 and 1963–64 (T5.1; R13, 14; C1–3, 2–4).

EXTENT OF PRIMARY AESTHETIC HABITAT

In 1963–64 the PAH covered 5 percent of Midwest's and 7.1 percent of Yoredale's total habitat (T5.1; R5; C3,4). This is approximately equivalent in Midwest to 100 nonrecurring, two-hour behavior settings—that is, to a twice-weekly series of one-night-stand concerts, plays, and exhibits [(T5.1; R4; C3)/0.05 (computed from T2.3)]—and in Yoredale to 150 such settings—that is, to a thrice-weekly music, drama, and art series.

Differences. Midwest's PAH is smaller than Yoredale's; in 1963–64 Midwest had 2.7 fewer cu of PAH (T5.1; R4; C3–4), amounting to 66 percent as many cu (T5.1; R4; C3/4) and to 2.1 fewer percent of the town's total habitat (T5.1; R5; C3–4).

Table 5.1
Aesthetics
Basic Habitat Data

	1954–55		1963–64	
Primary Habitat (PAH)	MW (1)	YD (2)	MW (3)	YD (4)
Extent				
(1) Behavior Settings per Year	58	59	75	79
(2) Mean BS per Day	4.4	5.0	5.8	11.8
(3) Mean BS per Hour	0.4	0.6	0.4	1.5
(4) Centiurbs (no.)	4.2	4.6	5.3	8.0
(5) Centiurbs (% of Town Total)	4.7%	5.1%	5.0%	7.1%
Erosion and Accretion				
Type of Change	Erosion from '54–55		Accretion to '63–64	
(6) Centiurbs (no.)	1.5	1.9	2.2	4.3
(7) Centiurbs (% of PAH)	35%	41%	41%	54%
Claims for Operatives				
(8) Number	1,316	802	2,247	1,418
(9) Number (% of Town Total)	24%	19%	22%	18%
Amount of Variety				
(10) Major Genotypes (no.)	9	10	9	10
(11) Total Genotypes (no.)	22	18	27	27
(12) Total Genotypes (% of Town Total)	13%	11%	14%	13%
Territorial Range				
(13) Centiurbs (no.)	57.0	58.9	75.3	81.9
(14) Centiurbs (% of Town Total)	64%	65%	70%	73%

Changes. Both towns' PAHs were larger in 1963–64 than in 1954–55. Midwest had 1.1 more cu of PAH (T5.1; R4; C3–1) in 1963–64, amounting to 126 percent as many cu (T5.1; R4; C3/1) and to 0.3 more percent of the town's total habitat (T5.1; R5; C3–1). Yoredale had 3.4 more cu of PAH (T5.1; R4; C4–2), amounting to 174 percent as many cu (T5.1; R4; C4/2) and to 2.0 more percent of the town's total habitat (T5.1; R5; C4–2).

Processes of change. More than 34 percent of the towns' 1954–55 PAHs were eroded before 1963–64, and more than 40 percent of their 1963–64 PAHs were accreted after 1954–55 (T5.1; R7; C1, 2 and 3, 4). Both erosion and accretion were smaller in Midwest than in Yoredale; 6 fewer percent of Midwest's 1954–55 PAH was eroded (T5.1; R7; C1–2), and 13 fewer percent of its 1963–64 PAH was accreted (T5.1; R7; C3–4). The reverse is true for the towns' total habitats; more of Midwest's than of Yoredale's habitat was both eroded and accreted (T3.2; R1, 5; Cl, 2).

CLAIMS FOR OPERATIVES WITHIN PRIMARY
AESTHETIC HABITAT

If all behavior settings within the towns' PAHs were to function simultaneously in 1963–64, it would require 2247 persons in Midwest and 1418 persons in Yoredale to carry out essential operations (T5.1; R8; C3, 4); these are the numbers of claims for operatives (positions of responsibility) within the towns' PAHs. Claims for PAH operatives are much greater than claims for operatives in general, on a centiurb basis; there are 424 claims for operatives per cu of Midwest's PAH (T5.1; R8/4; C3), compared with 96 for the whole habitat (T3.3; R2; C3)—that is, 442 percent as many—and there are 177 per cu of Yoredale's PAH (T5.1; R8/4; C4), compared with 69 for the whole habitat (T3.3; R2; C4)—257 percent as many. In 1963–64 the PAHs contained 22 and 24 percent of the total habitat-claims for operatives (T5.1; R9; C3,4); whereas, as we have seen, they comprised only 5.0 and 7.1 percent of the towns' total habitats (T5.1; R5; C3,4). The towns' PAHs are rich in positions of responsibility.

Differences. Midwest has more habitat-claims for PAH operatives than Yoredale. In 1963–64 it had 829 more such claims than Yoredale (T5.1; R8; C3–4), amounting to 158 percent as many (T5.1; R8; C3/4), to 240 percent as many per cu of PAH [T5.1; (R8/4; C3)/(R8/4; C4)], to 250 percent as many per town inhabitant [(T5.1; R8; C3)/(T3.4; R1; C3) ÷ (T5.1; R8; C4)/(T3.4; R1; C4)], and to 4 more percent of the town's total claims for operatives (T5.1; R9; C3–4).

Changes. Both towns had more PAH claims for operatives in 1963–64 than in 1954–55. Midwest had 931 more such claims in 1963–64 (T5.1; R8; C3–1), amounting to 171 percent as many (T5.1; R8; C3/1), to 135 percent as many per cu of PAH [T5.1; (R8/4; C3)/(R8/4; C1)], and to 147 percent as many per town inhabitant [(T5.1; R8; C3)/(T3.4; R1; C3) ÷ (T5.1; R8; C1)/(T3.4; R1; C1)], but to 2 fewer percent of the town's total claims for operatives (T5.1; R9; C3–1).

Yoredale had 616 more such claims (T5.1; R8; C4–2), amounting to 177 percent as many (T5.1; R8; C4/2), to 102 percent as many per cu of PAH [T5.1; (R8/4; C4)/(R8/4; C2)], and to 175 percent as many per town inhabitant [(T5.1; R8; C4)/(T3.4; R1; C4) ÷ (T5.1; R8; C2)/(T3.4; R1; C2)], but to 1 fewer percent of the town's total claims (T5.1; R9; C4–2).

VARIETY WITHIN PRIMARY AESTHETIC HABITAT

There is more variety within the two towns' PAHs than expected on the basis of extent. In 1963–64 Midwest's PAH, only 5 percent of the town's total habitat, was the locus of 14 percent of its behavior-setting genotypes (T5.1; R5, 12; C3); and Yoredale's PAH, 7.1 percent of total habitat, was the locus of 13 percent of its genotypes (T5.1; R5, 12; C4).

If Midwest and Yoredale were to display simultaneously in 1963–64 the complete range of behavior setting programs within their PAHs, both would require 27 different halls and exhibit rooms with their appropriate facilities, 27 differently trained and experienced casts of performers and exhibitors, and 27 different experts as directors, teachers, and so forth (T5.1; R11; C3, 4).

Differences. The amount of variety within the two towns' PAHs is similar. In 1963–64 Midwest had the same number of genotypes as Yoredale (T5.1; R11; C3–4), amounting to 100 percent as many (T5.1; R11; C3/4) and to 1 more percent of Midwest's than of Yoredale's total genotypes (T5.1; R12; C3–4).

Changes. The aesthetic variety of the two towns was greater in 1963–64 than in 1954–55. Midwest had 5 more genotypes (T5.1; R11; C3–1), amounting to 123 percent as many (T5.1; R11; C3/1) and to 1 more percent of the town's total genotypes (T5.1; R12; C3–1). Yoredale had 9 more genotypes (T5.1; R11; C4–2), amounting to 150 percent as many (T5.1; R11; C4/2) and to 2 more percent of the town's total genotypes (T5.1; R12, C4–2).

NATURE, COMMONALITY, AND DISTINCTIVENESS OF
PRIMARY AESTHETIC HABITAT

The major aesthetic genotypes of the towns' PAHs have a high degree of commonality (Table 5.2). Of Midwest's 9 and Yoredale's 10 major aesthetic genotypes in 1963–64, 7 were both common (category 1) and major—that is, they comprised 3 or more percent of the aesthetic habitat in both survey years (T5.2; R16, 17, 18, 20, 22, 23, 25; C1 to 4). In addition, 3 genotypes were common in both years but they are not major aesthetic genotypes: Church Weddings, Home Economics Competitions, and Church Funeral Services. These 10 genotypes identify the stable, common aesthetic habitats of Midwest and Yoredale in 1963–64—that is, the habitats present in both towns since 1954–55. Their number and extent show that there is greater commonality within them than within the towns' total habitats. In 1963–64 common genotypes accounted for 37 percent of the aesthetic genotypes of both towns, compared with 33 percent commonality for Midwest's and 31 percent for Yoredale's total genotypes (T4.2; R1; C5, 7). In terms of centiurbs, these common aesthetic genotypes embraced 78 percent of Midwest's and 71 percent of Yoredale's PAH, compared with 55 percent and 57 percent commonality, respectively, for the towns' total habitats (computed from T4.2; R1; C6, 8).

The common aesthetic genotypes consist largely of the performing arts (with musical performances predominant), followed by dramatic programs, libraries, worship services, religious ceremonies, and home-decorating services.

Although common genotypes dominate the towns' PAHs, each town has its distinctive aesthetic resources, reported in Table 5.3. In Midwest there are occasions for honoring persons in attractive settings (T5.3; R1, 12, 13; C1) and for displaying aesthetic achievements (T5.3; R2, 14, 17, 18; C1); only two of Midwest's 9 distinctive aesthetic genotypes do not have one or the other of these attributes: Landscaping and Floriculture Classes, and Painting Classes (T5.3; R15, 16; C1). Yoredale's distinctive aesthetic genotypes predominantly provide training and materials for engaging in crafts and hobbies (T5.3; R3 to 7, 9 to 12; C2); only one differs: Excursions and Sightseeing Trips (T5.3; R8; C2).

GENOTYPE SITES OF CHANGE IN
PRIMARY AESTHETIC HABITAT

There were 6 major and minor genotype sites of substantial change in Midwest's PAH between the survey years; 5 were sites of sub-

Table 5.2
Aesthetics
Variety Within the Towns' Primary Aesthetic Habitats
Major Genotypes in at Least One Town in One Year

	Percent of PAH			
	1954–55		1963–64	
	MW (1)	YD (2)	MW (3)	YD (4)
(1) Antique Shops	0	10.1	0	5.5
(2) Art Classes, Genl.	0	0	1.5	3.6
(3) Funeral Servs., Church	3.8	4.5	3.0	2.0
(4) [a] Libraries	4.0	6.1	3.6	7.4
(5) [a] Music Classes, Instrum.	7.4	9.8	15.6	6.3
(6) [a] Music Classes, Vocal	21.1	9.3	21.1	17.4
(7) Photog. Suppl. & Servs.	0	0.8	0	6.7
(8) [a] Plays & Dram. Progs.	14.5	9.8	12.8	8.0
(9) Progs. of Band Music	1.5	0	4.1	0
(10) [a] Progs. of Choral Music	5.9	6.5	3.7	4.4
(11) [a] Relig. Worship Servs.	9.5	26.2	10.6	10.7
(12) Upholst. Servs.	9.1	0	0	0
(13) [a] Wallpaper & Paint Servs.	4.0	3.2	3.3	11.7
(14) Weddings, Church	2.4	4.4	1.9	1.9

[a] Major genotypes in both towns and both years that are also common to the towns (category 1).

Table 5.3
Aesthetics
Distinctive Genotypes of the Towns' Primary Aesthetic Habitats, 1963–64

Commonality Category[a]		Midwest (1)	Yoredale (2)
(1)	7	Gift Showers	None
(2)		Piano Recitals	
(3)	6	None	Art Classes, Genl.
(4)			Basket-Mak'g Classes
(5)			Bookbind'g Classes
(6)			China-Paint'g Classes
(7)			Dancing Classes
(8)			Excurs'ns & Sightsee'g Trips
(9)			Metalwork Classes
(10)	5	None	Antique Shop
(11)			Upholst. Classes
(12)	4	Grad. & Prom. Cerems.	Stage Makeup Classes
(13)		Memorial Servs.	
(14)	3	Fashion Shows	Photog. Suppl. & Serv.
(15)		Landscap'g & Floricult.Classes	
(16)		Painting Classes	
(17)		Progs. of Band Music	
(18)		Public Speak'g & Drama Compets.	

[a] Genotypes are ordered from those that are unique to each town and environs (category 7) to those whose programs occur in the other town, but as components of different genotypes (category 3).

stantial increment (T5.4; R1, 2, 3, 8, 9; C1) and 1 of substantial decrement (T5.4; R12; C1). The increments involve the performing arts, with music predominant. Comparison of Table 5.4 with Table 5.2 shows that these increments are of a piece with the town's major aesthetic genotypes of 1954–55—that is, Midwest's aesthetic resources enlarged, but changed little in content, between the survey years.

The story is different for Yoredale. There were 12 genotype sites of substantial change in Yoredale's PAH (T5.3; C2); 11 were sites of substantial increment and 1 of substantial decrement. Most of the increments were not represented among the town's major aesthetic genotypes of 1954–55; Yoredale's aesthetic resources enlarged and changed in content.

CONTROL BY AUTHORITY SYSTEMS

Authority systems differ greatly in the extent to which they control the PAHs of the two towns. In 1963–64 Government Agencies controlled 7.7 percent of Midwest's and 4.0 percent of Yoredale's PAH, whereas Schools controlled 43.4 percent of Midwest's and 40.1 percent of Yoredale's PAH (T5.5; R3,5; C3,4). Churches, Government Agencies, and Schools control more of Midwest's than of Yoredale's PAH; Private Enterprises and Voluntary Associations control less (T5.5; R2 to 6; C3, 4).

Table 5.4
Aesthetics
Genotype Sites of Substantial[a] Changes in Extents of Primary Aesthetic Habitats
Between 1954–55 and 1963–64

		Midwest (1)	Yoredale (2)
(1)		Music Compets.	Art Classes, Genl.
(2)		Art Classes, Genl.	Basket-Mak'g Classes
(3)		Public Speak'g & Drama Compets.	Bookbind'g Classes
(4)	New Sites		China-Paint'g Classes
(5)			Metalwork Classes
(6)			Stage Makeup Classes
(7)			Upholst. Classes
(8)		Music Classes, Instrum.	Libraries
(9)	Enlarged Sites	Music Classes, Vocal	Music Classes, Vocal
(10)			Photog. Suppl. & Servs.
(11)			Wallpaper & Paint Serv.
(12)	Eroded Sites	Upholst. Servs.	
(13)	Reduced Sites	None	Relig. Worship Servs.

[a] A substantial change in the extent of a genotype between 1954–55 and 1963–64 involves one of the following: (a) a new genotype (one that occurred in 1963–64 but did not occur or did not have a prominent rating for the action pattern in 1954–55); (b) a completely eroded genotype (one that occurred in 1954–55 but did not occur or did not have a prominent rating for the action pattern in 1963–64); (c) a genotype 0.25 cu or more larger in 1963–64; (d) a genotype 0.25 cu or more smaller in 1963–64.

Extent of control of the towns' PAHs by authority systems changed much less in Midwest than in Yoredale between the survey years; and whereas the rank order of the authority systems did not change in Midwest, it changed greatly in Yoredale. The Schools of Yoredale increased their control of PAH from 7.1 percent in 1954–55 to 40.1 percent in 1963–64 (T5.5; R5; C2, 4), and the rank order of Schools in amount of control changed from last to first. This is further evidence, in addition to the greater expansion and turnover of Yoredale's PAH, that there is great aesthetic ferment in Yoredale. And the data on authority system control show that the preeminent single locus of this ferment is in the town's schools. Between the survey years, a new secondary school to serve the town and the surrounding rural area was established. As a result of these differential changes, Midwest and Yoredale were more similar in the authority system sources of their aesthetic habitats in 1963–64 than they were in 1954–55. Some of the aesthetic innovations of Yoredale's new school are indicated by the genotype sites of substantial increase in Yoredale's PAH (T5.4); all of the new genotypes, as well as the enlarged Libraries and Music Classes, are within the School authority system.

SPECIAL FEATURES

Aesthetics and Personal Appearance. The action pattern Aesthetics does not tell the whole story of the towns' habitat resources for beauty,

Table 5.5
Aesthetics
Control of Primary Aesthetic Habitats by Authority Systems
Percent of primary aesthetic habitats controlled by different authority systems

		1954–55		1963–64	
		MW (1)	YD (2)	MW (3)	YD (4)
(1)	Extent of PAH in cu	4.2	4.6	5.3	8.0
Percent of PAH controlled by:					
(2)	Churches	31.2	44.4	26.6	20.6
(3)	Govt. Agencies	9.0	7.2	7.7	4.0
(4)	Private Enterprises	21.8	24.2	15.6	26.9
(5)	Schools	32.9	7.1	43.4	40.1
(6)	Voluntary Assocs.	5.1	17.1	6.7	8.3

for it does not include personal beauty via clothing, grooming, and adornment. When we add to the towns' PAHs those behavior settings where Personal Appearance is prominent, we obtain the data of Table 5.6. Habitats with primary resources for environmental *or* personal beauty comprise 7.5 to 12 percent of the towns' habitats (T5.6; R2; C1 to 4). In 1963–64, about 1 in 13 of the behavior settings at hand for Midwesterners, and about 1 in 8 of those at hand for Dalesmen were beauty-enhancing. Total beauty-enhancing resources were greater in Yoredale than in Midwest in both years (T5.6; R1; C2–1, 4–3); they were 158 percent as great in 1963–64 (T5.6; R1; C4/3). These resources increased in extent in both towns between 1954–55 and 1963–64 at about the same rate as the towns' total habitats; all beauty-enhancing resources of the towns constituted roughly the same percentages of their total habitats in both years (T5.6; R2; C3–1, 4–2).

Landscape and architecture. The towns' aesthetic habitats involve landscape and architecture in different ways. Yoredale's aesthetic superiority to Midwest rests to some degree upon its scenic landscape and the beauty of its architecture; both are inherited from past times, but they both instigate attention, appreciation, and maintenance from the present inhabitants, thus contributing to the aesthetic ratings of the behavior settings into which they are incorporated.

Some buildings in Yoredale and environs are so architecturally noteworthy, and some of the surrounding region is so attractive, that they are sources of economic strength via the tourists they attract. There are therefore both aesthetic and economic reasons for maintaining the town's settings in aesthetic harmony with the whole area. In fact, building ordinances establish aesthetic as well as health and safety standards for new and altered buildings. Midwest's heritage includes no buildings as aesthetically noteworthy as some of Yoredale's, and its surrounding landscape has fewer scenic features than that surrounding Yoredale. Midwest's PAH does not involve in any significant degree attention to, appreciation of, or maintenance of an aesthetic inheritance, or the establishment of new settings in harmony with it.

Table 5.6
Aesthetics and Personal Appearance
Extents of Primary Aesthetic and Personal Appearance
Habitats

| | Extents of All Beauty-Enhancing Habitats | | | |
| | 1954–55 | | 1963–64 | |
	MW (1)	YD (2)	MW (3)	YD (4)
(1) No. of cu	6.8	9.6	8.5	13.5
(2) Percent of habitat	7.5%	10.7%	7.9%	12.0%

The differences between the towns in these respects are illustrated by their parks. In both towns, parks are behavior settings with aesthetic ratings in the prominent or secondary range. The programs of Yoredale's parks involve the study, appreciation, and maintenance of long-established plantings of trees and shrubs, stone walls, and seats where the views are best; the creation of new parks and park programs is secondary. Midwest's park programs, on the other hand, primarily involve establishing rather than maintaining aesthetic settings: planning a park landscape, making the plantings, building the fences.

Whereas for the present inhabitants of Yoredale the *maintenance* of an inherited aesthetic milieu is dominant, for the present inhabitants of Midwest the *creation* of an aesthetic milieu is dominant. The standing patterns of many of Yoredale's aesthetic behavior settings appear to originate in their persisting milieux (solid buildings and walls, old plantings, unalterable hills and dales), whereas they appear to originate in the inhabitants of Midwest's aesthetic settings.

Autonomy. Aesthetic resources are entirely regional and local in Midwest; all of its PAH is controlled within the town and the surrounding rural region (High and Medium local autonomy). In contrast, 28 percent of Yoredale's PAH is under the aegis of more distant authorities (Low local autonomy).

Business

DEFINITION

The action pattern Business is present within a behavior setting to the extent that the concrete occurrences which constitute the program of the setting involve one or more of the following: exchanging goods, services, or privileges for money; supplying materials for buying and selling in other settings; evaluating and appreciating the values of business; learning and teaching how to buy and sell. It should be noted that paying and receiving wages are not components of Business; the action pattern Professional Involvement deals with these behavior setting attributes.

Business is *prominent* in a behavior setting if most of its standing pattern consists of occurrences with one or more of the defining attributes stated above. This is true, for example, of the genotypes Grocery Stores and Insurance Offices. However, if much of the standing pattern of a setting is far removed from the exchange transaction, Business is *not* prominent, even if payment is obligatory. Dinners and Banquets are examples; much of their standing patterns involve preparing and eating food, conversing, and presenting and listening to the program; purchasing the privilege of inhabiting the setting is only a small part of the total pattern of Dinners and Banquets, so Business is a *secondary* attribute. Business is *absent* from a setting if no purchase or fee is required in order to participate completely in its standing pattern.

The behavior settings where Business is prominent constitute a town's *primary business habitat* (PBH), its primary habitat resources for business behavior. Those settings where Business is prominent *or* secondary comprise the *territorial range* of Business.

Basic data for Business are presented in Table 5.7; the report for Aesthetics provides a key to the location of particular data in this table.

SALIENT FINDINGS

The territorial range of Business extends over 58 to 70 percent of the towns' habitats. Habitats where resources for business behavior are prominent (PBH) comprise 17 to 28 percent of the total habitats.

Table 5.7
Business
Basic Habitat Data

	1954–55		1963–64	
Primary Habitat (PBH)	MW (1)	YD (2)	MW (3)	YD (4)
Extent				
(1) Behavior Settings per Year	62	85	63	102
(2) Mean BS per Day	36.1	42.6	27.4	54.7
(3) Mean BS per Hour	12.3	11.7	9.4	15.2
(4) Centiurbs (no.)	23.1	25.0	18.3	31.9
(5) Centiurbs (% of Town Total)	25.7%	27.8%	17.1%	28.3%
Erosion and Accretion				
Type of Change	Erosion from '54–55		Accretion to '63–64	
(6) Centiurbs (no.)	9.1	2.9	7.1	6.7
(7) Centiurbs (% of PBH)	39%	12%	39%	21%
Claims for Operatives				
(8) Number	238	483	313	525
(9) Number (% of Town Total)	4%	12%	3%	7%
Amount of Variety				
(10) Major Genotypes (no.)	10	12	12	14
(11) Total Genotypes (no.)	33	37	30	46
(12) Total Genotypes (% of Town Total)	19%	22%	15%	22%
Territorial Range (TR)				
(13) Centiurbs (no.)	58.2	63.4	62.0	73.2
(14) Centiurbs (% of Town Total)	65%	70%	58%	65%

Midwest's PBH is smaller than Yoredale's; PBH was smaller in Midwest, but larger in Yoredale, in 1963–64 than in 1954–55. Habitat-claims for operatives within the towns' PBHs constitute 3 to 12 percent of their total claims for operatives. Midwest has fewer claims for business operatives than Yoredale, and both towns had more such claims in 1963–64 than in 1954–55. There is less variety within Midwest's PBH than within Yoredale's; PBH variety decreased between the survey years in Midwest and increased in Yoredale.

TERRITORIAL RANGE OF BUSINESS

Business action patterns were regularly present in some degree in roughly 60 to 70 percent of the towns' habitats; conversely, about 30 to 40 percent of their habitats are free. The TR of Business extends over fewer centiurbs and smaller percentages of Midwest's than of Yoredale's habitat; and between the survey years, it increased in centiurbs of extent and decreased in percentages of the habitats of both towns.

EXTENT OF PRIMARY BUSINESS HABITAT

In 1963–64 the PBH covered 17 percent of Midwest's and 28 percent of Yoredale's total habitat. This is approximately equivalent in Midwest to 36 regular behavior settings that occur six days a week for eight hours a day—that is, to 36 grocery stores, sales routes, insurance offices, and so forth—and in Yoredale to about 64 regular behavior settings.

Differences. Midwest's PBH is smaller than Yoredale's; in 1963–64 Midwest had 13.6 fewer cu of PBH, amounting to 57 percent as many cu and to 11.2 fewer percent of the town's total habitat.

Changes. Midwest's PBH was smaller, and Yoredale's was larger, in 1963–64 than in 1954–55. Midwest had 4.8 fewer cu of PBH in 1963–64, amounting to 79 percent as many cu and to 8.6 fewer percent of the town's total habitat. Yoredale had 6.9 more cu of PBH, amounting to 128 percent as many cu and to 0.5 more percent of the town's total habitat.

Processes of change. More than 12 percent of the towns' 1954–55 PBHs were eroded before 1963–64, and more than 21 percent of their 1963–64 PBHs were accreted after 1954–55. Both erosion and accretion were greater in Midwest than in Yoredale; 27 more percent of Midwest's 1954–55 PBH was eroded, and 18 more percent of its 1963–64 PBH was accreted. The same is true for the towns' total habitats; more of Midwest's than of Yoredale's habitat was both eroded and accreted.

CLAIMS FOR OPERATIVES WITHIN PRIMARY
BUSINESS HABITAT

If all behavior settings within the towns' PBHs were to function simultaneously in 1963–64, it would require 313 persons in Midwest and 525 persons in Yoredale to carry out essential operations. Claims for PBH operatives are much less than claims for operatives in general, on a centiurb basis; there are 17.1 claims for operatives per cu of

Midwest's PBH, compared to 96 for the whole habitat—that is, 18 percent as many—and there are 16.5 per cu of Yoredale's PBH, compared to 69 for the whole habitat—24 percent as many. In 1963–64 the PBHs contained only 3 and 7 percent of the total habitat-claims for operatives; whereas, as we have seen, they comprised 17 and 28 percent of the towns' total habitats. The towns' PBHs are meager in positions of responsibility.

Differences. Midwest has fewer habitat-claims for PBH operatives than Yoredale. In 1963–64 it had 212 fewer such claims than Yoredale, amounting to 60 percent as many, to 104 percent as many per cu of PBH, to 94 percent as many per town inhabitant, and to 4 fewer percent of the town's total claims for operatives.

Changes. Both towns had more PBH claims for operatives in 1963–64 than in 1954–55. Midwest had 75 more such claims in 1963–64, amounting to 131 percent as many, to 166 percent as many per cu of PBH, and to 113 percent as many per town inhabitant, but to 1 less percent of the town's total claims for operatives. Yoredale had 42 more such claims, amounting to 109 percent as many, to 117 percent as many per cu of PBH, and to 108 percent as many per town inhabitant, but to 5 less percent of the town's total claims.

VARIETY WITHIN PRIMARY BUSINESS HABITAT

There is somewhat less variety within the two towns' PBHs than expected on the basis of extent. In 1963–64 Midwest's PBH, 17 percent of the town's total habitat, was the locus of 15 percent of its behavior setting genotypes; Yoredale's PBH, 28 percent of total habitat, was the locus of 22 percent of its genotypes.

If Midwest and Yoredale were to display simultaneously in 1963–64 the complete range of behavior setting programs within their PBHs, Midwest would require 30 different halls and exhibit rooms with their appropriate facilities, 30 differently trained and experienced staffs of clerks and secretaries, and 30 different experts as proprietors and managers; and Yoredale would require 46 different halls and staffs.

Differences. There is less variety within Midwest's PBH than within Yoredale's. In 1963–64 Midwest had 16 fewer genotypes than Yoredale, amounting to 65 percent as many and to 7 fewer percent of Midwest's than of Yoredale's total genotypes.

Changes. Midwest's business variety was smaller and Yoredale's was larger in 1963–64 than 1954–55. Midwest had 3 fewer genotypes in 1963–64, amounting to 91 percent as many and to 4 fewer percent of the town's total genotypes. Yoredale had 9 more genotypes, amounting to 124 percent as many and to the same percent of the town's total genotypes.

NATURE, COMMONALITY, AND DISTINCTIVENESS OF
PRIMARY BUSINESS HABITAT

The towns' major business habitats have a low degree of commonality (Table 5.8). Of Midwest's 12 and Yoredale's 14 major business

Table 5.8
Business
Variety Within the Towns' Primary Business Habitats
Major Genotypes in at Least One Town in One Year

	Percent of PBH			
	1954–55		1963–64	
	MW (1)	YD (2)	MW (3)	YD (4)
(1) Accountants Offices	0	3.9	0	3.0
(2) Animal Feed Mills	0	0	3.3	0
(3) Animal Feed Stores	4.8	0	2.9	0
(4) Attorneys Offices	7.9	0	9.3	0
(5) Bakeries	0	2.0	0	3.0
(6) Banks, Comm'l	2.0	3.4	2.3	3.0
(7) Butcher Shops	0	6.2	0	5.2
(8) Chemists Shops	0	3.7	0	3.1
(9) Clothiers & Dry Goods Stores	2.6	9.6	3.1	7.1
(10) Comm'l Company Offices	1.9	2.2	2.3	5.9
(11) Commiss'n Agents (Betting)	0	3.8	0	4.3
(12) Confectnrs. & Statnrs.	0	6.1	0	3.5
(13) Deliv. & Collect. Routes	3.7	1.5	1.1	0.9
(14) Drugstores	6.2	0	3.3	0
(15) Elect. Appl. & Servs.	0	0	0	4.0
(16) Farm Implement Ag'cies	4.9	0.2	2.1	0.6
(17) Govt. Record Offices	2.1	0	4.7	0
(18) [a] Grocery Stores	13.9	20.0	7.3	16.5
(19) Hardware (Ironmongers) Stores	2.5	3.7	5.6	2.9
(20) [a] Insur. Offices & Sales Routes	5.7	3.2	4.2	3.8
(21) Lumberyards	4.3	0	5.4	0
(22) Real Estate Agents	3.9	0	2.6	0
(23) Sales Routes: Cosmetics, etc.	1.1	0	3.4	0.7
(24) Service Stations	7.9	0	15.3	0
(25) Shoe Stores	0	3.6	0	3.4
(26) Solicitors Offices	0	3.4	0	2.5
(27) Variety Stores	4.6	0	3.1	0

[a] Major genotypes in both towns and both years that are also common to the towns (category 1).

genotypes in 1963–64, only 2, Grocery Stores and Insurance Offices, were both common and major in both survey years. In addition, the following 5 genotypes were common but not major business genotypes in both years: Auction Sales of Household Furnishings and General Merchandise, Clothiers and Dry Goods Stores (Drapers), Delivery and Collection Routes, Food and Rummage Sales, and Hardware Stores (Ironmongers). These 7 genotypes identify the stable, common business habitats of Midwest and Yoredale in 1963–64 — that is, the habitats present in both towns since 1954–55. From the number and extent of these common business genotypes, we discover that the towns have less commonality within their PBHs than within their total habitats. In 1963–64, 23 percent of Midwest's business genotypes were common to the towns, compared with 33 percent of its total genotypes; 15 percent of Yoredale's business genotypes were common, compared with 31 percent of its total genotypes. In terms of centiurbs, these common business genotypes embraced 24 percent of Midwest's PBH, compared with 55 percent of its total habitat, and 32 percent of Yoredale's PBH, compared with 57 percent of its total habitat.

Business genotypes that are not common to the towns, that are distinctive, are obviously important (Table 5.9). For example, coal can be purchased in Yoredale but not in Midwest; one cannot have grain ground for animal feed in Yoredale, but can in Midwest; and one cannot place a bet in a public setting in Midwest, but can in Yoredale. However, most of the 48 distinctive business genotypes involve materials, services, or processes that occur in some form in the other town;

Table 5.9
Business
Distinctive Genotypes, 1963–64

Commonality Category[a]		Midwest (1)	Yoredale (2)
(1)	7	Sales Prom. & Patron Att. Open.	Commiss'n Agents (Betting)
(2)			Markets, Public
(3)			Sales Routes, Fish
(4)	6	Animal Feed Mills	Coal Depots & Deliv.
(5)		Audit & Investig. Co.	Egg-Pack'g Plants
(6)	5	Animal Feed Stores	Auction Sales, Livestock
(7)	4	Attorneys Offices	Accountants Offices
(8)		Banks	Bakeries
(9)		Comm'l Company Offices	Banks, Comm'l
(10)		Farm Implement Ag'cies	Comm'l Company Offices
(11)		Furniture Stores	Estate Agents Offices
(12)		Govt. Offices: Bus. & Records	Freight Truck Lines
(13)		Newspaper & Print'g Plants	Milk Bottl'g & Deliv.
			Shoe Stores
(14)		Sav'gs Stamp Sales Stands	Solicitors Offices
(15)	3	Drugstores	Auction Sales, Real Estate
(16)		Fireworks Sales Stands	Banks, Saving's
(17)		Lumberyards	Butcher Shops
(18)		Real Estate Agents	Chemists
(19)		Service Stations	Cleaners, Dry Cleaning Depots
(20)		Tank Truck Lines	Confectnrs. & Statnrs.
(21)		Variety Stores	Crockery Shops
(22)			Elect. Appl. & Serv.
(23)			Farm Implement
(24)			Household Furns.
(25)			Needlecraft Mat'ls Shops
(26)			Photog. Suppl. & Serv.
(27)			Post Offices and Statnrs. Shops
(28)			Tax Assess (Rating) & Collect Offices

[a] Genotypes are ordered from those unique to each town and environs (category 7) to those whose programs occur in the other town but as components of different genotypes (category 3).

they are differently distributed among the business settings, or they involve technically different procedures. For example, Butcher Shops
comprise a distinct, primary business genotype in Yoredale, but in
Midwest the butcher-shop program is a subordinate synomorph of the
genotype Grocery Stores. The subordinate synomorph Newsstand
occurs in Yoredale as a part of the single genotype Confectioners and
Stationers Shops, but it occurs in Midwest as parts of two genotypes:
Drugstores and Restaurants. The fact that most primary business genotypes are neither predominantly common to the towns nor unique to
one town, that they are distinctive, gives each town's primary business
habitat a particular fascination to visitors from the other type of environment; business settings are familiar, yet they are surprising in unexpected ways.

In this connection it should be noted that Midwesterners would
meet more surprises in Yoredale's business settings than would Dalesmen in Midwest's business settings: Midwest has 1 instead of 3 unique
business genotypes (category 7), and 23 percent instead of 15 percent of
its primary business genotypes are common to the towns. We have seen
that the action pattern Aesthetics is different in these respects. One is almost equally "at home" in most of the towns' aesthetic genotypes, in
Church Weddings, Libraries, and Programs of Vocal Music, for example; but one is not equally "at home" in most business genotypes, in
the Drugstores of Midwest and the Chemist Shops of Yoredale, or in
the Attorneys' Offices of Midwest and the Solicitors' Offices of Yoredale.

GENOTYPE SITES OF CHANGE IN
PRIMARY BUSINESS HABITAT

The genotype sites of substantial change in the towns' PBHs
reveal some details of the disturbance and decline of Midwest's PBH
and of the stability and expansion of Yoredale's (Table 5.10). There
were 19 genotype sites of substantial change in Midwest's PBH; 11 of
these were sites of decrement (3 eroded and 8 reduced sites) and 8 of
increment (3 new and 5 enlarged sites). Some of the changes in Midwest's PBH are connected with changes in agriculture, enlargement of
farms, increase in the complexity and cost of farm machinery, changes
in animal nutrition, and changes in farm financing. Changes in agriculture are factors in the decline of Midwest's Machinery Repair Shops,
Animal Feed Stores, and Farm Implement Agencies, and in the increment of its Animal Feed Mills and Government Record and Business
Offices. The last reflects greater farm financing by federal government
agencies. Other changes in Midwest's PBH are connected with widespread changes in the techniques and economics of retail distribution.
The declines of Garages, Delivery and Collection Routes, Drugstores,
and Grocery Stores are associated with increased self-service, increased
central packaging of products, and increased capital requirements.
These, in turn, have resulted in increased consolidation of business settings. A widespread depressing influence on the extent of Midwest's

Table 5.10
Business
Genotype Sites of Substantial[a] Changes in Extents of Primary Business Habitats
Between 1954–55 and 1963–64

		Midwest (1)	Yoredale (2)
(1)	New Sites	Animal Feed Mills	Egg-Pack'g Plants
(2)		Audit & Investig. Co.	
(3)		Jewelry Stores	
(4)	Enlarged Sites	Govt. Offices: Bus. & Records	Bakeries
(5)			Comm'l Company Offices
(6)		Hardware Stores	Commiss'n Agents
(7)		Sales Prom. Openings	Elect. Suppl. & Serv.
(8)			Grocery Stores
(9)		Sales Routes: Cosmetics, Magazines, etc.	Insur. Offices & Sales Routes
(10)		Service Stations	Restaurants
(11)	Eroded Sites	Garages	
(12)		Ice Depots	None
(13)		Machin'y Repair Shops	
(14)	Reduced Sites	Animal Feed Stores	Confectnrs. Statnrs.
(15)		Deliv. & Collect. Routes	Coal Depots and Deliv'y
(16)		Drugstores	
(17)		Farm Implement Ag'cies	
(18)		Grocery Stores	
(19)		Insur. Offices & Sales Routes	
(20)		Real Estate Agents	
(21)		Variety Stores	

[a] See footnote a, Table 5.4.

primary habitat resources for Business was a general reduction in the length of business hours between 1954–55 and 1963–64. In 1954–55 Midwest was a "Saturday night" town, with many businesses open until 9:30; by 1963–64 this had ceased. In 1954–55 government settings occurred weekly for 44 hours and on 6 days; in 1963–64 they occurred 40 hours and on 5 days per week.

There were 10 genotype sites of substantial change in Yoredale's PBH; 8 of these were sites of increment (1 new and 7 enlarged), and 2 of decrement (both were reduced sites). Fundamental changes in agriculture and retail trade similar to those in Midwest undoubtedly occurred in Yoredale between 1955 and 1963, but to a smaller extent, and their effects were attenuated by a general expansion of retail trade based to some degree on tourism, reflected in the expanded Bakeries, Commission Agents, Grocery Stores, and Restaurants. To some degree modernization of dwellings within the town and district is the basis for the enlargement of Commercial Company Offices (mostly building firms) and of Electrical Supply and Service Companies. The decline in the genotype Coal Depots and Delivery Services is a consequence of the increasing use of electricity, gas, and oil for domestic heating.

CONTROL BY AUTHORITY SYSTEMS

Over 90 percent of the PBHs of both towns are under the control of Private Enterprise authority systems (Table 5.11). There are only small differences between the towns and between the years in extent of control by different authority systems; the largest differences occur in 1963–64, when the extent of control of the PBH by Private Enterprise authority systems was less in Midwest than in Yoredale by 4.6 percentage points, and control by Government Agencies was greater in Midwest by 3.5 percentage points. The greatest differences between the years occurred in Midwest; control of the PBH by Private Enterprise was 5 percentage points less in 1963–64, and control by Government Agencies was 3.2 percentage points greater in 1963–64.

SPECIAL FEATURES

Free and voluntary habitats. People without money are severely restricted in both towns; money is required for full participation in the 58 to 70 percent of the towns' habitats within the territorial range of Business (Table 5.7). For a Midwesterner with no money in his pocket in 1963–64, 42 percent (45 cu) of the town's habitat was open to him, whereas a penniless Dalesman had access to 35 percent (39.8 cu) of Yoredale's habitat. The inhabitants of both towns had more free territory in 1963–64 than in 1954–55: 9.2 cu more in Midwest, and 8.2 cu more in Yoredale.

But not all the town's free (nonbusiness) habitats are without financial constraints. Payment of wages to operatives often does not occur within the settings where the wages are earned; the schoolteacher is not paid in the classroom where he teaches, nor the pastor in the worship service where he preaches. For this reason, wages are covered separately by the action pattern Professional Involvement. When we remove from the towns' free habitats the behavior settings where performers are paid—that is, where Professional Involvement is prominent or secondary—the completely *free and voluntary* parts of the towns remain—that is, the parts where no inhabitant pays or is paid.

Table 5.11
Control of Primary Business Habitats by Authority Systems
Percent of primary business habitats controlled by different authority systems

		1954–55		1963–64	
		MW (1)	YD (2)	MW (3)	YD (4)
(1)	Extent of PBH in cu	23.1	25.0	18.3	31.9
	Percent of PBH controlled by:				
(2)	Church Authority System	0.9	0.4	0.0	0.3
(3)	Govt. Agency System	2.1	1.8	5.3	1.8
(4)	Private Enterprise System	95.9	96.0	90.9	95.5
(5)	School Authority System	0.4	0.0	2.9	1.1
(6)	Voluntary Assn. System	0.6	1.8	0.9	1.3

The free *and* voluntary habitats of the towns are much smaller than their free habitats alone; the free and voluntary habitats extend over 4.3 to 10.6 percent of the towns' total habitats (Table 5.12), whereas the free habitats alone cover 30 to 42 percent (Table 5.7). Midwest's free and voluntary habitat is larger and more varied than Yoredale's; in 1963–64 it was 6.6 cu (138 percent) greater in extent and had 26 (120 percent) more genotypes than Yoredale's.

Free and voluntary habitats increased in extent and variety in Midwest and decreased in Yoredale between the survey years. In Midwest the increase was 3.1 cu (37 percent) and 7 genotypes (17 percent); in Yoredale the decrement was 1.5 cu (24 percent) and 5 genotypes(19 percent). Midwest's superiority over Yoredale with respect to free and voluntary habitat was greater in all respects (centiurbs, percentage points, and variety) in 1963–64 than in 1954–55.

Major genotype sites of free and voluntary habitats common to Midwest and Yoredale in both years are Business Meetings, Parks and Playgrounds, Parties, Plays and Programs, Vocal Music Classes (Church Choir Practice), Religion Classes, Religious Fellowship Meetings, Religion Study Groups, Religious Worship Services, and Solicitation of Funds. Those unique to one town are Card Parties, Baseball Games, and Picnics in Midwest; and Badminton Games, Billiard Games, and Cricket Games in Yoredale.

It should be pointed out that although exchange of money is not obligatory in any of the free behavior settings, money is exchanged voluntarily in some of them—for example, Religious Worship Services and Solicitation of Funds.

Professionally operated business. For comparison with the towns' free and voluntary habitats, we give in Table 5.13 data on habitats where both Business and Professional Involvement are prominent. These are the predominantly business parts of the towns, where goods, services, and privileges are exchanges for money and where wages are paid operatives. They are only a little smaller in extent and variety than the towns' PBHs (Table 5.7), and the differences between the towns and years are essentially the same as for the towns' PBHs. Professionally operated business habitats exceed free and voluntary habitats in extent in both towns, but much more so in Yoredale than in Midwest; in

Table 5.12
Business
Extent and Variety of Free and Voluntary Habitats

	1954–55		1963–64	
	Midwest (1)	Yoredale (2)	Midwest (3)	Yoredale (4)
Measures of Extent and Variety				
(1) No. of centiurbs	8.3	6.3	11.4	4.8
(2) Percent of total habitat	9.3%	7.0%	10.6%	4.3%
(3) No. of genotypes	41	27	48	22

Table 5.13
Business
Extent and Variety of Professionally Operated
Primary Business Habitats

	1954–55		1963–64	
	Midwest (1)	Yoredale (2)	Midwest (3)	Yoredale (4)
Measures of Extent and Variety				
(1) No. of centiurbs	22.5	24.6	17.4	30.8
(2) Percent of total habitat	25.1%	27.3%	16.2%	27.3%
(3) No. of genotypes	29	34	25	41

1963–64, the professional business habitat was greater than the free and voluntary habitat by factors of 6.4 in Yoredale and 1.5 in Midwest (T5.13; R1; C3,4/T5.12; R1; C3,4).

Autonomy. More of Midwest's than of Yoredale's PBH is controlled within the town or surrounding rural region; in fact, only 3.8 percent of Midwest's PBH is under the aegis of distant authorities, whereas this is the case for 22.8 percent of Yoredale's PBH.

Education

DEFINITION

The action pattern Education is present within a behavior setting to the extent that the occurrences which constitute the program of the setting involve: formal teaching and learning; providing materials for teaching or learning in other settings; evaluating and appreciating education; teaching and learning how to educate. The action pattern Education does not include incidental teaching and learning.

Education is *prominent* in behavior settings if most of their standing patterns foster education via occurrences of the kinds specified above. The operatives within settings where Education is prominent are often professionally trained teachers, and they are always persons who possess special programs for imparting designated information or skills; they always inhabit zones 4, 5, or 6 of the setting, thereby controlling all or part of it. Two examples of behavior settings where Education is prominent are Elementary School Basic Classes and Religion Classes (Sunday School Classes). Education is *secondary* in behavior settings if some but less than 80 percent of their standing patterns foster education; for example, Drugstores in Midwest sell school supplies, Parents Association Meetings in Yoredale appraise educational programs. Education is *absent* from behavior settings if there is no teaching by an officially designated teacher, no learning by an officially designated pupil, or no appraisal or support for such programs in other settings; this is true, for example, of Barbershops in Midwest and Darts Games in Yoredale.

The behavior settings where Education is prominent constitute a town's *primary educational habitat* (PEH), its primary habitat resources for educational behavior. Settings where it occurs in some degree constitute the *territorial range* of Education.

Basic data for Education are presented in Table 5.14; the report for Aesthetics provides a key to the location of particular data in this table.

SALIENT FINDINGS

The territorial range of Education extends over 21 to 36 percent of the towns' habitats. Habitats with prominent resources for educational behavior (PEH) comprise 5 to 15 percent of the total habitats; Midwest's PEH is larger than Yoredale's, and the PEH was larger in both towns in 1963–64 than in 1954–55. Habitat-claims for operatives within the towns' PEHs constitute 3 to 4 percent of their total claims for operatives; Midwest has more claims for educational operatives than Yoredale does, and both towns had more such claims in 1963–64 than in 1954–55. Midwest's PEH had greater variety than Yoredale's in 1954–55 and less in 1963–64; PEH variety increased between the survey years in both towns.

Table 5.14
Education
Basic Habitat Data

	1954–55		1963–64	
Primary Habitat (PEH)	MW (1)	YD (2)	MW (3)	YD (4)
Extent				
(1) Behavior Settings per Year	96	43	144	130
(2) Mean BS per Day	15.7	7.8	29.2	25.8
(3) Mean BS per Hour	2.0	0.8	3.1	2.2
(4) Centiurbs (no.)	10.1	4.6	16.5	14.2
(5) Centiurbs (% of Town Total)	11.2%	5.1%	15.4%	12.6%
Erosion and Accretion Type of Change	Erosion from '54–55		Accretion to '63–64	
(6) Centiurbs (no.)	2.1	1.9	6.8	11.4
(7) Centiurbs (% of PEH)	21%	41%	41%	80%
Claims for Operatives				
(8) Number	228	168	331	302
(9) Number (% of Town Total)	4%	4%	3%	4%
Amount of Variety				
(10) Major Genotypes (no.)	8	8	7 ·	11
(11) Total Genotypes (no.)	26	15	37	43
(12) Total Genotypes (% of Town Total)	15%	9%	19%	20%
Territorial Range (TR)				
(13) Centiurbs (no.)	24.8	18.8	39.1	34.2
(14) Centiurbs (% of Town Total)	28%	21%	36%	30%

TERRITORIAL RANGE OF EDUCATION

Educational action patterns are regularly present in some degree in about one-quarter to one-third of the towns' habitats; and conversely, approximately two-thirds to three-quarters of the towns' habitats are without educational components. The TR of Education extends over more centiurbs and greater percentages of Midwest's than of Yoredale's habitat; it increased in extent in both towns between 1954–55 and 1963–64.

EXTENT OF PRIMARY EDUCATIONAL HABITAT

In 1963–64 the PEH covered 15.4 percent of Midwest's and 12.6 percent of Yoredale's total habitat, approximately equivalent in Midwest to 33 regular behavior settings that occur six days a week for eight hours a day, and in Yoredale to 28 regular settings. In terms of occasional settings, Midwest's PEH is about equivalent to 330 one-hour meetings of different classes, and Yoredale's PEH is approximately equivalent to 284 such classes.

Differences. Midwest's PEH is larger than Yoredale's; in 1963–64 Midwest had 2.3 more cu of PEH, amounting to 116 percent as many cu and to 2.8 more percent of the town's total habitat.

Changes. The towns' PEHs were larger in 1963–64 than in 1954–55. Midwest had 6.4 more cu of PEH in 1963–64, amounting to 163 percent as many cu and to 4.2 more percent of the town's total habitat. Yoredale had 9.6 more cu of PEH, amounting to 309 percent as many cu and to 7.5 more percent of the town's total habitat.

Processes of change. More than one-fifth of the towns' 1954–55 PEHs were eroded before 1963–64, and more than two-fifths of their 1963–64 PEHs were accreted after 1954–55. Both erosion and accretion were smaller in Midwest than in Yoredale; 20 fewer percent of Midwest's 1954–55 PEH was eroded, and 39 fewer percent of its 1963–64 PEH was accreted. The reverse is true for the towns' total habitats; more of Midwest's than of Yoredale's habitat was both eroded and accreted.

CLAIMS FOR OPERATIVES WITHIN PRIMARY
EDUCATIONAL HABITAT

If all behavior settings within the towns' PEHs were to function simultaneously in 1963–64, it would require 331 persons in Midwest and 302 persons in Yoredale to carry out essential operations. Claims for PEH operatives are much smaller than claims for operatives in general, on a centiurb basis; there are 20 claims for operatives per cu of Midwest's PEH, compared with 96 for the whole habitat,—that is, 21 percent as many—and there are 21 per cu of Yoredale's PEH, compared with 69 for the whole habitat—30 percent as many. In 1963–64 the PEHs contained only 3 and 4 percent of the total habitat-claims for operatives; whereas, as we have seen, they comprised 15.4 and 12.6 percent of the towns' total habitats. The towns' PEHs are low in positions of responsibility.

Differences. Midwest has more habitat-claims for PEH operatives than Yoredale. In 1963–64 it had 29 more such claims than Yoredale, amounting to 110 percent as many, to 94 percent as many per cu of PEH, to 173 percent as many per town inhabitant, and to 1 fewer percent of the town's total claims for operatives.

Changes. Both towns had more PEH claims for operatives in 1963–64 than in 1954–55. Midwest had 103 more such claims in 1963–64, amounting to 145 percent as many, to 89 percent as many per cu of PEH, to 125 percent as many per town inhabitant, and to 1 fewer percent of the town's total claims for operatives. Yoredale had 134 more such claims, amounting to 180 percent as many, to 58 percent as many per cu of PEH, to 178 percent as many per town inhabitant, and to the same percentage of the town's total claims as in 1954–55.

VARIETY WITHIN PRIMARY EDUCATIONAL HABITATS

There is more variety within the two towns' PEHs than expected on the basis of extents. In 1963–64 Midwest's PEH, 15 percent of the town's total habitat, was the locus of 19 percent of its behavior setting genotypes; Yoredale's PEH, 12 percent of total habitat, was the locus of 20 percent of its genotypes.

If Midwest and Yoredale were to display simultaneously in 1963–64 the complete range of behavior setting programs within their PEHs, Midwest would require 37 different halls and classrooms with their appropriate facilities, and 37 differently trained and experienced teachers; Yoredale would require 43 different rooms and teachers.

Differences. There is less variety within Midwest's PEH than within Yoredale's. In 1963–64 Midwest had 6 fewer genotypes than Yoredale, amounting to 86 percent as many and to 1 fewer percent of Midwest's than of Yoredale's total genotypes.

Changes. The educational variety of the towns was greater in 1963–64 than in 1954–55. Midwest had 11 more genotypes in 1963–64, amounting to 142 percent as many and to 4 more percent of the town's total genotypes. Yoredale had 28 more genotypes, amounting to 287 percent as many and to 11 more percent of the town's total genotypes.

NATURE, COMMONALITY, AND DISTINCTIVENESS OF
PRIMARY EDUCATIONAL HABITATS

The towns' major educational genotypes have a medium degree of commonality (Table 5.15). Of Midwest's 7 and Yoredale's 11 major educational genotypes in 1963–64, 4 were both common and major in both survey years. In addition, the following 5 genotypes were common but not major educational genotypes in both years: Libraries, Business Meetings, Discussion Meetings, Physical Education Classes, and Sewing and Dressmaking Classes. These 9 genotypes identify the stable, common educational habitats of Midwest and Yoredale. Their number and extent show that there is less commonality within them than within the towns' total habitats. In 1963–64 common genotypes accounted for

Table 5.15
Education
Variety Within the Towns' Primary Education Habitats
Major Genotypes in at Least One Town in One Year

	Percent of PEH			
	1954–55		1963–64	
	MW (1)	YD (2)	MW (3)	YD (4)
(1) Cooking Classes	2.0	0	0.9	3.1
(2) *a* Elem. School Basic Classes	20.0	33.0	18.1	13.5
(3) English Classes	2.2	0	1.4	6.9
(4) Exams, Standardized	0	1.1	1.1	3.7
(5) Home Ec. Classes	3.1	1.5	1.9	0
(6) Horticulture Classes	0	3.4	0	0.4
(7) Mathematics Classes	2.1	0	1.4	5.8
(8) Meetings, Business	5.0	1.1	2.3	0.4
(9) *a* Music Classes, Instrum.	3.1	9.8	5.0	3.1
(10) *a* Music Classes, Vocal	8.9	11.0	6.8	9.3
(11) Phys. & Biol. Sci. Classes	3.4	0	2.1	0
(12) Science Classes, Genl.	0	0	0	3.0
(13) Phys. Ed. Classes	2.7	9.1	10.8	9.5
(14) *a* Relig. Classes	18.5	11.2	18.7	5.5
(15) Relig. Study Groups	0	0	3.4	0.4
(16) School Admin. Offices	8.3	0	4.5	2.3
(17) Sewing & Dressmak'g Classes	2.1	8.2	1.0	3.4
(18) Woodwork'g Classes	2.3	5.1	1.3	1.9

a Major genotypes in both towns and both years that are also common to the towns (category 1).

24 percent of Midwest's and 21 percent of Yoredale's total educational genotypes, compared with 33 percent commonality for Midwest's and 31 percent for Yoredale's total genotypes. In terms of centiurbs, these common educational genotypes embraced 65 percent of Midwest's and 47 percent of Yoredale's PEH, compared with 55 percent and 57 percent commonality, respectively, for the towns' total habitats.

The common educational genotypes consist largely of the Basic Elementary Classes, Music Classes, and Religion Classes, followed by those mentioned above.

The distinctive genotypes of the towns (Table 5.16) indicate Midwest has educational services for deviant children that are not present in Yoredale, via the genotypes Psychological Services, Retarded Children's Classes, and Speech Therapy Classes, and that Yoredale has many educational genotypes with subject-matter content that do not occur in Midwest, such as Classes in Bookbinding, Dancing, French, German, Metalwork, Military Training, Upholstering, and Nature Study. Most of the other distinctive educational genotypes result from different distribution of similar educational programs among behavior settings.

Table 5.16
Education
Distinctive Genotypes, 1963–64

Commonality Category[a]		Midwest (1)	Yoredale (2)
(1)	7	None	None
(2)	6	Latin Classes	Art Classes, Genl
(3)		Psychol. Serv. Offices	Bookbind'g Classes
(4)		Retarded Chil. Classes	Dancing Classes
(5)		Speech Therapy Servs.	French Classes
(6)		Welfare Workers Classes	German Classes
(7)			Metalwork Classes
(8)			Military Trng. Classes
(9)	5	Agric. Advisors Offices	Upholst. Classes
(10)		Club Offices Trng. Classes	
(11)	4	Kindergarten Classes	Geography Classes
(12)		Motor Veh. Oper. Classes	Nature Study Classes
(13)		Phys. & Biol. Sci. Classes	School Admin. Offices
(14)		School Admin. Offices	
(15)		Soc. Sci. Classes	
(16)	3	Comml. Classes	History Classes
(17)		Landscap'g & Floricult. Classes	Horticulture Classes
(18)		Painting Classes	Motor Veh. Oper. Classes
(19)		Progs. of Band Music	School Enq. (Truant) Offices
(20)		Woodwork'g & Machine Shop Classes	Science Classes
(21)			Shorthand Classes
(22)			Tech. Drawing Classes
(23)			Typing Classes
(24)			Voc. Counsel'g Serv.
(25)			Woodwork'g Classes

[a] Genotypes are ordered from those that are unique to each town and environs (category 7) to those whose programs occur in the other town but as components of different genotypes (category 3).

GENOTYPE SITES OF CHANGE IN PRIMARY
EDUCATIONAL HABITAT

There were 17 genotype sites of substantial change in Midwest's PEH, 15 of them sites of increment; there were 29 sites of substantial change in Yoredale's PEH, all of them sites of increment (Table 5.17). More than twice as many new educational programs were introduced into Yoredale as into Midwest. Subject-matter content, such as Agronomy, Art, and Bookbinding, characterizes most of Yoredale's new educational genotypes, whereas educational services and methods, such as Agricultural Advisors' Offices, Standardized Examinations, and Speech Therapy Classes, characterize Midwest's innovations.

CONTROL BY AUTHORITY SYSTEMS

The towns differ greatly in the extent to which their PEHs are controlled by the different authority systems (Table 5.18). Schools domi-

Table 5.17
Education
Genotype Sites of Substantial[a] Changes in Extents of Primary Education Habitats
Between 1954–55 and 1963–64

		Midwest (1)	Yoredale (2)
(1)		Agric. Advisors Offices	Agronomy Classes
(2)		Exams, Standardized	Art Classes, Genl.
(3)		Kindergarten Classes	Athl. Equipm't Rooms
(4)		Libraries	Bookbind'g Classes
(5)		Motor Veh. Oper. Classes	Cooking Classes
(6)		Painting Classes	Educ. Methods Classes
(7)		Psychol. Serv. Offices	English Classes
(8)		Relig. Study Groups	French Classes
(9)		Retarded Chil. Classes	Geography Classes
(10)		Speech Therapy Serv.	German Classes
(11)		Welfare Workers Classes	History Classes
(12)			Libraries (School)
(13)	New Sites		Math Classes
(14)			Metalwork Classes
(15)			Motor Veh. Oper. Classes
(16)			Relig. Study Groups
(17)			School Admin. Offices
(18)			Science Classes, Genl.
(19)			Shorthand Classes
(20)			Swimming Classes
(21)			Tech. Drawing Classes
(22)			Typing Classes
(23)			Upholst. Classes
(24)			Voc. Counsel'g Classes
(25)		Elem. School Basic Classes	Elem. School Basic Classes
(26)	Enlarged Sites	Music Classes, Instrum.	Exams, Standardized
(27)		Phys. Ed. Classes	Music Classes, Vocal
(28)		Relig. Classes	Phys. Ed. Classes
(29)			Relig. Classes
(30)	Eroded Sites	Agric. Econ. Classes	
(31)		Farm Practices Classes	None
	Reduced Sites	None	None

[a] See footnote a, Table 5.4.

nate the PEHs of both towns but are less dominant in Midwest than in Yoredale. In 1963–64, 59 percent of Midwest's and 90 percent of Yoredale's PEHs were controlled by Schools. Churches and Government Agencies contributed more to education in Midwest than in Yoredale. Of the primary educational behavior settings at hand in 1963–64, 26 percent were controlled by Churches in Midwest and 5 percent in Yoredale; 9 percent were controlled by Government Agencies in Midwest and none in Yoredale. Private Enterprises and Voluntary Associations, between them, controlled fewer than 6 percent of the educational settings in each town in 1963–64.

The years differ too in extent to which educational habitats were controlled by the different authority systems. The greatest differences occurred in Yoredale, where control by Schools increased from 70 to 90 percent and control by Churches decreased from 13 to 5 percent. It is clear that, with the establishment of the new school in Yoredale, a different pattern of control of the town's educational habitat emerged; the dominance of Schools increased and the influence of Churches, Private Enterprises, and Voluntary Associations consequently receded. In 1954–55 these last three authority systems controlled 30 percent of Yoredale's educational habitat; in 1963–64 they controlled 10 percent of it. The change within Midwest in the pattern of control by authority systems was much less than in Yoredale. The greatest changes were an increase in the extent of the PEH under the aegis of Midwest's churches, from 21.2 to 26.4 percent, and a decrease in the extent of control by Government Agencies, from 16.9 to 9.5 percent.

SPECIAL FEATURES

A decade of change. The period between the surveys was one of great increase in educational habitat resources in both towns; increments in territorial range, extent of primary habitat, and amount of variety were greater, proportionately, than in these dimensions of the towns' total habitats, and increments in claims for operatives were in line with the towns' total increments on this dimension. Yoredale was far behind Midwest in 1954–55 in habitat resources for education, but its increments on all dimensions were greater, so that the two towns' habitat resources for Education were more similar in 1963–64. In territorial range, Midwest's educational habitat changed from 132 percent of Yoredale's in 1954–55 to 116 percent in 1963–64; in extent of PEH, from 220 percent to 116 percent; in habitat-claims for operatives, from 163 percent to 110 percent; and in variety, from 176 percent of Yoredale's in 1954–55 to 86 percent in 1963–64.

Table 5.18
Education
Control of Educational Habitats by Authority Systems
Percent of primary educational habitats controlled by
different authority systems

		1954–55		1963–64	
		MW (1)	YD (2)	MW (3)	YD (4)
(1)	Extent of PEH in cu	10.1	4.6	16.5	14.2
Percent of PEH controlled by:					
(2)	Churches	21.2	13.0	26.4	4.8
(3)	Govt. Agencies	16.9	0.0	9.5	0.0
(4)	Private Enterprises	3.2	9.8	3.8	2.1
(5)	Schools	56.3	70.4	58.8	89.6
(6)	Voluntary Assns.	2.4	6.8	1.6	3.5

Education is one of the two action pattern habitats where both erosion and accretion were greater in Yoredale than in Midwest (Aesthetics is the other); 41 percent of Yoredale's and 21 percent of Midwest's 1954–55 PEH were dismantled, and 80 percent of Yoredale's and 41 percent of Midwest's PEH were inaugurated between the survey years. The period under consideration is one of educational renovation in Yoredale and of steady renewal and growth in Midwest. These differences between the towns are well represented by their new schools. Yoredale's new school includes a new, modern building, a new staff, a new student body, and a new curriculum; it is a unit of new educational system devised, financed, and established from County Hall, beyond the borders of the Dale region. Midwest's new school includes a new, modern building too, with some staff additions, a slightly enlarged student body, and a few additions to the curriculum; it is a phase in developing a system planned, largely financed, and established within the town and rural district, including citizen acceptance of local bonds to pay for the building.

Despite the increasing similarity of the towns' educational resources, important differences remained in 1963–64. Midwest had special educational services that were missing in Yoredale (such as Speech Therapy, Psychological Services, Classes for the Retarded), and Yoredale taught a greater variety of subjects than Midwest (such as Foreign Language Classes and Craft Classes). The place of Religion Classes in the towns' PEHs differs greatly; they are major educational genotypes in both towns, but in Midwest they are all within the Church authority system and in Yoredale most are within the School authority system; Religious Instruction is a regular part of the curricula of both the state and Roman Catholic schools.

Autonomy. The educational enterprises of the towns differ greatly in the geographical loci of their control. In 1963–64 these percentages were:

	MW	YD
Locally controlled (High local autonomy)	22.9	4.7
Regionally controlled (Medium local autonomy)	76.6	25.4
Controlled from a distance (Low local autonomy)	0.6	69.7

Education is a regional and local responsibility in Midwest, and a county (equivalent to state in Midwest) and national responsibility in Yoredale. The school patrons of both towns come from the town, district, and region; in Midwest the inhabitants of these locales control almost all of the PEH, but in Yoredale they control less than one-third of it.

Government

DEFINITION

The action pattern Government is present within a behavior setting to the extent that concrete occurrences within the setting implement or resist the making, interpretation, and execution of laws and regulations by governmental agencies. This action pattern may involve: engaging in civic affairs; supplying material and behavior objects for governmental programs; learning and teaching about government and legal procedures; appraising governmental policies and officials.

Government is *prominent* within a behavior setting if 80 percent or more of its program involves occurrences of the kinds stated above. It may be prominent in private-enterprise settings, such as lawyers' and solicitors' offices, as well as in officially public settings such as city and parish council meetings. Important genotypes where the action pattern Government is prominent are identified in Table 5.20. The action pattern Government is *secondary* within a setting if government-connected occurrences are greater in degree than the general police surveillance which applies to all settings, but less than the degree defined for settings where Government is prominent—for example, Church Worship Services that regularly include prayers for the President, Queen, or other government officials, and Barbershops which operate in accordance with sanitary regulations prescribed by a government bureau. Government is *absent* from a setting if there are no regular, government-related occurrences; examples are a Newspaper Delivery Route and a Sunday School Class.

It should be especially noted that Government is not prominent within most behavior settings within School authority systems—that is, settings under the aegis of Midwest's school board and of Yoredale's headmasters and school managers. A School Board Meeting and a School Managers' Meeting are primary Government settings (their members are government functionaries, and the action pattern Government is prominent), but School Classes are not classified as primary Government settings unless they receive Government rating for teaching and learning (for example, a Civics Class); Government is secondary in other school settings.

The behavior settings where Government is prominent constitute a town's *primary governmental habitat* (PGH), its primary habitat resources for governmental behavior. Settings where it is present in some degree comprise the *territorial range of Government*.

Basic data for Government are presented in Table 5.19; the report for Aesthetics provides a key to the location of particular data in this table.

SALIENT FINDINGS

The territorial range of Government extends over 70 to 86 percent of the towns' habitats. Habitats with prominent resources for governmental behavior (PGH) comprise 8 to 16 percent of the total habitats. Midwest's PGH is larger than Yoredale's, and the PGH of each town was slightly larger in 1963–64 than in 1954–55. Habitat-claims for operatives within the towns' PGHs constitute 3 to 5 percent of their total claims for operatives; Midwest has more claims for government operatives than Yoredale, and both towns had more such claims in 1963–64

Table 5.19
Government
Basic Habitat Data

Primary Habitat (PGH)	1954–55		1963–64	
	MW (1)	YD (2)	MW (3)	YD (4)
Extent				
(1) Behavior Settings per Year	59	31	69	46
(2) Mean BS per Day	21.7	11.7	23.6	12.8
(3) Mean BS per Hour	7.0	3.9	6.8	3.6
(4) Centiurbs (no.)	14.5	7.9	15.3	8.6
(5) Centiurbs (% of Town Total)	16.1%	8.8%	14.2%	7.6%
Erosion and Accretion				
Type of Change	Erosion from '54–55		Accretion to '63–64	
(6) Centiurbs (no.)	0.9	0.9	2.2	1.2
(7) Centiurbs (% of PGH)	6%	12%	14%	14%
Claims for Operatives				
(8) Number	277	151	327	248
(9) Number (% of Town Total)	5%	4%	3%	3%
Amount of Variety				
(10) Major Genotypes (no.)	14	13	9	14
(11) Total Genotypes (no.)	26	22	27	27
(12) Total Genotypes (% of				
Town Total)	15%	13%	14%	13%
Territorial Range (TR)				
(13) Centiurbs (no.)	68.1	72.6	75.5	97.2
(14) Centiurbs (% of Town Total)	76%	81%	70%	86%

than in 1954–55. The towns had similar amounts of variety within their PGHs; variety increased slightly between the survey years in both towns.

TERRITORIAL RANGE OF GOVERNMENT

Governmental action patterns are regularly present in some degree in 70 to 86 percent of the towns' habitats; and conversely, 14 to 30 percent of the towns' habitats are without governmental components. The TR of Government extends over fewer centiurbs and smaller percentages of Midwest's than of Yoredale's habitat; it increased in extent in both towns between 1954–55 and 1963–64, but more so in Yoredale than in Midwest.

EXTENT OF PRIMARY GOVERNMENTAL HABITAT

In 1963–64 the PGH covered 14.2 percent of Midwest's and 7.6 percent of Yoredale's total habitat, approximately equivalent in Midwest to 31 regular behavior settings that occur six days a week for eight hours a day, and in Yoredale to 17 regular settings. In terms of occasional settings, Midwest's PGH is about equivalent to 306 one-hour meetings of different committees, and Yoredale's is equivalent to 172 occasional settings.

Differences. Midwest's PGH is larger than Yoredale's; in 1963–64

Midwest had 6.7 more cu of PGH, amounting to 178 percent as many cu and to 6.6 more percent of the town's total habitat.

Changes. The towns' PGHs were larger in 1963–64 than in 1954–55. Midwest had 0.8 more cu of PGH in 1963–64, amounting to 105 percent as many cu but to 1.9 fewer percent of the town's total habitat. Yoredale had 0.7 more cu of PGH, amounting to 109 percent as many cu but to 1.2 fewer percent of the town's total habitat.

Processes of change. Less than 13 percent of the towns' 1954–55 PGHs were eroded before 1963–64, and 14 percent of their 1963–64 PGHs were accreted after 1954–55. Erosion was smaller in Midwest than in Yoredale, and accretion was equal in the two towns; 6 fewer percent of Midwest's than of Yoredale's 1954–55 PGH was eroded, and the same percentage of the towns' 1963–64 PGHs was accreted. This differs from the towns' total habitats; more of Midwest's than of Yoredale's habitat was both eroded and accreted.

CLAIMS FOR OPERATIVES WITHIN PRIMARY
GOVERNMENTAL HABITAT

If all behavior settings within the towns' PGHs were to function simultaneously in 1963–64, it would require 327 persons in Midwest and 248 persons in Yoredale to carry out essential operations. Claims for PGH operatives are much smaller than claims for operatives in general, on a centiurb basis; there are 21 claims for operatives per cu of Midwest's PGH, compared with 96 for the whole habitat—that is, 22 percent as many—and there are 29 claims per cu of Yoredale's PGH, compared with 69 for the whole habitat—42 percent as many. The towns' PGHs contain only 3 percent of their total habitat-claims for operatives; whereas, as we have seen, they comprise 14.2 percent (Midwest) and 7.6 percent (Yoredale) of the towns' total habitats. The towns' PGHs are relatively low in positions of responsibility.

Differences. Midwest has more habitat-claims for PGH operatives than Yoredale. In 1963–64 it had 79 more such claims than Yoredale, amounting to 132 percent as many, to 74 percent as many per cu of PGH, to 208 percent as many per town inhabitant, and to the same percentage of the town's total claims for operatives.

Changes. Both towns had more PGH claims for operatives in 1963–64 than in 1954–55. Midwest had 50 more such claims in 1963–64, amounting to 118 percent as many, to 112 percent as many per cu of PGH, and to 102 percent as many per town inhabitant, but to 2 fewer percent of the town's total claims for operatives. Yoredale had 97 more such claims, amounting to 164 percent as many, to 151 percent as many per cu of PGH, to 163 percent as many per town inhabitant, but to 1 fewer percent of the town's total claims for operatives.

VARIETY WITHIN PRIMARY GOVERNMENTAL HABITAT

There was as much variety within Midwest's PGH as expected on the basis of extent, but in Yoredale there was more than expected. In

1963–64 Midwest's PGH, 14 percent of its total habitat, was the locus of 14 percent of its behavior setting genotypes; Yoredale's PGH, 8 percent of its total habitat, was the locus of 13 percent of its genotypes.

If Midwest and Yoredale were to display simultaneously in 1963–64 the complete range of behavior setting programs within their PGHs, both would require 27 different offices and meeting rooms with their appropriate facilities, 27 differently trained and experienced staffs of operators, and 27 different experts as executives.

Differences. The amount of variety within the two towns' PGHs is similar. In 1963–64 Midwest had the same number of genotypes as Yoredale, amounting to 100 percent as many and to 1 more percent of Midwest's than of Yoredale's total genotypes.

Changes. The governmental variety within the towns was slightly greater in 1963–64 than in 1954–55. Midwest had 1 more genotype in 1963–64, amounting to 104 percent as many but to 1 fewer percent of the town's total genotypes. Yoredale had 5 more genotypes, amounting to 123 percent as many and to the same percentage of the town's total genotypes.

NATURE, COMMONALITY, AND DISTINCTIVENESS OF
PRIMARY GOVERNMENTAL HABITAT

The towns' major governmental genotypes have a low degree of commonality (Table 5.20). Of Midwest's 9 and Yoredale's 14 major governmental genotypes in 1963–64, only 1 — Machinery Repair Shops — was both common and major in both survey years. In addition, 4 genotypes were common but not major governmental genotypes in both years: Elections (Polling Places), Fire Stations, Business Meetings, and Civil Weddings. These 5 genotypes identify the stable, common governmental habitats of Midwest and Yoredale. Their number and extent show that there is less commonality within them than within their total habitats. In 1963–64 common genotypes accounted for 18.5 percent of the governmental genotypes of both towns, compared with 33 percent commonality for Midwest's and 31 percent for Yoredale's total genotypes. In terms of centiurbs, these common governmental genotypes comprised 19 percent of Midwest's and 15 percent of Yoredale's PGH, compared with 55 percent and 57 percent commonality, respectively, for the towns' total habitats.

The finding that relatively few governmental genotypes are common to the towns means that the governmental genotypes that are not common, but distinctive, are very important (Table 5.21). Most PGH genotypes of Midwest and Yoredale are partly common to both (commonality categories 3 and 4); major instances are Attorneys' Offices (MW) and Solicitors' Offices (YD), Government Records Offices of both towns, Sheriffs' Offices (MW) and Police Stations (YD), Post Offices (MW) and Post Offices and Stationers and Sorting Post Offices (YD). The PGHs of Midwest and Yoredale are tantalizing mixes of the familiar and the strange to intertown visitors.

Table 5.20
Government
Variety Within the Towns' Primary Government Habitats
Major Genotypes in at Least One Town in One Year

	Percent of PGH			
	1954–55		1963–64	
	MW (1)	YD (2)	MW (3)	YD (4)
(1) Abstract Co. Offices	3.5	0	3.3	0
(2) Accountants Offices	0	12.5	0	11.0
(3) Agric. Advisors Offices	3.4	0	2.8	0
(4) Attorneys Offices	12.6	0	11.1	0
(5) Civil Engnr. & Public Health Offices	0	5.8	0	3.3
(6) Civil Engineers Offices	3.4	0	2.8	0
(7) Govt. Bus. & Record Offices	22.4	4.6	21.8	1.4
(8) Health Dept. Offices	0	5.8	0	4.8
(9) Jails	8.6	0	8.2	0
(10) Judges Chambers	4.4	0	3.6	0
(11) [a] Machin'y Repair Shops	4.0	3.8	6.0	5.7
(12) Meetings, Business	6.9	2.8	8.5	6.3
(13) Physicians Offices	0	0	0	4.6
(14) Police Stations	0	13.3	0	7.9
(15) Post Offices	4.2	0	4.0	0
(16) Post Offices and Statnrs	0	6.1	0	5.5
(17) Post Offices, Sorting	0	7.3	0	9.6
(18) Railway Freight Stations	0	6.3	0	5.8
(19) Railway Maint. Shops	0	6.3	0	0
(20) School Admin. Offices	5.8	0	4.4	3.8
(21) Sewage Disposal Plants	0	7.0	0	3.2
(22) Sheriffs Offices	3.0	0	2.8	0
(23) Soil Conserv. Serv. Offices	3.0	0	2.8	0
(24) Solicitors Offices	0	10.7	0	9.3
(25) Tax Assessm't Offices	0	5.8	0	5.3
(26) Welfare Offices	3.4	0	2.8	0

[a] Major genotypes in both towns and both years that are also common to the towns (category 1).

GENOTYPE SITES OF CHANGE IN
PRIMARY GOVERNMENTAL HABITAT

There were 8 genotype (both major and minor) sites of substantial change in Midwest's PGH (Table 5.22); 6 of these were sites of increment (4 new and 2 enlarged), and 2 of decrement (both were eroded genotypes). There were also 8 genotype sites of substantial change in Yoredale's PGH, 5 of them sites of increment (3 new and 2 enlarged), and 3 of decrement (1 eroded and 2 reduced in extent). In each town 3 of the new sites introduced entirely new primary governmental programs: Motor Vehicle Operators' Classes and Examinations, Water Supply Plants, and Welfare Workers' Classes, in Midwest; and Military Communications Demonstrations, Motor Vehicle Operators' Classes, and School Administrators' Offices, in Yoredale. A single pri-

Table 5.21
Government
Distinctive Genotypes, 1963–64

Commonality Category[a]		Midwest (1)	Yoredale (2)
(1)	7	None	None
(2)	6	Judges Chambers	Military Communica'ns Demons.
(3)		Welfare Workers Classes	Military Train'g Classes
(4)	5	Agric. Advisors Offices	Railway Freight Stations
(5)		Water Supply Plants	
(6)		Weed Inspctrs Offices	
(7)	4	Abstract & Title Co.	Accountants Offices
(8)		Attorney's Offices	Civil Engnrg & Public Health
(9)		Civil Engineers Offices	Court Sessions, Magistr. Courts
(10)		Court Sessions, County	Govt. Bus. & Record Offices
(11)		Court Sessions, Dist.	Health Dept. Offices
(12)		Govt. Bus. & Record Offices	School Admin. Offices
(13)		Jails	Sewage Disposal Plants
(14)		Motor Veh. Oper. Classes	Solicitors Offices
(15)		School Admin. Offices	
(16)		Sheriffs Offices	
(17)		Soil Conserv. Serv. Offices	
(18)	3	Post Offices	Elections, Vote Counts
(19)		Welfare Offices	Motor Veh. Oper. Classes
(20)			Police Stations
(21)			Post Offices & Statnrs Shops
(22)			Post Offices, Sorting
(23)			School Enq. (Truant) Office
(24)			Tax Assess & Collect Office

[a] Genotypes are ordered from those that are unique to each town and environs (category 7) to those whose programs occur in the other town but as components of different genotypes (category 3).

mary governmental site became extinct in each town: Farm Practices Classes in Midwest and Railway Maintenance Shops in Yoredale.

Several substantial changes in the genotype sites of the towns' PGHs are closely related to technological changes: Motor Vehicle Operators' Classes and Examinations, Water Supply Plants, and Machinery Repair Shops, in Midwest; and Military Communications Demonstrations, Motor Vehicle Operators' Classes, Railway Maintenance Shops, and Sewage Disposal Plants, in Yoredale. The remaining changes in both towns have their roots in social and ideological changes and are often consequences of changes in the organization of continuing governmental programs.

We conclude that the primary governmental resources of the towns changed little between 1955 and 1963, that the data provide little evidence of innovative changes in the towns' PGHs, and that an important number of the changes are connected rather directly with technological changes in connection with motor vehicles, railroads, water supplies, and sewage disposal.

Table 5.22
Government
Genotype Sites of Substantial[a] Changes in Extents of Primary Government Habitats
Between 1954–55 and 1963–64

		Midwest (1)	Yoredale (2)
(1)		Court Sessions, County	Military Communicat'ns Demons.
(2)	New Sites	Motor Veh. Oper. Classes	Motor Veh. Oper. Classes
(3)		Water Supply Plants	School Admin. Offices
(4)		Welfare Workers Classes	
(5)	Enlarged Sites	Machin'y Repair Shops	Meetings, Business
(6)		Meetings, Business	Post Offices, Sorting
(7)	Eroded Sites	Court Sessions, Justice of Peace	Railway Maint. Shops
(8)		Farm Pract. Classes	
(9)	Reduced Sites	None	Police Stations
(10)			Sewage Disposal Plants

[a] See footnote a, Table 5.4.

CONTROL BY AUTHORITY SYSTEMS

Not unexpectedly, the data show that the PGHs of both towns are predominantly controlled by Government Agencies; the concentration is greatest in Midwest in 1954–55, where 75 percent of the PGH is controlled by Government Agencies, and none by Churches or Voluntary Associations (Table 5.23). In both years, more of Midwest's than of Yoredale's PGH was controlled by Government Agencies and Schools, and less by Private Enterprises. Examples of behavior settings where Government is prominent but under the aegis of Private Enterprises in Yoredale are: Accountants' Offices, Post Offices and Stationers, Solicitors' Offices, and Physicians' Offices.

The pattern of control by authority systems did not change greatly between 1954–55 and 1963–64. The relative extent of control by Government Agencies and by Private Enterprises was slightly reduced in both towns, and control by Schools increased in both towns. The greatest change is the greater control of PGH by the School authority systems of Yoredale.

SPECIAL FEATURES

Prominence and ubiquity of government. Midwest is more of a governmental center than Yoredale; the programs of about one-seventh of the behavior settings at hand in Midwest are involved primarily with governmental affairs (Attorneys' Offices, Government Record Offices, Judges' Chambers, Advisory Committee Meetings, Abstract Company Offices, and so forth), whereas this is the case for only about one-thirteenth of Yoredale's settings (T5.19; R5; C4,5). At the same time, Midwest has more government-free regions than Yoredale; the programs of

Table 5.23
Government
Control of Government Habitats by Authority Systems
Percent of primary governmental habitats controlled
by different authority systems

	1954–55		1963–64	
	MW (1)	YD (2)	MW (3)	YD (4)
(1) Extent of PGH in cu	14.5	7.9	15.3	8.6
Percent of PGH controlled by:				
(2) Churches	0.0	0.0	0.0	0.6
(3) Govt. Agencies	75.3	68.2	74.7	62.8
(4) Private Enterprises	16.2	29.4	14.5	25.8
(5) Schools	8.5	1.4	10.2	8.6
(6) Voluntary Assns.	0.0	1.0	0.6	2.1

approximately one-third of Midwest's behavior settings are without governmental involvement of any kind (Piano Recitals, Card Club Meetings, Church Choir Practice, Sewing Services, and so forth), whereas, this is the case for only about one-seventh of Yoredale's settings (T5.19; R14; C3,4). The action pattern Government is more widely prominent in Midwest, but it is more nearly ubiquitous in Yoredale.

Autonomy. More of Midwest's than of Yoredale's PGH is locally controlled, and less is controlled from state (county) and national levels, as the following tabulation shows. Percentages of PGH of:

	MW	*YD*
High local autonomy	20	2
Medium local autonomy	49	39
Low local autonomy	30	59

Converted to centiurbs, PGH behavior settings that are controlled within the town or the immediately surrounding rural district (High local autonomy) comprise 3.1 of Midwest's 107 cu of habitat and 0.2 of Yoredale's 113 cu of habitat. The towns' local governmental habitats consist of board and committee meetings; in Midwest there are City Council Meetings, Library Board Meetings, Cemetery District Board Meetings, Volunteer Fire Brigade Meetings and Runs; in Yoredale there are Parish Council Meetings. In addition, there are local private offices in both towns that deal with governmental affairs, such as Autorneys' and Solicitors' Offices and Abstract and Accountants' Offices. In Midwest, local government settings have control, including taxing power, of the town's sewage system, fire station, library, cemetery, local police, and zoning. In Yoredale local government settings deal with the town's street lights, footpaths, cemetery, market place, and parking lot.

Governmental settings that are controlled within the town, district, or region (High and Medium local autonomy) embrace 10.7 cu in Midwest and 3.6 in Yoredale. These are the governmental habitats whose policies, schedules, finances (taxes, membership fees), operatives (paid professionals), and membership rules (eligibility) are determined by people of the town and county or dale whose representatives meet together face-to-face. These governmental settings have more nearly equivalent powers in Midwest and Yoredale, though the targets of their power differ greatly. The Midwest County Commissioners levy taxes within limits imposed by the state and national government for the support of: county police, court, and jail; county roads, public health service, public welfare service. The Yoredale Rural District Council imposes taxes, rates, and scales within limits imposed by the county and national government for the support of public housing, sewage, and water systems, and public health service.

Governmental settings that are controlled by directives from beyond the county or dale in Topeka (capital) or Northallerton (County Hall), in Kansas City or Leeds, in Washington or London (Low local autonomy), comprise 4.6 cu in Midwest and 5.1 cu in Yoredale. Local government is more pervasive in Midwest than in Yoredale.

Nutrition

DEFINITION

The action pattern Nutrition is present within a behavior setting to the extent that the concrete occurrences which constitute its program involve eating or drinking for nutritional purposes (including consuming soft drinks and alcoholic beverages). Nutritional occurrences may take the form of: eating, drinking, and preparing and serving food in the setting; providing food, drink, and utensils for eating in another setting; evaluating nutrition, ways of preparing or serving food, and persons who prepare and serve meals; teaching and learning ways of preparing and serving food.

Nutrition is *prominent* within a behavior setting if 80 percent or more of its standing pattern involves occurrences of the kinds specified above — for example, in Restaurants and Grocery Stores. Nutrition is *secondary* if some, but less than 80 percent of the standing pattern of the setting, is made up of nutritional occurrences, as in Bridge Club Meetings where refreshments are regularly served. Nutrition is *absent* from a setting if no components of its standing pattern regularly involve eating and drinking, food preparation, and so forth.

The behavior settings where Nutrition is prominent constitute a town's *primary nutritional habitat* (PNH), its primary habitat resources for nutritional behavior. Settings where Nutrition is present in some degree comprise the *territorial range of nutrition*.

Basic data for Nutrition are presented in Table 5.24; the report for Aesthetics provides a key to the location of particular data in this table.

SALIENT FINDINGS

The territorial range of nutrition extends over 44 to 70 percent of the towns' habitats. Habitats where resources for Nutrition are prominent (PNH) comprise 7 to 19 percent of the towns' habitats. Midwest's PNH is smaller than Yoredale's, and the PNH was smaller in Midwest and larger in Yoredale in 1963–64 than in 1954–55. Habitat-claims for operatives within the towns' PNHs constitute 5 to 7 percent of their total claims for operatives; Midwest had fewer claims for nutrition operatives than Yoredale in 1954–55 and more in 1963–64; and both towns had more such claims in 1963–64 than in 1954–55. There is less variety within Midwest's PNH; variety increased between the survey years in both towns.

TERRITORIAL RANGE OF NUTRITION

Nutritional action patterns are regularly present to some degree in 44 to 70 percent of the towns' habitats; and conversely, 30 to 56 percent of the towns' habitats are without nutritional components. The TR of Nutrition extends over fewer centiurbs and smaller percentages of Midwest's than of Yoredale's habitat; it increased in extent in both towns between 1954–55 and 1963–64, but more so in Midwest than in Yoredale.

EXTENT OF PRIMARY NUTRITIONAL HABITAT

In 1963–64 the PNH covered 7 percent of Midwest's and 16.5 percent of Yoredale's total habitat, approximately equivalent in Midwest to 15

Table 5.24
Nutrition
Basic Habitat Data

		1954–55		1963–64	
Primary Habitat (PNH)		MW (1)	YD (2)	MW (3)	YD (4)
	Extent				
(1)	Behavior Settings per Year	36	46	52	65
(2)	Mean BS per Day	10.0	29.6	8.7	31.8
(3)	Mean BS per Hour	3.8	8.6	3.0	8.6
(4)	Centiurbs (no.)	7.7	17.2	7.4	18.6
(5)	Centiurbs (% of Town Total)	8.5%	19.1%	6.9%	16.5%
	Erosion and Accretion				
	Type of Change	Erosion from '54–55		Accretion to '63–64	
(6)	Centiurbs (no.)	3.1	2.6	2.5	4.3
(7)	Centiurbs (% of PNH)	40%	15%	33%	23%
	Claims for Operatives				
(8)	Number	288	305	528	466
(9)	Number (% of Town Total)	5%	7%	5%	6%
	Amount of Variety				
(10)	Major Genotypes (no.)	4	7	7	7
(11)	Total Genotypes (no.)	11	18	17	23
(12)	Total Genotypes (% of Town Total)	6%	11%	9%	11%
	Territorial Range (TR)				
(13)	Centiurbs (no.)	39.2	63.0	52.5	73.4
(14)	Centiurbs (% of Town Total)	44%	70%	49%	65%

regular behavior settings that occur six days a week for eight hours a day, and in Yoredale to 37 regular settings.

Differences. Midwest's PNH is smaller than Yoredale's; in 1963–64 Midwest had 11.2 fewer cu of PNH, amounting to 40 percent as many cu and to 9.6 fewer percent of the town's total habitat.

Changes. Midwest's PNH was smaller in 1963–64 than in 1954–55, and Yoredale's was larger. Midwest had 0.3 fewer cu of PNH in 1963–64, amounting to 96 percent as many cu and to 1.6 fewer percent of the town's total habitat. Yoredale had 1.4 more cu of PNH, amounting to 108 percent as many cu and to 2.6 fewer percent of the town's total habitat.

Processes of change. More than one-sixth of the towns' 1954–55 PNHs were eroded before 1963–64, and more than one-fifth of their 1963–64 PNHs were accreted after 1954–55. Both erosion and accretion were greater in Midwest; 25 more percent of Midwest's than of Yoredale's 1954–55 PNH was eroded, and 10 more percent of its 1963–64 PNH was accreted. The same is true for the towns' total habitats; more of Midwest's than of Yoredale's habitat was both eroded and accreted.

CLAIMS FOR OPERATIVES WITHIN PRIMARY
NUTRITIONAL HABITAT

If all behavior settings within the towns' PNHs were to function simultaneously in 1963–64, it would require 528 persons in Midwest and 466 persons in Yoredale to carry out essential operations. Claims for PNH operatives are smaller than claims for operatives in general, on a centiurb basis; there are 71 claims for operatives per cu of Midwest's PNH, compared with 96 for the whole habitat—that is, 74 percent as many—and there are 25 claims per cu of Yoredale's PNH, compared with 69 for the whole habitat—36 percent as many. In 1963–64 the towns' PNHs contained 5 and 6 percent of their total habitat-claims for operatives; whereas, as we have seen, they comprised 7 and 16.5 percent of the towns' total habitats. The towns' PNHs are relatively meager in positions of responsibility.

Differences. Midwest has more habitat-claims for PNH operatives than Yoredale. In 1963–64 it had 62 more such claims than Yoredale, amounting to 113 percent as many, to 285 percent as many per cu of PNH, to 179 percent as many per town inhabitant, and to 1 fewer percent of the town's total claims for operatives.

Changes. Both towns had more PNH claims for operatives in 1963–64 than in 1954–55. Midwest had 240 more such claims in 1963–64, amounting to 183 percent as many, to 191 percent as many per cu of PNH, and to 158 percent as many per town inhabitant, but to the same percentage of the town's total claims for operatives. Yoredale had 161 more such claims, amounting to 153 percent as many, to 141 percent as many per cu of PNH, and to 152 percent as many per town inhabitant, but to 1 fewer percent of the town's total claims for operatives.

There is somewhat more variety within Midwest's PNH, and somewhat less within Yoredale's, than expected on the basis of extent. In 1963–64 Midwest's PNH, 7 percent of its total habitat, was the locus of 9 percent of its behavior setting genotypes; Yoredale's PNH, 16.5 percent of its total habitat, was the locus of 11 percent of its genotypes.

If Midwest and Yoredale were to display simultaneously in 1963–64 the complete range of behavior setting programs within their PNHs, Midwest would require 17 different facilities, 17 differently trained and experienced staffs of clerks, cooks, waiters, and so forth, and 17 different experts as managers; and Yoredale would require 23 different halls, staffs, and leaders.

Differences. There is less variety within Midwest's PNH than within Yoredale's. In 1963–64 Midwest had 6 fewer genotypes than Yoredale, amounting to 74 percent as many and to 2 fewer percent of Midwest's than of Yoredale's total genotypes.

Changes. There was more variety within the towns' PNHs in 1963–64 than in 1954–55. Midwest had 6 more genotypes in 1963–64, amounting to 154 percent as many and to 3 more percent of the town's total genotypes. Yoredale had 5 more genotypes, amounting to 128 percent as many and to the same percentage of the town's total genotypes.

NATURE, COMMONALITY, AND DISTINCTIVENESS OF
PRIMARY NUTRITIONAL HABITAT

The towns' major nutritional genotypes have a rather low degree of commonality (Table 5.25). Of Midwest's 9 and Yoredale's 11 major nutritional genotypes in 1963–64, only 2 — Grocery Stores and Restaurants — were both common and major in both survey years. In addition, 2 genotypes common in both years were not major nutritional genotypes: Dinners and Banquets, and Food and Rummage Sales. These 4 genotypes identify the stable, common nutritional habitats of Midwest and Yoredale. In terms of number of genotypes, there is less commonality within the towns' PNHs than within their total habitats. In 1963–64 common genotypes accounted for 23 percent of Midwest's and 17 percent of Yoredale's nutritional genotypes, compared with 33 percent commonality for Midwest's and 31 percent for Yoredale's total genotypes. But in terms of centiurbs, the common nutritional genotypes comprised 67 percent of Midwest's and 42 percent of Yoredale's PNH, compared with 55 percent and 57 percent commonality, respectively, for the town's total habitats.

Yoredale has a more distinctive nutritional habitat than Midwest — 11 vs. 6 distinctive genotypes — and some of Yoredale's distinctive nutritional genotypes are extensive: Darts Games, Fish and Chips Shops, Public Markets, Bakeries, Pubs, Butcher Shops (Table 5.26). Aside from Taverns, Midwest's distinctive nutritional genotypes are of small extent. In all, Yoredale's distinctive nutritional genotypes comprise 58 percent of its PNH, whereas Midwest's comprise only 33 per-

Table 5.25
Nutrition
Variety Within the Towns' Primary Nutritional Habitats
Major Genotypes in at Least One Town in One Year

	Percentage of PNH			
	1954–55		1963–64	
	MW (1)	YD (2)	MW (3)	YD (4)
(1) Bakeries	0	2.9	0	5.2
(2) Butcher Shops	0	9.0	0	8.9
(3) Confectnrs & Statnrs	0	8.9	0	0
(4) Deliv. & Collect'n Routes	9.2	0	4.3	0
(5) Dinners & Banquets	2.0	0.3	5.5	0.6
(6) Fish & Chips Shops	0	5.5	0	2.2
(7) Food & Rummage Sales	3.9	0.3	4.1	0.3
(8) [a] Grocery Stores	42.0	29.0	18.0	28.4
(9) Milk Deliv. Serv.	0	8.3	0	6.6
(10) Milk Collect'n Plants	0	2.9	0	3.3
(11) Pubs & Dining Rooms	0	18.1	0	14.4
(12) [a] Restaurants	32.8	8.4	40.2	12.7
(13) Taverns	2.1	0	9.9	0
(14) Water Supply Plants	0	0	4.0	0

[a] Major genotypes in both towns and both years that are also common to the towns (category 1).

Table 5.26
Nutrition
Distinctive Genotypes, 1963–64

Commonality Category[a]		Midwest (1)	Yoredale (2)
(1)	7	Ice Cream Socials	Darts Games
(2)		Sales Prom. Openings	Fish & Chips Shops
(3)			Markets, Public
(4)			Sales Routes, Fish
(5)	6	None	Egg-Pack'g Plants
(6)			Milk Collect'n Plants
(7)	5	Water Supply Plants	None
(8)	4	Taverns	Bakeries
(9)			Milk Bottl'g & Deliv. Serv.
(10)			Pubs & Dining Rooms
(11)	3	Bakery Serv., to Order	Butcher Shops
(12)		Picnics	Kitchens, Institutnl

[a] Genotypes are ordered from those that are unique to each town and environs (category 7) to those whose programs occur in the other town but as components of different genotypes (category 3).

cent of its PNH. Midwest's PNH is smaller and less distinctive than Yoredale's.

GENOTYPE SITES OF CHANGE IN PRIMARY
NUTRITIONAL HABITAT

There were 6 genotype sites of substantial change in Midwest's PNH between the survey years; 5 of these were sites of increment, and 1 a reduced site (Table 5.27). There were 10 sites of substantial change in Yoredale's PNH, 6 of them increments and 4 decrements. Most of the changes in the towns' nutritional habitats are linked with technological and economic changes. In Midwest, the new Water Supply Plant is a resultant of widespread changes in the water resources of the Midwest region (the water table is falling); in water standards and technology (purification), and in fire insurance rates (without an adequate water supply, rates become burdensome). The demise of Garden Allotments and Slaughterhouses in Yoredale is similarly related to changes in the economics and technology of food processing and distribution. Yoredale's new Cooking Classes and enlarged Institutional Kitchens are resultants of the new school.

CONTROL BY AUTHORITY SYSTEMS

Private Enterprises dominate the PNHs of both towns, but they are less dominant in Midwest than in Yoredale (T5.28). Churches and Schools have substantially greater control of Midwest's than of Yoredale's nutritional habitat. The churches of Midwest have more Dinners and Banquets for their members than do those of Yoredale, and in addition many dinners are served by the women's organizations for non-church groups, as a public service in view of the town's limited restau-

Table 5.27
Nutrition
Genotype Sites of Substantial[a] Changes in Extents of Primary Nutritional Habitats
Between 1954–55 and 1963–64

		Midwest (1)	Yoredale (2)
(1)	New Sites	Water Supply Plants	Cooking Classes
(2)		Picnics	Egg-Pack'g Plants
(3)		Dinners & Banquets	Bakeries
(4)	Enlarged	Taverns	Grocery Stores
(5)	Sites	Restaurants	Institutnl Kitchens
(6)			Restaurants
(7)	Eroded	None	Garden Allotments
(8)	Sites		Slaughterhouses
(9)	Reduced	Grocery Stores	Fish & Chips Shops
(10)	Sites		Pubs & Dining Rooms

[a] See footnote a, Table 5.4.

Table 5.28
Nutrition
Control of Nutritional Habitats by Authority Systems
Percent of primary nutritional habitats
controlled by different authority systems

		1954–55		1963–64	
		MW (1)	YD (2)	MW (3)	YD (4)
(1)	Extent of PNH in cu	7.7	17.2	7.4	18.6
Percent of PNH controlled by:					
(2)	Churches	3.3	0.0	6.1	0.8
(3)	Govt. Agencies	2.6	2.2	7.4	1.2
(4)	Private Enterprises	78.2	88.4	64.2	85.9
(5)	Schools	12.0	2.6	12.6	6.9
(6)	Voluntary Assns.	3.9	6.7	9.6	5.1

rants and as a way of raising money for church projects. Government Agencies are involved in the nutritional habitat of Midwest in 1963–64 via the Agricultural Extension Service, which conducts many classes, demonstrations, and lectures on food preparation and nutrition. Many equivalent settings of Yoredale are under the aegis of Voluntary Associations (such as the Women's Institute and Young Farmers).

SPECIAL FEATURES

Autonomy. The towns' habitat resources for nutrition are largely controlled locally; 74.3 percent of Midwest's PNH and 61.8 percent of Yoredale's PNH are controlled within the town or immediately surrounding rural district. This compares with 43.6 and 30.9 percent, respectively, for the whole habitats of Midwest and Yoredale. No other action pattern habitat has more local autonomy in Midwest and only 1 (Personal Appearance) has more in Yoredale.

Personal Appearance

DEFINITION

The action pattern Personal Appearance is present within a behavior setting to the extent that the concrete occurrences which constitute its program improve personal appearance via clothing, grooming, or adornment. Such occurrences may take the form of: getting well-dressed, well-groomed, looking one's best; supplying materials for enhancing personal appearance; displaying and evaluating well-dressed persons or equipment for grooming; teaching and learning ways and means of improving personal appearance.

Personal Appearance is *prominent* within a behavior setting if 80 percent or more of its standing pattern displays dress and adornment or enhances personal appearance within other settings. For example, in behavior settings of the genotypes Barbershops (Men's Hairdressers) and Beauty Shops (Ladies' Hairdressers), Personal Appearance is prominent because almost all components of the settings contribute toward improvement of the grooming of most of the inhabitants; Personal Appearance is prominent in settings of the genotype Church Weddings because most of the program involves display of dress and adornment achieved in other settings. Personal Appearance is a *secondary* attribute of a setting if some but less than 80 percent of its standing pattern contributes to or displays enhanced personal appearance. Personal Appearance is *absent* from a behavior setting if the program regularly involves no appreciation or enhancement of personal appearance—as, for example, in most settings of the genotypes Fire Drills and Dairy Barns.

The behavior settings where Personal Appearance is prominent constitute a town's *primary habitat for personal appearance* (PPAH), and the settings where Personal Appearance is present in some degree, primary or secondary, comprise its *territorial range*.

Basic data for Personal Appearance are presented in Table 5.29; the report for Aesthetics provides a key to the location of particular data in this table.

SALIENT FINDINGS

The territorial range of Personal Appearance extends over 24 to 37 percent of the towns' habitats. Habitats where resources for the enhancement or display of Personal Appearance are prominent (PPAH) comprise 3 to 6 percent of the towns' habitats. Midwest's PPAH is smaller than Yoredale's, and the PPAH of both towns was larger in 1963–64 than in 1954–55. Habitat-claims for operatives within the towns' PPAHs comprise 1 to 14 percent of their total claims for operatives; Midwest has more claims for personal appearance operatives than Yoredale does, and Midwest had more and Yoredale fewer such claims in 1963–64 than in 1954–55. There is greater variety within Midwest's PPAH; variety increased between the survey years in Midwest and declined in Yoredale.

TERRITORIAL RANGE OF PERSONAL APPEARANCE

Personal Appearance action patterns are regularly present to some degree in roughly one-fourth to one-third of the towns' habitats; and conversely, about two-thirds to three-quarters of the towns' habitats are without components for the enhancement or display of personal beauty. In 1963–64 the TR of Personal Appearance extended over fewer centiurbs and a smaller percentage of Midwest's than of Yoredale's habitat; it increased in both towns between the survey years, but much more so in Yoredale than in Midwest.

EXTENT OF PRIMARY PERSONAL APPEARANCE HABITAT

In 1963–64 the PPAHs covered 3.3 percent of Midwest's and 5.1 percent of Yoredale's total habitat, approximately equivalent in Midwest to 7 regular behavior settings, such as Barbershops and Clothiers, that occur six days a week for eight hours a day, and in Yoredale to 11 regular settings. In terms of one-hour occasional settings, such as Fashion Shows and Parades, Midwest's PPAH is approximately equivalent to 70 and Yoredale's to 114 different settings.

Differences. Midwest's PPAH is smaller than Yoredale's; in 1963–64 Midwest had 2.2 fewer cu of PPAH, amounting to 61 percent as many cu and to 1.8 fewer percent of the town's total habitat.

Changes. Both towns' PPAHs were larger in 1963–64 than in 1954–55. Midwest had 0.6 more cu of PPAH in 1963–64, amounting to 121 percent as many cu and to 0.1 more percent of the town's total habitat. Yoredale had 0.4 more cu of PPAH, amounting to 107 percent as many cu but to 0.8 fewer percent of the town's total habitat.

Processes of change. More than one-fifth of the towns' 1954–55 PPAHs were eroded before 1963–64, and more than one-fifth of their 1963–64 PPAHs were accreted after 1954–55. Erosion was smaller and accretion was greater in Midwest than in Yoredale; 7 fewer percent of Midwest's 1954–55 PPAH was eroded, and 12 more percent of its 1963–64 PPAH was accreted. This differs from the towns' total habitats; more of Midwest's than of Yoredale's habitat was both eroded and accreted.

CLAIMS FOR OPERATIVES WITHIN PRIMARY
PERSONAL APPEARANCE HABITAT

If all behavior settings within the towns' PPAHs were to function simultaneously in 1963–64, it would require 774 persons in Midwest and only 86 persons in Yoredale to carry out essential operations. Claims for PPAH operatives are greater in Midwest and smaller in Yoredale than claims for operatives in general, on a centiurb basis. There are 221 claims for operatives per cu of Midwest's PPAH, compared with 96 for the whole habitat—that is, 231 percent as many—and there are 15 claims per cu of Yoredale's PPAH, compared with 69 for the whole habitat—22 percent as many. In 1963–64 Midwest's PPAH contained 8 percent of its total habitat-claims for operatives, whereas it comprised 3.3 percent of both towns' total habitats; Midwest's PPAH is rich in positions of responsibility. The reverse is true for Yoredale; its PPAH contained only 1 percent of its total habitat-claims for operatives, and comprised 5.1 percent of its total habitat.

Differences. Midwest has more habitat-claims for PPAH operatives than Yoredale. In 1963–64 it had 688 more such claims than Yoredale, amounting to 900 percent as many, to 1,466 percent as many per cu of PPAH, to 1,420 percent as many per town inhabitant, and to 7 more percent of the town's total claims for operatives.

Changes. Midwest had more and Yoredale had fewer PPAH claims for operatives in 1963–64 than in 1954–55. Midwest had 34 more such claims in 1963–64, amounting to 105 percent as many, to 87 percent as many per cu of PPAH, to 90 percent as many per town inhabitant, and to 6 fewer percent of the town's total claims for operatives. Yoredale had 298 fewer such claims, amounting to 22 percent as many, to 21 per-

Table 5.29
Personal Appearance
Basic Habitat Data

Primary Habitat (PPAH)	1954–55		1963–64	
	MW (1)	YD (2)	MW (3)	YD (4)
Extent				
(1) Behavior Settings per Year	19	23	23	21
(2) Mean BS per Day	3.5	8.4	4.4	9.6
(3) Mean BS per Hour	1.2	2.4	1.5	2.7
(4) Centiurbs (no.)	2.9	5.3	3.5	5.7
(5) Centiurbs (% of Town Total)	3.2%	5.9%	3.3%	5.1%
Erosion and Accretion Type of Change	Erosion from '54–55		Accretion to '63–64	
(6) Centiurbs (no.)	0.6	1.4	1.2	1.3
(7) Centiurbs (% of PPAH)	20%	27%	35%	23%
Claims for Operatives				
(8) Number	740	384	774	86
(9) Number (% of Town Total)	14%	9%	8%	1%
Amount of Variety				
(10) Major Genotypes (no.)	8	6	7	5
(11) Total Genotypes (no.)	14	11	15	8
(12) Total Genotypes (% of Town Total)	8%	6%	8%	4%
Territorial Range (TR)				
(13) Centiurbs (no.)	26.3	22.0	31.8	41.6
(14) Centiurbs (% of Town Total)	29%	24%	30%	37%

cent as many per cu of PPAH, to 22 percent as many per town inhabitant, and to 6 fewer percent of the town's total claims for operatives.

VARIETY WITHIN PRIMARY PERSONAL APPEARANCE HABITAT

There is more variety within Midwest's PPAH than expected on the basis of extent; in 1963–64 its PPAH, 3 percent of its total habitat, was the locus of 8 percent of its behavior setting genotypes. Yoredale's PPAH is somewhat less varied than expected; its PPAH comprised 5 percent of its total habitat and was the locus of 4 percent of its genotypes in 1963–64.

If Midwest and Yoredale were to display simultaneously in 1963–64 the complete range of behavior setting programs within their PPAHs, Midwest would require 15 different shops, stores, and halls with their appropriate facilities, 15 differently trained and experienced staffs, and 15 different experts as executives; Yoredale would require 8 different halls, staffs, and leaders.

Differences. There is more variety within Midwest's PPAH than within Yoredale's. In 1963–64 Midwest had 7 more genotypes than Yoredale, amounting to 187 percent as many and to 4 more percent of Midwest's than of Yoredale's total genotypes.

Changes. There was a little more variety within Midwest's PPAH, and a little less within Yoredale's, in 1963–64 than in 1954–55. Midwest had 1 more genotype in 1963–64, amounting to 107 percent as many and to the same percentage of the town's total genotypes; Yoredale had 3 fewer genotypes, amounting to 73 percent as many and to 2 fewer percent of the town's total genotypes.

NATURE, COMMONALITY, AND DISTINCTIVENESS OF PRIMARY
PERSONAL APPEARANCE HABITAT

The two towns' major personal appearance genotypes have a rather high degree of commonality (Table 5.30). Of Midwest's 7 and Yoredale's 5 major personal appearance genotypes in 1963–64, 3 were both common and major in both survey years: Barbershops, Beauty Shops, and Clothiers and Dry Goods Stores. In addition, 2 genotypes common in both years were not major personal-appearance genotypes: Sewing and Dressmaking Classes, and Church Weddings. These 5 genotypes comprise the stable, common habitats of Midwest and Yoredale that regularly enhance or display Personal Appearance. Their number and extent show that there is as much or more commonality within the towns' PPAHs as within their total habitats. In 1963–64 common genotypes accounted for 33 percent of Midwest's and 62 percent of Yoredale's personal-appearance genotypes, compared with 33 percent commonality for Midwest's and 31 percent for Yoredale's total genotypes; in terms of centiurbs, they comprised 61 percent of Midwest's and 91 percent of Yoredale's PPAH, compared with 55 percent and 57 percent commonality, respectively, for the towns' total habitats. These common genotypes consist mainly of settings for the enhancement of Personal

Table 5.30
Personal Appearance
Variety Within the Towns' Primary Personal Appearance Habitats
Major Genotypes in at Least One Town in One Year

| | Percent of PPAH | | | |
| | 1954–55 | | 1963–64 | |
	MW (1)	YD (2)	MW (3)	YD (4)
(1) [a] Barbershops (Men's)	29.6	16.9	21.7	9.8
(2) [a] Beauty Shops (Ladies')	17.4	19.1	17.0	24.6
(3) [a] Clothiers & Dry Goods Stores	21.0	40.3	16.2	46.8
(4) Knitting Classes & Serv.	0	6.7	4.1	0
(5) Needlecraft Shops	0	0	0	7.2
(6) Parades	3.5	1.9	5.7	0
(7) Programs of Choral Music	3.5	0	0	0
(8) Sales Routes: Cosmetics, etc.	7.0	0	7.5	0
(9) Sewing & Dressmak'g Classes	3.6	2.6	2.9	7.0
(10) Sewing Serv.	0	5.9	12.1	0
(11) Weddings, Church	3.6	3.8	2.8	2.7

[a] Major genotypes in both towns and both years that are also common to the towns (category 1).

Table 5.31
Personal Appearance
Distinctive Genotypes, 1963–64

Commonality Category[a]		Midwest (1)	Yoredale (2)
(1)	7	None	None
(2)	6	None	None
(3)	5	None	None
(4)	4	Grad. & Prom. Cerems.	Stage Makeup Classes
(5)	3	Fashion Shows	Needlecraft Mat'ls Shops

[a] Genotypes are ordered from those that are unique to each town and environs (category 7) to those whose programs occur in the other town but as components of different genotypes (category 3).

Appearance and secondarily of settings for the display of Personal Appearance.

The towns have few distinctive genotypes for the enhancement or display of Personal Appearance (Table 5.31). Midwest has 2 distinctive genotypes for display, and Yoredale has 2 for enhancement.

GENOTYPE SITES OF CHANGE IN PRIMARY
PERSONAL APPEARANCE HABITAT

In Midwest, only 2 genotypes were sites of substantial change in PPAH between 1954–55 and 1963–64; both were sites of increment, and both involve the enhancement of Personal Appearance (Table 5.32). There were 6 genotype sites of substantial change in Yoredale's PPAH, 2 of them increments — both for enhancement — and 4 decrements, 3 for enhancement and 1 for display.

CONTROL BY AUTHORITY SYSTEMS

The PPAHs of both towns are dominated by Private Enterprises; more than three-quarters are controlled by such private undertakings as Barbershops, Clothiers and Dry Goods Stores, and Knitting Classes (Table 5.33). Private Enterprises are somewhat less dominant in Midwest than in Yoredale; in 1963–64 Midwest's Government Agencies, via the Agricultural Extension Service, controlled almost 6 percent of its PPAH, in the form of sewing classes and fashion shows. There is no government sponsorship of the PPAH of Yoredale.

SPECIAL FEATURES

Model settings. The data show that behavior settings where Personal Appearance is prominent are less extensive in Midwest than in Yoredale (comprising 61 percent as many centiurbs in Midwest in 1963–64) but that the number of habitat-claims for operatives within these settings is much greater (by a factor of 9) in Midwest. These differences are in line with those for the towns' total habitats — fewer centiurbs of habitat, but more habitat-claims for operatives, in Midwest

Table 5.32
Personal Appearance
Genotype Sites of Substantial[a] Changes in Extents of
Primary Personal Appearance Habitats Between 1954–55 and 1963–64

		Midwest (1)	Yoredale (2)
(1)	New Sites	Knitting Classes & Serv.	
(2)		Sewing Serv.	
(3)	Enlarged Sites	None	Beauty Shops
(4)			Clothiers & Dry Goods Stores
(5)	Eroded Sites	None	Knitting Serv.
(6)			Parades
(7)			Sewing Serv.
(8)	Reduced Sites	None	Barbershops

[a] See footnote *a*, Table 5.4.

than in Yoredale—but here the differences are greatly magnified. Midwest's PPAH comprises 3.3 percent of its total habitat and has 8 percent of its total habitat-claims for operatives, whereas Yoredale's PPAH comprises 5.1 percent of its total habitat and has only 1 percent of its habitat-claims. The general difference between the towns in these respects is exemplified by their distinctive personal-appearance genotypes (Table 5.31), Graduation and Promotion Ceremonies and Fashion Shows in Midwest and Stage Makeup Classes and Needlecraft Materials Shops in Yoredale. Graduation and Promotion Ceremonies and Fashion Shows have a habitat-claim for every graduate and every exhibitor; in 1963–64 there were 93 habitat-claims in these 2 genotypes which are, however, only 0.15 cu in extent. But Stage Makeup Classes and Needlecraft Materials Shops have relatively few habitat-claims for operatives; in 1963–64 there were only 4 habitat-claims in these 2 genotypes which were 0.47 cu in extent.

By and large, Midwesterners display themselves in their finery within occasional settings as operatives. Parades are an example; there were four costume and fancy-uniform parades in Midwest in 1963–64 (Halloween Celebration Parade, Old Settlers' Reunion Pet Parade, and two High School Band Parades) with 340 habitat-claims for operatives. There were no parades in Yoredale. On the other hand, there are few settings in Midwest whose programs call for more than informal dress by members; most of these are Lodge Meetings.

By and large, Dalesmen display themselves in their finery in occasional settings as members. Dinner-dances are an example; there were 14 dinner-dances in Yoredale in 1963–64 and only 1 in Midwest. On the other hand, there are few settings in Yoredale whose programs call for many dressed for display; the most notable is Weddings, where all members of the wedding party are operatives. Weddings had 56 habitat-claims for operatives in Yoredale in 1963–64 and 98 in Midwest. The great decline in claims for operatives within Yoredale's PPAH

Table 5.33
Personal Appearance
Control of Personal Appearance Habitats by Authority Systems
Percent of primary personal appearance habitats
controlled by different authority systems

		1954–55		1963–64	
		MW (1)	YD (2)	MW (3)	YD (4)
(1)	Extent of PPAH in cu	2.9	5.3	3.5	5.7
	Percent of PPAH controlled by:				
(2)	Churches	3.6	3.8	2.8	2.7
(3)	Govt. Agencies	5.4	0.9	5.8	0
(4)	Private Enterprises	77.2	88.9	78.7	88.4
(5)	Schools	12.1	2.6	8.5	7.0
(6)	Voluntary Assns.	1.7	3.8	4.2	1.9

(from 384 in 1954–55 to 86 in 1963–64) was due to the discontinuance of a single setting with a fancy-dress children's parade and costume contest, Children's Gala Day. The demise of this setting was greatly regretted by some, who often expressed the view, however, that "it was just too much work"; others felt that children have sufficient other treats in these times.

Autonomy. Both towns' habitat resources for Personal Appearance are largely locally controlled, Yoredale's more so than Midwest's. Almost two-thirds (64.6 percent) of Yoredale's PPAH and more than half (55.2 percent) of Midwest's PPAH are controlled within the town and rural districts. No other action pattern habitat has greater local autonomy in Yoredale, and only 2 have greater local autonomy in Midwest.

Physical Health

DEFINITION

The action pattern Physical Health is present within a behavior setting to the extent that the concrete occurrences which constitute the program of the setting improve physical health. Such occurrences may take the form of: caring medically for people or promoting physical health in any way, including athletic activities to improve health; supplying medicines, equipment, books, and money to promote health in other settings; judging and recognizing health via physical examinations and awards for physical prowess; teaching and learning ways of improving health.

Physical Health is *prominent* in a behavior setting if 80 percent or more of its standing pattern promotes health within it or in other settings. Examples are Doctors' Offices and Solicitation of Funds for organizations such as the Tuberculosis Association. Physical Health is *secondary* if some but less than 80 percent of the standing pattern of a setting contributes to health—as, for example, in Scout Meetings. Physical Health is *absent* from a behavior setting if its program regularly has no direct connection with health.

The behavior settings of a town where Physical Health is prominent constitute its *primary physical health habitat* (PHH), its primary habitat resources for the improvement of health. Settings where the action pattern Physical Health is prominent or secondary comprise its *territorial range*.

Basic data for Physical Health are presented in Table 5.34; the report for Aesthetics provides a key to the location of particular data in this table.

SALIENT FINDINGS

The territorial range of Physical Health extends over 15 to 21 percent of the towns' habitats. Habitats where resources for improving health are prominent (PHH) comprise 2 to 5 percent of the towns' habitats. Midwest's PHH is smaller than Yoredale's, and the PHHs of both towns were larger in 1963–64 than in 1954–55. Habitat-claims for operatives within the towns' PHHs constitute no more than 2 percent of their total claims for operatives; Midwest has fewer claims for health operatives than Yoredale, and both towns had more such claims in

Table 5.34
Physical Health
Basic Habitat Data

	1954–55		1963–64	
Primary Habitat (PHH)	MW (1)	YD (2)	MW (3)	YD (4)
Extent				
(1) Behavior Settings per Year	10	24	20	50
(2) Mean BS per Day	3.4	6.0	6.4	10.3
(3) Mean BS per Hour	0.7	1.6	0.4	1.6
(4) Centiurbs (no.)	1.9	4.0	2.8	6.3
(5) Centiurbs (% of Town Total)	2.1%	4.5%	2.6%	5.5%
Erosion and Accretion				
Type of Change	Erosion from '54–55		Accretion to '63–64	
(6) Centiurbs (no.)	1.3	0.4	2.2	2.7
(7) Centiurbs (% of PHH)	69%	10%	77%	44%
Claims for Operatives				
(8) Number	23	77	44	161
(9) Number (% of Town Total)	0.4%	2%	0.4%	2%
Amount of Variety				
(10) Major Genotypes (no.)	5	7	5	9
(11) Total Genotypes (no.)	6	11	8	15
(12) Total Genotypes (% of Town Total)	3%	6%	4%	7%
Territorial Range (TR)				
(13) Centiurbs (no.)	15.6	13.2	23.0	21.9
(14) Centiurbs (% of Town Total)	17%	15%	21%	19%

1963–64 than in 1954–55. Midwest's PHH is less varied than Yoredale's; variety increased in both towns between the survey years.

TERRITORIAL RANGE OF PHYSICAL HEALTH

The territorial range of Physical Health extends over 15 to 21 percent of the towns' total habitats; and conversely, 79 to 85 percent of the towns' habitats are without health components. The TR of Physical Health is smaller in Midwest than Yoredale, and it increased in both towns between 1954–55 and 1963–64.

EXTENT OF PRIMARY HEALTH HABITAT

In 1963–64 the PHHs covered 2.6 percent of Midwest's and 5.5 percent of Yoredale's total habitat, approximately equivalent in Midwest to 6 regular behavior settings, such as Dentists' and Doctors' Offices, that occur six days a week for eight hours a day, and in Yoredale to 13 regular settings.

Differences. Midwest's PHH is smaller than Yoredale's; in 1963–64 Midwest had 3.5 fewer cu of PHH, amounting to 44 percent as many cu and to 2.9 fewer percent of the town's total habitat.

Changes. Both towns' PHHs were larger in 1963–64 than in 1954–55. Midwest had 0.9 more cu of PHH in 1963–64, amounting to 147 percent as many cu and to 0.5 more percent of the town's total habitat. Yoredale had 2.3 more cu of PHH amounting to 157 percent as many cu and to 1.0 more percent of the town's total habitat.

Processes of change. Both erosion and accretion of the PHH were greater in Midwest than in Yoredale; 59 more percent of Midwest's than of Yoredale's 1954–55 PHH was eroded, and 33 more percent of its 1963–64 PHH was accreted. The same is true for the towns' total habitats; more of Midwest's than of Yoredale's habitat was both eroded and accreted.

CLAIMS FOR OPERATIVES WITHIN PRIMARY HEALTH HABITAT

If all behavior settings within the towns' PHHs were to function simultaneously in 1963–64, it would require 44 persons in Midwest and 161 persons in Yoredale to carry out essential operations. Claims for PHH operatives are much less than claims for operatives in general, on a centiurb basis; there are 16 claims for operatives per cu of Midwest's PHH, compared with 96 for the whole habitat—that is, 17 percent as many—and there are 26 per cu of Yoredale's PHH, compared with 69 for the whole habitat—38 percent as many. In 1963–64, the towns' PHHs contained 0.4 and 2.0 percent of their total habitat-claims for operatives; whereas, as we have seen, they comprised 2.6 and 5.5 percent of the towns' total habitats. The towns' PHHs are relatively meager loci of positions of responsibility.

Differences. Midwest has fewer habitat-claims for PHH operatives than Yoredale. In 1963–64 it had 117 fewer such claims than Yoredale, amounting to 27 percent as many, to 61 percent as many per cu of

PHH, to 43 percent as many per town inhabitant, and to 1.6 fewer percent of the town's total claims for operatives.

Changes. Both towns had more PHH claims for operatives in 1963–64 than in 1954–55. Midwest had 21 more such claims in 1963–64 amounting to 191 percent as many, to 130 percent as many per cu of PHH, and to 165 percent as many per town inhabitant, but to the same percentage of the town's total claims for operatives. Yoredale had 84 more such claims, amounting to 209 percent as many, to 133 percent as many per cu of PHH, and to 207 percent as many per town inhabitant, but to the same percentage of the town's total claims.

VARIETY WITHIN PRIMARY HEALTH HABITAT

There is more variety within the two towns' PHHs than expected on the basis of extent. In 1963–64 Midwest's PHH, 2.6 percent of its total habitat, was the locus of 4 percent of its genotypes; Yoredale's PHH, 5.5 percent of its total habitat, was the locus of 7 percent of its genotypes.

If Midwest and Yoredale were to display simultaneously in 1963–64 the complete range of behavior setting programs within their PHHs, Midwest would require 8 different offices, laboratories, and exhibit rooms with their appropriate facilities, 8 differently trained and experienced staffs, and 8 different experts; and Yoredale would require 15 different rooms, staffs, and leaders.

Differences. There is less variety within Midwest's PHH than within Yoredale's. In 1963–64 Midwest had 7 fewer genotypes than Yoredale, amounting to 53 percent as many and to 3 fewer percent of Midwest's than of Yoredale's total genotypes.

Changes. The variety within the towns' PHHs was greater in 1963–64 than in 1954–55. Midwest had 2 more genotypes in 1963–64, amounting to 133 percent as many and to 1 more percent of the town's total genotypes. Yoredale had 4 more genotypes, amounting to 136 percent as many and to 1 more percent of the town's total genotypes.

NATURE, COMMONALITY, AND DISTINCTIVENESS OF
PRIMARY HEALTH HABITAT

There is a low degree of commonality between the two towns' PPHs (Table 5.35). Of Midwest's 5 and Yoredale's 9 major health genotypes in 1963–64, only 2 were both common and major in both years: Dentists' Offices and Services, and Physical Education Classes. These comprise the stable, common health genotypes of the towns, for there were no minor health genotypes common to the towns in both years. In 1963–64 these stable, common health genotypes amounted to only 25 percent of Midwest's and 13 percent of Yoredale's primary health genotypes, compared with 33 percent commonality for Midwest's and 31 percent for Yoredale's total genotypes. In terms of centiurbs, these common health genotypes comprised 78 percent of Midwest's and 36 percent of Yoredale's PHH, indicating that Midwest's PHH has more in

Table 5.35
Physical Health
Variety Within the Towns' Primary Physical Health Habitats
Major Genotypes in at Least One Town in One Year

	Percent of PHH			
	1954–55		1963–64	
	MW (1)	YD (2)	MW (3)	YD (4)
(1) Athl. Equip't Rooms	0	0	0	5.9
(2) Chemists Shops	0	23.2	0	16.1
(3) Chiropractors Offices	12.9	0	8.8	0
(4) [a] Dentists Serv.	20.0	14.4	14.3	9.7
(5) First Aid Classes & Demons.	0	0	0	3.6
(6) Health Dept. Offices	0	11.3	0	6.6
(7) Nurses Offices & Serv.	0	3.9	0	3.3
(8) Optometrists Offices	0	3.1	1.8	1.7
(9) Phys. & Biol. Sci. Classes	0	0	4.1	0
(10) [a] Phys. Ed. Classes	14.2	10.4	63.7	26.9
(11) Physicians Offices	44.3	28.1	0	17.3
(12) Solicitat'n of Funds	6.1	0	3.7	3.1

[a] Major genotypes in both towns and both years that are also common to the towns (category 1).

common with Yoredale's PHH than the 55 percent commonality for its total habitat, whereas Yoredale's PHH has less in common with Midwest's PHH than the 57 percent commonality for its total habitat. Besides the few genotypes common to both towns, Yoredale contains many more health resources than Midwest does.

The distinctive health resources of the towns are reported in Table 5.36. Yoredale, as noted, has more than Midwest; only 1 health

Table 5.36
Physical Health
Distinctive Genotypes, 1963–64

Commonality Category[a]	Midwest (1)	Yoredale (2)
(1) 7	Chiropractors Offices	None
(2) 6	None	Chiropodists Serv.
(3)		Military Train'g Classes
(4)		Nurses Offices' & Serv.
(5) 5	None	None
(6) 4	Phys. & Biol. Sci. Class	Health Dept. Offices
(7)		Opticians Offices
(8) 3	Optometrists Serv.	Chemists

[a] Genotypes are ordered from those that are unique to each town and environs (category 7) to those whose programs occur in the other town but as components of different genotypes (category 3).

Table 5.37
Physical Health
Genotype Sites of Substantial[a] Changes in Extents of
Primary Physical Health Habitats Between 1954–55 and 1963–64

		Midwest (1)	Yoredale (2)
(1)	New Sites {	Optometrists Serv.	Athl. Equip't Rooms
(2)			First Aid Classes & Demons.
(3)	Enlarged Sites	Phys. Ed. Classes	Phys. Ed. Classes
(4)	Eroded Sites	Physicians Offices	None
	Reduced Sites	None	None

[a] See footnote a, Table 5.4.

genotype — Chiropractors' Offices — is distinctive to Midwest, while 3 are unique to Yoredale: Chiropodists' Services, Military Training Classes, and Nurses' Offices. The remaining distinctive health genotypes either are partly common to the towns or are differently distributed across their behavior settings.

GENOTYPE SITES OF CHANGE IN PRIMARY HEALTH HABITAT

In each town 3 genotypes were sites of substantial change in PHH between the survey years (Table 5.37). Midwest lost its Physician's Office, gained Optometrist's Services, and increased the extent of its Physical Education Classes. Yoredale lost no health resources; its gains were all in connection with its new school, involving new resources for athletics, first aid, and physical education. There were no great health habitat innovations in either town; expansion in Yoredale was spread quite generally over its health facilities, while expansion in Midwest occurred despite the serious loss of the Physician's Office.

CONTROL BY AUTHORITY SYSTEMS

Yoredale's PHH is more broadly based within authority systems than Midwest's (Table 5.38). Midwest's PHH is dominated by its schools; less than 30 percent is controlled by Private Enterprises, Voluntary Associations, and Government Agencies. Although Yoredale's schools also have the greatest control of the town's PHH, more than half is under the aegis of other authority systems; both Government Agencies and Private Enterprises are more powerful in Yoredale than in Midwest. Between the survey years the percentage of the PHH controlled by the Schools increased greatly in both towns; control by Private Enterprises and Voluntary Associations declined in Midwest and increased in Yoredale.

SPECIAL FEATURES

Medical resources. The medical theories and technologies practiced in Midwest and Yoredale are almost identical, but the habitats that

Table 5.38
Physical Health
Control of Physical Health Habitats by Authority Systems
Percent of primary physical health habitats
controlled by different authority systems

		1954–55		1963–64	
		MW (1)	YD (2)	MW (3)	YD (4)
(1)	Extent of PHH in cu	1.9	4.0	2.8	6.3
	Percent of PHH controlled by:				
(2)	Churches	0.0	1.2	0.0	0.8
(3)	Govt. Agencies	0.0	59.0	1.8	19.8
(4)	Private Enterprises	74.4	26.2	21.3	32.8
(5)	Schools	14.2	10.4	71.3	42.8
(6)	Voluntary Assns.	11.4	3.2	5.6	3.7

provide these common resources of knowledge, apparatus, and skills differ greatly. In fact, the attributes of the towns' PHHs differ more than those of any other action pattern habitat. The data indicate that Midwest's PHH is smaller than Yoredale's, comprising 44 percent as many cu, 27 percent as many habitat-claims for operatives, and 53 percent as many genotypes in 1963–64. Midwest's PHH is also much less stable, 69 percent of its 1954–55 PHH being eroded, compared with 10 percent for Yoredale, and 77 percent compared with 44 percent of its 1963–64 habitat being accreted. And Midwest's PHH is controlled by different authority systems; Government Agencies control 1.8 percent, compared with 19.8 percent for Yoredale, and Schools control 71.3 percent compared with 47.8 percent.

Autonomy. The towns differ too in the autonomy of their PHHs. In 1963–64 these percentages were:

	MW	*YD*
Locally controlled (High local autonomy)	12.5	0
Regionally controlled (Medium local autonomy)	76.9	39.6
Controlled from a distance (Low local autonomy)	10.6	60.4

Almost 90 percent of Midwest's relatively meager PHH is controlled within Midwest County, a region of about 400 square miles, whereas only 40 percent of Yoredale's PHH is controlled within Westerdale, also a region of about 400 square miles. About 10 percent of Midwest's and 60 percent of Yoredale's PHHs are under the aegis of distant authorities.

Midwest's relatively limited, unstable, and local health resources are embedded within a larger health system it is unable to cope with. The existing state of affairs with respect to medical resources does not reveal the needs of the town's inhabitants as expressed individually or via behavior settings of the town; it indicates only the weakness of Midwest in relation to the larger medical system.

Professional Involvement

DEFINITION

The action pattern Professional Involvement is present within a behavior setting to the extent that the *operatives* of the setting (the inhabitants of penetration zones 4, 5, and 6) are paid rather than voluntary; the setting provides materials for professional operatives to function in other settings; professional operatives are evaluated; or the program of the setting consists of teaching and learning professional operations.

Professional Involvement is *prominent* if 80 percent or more of the standing pattern within the program and maintenance circuits of a behavior setting are implemented by paid operatives. This is true, for example, of most businesses. Professional Involvement is *secondary* if some but less than 80 percent of the operatives are paid rather than voluntary; this is true of most Church Worship Services, where the minister is paid and the other operatives (ushers, choir members, organist) are voluntary. Professional Involvement is *absent* from a setting if no operatives are paid for their services — for example, in Sunday School Classes.

The behavior settings where Professional Involvement is prominent constitute a town's *primary professional habitat* (PPH); the settings where Professional Involvement is present in some degree constitute its *territorial range*.

Basic data for Professional Involvement are presented in Table ɔ.39; the report for Aesthetics provides a key to the location of particular data in this table.

SALIENT FINDINGS

The territorial range of Professional Involvement extends over 84 ιo 92 percent of the towns' habitats. Habitats where Professional Involvement is prominent (PPH) comprise two-thirds to three-fourths of the towns' habitats. Midwest's PPH is smaller than Yoredale's, and the PPH of each town was larger in 1963–64 than in 1954–55. Habitat-claims for operatives within the towns' PPHs comprise 9 to 24 percent of their total claims for operatives; Midwest has fewer claims for professional operatives than Yoredale, and both towns had more such claims in 1963–64 than in 1954–55. There is more variety within Midwest's PPH than within Yoredale's; variety of professional habitats increased between the survey years in both towns.

TERRITORIAL RANGE OF PROFESSIONAL INVOLVEMENT

The territorial range of Professional Involvement extends over 84 to 92 percent of the towns' habitats; and conversely, 8 to 16 percent of the towns' habitats are without paid operatives. The TR of Professional Involvement extended over fewer centiurbs and smaller percentages of Midwest's than of Yoredale's habitat in 1963–64; the towns did not differ in this respect in 1954–55.

EXTENT OF PRIMARY PROFESSIONAL HABITAT

In 1963–64 the PPH covered 66 percent of Midwest's and 71 percent of Yoredale's total habitat, approximately equivalent in Midwest to 141 regular behavior settings that occur six days a week for eight hours a day, and in Yoredale to 161 regular settings.

Differences. Midwest's PPH is smaller than Yoredale's; in 1963–64 Midwest had 10.1 fewer cu of PPH, amounting to 87 percent as many cu and to 5.8 fewer percent of the town's total habitat.

Changes. Both towns' PPHs were larger in 1963–64 than in 1954–55. Midwest had 3.8 more cu of PPH in 1963–64, amounting to 106 percent as many cu but to 8.6 fewer percent of the town's total habitat. Yoredale had 9.9 more cu of PPH, amounting to 114 percent as many cu and to 7.0 fewer percent of the town's total habitat than in 1954–55.

Processes of change. More than 19 percent of the towns' 1954–55 PPHs were eroded before 1963–64, and more than 28 percent of their 1963–64 PPHs were accreted after 1954–55. Both erosion and accretion were greater in Midwest than in Yoredale; 16 more percent of Midwest's than of Yoredale's 1954–55 PPH were eroded, and 9 more percent of its 1963–64 PPH were accreted. The same is true for the towns'

Table 5.39
Professional Involvement
Basic Habitat Data

	1954–55		1963–64	
Primary Habitat (PPH)	MW (1)	YD (2)	MW (3)	YD (4)
Extent				
(1) Behavior Settings per Year	226	236	297	331
(2) Mean BS per Day	116.0	127.0	120.0	146.6
(3) Mean BS per Hour	30.6	31.7	30.0	32.7
(4) Centiurbs (no.)	66.6	70.6	70.4	80.5
(5) Centiurbs (% of Town Total)	74.2%	78.4%	65.6%	71.4%
Erosion and Accretion Type of Change	Erosion from '54–55		Accretion to '63–64	
(6) Centiurbs (no.)	23.0	13.4	26.4	22.8
(7) Centiurbs (% of PPH)	35%	19%	37%	28%
Claims for Operatives				
(8) Number	632	975	976	1,121
(9) Number (% of Town Total)	12%	24%	9%	14%
Amount of Variety				
(10) Major Genotypes (no.)	4	4	5	2
(11) Total Genotypes (no.)	112	106	132	128
(12) Total Genotypes (% of Town Total)	65%	63%	67%	60%
Territorial Range (TR)				
(13) Centiurbs (no.)	78.0	78.6	90.5	103.5
(14) Centiurbs (% of Town Total)	87%	87%	84%	92%

total habitats, where more of Midwest's than of Yoredale's habitat was both eroded and accreted.

CLAIMS FOR OPERATIVES WITHIN PRIMARY PROFESSIONAL HABITAT

If all behavior settings within the towns' PPHs were to function simultaneously in 1963–64, it would require 976 persons in Midwest and 1121 persons in Yoredale to carry out essential operations. Claims for PPH operatives are much fewer than claims for operatives in general, on a centiurb basis; there are 14 claims for operatives per cu of Midwest's PPH, compared with 96 for the whole habitat—that is, 15 percent as many—and there are 14 per cu of Yoredale's PPH, compared with 69 for the whole habitat—20 percent as many. In 1963–64 the towns' PPHs contained 9 and 14 percent of their total habitat-claims for operatives; whereas, as we have seen, they comprised 66 and 71 percent of the towns' total habitats. The towns' PPHs are not rich in positions of responsibility.

Differences. Midwest had fewer habitat-claims for professional operatives than Yoredale. In 1963–64 it had 145 fewer claims for PPH operatives than Yoredale, amounting to 87 percent as many, to 100 percent as many per cu of PPH, to 137 percent as many per town inhabitant, but to 5 fewer percent of the town's claims for operatives.

Changes. Both towns had more PPH claims for operatives in 1963–64 than in 1954–55. Midwest had 344 more such claims in 1963–64, amounting to 154 percent as many, to 146 percent as many per cu of PPH, to 133 percent as many per town inhabitant, but to 3 fewer percent of the town's total claims for operatives. Yoredale had 146 more such claims, amounting to 115 percent as many, to 101 percent as many per cu of PPH, to 114 percent as many per town inhabitant, but to 10 fewer percent of the town's total claims for operatives.

VARIETY WITHIN PRIMARY PROFESSIONAL HABITAT

There is about as much variety within Midwest's PPH as expected on the basis of extent, but less within Yoredale's. In 1963–64 Midwest's PPH, 66 percent of its total habitat, was the locus of 67 percent of the town's behavior setting genotypes; whereas Yoredale's PPH, 71 percent of its total habitat, was the locus of only 60 percent of its genotypes.

If Midwest and Yoredale were to display simultaneously in 1963–64 the complete range of behavior setting programs within their PPHs, Midwest would require 132 different offices and stores with their appropriate facilities, 132 differently trained and experienced staffs of operatives, and 132 different experts as managers; and Yoredale would require 128 different stores, staffs, and leaders.

Differences. There is more variety within Midwest's PPH than within Yoredale's. In 1963–64 Midwest had 4 more genotypes than Yoredale, amounting to 103 percent as many and to 7 more percent of Midwest's than of Yoredale's total genotypes.

Changes. The variety within the towns' PPHs was greater in

1963–64 than in 1954–55. Midwest had 20 more genotypes in 1963–64, amounting to 118 percent as many and to 2 more percent of the town's total genotypes. Yoredale had 22 more genotypes, amounting to 121 percent as many but to 3 fewer percent of the town's total genotypes.

NATURE AND COMMONALITY OF PRIMARY PROFESSIONAL HABITATS

The PPHs of Midwest and Yoredale have a relatively low degree of commonality (Table 5.40). Of Midwest's 5 and Yoredale's 2 major professional genotypes, none were common in both years. However, 27 professional genotypes were common but not major genotypes in both years. In 1963–64 the 27 stable, common genotypes amounted to 20 percent of Midwest's and to 21 percent of Yoredale's total professional genotypes, and they comprised 39 percent of Midwest's and 45 percent of Yoredale's total PPH. By both of these measures, the towns' commonality with respect to their PPHs is less than with respect to their total habitats — 33 percent for Midwest and 31 percent for Yoredale, in terms of genotypes, and 55 percent for Midwest and 57 percent for Yoredale, in terms of centiurbs.

GENOTYPE SITES OF CHANGE IN PRIMARY PROFESSIONAL HABITAT

The sites of substantial change in the towns' professional settings reveal the habitat loci of expansion and contraction in employment opportunities (Table 5.41). The numbers of genotypes where substantial changes occurred are almost identical in Midwest and Yoredale (40 and 39, respectively), but substantial expansion occurred in fewer of Midwest's than of Yoredale's professional genotypes (in 22 and 26, respectively), and substantial contraction occurred in more of Midwest's

Table 5.40
Professional Involvement
Variety Within the Towns' Primary Professional Involvement Habitats
Major Genotypes in at Least One Town in One Year

	Percent of PPH			
	1954–55		1963–64	
	MW (1)	YD (2)	MW (3)	YD (4)
(1) Classrooms, Freetime	2.0	1.2	3.6	1.1
(2) Clothiers & Dry Goods Stores	0.9	3.4	0.8	3.3
(3) Elem. School Basic Classes	3.0	2.1	4.2	2.4
(4) Govt. Record Offices	4.9	0.5	4.7	0.2
(5) Grocery Stores	4.8	7.0	1.9	6.6
(6) Hotels	2.6	4.2	1.3	2.9
(7) Machinery Repair Shops	4.4	1.1	1.3	1.2
(8) Pubs & Dining Rooms	0	3.2	0	2.9
(9) Restaurants	2.6	0.6	3.6	2.7
(10) Service Stations	2.7	0	4.0	0

Table 5.41
Professional Involvement
Genotype Sites of Substantial[a] Changes in Extents of
Primary Professional Habitats Between 1954–55 and 1963–64

		Midwest (1)	Yoredale (2)
(1)		Animal Feed Mills	Cooking Classes[b]
(2)		Audit & Investig. Co. Offices	Egg-Pack'g Plants
(3)		Cleaners & Dry Cleaning Plants	English Classes[b]
(4)		Day Care Homes & Nurseries	History Classes[b]
(5)		Excurs'ns & Sightsee'g Trips[b]	Math Classes[b]
(6)	New Sites	Factory Assembly Shops	Metalwork Classes[b]
(7)		Laundries, Self-Serv.	School Admin. Offices[b]
(8)		Parking Lots[b]	School Offices[b]
(9)		Psychol. Serv. Offices[b]	Science Classes[b]
(10)		Telephone Automatic Exchs.	School Staff Lounges[b]
(11)		Telephone Booths	
(12)		Water Supply Plants	
(13)		Build'g, Construct'n, & Repair Serv.	Bakeries
(14)		Classrooms, Freetime[b]	Beauty Shops
(15)		Elem. School Basic Classes[b]	Bus Stops
(16)		Hardware Stores	Carpenters & Joiners Serv.
(17)		Music Classes, Instrum.[b]	Clothiers & Dry Goods Stores
(18)		Phys. Ed. Classes[b]	Commercial Company Offices
(19)	Enlarged	Refuse-Hauling Serv.	Commission Agents Offices
(20)	Sites	Restaurants	Elem. School Basic Classes[b]
(21)		Sales Prom. Openings	Exams, Standardized[b]
(22)		Taverns	Garages
(23)			Grocery Stores
(24)			Ins. Offices & Sales Routes
(25)			Music Classes, Vocal[b]
(26)			Phys. Ed. Classes[b]
(27)			Restaurants
(28)			Wallpaper'g & Paint'g Serv.
(29)		Cream Collect Stations	Gas Works
(30)		Dairy Barns	Knitting Serv.
(31)	Eroded Sites	Physicians Offices	Movies
(32)		Shoe Repair Shops	Print Shops
(33)		Telephone Exchs.	Railway Maint. Shops
(34)		Upholst. Serv.	
(35)		Animal Feed Stores	Barbershops
(36)		Deliv. & Collect Routes	Confect'nrs & Stat'nrs Shops
(37)		Drug Stores	Deliv. & Collect Routes
(38)		Farm Implem't Agencies	Fish & Chips Shops
(39)		Grocery Stores	Hotels
(40)	Reduced	Hotels	Police Stations
(41)	Sites	Ins. Offices & Sales Routes	Sewage Disposal Plants
(42)		Laundry Serv.	Shoe Stores
(43)		Machin'y Repair Shops	
(44)		Real Estate Agents	
(45)		TV & Radio Repair Shops	
(46)		Variety Stores	

[a] See footnote a, Table 5.4.
[b] Genotypes within the School authority system.

than of Yoredale's professional genotypes (in 18 and 13, respectively). Inspection of the genotypes shows that the greater expansion of Yoredale's habitat with paid operatives is due entirely to the greater expansion of Yoredale's School-controlled habitat. There was substantial expansion in more of Midwest's than of Yoredale's nonschool, professional genotypes (15 vs. 13), and also substantial contraction in more of Midwest's than of Yoredale's nonschool genotypes (18 vs. 13). Outside of the schools, the number of expanding professional genotypes equals the number of diminishing genotypes within both towns.

CONTROL BY AUTHORITY SYSTEMS

Over half of the PPHs of both towns—that is, habitats with paid operatives—are controlled by Private Enterprises, over one-fifth are controlled by Schools, over one-tenth by Government Agencies, and less than 1 percent are under the aegis of Churches and Voluntary Associations (Table 5.42). A smaller proportion of Midwest's than of Yoredale's PPH is controlled by Private Enterprises, and more is controlled by both Government Agencies and Schools. So far as paid employment is concerned, Midwest is less a private-enterprise town and more a bureaucratic (government and school) town than Yoredale.

SPECIAL FEATURES

Volunteerism. It is important to note that the definition of Professional Involvement differs in important respects from the definitions of other action patterns. Professional Involvement refers to a particular attribute of the habitat-claims of a behavior setting—namely, the degree to which habitat-claims are implemented by paid operatives. A town's PPH consists of the behavior settings in which 80 percent or more of the operatives are paid, the TR of Professional Involvement embraces those settings where some operatives are paid, and the nonprofessional, or *voluntary*, habitat consists of those behavior settings with no paid operatives.

Table 5.42
Professional Involvement
Control of Professional Habitats by Authority Systems
Percent of primary professional habitats
controlled by different authority systems

		1954–55		1963–64	
		MW (1)	YD (2)	MW (3)	YD (4)
(1)	Extent of PPH in cu	66.6	70.6	70.4	80.5
	Percent of PPH controlled by:				
(2)	Churches	0.1	0.7	0.9	0.5
(3)	Govt. Agencies	19.2	14.2	17.0	11.2
(4)	Private Enterprises	65.5	74.9	55.6	66.9
(5)	Schools	15.1	9.2	26.1	21.0
(6)	Voluntary Ass'ns	0.1	1.1	0.4	0.4

Both towns implement most of the maintenance and program circuits of about two-thirds of their habitats by paid professionals (T5.39; R5; C3, 4). Within these professionally implemented habitats, the number of habitat-claims for operatives was identical in the two towns on a centiurb basis—14 per cu on the average (T5.39; R8/R4; C3, 4). In the remaining habitats of both towns—those with mixed, professional-voluntary, and entirely voluntary operatives—the number of claims for operatives was much greater, by factors of more than 14, than in the professionally operated habitats. But here Midwest had more habitat-claims for operatives than Yoredale did: 9244 vs. 6673 in all [(T3.3; R1; C3, 4) − (T5.39; R8; C3, 4)], amounting to 253 habitat-claims per cu in Midwest and 204 per cu in Yoredale. We conclude that somewhat more of Midwest's than of Yoredale's habitat is manned entirely by volunteers, or by volunteers and professionals (34 vs. 29 percent), and that within these nonprofessional habitats Midwest installs more operatives per cu, 124 percent as many. The chief entirely volunteer behavior settings of Midwest occur in these genotypes: Baseball Games, Business Meetings, Card Parties, Cultural Meetings, Lodge Meetings, Parks and Playgrounds, Religion Classes, Religious Study Groups, Scout Meetings, and Vocal Music Classes (Church Choir Practice). Yoredale's chief volunteer settings occur in: Badminton Games, Business Meetings, Cultural Meetings, Parks and Playgrounds, Parties, Religion Classes, and Solicitation of Funds.

Recreation

DEFINITION

The action pattern Recreation is present within a behavior setting to the extent that the concrete occurrences which constitute its program involve play and entertainment. Recreational occurrences may take the form of: playing or being entertained; supplying materials and objects for recreation in other settings; appreciating entertainment and entertainers; teaching and learning about ways of recreation.

Recreation is *prominent* in a behavior setting if 80 percent or more of its standing pattern consists of occurrences of the kind listed above—as for example, in settings of the genotypes Cricket Games and Athletic Equipment Rooms. Recreation is *secondary* in a behavior setting if some, but less than 80 percent of its program, is connected with playing, providing recreational materials, appreciating, or teaching and learning games and sports; this is the case with Scout Meetings and Hardware Stores, for example. Recreation is *absent* if none of the standing pattern of the setting regularly provides recreational opportunities—as, for example, with Latin Classes and Judges' Chambers.

The behavior settings where Recreation is prominent constitute a town's *primary recreational habitat* (PRH); those where Recreation is prominent or secondary constitute the *territorial range of Recreation.*

Basic data for Recreation are presented in Table 5.43; the report for Aesthetics provides a key to the location of particular data in this table.

SALIENT FINDINGS

The territorial range of Recreation extends over 58 to 65 percent of the towns' habitats. Habitats where resources for recreational behavior are prominent (PRH) comprise one-tenth to one-sixth of the towns' habitats. Midwest's PRH is smaller than Yoredale's, and the PRH of each town was larger in 1963–64 than in 1954–55. Habitat-claims for operatives within the towns' PRHs constitute over two-fifths of their total claims for operatives; Midwest has more claims for recreational operatives than Yoredale, and both towns had more such claims in 1963–64 than in 1954–55. In 1954–55 Midwest had more variety than Yoredale within its PRH and in 1963–64 it had less; variety increased in both towns between the survey years.

Table 5.43
Recreation
Basic Habitat Data

		1954–55		1963–64	
Primary Habitat (PRH)		MW (1)	YD (2)	MW (3)	YD (4)
	Extent				
(1)	Behavior Settings per Year	128	124	207	210
(2)	Mean BS per Day	8.8	14.6	10.9	19.6
(3)	Mean BS per Hour	1.1	3.7	2.0	3.3
(4)	Centiurbs (no.)	9.3	12.9	14.5	17.9
(5)	Centiurbs (% of Town Total)	10.3%	14.3%	13.5%	15.9%
	Erosion and Accretion Type of Change	Erosion from '54–55		Accretion to '63–64	
(6)	Centiurbs (no.)	3.1	5.5	8.1	10.0
(7)	Centiurbs (% of PRH)	33%	42%	56%	56%
	Claims for Operatives				
(8)	Number	2,500	1,753	4,532	4,188
(9)	Number (% of Town Total)	47%	42%	44%	54%
	Amount of Variety				
(10)	Major Genotypes (no.)	8	7	11	8
(11)	Total Genotypes (no.)	39	37	47	51
(12)	Total Genotypes (% of Town Total)	23%	22%	24%	24%
	Territorial Range (TR)				
(13)	Centiurbs (no.)	52.5	59.1	65.0	71.4
(14)	Centiurbs (% of Town Total)	58%	66%	61%	63%

TERRITORIAL RANGE OF RECREATION

The territorial range of Recreation extends over about three-fifths to two-thirds of the towns' habitats; and conversely, approximately one-third to two-fifths of the towns' habitats are without recreational components. The TR of Recreation extends over fewer centiurbs and smaller percentages of Midwest's than of Yoredale's habitat. It increased in centiurbs of extent in both towns between the survey years; percentagewise, it increased in Midwest but decreased in Yoredale.

EXTENTS OF PRIMARY RECREATIONAL HABITATS

In 1963–64 the PRH covered 13.5 percent of Midwest's and 15.9 percent of Yoredale's total habitat, approximately equivalent in Midwest to 29 regular behavior settings that occur six days a week for eight hours a day, and in Yoredale to 36 regular settings. In terms of occasional settings, Midwest's PRH is about equivalent to 290 different one-hour behavior settings and Yoredale's to 358 such settings.

Differences. Midwest's PRH is smaller than Yoredale's; in 1963–64 Midwest had 3.4 fewer cu of PRH, amounting to 81 percent as many cu and to 2.4 fewer percent of the town's total habitat.

Changes. Both towns' PRHs were larger in 1963–64 than in 1954–55. Midwest had 5.2 more cu in 1963–64, amounting to 156 percent as many cu and to 3.2 more percent of the town's total habitat. Yoredale had 5 more cu, amounting to 139 percent as many cu and to 1.6 more percent of the town's total habitat.

Processes of change. One-third or more of the towns' 1954–55 PRHs were eroded before 1963–64, and more than one-half of their 1963–64 PRHs were accreted after 1954–55. The rate of erosion was less in Midwest than in Yoredale, the rate of accretion was equal; 9 fewer percent of Midwest's than of Yoredale's 1954–55 PRH were eroded, and the same percentage of the towns' 1963–64 PRHs were accreted. This is different from the towns' total habitats; more of Midwest's than of Yoredale's habitat was both eroded and accreted.

CLAIMS FOR OPERATIVES WITHIN PRIMARY RECREATIONAL HABITAT

If all behavior settings within the towns' PRHs were to function simultaneously in 1963–64, it would require 4532 persons in Midwest and 4188 persons in Yoredale to carry out essential operations. Claims for PRH operatives are much greater, on a centiurb basis, than claims for operatives in general; there are 312 claims for operatives per cu of Midwest's PRH, compared with 96 for the whole habitat—that is, 325 percent as many—and there are 234 per cu of Yoredale's PRH, compared with 69 for the whole habitat—340 percent as many. The towns' PRHs contain 44 and 54 percent of their total habitat-claims for operatives; whereas, as we have seen, they comprise only 13.5 and 15.9 percent of the towns' total habitats. The towns' PRHs are relatively rich in positions of responsibility.

Differences. Midwest has more habitat-claims for recreational operatives than Yoredale. In 1963–64 it had 344 more such claims than Yoredale, amounting to 108 percent as many, to 133 percent as many per cu of PRH, and to 171 percent as many per town inhabitant, but to 10 fewer percent of the town's total claims for operatives.

Changes. Both towns have more PRH claims for operatives in 1963–64 than in 1954–55. Midwest had 2032 more such claims in 1963–64, amounting to 181 percent as many, to 116 percent as many per cu of PRH, and to 156 percent as many per town inhabitant, but to 3 fewer percent of the town's total claims for operatives. Yoredale had 2435 more such claims, amounting to 239 percent as many, to 172 percent as many per cu of PRH, to 237 percent as many per town inhabitant, and to 12 more percent of the town's total claims for operatives.

VARIETY WITHIN PRIMARY RECREATIONAL HABITAT

There is more variety within the towns' PRHs than expected on the basis of extent. In 1963–64 Midwest's PRH, 13.5 percent of its total habitat, was the locus of 24 percent of the town's behavior setting genotypes; Yoredale's PRH, 15.9 percent of its total habitat, was the locus of 24 percent of its genotypes.

If Midwest and Yoredale were to display simultaneously in 1963–64 the complete range of behavior setting programs within their PRHs, Midwest would require 47 different halls and playing fields with their appropriate facilities, 47 differently trained and experienced teams, and 47 different experts as coaches and managers; and Yoredale would require 51 different halls, fields, teams, and leaders.

Differences. There was more variety within Midwest's PRH than within Yoredale's in 1954–55, and less in 1963–64. In 1963–64 Midwest had 4 fewer genotypes than Yoredale, amounting to 92 percent as many and to the same percentage of Midwest's as of Yoredale's total genotypes.

Changes. There was more variety within the towns' PRHs in 1963–64 than in 1954–55. Midwest had 8 more genotypes in 1963–64, amounting to 120 percent as many and to 1 more percent of the town's total genotypes. Yoredale had 14 more genotypes, amounting to 138 percent as many and to 2 more percent of the town's total genotypes.

NATURE, COMMONALITY, AND DISTINCTIVENESS OF
PRIMARY RECREATIONAL HABITAT

The PRHs of Midwest and Yoredale have a relatively low degree of commonality and a high degree of uniqueness (Table 5.44). Of Midwest's 11 and Yoredale's 8 major recreational genotypes in 1963–64, only 2 — Parks and Playgrounds, and Parties — were common to the towns in both years. But in addition, 11 primary recreational genotypes were common though not major recreational genotypes in both years: Card Parties, Cultural Meetings, Dances, Dinners and Banquets, Dinners with Dances, Dinners with Recreational and Cultural Programs,

Table 5.44
Recreation
Variety Within the Towns' Primary Recreational Habitats
Major Genotypes in at Least One Town in One Year

| | Percent of PRH | | | |
| | 1954–55 | | 1963–64 | |
	MW (1)	YD (2)	MW (3)	YD (4)
(1) Baseball Games	2.8	0	5.8	0
(2) Basketball Games	8.7	0	5.5	0
(3) Billiard Parlors & Taverns	7.7	0	4.9	0
(4) Bowling Games, Tenpins	0	0	14.0	0
(5) Card Parties	6.4	5.5	3.2	1.4
(6) Commiss'n Agents (Betting)	0	7.5	0	7.7
(7) Dinners w/Dances	0.5	0.8	0.3	3.9
(8) Dinners w/Programs	4.3	2.7	3.1	3.9
(9) Excurs'ns & Sightsee'g Trips	2.2	2.8	3.2	5.6
(10) Moving Picture Shows	4.3	4.9	0.8	0
(11) [a] Parks & Playgrnds	9.5	16.4	8.9	8.3
(12) [a] Parties	9.6	4.6	5.9	5.6
(13) Phys. Ed. Classes	0	1.0	0	9.4
(14) Plays & Programs	7.1	3.1	3.5	2.6
(15) Pubs & Dining Rooms	0	24.1	0	15.0
(16) Taverns	1.7	0	5.0	0

[a] Major genotypes in both towns and both years that are also common to the towns (category 1).

Excursions and Sightseeing Trips, Parades, Programs of Choral Music, Social Meetings, Street Fairs. These 13 genotypes constituted the stable, common recreational habitats of the two towns in 1963–64; they amounted to 28 percent of Midwest's and to 25 percent of Yoredale's total recreational genotypes, and they comprised 37 percent of Midwest's and 37 percent of Yoredale's PRH. By both of these measures, commonality of the towns' stable PRHs is less than obtains for their total habitats — 33 percent for Midwest and 31 percent for Yoredale in terms of genotypes, and 55 percent for Midwest and 57 percent for Yoredale in terms of centiurbs of habitat.

Those recreational genotypes that are not common to the towns, the distinctive genotypes (Table 5.45), include an unusually large number of unique genotypes. Of the 20 recreational genotypes that are distinctive to Midwest, 14 are unique to it (categories 6 or 7); and among the 21 that are distinctive to Yoredale, 15 are unique to it.

GENOTYPE SITES OF CHANGE IN PRIMARY RECREATIONAL HABITAT

The sites of substantial change in the towns' PRHs (Table 5.46) reveal approximately equal recreational innovation in the towns, with 2 new sport-and-game genotypes in each: Golf and Bowling in Midwest, Rugby and Swimming in Yoredale. Midwest's innovations are under the aegis of Private Enterprise and Voluntary Association authority systems,

Table 5.45
Recreation
Distinctive Genotypes, 1963–64

Commonality Category[a]	Midwest (1)	Yoredale (2)
(1) 7	Baseball Games	Bonfires, Public
(2)	Basketball Games	Bowling Games (Lawn Bowling)
(3)	Charivaris	Commiss'n Agents (Betting)
(4)	Football Games	Cricket Games
(5)	Gift Showers	Darts Games
(6)	Hayrack Rides	Football (Rugby) Games
(7)	Horseshoe Pitch'g Contests	
(8)	Ice Cream Socials	
(9)	Sales Prom. Openings	
(10)	School Rallies	
(11) 6	Bowling Games, Tenpins.	Badminton Games
(12)	Golf Games	Chess Games
(13)	Roller-Skat'g Parties	Dancing Classes
(14)	Volleyball Games	Football (Soccer) Games
(15)		Hockey Games
(16)		Horse Races
(17)		Sports Days
(18)		Stamp Club Meet'gs
(19)		Swimming Compets.
(20) 5	Tractor-Pull'g Contests	Tennis Matches
(21) 4	Taverns	Billiards Games
(22)		Bingo Games
(23)		Pubs & Dining Rooms
(24) 3	Billiard Parlors & Taverns	Fund-Rais'g Socials
(25)	Fireworks Sales Stands	Horticult. Classes
(26)	Painting Classes	
(27)	Parties, Stag	
(28)	Picnics	
(29)	Progs. of Band Music	

[a] Genotypes are ordered from those that are unique to each town and environs (category 7) to those whose programs occur in the other town but as components of different genotypes (category 3).

and Yoredale's innovations are under the aegis of Schools (the new school). Common changes are the reduction and elimination of Moving Picture Shows and the expansion of Excursions and Sightseeing Trips; differential changes are the enlargement of Parks and Playgrounds in Midwest and their reduction in Yoredale.

CONTROL BY AUTHORITY SYSTEMS

Voluntary Associations were predominant in Midwest's PRH in 1963–64 followed by Schools, Private Enterprises, Churches, and Government Agencies (Table 5.47), whereas control of Yoredale's recreational habitat was divided almost equally between Schools and Voluntary Associations, followed by Private Enterprises, Government

Table 5.46
Recreation
Genotype Sites of Substantial[a] Changes in Extents of
Primary Recreational Habitats Between 1954–55 and 1963–64

		Midwest (1)	Yoredale (2)
(1)		Bowling Games, Tenpins	Athl. Equip't Rooms
(2)	New Sites	Golf Games	Football (Rugby) Games
(3)			Swimming Classes
(4)		Baseball Games	Commiss'n Agents (Betting)
(5)		Dinners & Banquets	Dinners w/Dances
(6)		Excurs'ns & Sightsee'g Trips	Dinners w/Recreatnl and Cult. Progs.
	Enlarged Sites		
(7)		Parks & Playgrounds	Excurs'ns & Sightsee'g Trips
(8)		Taverns	Parties
(9)		Track & Field Meets	Phys. Ed. Classes
(10)	Eroded Sites	None	Movies
(11)		Movies	Card Parties
(12)	Reduced Sites	Restaurants	Parks & Playgrds
(13)			Pubs & Dining Rooms

[a] See footnote *a*, Table 5.4.

Agencies, and Churches. In 1963–64 the greatest differences between the towns were in the greater control of recreation by Voluntary Associations in Midwest and the greater control by Private Enterprises and Government Agencies in Yoredale. Between the survey years, the relative authority of schools decreased in Midwest and increased in Yoredale, and the relative authority of voluntary associations increased in Midwest and decreased in Yoredale.

SPECIAL FEATURES

Distinctiveness of recreational resources. Of all the differential habitats we have studied, recreational habitats are the most distinctive to the towns. Midwest's 14 and Yoredale's 15 unique recreational genotypes in 1963–64 (Table 5.45, commonlity categories 6 and 7) exceed the number of unique genotypes in any other differential habitat. And of the genotypes unique to one town in both survey years, recreational genotypes make up 44 percent of those unique to Midwest and 50 percent of those unique to Yoredale, far greater percentages than obtain for any other differential habitat (Tables 4.4, 4.5).

Recreational resources. Midwest's recreational habitat is smaller than one would expect, on the basis of the two towns' total habitats. The dimensions for 1963–64 of Midwest's PRH, stated as a percentage of Yoredale's PRH (and in parentheses the dimensions of Midwest's total habitat as a percentage of Yoredale's total habitat) are: Territorial Range, 91 (95); Primary Habitat, 81 (95); Total Habitat-Claims for Operatives, 108 (132); Habitat-Claims per Town Inhabitant, 171 (208); Variety, 92 (93). On all habitat dimensions, Midwest's PRH is smaller

Table 5.47
Recreation
Control of Recreational Habitats by Authority Systems
Percent of primary recreational habitats
controlled by different authority systems

| | 1954–55 | | 1963–64 | |
	MW (1)	YD (2)	MW (3)	YD (4)
(1) Extent of PRH in cu	9.3	12.9	14.5	17.9
Percent of PRH controlled by:				
(2) Churches	6.1	4.2	7.4	5.2
(3) Govt. Agencies	4.0	13.0	3.3	8.0
(4) Private Enterprises	20.0	32.0	16.2	24.8
(5) Schools	41.9	9.7	28.2	31.6
(6) Voluntary Assns.	28.0	41.1	44.9	30.4

relative to Yoredale's PRH than is its total habitat relative to Yoredale's total habitat. Midwest devotes less of its total habitat resources to recreation than Yoredale does.

Religion

DEFINITION

The action pattern Religion is present within a behavior setting to the extent that the concrete occurrences which constitute the program of the setting: are religious actions; supply religious objects or materials for religious actions in other settings; evaluate religion; or involve teaching and learning about religion.

Religion is *prominent* in a behavior setting if 80 percent or more of its program consists of occurrences of the kind listed above—as, for example, Worship Services and Religious Education Classes. Religion is *secondary* if some, but less than 80 percent, of a setting's standing pattern regularly consists of religious actions or involves religious materials—as for example, meetings which are opened with prayer or stores that sell Bibles or religious symbols. Religion is *absent* from a setting if none of its standing pattern regularly involves religious occurrences or objects, as is true of Post Offices and Mathematics Classes.

The behavior settings where Religion is prominent constitute a towns *primary religious habitat* (PRlH); those where Religion is prominent or secondary constitute the *territorial range of Religion*. Basic data for Religion are presented in Table 5.48; the report for Aesthetics provides a key to the location of particular data in this table.

SALIENT FINDINGS

The territorial range of Religion extends over 13 to 18 percent of the towns' habitats. Habitats where resources for religious behavior are prominent (PR1H) comprise 4 to 8.5 percent of the towns' habitats.

Table 5.48
Religion
Basic Habitat Data

Primary Habitat (PRIH)	1954–55		1963–64	
	MW (1)	YD (2)	MW (3)	YD (4)
Extent				
(1) Behavior Settings per Year	72	56	137	56
(2) Mean BS per Day	4.5	7.9	8.8	7.4
(3) Mean BS per Hour	0.2	0.3	0.4	0.4
(4) Centiurbs (no.)	4.7	4.8	9.1	4.7
(5) Centiurbs (% of Town Total)	5.2%	5.3%	8.5%	4.2%
Erosion and Accretion				
Type of Change	Erosion from '54–55		Accretion to '63–64	
(6) Centiurbs (no.)	1.9	1.5	6.0	2.0
(7) Centiurbs (% of PRIH)	39%	32%	66%	43%
Claims for Operatives				
(8) Number	872	578	1,095	655
(9) Number (% of Town Total)	16%	14%	11%	8%
Amount of Variety				
(10) Major Genotypes (no.)	8	9	8	8
(11) Total Genotypes (no.)	14	12	14	15
(12) Total Genotypes (% of Town Total)	8%	7%	7%	7%
Territorial Range (TR)				
(13) Centiurbs (no.)	14.3	11.7	19.8	15.5
(14) Centiurbs (% of Town Total)	16%	13%	18%	14%

Midwest's PR1H was smaller than Yoredale's in 1954–55 and larger in 1963–64; Midwest's PR1H was larger and Yoredale's was smaller in 1963–64 than in 1954–55. Habitat-claims for operatives within the towns' PR1Hs constitute 8 to 16 percent of their total claims for operatives; Midwest has more claims for religious operatives than Yoredale, and both towns had more such claims in 1963–64 than in 1954–55. The towns are similar in the amount of variety within their PR1Hs; variety did not change between the survey years in Midwest, it increased in Yoredale.

TERRITORIAL RANGE OF RELIGION

The territorial range of Religion extends over 13 to 18 percent of the towns' habitats; and conversely, 82 to 87 percent of the towns' habitats are without religious components. The TR of Religion extends over more centiurbs and greater percentages of Midwest's than of Yoredale's habitat, and increased between the survey years in both respects in both towns.

EXTENT OF PRIMARY RELIGIOUS HABITATS

In 1963–64 the PRlH covered 8.5 percent of Midwest's and 4.2 percent of Yoredale's total habitats, approximately equivalent in Midwest to 182 nonrecurring one-hour religious meetings, and in Yoredale to 94 such meetings.

Differences. Midwest's PRlH was larger than Yoredale's in 1963–64; Midwest had 4.4 more cu of PRlH, amounting to 194 percent as many cu and to 4.3 more percent of the town's total habitat.

Changes. Midwest's PRlH was larger in 1963–64 than in 1954–55, and Yoredale's was smaller. Midwest had 4.4 more cu of PRlH in 1963–64, amounting to 194 percent as many cu and to 3.3 more percent of the town's total habitat than in 1954–55. Yoredale had 0.1 fewer cu of PRlH, amounting to 98 percent as many cu and to 1.1 fewer percent of the town's total habitat.

Processes of change. More than 30 percent of the towns' 1954–55 PRlHs were eroded before 1963–64, and more than 40 percent of their 1963–64 PRlHs were accreted after 1954–55. Both erosion and accretion were greater in Midwest than in Yoredale; 7 more percent of Midwest's 1954–55 PRlH were eroded, and 23 more percent of its 1963–64 PRlH were accreted. The same is true for the towns' total habitats; more of Midwest's than of Yoredale's habitat was both eroded and accreted.

CLAIMS FOR OPERATIVES WITHIN PRIMARY RELIGIOUS HABITAT

If all behavior settings within the towns' PRlHs were to function simultaneously in 1963–64, it would require 1095 persons in Midwest and 655 persons in Yoredale to carry out essential operations. Claims for PRlH operatives are greater, on a centiurb basis, than claims for operatives in general; there are 120 claims for operatives per cu of Midwest's PRlH, compared with 96 for the whole habitat—that is, 125 percent as many —and there are 139 per cu of Yoredale's PRlH, compared with 69 for the whole habitat—201 percent as many. The towns' PRlHs contain 11 and 8 percent of their total habitat-claims for operatives; whereas, as we have seen, they comprise 8.5 and 4.2 percent of the towns' total habitats. The towns' PRlHs are relatively rich in positions of responsibility.

Differences. Midwest has more habitat-claims for PRlH operatives than Yoredale. In 1963–64 it had 440 more such claims than Yoredale, amounting to 167 percent as many, to 86 percent as many per cu of PRlH, to 264 percent as many per town inhabitant, and to 3 more percent of the town's total claims for operatives.

Changes. Both towns had more PRlH claims for operatives in 1963–64 than in 1954–55. Midwest had 223 more such claims in 1963–64 amounting to 126 percent as many, to 65 percent as many per cu of PRlH, and to 108 percent as many per town inhabitant, but to 5 fewer percent of the town's total claims for operatives. Yoredale had 77 more such claims, amounting to 113 percent as many, to 116 percent as many per cu of PRlH, and to 112 percent as many per town inhabitant, but to 6 fewer percent of the town's total claims for operatives.

VARIETY WITHIN PRIMARY RELIGIOUS HABITAT

There was less variety within Midwest's PRlH than expected on the basis of extent, and more in Yoredale's. In 1963–64 Midwest's PRlH, 8.5 percent of its total habitat, was the locus of 7 percent of the town's total genotypes; whereas Yoredale's PRlH, 4.2 percent of its total habitat, also contained 7 percent of the town's total genotypes.

If Midwest and Yoredale were to display simultaneously in 1963–64 the complete range of behavior setting programs within their PRlHs, Midwest would require 14 different sanctuaries and rooms with their appropriate facilities, 14 differently trained and experienced staffs of operatives, and 14 different leaders; and Yoredale would require 15 different halls, staffs, and leaders.

Differences. There was more variety within Midwest's PRlH than within Yoredale's in 1954–55, and less in 1963–64. In 1963–64 Midwest had 1 fewer genotype than Yoredale, amounting to 93 percent as many and to the same percentage of Midwest's as of Yoredale's total genotypes.

Changes. The religious variety of Midwest did not change; Yoredale's increased in extent between 1954–55 and 1963–64. Midwest had the same number of genotypes in 1963–64 as in 1954–55, amounting to 100 percent as many and to 1 fewer percent of the town's total genotypes. Yoredale had 3 more genotypes, amounting to 125 percent as many and to the same percentage of the town's total genotypes.

NATURE, COMMONALITY, AND DISTINCTIVENESS OF
PRIMARY RELIGIOUS HABITAT

The PRlHs of Midwest and Yoredale have a high degree of commonality (Table 5.49). Of Midwest's 8 and Yoredale's 8 major religious genotypes in 1963–64, only 2 were in both towns in both years: Religion Classes and Religious Worship Services. But in addition, 8 primary religious genotypes are common though not major religious genotypes in both years; Business Meetings, Church Weddings, Funeral Services, Plays and Programs, Programs of Choral Music, Religious Fellowship Meetings, Religious Prayer and Meditation Services, and Vocal Music Classes. These 10 genotypes constituted the stable, common religious habitat of the towns in 1963–64; they amounted to 71 percent of Midwest's and to 67 percent of Yoredale's total religious genotypes, and they comprised 79 percent of each town's PRlH. By both of these measures, commonality of religious habitats is greater than commonality of total habitats—33 percent of Midwest's and 31 percent of Yoredale's total genotypes, and 55 percent of Midwest's and 57 percent of Yoredale's total centiurbs of habitat. Worship Services and Religion Classes together comprise about half the PRlHs of both towns, but the former are

Table 5.49
Religion
Variety Within the Towns' Primary Religious Habitats
Major Genotypes in at Least One Town in One Year

	Percent of PRIH			
	1954–55		1963–64	
	MW (1)	YD (2)	MW (3)	YD (4)
(1) Confessions	0	6.0	0	6.0
(2) Funeral Servs., Church	3.4	4.3	1.7	3.3
(3) Meetings, Business	11.5	5.4	13.9	1.1
(4) Music Classes, Vocal	4.4	1.7	3.8	3.8
(5) Pastors Studies	0	0	3.6	0
(6) Plays & Programs	3.2	3.2	3.8	2.1
(7) Progs. of Choral Music	3.2	4.2	1.1	3.2
(8) [a] Relig. Classes	41.3	15.3	34.9	20.3
(9) Relig. Study Groups	0	0	14.8	8.2
(10) Relig. Fellowship Meet'gs	7.2	5.2	0	2.3
(11) Relig. Prayer & Medit. Servs.	1.1	16.3	4.2	15.3
(12) [a] Relig. Worship Servs.	17.5	36.3	15.4	29.0

[a] Major genotypes in both towns and both years that are also common to the towns (category 1).

more pervasive in Yoredale and the latter in Midwest. Business Meetings are more extensive in Midwest, indicating that Midwest's churches function much more via committees than Yoredale churches.

The dominance of the common religious habitat of the towns is emphasized by the meager list of the towns' distinctive religious genotypes in Table 5.50. There are no unique religous genotypes in either town.

GENOTYPE SITES OF CHANGE IN PRIMARY RELIGIOUS HABITAT

The sites of substantial changes in the towns' PRlHs reflect the general expansion of Midwest's PRlH between the survey years, and the

Table 5.50
Religion
Distinctive Genotypes, 1963–64

Commonality Category[a]		Midwest (1)	Yoredale (2)
(1)	7	None	None
(2)	6	None	None
(3)	5	None	Confess'ns, Rom. Cath.
(4)	4	Grad. & Prom. Cerems.	None
(5)		Memor'l Servs.	
(6)	3	Pastors Studies	Baptism Servs.

[a] Genotypes are ordered from those that are unique to each town and environs (category 7) to those whose programs occur in the other town but as components of different genotypes (category 3).

Table 5.51
Religion
Genotype Sites of Substantial[a] Changes in Extents of
Primary Religious Habitats between 1954–55 and 1963–64

		Midwest (1)	Yoredale (2)
(1)	New Sites	Relig. Study Groups	Relig. Study Groups
(2)		Business Meetings	
(3)	Enlarged	Relig. Classes	None
(4)	Sites	Relig. Prayer & Medit. Servs.	
(5)		Relig. Worship Servs.	
(6)	Eroded Sites	Relig. Fellowship Meet'gs	
(7)	Reduced Sites	None	Relig. Worship Servs.

[a] See footnote a, Table 5.4.

stability of Yoredale's (Table 5.51). A new common religious genotype appeared in both towns: Religion Study Groups, where a number of persons study a religious subject, taking joint or rotating responsibility for leading and teaching. Another common change in the towns' religious habitats was the decline of Religious Fellowship Meetings; they eroded in Midwest, and they declined, though not substantially, in Yoredale. The initiation of Religion Study Groups and the contraction of Religious Fellowship Meetings (which have many social components) indicate a shift in the primary religious habitats of both towns from a social to a more intellectual emphasis. Other changes between the survey years were, in Midwest, an expansion of its core religious genotypes (Religion Classes, Prayer Services, Worship Services, and Business Meetings), and in Yoredale a small reduction of Worship Services.

CONTROL BY AUTHORITY SYSTEMS

Not surprisingly, the PRlHs of both towns are dominated by Church authority systems (Table 5.52). However, the supremacy of the church was less complete in Yoredale than in Midwest, especially in 1963–64. Religion Classes are a regular part of the curriculum of the Yoredale schools, and, after the establishment of the new secondary school, they controlled 17 percent of the town's PRlH.

SPECIAL FEATURES

Equivalence of religious resources. Of all the differential habitats we have identified, religious habitats are the most similar within the two towns. No religious genotype is unique to either town, whereas the common ones constitute 71 percent of Midwest's and 67 percent of Yoredale's total religious genotypes, and comprise 79 percent of the PRlH of each town.

Religious resources. Midwest's religious habitat is larger than one would expect on the basis of the two towns' total habitats. The dimen-

Table 5.52
Religion
Control of Religion Habitats by Authority Systems
Percent of primary religious habitats
controlled by different authority systems

		1954–55		1963–64	
		MW (1)	YD (2)	MW (3)	YD (4)
(1)	Extent of PRIH in cu	4.7	4.8	9.1	4.7
	Percent of PRIH controlled by:				
(2)	Churches	93.2	90.7	98.4	79.6
(3)	Govt. Agencies	0.0	0.0	0.0	2.3
(4)	Private Enterprises	0.0	0.0	0.0	0.0
(5)	Schools	2.1	8.2	1.1	17.0
(6)	Voluntary Assns.	4.7	1.0	0.5	1.1

sions for 1963–64 of Midwest's PRlH, stated as a percentage of Yoredale's PRlH (and in the parentheses the dimensions of Midwest's total habitat as a percentage of Yoredale's total habitat) are: Territorial Range, 127 (95); Primary Habitat, 194 (95); Habitat-Claims for Operatives, 167 (132); Habitat-Claims per Town Inhabitant, 264 (208); Variety, 93 (93). On all habitat dimensions except Variety, Midwest's PRIH is larger relative to Yoredale's PRlH than is its total habitat relative to Yoredale's total habitat. Midwest devotes more of its total habitat resources to religion than Yoredale does.

Social Contact

DEFINITION

The action pattern Social Contact is present within a behavior setting to the extent that the concrete occurrences which constitute the standing pattern of the setting involve: social interactions; providing equipment and material for engaging in social interaction in other settings; evaluating social persons and sociability; or teaching and learning social techniques.

Social Contact is *prominent* in a behavior setting if 80 percent or more of its program consists of occurrences of the kinds listed above—as, for example, in Worship Services and Card Parties. Social Contact is *secondary* if some, but less than 80 percent, of a setting's program consists of social occurrences; this is the case with Libraries and Beauty Shops. Social Contact is *absent* if the program of a setting does not regularly involve social interaction; but in fact, this does not occur in either Midwest or Yoredale.

The settings where Social Contact is prominent constitute a town's *primary social habitat* (PSH); those where Social Contact is prominent or secondary constitute the *territorial range* of Social Contact.

Basic data for Social Contact are presented in Table 5.53; the

Table 5.53
Social Contact
Basic Habitat Data

	1954–55		1963–64	
Primary Habitat (PSH)	MW (1)	YD (2)	MW (3)	YD (4)
Extent				
(1) Behavior Settings per Year	468	369	754	630
(2) Mean BS per Day	68.9	63.1	79.2	103.0
(3) Mean BS per Hour	16.4	14.2	13.7	18.9
(4) Centiurbs (no.)	54.1	45.8	67.9	72.1
(5) Centiurbs (% of Town Total)	60.2%	51.0%	63.2%	63.9%

Erosion and Accretion				
Type of Change	Erosion from '54–55		Accretion to '63–64	
(6) Centiurbs (no.)	17.7	12.1	31.1	35.0
(7) Centiurbs (% of PSH)	33%	26%	46%	48%

Claims for Operatives				
(8) Number	5,072	3,658	9,817	7,257
(9) Number (% of Town Total)	95%	89%	96%	93%

Amount of Variety				
(10) Major Genotypes (no.)	7	8	5	4
(11) Total Genotypes (no.)	129	110	143	170
(12) Total Genotypes (% of Town Total)	75%	65%	72%	80%

Territorial Range (TR)				
(13) Centiurbs (no.)	89.8	90.0	107.4	112.8
(14) Centiurbs (% of Town Total)	100%	100%	100%	100%

report for Aesthetics provides a key to the location of particular data in this table.

SALIENT FINDINGS

The territorial range of social contact extends over the towns' entire habitats. Habitats where resources for social behavior are prominent (PSH) comprise approximately one-half to two-thirds of the towns' habitats. Midwest's PSH was larger than Yoredale's in 1954–55 and smaller in 1963–64; each town's PSH was larger in 1963–64 than in 1954–55. Habitat-claims for operatives that are located within the towns' PSHs constitute 89 to 96 percent of their total claims for operatives; Midwest has more claims for social operatives than Yoredale, and both towns had more such claims in 1963–64 than in 1954–55. There was more variety within Midwest's than within Yoredale's PSH in 1954–55, and less in 1963–64; variety increased between the survey years in both towns.

TERRITORIAL RANGE OF SOCIAL CONTACT

None of the town's habitats are without social components; and conversely, the TR of Social Contact extends over 100 percent of the habitats of both towns.

EXTENT OF PRIMARY SOCIAL HABITAT

In 1963–64 the PSH covered 63.2 percent of Midwest's and 63.9 percent of Yoredale's total habitat, approximately equivalent in Midwest to 136 regular behavior settings that occur six days a week for eight hours a day, and in Yoredale to 144 such regular settings. In terms of occasional settings, Midwest's PSH is equivalent to 1358 different, non-recurring, one-hour committee meetings, and Yoredale's to 1442 such occasional settings.

Differences. Midwest's PSH was smaller than Yoredale's in 1963–64; Midwest had 4.2 fewer cu of PSH, amounting to 94 percent as many cu and to 0.7 fewer percent of the town's total habitat.

Changes. Both towns' PSHs were larger in 1963–64 than in 1954–55. Midwest had 13.8 more cu of PSH in 1963–64, amounting to 125 percent as many cu and to 3.0 more percent of the town's total habitat. Yoredale had 26.3 more cu of PSH, amounting to 157 percent as many cu and to 12.9 more percent of the town's total habitat.

Processes of change. More than one-quarter of the towns' 1954–55 PSHs were eroded before 1963–64, and almost one-half of their 1963–64 PSHs were accreted after 1954–55. Erosion was greater in Midwest than in Yoredale, and accretion was less; 7 more percent of Midwest's 1954–55 PSH was eroded, and 2 fewer percent of its 1963–64 PSH was accreted. This is different from the towns' total habitats; more of Midwest's than of Yoredale's habitat was both eroded and accreted.

CLAIMS FOR OPERATIVES WITHIN PRIMARY SOCIAL HABITAT

If all behavior settings within the towns' PSHs were to function simultaneously in 1963–64, it would require 9817 persons in Midwest and 7257 persons in Yoredale to carry out essential operations. Claims for PSH operatives are greater, on a centiurb basis, than claims for operatives in general; there are 145 claims for operatives per cu of Midwest's PSH, compared with 96 for the whole habitat—that is, 151 percent as many—and there are 101 per cu of Yoredale's PSH, compared with 69 for the whole habitat—146 percent as many. The towns' PSHs contain 96 and 93 percent of their total habitat-claims for operatives; whereas, as we have seen, they comprise 63 and 64 percent of the towns' total habitats. The towns' PSHs are relatively rich in positions of responsibility.

Differences. Midwest has more habitat-claims for PSH operatives than Yoredale. In 1963–64 it had 2560 more such claims than Yoredale, amounting to 135 percent as many, to 144 percent as many per cu of PSH, to 213 percent as many per town inhabitant, and to 3 more percent of Midwest's than of Yoredale's claims for operatives.

Changes. Both towns had more PSH claims for operatives in 1963–64 than in 1954–55. Midwest had 4745 more such claims in 1963–64, amounting to 194 percent as many, to 154 percent as many per cu of PSH, to 167 percent as many per town inhabitant, and to 1 more percent of the town's total claims for operatives. Yoredale had 3599 more such claims amounting to 198 percent as many, to 126 percent as many per cu of PSH, to 197 percent as many per town inhabitant, and to 4 more percent of the town's total claims for operatives.

VARIETY WITHIN PRIMARY SOCIAL HABITAT

There is more variety within the towns' PSHs than expected on the basis of extent. In 1963–64 Midwest's PSH, 63.2 percent of its total habitat, was the locus of 72 percent of its genotypes; and Yoredale's PSH, 63.9 percent of its total habitat, was the locus of 80 percent of its genotypes.

If Midwest and Yoredale were to display simultaneously in 1963–64 the complete range of behavior setting programs within their PSHs, Midwest would require 143 different halls, classrooms, sanctuaries, offices, and so forth, with their appropriate facilities, 143 differently trained and experienced staffs of operatives, and 143 different experts as teachers, chairmen, M.C.s, and so forth; and Yoredale would require 170 different halls, staffs, and leaders.

Differences. There is less variety within Midwest's PSH than within Yoredale's. In 1963–64 Midwest had 27 fewer social genotypes than Yoredale, amounting to 84 percent as many and to 8 fewer percent of Midwest's than of Yoredale's total genotypes.

Changes. There was more variety within both towns' PSHs in 1963–64 than in 1954–55. Midwest had 14 more genotypes in 1963–64, amounting to 111 percent as many but to 3 fewer percent of the town's total genotypes. Yoredale had 60 more genotypes, amounting to 154 percent as many and to 15 more percent of the town's total genotypes.

Because of the ubiquitousness of the action pattern Social Contact across the habitats of both towns and its widespread occurrence, we do not report the degree of commonality of the towns' social habitats, the genotype sites of PSH change, or the control of the social habitat by authority systems; these data for the towns' total habitats appear to apply with sufficient adequacy to their social habitats. Those interested in a study of the fine structure of the social habitats of Midwest and Yoredale may refer to Barker and Barker (1963).

Summary

In the preceding sections we have separately presented information on each of the 11 action pattern habitats. We present here graphic overviews of the extent of these differential habitats of Midwest and Yoredale in 1963–64 and of changes in them between 1954–55 and 1963–64 by four habitat-size measures: Territorial Range (cu), Primary Habitat Extent (cu), Claims for Operatives (no.), and Variety (no. of genotypes). These summary data are reported graphically in Figures 5.1, 5.2, 5.3 and 5.4. In Figure 5.5 we summarize the Autonomy data for the primary action pattern habitats.

Each of the 4 size graphs has two parts: Part A shows a pair of curves representing habitat size in Midwest and in Yoredale across the differential habitats, arranged in order of increasing size in Midwest; Part B shows, with another pair of curves, change data for the habitats as the ratio of the appropriate 1963–64 value to the corresponding 1954–55 value in each town. Although we have chosen to present these data in the form of continuous line curves, there is no continuity across the 11 habitats—the action patterns are discrete qualities of the towns' habitats, and the curves should therefore be understood as diagrams representing the extent of these discrete qualities. This mode of presentation reveals the differences and changes in extent more clearly than do bar graphs or other representations that we have tried. The reader should remember that the order of the action patterns on the abscissa, and the scales used on the ordinate, are not constant across the four figures.

The reader should bear in mind as he studies the figures the important overall differences that we have seen earlier (Chapters 3 and 4) between the towns in these measures: in 1963–64, total centiurbs were 107 in Midwest and 113 in Yoredale; total habitat-claims were 10,220 in Midwest and 7764 in Yoredale; total genotypes were 198 in Midwest and 213 in Yoredale. These differences led us at first to transform the data on extent of the differential habitats into percentages of town totals. But when these percentages were plotted, the resulting figures did not truly reflect the extent of the differential habitat resources of the

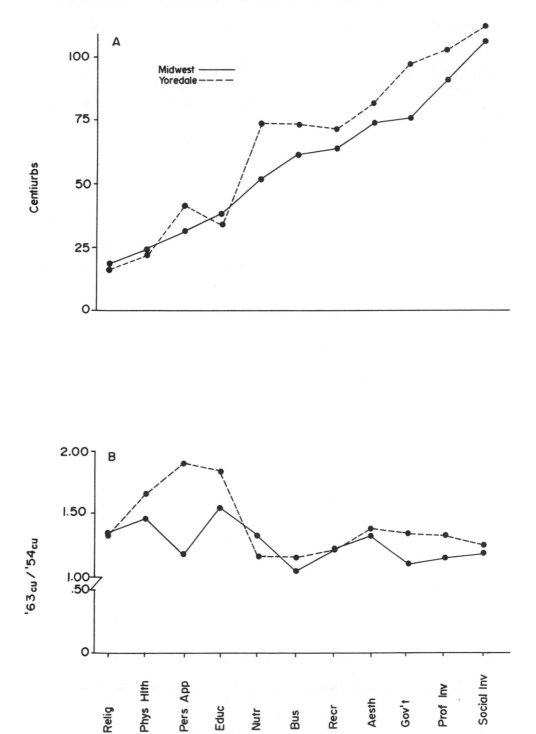

FIGURE 5.1.   Territorial Range of Action Pattern Habitats. A: centiurbs of habitat, 1963–64; B: change in centiurbs of habitat, $'63_{cu}/'54_{cu}$.

towns as they existed for the towns' inhabitants. For example, Figure 5.3A shows that Midwest's primary Education habitat had more habitat-claims for operatives (331) than Yoredale's (302); as percentages of the towns' total habitat-claims (10,220 and 7764), however, this relation is reversed; Midwest's equals 3.2 percent and Yoredale's equals 3.9 percent. But the essential fact is that Midwest's primary Education habitat makes more demands on its inhabitants than Yoredale's does. For this purpose, the actual number of habitat-claims for operatives is the better measure.

TERRITORIAL RANGE OF ACTION PATTERN HABITATS

The action patterns vary greatly in TR (Figure 5.1A). In 1963–64 the smallest (Religion), the median (Business), and the largest (Social Contact) had TRs in proportions of approximately 1:3:5 in Midwest and 1:5:7 in Yoredale. The most widely dispersed action pattern quality of each town was 5 times or more as widespread as the least widely dispersed.

Differences. We note first an important similarity between the towns. The order of the action patterns in 1963–64 was the same, with one exception: Personal Appearance and Education were third and fourth in Midwest, and fourth and third in Yoredale. So we find that within these rural towns of the United States and England, the habitat qualities we have studied are ordered almost identically in extent of dispersal across the towns.

But there are differences. The TR of 8 of the action patterns was smaller in Midwest, as would be expected if they have the same relation as does Midwest's total habitat to Yoredale's — namely, 95 percent as extensive. However, Nutrition, Personal Appearance, Government, and Business were proportionally more deficient than those in Midwest, with percentages (MW/YD times 100) of 65, 75, 77 and 85, respectively; and Religion, Education, and Physical Health occurred more widely in Midwest than in Yoredale.

Changes. The TR of all action patterns of both towns increased from 1954–55 to 1963–64, and the change ratios (1963/1954) were generally greater in Yoredale (Figure 5.1B). This is in line with the changes in the towns' total habitats, where the ratios were 1.25 for Yoredale and 1.19 for Midwest. However the TRs of Physical Health, Personal Appearance, and Education in Yoredale and of Education in Midwest increased at much greater rates than did the towns' total habitats.

EXTENT OF PRIMARY ACTION PATTERN HABITATS

The primary habitats of action patterns vary more in extent than do their TRs (Figure 5.2A). In 1963–64 Midwest's smallest (Physical Health), median (Recreation), and largest (Professional Involvement) primary habitats had approximate proportions of 1:5:25; and Yoredale's smallest (Religion), median (Education), and largest (Professional Involvement) had approximate proportions of 1:3:17.

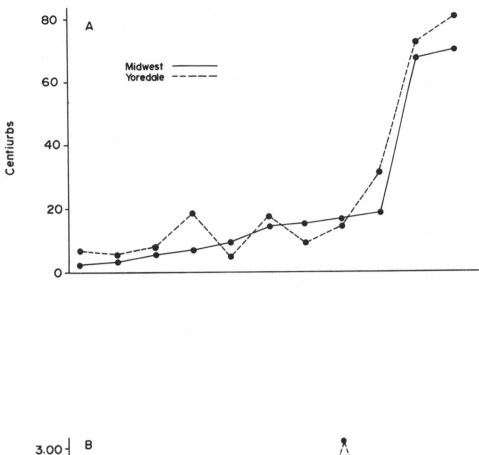

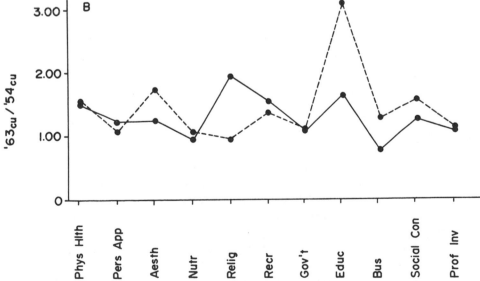

FIGURE 5.2. Extent of Primary Action Pattern Habitats. A: centiurbs of habitat, 1963–64; B: change in centiurbs of Habitat, $'63_{cu}/'54_{cu}$.

Differences. In line with Midwest's smaller total habitat, 8 of its primary action pattern habitats were smaller than their Yoredale counterparts in 1963–64. But 3 were larger: Religion, Government, and Education. The superiority of Government as a primary habitat in Midwest is particularly impressive in view of its inferiority in TR. Midwest is indeed a greater seat of government than Yoredale, but Government is less pervasive in Midwest. Midwest's greatest inferiorities — or, conversely, Yoredale's greatest superiorities — occur in the primary habitats for Business, Nutrition, and Professional Involvement. Habitat resources for Religion and Education are more widely present and prominent in Midwest, and those for Business and Nutrition are more widely present and prominent in Yoredale; habitat resources for Government are more widely present but less widely prominent in Yoredale, and those for Health are more widely present but less widely prominent in Midwest.

Changes. Between 1954–55 and 1963–64 the qualities of the towns as environments for molar actions were altered by habitat changes (Figure 5.2B). Common to the towns were increases in their primary Education, Physical Health, Recreation, Aesthetics, and Social Contact habitats at greater rates than those for the towns' total habitats. Common too were changes in primary Nutrition, Professional Involvement, and Government habitats at rates that did not keep pace with the towns' total habitats. The towns changed differentially with respect to primary resources for Business, which fell behind in Midwest and more than held its own in Yoredale, and for Religion, which moved ahead in Midwest and fell behind in Yoredale. The greatest decrement occurred in the primary Business habitat of Midwest, which was 79 percent as extensive in 1963–64 as in 1954–55. The greatest increment occured in the primary Education habitat of Yoredale, which more than tripled in extent between the survey years, largely as a function of the establishment in Yoredale of the new County Modern School.

CLAIMS FOR OPERATIVES WITHIN PRIMARY
ACTION PATTERN HABITATS

Claims for operatives within the primary action pattern habitats vary more than do territorial range or the extent of the primary habitats (Figure 5.3A). In 1963–64 Midwest's primary habitats with the smallest (Physical Health), median (Personal Appearance), and largest (Social Contact) number of claims for operatives had approximate proportions of $1:18:223$; and Yoredale's smallest (Personal Appearance), median (Business), and largest (Social Contact) had approximate proportions of $1:6:84$.

Differences. In line with Midwest's greater total number of habitat-claims for operatives, 132 percent as many, 8 of its primary action pattern habitats had more claims for operatives than Yoredale's in 1963–64. Midwest's superiority was greatest in claims for operatives to man its habitats where Personal Appearance, Aesthetics, Religion, and

Social Contact were prominent. Yoredale exceeded Midwest in claims for operatives to man its habitats were Physical Health, Business, and Professional Involvement were prominent.

Changes. In both towns, increases in claims for operatives were relatively great for habitats where Physical Health, Recreation, and Social Contact were prominent; they were small where Personal Appearance was prominent—in fact, they declined in Yoredale (Figure 5.3B). Differences between the towns are found chiefly in Midwest's more rapid rate of increase in habitat-claims for Professional, Nutrition, and Business operatives, and in Yoredale's greater rate of increase in claims for Recreation, Government, and Education operatives.

VARIETY WITHIN PRIMARY ACTION PATTERN HABITATS

Variety differs within the primary action pattern habitats in about the same proportions as extent (Figure 5.4A). In 1963–64 Midwest's habitats with the smallest (Physical Health), median (Aesthetics), and largest (Social Contact) number of genotypes had approximate proportions of 1 : 3 : 18; and Yoredale's smallest (Personal Appearance), median (Aesthetics), and largest (Social Contact) had approximate proportions of 1 : 3 : 21.

Differences. In line with Yoredale's greater total variety—108 percent as many genotypes—7 of its primary action pattern habitats had more variety than did Midwest's, 2 were equal (Aesthetics, Government), and 2 had less variety (Personal Appearance, Professional Involvement). Yoredale's superiority was greatest within the primary Physical Health, Business, and Nutrition habitats.

Changes. Common to the two towns were a relatively great increase in variety between the survey years within the primary Education habitat and little change (a small increase in Midwest, a decrement in Yoredale) in the primary Personal Appearance habitat (Figure 5.4B). Personal Appearance is the only action pattern where variety did not increase in Yoredale, whereas there were 3 in Midwest: Physical Health, Religion, and Business. The increase in primary habitat variety was greater in Yoredale than in Midwest for 9 of the 11 action patterns. This increase is in line with the change within the towns' total habitats, where variety increased 19 percent in Midwest and 25 percent in Yoredale.

AUTONOMY OF ACTION PATTERN HABITATS

The degrees to which primary action pattern habitats are locally controlled within the town or contiguous rural district (High local autonomy), regionally controlled within the surrounding rural region (Medium local autonomy), or controlled from a distance beyond the town, district, and region (Low local autonomy) are reported for 1963–64 in Figure 5.5 in terms of percentages of habitats measured in centiurbs. Action patterns are ordered from left to right along the ab-

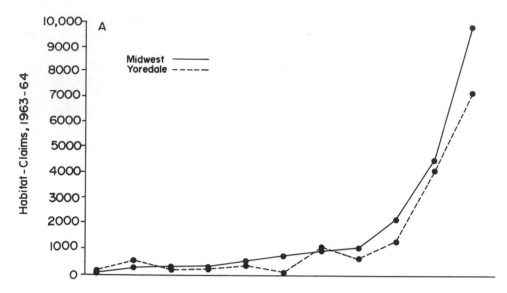

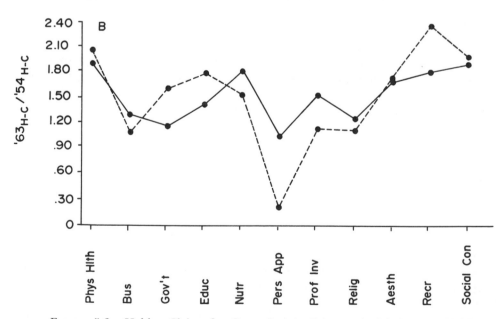

FIGURE 5.3.   Habitat-Claims for Operatives in Primary Action Pattern Habitats. A: number of habitat-claims, 1963–64; B: change in habitat-claims, $'63_{H\text{-}C}/'54_{H\text{-}C}$.

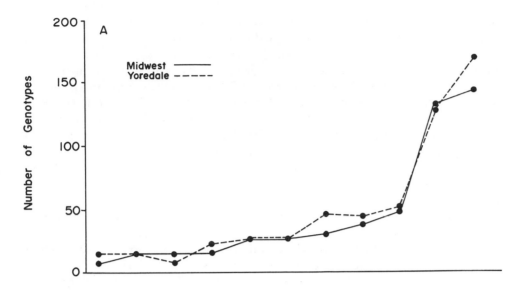

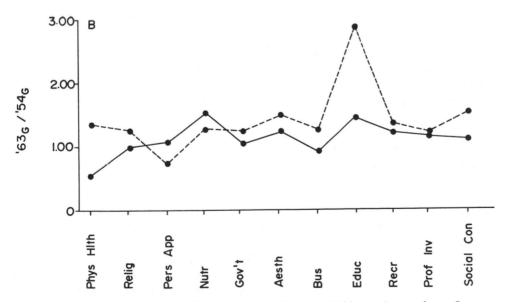

FIGURE 5.4.   Variety in Primary Action Pattern Habitats. A: number of genotypes, 1963–64; B: change in number of genotypes, $'63_G/'54_G$.

scissa by increasing extent of local control in Midwest. (See notes regarding graphic presentations in the first pages of this chapter.)

High local autonomy. Extent of local control varies greatly across primary action pattern habitats (Figure 5.5A). In Midwest it ranges from 12 percent for Physical Health to 74 percent for Nutrition, and in Yoredale from zero percent for Physical Health to 65 percent for Personal Appearance. On the basis of the extent of local control of the towns' total habitats, where the MW/YD ratio of percentages is 1.4 (T6.6; R5; C3/4), we expect local control to be more extensive in Midwest than in Yoredale and to hold for 9 of the 11 action patterns. However, Midwest's superiority to Yoredale is much greater than expected for Physical Health, Government, Education, Religion, and Recreation, and Midwest is inferior to Yoredale in local control of Business and Personal Appearance.

Medium local autonomy. Regional control of primary action pattern habitats varies less than does local control (Figure 5.5B). The range in Midwest is from 21 percent for Nutrition to 77 percent for Physical Health, and in Yoredale from 23 percent for Nutrition to 46 percent for Recreation. Regional control, like local control, is more extensive in Midwest than in Yoredale for 9 of the 11 action patterns, as expected on the basis of its extent in the towns' total habitats, where the MW/YD ratio of percentages is 1.3 (T6.8; R5; C3/4). However, Midwest's superiority is greater than expected for Physical Health and Education, and Midwest is inferior to Yoredale in extent of regional control of Recreation and Nutrition.

Low local autonomy. Control from a distance varies greatly across the primary action pattern habitats of Midwest and Yoredale (Figure 5.5C). The range in Midwest is from zero distant control for Aesthetics and Personal Appearance to 30 percent for Government, and in Yoredale from 7 percent for Personal Appearance to 70 percent for Education. Distant control is less extensive in Midwest than in Yoredale, as expected on the basis of its extent in the towns' total habitats, where the MW/YD ratio of percentages is 0.25 (T6.10; R5; C3/4). However, Midwest's inferiority in percentage of habitat controlled from beyond the surrounding district and region is much greater than expected for Education, Religion, and Recreation. Only in Midwest's primary habitats for Health and Government does distant control exceed 10 percent, whereas it does in all of Yoredale's primary habitats except Personal Appearance.

BEHAVIOR MECHANISM HABITATS

We have investigated 4 behavior mechanism qualities of the towns' habitats: Affective Behavior, Gross Motor Activity, Manipulation, and Talking. Our data bear upon such issues as the degree to which Midwest and Yoredale differ in habitat resources for the occurrence of, say, running, lifting, bending, kneeling, wrestling, walking,

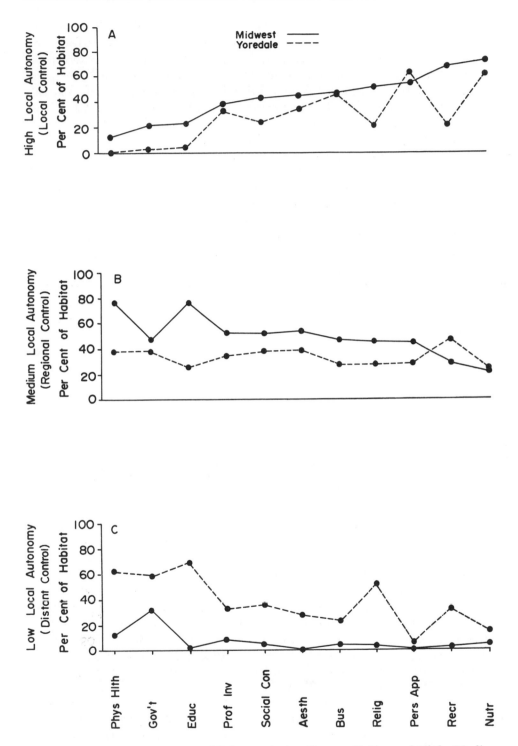

FIGURE 5.5. Percentage of Primary Action Pattern Habitats of High, Medium, and Low Local Autonomy, 1963–64.

throwing, and so forth—that is, Gross Motor Activity. Habitat resources for Gross Motor Activity are provided by Physical Education
Classes, Dances, Garages, Trafficways, and Parks and Playgrounds,
among others. In raising this issue (and others like it), we have presumed that if habitats of the towns differ in this respect, it makes a difference in the behavior of their human inhabitants, in somewhat the
same way that a hilly pasture and a level pasture make a difference in
the behavior of the animals pastured in them.

As with action pattern habitats, behavior mechanism habitats are
not mutually exclusive—Football Games provide resources for both
Gross Motor Activity and Talking, for example—and measures of the
extent of behavior mechanism habitats imply nothing directly with
respect to the amount of the appropriate behavior that occurs within
them. But there is an important difference: behavior mechanism habitats have no obvious relation to the goal-directedness of the actions occurring within them. Habitats with prominent resources for Talking,
for example, may have resources for the achievement of aesthetic goals
(Choral Concerts), governmental goals (Court Sessions), personal
appearance goals (Beauty Shops), recreational goals (Darts Games), or
religious goals (Worship Services).

Summaries of the data for behavior mechanism hatitats are presented in Figures 5.6 to 5.10.

Affective Behavior

DEFINITION

Affective Behavior is present within a behavior setting to the extent that the concrete occurrences which constitute its program involve
inhabitants in the overt expression of feelings and emotions.

Affective Behavior is *prominent* in a behavior setting if most of its
standing pattern includes overt expression of emotion by the setting's
inhabitants. For example, in most behavior settings of the genotype
Basketball Games (in Midwest) or Cricket Games (in Yoredale), Affective Behavior is prominent because the overt expression of emotion is
widespread among the inhabitants, with a high frequency of occurrence
throughout the duration of setting. Affective Behavior is *secondary*
within a setting if some, but less than 80 percent, of the standing pattern involves overt expression of emotion. Affective Behavior is *absent*
from a setting if no components of the standing pattern regularly involve the overt expression of emotion—for example, in Garages, and
Woodworking and Machine Shop Classes.

The behavior settings where Affective Behavior is prominent
constitute a town's *primary affective habitat* (PAfH); those where Affective
Behavior is regularly present in some degree constitute the *territorial
range* of Affective Behavior.

Basic data for affective Behavior are presented in Table 5.54; the

Table 5.54
Affective Behavior
Basic Habitat Data

	1954–55		1963–64	
	MW (1)	YD (2)	MW (3)	YD (4)
Primary Habitat (PAfH)				
Extent				
(1) Behavior Settings per Year	132	101	184	129
(2) Mean BS per Day	12.0	9.1	18.1	9.1
(3) Mean BS per Hour	1.1	1.4	1.5	0.9
(4) Centiurbs (no.)	10.2	8.3	14.4	9.2
(5) Centiurbs (% of Town Total)	11.4%	9.2%	13.4%	8.2%
Erosion and Accretion Type of Change	Erosion from '54–55		Accretion to '63–64	
(6) Centiurbs (no.)	2.2	3.5	7.1	4.8
(7) Centiurbs (% of PAfH)	21%	42%	49%	51%
Claims for Operatives				
(8) Number	2,778	1,771	4,930	3,414
(9) Number (% of Town Total)	52%	43%	48%	44%
Amount of Variety				
(10) Major Genotypes (no.)	10	10	10	8
(11) Total Genotypes (no.)	45	34	55	37
(12) Total Genotypes (% of Town Total)	26%	20%	28%	17%
Territorial Range (TR)				
(13) Centiurbs (no.)	46.0	42.4	55.3	59.9
(14) Centiurbs (% of Town Total)	51%	47%	52%	53%

report for Aesthetics provides a key to the location of particular data in this table.

SALIENT FINDINGS

The territorial range of Affective Behavior covers just over half of the towns' habitats. Habitats where resources for Affective Behavior are prominent (PAfH) comprise 8 to 13 percent of the towns' habitats. Midwest's PAfH is larger than Yoredale's, and the PAfH of both towns was larger in 1963–64 than in 1954–55. Habitat-claims for operatives within the towns' PAfHs are 43 to 52 percent of their total claims for operatives; Midwest has more claims for PAfH operatives than Yoredale, and both towns had more in 1963–64 than in 1954–55. There is more variety within Midwest's than within Yoredale's PAfH; variety increased between the survey years in both towns.

TERRITORIAL RANGE OF AFFECTIVE BEHAVIOR

The territorial range of Affective Behavior extends over about one-half of the towns' habitats; and conversely, approximately one-half of their habitats are without regular affective components. The TR of Affective Behavior was slightly smaller in Midwest than in Yoredale in 1963–64; it increased in both towns between the survey years, more so in Yoredale than in Midwest.

EXTENT OF PRIMARY AFFECTIVE HABITAT

Midwest's PAfH in 1963–64 was approximately equivalent to 288 occasional settings such as Parties, or Plays and Programs; and Yoredale's was equivalent to 184 occasional settings. PAfHs cover 13.4 percent of Midwest's and 8.2 percent of Yoredale's total habitats.

Differences. Midwest's PAfH is larger than Yoredale's; in 1963–64 Midwest had 5.2 more cu of PAfH, amounting to 156 percent as many cu and to 5.2 more percent of the town's total habitat.

Changes. Both towns' PAfHs were larger in 1963–64 than in 1954–55. Midwest had 4.2 more cu of PAfH in 1963–64, amounting to 141 percent as many cu and to 2 more percent of the town's total habitat. Yoredale had 0.9 more cu, amounting to 111 percent as many cu and to 1.0 fewer percent of the town's total habitat.

Processes of change. More than one-fifth of the towns' 1954–55 PAfHs were eroded before 1963–64, and about one-half of their 1963–64 PAfHs were accreted after 1954–55. Both erosion and accretion were less in Midwest than in Yoredale; 21 fewer percent of Midwest's 1954–55 PAfH was eroded, and 2 fewer percent of its 1963–64 PAfH was accreted. The opposite is true for the towns' total habitats; more of Midwest's than of Yoredale's habitat was both eroded and accreted.

CLAIMS FOR OPERATIVES WITHIN PRIMARY AFFECTIVE HABITAT

If all behavior settings within the towns' PAfHs were to function simultaneously in 1963–64, it would require 4930 persons in Midwest and 3414 persons in Yoredale to carry out essential operations. Claims for PAfH operatives are much greater than claims for operatives in general, on a centiurb basis; there are 342 claims for operatives per cu of Midwest's PAfH, compared with 96 for the whole habitat, and 371 per cu of Yoredale's PAfH, compared with 69 for the whole habitat. The towns' PAfHs contain 48 and 44 percent of their total habitat-claims for operatives; whereas, as we have seen, they comprise 13.4 and 8.2 percent of the towns' total habitats. The towns' PAfHs are rich in positions of responsibility.

Differences. Midwest has more habitat-claims for PAfH operatives than Yoredale. In 1963–64 it had 1516 more such claims than Yoredale, amounting to 144 percent as many, to 92 percent as many per cu of PAfH, to 228 percent as many per town inhabitant, and to 4 more percent of the town's total claims for operatives.

Changes. Both towns had more PAfH claims for operatives in 1963–64 than in 1954–55. Midwest had 2152 more such claims in

1963–64, amounting to 177 percent as many, to 126 percent as many per cu of PAfH, and to 153 percent as many per town inhabitant, but to 4 less percent of the town's total claims for operatives. Yoredale had 1643 more such claims, amounting to 193 percent as many, to 174 percent as many per cu of PAfH, to 191 percent as many per town inhabitant, and to 1 more percent of the town's total claims for operatives.

VARIETY WITHIN PRIMARY AFFECTIVE HABITAT

There was more variety within the two towns' PAfHs than expected on the basis of extent. In 1963–64 Midwest's PAfH, 13.4 percent of its total habitat, was the locus of 28 percent of the town's behavior setting genotypes; and Yoredale's PAfH, 9.2 percent of its total habitat, was the locus of 18 percent of its genotypes.

If Midwest and Yoredale were to display simultaneously in 1963–64 the complete range of behavior setting programs within their PAfHs, Midwest would require 55 different halls, playing fields, and meeting rooms with their appropriate facilities, 55 differently trained and experienced groups of operatives, and 55 different experts as coaches, instructors, group leaders, and so forth; and Yoredale would require 39 different halls, staffs of functionaries, and leaders.

Differences. There is more variety within Midwest's PAfH than within Yoredale's. In 1963–64 Midwest had 18 more genotypes than Yoredale, amounting to 148 percent as many and to 11 more percent of Midwest's than of Yoredale's total genotypes.

Changes. There was more variety within the town's PAfHs in 1963–64 than in 1954–55. Midwest had 10 more genotypes in 1963–64, amounting to 122 percent as many and to 2 more percent of the town's total genotypes. Yorcdale had 3 more genotypes, amounting to 109 percent as many and to 2 less percent of the town's total genotypes.

NATURE OF PRIMARY AFFECTIVE HABITAT

An overview of the towns' habitat resources for Affective Behavior in 1963–64 is provided by this sample of genotypes: (*a*) Major genotypes of MW's PAfH that do not occur in YD's PAfH: Baseball Games, Basketball Games, Judges' Chambers, Day Care Homes and Nurseries. (*b*) Major genotype of MW's PAfH that is a minor genotype of YD's PAfH: Physical Education classes. (*c*) Major genotypes of both MW's and YD's PAfHs: Plays and Programs, Parks and Playgrounds, Religious Worship Services, Parties. (*d*) Major genotype of YD's PAfH that is a minor genotype of MW's PAfH: Vocal Music Classes. (*e*) Major genotypes of YD's PAfH that do not occur in MW's PAfH: Darts Games, Cricket Games.

CONTROL BY AUTHORITY SYSTEMS

In 1963–64 almost half the PAfHs of both towns were under the aegis of School authority systems, with Voluntary Associations and Churches next in order of breadth of influence (Table 5.55). Private En-

Table 5.55
Affective Behavior
Control of Affective Habitats by Authority Systems
Percent of primary affective habitats
controlled by different authority systems

		1954–55		1963–64	
		MW (1)	YD (2)	MW (3)	YD (4)
(1)	Extent of PAfH in cu	10.2	8.3	14.4	9.2
Percent of PAfH controlled by:					
(2)	Churches	16.0	26.7	16.3	16.7
(3)	Govt. Agencies	17.8	18.2	13.6	9.9
(4)	Private Enterprises	5.2	8.2	5.3	3.9
(5)	Schools	47.9	21.8	48.1	45.1
(6)	Voluntary Assns.	13.1	25.1	16.7	24.5

terprises were least involved, controlling 5.3 and 3.9 percent of the PAfHs of Midwest and Yoredale, respectively.

Gross Motor Activity

DEFINITION

Gross Motor Activity is present within a behavior setting to the extent that the concrete occurrences which constitute its program require inhabitants to utilize movements of large muscles, limbs, and the trunk of the body.

Gross Motor Activity is *prominent* in a behavior setting if most of its standing pattern involves the use of large muscles, limbs, and the body trunk in implementing the program of the setting. For example, in most behavior settings of the genotype Parks and Playgrounds, Gross Motor Activity is prominent because most of the concrete occurrences that make up the programs of these settings involve persons in activities which utilize large muscle movements—running, jumping, swinging, throwing. Gross Motor Activity is *secondary* if some, but less than 80 percent, of the setting's standing pattern involves use of large muscle movements; this is true, for example, of Libraries, TV and Radio Repair Shops, and Food and Rummage Sales. Gross Motor Activity is *absent* from a setting if no components of the standing pattern regularly involve inhabitants in the use of large muscle movements—as, for example, in Latin Classes and Business Meetings.

The behavior settings where Gross Motor Activity is prominent constitute a town's *primary gross motor habitat* (PGMH); those where Gross Motor Activity is regularly present in some degree comprise the *territorial range* of Gross Motor Activity.

Basic data for Gross Motor Activity are presented in Table 5.56; the report for Aesthetics provides a key to the location of particular data in this table.

Table 5.56
Gross Motor Activity
Basic Habitat Data

Primary Habitat (PGMH)	1954–55		1963–64	
	MW (1)	YD (2)	MW (3)	YD (4)
Extent				
(1) Behavior Settings per Year	153	153	181	200
(2) Mean BS per Day	58.8	55.1	47.7	50.0
(3) Mean BS per Hour	14.4	14.3	10.6	11.6
(4) Centiurbs (no.)	34.5	33.6	29.7	32.2
(5) Centiurbs (% of Town Total)	38.4%	37.3%	27.7%	28.5%
Erosion and Accretion Type of Change	Erosion from '54–55		Accretion to '63–64	
(6) Centiurbs (no.)	15.3	6 7	15.1	9.4
(7) Centiurbs (% of PGMH)	44%	20%	51%	29%
Claims for Operatives				
(8) Number	1,785	1,993	3,051	4,101
(9) Number (% of Town Total)	33%	48%	30%	53%
Amount of Variety				
(10) Major Genotypes (no.)	12	10	8	10
(11) Total Genotypes (no.)	64	67	63	77
(12) Total Genotypes (% of Town Total)	37%	40%	32%	36%
Territorial Range (TR)				
(13) Centiurbs (no.)	62.9	72.1	65.6	88.0
(14) Centiurbs (% of Town Total)	70%	80%	61%	78%

SALIENT FINDINGS

The territorial range of Gross Motor Activity comprises three-fifths to four-fifths of the towns' habitats. Habitats where resources for Gross Motor Activity are prominent (PGMH) comprise 28 to 38 percent of the towns' habitats. Midwest and Yoredale differed little in PGMH in 1963–64, and PGMH in both towns was smaller in 1963–64 than in 1954–55. Habitat-claims for operatives within the towns' PGMHs constitute 30 to 53 percent of their total claims for operatives; Midwest has fewer claims for PGMH operatives than Yoredale, and both towns had more in 1963–64 than in 1954–55. There is less variety within Midwest's than within Yoredale's PGMH; variety decreased between the survey years in Midwest, but increased in Yoredale.

TERRITORIAL RANGE OF GROSS MOTOR ACTIVITY

The territorial range of Gross Motor Activity extends over about three-fifths to four-fifths of the towns' habitats; and conversely, approximately one-fifth to two-fifths of the towns' habitats are without gross motor components. The TR of Gross Motor Activity is smaller in Midwest than in Yoredale; it increased in both towns between the survey years, but it decreased as percentages of the towns' total habitats.

EXTENT OF PRIMARY GROSS MOTOR HABITAT

Midwest's PGMH in 1963–64 was approximately equivalent to 59 regular behavior settings that occur six days a week for eight hours a day, such as Midwest Lumberyard and Bethels Service Station; and Yoredale's PGMH was equivalent to 64 regular settings. PGMHs cover 27.7 percent of Midwest's and 28.5 percent of Yoredale's total habitats.

Differences. Midwest's PGMH is smaller than Yoredale's; in 1963–64 Midwest had 2.5 fewer cu of PGMH, amounting to 92 percent as many cu and to 0.8 fewer percent of the town's total habitat.

Changes. Both towns' PGMHs were smaller in 1963–64 than in 1954–55. Midwest had 4.8 fewer cu of PGMH in 1963–64, amounting to 86 percent as many cu and to 10.7 fewer percent of the town's total habitat. Yoredale had 1.4 fewer cu, amounting to 96 percent as many cu and to 8.8 fewer percent of the town's total habitat.

Processes of change. More than one-fifth of the towns' 1954–55 PGMHs were eroded before 1963–64, and 29 percent or more of their 1963–64 PGMHs were accreted after 1954–55. Both erosion and accretion were greater in Midwest than in Yoredale; 24 more percent of Midwest's 1954–55 PGMH was eroded, and 22 more percent of its 1963–64 PGMH was accreted. The same is true for the towns' total habitats; more of Midwest's than of Yoredale's habitat was both eroded and accreted.

CLAIMS FOR OPERATIVES WITHIN PRIMARY
GROSS MOTOR HABITAT

If all behavior settings within the towns' PGMHs were to function simultaneously in 1963–64, it would require 3051 persons in Midwest and 4101 persons in Yoredale to carry out essential operations. Claims for PGMH operatives are greater than claims for operatives in general on a centiurb basis; there are 103 claims for operatives per cu of Midwest's PGMH, compared with 96 for the whole habitat, and there are 127 per cu of Yoredale's PGMH, compared with 69 for the whole habitat. The towns' PGMHs contain 30 and 53 percent of their total habitat-claims for operatives; whereas, as we have seen, they comprise only 27.7 and 28.5 percent of the towns' total habitats. The towns' PGMHs are relatively rich in positions of responsibility.

Differences. Midwest has fewer habitat-claims for PGMH operatives than Yoredale. In 1963–64 it had 1050 fewer such claims, amounting to 74 percent as many, to 81 percent as many per cu of PGMH, to 117 percent as many per town inhabitant, and to 23 fewer percent of the town's total claims for operatives.

Changes. Both towns had more PGMH claims for operatives in 1963–64 than in 1954–55. Midwest had 1266 more such claims, in 1963–64, amounting to 171 percent as many, to 198 percent as many per cu of PGMH, and to 147 percent as many per town inhabitant, but to 3 fewer percent of the town's total claims for operatives. Yoredale had 2108 more such claims, amounting to 206 percent as many, to 215 percent as many per cu of PGMH, to 204 percent as many per town inhabitant, and to 5 more percent of the town's total claims for operatives.

VARIETY WITHIN PRIMARY GROSS MOTOR HABITAT

There was somewhat more variety within the two towns' PGMHs than expected on the basis of extent. In 1963–64 Midwest's PGMH, 27.7 percent of its total habitat, was the locus of 32 percent of the town's behavior setting genotypes; and Yoredale's PGMH, 28.5 percent of its total habitat, was the locus of 37 percent of its genotypes.

If Midwest and Yoredale were to display simultaneously in 1963–64 the complete range of behavior setting programs within their PGMHs, Midwest would require 63 different stores, shops, playing fields, and so forth, with their appropriate facilities, 63 differently trained and experienced groups of operatives, and 63 different experts as supervisors, instructors, and coaches; and Yoredale would require 78 different stores, playing fields, and so forth, with their staffs of functionaries and leaders.

Differences. There is less variety within Midwest's PGMH than within Yoredale's. In 1963–64 Midwest had 14 fewer genotypes than Yoredale, amounting to 82 percent as many and to 4 fewer percent of Midwest's than of Yoredale's total genotypes.

Changes. There was slightly less variety in Midwest's PGMH and more in Yoredale's in 1963–64 than in 1954–55. Midwest had 1 less genotype in 1963–64, amounting to 98 percent as many and to 5 fewer percent of the town's total genotypes. Yoredale had 10 more genotypes, amounting to 115 percent as many but to 4 fewer percent of the town's total genotypes.

NATURE OF PRIMARY GROSS MOTOR ACTIVITY HABITAT

An overview of the towns' habitat resources for Gross Motor Activity in 1963–64 is provided by this sample of genotypes: (*a*) Major genotypes of MW's PGMH that do not occur in YD's PGMH: Lumberyards, Service Stations. (*b*) Major genotypes of MW's PGMH that are minor genotypes of YD's PGMH: Building, Construction, and Repair Services; Delivery and Collection Routes. (*c*) Major genotypes of both MW's and YD's PGMHs: Garages, Grocery Stores, Parks and Playgrounds, Physical Education Classes. (*d*) Major genotypes of YD's PGMH that are minor genotypes of MW's PGMH: Hallways, Machinery Repair Shops. (*e*) Major genotypes of YD's PGMH that do not occur in MW's PGMH: Hotels, Milk Bottling and Delivery Services, Trafficways.

CONTROL BY AUTHORITY SYSTEMS

In 1963–64 Private Enterprises dominated the PGMHs of both towns, controlling three-fifths of Midwest's and almost one-half of Yore-

Table 5.57
Gross Motor Activity
Control of Gross Motor Habitats by Authority Systems
Percent of primary gross motor habitats
controlled by different authority systems.

		1954–55		1963–64	
		MW (1)	YD (2)	MW (3)	YD (4)
(1)	Extent of PGMH in cu	34.5	33.6	29.7	32.2
Percent of PGMH controlled by:					
(2)	Churches	0.4	1.2	2.4	2.0
(3)	Govt. Agencies	13.6	18.2	7.6	14.9
(4)	Private Enterprises	67.0	61.8	60.0	48.7
(5)	Schools	13.9	9.8	21.0	24.4
(6)	Voluntary Assns.	5.1	9.0	9.0	10.0

dale's PGMH (Table 5.57). However, less of Yoredale's than of Midwest's PGMH is under the aegis of Private Enterprises, and more is under the aegis of its Government Agencies.

Manipulation

DEFINITION

Manipulation is present in a behavior setting to the extent that the concrete occurrences which constitute the program require the inhabitants to utilize their hands in grasping, holding, pushing, pulling, tapping, clapping and manipulating objects or materials.

Manipulation is *prominent* in a behavior setting if most of its standing pattern involves use of the hands in implementing the program of the setting. For example, in most behavior settings of the genotype Restaurants, Manipulation is prominent because most of the concrete occurrences that make up the programs of these settings involve persons in activities which require hand movements—cooking, serving, eating, writing checks, making change. Manipulation is *secondary* if some, but less than 80 percent, of the setting's standing pattern involves use of hand movements; this is true, for example, of Attorneys' Offices, Plays and Programs, and Rotary Club Meetings. Manipulation is *absent* from a setting if no components of the standing pattern regularly involve inhabitants in the use of the hands; this is true, for example, of Hallways and Lodge Meetings.

The behavior settings where Manipulation is prominent constitute town's *primary manipulation habitat* (PMH); those where Manipulation is present in some degree comprise the *territorial range* of Manipulation.

Basic data for Manipulation are presented in Table 5.58; the report for Aesthetics provides a key to the location of particular data in this table.

Table 5.58
Manipulation
Basic Habitat Data

Primary Habitat (PMH)	1954–55		1963–64	
	MW (1)	YD (2)	MW (3)	YD (4)
Extent				
(1) Behavior Settings per Year	134	129	164	173
(2) Mean BS per Day	56.7	60.6	49.0	52.5
(3) Mean BS per Hour	15.0	15.0	13.2	13.7
(4) Centiurbs (no.)	33.7	34.4	31.8	33.4
(5) Centiurbs (% of Town				
Total)	37.5%	38.2%	29.6%	29.6%
Erosion and Accretion				
Type of Change	Erosion from '54–55		Accretion to '63–64	
(6) Centiurbs (no.)	16.8	7.1	15.3	10.2
(7) Centiurbs (% of PMH)	50%	21%	48%	30%
Claims for Operatives				
(8) Number	1,177	1,165	2,630	1,990
(9) Number (% of Town				
Total)	22%	28%	26%	26%
Amount of Variety				
(10) Major Genotypes (no.)	11	9	7	7
(11) Total Genotypes (no.)	62	64	65	78
(12) Total Genotypes (% of				
Town Total)	36%	38%	33%	37%
Territorial Range (TR)				
(13) Centiurbs (no.)	69.1	69.9	77.9	98.7
(14) Centiurbs (% of Town Total)	77%	78%	73%	88%

SALIENT FINDINGS

The territorial range of Manipulation extends over 73 to 88 percent of the towns' total habitats. Habitats where resources for Manipulation are prominent (PMH) comprise 30 to 38 percent of the towns' habitats. Midwest's PMH is smaller than Yoredale's, and the PMH was smaller in both towns in 1963–64 than in 1954–55. Habitat-claims for operatives in the towns' PMHs are 22 to 28 percent of their total claims for operatives; Midwest has more claims for PMH operatives than Yoredale, and both towns had more in 1963–64 than in 1954–55. There is less variety within Midwest's than within Yoredale's PMH; variety increased between the survey years in both towns.

TERRITORIAL RANGE OF MANIPULATION

The territorial range of Manipulation extends over about three-quarters to seven-eighths of the towns' habitats; and conversely, approximately one-eighth to one-quarter of the towns' habitats are without manipulation components. The TR of Manipulation is greater in Midwest than in Yoredale.

EXTENT OF PRIMARY MANIPULATION HABITAT

Midwest's PMH in 1963–64 was approximately equivalent to 63 regular behavior settings that occur six days a week for eight hours a day, such as Eggleston Garage and Service Station; and Yoredale's PMH was equivalent to 66 regular settings. PMHs cover 29.6 percent of the total habitats of both towns.

Differences. Midwest's PMH is smaller than Yoredale's; in 1963–64 Midwest had 1.6 fewer cu of PMH, amounting to 95 percent as many cu and to the same percentage of the town's total habitat.

Changes. Both towns' PMHs were smaller in 1963–64 than in 1954–55. Midwest had 1.9 fewer cu in 1963–64, amounting to 94 percent as many cu and to 7.9 fewer percent of the town's total habitat. Yoredale had 1.0 fewer cu, amounting to 97 percent as many cu and to 8.6 fewer percent of the town's total habitat.

Processes of change. More than one-fifth of the towns' 1954–55 PMHs were eroded before 1963–64, and more than three-tenths of their 1963–64 PMHs were accreted after 1954–55. Both erosion and accretion were greater in Midwest than in Yoredale; 29 more percent of Midwest's 1954–55 PMH was eroded, and 18 more percent of its 1963–64 PMH was accreted. The same is true for the towns' total habitats; more of Midwest's than of Yoredale's habitat was both eroded and accreted.

CLAIMS FOR OPERATIVES WITHIN PRIMARY MANIPULATION HABITAT

If all behavior settings within the towns' PMHs were to function simultaneously in 1963–64, it would require 2630 persons in Midwest and 1990 persons in Yoredale to carry out essential operations. Claims for PMH operatives are fewer than claims for operatives in general, on a centiurb basis; there are 83 claims for operatives per cu of Midwest's PMH, compared with 96 for the whole habitat, and 60 per cu of Yoredale's PMH, compared with 69 for the whole habitat. Each town's PMH contains 26 percent of its total habitat-claims for operatives; whereas, as we have seen, they comprise more than 30 percent of each town's total habitat. The towns' PMHs are lean in positions of responsibility.

Differences. Midwest has more habitat-claims for PMH operatives than Yoredale. In 1963–64 it had 640 more such claims than Yoredale, amounting to 132 percent as many, to 139 percent as many per cu of PMH, to 209 percent as many per town inhabitant, and to the same percentage of the town's total claims for operatives.

Changes. Both towns had more PMH claims for operatives in 1963–64 than in 1954–55. Midwest had 1453 more such claims in 1963–64, amounting to 223 percent as many, to 237 percent as many per cu of PMH, to 192 percent as many per town inhabitant, and to 4 more percent of the town's total claims for operatives. Yoredale had 325 more such claims, amounting to 171 percent as many, to 176 percent as many per cu of PMH, and to 170 percent as many per town inhabitant, but to 2 fewer percent of the town's total claims for operatives.

VARIETY WITHIN PRIMARY MANIPULATION HABITAT

There was somewhat more variety within the two towns' PMHs than expected on the basis of extent. In 1963–64 Midwest's PMH, 29.6 percent of its habitat, was the locus of 33 percent of the town's behavior setting genotypes; and Yoredale's PMH, 29.6 percent of its total habitat, was the locus of 37 percent of its genotypes.

If Midwest and Yoredale were to display simultaneously in 1963–64 the complete range of behavior setting programs within their PMHs, Midwest would require 65 different offices and meeting rooms with their appropriate facilities, 65 differently trained and experienced groups of operatives, and 65 different experts as supervisors, instructors, coaches, and so forth; and Yoredale would require 78 different rooms, staffs of functionaries, and leaders.

Differences. There is less variety within Midwest's PMHs than within Yoredale's. In 1963–64 Midwest had 13 fewer genotypes than Yoredale, amounting to 83 percent as many and to 4 fewer percent of Midwest's than of Yoredale's total genotypes.

Changes. There was more variety within the towns' PMH in 1963–64 than in 1954–55. Midwest had 3 more genotypes in 1963–64, amounting to 105 percent as many and to 3 fewer percent of the town's total genotypes. Yoredale had 14 more genotypes, amounting to 122 percent as many and to 1 fewer percent of the town's total genotypes.

NATURE OF PRIMARY MANIPULATION HABITAT

An overview of the towns' habitat resources for Manipulation in 1963–64 is provided by this sample of genotypes: (*a*) Major genotypes of MW's PMH that do not occur in YD's PMH: Delivery and Collection Routes, Lumberyards, Service Stations. (*b*) There are no major geno-

Table 5.59
Manipulation
Control of Manipulation Habitats by Authority Systems
Percent of primary manipulation habitats
controlled by different authority systems

		1954–55		1963–64	
		MW (1)	YD (2)	MW (3)	YD (4)
(1)	Extent of PMH in cu	33.7	34.4	31.8	33.4
	Percent of PMH controlled by:				
(2)	Churches	0.5	0.0	1.3	1.1
(3)	Govt. Agencies	6.5	9.7	7.6	12.9
(4)	Private Enterprises	78.2	76.9	74.8	61.5
(5)	Schools	12.1	7.9	12.9	18.9
(6)	Voluntary Assns.	2.6	5.5	3.3	5.6

types of MW's PMH that are minor genotypes of YD's PMH. (*c*) Major genotypes of both MW's and YD's PMHs: Building, Construction, and Repair Services; Garages; Grocery Stores; Restaurants. (*d*) Major genotype of YD's PMH that is a minor genotype of MW's PMH: Physical Education Classes. (*e*) Major genotype of YD's PMH that does not occur in MW's PMH: Milk Bottling and Delivery Services.

CONTROL BY AUTHORITY SYSTEMS

In 1963–64 the Private Enterprises of both towns dominated their PMHs, more so in Midwest than in Yoredale (Table 5.59). Of all the authority systems, Churches were least involved with manipulation.

Talking

DEFINITION

Talking is present in a behavior setting to the extent that the concrete occurrences which constitute its program involve inhabitants in verbal behavior—talking, singing, yelling, crying, cheering.

Talking is *prominent* in a behavior setting if most of its standing pattern involves talking or some other form of verbalization in implementing the program of the setting. For example, in most behavior settings of the genotype Business Meetings or Vocal Music Classes, Talking is prominent because most of the concrete occurrences that make up the programs of these settings involve the inhabitants in verbalizing in one form or another—discussing, presenting reports, singing. Talking is *secondary* if some, but less than 80 percent, of the setting's standing pattern involves verbal behavior—as, for example, with Cemeteries or Fire Drills. Talking is *absent* from a setting if no components of the standing pattern regularly involve inhabitants in verbalization; this is true, for example, of Bus Stops and Moving Picture Shows.

The behavior settings of a town where Talking is prominent constitute its *primary talking habitat* (*PTH*); those where Talking is present in some degree comprise the *territorial range* of Talking.

Basic data for Talking are presented in Table 5.60; the report for Aesthetics provides a key to the location of particular data in the table.

SALIENT FINDINGS

The territorial range of Talking extends over 83 to 88 percent of the towns' total habitats. Habitats where resources for talking behavior are prominent (PTH) comprise 12 to 18 percent of the towns' habitats. Midwest's PTH is smaller than Yoredale's, and the PTH was smaller in Midwest and larger in Yoredale in 1963–64 than in 1954–55. Habitat-claims for operatives within the towns' PTHs constitute 42 to 55 percent of their total claims for operatives; Midwest has more claims for PTH operatives than Yoredale, and both towns had more in 1963–64 than in 1954–55. The towns are similar in the amount of variety within their

Table 5.60
Talking
Basic Habitat Data

	1954–55		1963–64	
Primary Habitat (PTH)	MW (1)	YD (2)	MW (3)	YD (4)
Extent				
(1) Behavior Settings per Year	189	127	181	192
(2) Mean BS per Day	17.5	18.1	12.7	21.1
(3) Mean BS per Hour	3.3	4.1	1.4	3.2
(4) Centiurbs (no.)	16.4	14.2	13.1	17.2
(5) Centiurbs (% of Town Total)	18.2%	15.8%	12.2%	15.2%
Erosion and Accretion Type of Change	Erosion from '54–55		Accretion to '63–64	
(6) Centiurbs (no.)	6.2	5.2	5.2	8.8
(7) Centiurbs (% of PTH)	38%	37%	40%	51%
Claims for Operatives				
(8) Number	2,939	2,064	4,276	3,287
(9) Number (% of Town Total)	55%	50%	42%	42%
Amount of Variety				
(10) Major Genotypes (no.)	13	8	11	10
(11) Total Genotypes (no.)	60	45	53	54
(12) Total Genotypes (% of Town Total)	35%	27%	27%	25%
Territorial Range (TR)				
(13) Centiurbs (no.)	78.1	74.7	94.1	99.8
(14) Centiurbs (% of Town Total)	87%	83%	88%	88%

PTHs; variety decreased in Midwest and increased in Yoredale between the survey years.

TERRITORIAL RANGE OF TALKING

The territorial range of Talking extends over about five-sixths to eight-ninths of the towns' habitats; and conversely, approximately one sixth to one-ninth of the towns' habitats are without regular talking components. In 1963–64, the TR of Talking was smaller in Midwest than in Yoredale, in terms of centiurbs, but it was equal in the two towns in terms of percentages of total habitats.

EXTENT OF PRIMARY TALKING HABITAT

Midwest's PTH in 1963–64 was approximately equivalent to 260 nonrecurring, two-hour occasional settings such as Dinner Dances, Parties, Plays and Programs; and Yoredale's PTH was equivalent to about 340 occasional settings. PTHs cover 12.2 percent of Midwest's and 15.2 percent of Yoredale's total habitats.

Differences. Midwest's PTH is smaller than Yoredale's; in 1963–64

Midwest had 4.1 fewer cu of PTH, amounting to 76 percent as many cu and to 3.0 fewer percent of the town's total habitat.

Changes. The PTH was smaller in Midwest and larger in Yoredale in 1963–64 than in 1954–55. Midwest had 3.3 fewer cu in 1963–64, amounting to 80 percent as many cu and to 6 fewer percent of the town's total habitat. Yoredale had 3 more cu, amounting to 121 percent as many cu and to 0.6 fewer percent of the town's total habitat.

Processes of change. More than 36 percent of the towns' 1954–55 PTHs was eroded before 1963–64, and more than 39 percent of their 1963–64 PTHs was accreted after 1954–55. Erosion was greater in Midwest, and accretion was greater in Yoredale: 1 more percent of Midwest's 1954–55 PTH was eroded, and 11 fewer percent of its 1963–64 PTH was accreted. This differs from the towns' total habitats; more of Midwest's than of Yoredale's habitat was both eroded and accreted.

CLAIMS FOR OPERATIVES WITHIN PRIMARY TALKING HABITAT

If all behavior settings within the towns' PTHs were to function simultaneously in 1963–64, it would require 4276 persons in Midwest and 3287 persons in Yoredale to carry out essential operations. Claims for PTH operatives are much greater than claims for operatives in general, on a centiurb basis; there are 326 claims for operatives per cu of Midwest's PTH, compared with 96 for the whole habitat, and 191 per cu of Yoredale's PTH, compared with 69 for the whole habitat. Each town's PTH contains 42 percent of its total habitat-claims for operatives; whereas, as we have seen, they comprise 12.2 and 15.2 percent of the towns' total habitats. The towns' PTHs are rich in positions of responsibility.

Differences. Midwest has more habitat-claims for PTH operatives than Yoredale. In 1963–64 it had 989 more such claims than Yoredale, amounting to 130 percent as many, to 171 percent as many per cu of PTH, to 205 percent as many per town inhabitant, and to the same percentage of the town's total claims for operatives.

Changes. Both towns had more PTH claims for operatives in 1963–64 than in 1954–55. Midwest had 1337 more such claims in 1963–64, amounting to 145 percent as many, to 182 percent as many per cu of PTH, and to 125 percent as many per town inhabitant, but to 13 fewer percent of the town's total claims for operatives. Yoredale had 1223 more such claims, amounting to 159 percent as many, to 131 percent as many per cu of PTH, to 158 percent as many per town inhabitant, but to 8 fewer percent of the town's total claims for operatives.

VARIETY WITHIN PRIMARY TALKING HABITAT

There was more variety within both towns' PTHs than expected on the basis of extent. In 1963–64 Midwest's PTH, 12.2 percent of its habitat, was the locus of 27 percent of the town's behavior setting genotypes; and Yoredale's PTH, 15.2 percent of its total habitat, was the locus of 25 percent of its genotypes.

If Midwest and Yoredale were to display simultaneously in 1963–64 the complete range of behavior setting programs within their PTHs, Midwest would require 53 different halls and meeting rooms with their appropriate facilities, 53 differently trained and experienced groups of operatives, and 53 different experts as speakers, masters of ceremony, group leaders, and so forth; and Yoredale would require 54 different halls, staffs of functionaries, and leaders.

Differences. There was slightly less variety within Midwest's PTH than within Yoredale's. In 1963–64 Midwest had 1 less genotype than Yoredale, amounting to 98 percent as many and to 2 more percent of Midwest's than of Yoredale's total genotypes.

Changes. There was less variety within Midwest's PTH and more within Yoredale's in 1963–64 than in 1954–55. Midwest had 7 fewer genotypes in 1963–64, amounting to 88 percent as many and to 8 fewer percent of the town's total genotypes. Yoredale had 9 more genotypes, amounting to 120 percent as many and to 2 fewer percent of the town's total genotypes.

NATURE OF PRIMARY TALKING HABITATS

An overview of the towns' habitat resources for Talking in 1963–64 is provided by this sample of their talking genotypes selected and arranged as indicated: (*a*) Major genotypes of MW's PTH that do not occur in YD's PTH: Baseball Games, Basketball Games, Beauty Shops, Taverns. (*b*) Major genotypes of MW's PTH that are minor genotypes of YD's PTH: Cultural Meetings, Plays and Programs, Restaurants. (*c*) Major genotypes of both MW's and YD's PTHs: Business Meetings, Vocal Music Classes, Parks and Playgrounds, Parties, Religious Worship Services. (*d*) Major genotypes of YD's PTH that are minor genotypes of MW's PTH: Dinners with Dances, Physical Education Classes (*e*) Major

Table 5.61
Talking
Control of Talking Habitats by Authority Systems
Percent of primary talking habitats
controlled by different authority systems.

		1954–55		1963–64	
		MW (1)	YD (2)	MW (3)	YD (4)
(1)	Extent of PTH in cu	16.4	14.2	13.1	17.2
Percent of PTH controlled by:					
(2)	Churches	18.1	14.6	15.9	11.6
(3)	Govt. Agencies	6.7	11.8	3.4	8.8
(4)	Private Enterprises	22.7	31.4	13.4	24.6
(5)	Schools	31.0	13.9	44.1	34.2
(6)	Voluntary Assns.	21.5	28.4	23.3	20.8

genotypes of YD's PTH that do not occur in MW's PTH: Commission Agents Offices (Betting), Pubs and Dining Rooms.

CONTROL BY AUTHORITY SYSTEMS

Schools controlled more and Government Agencies less of the PTHs of both towns in 1963–64 than did any other authority system (Table 5.61).

Summary

In this section we present overviews of the data for behavior mechanisms in accordance with the procedures followed in the summary of the data for action patterns. The reader may find it helpful to review the explanatory comments given there. The data are shown in Figures 5.6, 5.7, 5.8, and 5.9, which correspond to the four measures of habitat size: Territorial Range, Primary Habitat Extent, Claims for Operatives, and Variety. In Figure 5.10 we summarize the Autonomy data for the behavior mechanism habitats.

TERRITORIAL RANGE OF BEHAVIOR MECHANISM HABITATS

In 1963–64 the rank order of behavior mechanism habitats by TR was the same in both towns (Figure 5.6A). Talking occurs regularly in some degree in almost all behavior settings of both towns; its TR, the largest of the 4, is almost twice that of Affective Behavior, the smallest, which is regularly programed in a little more than half of both towns' habitats.

Differences. The TRs of Midwest's behavior mechanism habitats are all smaller than Yoredale's; Gross Motor Activity and Manipulation have the largest deficiencies.

Changes. The TRs of all behavior mechanism habitats of both towns increased from 1954–55 to 1963–64 (Figure 5.6B); Gross Motor Activity increased the least. Midwest's increments were all smaller than Yoredale's; in fact, only Talking exceeded the rate of increase of Midwest's total habitat, whereas Talking, Manipulation, and Affective Behavior all expanded at faster rates than did Yoredale's total habitat.

EXTENT OF PRIMARY BEHAVIOR MECHANISM HABITATS

In 1963–64 in both towns those habitats where Manipulation and Gross Motor Activity were prominent had roughly twice the extent of Talking and Affective Behavior, the smallest primary behavior mechanism habitats (Figure 5.7A). Recalling that Talking had the largest TR in both towns, we note with interest that its primary habitat is small in both towns; Talking occurs widely across the behavior settings of both towns, but it achieves prominence in relatively few settings of either town.

Differences. Primary habitat resources for Affective Behavior are more extensive in Midwest than in Yoredale, whereas the opposite

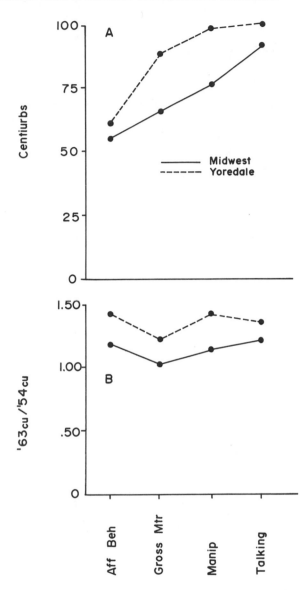

FIGURE 5.6. Territorial Range of Behavior Mechanism Habitats. A: centiurbs of habitat, 1963–64; B: change in centiurbs of habitat, $'63_{cu}/'54_{cu}$.

relation holds for all other primary behavior mechanism habitats. Although none of these differences appears impressively large, Midwest's primary habitat for Affective Behavior is 150 percent as large as Yoredale's, and its primary habitat for Talking is 75 percent as large, whereas its total habitat is 95 percent as extensive as Yoredale's total habitat. In brief, Midwest's habitat provides fewer primary resources than Yoredale's does for Gross Motor Activity, Manipulation, and Talking, and more for Affective Behavior.

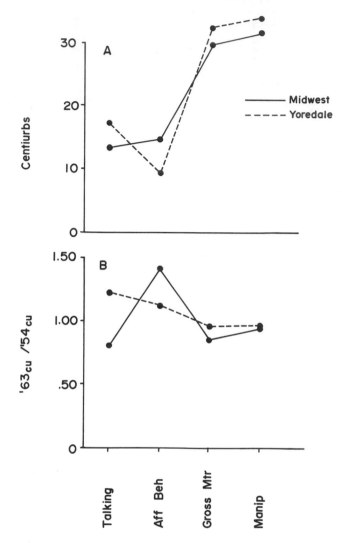

FIGURE 5.7. Extent of Primary Behavior Mechanism Habitats. A: centiurbs of habitat, 1963–64; B: change in centiurbs of habitat, $'63_{cu}/'54_{cu}$.

Changes. Only 1 of the 4 primary behavior mechanism habitats increased in extent between the survey years in Midwest — Affective Behavior — and only 2 did so in Yoredale — Affective Behavior and Talking. Of these, only Midwest's primary Affective Behavior habitat increased at as fast a rate as the town's total habitat. The largest differences between the towns in rate of change occurred in the primary habitats for Talking, which decreased in Midwest and increased in Yoredale, and for Affective Behavior, which increased more sharply in Midwest than in Yoredale.

CLAIMS FOR OPERATIVES WITHIN PRIMARY
BEHAVIOR MECHANISM HABITATS

The primary behavior mechanism habitats with the most habitat-claims for operatives — Affective Behavior in Midwest, Gross Motor Activity in Yoredale — have about twice the number of claims as the one with the fewest — Manipulation in each town (Figure 5.8A). The rank

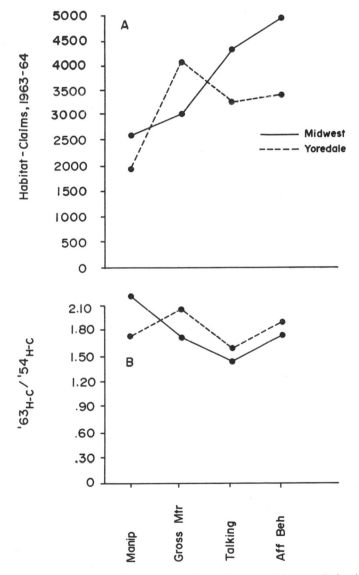

FIGURE 5.8.   Habitat-Claims for Operatives in Primary Behavior Mechanism Habitats. A: number of habitat-claims, 1963–64; B: change in habitat-claims, $'63_{H-C}/'54_{H-C}$.

order of the habitats with respect to number of claims for operatives is quite different; only that for Manipulation is the same, being lowest in both towns.

Differences. Midwest's overall superiority to Yoredale in number of habitat-claims (32 percent) is not distributed evenly across the 4 behavior mechanism habitats; it is heavily concentrated in the habitat where Affective Behavior is prominent, and Midwest has a great deficit in claims for Gross Motor operatives.

Changes. The very substantial increases between survey years in

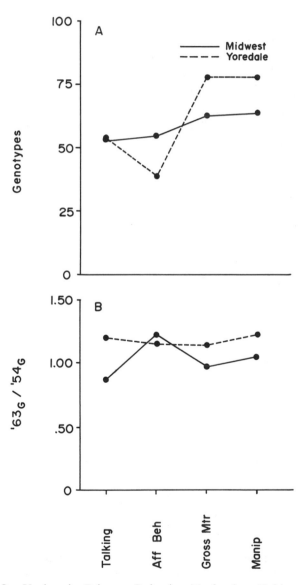

FIGURE 5.9.   Variety in Primary Behavior Mechanism Habitats. A: number of genotypes, 1963–64; B: change in number of genotypes, $'63_G/'54_G$.

total habitat-claims for operatives (91 percent in Midwest, 88 percent in Yoredale) did not occur uniformly across the behavior mechanism habitats. In Midwest only Manipulation and in Yoredale only Gross Motor Activity expanded at rates well above those for the towns' total habitats; Talking lagged behind in both towns.

VARIETY WITHIN PRIMARY BEHAVIOR MECHANISM HABITATS

In 1963–64 the amount of variety across the 4 differential habitats varied little in Midwest but was considerable in Yoredale (Figure 5.9A).

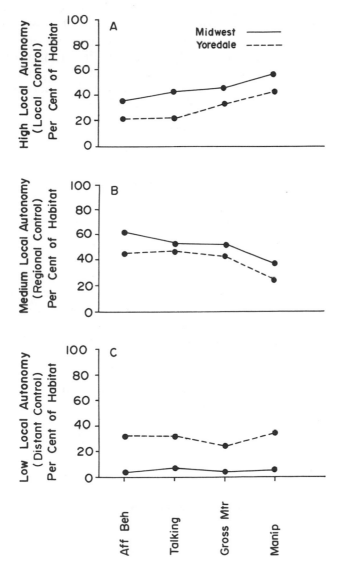

FIGURE 5.10. Percentage of Primary Behavior Mechanism Habitats of High, Medium, and Low Local Autonomy, 1963–64.

Differences. Yoredale's primary habitat for Affective Behavior has much less variety, and its primary habitats for Gross Motor Activity and Manipulation have substantially more variety than do Midwest's corresponding habitats.

Changes. In general, the towns' greater total habitat variety in 1963–64 than in 1954–55 did not occur in the separate behavior mechanism habitats. Only Affective Behavior in Midwest increased at as great a rate as the town's total habitat, and none did so in Yoredale. In Midwest, moreover, Talking and Gross Motor Activity had fewer genotypes in 1963–64 than in 1954–55. These differential habitats show less increase in variety in Midwest than in Yoredale in every case except the primary habitat for Affective Behavior, in which Midwest's variety increased at a rate only slightly faster than did Yoredale's. Midwest's greatest deficiency compared with Yoredale on this dimension occurs in the primary habitat for Talking, in which Midwest's variety decreased substantially between the survey years and Yoredale's increased at a rate only slightly below that of Yoredale's total habitat.

AUTONOMY OF BEHAVIOR MECHANISM HABITATS

The degrees to which the primary behavior mechanism habitats of Midwest and Yoredale were locally controlled (High local autonomy), regionally controlled (Medium local autonomy), or controlled from a distance (Low local autonomy) are reported for 1963–64 in Figure 5.10 in accordance with the procedures outlined in connection with action pattern habitats.

We note first that the three degrees of autonomy vary much less across behavior mechanisms than across action patterns (Figure 5.5). The greatest variation here occurs in regional control in Yoredale, where 25 percent of the Manipulation habitat and 49 percent of the Talking habitat are controlled in the region surrounding the town. A second noteworthy fact is that differences between Midwest and Yoredale are surprisingly uniform across the behavior mechanism habitats, approximating in all cases the differences that obtain for the towns' total habitats, reported in Chapter 6. The greater extent of local and regional control and the lesser extent of distant control of Midwest's than of Yoredale's total habitat hold to approximately the same degrees across all the behavior mechanism habitats.

CHAPTER **6**

Qualities of the Towns as Habitats II

Authority System, Autonomy,
Attendance and Beneficence Habitats

༄༄༄༄༄༄༄༄༄༄༄༄༄༄༄༄༄༄༄༄༄༄༄༄

In this chapter we continue the description of the towns as habitats. Most of the measures used in Chapter 5 are reported here, but there is one important difference in the analysis: within a class of differential habitats, such as authority systems, a given behavior setting has only one attribute. For example, a setting of the Church authority system is not also of the School authority system. Thus in this chapter, the measures of extent of all the differential habitats of a class sum to the extent of the town's total habitat. And because settings do not possess habitat attributes in different degrees, there is only one measure of extent in centiurbs rather than the two, territorial range and primary habitat, as reported for the differential habitats in Chapter 5. Therefore, in the basic data on habitat extent in centiurbs we report only one value for a differential habitat.

In the interest of brevity, data on the attendance and beneficence attributes are reported only by narrative and graphic summaries.

193

AUTHORITY SYSTEM HABITATS

We have investigated the extent to which the programs of the towns' behavior settings are controlled by 5 classes of executive settings: Churches, Government Agencies (other than Schools), Private Enterprises, Schools, and Voluntary Associations. We have made these analyses on the assumption that differences in the extents to which these different classes of executive settings control the towns' habitats constitute significant differences for inhabitant behavior. We assume, for example, that among all behavior settings of the genotype Parties, the programs of those under the aegis of Churches are different in common, subtle ways from those under the aegis of nonchurch Voluntary Associations. One clear difference is that the influence routes to be followed in effecting changes in habitats vary according to their authority system affiliations. Persons interested in the relative power of Churches, Government Agencies, and so forth, over the towns' habitats will find the data directly meaningful.

In Chapter 5 we reported the extents to which the various action pattern and behavior mechanism habitats are controlled by different authority systems. Here we report similar data for the towns' entire habitats.

Church Authority System

DEFINITION

Behavior settings controlled by central administrative settings of churches make up a town's Church authority system habitat (Church habitat). Definitions and illustrations of authority systems are given in Chapter 2.

Basic data for Church habitat are presented in Table 6.1; the report for Aesthetics provides a key to the location of particular data in this table.

SALIENT FINDINGS

The Church habitats of Midwest and Yoredale comprise 6 to 11 percent of the towns' total habitats. Midwest's Church habitat is larger than Yoredale's, and the Church habitats of both towns were larger in 1963–64 than in 1954–55. The towns' Church habitats contain 11 to 21 percent of their total habitat-claims for operatives; Midwest's Church habitat has more such claims than Yoredale's, and both towns had more in 1963–64 than in 1954–55. The towns are similar in the amount of variety within their Church habitats; variety increased between the survey years in both towns.

EXTENT OF CHURCH HABITAT

Midwest's Church habitat in 1963–64 was approximately equivalent to 244 occasional behavior settings—such as Church Weddings,

Table 6.1
Church Authority System
Basic Habitat Data

	1954–55		1963–64	
Extent of Habitat	MW (1)	YD (2)	MW (3)	YD (4)
(1) Behavior Settings per Year	103	78	193	94
(2) Mean BS per Day	4.9	7.1	10.0	6.3
(3) Mean BS per Hour	0.2	0.3	0.6	0.3
(4) Centiurbs (no.)	6.4	5.7	12.2	6.3
(5) Centiurbs (% of Town Total)	7.1%	6.3%	11.4%	5.6%
Erosion and Accretion				
Type of Change	Erosion from '54–55		Accretion to '63–64	
(6) Centiurbs (no.)	2.5	2.0	8.0	2.9
(7) Centiurbs (% of Church				
Habitat)	39%	36%	66%	46%
Claims for Operatives				
(8) Number	1,139	634	1,682	831
(9) Number (% of Town Total)	21%	15%	16%	11%
Amount of Variety				
(10) Major Genotypes (no.)	6	10	8	10
(11) Total Genotypes (no.)	27	18	31	28
(12) Total Genotypes (% of				
Town Total)	16%	11%	16%	13%

Worship Services, Youth Parties, Dinners—and Yoredale's was equivalent to 126 occasional settings. The Church habitat extends over 11.4 percent of Midwest's and 5.6 percent of Yoredale's total habitats.

Differences. Midwest's Church habitat is larger than Yoredale's; in 1963–64 Midwest had 5.9 more cu of Church habitat than Yoredale, amounting to 190 percent as many cu and to 5.8 more percent of the town's total habitat.

Changes. Both towns' Church habitats were larger in 1963–64 than in 1954–55. Midwest's had 5.8 more cu in 1963–64, amounting to 191 percent as many cu and to 4.3 more percent of the town's total habitat. Yoredale's had 0.6 more cu, amounting to 110 percent as many cu and to 0.7 fewer percent of the town's total habitat.

Processes of change. More than one-third of the towns' 1954–55 Church habitats were eroded before 1963–64, and more than two-fifths of the 1963–64 habitats were accreted after 1954–55. Both erosion and accretion were greater in Midwest than in Yoredale; 4 more percent of Midwest's 1954–55 Church habitat was eroded, and 19 more percent of its 1963–64 Church habitat was accreted. The same is true for the towns' total habitats; more of Midwest's than of Yoredale's habitat was both eroded and accreted.

CLAIMS FOR OPERATIVES WITHIN CHURCH HABITAT

If all behavior settings within the towns' Church habitats were to function simultaneously in 1963–64, it would require 1682 persons in

Midwest and 831 persons in Yoredale to carry out essential operations. Claims for Church operatives are greater than claims for operatives in general, on a centiurb basis; there are 138 claims for operatives per cu of Midwest's Church habitat, compared with 96 for the whole habitat, and 132 per cu of Yoredale's Church habitat, compared with 69 for the whole habitat. The towns' Church habitats contain 16 and 11 percent of their total habitat-claims for operatives; whereas, as we have seen, they comprise 11.4 and 5.6 percent of the towns' total habitats. The towns' Church authority system habitats are relatively rich in positions of responsibility.

Differences. Midwest has more habitat-claims for Church operatives than Yoredale. In 1963–64 it had 851 more such claims than Yoredale, amounting to 202 percent as many, to 104 percent as many per cu of Church habitat, to 319 percent as many per town inhabitant, and to 5 more percent of Midwest's than of Yoredale's claims for operatives.

Changes. Both towns had more claims for Church operatives in 1963–64 than in 1954–55. Midwest had 543 more such claims in 1963–64, amounting to 148 percent as many, to 77 percent as many per cu of Church habitat, and to 127 percent as many per town inhabitant, but to 5 fewer percent of the town's total claims for operatives. Yoredale had 197 more such claims, amounting to 131 percent as many, to 119 percent as many per cu of Church habitat, and to 130 percent as many per town inhabitant, but to 4 fewer percent of the town's total claims for operatives.

VARIETY WITHIN CHURCH HABITAT

If Midwest and Yoredale were to display simultaneously in 1963–64 the complete range of behavior setting programs within their Church habitats, Midwest would require 31 different halls and meeting rooms with their appropriate facilities, 31 differently trained and experienced staffs, and 31 different experts as chairmen, presidents, directors; and Yoredale would require 28 different halls, staffs of functionaries, and leaders.

Differences. There is more variety within Midwest's Church habitat than within Yoredale's. In 1963–64 Midwest had 3 more genotypes than Yoredale, amounting to 111 percent as many and to 3 more percent of Midwest's than of Yoredale's total genotypes.

Changes. There was more Church habitat variety in both towns in 1963–64 than in 1954–55. Midwest had 4 more genotypes in 1963–64, amounting to 115 percent as many and to the same percentage of the town's total genotypes. Yoredale had 10 more genotypes, amounting to 156 percent as many and to 2 more percent of the town's total genotypes.

NATURE OF CHURCH HABITAT

An overview of the towns' habitat resources under the aegis of Churches in 1963–64 is provided by this sample of genotypes. (*a*) Major genotypes of MW's Church habitat that do not occur in YD's: None. (*b*) Major genotypes of MW's Church habitat that are minor genotypes of YD's: Vocal Music Classes, Plays and Programs, Religious Fellowship Meetings. (*c*) Major genotypes of both MW's and YD's Church habitats: Business Meetings, Religion Classes, Religion Study Groups, Religious Prayer and Meditation Services, Religious Worship Services. (*d*) Major genotypes of YD's Church habitat that are minor genotypes of MW's: Excursions and Sightseeing Trips, Parties, Solicitation of Funds. (*e*) Major genotypes of YD's Church habitat that do not occur in MW's: Roman Catholic Confessions, Food and Rummage Sales.

These data indicate that some parts of the towns' habitats under the aegis of Churches consist of genotypes without prominent religious elements, such as excursions, parties, and food sales. The data indicate, too, that a large core of the genotypes under Church jurisdiction is common to the towns, and that Midwest has no unique Church-controlled genotype.

Government Agency Authority System

DEFINITION

Behavior settings controlled by executive settings of town, county, state, or federal governments (except School controlled settings) make up a town's Government Agency authority system habitat (Government Agency habitat). Definitions and illustrations of authority systems are given in Chapter 2.

Basic data for Government Agency habitats are presented in Table 6.2; the report for Aesthetics provides a key to the location of particular data in this table.

SALIENT FINDINGS

Habitats under the control of Government Agencies comprise 11 to 19 percent of the towns' total habitats. Midwest's Government Agency habitat is larger than Yoredale's, and the Government Agency habitats of both towns underwent little change between the survey years. The towns' Government Agency authority systems contain 5 to 10 percent of their total habitat-claims for operatives; Midwest's Government Agency habitat has more such claims than Yoredale's, and both towns had more in 1963–64 than in 1954–55. There is more variety within Midwest's than within Yoredale's Government Agency habitat; variety increased between the survey years in both towns.

EXTENT OF GOVERNMENT AGENCY HABITAT

Midwest's Government-controlled habitat in 1963–64 was approximately equivalent to 35 regular behavior settings that occur six days a week for eight hours a day—such as County Clerk's Office and Sorting Post Office—and Yoredale's was equivalent to 25 regular settings. Or, Midwest's Government Agency habitat was equivalent to 350

Table 6.2
Government Agency Authority System
Basic Habitat Data

Extent of Habitat	1954–55		1963–64	
	MW (1)	YD (2)	MW (3)	YD (4)
(1) Behavior Settings per Year	97	50	114	59
(1) Mean BS per Day	23.0	18.6	22.5	16.4
(3) Mean BS per Hour	7.2	6.7	7.1	6.0
(4) Centiurbs (no.)	16.9	13.1	17.5	12.4
(5) Centiurbs (% of Town Total)	18.8%	14.5%	16.3%	10.9%
Erosion and Accretion Type of Change	Erosion from '54–55		Accretion to '63–64	
(6) Centiurbs (no.)	2.8	2.1	3.5	1.1
(7) Centiurbs (% of Govt. Agency Habitat)	16%	16%	20%	9%
Claims for Operatives				
(8) Number	529	230	740	416
(9) Number (% of Town Total)	10%	6%	7%	5%
Amount of Variety				
(10) Major Genotypes (no.)	8	14	8	14
(11) Total Genotypes (no.)	47	35	52	41
(12) Total Genotypes (% of Town Total)	27%	21%	26%	19%

occasional settings—such as, City Council Meeting, County Commissioners' Meeting—and Yoredale's to 248 occasional settings. The Government Agency habitats cover 16.3 percent of Midwest's and 10.9 percent of Yoredale's total habitats.

Differences. Midwest's Government Agency habitat is larger than Yoredale's; in 1963–64 Midwest had 5.1 more cu of Government Agency habitat than Yoredale, amounting to 141 percent as many cu and to 5.4 more percent of the town's total habitat.

Changes. The two towns' Government Agency habitats changed little between the survey years. In 1963–64 Midwest's had 0.6 more cu than in 1954–55, amounting to 104 percent as many cu and to 2.5 fewer percent of the town's total habitat. Yoredale's had 0.7 fewer cu, amounting to 95 percent as many cu and to 3.6 fewer percent of the town's total habitat.

Processes of change. Less than one-fifth of the towns' 1954–55 Government Agency habitats were eroded before 1963–64, and one-fifth or less of the 1963–64 habitats were accreted after 1954–55. Both erosion and accretion of government habitats were greater in Midwest than in Yoredale; 1 more percent of Midwest's 1954–55 Government Agency habitat was eroded, and 10 more percent of its 1963–64 Government habitat was accreted. The same is true for the towns' total habitats; more of Midwest's than of Yoredale's habitat was both eroded and accreted.

If all behavior settings within the towns' Government Agency habitats were to function simultaneously in 1963–64, it would require 740 persons in Midwest and 416 persons in Yoredale to carry out essential operations. Claims for Government operatives are less than claims for operatives in general, on a centiurb basis; there are 42 claims for operatives per cu of Midwest's Government Agency habitat, compared with 96 for the whole habitat, and there are 34 per cu of Yoredale's, compared with 69 for the whole habitat. The towns' Government Agency habitats contain 7 and 5 percent of their total habitat-claims for operatives; whereas, as we have seen, they comprise 16.3 and 10.9 percent of the towns' total habitats. Government Agency habitats are poor in positions of responsibility.

Differences. Midwest has more habitat-claims for Government Agency operatives than Yoredale. In 1963–64 it had 324 more such claims than Yoredale, amounting to 178 percent as many, to 126 percent as many per cu of government habitat, to 281 percent as many per town inhabitant, and to 2 more percent of Midwest's than of Yoredale's claims for operatives.

Changes. Both towns had more claims for Government Agency operatives in 1963–64 than in 1954–55. Midwest had 211 more such claims in 1963–64, amounting to 140 percent as many, to 135 percent as many per cu of government habitat, and to 120 percent as many per town inhabitant, but to 3 fewer percent of the town's total claims for operatives. Yoredale had 186 more such claims, amounting to 181 percent as many, to 191 percent as many per cu of government habitat, and to 180 percent as many per town inhabitant, but to 1 fewer percent of the town's total claims for operatives.

If Midwest and Yoredale were to display simultaneously in 1963–64 the complete range of behavior setting programs within their Government Agency habitats, Midwest would require 52 different offices and meeting rooms with their appropriate facilities, 52 differently trained and experienced staffs, and 52 different experts as managers, directors, commissioners, and so forth; and Yoredale would require 41 different places, staffs of functionaries, and leaders.

Differences. There is more variety within Midwest's Government Agency habitat than within Yoredale's. In 1963–64 Midwest had 11 more genotypes than Yoredale, amounting to 127 percent as many and to 7 more percent of Midwest's than of Yoredale's total genotypes.

Changes. There was more Government Agency habitat variety in both towns in 1963–64 than in 1954–55. Midwest had 5 more genotypes in 1963–64, amounting to 111 percent as many and to 1 fewer percent of the town's total genotypes. Yoredale had 6 more genotypes, amounting to 117 percent as many and to 2 fewer percent of the town's total genotypes.

NATURE OF GOVERNMENT AGENCY HABITAT

An overview of the towns' habitat resources under the aegis of Government Agencies in 1963–64 is provided by this sample of genotypes: (*a*) Major genotypes of MW's Government Agency habitat that do not occur in YD's: Jails, Judges Chambers, General Post Offices. (*b*) Major genotypes of MW's Government Agency habitat that are minor genotypes of YD's: Government Business and Records Offices. (*c*) Major genotypes of both MW's and YD's Government habitats: Hallways, Machinery Repair Shops, Business Meetings, Trafficways. (*d*) Major genotypes of YD's Government Agency habitat that are minor genotypes of MW's: Cemeteries, Parks and Playgrounds. (*e*) Major genotypes of YD's Government Agency habitat that do not occur in MW's: Health Department Offices, Nursing Homes, Physicians Offices, Police Stations, Sorting Post Offices, Railway Freight Offices, Tax Assessment and Collection Offices, Telephone Kiosks.

These data spell out the greater distinctiveness of Yoredale's Government Agency authority system. Eight genotypes within the habitat controlled by the executive settings of Yoredale's Government habitat are entirely absent from Midwest's Government authority system; they cover health, welfare, transportation, and communication services that are within other authority systems in Midwest.

Private Enterprise Authority System

DEFINITION

Behavior settings operated by private citizens in order to make a living constitute a town's Private Enterprise authority system habitat (Private Enterprise habitat). Definitions and illustrations of authority systems are given in Chapter 2.

Basic data for Private Enterprise habitats are presented in Table 6.3; the report for Aesthetics provides a key to the location of particular data in this table.

SALIENT FINDINGS

The Private Enterprise habitats of Midwest and Yoredale comprise 38 to 60 percent of the towns' total habitats. Midwest's Private Enterprise habitat is smaller than Yoredale's, and Midwest's decreased while Yoredale's increased slightly between 1954–55 and 1963–64. The towns' Private Enterprise habitats contain 4 to 17 percent of their total habitat-claims for operatives; Midwest's Private Enterprise habitat has fewer such claims than Yoredale's, and the number increased in Midwest but decreased in Yoredale between the survey years. The towns are similar in the amount of variety within their Private Enterprise habitats; there was little change between the survey years in either town.

Table 6.3
Private Enterprise Authority System
Basic Habitat Data

Extent of Habitat	1954–55		1963–64	
	MW (1)	YD (2)	MW (3)	YD (4)
(1) Behavior Settings per Year	122	161	132	163
(2) Mean BS per Day	76.1	98.2	65.7	102.4
(3) Mean BS per Hour	21.7	24.7	20.1	25.7
(4) Centiurbs (no.)	44.0	53.7	41.0	55.7
(5) Centiurbs (% of Town Total)	49.0%	59.7%	38.0%	49.4%
Erosion and Accretion				
Type of Change	Erosion from '54–55		Accretion to '63–64	
(6) Centiurbs (no.)	21.2	11.3	19.2	11.1
(7) Centiurbs (% of Priv. Enterprise Habitat)	48%	21%	47%	20%
Claims for Operatives				
(8) Number	312	687	450	645
(9) Number (% of Town Total)	6%	17%	4%	8%
Amount of Variety				
(10) Major Genotypes (no.)	9	5	7	6
(11) Total Genotypes (no.)	65	73	70	71
(12) Total Genotypes (% of Town Total)	38%	43%	35%	33%

EXTENT OF PRIVATE ENTERPRISE HABITAT

Midwest's Private Enterprise habitat in 1963–64 was approximately equivalent to 82 regular behavior settings that occur six days a week for eight hours a day, such as Ellsons Drugstore and Wiley Attorneys Office, and Yoredale's was equivalent to 111 regular settings. Private Enterprise habitats cover 38 percent of Midwest's and 49.4 percent of Yoredale's total habitats.

Differences. Midwest's Private Enterprise habitat is smaller than Yoredale's; in 1963–64 Midwest had 14.7 fewer cu of Private Enterprise habitat than Yoredale, amounting to 74 percent as many cu and to 11.4 fewer percent of the town's total habitat.

Changes. Midwest's Private Enterprise habitat decreased and Yoredale's increased between the survey years. In 1963–64 Midwest's had 3.0 fewer cu than in 1954–55, amounting to 93 percent as many cu and to 11.0 fewer percent of the town's total habitat. Yoredale's had 2.0 more cu, amounting to 104 percent as many cu and to 10.3 fewer percent of the town's total habitat.

Processes of change. More than one-fifth of the towns' 1954–55 Private Enterprise habitats were eroded before 1963–64, and one-fifth or more of the 1963–64 habitats were accreted after 1954–55. Both erosion and accretion were greater in Midwest than in Yoredale; 27 more percent of Midwest's 1954–55 Private Enterprise habitat was eroded, and

27 more percent of its 1963–64 Private Enterprise habitat was accreted. The same is true for the towns' total habitats; more of Midwest's than of Yoredale's habitat was both eroded and accreted.

CLAIMS FOR OPERATIVES WITHIN PRIVATE ENTERPRISE HABITAT

If all behavior settings within the towns' Private Enterprise habitats were to function simultaneously in 1963–64, it would require 450 persons in Midwest and 645 persons in Yoredale to carry out essential operations. Claims for Private Enterprise operatives are much less than claims for operatives in general, on a centiurb basis; there are 11 claims for operatives per cu of Midwest's Private Enterprise habitat, compared with 96 for the whole habitat, and 12 per cu of Yoredale's, compared with 69 for the whole habitat. The towns' Private Enterprise habitats contain 4 and 8 percent of their total habitat-claims for operatives; whereas, as we have seen, they comprise 38 and 49.4 percent of the towns' total habitats. The towns' Private Enterprise habitats are extremely poor in positions of responsibility.

Differences. Midwest has fewer claims for Private Enterprise operatives than Yoredale. In 1963–64 it had 195 fewer such claims than Yoredale, amounting to 70 percent as many, to 95 percent as many per cu of Private Enterprise habitat, to 110 percent as many per town inhabitant, and to 4 fewer percent of Midwest's than of Yoredale's claims for operatives.

Changes. Midwest had more and Yoredale had fewer claims for Private Enterprise operatives in 1963–64. Midwest had 138 more such claims in 1963–64, amounting to 144 percent as many, to 155 percent as many per cu of Private Enterprise habitat, and to 124 percent as many per town inhabitant, but to 2 fewer percent of the town's total claims for operatives. Yoredale had 42 fewer such claims, amounting to 94 percent as many, to 90 percent as many per cu of Private Enterprise habitat, to 93 percent as many per town inhabitant, and to 9 fewer percent of the town's total claims for operatives.

VARIETY WITHIN PRIVATE ENTERPRISE HABITAT

If Midwest and Yoredale were to display simultaneously in 1963–64 the complete range of behavior setting programs within their Private Enterprise habitats, Midwest would require 70 different halls and exhibit rooms with their appropriate facilities, 70 differently trained and experienced staffs, and 70 different experts as operators, managers, salesmen, and so forth, and Yoredale would require 71 different places, staffs of functionaries, and leaders.

Differences. There is very slightly less variety within Midwest's Private Enterprise habitat than within Yoredale's. In 1963–64 Midwest had 1 less genotype than Yoredale, amounting to 99 percent as many and to 2 more percent of Midwest's than of Yoredale's total genotypes.

Changes. Midwest's Private Enterprise variety was greater in 1963–64 than in 1954–55, and Yoredale's was less. Midwest had 5 more genotypes in 1963–64, amounting to 108 percent as many and to 3 fewer percent of the town's total genotypes. Yoredale had 2 fewer genotypes, amounting to 97 percent as many and to 10 fewer percent of the town's total genotypes.

NATURE OF PRIVATE ENTERPRISE HABITAT

An overview of the towns' habitat resources for Private Enterprise in 1963–64 is provided by this sample of genotypes. (*a*) Major genotypes of MW's Private Enterprise habitat that do not occur in Yd's: Attorneys Offices, Self-Service Laundries. (*b*) Major genotypes of MW's Private Enterprise habitat that are minor genotypes of YD's: Building, Construction, and Repair Services; Delivery and Collection Routes. (*c*) Major genotypes of both MW's and Yd's Private Enterprise habitats: Grocery Stores, Restaurants. (*d*) Major genotypes of YD's Private Enterprise habitat that are minor genotypes of MW's: Clothiers and Dry Goods Stores, Commercial Company Offices, Hotels. (*e*) Major genotype of YD's Private Enterprise habitat that does not occur in MW's: Pubs and Dining Rooms.

School Authority System

DEFINITION

Behavior settings operated by private or public educational agencies make up a town's School authority system habitat (School habitat). Definitions and illustrations of authority systems are given in Chapter 2.

Basic data for School habitats are presented in Table 6.4. The report for Aesthetics provides a key to the location of particular data in this table.

SALIENT FINDINGS

The School habitats of Midwest and Yoredale comprise 8 to 26 percent of the towns' total habitats. Midwest's School habitat was smaller than Yoredale's in 1963–64, and the School habitats of both towns were larger in 1963–64 than in 1954–55. The towns' School habitats contain 12 to 42 percent of their total habitat-claims for operatives; Midwest's School habitat has more such claims than Yoredale's, and both towns had more in 1963–64 than in 1954–55. There was less variety within Midwest's than within Yoredale's School habitat in 1963–64; variety increased between the survey years in both towns.

EXTENT OF SCHOOL AUTHORITY SYSTEM HABITAT

Midwest's School habitat in 1963–64 was approximately equivalent to 50 regular behavior settings that occur six days a week for eight hours a day—such as High School Principal's Office and Elementary School Hallways—and Yoredale's was equivalent to 58 regular settings.

Table 6.4
School Authority System
Basic Habitat Data

		1954–55		1963–64	
Extent of Habitat		MW (1)	YD (2)	MW (3)	YD (4)
(1)	Behavior Settings per Year	146	55	233	281
(2)	Mean BS per Day	28.1	14.0	41.8	48.9
(3)	Mean BS per Hour	2.9	1.8	4.2	4.7
(4)	Centiurbs (no.)	16.1	7.5	24.8	29.2
(5)	Centiurbs (% of Town Total)	18.0%	8.3%	23.1%	25.9%
Erosion and Accretion	Type of Change	Erosion from '54–55		Accretion to '63–64	
(6)	Centiurbs (no.)	2.5	1.8	8.9	23.5
(7)	Centiurbs (% of School Habitat)	16%	24%	36%	80%
Claims for Operatives					
(8)	Number	2,073	517	3,999	3,246
(9)	Number (% of Town Total)	39%	12%	39%	42%
Amount of Variety					
(10)	Major Genotypes (no.)	10	10	8	6
(11)	Total Genotypes (no.)	55	24	68	87
(12)	Total Genotypes (% of Town Total)	32%	14%	34%	41%

Or, Midwest's School authority system habitat was equivalent to 496 occasional settings—such as High School District Music Festival and High School Freshman Aptitude Test—and Yoredale's to 584 occasional settings. School habitats cover 23.1 percent of Midwest's and 25.9 percent of Yoredale's total habitats.

Differences. Midwest's School habitat was smaller than Yoredale's in 1963–64, when Midwest had 4.4 fewer cu of School habitat than Yoredale, amounting to 85 percent as many cu and to 2.8 fewer percent of the town's total habitat.

Changes. Both towns' School habitats were larger in 1963–64 than in 1954–55. Midwest's had 8.7 more cu in 1963–64, amounting to 154 percent as many cu and to 5.1 more percent of the town's total habitat. Yoredale's had 21.7 more cu, amounting to 389 percent as many cu and to 17.6 more percent of the town's total habitat.

Processes of change. Less than one-quarter of the towns' 1954–55 School habitats were eroded before 1963–64, and more than one-third of the 1963–64 habitats were accreted after 1954–55. Both erosion and accretion were less in Midwest than in Yoredale; 9 fewer percent of Midwest's 1954–55 School habitat was eroded, and 44 fewer percent of its 1963–64 School habitat was accreted. The opposite is true for the towns' total habitats; more of Midwest's than of Yoredale's habitat was both eroded and accreted.

CLAIMS FOR OPERATIVES WITHIN SCHOOL HABITAT

If all behavior settings within the towns' School habitats were to function simultaneously in 1963–64, it would require 3999 persons in Midwest and 3246 persons in Yoredale to carry out essential operations. Claims for school operatives are greater than claims for operatives in general, on a centiurb basis; there are 161 claims for operatives per cu of Midwest's School habitat, compared with 96 for the whole habitat, and 111 per cu of Yoredale's, compared with 69 for the whole habitat. The towns' School habitats contain 39 and 42 percent of their total habitat-claims for operatives; whereas, as we have seen, they comprise 23.1 and 25.9 percent of the towns' total habitats. The towns' School habitats are rich in positions of responsibility.

Differences. Midwest has more habitat-claims for School operatives than Yoredale. In 1963–64 it had 753 more such claims than Yoredale, amounting to 123 percent as many, to 145 percent as many per cu of School habitat, and to 194 percent as many per town inhabitant, but to 3 fewer percent of Midwest's than of Yoredale's claims for operatives.

Changes. Both towns had more claims for School operatives in 1963–64 than in 1954–55. Midwest had 1926 more such claims in 1963–64, amounting to 193 percent as many, to 125 percent as many per cu of School habitat, to 166 percent as many per town inhabitant, and to the same percentage of the town's total claims for operatives. Yoredale had 2729 more such claims amounting to 628 percent as many, to 161 percent as many per cu of School habitat, to 623 percent as many per town inhabitant, and to 30 more percent of the town's total claims for operatives.

VARIETY WITHIN SCHOOL HABITAT

If Midwest and Yoredale were to display simultaneously in 1963–64 the complete range of behavior-setting programs within their School habitats, Midwest would require 68 different halls and classrooms with their appropriate facilities, 68 differently trained and experienced staffs, and 68 different experts as teachers, principals, chairmen, and so forth; and Yoredale would require 87 different halls, staffs of functionaries, and leaders.

Differences. There was less variety within Midwest's School habitat than within Yoredale's in 1963–64, when Midwest had 19 fewer genotypes than Yoredale, amounting to 78 percent as many and to 7 fewer percent of Midwest's than of Yoredale's total genotypes.

Changes. There was more School habitat variety in both towns in 1963–64 than in 1954–55. Midwest had 13 more genotypes in 1963–64, amounting to 124 percent as many and to 2 more percent of the town's total genotypes. Yoredale had 63 more genotypes, amounting to 362 percent as many and to 27 more percent of the town's total genotypes.

An overview of the towns' habitat resources for the School authority system in 1963–64 is provided by this sample of genotypes. (*a*) Major genotype of MW's School habitat that does not occur in YD's: Basketball Games. (*b*) Major genotypes of MW's School habitat that are minor genotypes of YD's: Business Meetings, Plays and Programs, School Administrators Offices. (*c*) Major genotypes of both MW's and YD's School habitats: Classrooms, Freetime; Basic Elementary School Classes, Vocal Music Classes, Physical Education Classes. (*d*) Major genotype of YD's School habitat which is a minor genotype of MW's: English Classes. (*e*) Major genotypes of YD's School habitat that do not occur in MW's: None.

Voluntary Association Authority System

DEFINITION

Behavior settings which are not included in any of the other four authority system habitats (Church, Government Agency, Private Enterprise, and School) make up the town's Voluntary Association authority system habitat (Voluntary Association habitat). They are predominantly under the aegis of recreational, cultural, and service organizations.

Basic data for Voluntary Association habitats are presented in Table 6.5; the report for Aesthetics provides a key to the location of particular data in this table.

SALIENT FINDINGS

The Voluntary Association habitats of Midwest and Yoredale comprise 7 to 11 percent of the towns' total habitats. Midwest's Voluntary Association habitat is larger than Yoredale's, and Midwest's increased in extent while Yoredale's decreased between 1954–55 and 1963–64. The towns' Voluntary Association habitats contain 24 to 50 percent of their total habitat-claims for operatives; Midwest's has more such claims than Yoredale's, and both towns had more in 1963–64 than in 1954–55. There is less variety within Midwest's than within Yoredale's Voluntary Association habitat; variety increased between the survey years in both towns.

EXTENT OF VOLUNTARY ASSOCIATION HABITAT

Midwest's Voluntary Association habitat in 1963–64 was approximately equivalent to 246 occasional behavior settings—such as Rotary Club Meeting and City Park Volunteer Work Group—and Yoredale's was equivalent to 186 occasional settings. Voluntary Association habitats cover 11.4 percent of Midwest's and 8.2 percent of Yoredale's total habitats.

Table 6.5
Voluntary Association Authority System
Basic Habitat Data

Extent of Habitat	1954–55		1963–64	
	MW (1)	YD (2)	MW (3)	YD (4)
(1) Behavior Settings per Year	108	160	212	161
(2) Mean BS per Day	3.8	5.9	5.7	4.2
(3) Mean BS per Hour	0.4	0.8	0.6	0.5
(4) Centiurbs (no.)	6.5	10.0	12.3	9.3
(5) Centiurbs (% of Town Total)	7.2%	11.1%	11.4%	8.2%
Erosion and Accretion Type of Change	Erosion from '54–55		Accretion to '63–64	
(6) Centiurbs (no.)	2.7	5.1	8.1	5.0
(7) Centiurbs (% of Volun. Assn. Habitat)	42%	51%	66%	54%
Claims for Operatives				
(8) Number	1,307	2,055	3,349	2,626
(9) Number (% of Town Total)	24%	50%	33%	34%
Amount of Variety				
(10) Major Genotypes (no.)	9	6	12	7
(11) Total Genotypes (no.)	38	55	48	60
(12) Total Genotypes (% of Town Total)	22%	33%	24%	28%

Differences. Midwest's Voluntary Association habitat is larger than Yoredale's; in 1963–64 Midwest had 3 more cu of Voluntary Association habitat than Yoredale, amounting to 132 percent as many cu and to 3.2 more percent of the town's total habitat.

Changes. Midwest's Voluntary Association habitat was larger, and Yoredale's was slightly smaller, in 1963–64 than in 1954–55. Midwest's had 5.8 more cu in 1963–64, amounting to 189 percent as many cu and to 4.2 more percent of the town's total habitat. Yoredale's had 0.7 fewer cu, amounting to 93 percent as many cu and to 2.9 fewer percent of the town's total habitat.

Processes of change. More than two-fifths of the towns' 1954–55 Voluntary Association habitats were eroded before 1963–64, and more than half of the 1963–64 habitats were accreted after 1954–55. Erosion was less and accretion was greater in Midwest than in Yoredale; 10 fewer percent of Midwest's 1954–55 Voluntary Association habitat was eroded, and 12 more percent of its 1963–64 habitat was accreted. This differs from the towns' total habitats; more of Midwest's than of Yoredale's habitat was both eroded and accreted.

CLAIMS FOR OPERATIVES WITHIN VOLUNTARY ASSOCIATION HABITAT

If all behavior settings within the towns' Voluntary Association habitats were to function simultaneously in 1963–64, it would require 3349 persons in Midwest and 2626 persons in Yoredale to carry out essential operations. Claims for Voluntary Association operatives are much greater than claims for operatives in general, on a centiurb basis; there are 272 claims per cu of Midwest's Voluntary Association habitat, compared with 96 for the whole habitat, and 282 per cu of Yoredale's, compared with 69 for the whole habitat. The towns' Voluntary Association habitats contain 33 and 34 percent of their total habitat-claims for operatives; whereas, as we have seen, they comprise 11.4 and 8.2 percent of the towns' total habitats. The towns' Voluntary Association habitats are extremely rich in positions of responsibility.

Differences. Midwest has more habitat-claims for Voluntary Association operatives than Yoredale. In 1963–64 it had 723 more such claims than Yoredale, amounting to 127 percent as many, to 96 percent as many per cu of Voluntary Association habitat, and to 201 percent as many per town inhabitant, but to 1 fewer percent of Midwest's than of Yoredale's claims for operatives.

Changes. Both towns had more habitat-claims for Voluntary Association operatives in 1963–64 than in 1954–55. Midwest had 2042 more such claims in 1963–64, amounting to 256 percent as many, to 135 percent as many per cu of Voluntary Association habitat, to 221 percent as many per town inhabitant, and to 9 more percent of the town's total claims for operatives. Yoredale had 571 more such claims, amounting to 128 percent as many, to 137 percent as many per cu of Voluntary Association habitat, and to 127 percent as many per town inhabitant, but to 16 fewer percent of the town's total claims for operatives.

VARIETY WITHIN VOLUNTARY ASSOCIATION HABITAT

If Midwest and Yoredale were to display simultaneously in 1963–64 the complete range of behavior setting programs within their Voluntary Association habitats, Midwest would require 48 different halls and exhibit rooms with their appropriate facilities, 48 differently trained and experienced staffs, and 48 different experts as chairmen, presidents, masters of ceremony, and so forth; and Yoredale would require 59 different halls, staffs of functionaries, and leaders.

Differences. There is less variety within Midwest's Voluntary Association habitat than within Yoredale's. In 1963–64 Midwest had 11 fewer genotypes than Yoredale, amounting to 81 percent as many and to 4 fewer percent of Midwest's than of Yoredale's total genotypes.

Changes. There was more Voluntary Association habitat variety in both towns in 1963–64 than in 1954–55. Midwest had 10 more genotypes in 1963–64, amounting to 126 percent as many and to 2 more percent of the town's total genotypes. Yoredale had 4 more genotypes, amounting to 107 percent as many but to 5 fewer percent of the town's total genotypes.

NATURE OF VOLUNTARY ASSOCIATION HABITAT

An overview of the towns' habitat resources for Voluntary Associations in 1963–64 is provided by this sample of genotypes. (*a*) Major genotypes of MW's Voluntary Association habitat that do not occur in YD's: Baseball Games, Bowling Games (Ten Pins), Dinners with Business Meetings, Golf Games. (*b*) Major genotypes of MW's Voluntary Association habitat that are minor genotypes of YD's: Card Parties, Dinners and Banquets, Lodge Meetings, Scout Meetings. (*c*) Major genotypes of both MW's and YD's Voluntary Association habitats: Dinners with Programs, Business Meetings, Cultural Meetings, Parks and Playgrounds. (*d*) Major genotypes of YD's Voluntary Association habitat that are minor genotypes of MW's: Excursions and Sightseeing Trips, Solicitation of Funds. (*e*) Major genotypes of YD's Voluntary Association habitat that do not occur in MW's: Darts Games, Dinners with Dances.

Summary

In the preceding sections we separately presented information on each of the 5 authority system habitats. We present here graphic overviews of these differential habitats in 1963–64 and changes in them between 1954–55 and 1963–64 by three measures: Extent in centiurbs, number of Habitat-Claims for Operatives, and Variety as indicated by number of genotypes. The graphic presentations and discussions follow the format described in the summary section for action pattern habitats; the reader may find it helpful to review the explanations and cautions given in that section for interpreting them.

EXTENT OF AUTHORITY SYSTEM HABITATS

Extents of the authority system habitats range in order in both towns from Church habitat—constituting about one-tenth of Midwest's and one-twentieth of Yoredale's total habitat—through Voluntary Association, Government Agency, and School habitats, to the Private Enterprise habitat, which includes almost two-fifths of Midwest's and nearly half of Yoredale's total habitat (Figure 6.1A). Private Enterprise is preeminent; it exceeds the next in size, Schools, by a factor of 1.5 in Midwest and almost 2 in Yoredale, and it exceeds the smallest, Churches, by a factor of more than 3 in Midwest and almost 9 in Yoredale. In terms of the centiurb measure of extent the "at-handness" of the habitat resources of the towns is greater for habitats controlled by Private Enterprises and smaller for habitats controlled by Churches than for those under the aegis of other authority systems.

Differences. The curves reveal a remarkably similar pattern within the two towns; however, there are important differences. Although Midwest's total habitat in 1963–64 was smaller than Yoredale's (95 percent as large), 3 of the 5 authority systems were larger in Midwest: Church habitat was 194 percent as large, Government habitat was 141 percent as large, and Voluntary Association habitat was 132 percent as large. The other authority systems were smaller than expected on the basis of the towns' total habitats: School habitat was 85 percent as large,

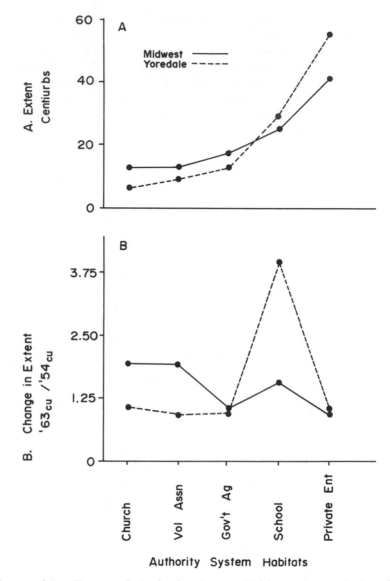

FIGURE 6.1. Extent of Authority System Habitats. A: centiurbs of habitat, 1963–64; B: change in centiurbs of habitat, $'63_{cu}/'54_{cu}$.

and Private Enterprise habitat was 74 percent as large in Midwest as in Yoredale. Thus Midwest was relatively better endowed than Yoredale with habitat resources controlled by its Churches, Voluntary Associations, and Government Agencies, but deficient in behavior settings under the aegis of Schools and Private Enterprises.

   Changes. The most impressive change is the dramatic increase in Yoredale's School habitat, nearly quadrupled between 1954–55 and 1963–64 (Figure 6.1B). The habitats controlled by Yoredale's Churches and Private Enterprises increased, but at rates below that for the town as a whole, and those controlled by Government Agencies and Voluntary Associations decreased slightly. Midwest's habitats controlled by Churches, Voluntary Associations, and Schools increased at rates well above that of the town as a whole, and the habitat controlled by Government Agencies held its own, leaving only the Private Enterprise habitat showing a small decrease in size from 1954–55.

CLAIMS FOR OPERATIVES WITHIN AUTHORITY SYSTEM HABITATS

Number of habitat-claims for operatives varies greatly across authority system habitats; the one with the greatest number exceeded the one with the smallest number in 1963–64 by factors of 9 in Midwest and 8 in Yoredale (Figure 6.2A).

Differences. The rank order of the authority systems in 1963–64 was the same in both towns, except for the two smallest: Government Agencies had the fewest claims in Yoredale, and Private Enterprises had the fewest in Midwest. Schools had the most habitat-claims in both towns. Midwest's overall superiority to Yoredale (MW/YD times 100 equals 132) was reflected in similar or greater superiority in all the authority systems except Private Enterprises, in which Midwest had only 70 percent as many habitat-claims as did Yoredale. Midwest's superiority to Yoredale was greatest in Churches and Government Agencies, where Midwest had 2 and 1.78 times, respectively, as many claims as Yoredale.

Changes. The most striking change is the more than sixfold increase in the number of habitat-claims in Yoredale's School habitat. This is the only authority system in Yoredale which increased at a much faster rate than the town as a whole. Claims for operatives also burgeoned in Midwest's Voluntary Association habitat. The other authority systems of the towns increased at rates at or below those for the towns as wholes.

VARIETY WITHIN AUTHORITY SYSTEM HABITATS

Variety is smallest within the Church authority systems of both towns; it is greatest within the Schools of Yoredale — 3 times as great as in the Churches — and within the Private Enterprises of Midwest — 2 times as great as in the Churches.

Differences. Midwest's overall deficiency relative to Yoredale in amount of variety (MW/YD times 100 equals 93 percent) in 1963–64 was not reflected evenly across the 5 authority systems; only 2, Schools and Voluntary Associations, had deficiencies as great as or greater than that of its total habitat, whereas Midwest's Churches and Government Agencies controlled more genotypes than did their Yoredale counterparts. Midwest's superior resources in settings controlled by Churches and Government Agencies were clearly evident in terms of variety, as in other measures.

Changes. The big change was in Yoredale's School habitat, which in 1963–64 had 362 percent as much variety as in 1954–55 (Figure

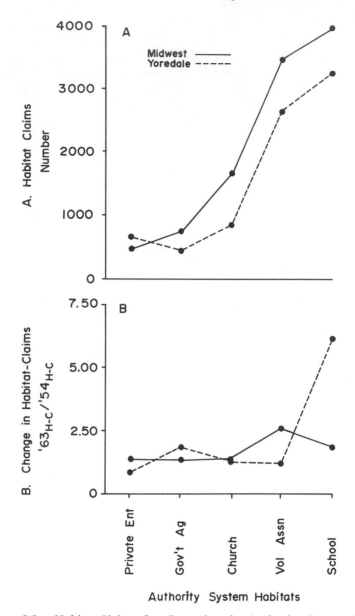

FIGURE 6.2.   Habitat-Claims for Operatives in Authority System Habitats. A: habitat-claims, 1963–64; B: change in habitat-claims, $'63_{H-C}/'54_{H-C}$.

6.3B). This is in line with the increases in the other measures of Yoredale's Schools. Variety also increased more within Yoredale's Church-controlled habitat than within the town's total habitat. In Midwest all 5 authority system habitats increased in variety at rates which deviate only slightly from that for the town's total habitat.

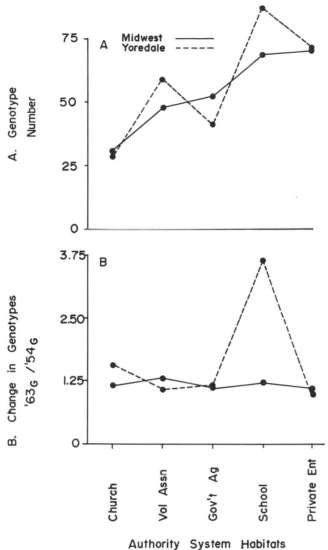

FIGURE 6.3.   Variety in Authority System Habitats. A: number of genotypes, 1963–64; B; change in number of genotypes, $'63_G/'54_G$.

AUTONOMY OF AUTHORITY SYSTEM HABITATS

The degrees to which the 5 authority system habitats of Midwest and Yoredale in 1963–64 were of High, Medium, or Low local autonomy are presented here in the format followed for action pattern habitats: by curves representing percentages of authority system habitats, measured in centiurbs (Figure 6.4).

High local autonomy. Extent of local control varies greatly across

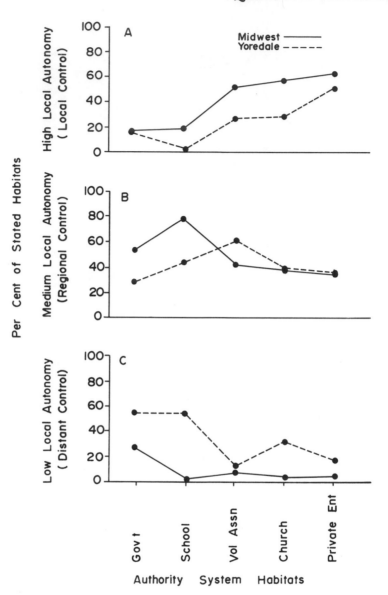

FIGURE 6.4. Percentage of Authority System Habitats, in Centiurbs, of High, Medium, and Low Local Autonomy, 1963–64.

the towns' authority system habitats (Figure 6.4A). In Midwest it ranges from 19 percent of Government Agency to 62 percent of Private Enterprise habitats, and in Yoredale from 2 percent of School to 50 percent of Private Enterprise habitats. On the basis of extent of local control of the towns' total habitats, where the MW/YD ratio of percentages is 1.4, we expect local control to be more extensive within Midwest than within Yoredale. And this is true for all authority system habitats. However, Midwest's superiority in this respect is much greater than expected within School, Voluntary Association, and Church habitats, and it is less than expected within the Government Agency habitat. Local control of Government Agency and School habitats is less than expected in both towns.

Medium local autonomy. Regional control of authority system habitats varies less across the towns than does local control (Figure 6.4B). The greatest range is from 33 percent of Midwest's Private Enterprise habitat to 79 percent of its School habitat. On the basis of the extent of regional control in the towns' total habitats, where the MW/YD ratio of percentages is 1.3, we expect regional control of authority systems to be more extensive within Midwest than within Yoredale. But this is the case only for Government Agency and School habitats; smaller percentages of Voluntary Association, Church, and Private Enterprise habitats are regionally controlled in Midwest than in Yoredale.

Low local autonomy. Control from a distance varies greatly across the two towns' authority system habitats (Figure 6.4C). The range in Midwest is from 1 percent of School to 28 percent of Government Agency habitats, and in Yoredale from 17 percent of Private Enterprise to 57 percent of School habitats. Distant control is less extensive in Midwest than in Yoredale within all authority systems, as expected on the basis of extent in the towns' total habitats, where the MW/YD ratio of percentages is 0.25. However, there is much less control from state and national levels than expected within Midwest's School and Church habitats.

From these data we learn that local control is more extensive and distant control is less extensive in Midwest than in Yoredale across all authority system habitats and that these differences are greatest in School and Church habitats.

AUTONOMY HABITATS

The reports for the differential action pattern, behavior mechanism, and authority system habitats have included data on the extent to which they are controlled locally (High local autonomy), regionally (Medium local autonomy), and from a distance (Low local autonomy). Here we present the basic autonomy data for the towns' total habitats.

The autonomy measures were developed on the assumption that it makes a difference to the behavior and experience of the towns' inhabitants whether decisions with respect to officers, membership rules, agendas, meeting places, space, equipment, budgets, and so forth of the settings they inhabit are made nearby, where the inhabitants can continually participate directly, or whether directives come from headquarters at distances (in Topeka or Northallerton, St. Louis or Manchester, Washington or London), where continual, direct participation is not possible. Geographical closeness of habitat control-centers is judged to be positively correlated with power of inhabitants over their habitats.

The habitats with High, Medium, or Low local autonomy are mutually exclusive.

High Local Autonomy

DEFINITION

A habitat with High local autonomy consists of behavior settings for which appointment of leaders, admission of members, determination of fees and prices, and establishment of policies and programs are controlled largely by sources located within the setting, the town, or the circumjacent School District (MW) or Rural District (YD). These are the towns' *locally controlled* habitats.

Basic data for High local autonomy are presented in Table 6.6; the report for Aesthetics serves as a key to the location of particular data in this table.

SALIENT FINDINGS

The locally controlled habitats of Midwest and Yoredale comprise 31 to 47 percent of their total habitats. Midwest's is larger than Yoredale's, and it increased in extent, while Yoredale's decreased between 1954–55 and 1963–64. Locally controlled habitats contain 18 to 48 percent of the towns' total habitat-claims for operatives; Midwest has more

Table 6.6
High Local Autonomy
Basic Habitat Data

		1954–55		1963–64	
Extent of Habitat		MW (1)	YD (2)	MW (3)	YD (4)
(1)	Behavior Settings per Year	277	197	409	163
(2)	Mean BS per Day	63.5	57.5	56.9	55.7
(3)	Mean BS per Hour	15.3	14.7	14.5	14.9
(4)	Centiurbs (no.)	42.5	36.7	46.8	34.8
(5)	Centiurbs (% of Town Total)	47.4%	40.7%	43.6%	30.9%
Erosion and Accretion					
	Type of Change	Erosion from '54–55		Accretion to '63–64	
(6)	Centiurbs (no.)	19.5	11.3	24.0	9.1
(7)	Centiurbs (% of Locally Controlled Habitat)	46%	31%	51%	26%
Claims for Operatives					
(8)	Number	2,557	1,491	4,290	1,378
(9)	Number (% of Town Total)	48%	36%	42%	18%
Amount of Variety					
(10)	Major Genotypes (no.)	8	9	6	11
(11)	Total Genotypes (no.)	98	72	120	69
(12)	Total Genotypes (% of Town Total)	57%	43%	61%	32%

such claims than Yoredale, and it had more in 1963–64 than in 1954–55, whereas claims in Yoredale's locally controlled habitat diminished between the survey years. There is more variety within Midwest's locally controlled habitat than within Yoredale's; variety increased in Midwest and decreased in Yoredale between the survey years.

EXTENT OF HABITAT WITH HIGH LOCAL AUTONOMY

Midwest's locally controlled habitat covered 43.6 percent of its total habitat in 1963–64 and was approximately equivalent to 94 regular behavior settings that occur six days a week for eight hours a day — such as Attorneys' Offices and Building, Construction, and Repair Services. Yoredale's covered 30.9 percent of its total habitat and was equivalent to 70 regular settings.

Differences. Midwest's locally controlled habitat is larger than Yoredale's; in 1963–64 it had 12.0 more cu than Yoredale's, amounting to 134 percent as many cu and to 12.7 more percent of the town's total habitat.

Changes. Midwest's locally controlled habitat was larger, and Yoredale's was smaller, in 1963–64 than in 1954–55. Midwest's had 4.3 more cu in 1963–64, amounting to 110 percent as many cu and to 3.8 fewer percent of the town's total habitat. Yoredale's had 1.9 fewer cu, amounting to 95 percent as many cu and to 9.8 fewer percent of the town's total habitat.

Processes of change. More than three-tenths of the towns' 1954–55 locally controlled habitats were eroded before 1963–64, and more than one-quarter of the 1963–64 habitats were accreted after 1954–55. Both erosion and accretion were greater in Midwest than in Yoredale; 15 more percent of Midwest's 1954–55 locally controlled habitat was eroded, and 25 more percent of its 1963–64 locally controlled habitat was accreted. The same is true for the towns' total habitats; more of Midwest's than of Yoredale's habitat was both eroded and accreted.

CLAIMS FOR OPERATIVES WITHIN HABITAT
WITH HIGH LOCAL AUTONOMY

If all behavior settings within the towns' locally controlled habitats had been functioning simultaneously in 1963–64, it would have required 4290 persons in Midwest and 1378 persons in Yoredale to carry out essential operations. These are the numbers of positions involving responsibilities that must be shouldered without directives from outside the town or immediately surrounding district. Claims for operatives of locally controlled habitats are fewer than claims for operatives in general, on a centiurb basis; there are 92 such claims per cu in Midwest, compared with 96 for the whole habitat, and 40 per cu in Yoredale, compared with 69 for the whole habitat. The towns' locally controlled habitats are not rich in positions of responsibility, particularly in Yoredale.

Differences. Midwest's locally controlled habitat has more claims

for operatives than Yoredale's. In 1963–64 Midwest had 2912 more
such claims than Yoredale, amounting to 311 percent as many, to 231
percent as many per cu of locally controlled habitat, to 491 percent
as many per town inhabitant, and to 24 more percent of Midwest's
than of Yoredale's total claims for operatives.

Changes. Midwest's locally controlled habitat had more claims for
operatives, and Yoredale's had fewer in 1963–64 than in 1954–55.
Midwest had 1733 more such claims in 1963–64, amounting to 168 percent as many, to 152 percent as many per cu of locally controlled habitat, and to 141 percent as many per town inhabitant, but to 6 less percent
of the town's total claims for operatives. Yoredale had 113 fewer such
claims, amounting to 92 percent as many, to 85 percent as many per cu
of locally controlled habitat, to 92 percent as many per town inhabitant,
and to 18 less percent of the town's total claims for operatives.

VARIETY WITHIN HABITAT WITH HIGH LOCAL AUTONOMY

If Midwest and Yoredale were to display simultaneously in
1963–64 the complete range of behavior setting programs within their
locally controlled habitats, Midwest would require 120 different halls
and exhibit rooms with their appropriate facilities, 120 differently
trained and experienced staffs and 120 different experts as operators,
managers, chairmen, and so forth; and Yoredale would require 69 different halls, staffs of functionaries, and leaders.

Differences. There is more variety within Midwest's locally controlled habitat than within Yoredale's. In 1963–64 Midwest had 51 more
genotypes than Yoredale, amounting to 174 percent as many and to 29
more percent of Midwest's than of Yoredale's total genotypes.

Changes. Variety within the towns' locally controlled habitats increased in Midwest, and decreased in Yoredale, between the survey

Table 6.7
High Local Autonomy
Control of High Local Autonomy Habitats by Authority Systems
Percent of High local autonomy habitats
controlled by different authority systems

		1954–55		1963–64	
		MW (1)	YD (2)	MW (3)	YD (4)
(1)	Extent of High local autonomy habitat in cu	42.5	36.7	46.8	34.8
	Percent of High local autonomy habitat controlled by:				
(2)	Churches	11.5	7.3	15.2	5.4
(3)	Govt. Agencies	6.2	4.4	7.2	6.5
(4)	Priv. Enterprises	68.1	76.0	53.9	80.0
(5)	Schools	7.0	0.1	10.4	1.1
(6)	Voluntary Assns.	7.1	12.1	13.3	7.0

years. Midwest had 22 more genotypes in 1963–64 than in 1954–55, amounting to 122 percent as many and to 4 more percent of the town's total genotypes. Yoredale had 3 fewer genotypes, amounting to 96 percent as many and to 11 fewer percent of the town's total genotypes.

CONTROL BY AUTHORITY SYSTEMS

More than half the locally controlled habitats of both towns are under the aegis of Private Enterprises, but Private Enterprises are more dominant in Yoredale than in Midwest, whereas Churches, Schools, and Voluntary Associations are locally more powerful in Midwest than in Yoredale (Table 6.7). Between the survey years Midwest's Churches, Schools, and Voluntary Associations gained local power, and its Private Enterprises lost local power, whereas Yoredale's Churches and Voluntary Associations lost local power and Private Enterprises gained.

Medium Local Autonomy

DEFINITION

A habitat with Medium local autonomy consists of behavior settings for which appointment of leaders, admission of members, determination of fees and prices, and establishment of policies and programs are controlled largely by sources located outside the town and district but within the surrounding region. These are the towns' *regionally controlled* habitats.

Basic data for Medium local autonomy are presented in Table 6.8; the report for Aesthetics serves as a key to the location of particular data in this table.

SALIENT FINDINGS

The regionally controlled habitats of Midwest and Yoredale comprise 37 to 48 percent of the towns' total habitats. Midwest's is larger than Yoredale's, and both were larger in 1963–64 than in 1954–55. Regionally controlled habitats contain 46 to 53 percent of the towns' total habitat-claims for operatives; Midwest has more such claims than Yoredale, and both towns had more in 1963–64 than in 1954–55. The towns are similar in the amount of variety within their regionally controlled habitats; variety increased between the survey years in both towns.

EXTENT OF HABITAT WITH MEDIUM LOCAL AUTONOMY

Midwest's regionally controlled habitat covered 48.5 percent of its total habitat in 1963–64 and was approximately equivalent to 120 regular behavior settings that occur five days a week for eight hours a day—such as County Clerk's Office and Register of Deeds Office. Yoredale's covered 37.4 percent of its total habitat and was equivalent to 84 regular settings.

Table 6.8
Medium Local Autonomy
Basic Habitat Data

Extent of Habitat	1954–55		1963–64	
	MW (1)	YD (2)	MW (3)	YD (4)
(1) Behavior Settings per Year	255	211	399	315
(2) Mean BS per Day	62.6	54.0	77.7	64.4
(3) Mean BS per Hour	13.6	11.7	15.7	12.9
(4) Centiurbs (no.)	39.6	33.7	52.1	42.2
(5) Centiurbs (% of Town Total)	44.1%	37.5%	48.5%	37.4%
Erosion and Accretion Type of Change	Erosion from '54–55		Accretion to '63–64	
(6) Centiurbs (no.)	8.7	7.2	19.8	15.8
(7) Centiurbs (% of Regionally Controlled Habitat)	22%	21%	38%	37%
Claims for Operatives				
(8) Number	2,451	2,040	5,430	4,091
(9) Number (% of Town Total)	46%	49%	53%	53%
Amount of Variety				
(10) Major Genotypes (no.)	12	8	6	6
(11) Total Genotypes (no.)	90	89	112	119
(12) Total Genotypes (% of Town Total)	53%	53%	57%	56%

Differences. Midwest's regionally controlled habitat is larger than Yoredale's; in 1963–64 it had 9.9 more cu than Yoredale's, amounting to 123 percent as many cu and to 11.1 more percent of the town's total habitat.

Changes. Both towns' regionally controlled habitats were larger in 1963–64 than in 1954–55. Midwest's had 12.5 more cu in 1963–64, amounting to 132 percent as many cu and to 4.4 more percent of the town's total habitat. Yoredale's had 8.5 more cu, amounting to 125 percent as many cu and to the same percentage of the town's total habitat.

Processes of change. About one-fifth of the towns' 1954–55 regionally controlled habitats were eroded before 1963–64, and almost two-fifths of the 1963–64 habitats were accreted after 1954–55.

CLAIMS FOR OPERATIVES WITHIN HABITAT
WITH MEDIUM LOCAL AUTONOMY

If all behavior settings within the towns' regionally controlled habitats had been functioning simultaneously in 1963–64, it would have required 5430 persons in Midwest and 4091 persons in Yoredale to carry out essential operations. Claims for these operatives are greater than claims for operatives in general, on a centiurb basis; there are 104 such claims per cu in Midwest compared with 96 for the whole habitat, and 97 per cu in Yoredale compared with 69 for the whole habitat. Regionally controlled habitats contain 53 percent of both towns' total habitat-claims for operatives; whereas, as we have seen, they comprise 48.5 and 37.4 percent of the towns' total habitats. The towns' regionally controlled habitats are above average in positions of responsibility, more so in Yoredale than in Midwest.

Differences. Midwest's regionally controlled habitat has more claims for operatives than Yoredale's. In 1963–64 it had 1339 more such claims than Yoredale, amounting to 133 percent as many, to 107 percent as many per cu of regionally controlled habitat, to 209 percent as many per town inhabitant, and to the same percentage of Midwest's as of Yoredale's total claims for operatives.

Changes. Both towns had more claims for operatives within their regionally controlled habitats in 1963–64 than in 1954–55. Midwest had 2979 more such claims in 1963–64, amounting to 221 percent as many, to 168 percent as many per cu, of regionally controlled habitat, to 191 percent as many per town inhabitant, and to 7 more percent of the town's total claims for operatives. Yoredale had 2051 more such claims, amounting to 200 percent as many, to 160 percent as many per cu, of regionally controlled habitat, to 199 percent as many per town inhabitant, and to 3 more percent of the town's total claims for operatives.

VARIETY WITHIN HABITAT WITH MEDIUM LOCAL AUTONOMY

If Midwest and Yoredale were to display simultaneously in 1963–64 the complete range of behavior setting programs with Medium local autonomy, Midwest would require 112 different halls and exhibit rooms with their appropriate facilities, 112 differently trained and experienced staffs, and 112 different experts as operators, managers, presidents, and so forth; and Yoredale would require 119 different halls, staffs of functionaries, and leaders.

Differences. There is less variety within Midwest's regionally controlled habitat than within Yoredale's. In 1963–64 Midwest had 7 fewer genotypes than Yoredale, amounting to 94 percent as many and to 1 more percent of Midwest's than of Yoredale's total genotypes.

Changes. There was more variety within the towns' habitats with Medium local autonomy in 1963–64 than in 1954–55. Midwest had 22 more genotypes in 1963–64, amounting to 124 percent as many and to 4 more percent of the town's total genotypes. Yoredale had 30 more genotypes, amounting to 134 percent as many and to 3 more percent of the town's total genotypes.

CONTROL BY AUTHORITY SYSTEMS

Control from the regions surrounding the towns is channeled chiefly through the School authority system of Midwest and the Private Enterprise authority system of Yoredale, and secondarily through the Private Enterprises of Midwest and the Schools of Yoredale (Table 6.9). Approximately two-thirds of the town's regionally controlled habitats are under the aegis of these two authority systems.

Table 6.9
Medium Local Autonomy
Control of Medium Local Autonomy Habitats by Authority Systems
Percent of Medium local autonomy habitats
controlled by different authority systems

	1954–55		1963–64	
	MW (1)	YD (2)	MW (3)	YD (4)
(1) Extent of Medium local autonomy habitat in cu	39.6	33.7	52.1	42.3
Percent of Medium local autonomy habitat controlled by:				
(2) Churches	3.7	3.7	9.1	5.9
(3) Govt. Agencies	27.1	13.0	17.9	8.2
(4) Priv. Enterprises	29.8	48.5	25.8	43.6
(5) Schools	32.1	20.9	37.8	29.1
(6) Voluntary Assns.	7.3	13.9	9.5	13.2

Low Local Autonomy

DEFINITION

A habitat with Low local autonomy consists of behavior settings for which appointment of leaders, admission of members, determination of fees and prices, and establishment of policies and programs are controlled largely by sources located beyond the town, beyond the surrounding district, and beyond the surrounding region — at the state and national levels in the case of Midwest and at the county and national levels in the case of Yoredale. These habitats are *controlled from a distance.*

Basic data on Low local autonomy habitats are presented in Table 6.10; the report for Aesthetics provides a key to the location of particular data in this table.

SALIENT FINDINGS

The habitats of Midwest and Yoredale that are controlled from a distance comprise 8 to 32 percent of the towns' total habitats. Distant control is less extensive in Midwest than in Yoredale, and it increased in both towns between the survey years. Habitats controlled from a distance contain 5 to 29 percent of the towns' total habitat-claims for operatives; Midwest has fewer such claims than Yoredale, and both towns had more in 1963–64 than in 1954–55. There is less variety within Midwest's than within Yoredale's habitat with Low local autonomy; variety increased between the survey years in both towns.

EXTENT OF HABITAT WITH LOW LOCAL AUTONOMY

Midwest's habitat controlled from a distance covered 7.9 percent of its total habitat in 1963–64 and was approximately equivalent to 17

Table 6.10
Low Local Autonomy
Basic Habitat Data

Extent of Habitat	1954–55		1963–64	
	MW (1)	YD (2)	MW (3)	YD (4)
(1) Behavior Settings per Year	44	96	76	280
(2) Mean BS per Day	9.7	32.3	11.2	58.0
(3) Mean BS per Hour	3.4	7.9	2.3	9.4
(4) Centiurbs (no.)	7.6	19.6	8.5	35.7
(5) Centiurbs (% of Town Total)	8.5%	21.8%	7.9%	31.7%
Erosion and Accretion				
Type of Change	Erosion from '54–55		Accretion to '63–64	
(6) Centiurbs (no.)	3.5	3.8	4.0	18.8
(7) Centiurbs (% of Distantly Controlled Habitat	46%	19%	52%	53%
Claims for Operatives				
(8) Number	352	592	500	2,295
(9) Number (% of Town Total)	7%	14%	5%	29%
Amount of Variety				
(10) Major Genotypes (no.)	10	11	11	3
(11) Total Genotypes (no.)	30	62	31	115
(12) Total Genotypes (% of Town Total)	17%	37%	16%	54%

regular behavior settings that occur six days a week for eight hours a day — such as Post Offices and Automatic Telephone Exchanges. Yoredale's covered 31.7 percent of its total habitat and was equivalent to 71 regular settings such as Commercial Banks and Police Stations.

Differences. Midwest's habitat controlled from a distance is smaller than Yoredale's; in 1963–64 it had 27.2 fewer cu, amounting to 24 percent as many cu and to 23.8 fewer percent of the town's total habitat.

Changes. Habitats controlled from a distance were larger in both towns in 1963–64 than in 1954–55. Midwest's had 0.9 more cu in 1963–64, amounting to 112 percent as many cu and to 0.5 fewer percent of the town's total habitat. Yoredale's had 16.1 more cu, amounting to 182 percent as many cu and to 9.9 more percent of the town's total habitat.

Processes of change. More than one-sixth of the towns' 1954–55 habitats controlled from a distance were eroded before 1963–64, and about half of the 1963–64 habitats were accreted after 1954–55. Erosion was greater and accretion was less in Midwest than in Yoredale; 27 more percent of Midwest's 1954–55 distantly controlled habitat was eroded, and 6 fewer percent of its 1963–64 distantly controlled habitat was accreted. This differs from the towns' total habitats; more of Midwest's than of Yoredale's habitat was both eroded and accreted.

CLAIMS FOR OPERATIVES WITHIN HABITAT
WITH LOW LOCAL AUTONOMY

If all behavior settings within the towns' habitats controlled from
a distance were to function simultaneously in 1963–64, it would require
500 persons in Midwest and 2295 persons in Yoredale to carry out essential operations. Claims for these operatives are fewer than claims for
operatives in general, on a centiurb basis; there are 59 such claims per
cu in Midwest, compared with 96 for the whole habitat, and 64 per cu in
Yoredale, compared with 69 for the whole habitat. The habitats controlled from a distance contain 5 and 29 percent of the towns' total
habitat-claims for operatives; whereas, as we have seen, they comprise
7.9 and 31.7 percent of the towns' total habitats. The towns' distantly
controlled habitats are poor in positions of responsibility.

Differences. Midwest's distantly controlled habitat has fewer claims
for operatives than Yoredale's. In 1963–64 it had 1795 fewer such
claims than Yoredale, amounting to 22 percent as many, to 91 percent
as many per cu of habitat controlled from a distance, to 34 percent as
many per town inhabitant, and to 24 fewer percent of Midwest's than of
Yoredale's total claims for operatives.

Changes. Both towns had more habitat-claims for operatives
within their distantly controlled habitats in 1963–64 than in 1954–55.
Midwest had 148 more such claims in 1963–64, amounting to 142 percent as many, to 127 percent as many per cu of distantly controlled habitat, to 122 percent as many per town inhabitant, but to 2 fewer percent
of the town's total claims for operatives. Yoredale had 1703 more such
claims, amounting to 388 percent as many, to 213 percent as many per
cu of distantly controlled habitat, to 385 percent as many per town
inhabitant, and to 15 more percent of the town's total claims for operatives.

VARIETY WITHIN HABITAT WITH LOW LOCAL AUTONOMY

If Midwest and Yoredale were to display simultaneously in
1963–64 the complete range of behavior setting programs with Low
local autonomy, Midwest would require 31 different halls and exhibit
rooms with their appropriate facilities, 31 differently trained and experienced staffs and 31 different experts as chairmen, directors, operators,
and so forth; and Yoredale would require 115 different halls, staffs of
functionaries, and leaders.

Differences. There is less variety within Midwest's habitat controlled from a distance than within Yoredale's. In 1963–64 Midwest had
84 fewer genotypes than Yoredale, amounting to 27 percent as many
and to 38 fewer percent of Midwest's than of Yoredale's total genotypes.

Changes. Variety within habitats controlled from a distance increased between the survey years in both towns. Midwest had 1 more
genotype in 1963–64 than in 1954–55, amounting to 103 percent as
many and to 1 fewer percent of the town's total genotypes. Yoredale

Table 6.11
Low Local Autonomy
Control of Low Local Autonomy Habitats by Authority Systems
Percent of Low local autonomy habitats
controlled by different authority systems

	1954–55		1963–64	
	MW (1)	YD (2)	MW (3)	YD (4)
(1) Extent of Low local autonomy Habitat in cu	7.6	19.6	8.5	35.7
Percent of Low local autonomy habitat controlled by:				
(2) Churches	0.0	9.0	4.0	5.5
(3) Govt. Agencies	45.6	36.2	56.4	18.6
(4) Priv. Enterprises	41.4	48.5	23.6	26.3
(5) Schools	5.7	2.0	2.9	46.2
(6) Voluntary Assns.	7.2	4.3	13.0	3.5

had 53 more genotypes, amounting to 185 percent as many and to 17 more percent of the town's total genotypes.

CONTROL BY AUTHORITY SYSTEMS

In 1963–64 Midwest's small habitat with Low local autonomy was dominated by Government Agencies, followed by Private Enterprises and Voluntary Associations (Table 6.11). Schools are predominant in Yoredale's distantly controlled habitat, followed by Private Enterprises and Government Agencies. Within the habitats mainly controlled from beyond the towns and their surrounding districts and regions, Government Agencies are more dominant in Midwest and Schools are much more dominant in Yoredale.

The preeminent change between the survey years is that Yoredale's School authority system, last among the 5 authority systems in extent of control over the town's distantly controlled habitat in 1954–55, was first in 1963–64. The greatest change in Midwest was the decline in the relative importance of Private Enterprises in the town's habitat controlled from a distance.

Summary

In the preceding sections we separately presented detailed information on each of the three autonomy habitats. We present here graphic overviews of the extents of these habitats in 1963–64 and of changes in them between 1954–55 and 1963–64 by three measures: extent in centiurbs, number of habitat-claims for operatives, and variety as indicated by number of genotypes. The graphic presentations and discussions follow the format described in the summary section on action pattern habitats; the reader may find it helpful to review the explana-

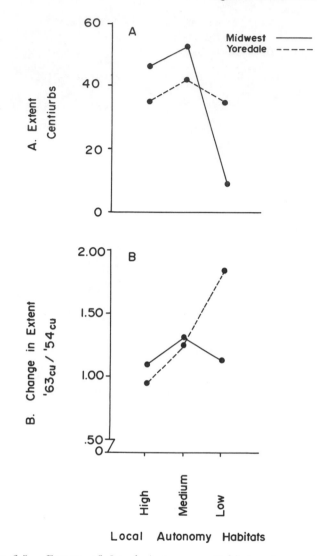

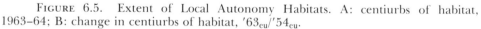

Local Autonomy Habitats

FIGURE 6.5. Extent of Local Autonomy Habitats. A: centiurbs of habitat, 1963–64; B: change in centiurbs of habitat, $'63_{cu}/'54_{cu}$.

tions and cautions given in that section for interpreting these graphic presentations. It should be noted, however, that here the differential habitats are shown in the same sequence on all three graphs, rather than in order of increasing size in Midwest.

EXTENT OF AUTONOMY HABITATS

Extents of the autonomy habitats vary greatly within and between the towns (Figure 6.5A). One generalization may be made, however: regional control (Medium local autonomy) is more extensive than either local control (High local autonomy) or distant control (Low local autonomy) in both towns.

Differences. In 1963–64 Yoredale's total habitat was divided more evenly among the three autonomy habitats than was Midwest's. The extents of distantly, regionally, and locally controlled habitats were proportionately 1.00:1.18:0.97 in Yoredale and 1.00:6.13:5.51 in Midwest. Midwest had much less distantly controlled habitat than Yoredale (24 percent as much), more regionally controlled habitat (123 percent as much), and more locally controlled habitat (134 percent as much). Midwest's distantly controlled habitat amounted to only 10 percent of its total habitat, whereas Yoredale's amounted to 32 percent of its total habitat.

Changes. Midwest's autonomy habitats increased between the survey years at rates which do not deviate markedly from the rate for the total town, whereas Yoredale's habitat controlled from a distance grew at a much faster rate than its total habitat, and its locally controlled habitat decreased (Figure 6.5B). Midwest's habitat remained relatively stable between the survey years with respect to the geographical loci of the controlling centers, but Yoredale's shifted strongly toward more control by centers beyond the surrounding district and region, at the county and national levels.

CLAIMS FOR OPERATIVES WITHIN AUTONOMY HABITATS

Comparison of these data (Figure 6.6A) with those presented above on extent in centiurbs (Figure 6.5A) reveals a strong similarity in the patterns, with the trends even more sharply accentuated here.

Differences. Claims for operatives were distributed more evenly across the autonomy habitats of Yoredale than of Midwest in 1963–64. In the distantly, regionally, and locally controlled habitats they were proportionately 1.00:1.78:0.61 in Yoredale and 1.00:10.86:8.58 in Midwest. Midwest's locally controlled habitat was about 3 times as rich as Yoredale's in claims for operatives, and its distantly controlled habitat was only about one-fifth as rich.

Changes. The trends noted in the data on extent are repeated here in more extreme form. Claims for operatives increased in each of Midwest's differential autonomy habitats at about the same rate as in its total habitat, but in Yoredale they increased within its distantly controlled habitat at double the rate of the town's total habitat, and they decreased within its locally controlled habitat. Over the decade Yoredale's positions of responsibility came increasingly under the aegis of authorities beyond the town, district, and region, whereas Midwest was much more stable in this respect.

VARIETY WITHIN AUTONOMY HABITATS

Differences. The greater importance of local control in Midwest than in Yoredale in 1963–64, as reported in the preceding sections, is obvious in the data on variety as well (Figure 6.7A). Midwest's locally controlled habitat was 174 percent as rich in variety as Yoredale's,

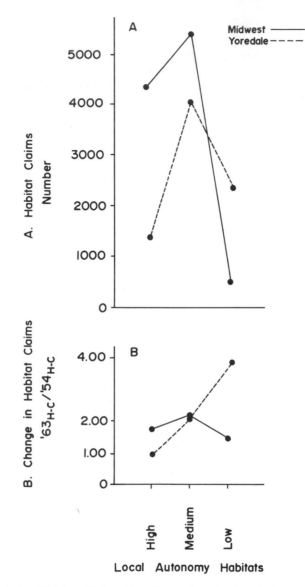

FIGURE 6.6.   Habitat-Claims for Operatives in Local Autonomy Habitats. A: number of habitat-claims, 1963–64; B: change in habitat-claims, $'63_{H-C}/'54_{H-C}$.

whereas its habitat controlled from a distance was only 27 percent as varied.

Changes. The change data are quite similar to those for the other two habitat dimensions. Number of genotypes increased in Midwest between 1954–55 and 1963–64 in each of the three differential autonomy habitats at rates which do not differ markedly from the rate for the whole town. In Yoredale, however, they increased in the habitat controlled from a distance at a rate much higher than that for the town as a whole, and in the locally controlled habitat there were fewer geno-

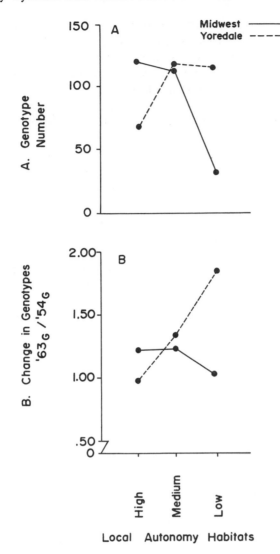

FIGURE 6.7. Variety in Local Autonomy Habitats. A: number of genotypes, 1963–64; B: change in number of genotypes, $'63_G/'54_G$.

types in 1963–64 than in 1954–55. So again we see the same trends discussed above: Yoredale shifted sharply away from local control between the survey years, while Midwest either did not change in this respect or moved toward increased control of its habitat resources at the local and regional levels.

ATTENDANCE HABITATS

Behavior settings differ in the degree to which they encourage or discourage entrance and participation by different persons and population subgroups. Children, for example, are required to attend school classes but are prohibited from entering meetings of the Yoredale Rural District Council. Because of our special interest in Midwest and Yoredale as habitats for children, we next report results of an analysis of the behavior settings of the towns in terms of their pressures upon two population subgroups: children and adolescents.

The definitions and procedures used in this analysis are those described in Barker (1968, pp. 70–75), under the title "Pressure." Five classes of behavior settings differing with respect to their pressures upon children and upon adolescents to attend (inhabit) them are identified: attendance *required,* attendance *encouraged,* behavior setting *neutral,* attendance *discouraged,* and attendance *prohibited.* The behavior settings falling into each of these categories are dealt with as a differential habitat. The ratings and analyses parallel those for the previously reported differential habitats. However, it has seemed possible to convey the findings of greatest interest by means of less detailed reports, so we present only the graphic summaries for 3 habitat dimensions: extent, habitat-claims for operatives, and variety. The figures are similar to those presented in the summary sections for the other differential habitats; the reader may find it helpful to review the explanatory comments given there. However, here the differential habitats are shown in the same sequence (required, encouraged, neutral, discouraged, prohibited) on all the graphs, rather than in order of increasing size in Midwest.

Output data for the attendance habitats are presented in Chapter 10.

Child Attendance Habitats

DEFINITIONS

Attendance required. These are the settings about which children have no choice. Children have to go to these settings; all the pressure of the family, in most cases, and if necessary of the police force of the community requires child attendance. These are, in Midwest and Yoredale, almost exclusively school settings.

Attendance encouraged. These settings bring pressure to bear upon the eligible children to attend, yet the children have some choice — for example, boys are invited but not required to participate in the setting Boy Scout Cub Pack Meeting. Children are singled out from other age groups as the special targets of attendance pressures generated by these settings — that is, the pressures apply specifically to children to a greater degree than to members of other age subgroups.

Neutral. These behavior settings generate no special pressures upon children either to enter or to stay out of them. Children as an age group are not singled out in any way as targets for special pressure to enter or not enter these settings. Examples are Trafficways and Grocery Stores.

Attendance discouraged. These behavior settings resist and discourage, but do not prohibit, the entrance and participation of children; they discriminate against children as an age group. For example, children are discouraged from entering Attorneys' Offices in Midwest and Commission (Betting) Agents' Offices in Yoredale.

Attendance prohibited. These behavior settings actively exclude children as an age group; pressures against entrance of children (except temporarily, in emergencies) are irresistible. The presence of children is not tolerated, for example, in Yoredale's Kings Arms Pub or Midwest's Odd Fellows Lodge Meeting.

EXTENT OF CHILD ATTENDANCE HABITATS

The general pattern of the extent of child attendance habitats is common to Midwest and Yoredale (Figure 6.8A). The habitat neutral to children is the largest in both towns; it comprised more than two-fifths of the total habitat of each town in 1963–64. The two attendance habitats on the negative side of neutral, those which discourage or prohibit child attendance, covered another two-fifths of the towns' total habitats; and the two positive habitats, those which require or encourage the attendance of children, made up the remaining one-fifth of the towns' total habitats.

Differences. Yoredale is more coercive toward children than is Midwest; more of its habitat requires or prohibits the attendance of children. Although the difference is not large in absolute terms (about 12 cu), it is twice as large as Yoredale's total habitat superiority over Midwest (6 cu). This difference becomes dramatic in light of the reversal in direction of the difference in the case of settings that encourage or discourage the attendance of children; about 12 cu more of Midwest's than of Yoredale's habitat exerts minimum to moderate pressure upon children to attend some settings and avoid others.

Changes. The increases between the survey years in extent of total habitat — 119 percent in Midwest, 125 percent in Yoredale — are not reflected evenly across the five child attendance habitats (Figure 6.8B). There were much greater increases in both towns in the habitat which requires the attendance of children and also in Midwest's habitats that encourage and prohibit their attendance.

CLAIMS FOR OPERATIVES WITHIN CHILD ATTENDANCE HABITATS

In both towns the largest number of claims for operatives is in the habitat neutral to children (Figure 6.9A); it accounts for about two-fifths of Midwest's and little more than one-third of Yoredale's total claims. Claims for operatives are low in habitats that discourage and prohibit children's attendance in both towns.

Differences. The greatest differences between the towns occur in habitats that require and encourage the attendance of children. Although Midwest's total habitat-claims for operatives were 132 percent of Yoredale's (Table 3.3), within the habitat that requires child atten-

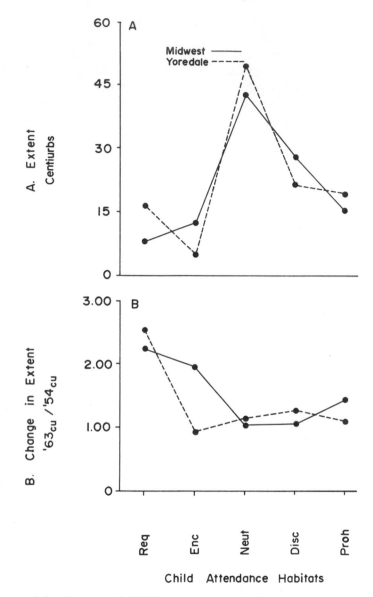

FIGURE 6.8.   Extent of Child Attendance Habitats. A: centiurbs of habitat, 1963–64; B: change in centiurbs of habitat, $'63_{cu}/'54_{cu}$.

dance it was only 43 percent of Yoredale's. An even larger difference in the opposite direction occurred in the habitat that encourages the attendance of children, where Midwest's claims were 350 percent of Yoredale's.

Changes. Most of these differential habitats grew in claims for operatives at rates near or somewhat below those for the towns' total habitats (191 percent in Midwest, 188 percent in Yoredale). In both

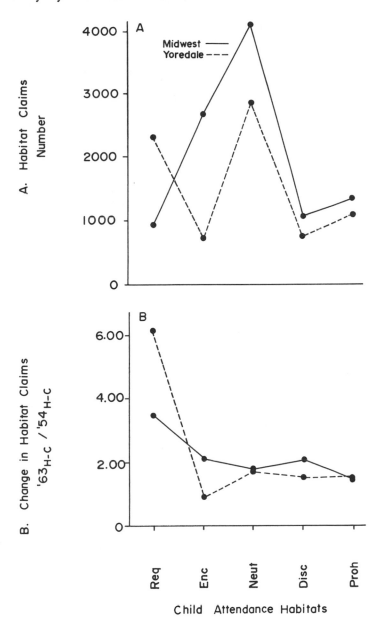

FIGURE 6.9. Habitat-Claims for Operatives in Child Attendance Habitats. A: number of habitat-claims, 1963–64; B: change in habitat-claims, $'63_{H-C}/'54_{H-C}$.

towns, however, there is the same outstanding exception: in the habitat where child attendance is required, Midwest had 358 percent as many claims for operatives in 1963–64 as in 1954–55, and Yoredale had 618 percent as many. These dramatic increases reflect the increased extent and vigor of the two towns' educational programs for their children.

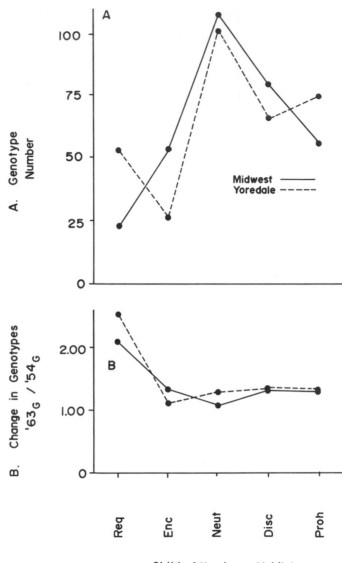

FIGURE 6.10.   Variety in Child Attendance Habitats. A: number of genotypes, 1963–64; B: change in number of genotypes, $'63_G/'54_G$.

VARIETY WITHIN CHILD ATTENDANCE HABITATS

On this habitat dimension, as on the two already considered, the habitat neutral to children is much larger than any other in both towns, containing about half of each town's genotypes (Figure 6.10A).

Differences. The greater coerciveness of Yoredale's behavior settings is reflected in many more genotypes in the most coercive child attendance habitats: attendance required and attendance prohibited.

Changes. Variety increased in all child attendance habitats in both towns (Figure 6.10B). By far the largest increases were in habitats that require the attendance of children; for Midwest there were 2 and for Yoredale 2.5 times as many genotypes in 1963–64 as in 1954–55.

Adolescent Attendance Habitats

We here present a summary of findings for the adolescent attendance habitats, using parallel definitions and following the general format of the section on child attendance habitats.

EXTENT OF ADOLESCENT ATTENDANCE HABITATS

The largest habitat in each town in 1963–64 was the one neutral to adolescents; it included about half the total habitat of each town (Figure 6.11A). On the positive side of neutral, the differential habitats which encourage and require adolescent participation covered nearly a third of the towns' total habitats; and on the negative side, those which discourage and prohibit adolescents made up just over one-fifth of the towns' total habitats.

Differences. The curves show that Midwest's overall deficiency in total habitat size (95 percent of Yoredale's) is not reflected evenly across the five habitats. Those involving strongest coercion upon adolescents to enter (attendance required) and to stay out (attendance prohibited) were much smaller in Midwest than in Yoredale, whereas those involving minimum to moderate pressure upon adolescents to enter (attendance encouraged) and to stay out (attendance discouraged) were larger. Thus while both towns bring to bear upon adolescents positive and negative pressures toward entrance and participation in behavior settings, strong pressures characterize much more of Yoredale's habitat. Midwest's adolescents more frequently than Yoredale's have the choice of entering behavior settings or not.

Changes. The increases between the survey years in extent of total habitat — 119 percent in Midwest, 125 percent in Yoredale — are not reflected evenly across the adolescent attendance habitats (Figure 6.11B). The habitat that requires adolescent attendance increased most in both towns, by factors of 2.4 in Midwest and 4.3 in Yoredale.

CLAIMS FOR OPERATIVES WITHIN ADOLESCENT
ATTENDANCE HABITATS

This habitat dimension is distributed very unevenly across the adolescent attendance habitats (Figure 6.12A).

Differences. Midwest's 32 percent overall superiority to Yoredale in habitat-claims for operatives was greatly exceeded in the habitat that encourages adolescent attendance; it was also exceeded in the habitat that discourages it. Midwest is deficient relative to Yoredale in claims for operatives in the habitat where adolescent attendance is required.

Changes. The most impressive finding is the large increase in claims for operatives within the habitats of both towns that require and

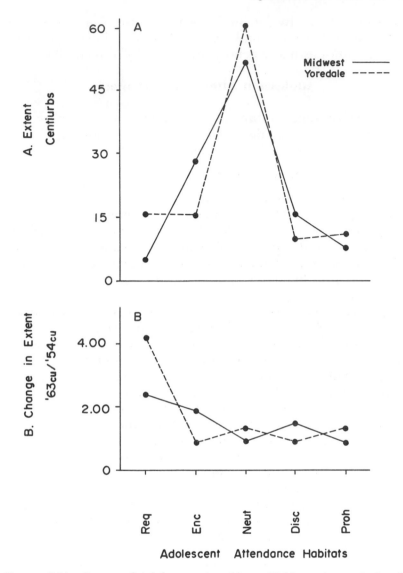

FIGURE 6.11. Extent of Adolescent Attendance Habitats. A: centiurbs of habitat, 1963–64; B: change in centiurbs of habitat, $'63_{cu}/'54_{cu}$.

encourage adolescent attendance (Figure 6.12B). In 1963–64 the required habitat was 386 percent as great in Midwest and 611 percent as great in Yoredale as in 1954–55; and the encouraged habitat was 252 percent as great in Midwest and 191 percent as great in Yoredale.

These findings closely parallel those reported above for the child attendance habitats (Figure 6.9B); they reveal the increased extent and vigor of the towns' educational programs in 1963–64, when there were many more educational settings rich in claims for operatives and requiring or encouraging the entrance and participation of the adolescents of both towns.

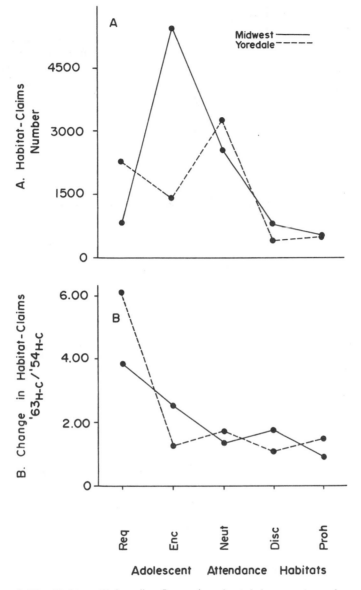

FIGURE 6.12. Habitat-Claims for Operatives in Adolescent Attendance Habitats. A: number of habitat-claims, 1963–64; B: change in habitat-claims, $'63_{H\text{-}C}/'54_{H\text{-}C}$.

VARIETY WITHIN ADOLESCENT ATTENDANCE HABITATS

In both towns the habitat neutral to adolescents has much greater variety than any other adolescent attendance habitat (Figure 6.13A).

Differences. Yoredale's greater coerciveness toward adolescents is again apparent in the larger number of genotypes within the habitat that requires adolescent attendance. In 1963–64 Midwest had only 42 percent as many such genotypes as did Yoredale. Midwest had more

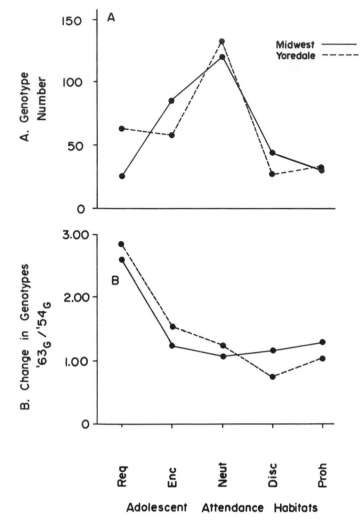

FIGURE 6.13. Variety in Adolescent Attendance Habitats. A: number of geno-types, 1963–64; B: change in number of genotypes, $'63_G/'54_G$.

variety than Yoredale in the habitats that encourage and discourage adolescent attendance.

Changes. In both towns the largest increases in variety occurred in the habitat that requires the attendance of adolescents. The rates of change for the other habitats do not differ markedly from the rates for the towns as wholes.

BENEFICENCE HABITATS

Most of the town's behavior settings serve all or several of the population subgroups equally, but some settings are designed to benefit particular subgroups selectively. Our special interest in the children and adolescents of Midwest and Yoredale led us to analyze the two towns' behavior settings to determine the frequency with which they are intended to benefit the child and adolescent inhabitants selectively.

Four categories of behavior settings are identified: children (adolescents) benefited directly, children (adolescents) benefited indirectly, setting neutral toward children (adolescents), and others benefited by children (adolescents). In the sections which follow, the behavior settings falling into each of these four categories are considered as an identifiable habitat. The ratings of behavior settings, data analyses, and tabulations for the differential child beneficence habitats follow the format described for the previously reported habitat qualities. However, in this case, as with attendance, it is possible to convey the findings of greatest interest by means of a less detailed report. We therefore present below only the graphic summaries similar to those given at the ends of the sections on the other attributes.

Output data for beneficence habitats are reported in Chapter 10.

Child Beneficence Habitats

DEFINITIONS

Children benefited directly. Behavior settings which serve the welfare of their child inhabitants make up this habitat, which is designed specifically to influence child inhabitants in a particular beneficial way, such as to educate, provide recreation for, entertain, or feed them. Two examples are a school class and a Cub Scout meeting. This habitat does not include settings which serve all age groups indiscriminately, such as most business settings; it is limited to those which benefit their child inhabitants selectively.

Children benefited indirectly. Behavior settings which promote the welfare of the child inhabitants of *other* behavior settings make up this habitat. It has no child members; rather, the settings which constitute it instigate, support, and control other settings that do benefit children. For example, Midwest's Elementary School Board has no child members, but its central purpose is to provide for the educational well-being of children in other behavior settings. This habitat does not include settings that, as only one function among others, foster children's behavior settings—for instance, the Women's Institute Meeting, which arranges a children's Christmas Party. Only adult settings which would cease if the child settings they foster should cease—such as Kindergarten Parents Association Meeting—are included in this habitat.

Unconcerned with children. Behavior settings whose primary purposes are not specifically related to the welfare of children as a group make up this habitat. It includes settings, such as stores, which are unselective with respect to children—that is, they have no more interest in children than in other population subgroups—and it also includes settings which focus specifically on the interests of other age groups, even to the point of discouraging or prohibiting entrance by children, such as High School Latin Classes.

Children benefit others. Behavior settings implemented by child operatives for the benefit of members of other age groups make up this habitat. The child inhabitants of its settings have responsible positions where they educate, entertain, provide recreation for, or otherwise benefit people of other age groups, as in the Elementary School Christmas Program.

EXTENT OF CHILD BENEFICENCE HABITATS

The extent of these differential habitats in 1963–64 varied greatly, with the habitat that provides no special benefits for children dominating both towns, and the habitat that directly benefits children next in extent (Figure 6.14A).

Differences. Midwest's total habitat was 95 percent as extensive as Yoredale's, but this relation was not uniform across the differential child beneficence habitats. Midwest's habitat that benefits children directly was 85 percent as large as Yoredale's, whereas its habitat where children benefit others, though small, was 11 times as large as Yoredale's. These findings indicate that Midwest provides its children with a smaller habitat devoted especially to their welfare than Yoredale does, but a larger habitat where they have the opportunity and power to benefit others.

Changes. Changes between the survey years were very uneven across the four child beneficence habitats (Figure 6.14B). Increases in the size of the habitats that benefit children directly occurred in both towns, and they were proportionally greater than the increases in the towns' total habitats. The habitat where children benefit others almost tripled in size in Midwest, but did not increase in Yoredale. The other child beneficence habitats failed to keep pace with the growth of the towns as wholes.

CLAIMS FOR OPERATIVES WITHIN CHILD BENEFICENCE HABITATS

The distribution of habitat-claims for operatives across these habitats in 1963–64 followed the general pattern noted above for habitat extent in centiurbs (Figure 6.15A).

Differences. Although overall Midwest had 132 percent as many claims for operatives as Yoredale did, the habitat that benefits children directly had less than half as many claims for operatives in Midwest as in Yoredale. Indeed, claims in this habitat amounted to over one-third of all Yoredale's claims for operatives, but to only one-eighth of Midwest's. This finding, that many more of Yoredale's than of Midwest's positions of responsibility and leadership occur in settings which directly serve children, provides evidence that Yoredale's child-rearing system differs from Midwest's by leaning more heavily upon special, child-centered behavior settings. This difference is indicated also by the data for the habitats where children serve others. This habitat had almost 9 times as many claims for operatives in Midwest as in Yoredale. Thus Midwest

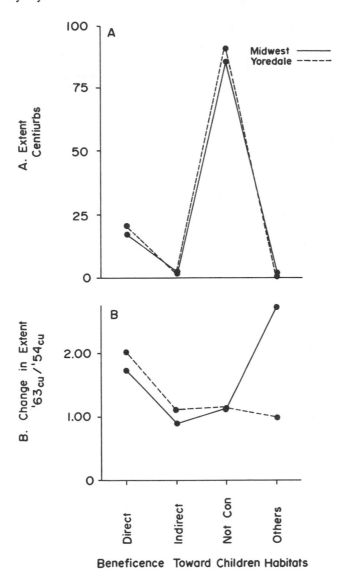

FIGURE 6.14.   Extent of Beneficence Toward Children Habitats. A: centiurbs of habitat, 1963–64; B: change in centiurbs of habitat, $'63_{cu}/'54_{cu}$.

children are placed in many more positions of responsibility than are Yoredale children in behavior settings which provide service, education, entertainment, or recreation for persons of other age groups. Yoredale prepares its children for life by education and socialization in special children's behavior settings, whereas Midwest depends less upon special children's settings and more upon involving children in the operation of the town's regular behavior settings.

Changes. Rate of change between the survey years varies greatly across the child beneficence habitats. In Midwest the rate of increase in

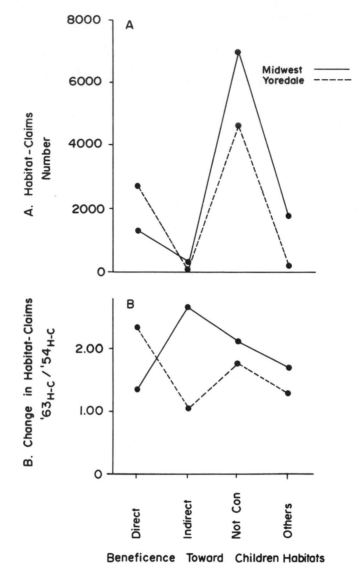

FIGURE 6.15.   Habitat-Claims for Operatives in Beneficence Toward Children Habitats. A: number of habitat-claims, 1963–64; B: change in habitat-claims, $'63_{H-C}/'54_{H-C}$.

claims for operatives in the habitat that directly benefits children was smaller than the rate for all the town's claims for operatives, and it was smaller than for any of the other beneficence habitats; the reverse was true in Yoredale (Figure 6.15B). In Midwest claims for operatives in the habitat where children benefit others almost kept pace with the rate of increase in the town's total claims for operatives, but in Yoredale they fell behind. Claims for operatives in the habitat that benefits children indirectly are so small that change data are not very meaningful.

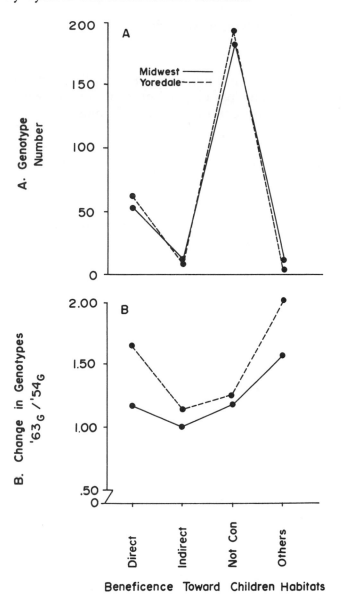

FIGURE 6.16. Variety in Beneficence Toward Children Habitats. A: number of genotypes, 1963–64; B: change in number of genotypes, $'63_G/'54_G$.

VARIETY WITHIN CHILD BENEFICENCE HABITATS

As with the measures of habitat extent and claims for operatives, measures of habitat variety are very different for the four child benefi-cence habitats (Figure 6.16A). The variety curves closely parallel the other curves; these data therefore further emphasize the significance of the findings discussed above.

Adolescent Beneficence Habitats

We here present a summary of the findings for adolescent beneficence habitats, using parallel definitions and following the general format of the section on child beneficence habitats.

EXTENT OF ADOLESCENT BENEFICENCE HABITATS

The extent of these habitats varies greatly in both towns, from less than 5 cu for the habitats that benefit adolescents indirectly and

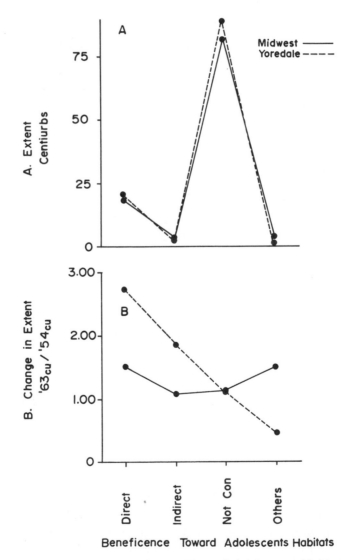

FIGURE 6.17.   Extent of Beneficence Toward Adolescents Habitats: A: centiurbs of habitat, 1963–64; B: change in centiurbs of habitat, $'63_{cu}/'54_{cu}$.

where adolescents benefit others to over 20 cu for the habitat that
benefits adolescents directly and over 75 cu for the habitat not concerned with adolescents (Figure 6.17A).

Differences. The order of the habitats is the same in the two towns,
but there are interesting differences in their extents. Contrary to expectations on the basis of the towns' total habitats—Midwest's 95 percent as
large as Yoredale's—Midwest's habitat that benefits adolescents directly
was 86 percent as large as Yoredale's, and its habitat where adolescents
benefit others was more than 6 times the size of its counterpart in

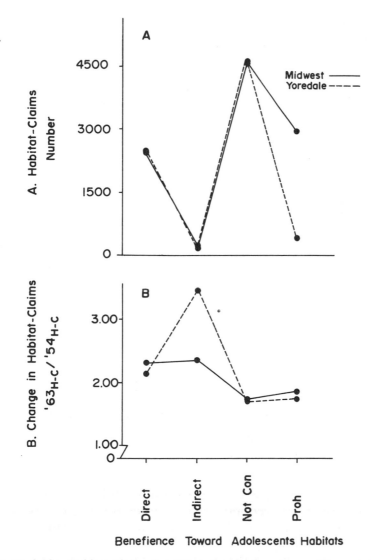

FIGURE 6.18. Habitat-Claims for Operatives in Beneficence Toward Adolescents
Habitats. A: number of habitat-claims, 1963–64; B: change in habitat-claims,
'63$_{H-C}$/'54$_{H-C}$.

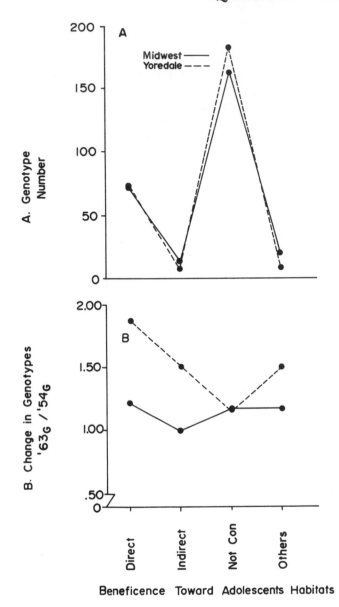

FIGURE 6.19. Variety in Beneficence Toward Adolescents Habitats. A: number of genotypes, 1963–64; B: change in number of genotypes, $'63_G/'54_G$.

Yoredale. These data indicate therefore that Midwest's adolescents, like its children, are more frequently integrated into regular behavior settings of the town and less often segregated into settings created especially for them than is the case in Yoredale.

Changes. Changes between the survey years were relatively uniform across Midwest's adolescent beneficence habitats (Figure 6.17B). All the habitats increased in extent; the one that benefits adolescents directly and the one where adolescents benefit others increased at somewhat greater rates than did Midwest's total habitat, the others at somewhat lesser rates. In Yoredale, however, there were great differences in the rates of change of these differential habitats; the habitat that benefits adolescents directly increased at more than double the rate of the town as a whole, and the habitat where adolescents benefit others declined in extent.

CLAIMS FOR OPERATIVES WITHIN ADOLESCENT
BENEFICENCE HABITATS

The distribution of claims for operatives across these habitats in 1963–64 follows the pattern reported above for habitat extent, with one exception noted below (Figure 6.18A).

Differences. Over all its habitat Midwest had 132 percent as many claims for operatives as Yoredale did; we find now that Midwest's superiority occurred almost entirely within its habitat where adolescents benefit others. In its behavior settings with claims for adolescent operatives Midwest provides more opportunities and obligations for important and responsible actions than Yoredale does.

Changes. With one exception, the change ratios across the four habitats do not deviate markedly from those for the towns as total habitats. The one exception is in Yoredale's habitat that benefits adolescents indirectly, which in 1963–64 had 345 percent as many claims for operatives as in 1954–55. This, together with the corresponding data on extent (Figure 6.18B), indicates an increase in the number of settings which plan for and control other settings benefiting adolescent inhabitants—such as Young Farmer's Club Advisory Committee Meeting, Secondary Modern School Managers' Meeting, and Parent-Teachers Association Meeting.

VARIETY WITHIN ADOLESCENT BENEFICENCE HABITATS

Differences in the amount of variety occurring within these habitats in 1963–64 (Figure 6.19A) have a marked correspondence with the findings for habitat extent; the patterns displayed by the two sets of curves are strikingly similar. These data therefore tend to confirm and increase our confidence in the findings presented and discussed above. The change ratios for Midwest do not differ widely from those for the town's whole habitat, but the increase in variety within habitats that benefit adolescents directly is much greater in Yoredale than that for Yoredale's total habitat.

CHAPTER 7

Behavior Setting Theory and Its Application to Midwest and Yoredale

This chapter deals with processes by which behavior settings form the behavior of their inhabitants to accord with their programs. It is a brief statement, with special reference to Midwest-Yoredale differences of some complicated and incompletely understood interdependences between habitat and behavior. These issues are considered more thoroughly in Barker (1968).

When a leaf is picked up by a dust devil, its motion results from forces in the dust devil interacting with properties of the leaf. One consequence may be the separation of the leaf from the dust devil—for example, if the leaf is too heavy—but while within the whirlwind the leaf responds in accordance with the pattern of resultant forces. Similarly, when a person is within the bounds of a behavior setting, he behaves in accordance with the resultants of its ongoing pattern of forces (their strength and direction) and his own properties (dispositions, skills, intentions). These may lead to his separation from the setting; but while he is within it the person behaves according to the resultant pattern of forces. This is the thesis of behavior setting theory.

The theory deals with only a few differences in the towns' habitats and in the behavior of their inhabitants; most of the findings have to stand as observed differences, without explanation. Even in the case of habitat differences that have understandable and predictable consequences for behavior, the question remains as to their sources: Is Midwest's smaller population, relative to its habitat and habitat-claims, an accident of history? Is this difference imposed by outside authorities? Is it an expression of the inhabitants' different personalities? We cannot follow the chains of causation beyond the restricted scope of our observations.

Observed Associations Between Behavior and Behavior Settings

We begin with the observation mentioned earlier, in Chapter 2, that particular types of behavior settings and particular kinds of behavior are commonly associated. For instance, in Midwest bowling occurs in Bowling Games, not in Worship Services; in Yoredale prescriptions are filled in Chemists' Shops, not in Betting Offices. These are analogous to the observation that indigenous redwood trees grow in redwood forests, not in palm groves; or that geese migrate in skeins of geese, not in flocks of blackbirds. Although some of these statements are verbal tautologies, they all refer to phenomena that pose difficult problems: Why is there no bowling in Worship Services (many bowlers attend Worship Services)? Why are prescriptions not filled in Betting Shops (some bettors need medicines)?

Obviously the answers involve many variables. The absence of redwoods from palm groves is undoubtedly connected with such phenomena as the ecosystems of redwood forests and palm groves: the reproduction, nutrition, and respiration of redwoods and palms, the physical state and chemistry of the soils of the areas, and the vegetative history of the regions. Similarly, to account for the occurrence of bowling in Bowling Games and its absence in Worship Services requires an understanding of such varied phenomena as the programs of Bowling Games and Worship Services, the interests and abilities of the inhabitants, the milieux of the settings (space, design, behavior objects), and the technological and cultural histories of the communities. Broad categories of knowledge such as these are certainly involved, and we have considerable understanding of some of them, but at the present time we can do little more than speculate about the nature and operation of many of the variables.

Nonetheless, the empirical association between types (genotypes) of behavior settings and kinds of behavior means that one can predict from a town's habitat, as indicated by the properties of its genotypes, the kinds of behavior that occur within it. The fact that there is the genotype Chiropractors' Offices in Midwest, and not in Yoredale, means that the behavior "getting a spinal adjustment" occurs in Midwest and does not occur in Yoredale; and we can predict that the inhabitants of Yoredale, via its genotype Cricket Games, engage in the behavior "attending cricket games," and that this behavior does not occur in Midwest, which does not have this genotype.

The association between behavior setting genotypes and kinds of behavior means, too, that the amount of habitat variety, as measured by number of behavior setting genotypes, is positively related to the amount of behavior diversity. The inhabitants of a town which contains a relatively large number of genotypes exhibit a greater diversity of behavior than do the inhabitants of a town with a relatively small number of genotypes. Analogously, a biogeographical region with many types of local environment (such as the Grand Canyon) has more diverse life forms than does a region with few types of local environment (such as the high prairies of western Kansas). The associations between genotypes and behavior are observed associations, not derived relationships. We shall now consider some associations between habitat and behavior that are of a different kind; the behavior in these cases is derived from (and explained by) the habitats.

Behavior Differences Based on
Habitat Differences

In considering the consequences for the behavior of the inhabitants of Midwest and Yoredale of certain differences in the habitats of the towns, we have the important advantage, emphasized in Chapter 2, that all the behavior·settings that constitute the habitats of Midwest and Yoredale have the same defining attributes. In this respect they are like protoplasmic cells, internal combustion engines, or gyroscopes; and the consequences of specified differences between cells, engines, scopes, or behavior settings can be considered without each time demonstrating the basic equivalence of the units compared.

We emphasize in the beginning that the behavior consequences we consider do not occur because the habitat differences involve psychological phenomena. The consequences occur because human components and their behavior are essential elements of the program and maintenance systems of the settings that constitute the towns' habitats, and these systems differ in Midwest and Yoredale; the inhabitants of Midwest and Yoredale, therefore, inevitably display any differences that are built into the habitats *of which they are components.* Some of these differences can be derived from the habitat differences via behavior setting theory. The terms *behavior settings* and, collectively, *habitat,* refer to an entire system; people-and-their-behavior constitute the human part of this system. We derive a part of the system—behaving people—from aspects of the whole system, as an engineer accounts for sparking sparkplugs from aspects of the overall engine design.

DERIVATIONS FROM PROGRAM AND MAINTENANCE CIRCUITS

The basic idea of behavior setting theory is that the inhabitants of behavior settings are one class of components, among other classes (nonhuman behavior objects), that make up the internal media of behavior settings. The number of available inhabitants of a behavior setting, relative to the optimal number, affects its operation—including, via sensors and feedback circuits, the strengths and directions of the forces acting upon its human components. One critical relationship is between number of inhabitants and the strength and range of directions of the forces acting upon them; *forces upon a town's inhabitants toward participation in the program and maintenance circuits of its behavior settings vary in mean strength per inhabitant, and in mean range of direction per inhabitant, inversely with the number of available inhabitants.* This relation holds when the number of inhabitants varies between the minimum number required to operate and maintain the setting at its lowest operating level and the optimal number required to operate and maintain it at its most effective level. To the degree therefore that Midwest and Yoredale differ within these limits in number of human components, there are predictable differences for their inhabitants.

Behavior settings are neutral with respect to the psychological processes by which their human components comply with their operating programs and their maintenance systems. In fact, if the habitats of Midwest and Yoredale were completely mechanized so that all program and maintenance actions were performed by machines, the machines would exhibit the same differences as the human components.

The processes by which the control mechanisms of behavior settings regulate forces upon their human components are various; there is a diversity of sensors and executive machinery by which behavior settings activate many of the psychological mechanisms of their human components. Internally, behavior settings are richly connected entities. While we shall not present here the operations of the behavior setting control mechanisms, so far as they are known, we shall present a paradigm that predicts and explicates the behavioral consequences of certain habitat differences after the control mechanisms have operated in accordance with the relation stated above.

The data have shown that Midwest has fewer inhabitants to provide human components for its behavior settings than Yoredale, that it has fewer per centiurb of habitat and fewer per habitat-claim for operatives (T3.4; R1, 2, 3; C1 to 4). The paradigm, presented in the chart in Figure 7.1, is stated in terms of differences between Midwest and Yoredale in human components per habitat-claim. The chart may be narrated as follows (the items of the paradigm to which the statements refer are designated in the parentheses):

Midwest's habitat, *in comparison with Yoredale's habitat*, has fewer human components per habitat-claim for operatives. Under these conditions, if the number of available human components is not fully adequate in both towns, the control units of Midwest's behavior settings generate more program forces per human component (forces upon inhabitants of all penetration zones of behavior settings toward implementing habitat-claims for operatives within (*a*) program circuits) in a greater range of directions (a_1), and more regular maintenance forces per human component (forces upon inhabitants of all penetration zones of behavior settings toward implementing habitat-claims for operatives within (b) maintenance circuits) in a greater range of directions (b_1). In spite of these compensatory adjustments, Midwest's behavior settings operate less effectively and with smaller margins of adequacy as habitats (a_2, b_2). They are in this respect, relative to Yoredale, like engines with fewer back-up circuits and spare parts. This results in more frequent and serious habitat deficiencies in Midwest (a_3, b_3), which instigate more, stronger, and more varied emergency maintenance forces (b_4). Because of observed habitat differences (b) and inferred differences (b_4), there are more frequent deviation-countering and less frequent vetoing maintenance forces in Midwest—that is, more centripetal forces (b_5); and because of differences (b_4, b_5), there are more induced maintenance forces—that is, more forces initiated by other human components (b_6). In the paradigm, the observed habitat differences (a and b) are structural differences, and according to the theory they generate dynamic and functional habitat differences (a_1 to a_3 and b_1 to b_6).

The dynamic habitat differences between the towns produce certain behavior differences in their human components. In the following statements, the action differences are listed and the habitat sources, as represented in Figure 7.1, are identified in the parentheses. Midwest's human components, in comparison with Yoredale's, exhibit on the average: (1) more, more vigorous, and more varied actions as program operatives (a_1); (2) more, more vigorous, and more varied actions as regular maintenance operatives (b_1); (3) more, more vigorous, and more varied actions as emergency maintenance operatives (b_4); (4) more deviation-countering and fewer vetoing actions—that is, more centripetal actions (b_5); and (5) more induced actions (b_6). These are the primary, predicted differences in behavior generated by the towns' habitats. They have, in turn, secondary consequences within the context of behavior settings; these are numbered 6 to 9 below.

Midwest's human habitat components (its inhabitants), in comparison with Yoredale's, exhibit on the average these behavior differences within the towns' program and maintenance circuits:

6. *Midwesterners are more frequently involved in difficult actions.* Inhabitants of both towns engage in actions that vary in difficulty, where difficulty is defined in terms of human abilities. The more difficult actions are those nearer the top of the inhabitants' ability ranges. The greater number of more vigorous and more varied actions by Midwesterners (primary action differences 1 to 3) overcome greater ability difficulties, so that Midwesterners more frequently function near the top of their abilities than Dalesmen.

7. *Midwesterners are more frequently involved in important actions.* The inhabitants of both towns engage in actions that vary in importance, where importance is defined as amount of impairment suffered by a set-

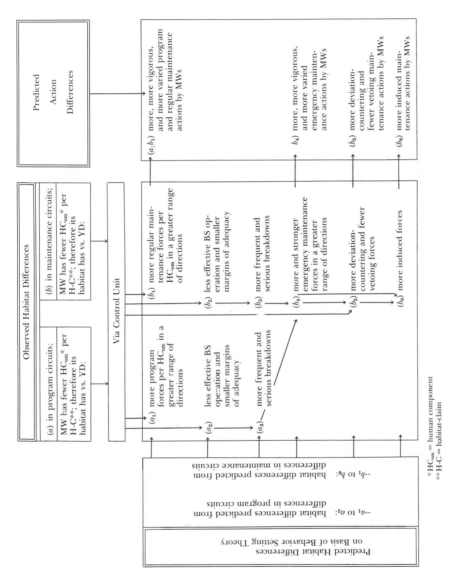

FIGURE 7.1. Paradigm of Behavior Setting Theory of Program and Maintenance Circuits as Applied to Midwest and Yoredale

ting when an inhabitant is inadequate or absent. The more important actions within a behavior setting occur in regions that are surrounded by ever stronger barriers to access. For example, whereas almost anyone can engage in window shopping—a relatively unimportant action to the functioning of a store—to act as a customer, a more important action, requires crossing more barriers (opening door, paying money); and to act as an employee, still more important to the functioning of the setting, requires crossing a still more resistant barrier (getting hired). Similarly there are more barriers to becoming Honorary Secretary of Yoredale's Bowling Club Meeting than to becoming a spectator or a member. The stronger and more varied program and maintenance actions of Midwesterners (primary action differences 1 to 3) overcome more of the barriers surrounding important action regions, so that Midwesterners more frequently enter these regions than Dalesmen.

8. *Midwesterners are engaged in a wider range of activities.* The inhabitants of both towns engage in a range of actions within particular behavior settings, and in actions within a variety of settings, but the greater number of more varied and vigorous actions by Midwesterners (primary action differences 1 to 3) extends their range within and among settings. For example, the proprietor of a store with a number of employees will on occasion serve customers, order supplies, balance the books. But the proprietor of a one-man or a two-man store, one with fewer human components per habitat-claim—of which there are more in Midwest—will regularly engage in these varied actions, and in addition he will have to sweep the floor and stock the shelves. Similarly, outside his store the Midwest proprietor will receive urgent invitations (pressures) from the settings of a number of organizations struggling for viability—the Chamber of Commerce, the Rotary Club, the Lions Club —whereas the Yoredale proprietor shares with a greater number of other proprietors less urgent invitations from about the same number of more stable settings. The Yoredale proprietor is the recipient of fewer and weaker invitations, and consequently he engages in behavior in fewer and less varied vocational and nonvocational settings.

9. *Midwesterners are more frequently involved in the operating zones of behavior settings.* Quantitative output differences 6, 7, and 8 result in an important qualitative difference: Midwesterners engage in more claim-operations in more settings, they carry more responsibilities than Dalesmen. Obstacles to entering central zones 4, 5, and 6 of both towns (the operating zones of officers, speakers, teachers, clerks, and so forth) are greater than obstacles to entering peripheral zones 1, 2, and 3 (the utility zones of visitors, customers, members), and it requires greater ability to function as an operative than as a member. The greater mean number of more vigorous actions by Midwesterners (primary action differences 1 to 3) impel them more frequently into operating zones of the town's settings where they are responsible functionaries and joint and single leaders.

PROBABLE PSYCHOLOGICAL CONSEQUENCES OF DIFFERENCES
IN PROGRAM AND MAINTENANCE CIRCUITS

We have emphasized that the nine primary and secondary differences in the actions of the towns' inhabitants have been derived from differences in the towns' habitats and do not identify the psychological phenomena involved. However, there are some highly *probable* psychological accompaniments of the predicted action differences. These are not derivations from behavior setting theory; they are based on common observations and empirical studies. In comparison with Dalesmen, Midwesterners, on the average, exhibit these differences:

10. *Midwesterners are less sensitive to, and less evaluative of, individual differences.* As a consequence, they are more tolerant of themselves and their associates, they have lower standards of adequate performance and lower tests for admission for behavior setting operatives.

11. *Midwesterners see themselves as having greater functional importance, as being more important people.* They more easily aspire to important and powerful positions. The inverse, which holds for Dalesmen vs. Midwesterners, deserves special emphasis: More of the able inhabitants of Yoredale have little functional importance within the town; they are unimportant to the continuance of the town as a human habitat, and so see themselves.

12. *Midwesterners are burdened with greater responsibilities.* More behavior settings and more people are dependent upon them.

13. *Midwesterners identify themselves and others more often in terms of the functions they perform and less often in terms of their personality attributes.*

14. *Midwesterners experience greater insecurity.* They are marginally adequate behavior setting operatives; both success and failure are more frequent.

15. *Midwesterners are more versatile, and so regard themselves.* They see themselves as able to carry out satisfactorily a greater variety of tasks.

16. *Midwesterners work harder in the public areas of the town.* They believe this to be necessary and good.

The objection may be made that some of the behavior differences derived from the habitat differences on the bases of the theory are so closely connected with the habitat differences that there is little increase in understanding. If there are three men in a setting who lift a weight, they "lift more" per man, on the average, than if there are four men in the setting who lift the weight. Is this more than physics? This criticism does not apply to most of the derivations; and where it does apply, it identifies an old problem in a new context — namely, how to deal simultaneously with two realms of phenomena, the physical and the psychological. This is the old problem of psychophysics in a new guise.

DERIVATIONS FROM GOAL SYSTEMS

According to the theory we have just presented, the behavior settings that constitute the habitat of a town "need" human components for their operation and maintenance as habitat units, and they have dynamic control mechanisms by which they incorporate the appropriate human components into their maintenance and program circuits. But this, of course, is not the only reason people inhabit behavior settings. Within penetration zones 1, 2, and 3, primarily, behavior settings provide goals that people "need" for their operation and maintenance as psychological units, and people have dynamic mechanisms (molar actions) by which they incorporate themselves into the goal circuits of behavior settings. In Figure 7.2 we present a paradigm of the goal systems of the towns which may be narrated as follows (with relevant paradigm items in the parentheses):

We assume that, en masse, the inhabitants of Midwest and Yoredale are equivalent with respect to their needs (w) and abilities (x), and that the habitats of the towns are equal with respect to the goals they provide (y). In consequence, the inhabitants of the towns have, on the average, equal motivation to behavior via equal skills with reference to equally attractive goals. And we observe that Midwest has fewer inhabitants than Yoredale to achieve satisfactions within the goal circuits of the town's behavior settings, fewer per centiurb of habitat (z). These attributes of the towns' inhabitants and goal systems have consequences for behavior output; we list them, like the other predictions from the theory, with the relevant attributes in parentheses.

17. *Mean behavior output per inhabitant within the goal systems* of the towns' behavior settings is equal in Midwest and Yoredale (w, x, y).

18. *Mean amount of behavior per centiurb of habitat within the goal circuits of the towns' behavior settings is smaller in Midwest than* in Yoredale (w, x, y, z).

As an illustration of consequences 17 and 18: If love of marching bands is equally distributed among Midwesterners and Dalesmen (w), if the towns' inhabitants are equally able to get out to see the parade (x), and if equally attractive bands parade the same number of times in the towns (y), then Midwesterners and Dalesmen will spend equal mean amounts of time as spectators of marching bands, and in 1963–64 this will produce fewer person-hours of spectator behavior in Midwest than in Yoredale (830/1310 equals 63 percent as many).

The question arises whether Midwest's fewer inhabitants do not have the possibility of getting a larger fair share of the town's limited resources. If, for example, half the inhabitants of the towns love marching bands and the standing space along the line of the march of the parade were equal in the towns, but less than the optimal amount for Yoredale's 655 spectators, Midwest's 415 spectators would have more spectator space than Yoredale spectators; behavioral consequences of crowding would appear in Yoredale but not in Midwest. In fact, how-

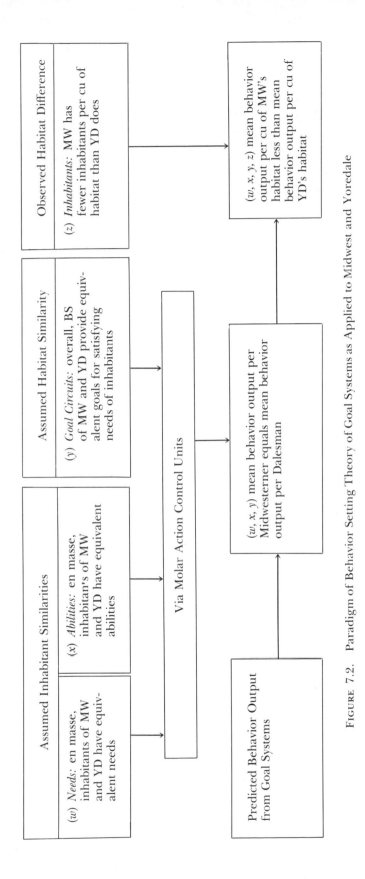

FIGURE 7.2. Paradigm of Behavior Setting Theory of Goal Systems as Applied to Midwest and Yoredale

ever, limited resources are not frequent in either town; most behavior settings of both towns can accommodate all potential inhabitants. There is one clear exception. Resources for engaging in the actions of operatives are limited in both towns by the programs of their behavior settings. Inhabitants are not free to enter behavior settings as operatives as they enter most settings as customers, audience members, and so forth. To the degree, therefore, that becoming an operative—such as a club secretary or a teacher—has goal properties for inhabitants, the inhabitants of Midwest have greater opportunities to become leaders and functionaries, to be people of power and importance, than Yoredale's inhabitants, but there is no crowding of the goal circuits of either town.

　　We shall consider some of these derivations further in Chapter 8, where predictions are checked against data. It must be emphasized, however, that we do not have data that are relevant to all derivations from the theory, and that the theory bears upon only a few of the findings of the study.

PART III

In this part we report the amounts of behavior that occur within the total habitats of the towns and also within their qualitatively different habitats, such as aesthetic or neutral-to-children habitats. The behavior outputs are reported for all inhabitants of the towns and for various subclasses of inhabitants. These data are analogous to those for the biomass produced by total prairie regions; by their qualitatively different parts, such as alkaline and permeable areas; and by different varieties of vegetation.

The data refer on the one hand to habitat phenomena—the behavior the towns induce in their human components—and on the other hand to psychological phenomena—the behavior the inhabitants of the towns transact in relation to the towns as habitats. Both views are legitimate within the theoretical frame of the research—namely, that behavior stands between the nonpsychological environment and the psychological person. Our language reflects this duality; in fact, we use two languages. In one we speak of the behavior the towns generate via their human components, in the other of the behavior the inhabitants carry out via the towns as habitats.

We favor the first language, where classes of behavior settings are the subjects and classes of human components are the objects of transitive verbs; thus sentences take the form "The towns' worship services produce hymn singing by the inhabitants." We favor this language because the habitat is the focus of our

BEHAVIOR OUTPUT OF
MIDWEST AND YOREDALE

꧁꧂꧁꧂꧁꧂꧁꧂꧁꧂꧁꧂꧁꧂꧁꧂꧁꧂꧁꧂꧁꧂꧁꧂

research, and also because it appears to us that the behavioral sciences have been dominated, and limited, by the second language, where classes of persons *are the subjects and classes of* behavior settings *are the objects of transitive verbs, and sentences take the form "People sing hymns in worship services."*

CHAPTER

Behavior Output of the Towns' Total Habitats

I n this chapter we present the behavior outputs of the towns' total habitats; outputs within differential habitats are reported in Chapters 9 and 10, and those via population subgroups are presented in Chapters 11 and 12.

We report five measures of behavior output: *person-hours* (P-H), *inhabitant-setting intersections* (ISI), *claim-operations* (C-O), *leader acts* (LA), and *leaders* (L). Of these, P-H is the most comprehensive; this measure includes the outputs of the goal circuits, the program circuits, and the maintenance circuits of the behavior settings comprising a designated habitat: it measures the habitat's total behavior product. The first four measures are reported for two classes of inhabitants: *all inhabitants* (both regular town residents, and visitors and commuters) and *town inhabitants* only. The single measure leaders (L) is reported for *town inhabitants* only. The resulting nine sets of data, and the terms and abbreviations identifying them, are: (*a*) *gross behavior product* (GBP), person-hours of behavior via all inhabitants; (*b*) *town behavior product* (TBP), person-hours of behavior via town inhabitants only; (*c*) *gross inhabitant-setting intersections* (GISI), number of inhabitant-setting intersections via all inhabitants; (*d*) *town inhabitant-setting intersections* (TISI), number of inhabitant-setting intersections via town inhabitants; (*e*) *gross claim-operations* (GC-O), claim-operations via all inhabitants; (*f*) *town claim-operations* (TC-O), claim-operations via town inhabitants only; (*g*) *gross leader acts* (GLA), leader acts via all inhabitants; (*h*) *town leader acts* (TLA), leader acts via town inhabitants; (*i*) *town leaders* (TL), town inhabitants who lead one or more settings.

The measures that are available for the two towns in different years are reported in Table 8.1; it will be noted that the data for 1963–64 are most extensive. It was stated earlier (Chapter 2) that the populations of the towns provide the best data regarding the relative numbers of inhabitants available for their public settings (inhabitants of penetration zone 0). For this reason, the towns' populations provide the best bases for the comparative study of the involvement of inhabitants in the towns' public habitats; therefore, although all data are reported in the tables, the discussions focus on the most adequate data, those for town inhabitants in 1963–64.

Narrative reports of differences and changes in output are made in both habitat language and psychological language. Two conventions are used: (1) In the habitat statements, differences and changes are reported in terms of quantitative data, and each finding is designated by a letter symbol: "Midwest produced (*d*) 125 percent as many P-H per inhabitant as Yoredale." This is repeated in psychological language, with corresponding habitat statement and data identified by letter symbol: "Midwesterners, on the average, engaged in appreciably more behavior in public habitat areas than Dalesmen (*d*)." (2) In the psychological narrative, the quantitative differences are transformed into verbal descriptions by the following adjectives for the designated (MW/YD)100 ratios: 99–101, equal, about the same; 97–98 and 102–103 slight, few; 94–96 and 104–106 somewhat; 85–93 and 107–115, more, less; 61–84 and 116–139, appreciable; and under 61 and over 139, much, great, many.

Person-Hours of Behavior

SALIENT FINDINGS

Midwest's total behavior output is smaller than Yoredale's; it is smaller per centiurb of habitat, but greater per town inhabitant. Midwest's output was greater in 1963–64 than in 1954–55, whereas Yoredale's was less.

PERSON-HOURS OF BEHAVIOR GENERATED BY TOTAL HABITAT

Midwest's GBP in 1963–64 was approximately equal to the behavior generated by 7 games of baseball with 60,000 spectators, players, and officials per game; Yoredale's GBP was about equivalent to the behavior output of 8 games of soccer with 100,000 fans and functionaries per game (T8.2; R1; C3, 4). Mean output per day in Midwest was 5125 P-H, approximately the amount of behavior generated by a single person in the waking hours of 10.5 months, or by a lunch-hour parade of 5000 persons. Yoredale's mean daily output of 7174 P-H was approximately equivalent to that generated in 14.8 months by a single person, or by a two-hour public rally of 3500 people.

Table 8.1
Available Measures of Behavior Outputs

| | 1954–55 | | 1963–64 | | 1967–68 | |
Measure	MW	YD	MW	YD	MW	YD
Gross Behavior Product (GBP)			X	X		
Town Behavior Product (TBP)	X	X	X	X		
Gross Inhabitant-Setting Intersections (GISI)			X	X		
Town Inhabitant-Setting Intersections (TISI)			X	X		
Gross Claim-Operations (GC-O)	X	X	X	X		
Town Claim-Operations (TC-O)	X	X	X	X		
Gross Claim-Leader Actions (GLA)			X	X		
Town Claim-Leader Actions (TLA)			X	X		
Town Leaders (TL)			X	X	X	X

More than half of the towns' GBPs are generated via town inhabitants. Midwest produces 1.1 million P-H via its 830 inhabitants, amounting to 60 percent of its GBP; Yoredale produces 1.4 million P-H via its 1310 inhabitants, amounting to 54 percent of its GBP (T8.2; R3; C3, 4). For Midwesterners this TBP amounts to 3 hours 44 minutes (224 minutes) per day, and for Dalesmen it amounts to 2 hours 58 minutes (178 minutes) per day (T8.2; R6; C3, 4). On the basis of a 16-hour waking day, Midwesterners spend 23 percent and Dalesmen 19 percent of their time in the public regions of the towns. If the town inhabitants who are prevented by incapacity from entering public habitats (estimated at 10 percent) are eliminated from the calculations, mean occupancy approaches one-quarter of the waking days of Midwesterners and one-fifth of the waking days of Dalesmen.

Differences. Midwest produces less behavior than Yoredale. In 1963–64 it produced, via town inhabitants, (a) 300,981 fewer P-H than Yoredale (T8.2; R3; C4-3), amounting to (b) 79 percent as much (T8.2; R3; C3/4) and to (c) 83 percent as much per cu of habitat (T8.2; R5; C3/4), but to (d) 125 percent as much per inhabitant (T8.2; R6; C3/4). Involved in Midwest's smaller TBP were these habitat differences: (e) fewer cu, 95 percent as many (T3.1; R1; C3/4); (f) less variety, 93 percent as varied (T4.1; R1; C3/4); (g) fewer town inhabitants, 63 percent as many (T3.4; R1; C3/4); and (h) fewer town inhabitants per cu of habitat, 67 percent as many (T3.4; R2; C3/4).

In psychological terms, these findings indicate that, *on the average,* Midwesterners *in comparison with Dalesmen* engaged in appreciably more behavior in public habitat areas (d), within settings where there was appreciably less behavior by fellow townsmen (c); they did this within a town where there was appreciably less behavior in its public regions (a, b), with somewhat fewer (e) and less diverse (f) resources for molar actions, and with appreciably fewer town inhabitants to take advantage of the opportunities and the duties the habitat provided (g, h).

The data for town inhabitants in 1954–55 (T8.2; R3, 6; C1/2) and for all inhabitants in 1963–64 (T8.2; R1, 2; C3/4) agree that Mid-

Table 8.2
Person-Hours of Behavior

	1954–55		1963–64	
	MW (1)	YD (2)	MW (3)	YD (4)
(1) Output via all inhabitants (GBP)			1,880,732	2,625,816
(2) Mean per cu of habitat			17,517	23,272
(3) Output via town inhabitants (TBP)	929,861	1,506,739	1,125,134	1,426,115
(4) Percent of GBP			60%	54%
(5) Mean per cu of habitat	10,351	16,742	10,479	12,640
(6) Mean per town inhabitant	1,300	1,159	1,356	1,089

west's total output of P-H and its output per centiurb were smaller than Yoredale's, but that its output per town inhabitant was greater.

Changes. Midwest produced more behavior in 1963–64 than in 1954–55. It produced, via town inhabitants, (*a*) 195,273 more P-H in 1963–64 (T8.2; R3; C3-1), amounting to (*b*) 121 percent as much (T8.2; R3; C3/1), to (*c*) 102 percent as much per cu of habitat (T8.2; R5; C3/1), and to (*d*) 104 percent as much per inhabitant (T8.2; R6; C3/1). Involved in Midwest's greater TBP in 1963–64 were these habitat differences: (*e*) a larger habitat, 119 percent as extensive (T3.1; R1; C3/1); (*f*) a more varied habitat, 116 percent as varied (T4.1; R1; C3/1); (*g*) more town inhabitants, 116 percent as many (T3.4; R1; C3/1); but (*h*) fewer inhabitants per cu, 98 percent as many (T3.4; R2; C3/1).

In psychological language, these findings indicate that, *on the average,* Midwesterners in 1963–64 *in comparison with 1954–55* engaged in somewhat more behavior in the town's public areas (*d*), within settings where there was slightly more behavior by Midwesterners (*c*); they did this in 1963–64 within a town where there was appreciably more behavior in its public regions (*a, b*), with appreciably more extensive (*e*) and diverse (*f*) resources for molar actions and appreciably more town inhabitants (*g*), but slightly fewer inhabitants in relation to the opportunities and duties the habitat provided (*h*).

Yoredale produced less behavior in 1963–64 than in 1954–55. It produced, via town inhabitants, (*a*) 80,625 fewer P-H in 1963–64 (T8.2; R3; C4-2), amounting to (*b*) 95 percent as much (T8.2; R3; C4/2), to (*c*) 75 percent as much per cu of habitat (T8.2; R5; C4/2), and to (*d*) 94 percent as much per inhabitant (T8.2; R6; C4/2). Involved in Yoredale's smaller TBP in 1963–64 were these habitat differences: (*e*) a larger habitat, 126 percent as extensive (T3.1; R1; C4/2); (*f*) a more varied habitat, 127 percent as varied (T3.1; R1; C4/2); (*g*) the same number of town inhabitants, 101 percent as many (T3.4; R1; C4/2); and (*h*) fewer inhabitants per cu, 81 percent as many (T3.4; R2; C4/2).

In psychological language, these findings indicate that, *on the average,* Yoredale's inhabitants in 1963–64 *in comparison with 1954–55* engaged in somewhat less behavior in the town's public areas (*d*), within settings where there was appreciably less behavior by Dalesmen (*c*); they did this in 1963–64 within a town where there was somewhat less activity in its public regions (*a, b*) with appreciably more extensive (*e*) and varied (*f*) resources for molar action and almost the same number of town inhabitants (*g*), but appreciably fewer in relation to the opportunities and duties the habitat provided (*h*).

Inhabitant-Setting Intersections

Number of inhabitant-setting intersections (ISI) is a less precise measure of total behavior output than P-H. It includes the outputs of goal, program, and maintenance circuits, but does not weight the intersection for hours of duration as P-H does: it is a simple enumeration of inhabitant-setting contacts. An ISI consists of a unique combination of *a particular behavior setting* in any of its occurrences and *a specific human component* in any penetration zone of the setting during one or more of its occurrences. If Jane White attends the Midwest Presbyterian Worship Service once during 1963–64, this is one ISI; if she attends the Methodist Church Worship Service thirty times during the year, this is also one ISI. The ISI of a behavior setting is the number of different persons who inhabit it during a year. For a town or part of a town the number of ISI is the sum of the ISI of all its behavior settings; it is equivalent, for example, to the number of class enrollments in a school. ISI and P-H are independently determined measures of the same phenomena, but they differ in precision. Intersection data are available for 1963–64 only.

SALIENT FINDINGS

Midwest's total output of ISI is smaller than Yoredale's; it is smaller per centiurb of habitat, but greater per town inhabitant.

INHABITANT-SETTING INTERSECTIONS GENERATED BY TOTAL HABITAT

Midwest's total ISI in 1963–64 by both town and out-of-town inhabitants were equivalent to 884 behavior settings (for instance, Election Polling Places) with a mean of 147 nonrepeating and nonduplicating inhabitants (in this case, voters) per setting; Yoredale's were equiv-

Table 8.3
Inhabitant-Setting Intersections

		1963–64	
		MW (1)	YD (2)
(1)	Output via all inhabitants (GISI)	130,080	238,619
(2)	Mean per cu of habitat	1,211	2,115
(3)	Output via town inhabitants (TISI)	50,809	76,592
(4)	Percent of GISI	39%	32%
(5)	Mean per cu of habitat	473	679
(6)	Mean per town inhabitant	61.2	58.5

alent to 758 settings with a mean of 302 inhabitants (T8.3; R1; C1, 2). Less than half the towns' total ISI were generated via town inhabitants (T8.3; R4; C1, 2).

If every Midwest inhabitant were to have entered every Midwest behavior setting at least once in 1963–64, there would have been 723,720 ISI via town inhabitants (number of behavior settings times number of town inhabitants); in fact, there were 50,809, amounting to 7 percent of the possible number. In Yoredale there were 992,980 potential ISI by town inhabitants; there were actually 76,592, amounting to 7.7 percent of the possible number (T8.3; R3; C1, 2). The mean number of settings that town inhabitants entered to form ISI was 61.2 (MW) and 58.5 (YD) (T8.3; R3; C1,2/T3.4; R1; C3,4); the mean number of hours of habitation per ISI was, for all inhabitants, 14.5 (MW) and 11.0 (YD) (T8.2; R1; C3,4/T8.3; R1; C1.2), and for town inhabitants it was 22.1 (MW) and 18.7 (YD) (T8.2; R3; C3,4/T8.3; R3; C1,2).

Differences. Midwest produces fewer ISI than Yoredale. In 1963–64 it produced, via town inhabitants: (*a*) 25,783 fewer ISI than Yoredale (T8.3; R3; C2-1), amounting to (*b*) 66 percent as many (T8.3; R3; C1/2), to (*c*) 70 percent as many per cu of habitat (T8.3; R5; C1/2), and to (*d*) 104 percent as many per inhabitant (T8.3; R6; C1/3).

In psychological language, these findings indicate that, *on the average,* Midwesterners *in comparison with Dalesmen* inhabited somewhat more public settings (*d*) with appreciably fewer fellow townsmen (*c*); they did this within a town where there were appreciably fewer contacts between the town's inhabitants and its behavior settings (*a, b*).

Midwest's output of ISI via all inhabitants was also less than Yoredale's, 55 percent as great (T8.3; R1; C1/2).

The ISI data verify the P-H data regarding the directions of all differences in the behavior outputs of the towns: both sets of data indicate that Midwest is inferior to Yoredale in total output and in output per centiurb, but superior in output per inhabitant. Midwest's inferiority to Yoredale in total output and in output per centiurb is greater, and its superiority in output per inhabitant is less, by ISI measures than by P-H measures. These differences occur because Midwesterners spend more time in the settings they intersect, 119 percent as many hours per ISI in the case of town inhabitants and 131 percent as many in the case of all inhabitants (T8.3; R3; C1/T8.2; R3; C3)/(T8.3; R3; C2/T8.2; R3; C4). On the average, Midwesterners enter more settings than Dalesmen (4 per cent more) and they stay longer (19 percent longer).

Claim-Operations

Number of claim-operations (C-O) is a measure of the essential operations required of a town's human components in the process of keeping its habitat habitable. In psychological language, it is a measure of the important and difficult actions, the responsibilities, a town's inhabitants perform in operating and maintaining the town as a human habitat.

SALIENT FINDINGS

Midwest's total output of C-O is greater than Yoredale's; it is greater per centiurb of habitat, and greater per town inhabitant. C-O increased in both towns between the survey years.

CLAIM-OPERATIONS GENERATED BY TOTAL HABITAT

The total number of C-O involved in the operation and maintenance of the public habitats of Midwest and Yoredale may be comprehended in some degree by imagining a social custom that limits a person to a single "tour of duty" (one C-O) during a year. By this custom, if Midwest inhabitant Walter Jones preaches at one or more occurrences of the behavior setting Presbyterian Worship Service, he cannot also preside at any club meeting, officiate at any game, or operate a stall at any school carnival: he cannot implement a habitat-claim for operatives in any other behavior setting. Such a single-tour-of-duty system would require 14,249 persons to implement the programs and maintain the milieu of the behavior settings that constituted Midwest's habitat in 1963–64; Yoredale's would require an implementing staff of 11,704 (T8.4; R1; C3,4). Under this system, the 830 Midwesterners could carry out 6 percent of their town's essential operational and maintenance tasks, and the 1310 Dalesmen could carry out 11 percent of them.

In fact, however, Midwesterners carried out 47 percent, and Dalesmen 36 percent, of their towns' C-O (T8.4; R4; C3,4). On the average, each of Midwest's inhabitants undertook responsibilities in 8 behavior settings directed toward the continuance of the town as a habitat (as teacher, secretary, choir member, umpire, and so forth), and each of Yoredale's inhabitants assumed similar responsibilities in 3.2 settings (T8.4; R6; C3,4). And it must be remembered that the behavior settings, and hence the tasks, may occur only once or they may recur on a number of days: teaching (by a substitute teacher) may occur in the Yoredale setting County Primary School Infants Academic Class on one or a few of the setting's occurrences, or it may occur (by the regular teacher) on 180 days; football umpiring may occur on one to 35 days; adjudicating musicianship may occur on one to three days.

Differences. Midwest generates more C-O than Yoredale. In 1963–64 it generated, via town inhabitants: (*a*) 2440 more TC-O than Yoredale (T8.4; R3; C3-4), amounting to (*b*) 158 percent as many (T8.4; R3; C3/4), to (*c*) 167 percent as many per cu (T8.4; R5; C3/4), to (*d*) 250 percent as many per inhabitant (T8.4; R6; C3/4), and to (*e*) a greater percentage of its ISI, greater by a factor of 2.4 (T8.4; R7; C3/4). Involved in Midwest's greater output of TC-O were these habitat differences: (*f*) more claims for operatives, 132 percent as many (T3.3; R1; C3/4); (*g*) fewer town inhabitants per cu, 67 percent as many (T3.4;

Table 8.4
Claim-Operations

		1954–55		1963–64	
		MW (1)	YD (2)	MW (3)	YD (4)
(1)	Output via all inhabitants (GC-O)	7,936	6,453	14,249	11,704
(2)	Mean per cu of habitat	88	72	133	104
(3)	Output via town inhabitants (TC-O)	4,173	3,055	6,642	4,202
(4)	Percent of GC-O	53%	47%	47%	36%
(5)	Mean per cu of habitat	46	34	62	37
(6)	Mean per town inhabitant	5.8	2.3	8.0	3.2
(7)	Percent of TISI			13.1%	5.5%

R2; C3/4); and (*h*) fewer town inhabitants per claim, 47 percent as many (T3.4; R3; C3/4).

In psychological language, these findings indicate that, *on the average,* Midwesterners *in comparison with Dalesmen* carried out many more responsible tasks, they worked harder (*d*) within settings where there was much more responsible activity by fellow townsmen (*c*); they did this within a town where there was much more responsible behavior by town inhabitants (*a, b, e*), an appreciably larger number of important and difficult tasks (*f*), appreciably fewer town inhabitants per setting to help carry them out (*g*), and many fewer inhabitants per task (*h*).

The data for town inhabitants in 1954–55 (T8.4; R3; C1/2) and for all inhabitants in both survey years (T8.4; R1; C1/2, 3/4), agree that Midwest's output of C-O was greater than Yoredale's.

Changes. Both towns produced more C-O in 1963–64. Midwest produced, via town inhabitants, (*a*) 2469 more TC-O than in 1954–55 (T8.4; R3; C3-1), amounting to (*b*) 159 percent as many (T8.4; R3; C3/1), (*c*) to 135 percent as many per cu of habitat (T8.4; R5; C3/1), and (*d*) to 138 percent as many per inhabitant (T8.4; R6; C3/1). Involved in Midwest's greater output of TC-O in 1963–64 were these habitat differences: (*e*) more habitat-claims for operatives, 191 percent as many (T3.3; R1; C3/1); (*f*) fewer town inhabitants per cu 98 percent as many (T3.4; R2; C3/1); and (*g*) fewer town inhabitants per habitat-claim for operatives, 61 percent as many (T3.4; R3; C3/1).

Yoredale produced, via town inhabitants: (*a*) 1147 more TC-O in 1963–64 than in 1954–55 (T8.4; R3; C4-2), amounting to (*b*) 137 percent as many (T8.4; R5; C4/2), to (*c*) 116 percent as many per cu of habitat (T8.4; R5; C4/2), and to (*d*) 139 percent as many per inhabitant (T8.4; R6; C4/2). Involved in Yoredale's greater output of TC-O in 1963–64 were these habitat differences: (*e*) more habitat-claims for operatives, 188 percent as many (T3.3; R1; C4/2); (*f*) fewer town inhabitants per cu, 81 percent as many (T3.4; R2; C4/2); and (*g*) fewer town inhabitants per habitat-claim for operatives, 54 percent as many (T3.4; R3; C4/2).

In psychological language, these findings indicate that, *on the average,* both Midwesterners and Dalesmen in 1963–64 *in comparison with 1954–55* carried out appreciably more tasks and duties per town inhabitant (*d*), in settings where the levels of such responsible behavior were appreciably higher than in 1954–55 (*c*). There was much more responsible behavior by town inhabitants in the public areas of Midwest and appreciably more in Yoredale (*a, b*); many more tasks and duties (*e*), with slightly fewer town inhabitants per setting in Midwest and appreciably fewer in Yoredale (*f*); and appreciably fewer inhabitants in Midwest and many fewer in Yoredale in relation to the number of tasks and duties (*g*).

The outputs of C-O via all inhabitants were also greater in 1963–64 than in 1954–55. In Midwest the 1963–64 output was 179 percent of the 1954–55 output, and in Yoredale it was 181 percent (T8.4; R1; C3/1, 4/2).

Leader Acts

Number of leader acts (LA) is a measure of the highest levels of difficult, important, and responsible actions a town's habitat generates via its human components.

SALIENT FINDINGS

Midwest's total output of leader acts is greater than Yoredale's; it is greater per centiurb of habitat, per town inhabitant, and per leader. (See Binding, 1969.)

LEADER ACTS GENERATED BY TOTAL HABITAT

A single-tour-of-leadership system would require 2104 persons to carry out the LA that occurred in Midwest in 1963–64, and 1673 persons in Yoredale (T8.5; R1; C1, 2): these are the numbers of unique person-setting-leader combinations (GLA) that occurred in the two towns. More than half the GLA are produced via town inhabitants

Table 8.5
Leader Acts

| | | 1963–64 ||
		MW (1)	YD (2)
(1)	Output via all inhabitants (GLA)	2,104	1,673
(2)	Mean per cu of habitat	20	15
(3)	Output via town inhabitants (TLA)	1,482	883
(4)	Percent of GLA	70%	53%
(5)	Mean per cu of habitat	14	8
(6)	Mean per town inhabitant	1.8	0.7

(TLA). On the average, TLA is 1.8 for each Midwesterner, and 0.7 for each Dalesmen.

Differences. Midwest generates more LA than Yoredale. In 1963–64 it generated, via town inhabitants: (*a*) 599 more TLA than Yoredale (T8.5; R3; C1-2), amounting to (*b*) 168 percent as many (T8.5; R3; C1/2), to (*c*) 175 percent as many per cu (T8.5; R5; C1/2), to (*d*) 257 percent as many per inhabitant (T8.5; R6; C1/2), and to (*e*) 129 percent as many per leader (T8.6; R5; C1/2).

In psychological language, we can say that, *on the average,* Midwesterners *in comparison with Dalesmen* carried out many more actions of highest responsibility in the town's public habitats (*d*), in settings where there were many more leader acts by town inhabitants (*c*); they did this within a town where there was a much greater total amount of such activity (*a, b*) by leaders who engaged in appreciably more leader actions (*e*).

Midwest also produced more LA than Yoredale via all inhabitants, 126 percent as many (T8.5; R1; C1/2), amounting to 133 percent as many per cu of habitat (T8.5; R2; C1/2).

Town Leaders

The percentage of a town's inhabitants who are leaders of one or more settings (TL) is a measure of the breadth of distribution of highest public responsibility among its inhabitants.

SALIENT FINDINGS

More, and a greater percentage, of Midwesterners than of Dalesmen were leaders in 1963–64, but they were less likely than Yoredale leaders to lead the same setting in a subsequent year.

LEADERS GENERATED BY TOTAL HABITAT

In Midwest and Yoredale, respectively, approximately 40 and 20 percent of town inhabitants were leaders; they led settings that comprised 80 and 75 percent of the towns' habitats; and they led 4 and 3 settings per year, on the average.

Differences. Midwest produces more leaders than Yoredale. In 1963–64 it produced (*a*) 77 more TL than Yoredale (T8.6; R1; C1-2), amounting to (*b*) 129 percent as many (T8.6; R1; C1/2), to (*c*) 145 percent as many per cu (T8.6; R2; C1/2), and to (*d*) 21 more percent of the town's inhabitants (T8.6; R4; C1-2); they led (*e*) 8 more percent of the town's habitat (T8.6; R5; C1-2) and (*f*) 1 more behavior setting per leader (T8.6; R6; C1-2).

In psychological language, these data indicate that, *on the average,* Midwesterners *in comparison with Dalesmen* were more likely to experience the rewards and burdens of leadership (*d*), within a town and within settings where more of their fellow townsmen were leaders (*a, b,*

Table 8.6
Town Leaders

		1963–64	
		Midwest (1)	Yoredale (2)
(1)	Town inhabitants who are leaders	339	262
(2)	Mean per cu of habitat	3.2	2.3
(3)	Mean per inhabitant	0.41	0.20
(4)	Percent of town inhabitants	41%	20%
(5)	Percent of habitat with town leaders	81%	73%
(6)	Mean leader acts per leader (settings led)	4.4	3.4

c); they led more of the town's habitat (*e*), and each leader led more settings (*f*).

Changes. Leaders were less stable in Midwest than in Yoredale
over the period 1963–64 to 1967–68. Midwest had (*a*) 87 percent as
many TL who led the same settings in both years (T8.7; R1; C1/2), (*b*)
71 percent as many cu of habitat with identical TL in both years (T8.7;
R3; C1/2), and (*c*) 144 percent as many cu of habitat with completely
different leaders in the two years (T8.7; R5; C1/2).

These data indicate that Midwest's leaders had less secure tenure
than did Yoredale's leaders (*a*) and that the members, clients, customers, assistants, functionaries, and guests of Midwest's behavior settings
experienced complete leader continuity in fewer settings (*b*) and completely new leadership in more settings (*c*) than did Dalesmen. Of every
100 leaders in 1963–64, 61 of Midwest's and 40 of Yoredale's did not
have leadership responsibility in the same settings three years later
(T8.7; R2; C1, 2). Of every 100 cu of behavior settings in 1963–64, the
inhabitants of 32 of Midwest's and 43 of Yoredale's experienced *no* leadership turnover in 1967–68 (T8.7; R4; C1, 2); and the inhabitants of 36
of Midwest's and 24 of Yoredale's experienced *complete* leadership turnover within the three-year period (T8.7; R6; C1, 2).

Table 8.7
Stability of Town Leaders (TL) between 1963–64 and 1967–68

	Midwest (1)	Yoredale (2)
TL who led the same settings in '63 and '67		
(1) Number	136	157
(2) Percent of 1963–64 TL	39%	60%
Habitat with identical TL in '63 and '67		
(3) Number of cu	35	49
(4) Percent of total '63 habitat with TL	32%	43%
Habitat with completely different TL in '63 and '67		
(5) Number of cu	39	26
(6) Percent of total '63 habitat with TL	36%	24%

Observed and Predicted Differences
and Changes in Behavior Output

DIFFERENCES: THEORY AND EVIDENCE

In its most general form, our theory (discussed in Chapter 7) states that mean number of human components per centiurb of habitat is inversely related to mean behavior output per component and directly related to mean output per centiurb of habitat. The data for 1963–64 are:

	MW	YD	(MW/YD)100
Town inhabitants per cu of habitat	7.8	11 6	67
Behavior (P-H) per town inhabitant	1,356	1,089	125
Behavior (P-H) per cu of habitat	10,479	12,639	83

The overall findings are in accord with the theory: Midwest has fewer human components per centiurb than does Yoredale; it generates more behavior per component and less per centiurb.

However, the theory goes further and identifies loci and processes by which the overall relations between habitat and output occur. The inverse relation between human components and output is a consequence of processes within penetration zones 4 to 6 of behavior settings, where the program and maintenance circuits function (the operating zones); the direct relation is largely a consequence of processes in penetration zones 1 to 3, where only goal circuits occur (the utility zones). (Zones are summarized in Table 2.4.) We have sought among the available data for evidence bearing upon the detailed features of the theory; however, the data have certain limitations that are explicated and assessed here where relevant.

Evidence pertaining to processes within operating zones. The most apposite data concerning the inverse relation within the operating zones of the towns' settings are, on the habitat side, mean number of inhabitants per habitat-claim for operatives and, on the output side, mean C-O per town inhabitant. The data for 1963–64 are:

	MW	YD	(MW/YD)100
Town inhabitants per habitat-claim	0.08	0.17	47
C-O per town inhabitant	8.0	3.2	250

Here we see, as the theory predicts, that Midwest, with fewer inhabitants per habitat-claim than Yoredale, produces more C-O per inhabitant (paradigm items a_1 to a_3 to b_4, Figure 7.1; output prediction 9). If Midwest's greater output of C-O were strictly inversely proportional to its smaller complement of inhabitants, it would produce 213 percent as many per inhabitant as Yoredale. We can only conjecture why the enhanced productivity occurs, but here is a possible source: The program and maintenance forces of the towns' behavior settings do not act upon town inhabitants only; in fact, town inhabitants implement only 47 percent of Midwest's and 36 percent of Yoredale's C-O (T8.4; R4; C3,4), so town inhabitants are a sample of all inhabitants to which the theory applies. Most of the towns' other operatives live in the surrounding districts and regions, where Midwest's inferiority to Yoredale in potential inhabitants per habitat-claim is still greater, by an unknown amount, than it is in town inhabitants (T3.4; R5; C3/4). According to the theory, therefore, Midwest should produce more than 213 percent as many C-O per inhabitant as Yoredale, by an unknown amount.

Mean LA per inhabitant provides a less adequate test of the theory than C-O, because we do not have the habitat measure the theory requires, habitat-claims for leaders. However, the assumption that the towns differ in this respect to about the same degree as they differ in habitat-claims for total operatives appears to be reasonable. The obtained ratio of 2.57 is, again, in line with the theory (T8.5; R6; C1/2). This is true too of the proportion of town inhabitants who become leaders; in 1963–64 Midwest exceeded Yoredale in this respect by a factor of 2.05.

Evidence pertaining to processes within utility zones. The theory as applied to the utility zones of Midwest and Yoredale asserts that a *direct* relation holds between mean number of human components per centiurb of habitat and mean behavior output per centiurb of habitat (paradigm items *w, x, y, z,* Figure 7.2; output prediction 18). The most pertinent available output data are mean P-H per centiurb of habitat. These data are not as adequate for testing this prediction as C-O are for testing the inverse prediction, because the P-H measure includes the outputs from the operating zones as well as from the utility zones. Nevertheless, the data have some value in the present connection; for 1963–64 they are:

	MW	YD	(MW/YD)100
Town inhabitants per cu of habitat	7.8	11.6	67
Behavior (P-H) per cu of habitat	10,479	12,639	83

Here we find, as the theory predicts, that Midwest's fewer inhabitants per centiurb produce fewer P-H per centiurb. If Midwest's smaller output were strictly directly proportional to its fewer inhabitants, it would produce 67 percent as many P-H per cu. Since these data include output from the towns' operating zones, where program and maintenance forces are greater on Midwesterners than on Dalesmen, we expect a deviation in the direction obtained. In fact, data on the expected extent of this deviation are available. Midwesterners on the average produce 125 percent as many P-H per inhabitant as Dalesmen, within all behavior setting zones (T8.2; R6; C3/4). Midwest's fewer inhabitants per centiurb, therefore, will produce 125 percent as much behavior per cu as is expected on the basis of their number alone, and 1.25 times 0.67 equals .837, essentially the obtained output of Midwest relative to the output of Yoredale.

Evidence from all measures of behavior output. The data we have thus far presented were selected as bearing most directly upon stated aspects of the theory. We now turn to all the evidence on behavior output. The four measures of the mean behavior outputs of the inhabitants of Midwest and Yoredale are inhabitant-setting intersections (ISI), person-hours of behavior (P-H), claim-operations (C-O), and leader acts (LA). By all these measures, the towns' outputs are in accord with the general theory; output per inhabitant is greater in Midwest than in Yoredale, as follows: ISI, 4 percent; P-H, 25 percent; C-O, 150 percent; LA, 157 percent.

We are interested in the reasons for the great differences in these measures of Midwest's superiority and especially in discovering whether the reasons are in accord with and support the theory or whether they are contrary to and weaken our evidence for it. The theory itself has something to say about why the measures vary; according to it, Midwest's superiority to Yoredale in output per inhabitant varies with (*a*) *the behavior setting zones that generate the output measured* and (*b*) *the outputs measured.* (See Table 2.4.)

With respect to the zones, the theory states that Midwest is less superior to Yoredale on measures of the outputs of both the utility and operating zones than on measures of operating zone outputs alone (output predictions 9 and 17). Since ISI and P-H measure outputs of all zones, we expect Midwest to be less superior to Yoredale on these measures than on C-O and LA, which measure outputs of operating zones only. C-O and LA eliminate data upon which, according to the theory, Midwest is not superior to Yoredale. On the basis of the general theory too, Midwest is more superior to Yoredale in output of LA (zones 5 and 6) than in outputs of all operating zones (zones 4 to 6).

With respect to the outputs measured, Midwest's superiority to Yoredale is less, according to the theory, on measures that enumerate only behavior setting entrances than on measures that include both entrances and hours of habitancy (output prediction 8). Since ISI, C-O, and LA are sums of settings entered, Midwest is less superior to Yoredale on these than on the P-H measure, which is the sum of the settings entered, weighted for hours of habitancy. ISI, C-O, and LA do not eliminate data upon which, according to the theory, Midwest's superiority to Yoredale is small (output of utility and operating zones), but they do not weight the outputs on which Midwest is superior as the P-H measure does (duration of habitancy). According to the theory, Midwest's superiority to Yoredale varies more across the different behavior setting zones measured— utility (zones 1 to 3), operating (zones 4 to 6), leader (zones 5 and 6)—than across the different behavior outputs measured—behavior setting entrances and hours of habitancy.

In Table 8.8 we give the predicted and obtained orders of Midwest's measured superiority to Yoredale. In column *a* the order of the output measures is based on the zones measured; in column *b* it is based on the outputs measured. The order in column *c* is based on the sums of the parenthetical weights in columns *a* and *b*, which express the

Table 8.8
Midwest's Superiority to Yoredale on the Basis of
Four Measures of Behavior Output

Relative order of Midwest's superiority to Yoredale in
mean output per town inhabitant

(a) order on basis of zone measured	(b) order on basis of output measured	(c) predicted order on basis of a and b	(d) order of obtained output (MW/YD)100
LA (5)*	P-H (3)*	LA (6)*	LA (257)
C-O (4)	ISI = C-O = LA (1)	C-O (5)	C-O (250)
ISI = P-H (1)		P-H (4)	P-H (125)
		ISI (2)	ISI (104)

* Presumed proportional superiority of Midwest on the stated measures.

presumed greater variation of Midwest's measured superiority across the zones measured and across the outputs measured: this is the predicted order of Midwest's measured superiority to Yoredale in output per inhabitant. In column *d* we give Midwest's superiority to Yoredale in mean output per town inhabitant by the four measures. The general expectation on the basis of the theory and the stated assumptions is verified.

In any case, the data of Table 8.8 show that Midwest is superior to Yoredale in behavior output per inhabitant by all measures; that its superiority is greatest within the highest performance zones (leadership zones), even when measured by one of the less discriminating measures, LA; and that its superiority is least within undifferentiated operating and utility zones when measured by one of the less discriminating measures, ISI.

CHANGES: THEORY AND EVIDENCE

Changes in Midwest's habitat and behavior between 1954–55 and 1963–64 are in accord with theoretical expectations in about the same degree as are the difference data. Proportional increases in Midwest's population and habitat extent kept pace almost exactly, so that the mean number of town inhabitants per centiurb of habitat in 1963–64 was 99 percent of the number in 1954–55. During this time behavior output in P-H per cu increased 2 percent, and in P-H per inhabitant increased 4 percent.

The increase in Midwest's population did not keep pace with the increase in its habitat-claims for operatives, so that the mean number of town inhabitants per habitat-claim declined over the decade:

	1954–55	1963–64	('63/'54)100
Town inhabitant per habitat-claim	0.13	0.08	61
C-O per town inhabitant	5.84	8.00	138

As the theory predicts, Midwest's fewer inhabitants per habitat-claim in 1963–64 produced more C-O per inhabitant. If Midwest's greater output in 1963–64 were strictly inversely proportional to its smaller number of human components, it would have produced 164 percent as many C-O per inhabitant in 1963–64 as in 1954–55.

Changes in output and habitat between the survey years in Yoredale were not in accord with theoretical expectations. The most general manifestation of the discrepancy is found in these dimensions: Yoredale's population in 1963–64 was 101 percent as extensive as in 1954–55, and its habitat was 125 percent as extensive; in consequence, inhabitants per cu of habitat were only 81 percent as great in 1963–64. According to the theory, this decrease should result in an increase in behavior output per inhabitant, whereas P-H of behavior per Yoredale inhabitant decreased to 94 percent of the 1954–55 figure.

The sources of these discrepancies are found almost entirely within the School authority system. Most of Yoredale's habitat increment in 1963–64 — 21.7 of the 23 cu of increment — was within the School authority system. In effect, the behavior settings under the aegis of Yoredale's School authority system constitute to a great degree a foreign closed system within the town, whereas the theory is based upon open communication between inhabitants and behavior settings. Aspects of the changes in the schools are presented in connection with the outputs of the differential program habitats (Chapters 9 and 10) and the differential subgroup habitats (Chapters 11 and 12), and are discussed in "Melting Pot and Enlightened Colonial Systems of Child-Rearing" (Chapter 13.)

Concluding Statement

The data show that Midwesterners are, on the average, busier in the public settings of the town than Dalesmen, especially in the difficult, important, and responsible undertakings of operatives (functionaries and leaders), where they are more than twice as active as Dalesmen. During a year Midwesterners lead in more different behavior settings than Dalesmen, but they do not retain their leadership positions as long; leadership turnover is greater in Midwest. Despite the greater busy-ness of Midwesterners in the public regions of the town, Midwest is not as busy a town as Yoredale. Midwesterners engage in 125 percent as much behavior as Dalesmen in settings where there is 83 percent as much going on.

The data are in accord with behavior setting theory, which asserts that the observed behavior differences result from differences in the towns' habitats, of which Midwesterners and Dalesmen are the essential human components.

Behavior Output of the Towns' Differential Habitats I

Action Pattern and Behavior Mechanism Habitats

We now turn to the amounts of behavior generated by parts of the towns' habitats that differ with respect to two classes of qualities: action patterns (11 qualities) and behavior mechanisms (4 qualities). These differential habitats are defined and their extents, human component requirements, and variety are reported in Chapter 5. A section of the present chapter is devoted to each differential habitat; graphic summaries of crucial findings are presented for each class of habitat.

We present here data on the person-hours (P-H) and the claim-operations (C-O) generated within each differential habitat. These data are given in detail in the tables for the primary habitats (where the quality is prominent). For the territorial ranges (where the attribute is present) only P-H of output are reported; they are given in the text as

percentages of the gross behavior products (GBP) of the towns. No effort is made to systematically relate habitat and behavior within the differential habitats in terms of behavior setting theory because frequently
there are special conditions for inhabitant eligibility. However, habitat
conditions with respect to extent, variety, and number of inhabitants are
reviewed in every case—in other words, relations between behavior and
habitat are described in some detail.

Before presenting the data, we wish to emphasize again that habitat attributes are by no means independent; all behavior settings have a
number of them. For example, many behavior settings of the genotype
Worship Services have both religious and aesthetic action pattern qualities; such settings, therefore, are parts of both the primary Religious
and the primary Aesthetic habitats of the towns, and they contribute to
the behavior outputs of both of these differential habitats.

Again, as with the data in Chapter 5, the action pattern Aesthetics serves as a key to the tabular location of the data of all differential
habitats; it also identifies for all of them corresponding habitat and
psychological statements regarding P-H of output.

BEHAVIOR OUTPUTS OF ACTION PATTERN HABITATS

Aesthetics

PERSON-HOURS OF BEHAVIOR GENERATED BY AESTHETIC HABITAT

Salient findings, 1963–64. Those parts of the towns' habitats that
have *some* aesthetic attributes—the territorial range of Aesthetics—
produced 75 percent of Midwest's and 84 percent of Yoredale's gross
behavior product (GBP), and the primary aesthetic habitats of the
towns (PAH) produced, respectively, 3.8 and 4.4 percent of their GBP
(T9.1; R2; C3, 4). The mean weekly PAH outputs per town inhabitant

Table 9.1
Aesthetics
Behavior Output of Primary Habitat: Person-Hours (P-H)

	1954–55		1963–64	
	Midwest (1)	Yoredale (2)	Midwest (3)	Yoredale (4)
Output via all inhabitants				
(1) Total P-H			71,696	114,798
(2) Percent of GBP			3.8%	4.4%
(3) Mean P-H per cu			13,437	14,414
Output via town inhabitants				
(4) Total P-H	30,708	47,098	38,806	63,823
(5) Percent of TBP	3.3%	3.1%	3.4%	4.5%
(6) Mean P-H per cu	7,252	10,233	7,273	8,013
(7) Mean P-H per town inhabitant	42.9	36.2	46.7	48.7

were 54 minutes per Midwesterner and 56 minutes per Dalesman
(T9.1; R7; C3, 4), which were 109 and 134 percent, respectively, of the
1954–55 outputs (T9.1; R7; C4/2). More than half the PAH outputs of
both towns—54 percent of Midwest's and 56 percent of Yoredale's—
were generated via town inhabitants (T9.1; R4/1; C3, 4).

Differences. Midwest's PAH produces less behavior than Yoredale's. In 1963–64 it produced, via town inhabitants, (*a*) 25,017 fewer
P-H of aesthetic behavior than Yoredale (T9.1; R4; C4-3), amounting to
(*b*) 61 percent as much (T9.1; R4; C3/4), to (*c*) 91 percent as much per
cu of PAH (T9.1; R6; C3/4), and to (*d*) 96 percent as much per inhabitant (T9.1; R7; C3/4). Involved in Midwest's lower aesthetic output were
these habitat differences: (*e*) a smaller PAH, 66 percent as extensive as
Yoredale's (T5.1; R4; C3/4); (*f*) an equally varied PAH, 100 percent as
varied (T5.1; R11; C3/4); (*g*) fewer town inhabitants, 63 percent as
many (T3.4; R1; C3/4); and (*h*) fewer town inhabitants per cu of PAH,
96 percent as many (T3.4, T5.1).

In psychological language, these findings indicate that in
1963–64, *on the average,* Midwesterners *in comparison with Dalesmen*
engaged in somewhat less behavior in the town's PAH (*d*), within settings where there was less aesthetic activity by Midwesterners (*c*); they
did this within a town where there was appreciably less such activity (*a*,
b), an appreciably smaller (*e*) but equally varied (*f*) aesthetic habitat, with
appreciably fewer town inhabitants to take advantage of the aesthetic
opportunities and carry out the aesthetic duties (*g*), and somewhat fewer
town inhabitants in relation to the aesthetic opportunities and duties (*h*).

Changes. Both towns' PAHs produced more behavior in 1963–64.
Midwest's produced, via town inhabitants, 8098 more P-H of aesthetic
behavior than in 1954–55 (T9.1; R4; C3-1), amounting to 126 percent
as much (T9.1; R4; C3/1), to 100 percent as much per cu of PAH (T9.1;
R6; C3/1), and to 109 percent as much per inhabitant (T9.1; R7; C3/1).
Involved in Midwest's greater aesthetic output in 1963–64 were these
habitat differences: a larger PAH, 126 percent as extensive as in
1954–55 (T5.1; R4; C3/1); a more varied PAH, 123 percent as varied
(T5.1; R11; C3/1); more town inhabitants, 116 percent as many (T3.4;
R1; C3/1); but fewer town inhabitants per cu of PAH, 92 percent as
many (T3.4, T5.1).

Yoredale's PAH produced, via town inhabitants, 16,725 more
P-H of aesthetic behavior in 1963–64 than in 1954–55 (T9.1; R4; C4-2),
amounting to 136 percent as much (T9.1; R4; C4/2), but to 78 percent
as much per cu of PAH (T9.1; R6; C4/2) and to 134 percent as much
per inhabitant (T9.1; R7; C4/2). Involved in Yoredale's greater aesthetic
output in 1963–64 were these habitat differences: a larger PAH, 174
percent as extensive as in 1954–55 (T5.1; R4; C4/2); a more varied
PAH, 150 percent as varied (T5.1; R11; C4/2); the same number of
town inhabitants, 101 percent as many (T3.4; R1; C4/2); but fewer town
inhabitants per cu of PAH, 58 percent as many (T3.4; T5.1).

CLAIM-OPERATIONS GENERATED BY PRIMARY AESTHETIC HABITAT

Salient findings, 1963–64. The total number of C-O generated by the towns' PAHs for cast members, ushers, directors, chorus members, ticket-takers, and so forth, was approximately equivalent to those produced by 100 different concert, drama, and art settings, with 26 operatives each in Midwest [(T9.2; R1; C3)/100] and 24 operatives each in Yoredale [(T9.2; R1; C4)/100]. The PAHs of both towns were more productive of responsible actions (C-O) than expected on the basis of either their extent or their output of P-H. Midwest's PAH in 1963–64 constituted 5.0 percent of its total habitat (T5.1; R5; C3), produced 3.8 percent of its GBP (T9.1; R2; C3), and generated 18.1 percent of its GC-O (T9.2; R2; C4); and Yoredale's PAH constituted 7.1 percent of its total habitat (T5.1; R5; C3), produced 4.4 percent of its GBP (T9.1; R2; C4), and generated 20.3 percent of its GC-O (T9.2; R2; C4). The mean yearly outputs per town inhabitant were 1.4 C-O per Midwesterner and 0.7 C-O per Dalesman, which were 110 and 121 percent, respectively, of 1954–55 outputs (T9.2; R7; C3/1, 4/2). Less than half of all aesthetic C-O—44 percent of Midwest's and 38 percent of Yoredale's—was generated via town inhabitants (T9.2; R4/1; C3, 4).

Differences. Midwest's PAH produces more C-O than Yoredale's. In 1963–64 it produced, via town inhabitants, 219 more C-O than Yoredale (T9.2; R4; C3-4), amounting to 124 percent as many (T9.2; R4; C3/4), to 185 percent as many per cu of PAH (T9.2; R6; C3/4), and to 196 percent as many per inhabitant (T9.2; R7; C3/4). Involved in Midwest's greater output of aesthetic C-O were these habitat differences: more PAH claims for operatives, 158 percent as many as Yoredale (T5.1; R8; C3/4); fewer town inhabitants, 63 percent as many (T3.4; R1; C3/4); and fewer town inhabitants per PAH claim, 40 percent as many (T3.4, T5.1).

Table 9.2
Aesthetics
Behavior Output of Primary Habitat: Claim-Operations (C-O)

	1954–55		1963–64	
	Midwest (1)	Yoredale (2)	Midwest (3)	Yoredale (4)
Output via all inhabitants				
(1) Total C-O	1,636	1,532	2,585	2,380
(2) Percent of Gross C-O	20.6%	23.7%	18.1%	20.3%
(3) Mean C-O per cu	386	333	484	299
Output via town inhabitants				
(4) Total C-O	893	749	1,135	916
(5) Percent of Town C-O	21.4%	24.5%	17.1%	21.8%
(6) Mean C-O per cu	211	163	213	115
(7) Mean C-O per town inhabitant	1.25	0.58	1.37	0.70

Changes. Both towns' PAHs produced more C-O in 1963–64. Midwest's produced, via town inhabitants, 242 more C-O than in 1954–55 (T9.2; R4; C3-1), amounting to 127 percent as many (T9.2; R4; C3/1), to 101 percent as many per cu of PAH (T9.2; R6; C3/1), and to 110 percent as many per inhabitant (T9.2; R7; C3/1). Involved in Midwest's greater output of aesthetic C-O in 1963–64 were these habitat differences: more PAH claims for operatives, 171 percent as many as in 1954–55 (T5.1; R8; C3/1); more town inhabitants, 116 percent as many (T3.4; R1; C3/1); and fewer town inhabitants per PAH claim, 68 percent as many (T3.4; R1; C3)/(T5.1; R8; C3) ÷ (T3.4; R1; C1)/(T5.1; R8; C1).

Yoredale's PAH produced, via town inhabitants, 167 more C-O in 1963–64 than in 1954–55 (T9.2; R4; C4-2), amounting to 122 percent as many (T9.2; R4; C4/2), to 71 percent as many per cu of PAH (T9.2; R6; C4/2), and to 121 percent as many per inhabitant (T9.2; R7; C4/2). Involved in Yoredale's greater output of aesthetic C-O in 1963–64 were these habitat differences: more PAH claims for operatives, 177 percent as many as in 1954–55 (T5.1; R8; C4/2); the same number of town inhabitants, 101 percent as many (T3.4; R1; C4/2); and fewer town inhabitants per PAH claim, 57 percent as many (T3.4; R1; C4)/(T5.1; R8; C4) ÷ (T3.4; R1; C2)/(T5.1; R8; C2).

BUSINESS

PERSON-HOURS OF BEHAVIOR GENERATED BY BUSINESS HABITAT

Salient findings, 1963–64. Those parts of the town's habitats that have some business attributes—the territorial range of Business—produced 57 percent of both Midwest's and Yoredale's GBP, and the primary business habitats of the towns (PBH) produced, respectively, 22 and 29 percent of their GBP. The mean weekly PBH outputs per town inhabitant were 6 hours, 54 minutes per Midwesterner and 6 hours, 30 minutes per Dalesman, which were 87 and 147 percent, respectively, of the 1954–55 outputs. More than half the PBH outputs of both towns—73 percent of Midwest's and 59 percent of Yoredale's—were generated via town inhabitants.

P-H data are reported in Table 9.3.

Differences. Midwest PBH produces less behavior than Yoredale's. In 1963–64 it produced, via town inhabitants, 144,862 fewer P-H of business behavior than Yoredale's, amounting to 67 percent as much, to 117 percent as much per cu of PBH, and to 106 percent as much per inhabitant. Involved in Midwest's smaller business output were these habitat differences: a smaller PBH, 57 percent as extensive as Yoredale's; a less varied PBH, 65 percent as varied; fewer town inhabitants, 63 percent as many; and more town inhabitants per cu of PBH, 110 percent as many.

In psychological language, these findings indicate that in 1963–64, *on the average,* Midwesterners *in comparison with Dalesmen*

Table 9.3
Business
Behavior Output of Primary Habitat: Person-Hours (P-H)

	1954–55		1963–64	
	Midwest (1)	Yoredale (2)	Midwest (3)	Yoredale (4)
Output via all inhabitants				
(1) Total P-H			406,625	756,034
(2) Percent of GBP			21.6%	28.8%
(3) Mean P-H per cu			22,199	23,670
Output via town inhabitants				
(4) Total P-H	294,143	295,602	298,411	443,273
(5) Percent of TBP	31.6%	19.6%	26.5%	31.1%
(6) Mean P-II per cu	12,760	11,828	16,291	13,878
(7) Mean P-H per town inhabitant	411	227	359	338

engaged in somewhat more behavior in the town's PBH, within settings where there was more business activity by Midwesterners; they did this within a town where there was appreciably less such activity, a much smaller and less varied business habitat, appreciably fewer town inhabitants to take advantage of the business opportunities and to carry out the business duties, and more inhabitants in relation to the business opportunities and duties.

Changes. Both towns, PBHs produced more behavior in 1963–64. Midwest's produced, via town inhabitants, 4268 more P-H of business behavior than in 1954–55, amounting to 101 percent as much, to 128 percent as much per cu of PBH, but to 87 percent as much per inhabitant. Involved in Midwest's greater business output in 1963–64 were these habitat differences: a smaller PBH, 79 percent as extensive as in 1954–55; a less varied PBH, 91 percent as varied; more town inhabitants, 116 percent as many, and more inhabitants per cu of PBH, 147 percent as many.

Yoredale's PBH produced, via town inhabitants, 147,671 more P-H of business behavior in 1963–64 than in 1954–55, amounting to 150 percent as much, to 117 percent as much per cu of PBH, and to 149 percent as much per inhabitant. Involved in Yoredale's greater business output in 1963–64 were these habitat differences: a larger PBH, 128 percent as extensive as in 1954–55; a more varied PBH, 124 percent as varied; the same number of town inhabitants, 101 percent as many; but fewer inhabitants per cu of PBH, 79 percent as many.

CLAIM-OPERATIONS GENERATED BY PRIMARY BUSINESS HABITAT

Salient findings, 1963–64. The total number of C-O generated by the towns' PBHs for secretaries, salesmen, managers, clerks, and so forth, was approximately equivalent to those produced by 100 different commercial settings with 5 operatives each in Midwest and 7 operatives

Table 9.4
Business
Behavior Output of Primary Habitat: Claim-Operations (C-O)

	1954–55		1963–64	
	Midwest (1)	Yoredale (2)	Midwest (3)	Yoredale (4)
Output via all inhabitants				
(1) Total C-O	271	513	495	746
(2) Percent of Gross C-O	3.4%	7.9%	3.5%	6.4%
(3) Mean C-O per cu	11.8	20.5	27.0	23.4
Output via town inhabitants				
(4) Total C-O	226	273	297	299
(5) Percent of Town C-O	5.4%	8.9%	4.5%	7.1%
(6) Mean C-O per cu	9.8	10.9	16.2	9.4
(7) Mean C-O per town inhabitant	0.32	0.21	0.36	0.23

each in Yoredale. The PBHs of both towns were less productive of responsible actions than expected on the basis of either their extent or their output of P-H. Midwest's PBH constituted 17.1 percent of its total habitat, produced 21.6 percent of its GBP, and generated 3.5 percent of its C-O; and Yoredale's PBH constituted 28.3 percent of its total habitat, produced 28.8 percent of its GBP, and generated 6.4 percent of its C-O. The mean yearly outputs per town inhabitant were 0.4 C-O per Midwest-erner and 0.2 C-O per Dalesman, which were 157 and 106 percent, respectively, of the 1954–55 outputs. There were 60 percent of Midwest's and 40 percent of Yoredale's business C-O generated via town inhabitants.

C-O data are reported in Table 9.4.

Differences. Midwest's PBH produces fewer C-O than Yoredale's. In 1963–64 it produced, via town inhabitants, 2 fewer C-O than Yoredale's, amounting to 100 percent as many, to 171 percent as many per cu of PBH, and to 157 percent as many per inhabitant. Involved in Midwest's smaller output of business C-O were these habitat differences: fewer PBH claims for operatives, 60 percent as many as Yoredale; fewer town inhabitants, 63 percent as many; and more inhabitants per PBH claim, 106 percent as many.

Changes. Both towns' PBHs produced more C-O in 1963–64. Midwest produced, via town inhabitants, 71 more than in 1954–55, amounting to 131 percent as many, to 165 percent as many per cu of PBH, and to 112 percent as many per inhabitant. Involved in Midwest's greater output of business C-O in 1963–64 were these habitat differences: more PBH claims for operatives, 132 percent as many as in 1954–55; more town inhabitants, 116 percent as many; but fewer inhabitants per PBH claim, 88 percent as many.

Yoredale's PBH produced via town inhabitants, 26 more C-O in 1963–64 than in 1954–55, amounting to 109 percent as many, to 86 percent as many per cu of PBH, and to 110 percent as many per inhabitant. Involved in Yoredale's output of business C-O in 1963–64 were these habitat differences: somewhat more PBH claims for operatives 109 percent as many as in 1954–55; the same number of town inhabitants, 101 percent as many; and fewer inhabitants per PBH claim, 92 percent as many.

Education

PERSON-HOURS OF BEHAVIOR GENERATED BY EDUCATIONAL HABITAT

Salient findings, 1963–64. Those parts of the towns' habitats that have some educational attributes—the territorial range of Education—produced 44 percent of Midwest's and 31 percent of Yoredale's GBP, and the primary educational habitats of the towns (PEH) produced, respectively, 23.6 and 15.2 percent of their GBP. The mean weekly PEH outputs per town inhabitant were 4 hours, 54 minutes per Midwesterner and 2 hours, 6 minutes per Dalesman, which were 163 and 94 percent, respectively, of the 1954–55 outputs. Less than half the PEH outputs of both towns—48 percent of Midwest's and 35 percent of Yoredale's—were generated via town inhabitants.

P-H data are reported in Table 9.5.

Differences. Midwest's PEH produces more behavior than Yoredale's. In 1963–64 it produced, via town inhabitants, 69, 918 more P-H of educational behavior than Yoredale's, amounting to 149 percent as much, to 129 percent as much per cu of PEH, and to 236 percent as much per inhabitant. Involved in Midwest's larger educational output were these habitat differences: a larger PEH, 116 percent as extensive as Yoredale's; a less varied PEH, 86 percent as varied; fewer town inhabitants, 63 percent as many; and fewer town inhabitants per cu of PEH, 54 percent as many.

Table 9.5
Education
Behavior Output of Primary Habitat: Person-Hours (P-H)

	1954–55		1963–64	
	Midwest (1)	Yoredale (2)	Midwest (3)	Yoredale (4)
Output via all inhabitants				
(1) Total P-H			443,673	399,732
(2) Percent of GBP			23.6%	15.2%
(3) Mean P-H per cu			26,862	28,099
Output via town inhabitants				
(4) Total P-H	111,562	149,094	211,174	141,256
(5) Percent of TBP	12.0%	9.9%	18.8%	9.9%
(6) Mean P-H per cu	11,057	32,594	12,786	9,930
(7) Mean P-H per town inhabitant	156.0	114.7	254.4	107.8

In psychological terms, these findings indicate that in 1963–64, *on the average,* Midwesterners *in comparison with Dalesmen* engaged in much more behavior in the town's PEH, within settings where there was more educational activity by Midwesterners; they did this within a town where there was much more such activity, an appreciably larger but less varied educational habitat, fewer town inhabitants to take advantage of the educational opportunities and carry out the educational duties, and many fewer inhabitants in relation to the educational opportunities and duties.

Changes. Midwest's PEH produced more behavior in 1963–64 than in 1954–55. It produced, via town inhabitants, 99,612 more P-H of educational behavior in 1963–64, amounting to 189 percent as much, to 116 percent as much per cu of PEH, and to 163 percent as much per inhabitant. Involved in Midwest's greater educational output in 1963–64 were these habitat differences: a larger PEH, 163 percent as extensive as in 1954–55; a more varied PEH, 142 percent as varied; more town inhabitants, 116 percent as many; and fewer inhabitants per cu of PEH, 71 percent as many.

Yoredale's PEH produced less behavior in 1963–64 than in 1954–55. It produced, via town inhabitants, 7838 fewer P-H of educational behavior, amounting to 95 percent as much, to 30 percent as much per cu of PEH, and to 94 percent as much per town inhabitant. Involved in Yoredale's smaller educational output in 1963–64 were these habitat differences: a larger PEH, 309 percent as extensive as in 1954–55; a more varied PEH, 287 percent as varied; almost the same number of town inhabitants, 101 percent as many; but fewer inhabitants per cu of PEH, 33 percent as many.

CLAIM-OPERATIONS GENERATED BY PRIMARY EDUCATIONAL HABITAT

Salient findings, 1963–64. The total number of C-O generated by the towns' PEHs for teachers, leaders, administrators, performers, and so forth, was approximately equivalent to those produced by 100 different educational settings with 4.5 operatives each in Midwest and 11 operatives each in Yoredale. The PEHs of both towns were less productive of responsible actions than expected on the basis of either their extents or their outputs of P-H. Midwest's PEH in 1963–64 constituted 15.4 percent of its total habitat, produced 23.6 percent of its GBP, and generated 3.2 percent of its C-O; and Yoredale's PEH constituted 12.6 percent of its total habitat, produced 15.2 percent of its GBP, and generated 9.6 percent of its C-O. The mean yearly outputs per town inhabitant were 0.28 C-O per Midwesterner and 0.15 C-O per Dalesman, which were 117 and 125 percent, respectively, of the 1954–55 outputs. There were 51 percent of Midwest's and 18 percent of Yoredale's educational C-O generated via town inhabitants.

C-O data are reported in Table 9.6.

Differences. Midwest's PEH produces more C-O than Yoredale's. In 1963–64 it produced, via town inhabitants, 27 more C-O than Yore-

Table 9.6
Education
Behavior Output of Primary Habitat: Claim-Operations (C-O)

| | 1954–55 | | 1963–64 | |
	Midwest (1)	Yoredale (2)	Midwest (3)	Yoredale (4)
Output via all inhabitants				
(1) Total C-O	260	728	454	1,129
(2) Percent of Gross C-O	3.3%	11.3%	3.2%	9.6%
(3) Mean C-O per cu	25.8	159.1	27.5	79.4
Output via town inhabitants				
(4) Total C-O	173	152	230	203
(5) Percent of Town C-O	4.1%	5.0%	3.5%	4.8%
(6) Mean C-O per cu	17.1	33.2	13.9	14.3
(7) Mean C-O per town inhabitant	0.24	0.12	0.28	0.15

dale's, amounting to 113 percent as many, to 97 percent as many per cu of PEH, and to 187 percent as many per town inhabitant. Involved in Midwest's greater output of educational C-O were these habitat differences: more PEH claims for operatives, 110 percent as many as Yoredale; fewer town inhabitants, 63 percent as many; and fewer town inhabitants per PEH claim, 58 percent as many.

Changes. Both towns' PEHs produced more C-O in 1963–64. Midwest's produced, via town inhabitants, 57 more C-O than in 1954–55, amounting to 133 percent as many, to 81 percent as many per cu of PEH, and to 117 percent as many per town inhabitant. Involved in Midwest's greater output of educational C-O in 1963–64 were these habitat differences: more PEH claims for operatives, 145 percent as many as in 1954–55; more town inhabitants, 116 percent as many; but fewer town inhabitants per PEH claim, 80 percent as many.

Yoredale's PEH produced, via town inhabitants, 51 more C-O in 1963–64 than in 1954–55, amounting to 133 percent as many, but to 43 percent as many per cu of PEH, and to 125 percent as many per inhabitant. Involved in Yoredale's greater output of educational C-O in 1963–64 were these habitat differences: more PEH claims for operatives, 180 percent as many as in 1954–55; about the same number of town inhabitants, 101 percent as many; but fewer town inhabitants per claim, 56 percent as many.

Government

PERSON-HOURS OF BEHAVIOR GENERATED BY GOVERNMENT HABITATS

Salient findings, 1963–64. Those parts of the towns' habitats that have some governmental attributes—the territorial range of Government—produced 88 percent of Midwest's and 96 percent of Yoredale's GBP, and the primary governmental habitats of the towns (PGH) produced, respectively, 11.6 and 5.0 percent of their GBP. The mean

Table 9.7
Government
Behavior Output of Primary Habitat; Person-Hours (P-H)

	1954–55		1963–64	
	Midwest (1)	Yoredale (2)	Midwest (3)	Yoredale (4)
Output via all inhabitants				
(1) Total P-H			218,643	131,007
(2) Percent of GBP			11.6%	5.0%
(3) Mean P-H per cu			14,322	15,299
Output via town inhabitants				
(4) Total P-H	98,437	75,451	122,524	89,355
(5) Percent of TBP	10.6%	5.0%	10.9%	6.3%
(6) Mean P-H per cu	6,800	9,576	8,026	10,435
(7) Mean P-H per town inhabitant	137.7	58.0	147.6	68.2

weekly PGH outputs per town inhabitant were 2 hours, 48 minutes per Midwesterner and 1 hour, 24 minutes per Dalesman, which were 107 and 118 percent, respectively, of the 1954–55 outputs. More than half the PGH outputs of both towns—56 percent of Midwest's and 68 percent of Yoredale—were generated via town inhabitants.

P-H data are reported in Table 9.7.

Differences. Midwest's PGH produces more behavior than Yoredale's. In 1963–64 it produced via town inhabitants, 33,169 more P-H of governmental behavior than Yoredale's, amounting to 137 percent as much, to 77 percent as much per cu of PGH, and to 216 percent as much per town inhabitant. Involved in Midwest's greater governmental output were these habitat differences: a larger PGH, 178 percent as extensive as Yoredale's; an equally varied PGH, 100 percent as varied; fewer town inhabitants, 63 percent as many; and fewer town inhabitants per cu of PGH, 36 percent as many.

In psychological terms, these findings mean that in 1963–64, *on the average,* Midwesterners *in comparison with Dalesmen* engaged in somewhat more behavior in the town's PGH, within settings where there was less governmental activity by Midwesterners; they did this within a town where there was appreciably more such activity, a much larger but equally varied governmental habitat, appreciably fewer town inhabitants to take advantage of the governmental opportunities and carry out the governmental duties, and many fewer town inhabitants in relation to the governmental opportunities and duties.

Changes. Both towns' PGHs produced more behavior in 1963–64. Midwest's produced, via town inhabitants, 24,087 more governmental P-H behavior than in 1954–55, amounting to 124 percent as much, to 118 percent as much per cu of PGH, and to 107 percent as much per inhabitant. Involved in Midwest's greater governmental output in 1963–64 were these habitat differences: a larger PGH, 105 percent as extensive as in 1954–55; a more varied PGH, 104 percent as varied; more town inhabitants, 116 percent as many; and more town inhabitants per cu of PGH, 110 percent as many.

Yoredale's PGH produced, via town inhabitants, 13,904 more P-H of governmental behavior in 1963–64 than in 1954–55, amounting to 118 percent as much, to 109 percent as much per cu of PGH, and to 118 percent as much per inhabitant. Involved in Yoredale's greater governmental output in 1963–64 were these habitat differences: a larger PGH, 109 percent as extensive as in 1954–55; a more varied PGH, 123 percent as varied; about the same number of town inhabitants, 101 percent as many; and fewer town inhabitants per cu of PGH, 93 percent as many.

CLAIM-OPERATIONS GENERATED BY PRIMARY GOVERNMENTAL HABITAT

Salient findings, 1963–64. The total number of C-O generated by the towns' PGHs for judges, secretaries, lawyers, constables, treasurers, and so forth, was approximately equivalent to those produced by 100 different government settings with 9 operatives each in Midwest and 5 operatives each in Yoredale. The PGHs of both towns were less productive of responsible actions than expected on the basis of either their extent or their output of P-H. Midwest's PGH in 1963–64 constituted 14.2 percent of its total habitat, produced 11.6 percent of its GBP, and generated 5 percent of its C-O; and Yoredale's PGH constituted 7.6 percent of its total habitat, produced 5 percent of its GBP, and generated 4.5 percent of its C-O. The mean yearly outputs per town inhabitant were 0.27 C-O per Midwesterner and 0.15 C-O per Dalesman, which were 112 and 214 percent, respectively, of the 1954–55 outputs. There were 32 percent of Midwest's and 37 percent of Yoredale's governmental C-O generated via town inhabitants.

C-O data are reported in Table 9.8.

Differences. Midwest's PGH produces more C-O than Yoredale's.

Table 9.8
Government
Behavior Output of Primary Habitat: Claim Operations (C-O)

	1954–55		1963–64	
	Midwest (1)	Yoredale (2)	Midwest (3)	Yoredale (4)
Output via all inhabitants				
(1) Total C-O	584	492	713	533
(2) Percent of Gross C-O	7.4%	7.6%	5.0%	4.5%
(3) Mean C-O per cu	40.3	62.4	46.7	62.2
Output via town inhabitants				
(4) Total C-O	173	92	228	199
(5) Percent of Town C-O	4.1%	3.0%	3.4%	4.7%
(6) Mean C-O per cu	11.9	11.7	14.9	23.2
(7) Mean C-O per town inhabitant	0.24	0.07	0.27	0.15

In 1963–64 it produced, via town inhabitants, 29 more C-O than Yore-dale's amounting to 115 percent as many, but to 64 percent as many per cu of PGH and to 180 percent as many per inhabitant. Involved in Midwest's greater output of governmental C-O were these habitat differences: more PGH claims for operatives, 132 percent as many as Yoredale; fewer town inhabitants, 63 percent as many; and fewer town inhabitants per PGH claim, 47 percent as many.

Changes. Both towns' PGHs produced more C-O in 1963–64. Midwest's produced, via town inhabitants, 55 more C-O than in 1954–55, amounting to 132 percent as many, to 125 percent as many per cu of PGH, and to 112 percent as many per inhabitant. Involved in Midwest's greater output of governmental C-O in 1963–64 were these habitat differences: more PGH claims for operatives, 118 percent as many as in 1954–55; more town inhabitants, 116 percent as many, and fewer town inhabitants per PGH claim, 97 percent as many.

Yoredale's PGH produced, via town inhabitants, 107 more C-O in 1963–64 than in 1954–55, amounting to 216 percent as many, to 198 percent as many per cu of PGH, and to 214 percent as many per inhabitant. Involved in Yoredale's greater output of governmental C-O in 1963–64 were these habitat differences: more PGH claims for operatives, 164 percent as many as in 1954–55; about the same number of town inhabitants, 101 percent as many; and fewer inhabitants per claim, 61 percent as many.

Nutrition

PERSON-HOURS OF BEHAVIOR GENERATED BY NUTRITION HABITAT

Salient findings, 1963–64. Those parts of the towns' habitats that have some nutritional attributes—the territorial range of Nutrition—produced 63 percent of Midwest's and 81 percent of Yoredale's GBP, and the primary nutritional habitats of the towns (PNH) produced, respectively, 12.2 and 24.0 percent of their GBP. The mean weekly PNH outputs per town inhabitant were 4 hours, 5 minutes per Midwesterner and 5 hours, 12 minutes per Dalesmen, which were 117 and 121 percent, respectively, of the 1954–55 outputs. More than half the PNH outputs of both towns—77 percent of Midwest's and 56 percent of Yoredale's—were generated via town inhabitants.

P-H data are reported in Table 9.9.

Differences. Midwest's PNH produces less behavior than Yoredale's. In 1963–64 it produced, via town inhabitants, 178,238 fewer P-H of nutritional behavior than Yoredale's, amounting to 50 percent as much, but to 125 percent as much per cu of PNH, and to 79 percent as much per inhabitant. Involved in Midwest's smaller nutritional output were these habitat differences: a smaller PNH, 40 percent as extensive as Yoredale's; less varied PNH, 74 percent as varied; fewer town inhabitants, 63 percent as many; and more town inhabitants per cu of PNH, 159 percent as many.

Table 9.9
Nutrition
Behavior Output of Primary Habitat: Person-Hours (P-H)

	1954–55		1963–64	
	Midwest (1)	Yoredale (2)	Midwest (3)	Yoredale (4)
Output via all inhabitants				
(1) Total P-H			229,644	631,267
(2) Percent of GBP			12.2%	24.0%
(3) Mean P-H per cu			31,053	33,902
Output via town inhabitants				
(4) Total P-H	129,745	354,304	176,492	354,730
(5) Percent of TBP	13.9%	23.5%	15.7%	24.9%
(6) Mean P-H per cu	16,952	20,659	23,866	19,051
(7) Mean P-H per town inhabitant	181.5	272.5	212.6	270.8

In psychological terms, these findings indicate that in 1963–64, *on the average,* Midwesterners *in comparison with Dalesmen* engaged in somewhat less behavior in the town's PNH, within settings where there was appreciably more nutritional activity by Midwesterners; they did this within a town where there was much less such activity, a smaller and less varied nutritional habitat, appreciably fewer town inhabitants to take advantage of the nutritional opportunities and carry out the nutritional duties, and many more town inhabitants in relation to the nutritional opportunities and duties.

Changes. Both towns' PNHs produced more behavior in 1963–64. Midwest's produced via town inhabitants, 46,747 more P-H of nutritional behavior than in 1954–55, amounting to 136 percent as much, to 141 percent as much per cu of PNH, and to 117 percent as much per inhabitant. Involved in Midwest's greater nutritional output in 1963–64 were these habitat differences: a smaller PNH, 96 percent as extensive as in 1954–55; a more varied PNH, 154 percent as varied; more town inhabitants, 116 percent as many; and more inhabitants per cu of PNH, 121 percent as many.

Yoredale's PNH produced, via town inhabitants, 426 more P-H of nutritional behavior in 1963–64 than in 1954–55, amounting to 100 percent as much, to 92 percent as much per cu of PNH, and to 99 percent as much per inhabitant. Involved in Yoredale's almost unchanged nutritional output in 1963–64 were these habitat differences: a larger PNH, 108 percent as extensive as in 1954–55, an appreciably more varied PNH, 128 percent as varied; almost the same number of town inhabitants, 101 percent as many; and fewer inhabitants per cu of PNH, 93 percent as many.

CLAIM-OPERATIONS GENERATED BY PRIMARY NUTRITIONAL HABITAT

Salient findings, 1963–64. The total number of C-O generated by the towns' PNHs for waiters, salesmen, publicans, grocers, workers at fund-raising dinners or teas, and so forth, was approximately equivalent to those produced by 100 different nutritional settings with 6 operatives each in Midwest and 9 operatives each in Yoredale. The PNHs of both towns were less productive of responsible actions than expected on the basis of either their extent or their output of P-H. Midwest's PNH in 1963–64 constituted 6.9 percent of its total habitat, produced 12.2 percent of its GBP, and generated 4.2 percent of its C-O; and Yoredale's PNH constituted 16.5 percent of its total habitat, produced 24 percent of its GBP, and generated 8.1 percent of its C-O. The mean yearly outputs per town inhabitant were 0.44 C-O per Midwesterner and 0.29 C-O per Dalesman, which were 142 and 181 percent, respectively, of the 1954–55 outputs. There were 60 percent of Midwest's and 41 percent of Yoredale's nutritional C-O generated via town inhabitants. This differs from P-H of nutritional behavior, where more than half was generated via the town inhabitants of both towns.

C-O data are reported in Table 9.10.

Differences. Midwest's PNH produces fewer C-O than Yoredale's. In 1963–64 it produced via town inhabitants, 23 fewer C-O than Yoredale's, amounting to 94 percent as many, but to 237 percent as many per cu of PNH and to 152 percent as many per inhabitant. Involved in Midwest's greater output of nutritional C-O were these habitat differences: more PNH claims for operatives 114 percent as many as Yoredale; fewer town inhabitants, 63 percent as many; and fewer town inhabitants per PNH claim, 56 percent as many.

Changes. Both towns' PNHs produced more C-O in 1963–64. Midwest's produced, via town inhabitants, 144 more than in 1954–55, amounting to 166 percent as many, to 172 percent as many per cu of PNH, and to 142 percent as many per inhabitant. Involved in Midwest's greater output of nutritional C-O in 1963–64 were these habitat differences: more PNH claims for operatives, 183 percent as many as in 1954–55; more town inhabitants, 116 percent as many; and fewer town inhabitants per PNH claim, 63 percent as many.

Table 9.10
Nutrition
Behavior Output of Primary Habitat: Claim-Operations (C-O)

	1954–55		1963–64	
	Midwest (1)	Yoredale (2)	Midwest (3)	Yoredale (4)
Output via all inhabitants				
(1) Total C-O	295	332	602	947
(2) Percent of Gross C-O	3.7%	5.1%	4.2%	8.1%
(3) Mean C-O per cu	38.5	19.4	81.4	50.9
Output via town inhabitants				
(4) Total C-O	219	206	363	386
(5) Percent of Town C-O	5.2%	6.7%	5.5%	9.2%
(6) Mean C-O per cu	28.6	12.0	49.1	20.7
(7) Mean C-O per town inhabitant	0.31	0.16	0.44	0.29

Yoredale's PNH produced via town inhabitants, 180 more C-O in 1963–64 than in 1954–55, amounting to 187 percent as many, to 172 percent as many per cu of PNH, and to 181 percent as many per inhabitant. Involved in Yoredale's output of nutritional C-O in 1963–64 were these habitat differences: more PNH claims for operatives, 153 percent as many as in 1954–55; about the same number of town inhabitants, 101 percent as many; and fewer inhabitants per claim, 66 percent as many.

Personal Appearance

PERSON-HOURS OF BEHAVIOR GENERATED BY
PERSONAL APPEARANCE HABITAT

Salient findings, 1963–64. Those parts of the towns' habitats that have some personal appearance attributes, — the territorial range of Personal Appearance — produced 25 percent of Midwest's and 33 percent of Yoredale's GBP, and the primary personal appearance habitats of the towns (PPAH) produced, respectively, 2.8 and 4.5 percent of their GBP. The mean weekly PPAH outputs per town inhabitant were 50 minutes per Midwesterner and 56 minutes per Dalesman, which were 87 and 107 percent, respectively, of the 1954–55 outputs. More than half the PPAH outputs of both towns — 68 percent of Midwest's and 54 percent of Yoredale's — were generated via town inhabitants.

P-H data are reported in Table 9.11.

Differences. Midwest's PPAH produces less behavior than Yoredale's. In 1963–64 it produced, via town inhabitants, 27,879 fewer P-H of PPAH than Yoredale's, amounting to 56 percent as much, to 91 percent as much per cu of PPAH, and to 89 percent as much per inhabitant. Involved in Midwest's smaller personal appearance output were these habitat differences: a smaller PPAH, 61 percent as extensive as Yoredale's; a more varied PPAH, 187 percent as varied, fewer town inhabitants, 63 percent as many; and more town inhabitants per cu of PPAH, 103 percent as many.

Table 9.11
Personal Appearance
Behavior Output of Primary Habitat: Person-Hours (P-H)

	1954–55		1963–64	
	Midwest (1)	Yoredale (2)	Midwest (3)	Yoredale (4)
Output via all inhabitants				
(1) Total P-H			52,982	117,538
(2) Percent of GBP			2.8%	4.5%
(3) Mean P-H per cu			14,948	20,461
Output via town inhabitants				
(4) Total P-H	35,570	59,194	35,895	63,774
(5) Percent of TBP	3.8%	3.9%	3.2%	4.5%
(6) Mean P-H per cu	12,380	11,166	10,128	11,102
(7) Mean P-H per town inhabitant	49.7	45.5	43.2	48.7

In psychological language, these findings indicates that in 1963–64, *on the average*, Midwesterners *in comparison with Dalesmen* engaged in somewhat less behavior in the town's PPAH, within settings where there was less personal appearance activity by Midwesterners; they did this within a town where there was much less such activity, a smaller but more varied personal appearance habitat, appreciably fewer town inhabitants to take advantage of the personal appearance opportunities and carry out the duties, and slightly more inhabitants in relation to the number of personal appearance opportunities and duties.

Changes. Both towns' PPAHs produced more behavior in 1963–64. Midwest's produced, via town inhabitants, 325 more P-H of personal appearance behavior than in 1954–55, amounting to 101 percent as much, to 82 percent as much per cu of PPAH and to 87 percent as much per inhabitant. Involved in Midwest's greater personal appearance output in 1963–64 were these habitat differences: a larger PPAH, 121 percent as extensive as in 1954–55; a more varied PPAH, 107 percent as varied; more town inhabitants, 116 percent as many; and fewer inhabitants per cu of PPAH, 96 percent as many.

Yoredale's PPAH produced, via town inhabitants, 4580 more P-H of dress, grooming and adornment behavior in 1963–64 than in 1954–55, amounting to 108 percent as much, to 99 percent as much per cu of PPAH, and to 107 percent as much per inhabitant. Involved in Yoredale's greater output in 1963–64 were these habitat differences: a larger PPAH, 107 percent as extensive as in 1954–55; a less varied PPAH, 73 percent as varied; almost the same number of town inhabitants, 101 percent as many; and fewer inhabitants per cu of PPAH, 94 percent as many.

CLAIM-OPERATIONS GENERATED BY PRIMARY
PERSONAL APPEARANCE HABITAT

Salient findings, 1963–64. The total number of C-O generated by the towns' PPAHs for beauty operators, fashion models, bridesmaids, paraders, and so forth, were approximately equivalent to those produced by 100 different personal appearance settings with 8 operatives each in Midwest and 1.33 operatives each in Yoredale. Midwest's PPAH was more productive and Yoredale's was less productive of responsible actions than expected on the basis of either their extent or their output of P-H. Midwest's PPAH in 1963–64 constituted 3.3 percent of its total habitat, produced 2.8 percent of its GBP, and generated 5.9 percent of its C-O; and Yoredale's PPAH constituted 5.1 percent of its total habitat, produced 4.5 percent of its GBP, and generated 1.2 percent of its C-O. The mean yearly outputs per town inhabitant were 0.44 C-O per Midwesterner and 0.06 C-O per Dalesman, which were 88 and 40 percent, respectively, of the 1954–55 outputs. There were 43 percent of Midwest's and 54 percent of Yoredale's personal appearance C-O generated via town inhabitants.

C-O data are reported in Table 9.12.

Table 9.12
Personal Appearance
Behavior Output of Primary Habitat: Claim-Operations (C-O)

	1954–55		1963–64	
	Midwest (1)	Yoredale (2)	Midwest (3)	Yoredale (4)
Output via all inhabitants				
(1) Total C-O	829	425	840	139
(2) Percent of Gross C-O	10.4%	6.6%	5.9%	1.2%
(3) Mean C-O per cu	288.5	80.2	237.0	24.2
Output via town inhabitants				
(4) Total C-O	359	196	363	75
(5) Percent of Town C-O	8.6%	6.4%	5.5%	1.8%
(6) Mean C-O per cu	125.0	37.0	102.4	13.0
(7) Mean C-O per town inhabitant	0.50	0.15	0.44	0.06

Differences. Midwest's PPAH produces more C-O than Yoredale's. In 1963–64 it produced, via town inhabitants, 288 more C-O than Yoredale's, amounting to 484 percent as many, to 788 percent as many per cu of PPAH, and to 733 percent as many per inhabitant. Involved in Midwest's greater output of personal appearance C-O were these habitat differences: more PPAH claims for operatives, 900 percent as many as Yoredale; fewer town inhabitants, 63 percent as many; and fewer town inhabitants per PPAH claim, 7 percent as many.

Changes. Midwest's PPAH produced more C-O in 1963–64 than in 1954–55, and Yoredale's PPAH produced less. Midwest's produced, via town inhabitants, 4 more C-O in 1963–64, amounting to 101 percent as many, to 82 percent as many per cu of PPAH, and to 88 percent as many per inhabitant. Involved in Midwest's greater output of personal appearance C-O in 1963–64 were these habitat differences: more PPAH claims for operatives, 105 percent as many as in 1954–55; more town inhabitants, 116 percent as many, and more town inhabitants per PPAH claim, 111 percent as many.

Yoredale's PPAH produced, via town inhabitants, 121 fewer C-O in 1963–64 than in 1954–55, amounting to 38 percent as many, to 35 percent as many per cu of PPAH, and to 40 percent as many per inhabitant. Involved in Yoredale's smaller output of personal appearance C-O in 1963–64 were these habitat differences: fewer PPAH claims for operatives, 22 percent as many as in 1954–55; about the same number of town inhabitants, 101 percent as many; and more inhabitants per claim, 450 percent as many.

Yoredale's marked decrease in C-O reflects in large measure the demise between the survey years of a single but important behavior setting, Gala Day, which involved many Yoredale residents in implementing C-O in this day-long setting where most of the children of the town were decked out in colorful and often original costumes.

Physical Health

PERSON-HOURS OF BEHAVIOR GENERATED BY
PHYSICAL HEALTH HABITAT

Salient findings, 1963–64. Those parts of the towns' habitats that
have some health attributes—the territorial range of Physical
Health—produced 36 percent of Midwest's and 17 percent of Yoredale's GBP, and the primary physical health habitats of the towns
(PHH) produced, respectively, 2.4 and 3.6 percent of their GBP. The
mean weekly physical health outputs per town inhabitant were 27
minutes per Midwesterner and 35 minutes per Dalesman, which were
150 and 98 percent, respectively, of the 1954–55 outputs. Less than half
the PHH outputs of both towns—44 percent of Midwest's and 43 percent of Yoredale's—were generated via town inhabitants.

P-H data are reported in Table 9.13.

Differences. Midwest's PHH produces less behavior than Yoredale's. In 1963–64 it produced, via town inhabitants, 20,530 fewer P-H
of PHH behavior than Yoredale's, amounting to 49 percent as much, to
109 percent as much per cu of PHH, and to 77 percent as much per
inhabitant. Involved in Midwest's smaller health output were these habitat differences: a smaller PHH, 44 percent as extensive as Yoredale's; a
less varied PHH, 53 percent as varied; fewer town inhabitants, 63 percent as many; and more town inhabitants per cu of PHH, 142 percent
as many.

In psychological language, these findings indicate that in
1963–64, *on the average,* Midwesterners *in comparison with Dalesmen*
engaged in somewhat less behavior in the town's PHH, within settings
where there was more health activity by Midwesterners; they did this
within a town where there was much less such activity, a smaller and less
varied health habitat, appreciably fewer town inhabitants to take advantage of the health opportunities and carry out the health duties, but

Table 9.13
Physical Health
Behavior Output of Primary Habitat: Person-Hours (P-H)

	1954–55		1963–64	
	Midwest (1)	Yoredale (2)	Midwest (3)	Yoredale (4)
Output via all inhabitants				
(1) Total P-H			45,298	94,539
(2) Percent of GBP			2.4%	3.6%
(3) Mean P-H per cu			16,187	15,115
Output via town inhabitants				
(4) Total P-H	11,398	40,548	19,720	40,250
(5) Percent of TBP	1.2%	2.7%	1.7%	2.8%
(6) Mean P-H per cu	5,970	10,064	7,047	6,435
(7) Mean P-H per town inhabitant	15.9	31.2	23.8	30.7

more inhabitants in relation to the physical health opportunities and duties.

Changes. Midwest's PHH produced more behavior in 1963–64 than in 1954–55, and Yoredale's produced less. Midwest's produced, via town inhabitants, 8322 more P-H of health behavior in 1963–64, amounting to 173 percent as much, to 118 percent as much per cu of PHH, and to 150 percent as much per inhabitant. Involved in Midwest's greater health output in 1963–64 were these habitat differences: a larger PHH, 147 percent as extensive as in 1954–55; a more varied PHH, 133 percent as varied; more town inhabitants, 116 percent as many; and fewer inhabitants per cu of PHH, 79 percent as many.

Yoredale's PHH produced slightly less behavior in 1963–64. It produced via town inhabitants, 298 fewer P-H of health behavior than in 1954–55, amounting to 99 percent as much, to 64 percent as much per cu of PHH, and to 98 percent as much per inhabitant. Involved in Yoredale's smaller health output in 1963–64 were these habitat differences: a larger PHH, 157 percent as extensive as in 1954–55; a more varied PHH, 136 percent as varied; about the same number of town inhabitants, 101 percent as many; and fewer inhabitants per cu of PHH, 64 percent as many.

CLAIM-OPERATIONS GENERATED BY PRIMARY
PHYSICAL HEALTH HABITAT

Salient findings, 1963–64. The total number of C-O generated by the towns' PHHs for dentists, pharmacists, teachers, clerks, doctors and so forth, were approximately equivalent to those produced by 50 different health settings with 1.25 operatives each in Midwest and 4 operatives each in Yoredale. Both towns PHHs were less productive of responsible actions than expected on the basis of either their extent or their output of P-H. Midwest's PHH in 1963–64 constituted 2.6 percent of its total habitat, produced 2.4 percent of its GBP, and generated 0.4 percent of its C-O; and Yoredale's PHH constituted 5.5 percent of its total habitat, produced 3.6 percent of its GBP, and generated 1.7 percent of its C-O. The mean yearly outputs per town inhabitant were 0.04 C-O per Midwesterner and 0.05 C-O per Dalesman, which were 80 and 167 percent, respectively, of the 1954–55 outputs. There were 59 percent of Midwest's and 35 percent of Yoredale's physical health C-O generated via town inhabitants.

C-O data are reported in Table 9.14.

Differences. Midwest's PHH produces fewer C-O than Yoredale's. In 1963–64 it produced, via town inhabitants, 34 fewer C-O than Yoredale, amounting to 52 percent as many, to 117 percent as many per cu of PHH, and to 80 percent as many per inhabitant. Involved in Midwest's smaller output of health C-O were these habitat differences: fewer PHH claims for operatives, 27 percent as many as Yoredale; fewer town inhabitants, 63 percent as many; and more town inhabitants per PHH claim, 232 percent as many.

Table 9.14
Physical Health
Behavior Output of Primary Habitat: Claim-Operations (C-O)

	1954–55		1963–64	
	Midwest (1)	Yoredale (2)	Midwest (3)	Yoredale (4)
Output via all inhabitants				
(1) Total C-O	48	84	63	200
(2) Percent of gross C-O	0.6%	1.3%	0.4%	1.7%
(3) Mean C-O per cu	25.1	20.8	22.5	32.0
Output via town inhabitants				
(4) Total C–O	35	44	37	71
(5) Percent of Town C-O	0.8%	1.4%	0.6%	1.7%
(6) Mean C-O per cu	18.3	10.9	13.2	11.3
(7) Mean C-O per town inhabitant	0.05	0.03	0.04	0.05

Changes. Both towns' PHHs produced more C-O in 1963–64. Midwest's produced, via town inhabitants, 2 more C-O than in 1954–55, amounting to 106 percent as many, to 72 percent as many per cu of PHH, and to 80 percent as many per inhabitant. Involved in Midwest's greater output of health C-O in 1963–64 were these habitat differences: more PHH claims for operatives, 191 percent as many as in 1954–55; more town inhabitants, 116 percent as many, and fewer town inhabitants per PHH claim, 61 percent as many.

Yoredale's PHH produced, via town inhabitants, 27 more C-O in 1963–64, amounting to 161 percent as many, to 104 percent as many per cu of PHH, and to 167 percent as many per inhabitant. Involved in Yoredale's greater output of health C-O in 1963–64 were these habitat differences: more PHH claims for operatives, 209 percent as many as in 1954–55; about the same number of town inhabitants, 101 percent as many, and fewer inhabitants per claim, 48 percent as many.

Professional Involvement

PERSON-HOURS OF BEHAVIOR GENERATED BY
PROFESSIONAL INVOLVEMENT HABITAT

Salient findings, 1963–64. Those parts of the towns' habitats that have some professional attributes — the territorial range of Professional Involvement — produced 96 percent of Midwest's and 97 percent of Yoredale's GBP, and the primary professional involvement habitats of the towns (PPH) produced respectively, 88.3 and 86.6 percent of their GBP. The mean daily professional involvement outputs per town inhabitant were 3 hours, 11 minutes per Midwesterner and 2 hours, 41 minutes per Dalesman, which were 110 and 92 percent, respectively, of the 1954–55 outputs. More than half the PPH outputs of both towns — 62 percent of Midwest's and 56 percent of Yoredale's — were generated via town inhabitants.

Table 9.15
Professional Involvement
Behavior Output of Primary Habitat: Person-Hours (P-H)

| | 1954–55 | | 1963–64 | |
	Midwest (1)	Yoredale (2)	Midwest (3)	Yoredale (4)
Output via all inhabitants				
(1) Total P-H			1,566,686	2,275,053
(2) Percent of GBP			83.3%	86.6%
(3) Mean P-H per cu			22,242	28,260
Output via town inhabitants				
(4) Total P-H	760,478	1,336,322	967,858	1,284,038
(5) Percent of TBP	81.8%	88.7%	86.0%	90.0%
(6) Mean P-H per cu	11,416	18,940	13,740	15,950
(7) Mean P-H per town inhabitant	1,064	1,028	1,166	980

P-H data are reported in Table 9.15.

Differences. Midwest's PPH produces less behavior than Yoredale's. In 1963–64 it produced, via town inhabitants, 316,180 fewer P-H than Yoredale's, amounting to 76 percent as much, to 86 percent as much per cu of PPH, but to 119 percent as much per inhabitant. Involved in Midwest's smaller professional output were these habitat differences: a smaller PPH, 87 percent as extensive as Yoredale's; a more varied PPH, 103 percent as varied; fewer town inhabitants, 63 percent as many; and fewer town inhabitants per cu of PPH, 72 percent as many.

In psychological language, these findings indicate that in 1963–64, *on the average,* Midwesterners *in comparison with Dalesmen* engaged in somewhat more behavior in the town's PPH, within settings where there was less professional activity by Midwesterners; they did this within a town where there was appreciably less such activity, a smaller and slightly more varied professional habitat, appreciably fewer town inhabitants to take advantage of the professional opportunities and carry out the duties, and appreciably fewer inhabitants in relation to the professional opportunities and duties.

Changes. Midwest's PPH produced more behavior in 1963–64 than in 1954–55, and Yoredale's produced less. Midwest's produced, via town inhabitants, 207,380 more P-H in 1963–64, amounting to 127 percent as much, to 120 percent as much per cu of PPH, and to 110 percent as much per town inhabitant. Involved in Midwest's greater professional output in 1963–64 were these habitat differences: a larger PPH, 106 percent as extensive as in 1954–55; a more varied PPH, 118 percent as varied; more town inhabitants, 116 percent as many; and more inhabitants per centiurb of PPH, 110 percent as many.

Yoredale's PPH produced somewhat less behavior in 1963–64. It produced, via town inhabitants, 52,284 fewer P-H than in 1954–55, amounting to 96 percent as much, to 84 percent as much per cu of

PPH, and to 92 percent as much per inhabitant. Involved in Yoredale's smaller professional output in 1963–64 were these habitat differences: a larger PPH, 114 percent as extensive as in 1954–55; a more varied PPH, 121 percent as varied; almost the same number of town inhabitants, 101 percent as many; and fewer inhabitants per cu of PPH, 88 percent as many.

CLAIM-OPERATIONS GENERATED BY PRIMARY
PROFESSIONAL INVOLVEMENT HABITAT

Salient findings, 1963–64. The total numbers of C-O generated by the towns' PPHs for teachers, clerks, secretaries, carpenters, and so forth, were approximately equivalent to those produced by 100 different professional settings with 14 operatives each in Midwest and 16 operatives each in Yoredale. Both towns' PPHs were less productive of responsible actions than expected on the basis of either their extent or their output of P-H. Midwest's PPH in 1963–64 constituted 65.6 percent of its total habitat, produced 83.3 percent of its GBP, and generated 10.2 percent of its C-O; and Yoredale's PPH constituted 71.4 percent of its total habitat, produced 86.6 percent of its GBP, and generated 14.1 percent of its C-O. The mean yearly outputs per town inhabitant were 0.99 C-O per Midwesterner and 0.55 C-O per Dalesman, which were 139 and 131 percent, respectively, of the 1954–55 outputs. There were 56 percent of Midwest's and 44 percent of Yoredale's professional involvement C-O generated via town inhabitants.

C-O data are reported in Table 9.16.

Differences. Midwest's PPH produces more C-O than Yoredale's. In 1963–64 it produced, via town inhabitants, 94 more C-O than Yoredale's, amounting to 113 percent as many, to 129 percent as many per cu of PPH, and to 180 percent as many per inhabitant. Involved in Midwest's greater output of professional C-O were these habitat differences: fewer PPH claims for operatives, 87 percent as many, as

Table 9.16
Professional Involvement
Behavior Output of Primary Habitat: Claim-Operations (C-O)

	1954–55		1963–64	
	Midwest (1)	Yoredale (2)	Midwest (3)	Yoredale (4)
Output via all inhabitants				
(1) Total C-O	860	1,093	1,452	1,654
(2) Percent of Gross C-O	10.8%	16.9%	10.2%	14.1%
(3) Mean C-O per cu	12.9	15.5	20.6	20.5
Output via town inhabitants				
(4) Total C-O	509	553	819	725
(5) Percent of Town C-O	12.2%	18.1%	12.3%	17.2%
(6) Mean C-O per cu	7.6	7.8	11.6	9.0
(7) Mean C-O per town inhabitant	0.71	0.42	0.99	0.55

Yoredale; fewer town inhabitants, 63 percent as many; and fewer town inhabitants per PPH claim, 73 percent as many.

Changes. Both towns' PPHs produced more C-O in 1963–64. Midwest's produced, via town inhabitants, 310 more C-O than in 1954–55, amounting to 161 percent as many, to 153 percent as many per cu of PPH, and to 139 percent as many per inhabitant. Involved in Midwest's greater output of professional C-O in 1963–64 were these habitat differences: more PPH claims for operatives, 154 percent as many as in 1954–55; more town inhabitants, 116 percent as many; and fewer town inhabitants per PPH claim, 75 percent as many.

Yoredale's PPH produced, via town inhabitants, 172 more C-O in 1963–64, amounting to 131 percent as many, to 115 percent as many per cu of PPH, and to 131 percent as many per inhabitant. Involved in Yoredale's greater output of professional C-O in 1963–64 were these habitat differences: more PPH claims for operatives, 115 percent as many as in 1954–55; about the same number of town inhabitants, 101 percent as many; and fewer inhabitants per claim, 88 percent as many.

Recreation

PERSON-HOURS OF BEHAVIOR GENERATED BY RECREATIONAL HABITAT

Salient findings, 1963–64. Those parts of the towns' habitats that have some recreational attributes—the territorial range of Recreation—produced 67 percent of Midwest's and 70 percent of Yoredale's gross behavior GBP, and the primary recreational habitats of the towns (PRH) produced, respectively, 13.9 and 13.1 percent of their GBP. The mean weekly recreational outputs per town inhabitant were 3 hours, 13 minutes per Midwesterner and 2 hours, 45 minutes per Dalesman, which were 91 and 71 percent, respectively, of the 1954–55 outputs. More than half the PRH outputs of both towns—53 percent of Midwest's and 54 percent of Yoredale's—were generated via town inhabitants.

P-H data are reported in Table 9.17.

Differences. Midwest's PRH produces less behavior than Yoredale's. In 1963–64 it produced, via its town inhabitants, 49,264 fewer P-H of recreational behavior than Yoredale's, amounting to 74 percent as much, to 91 percent as much per cu of PRH, and to 116 percent as much per inhabitant. Involved in Midwest's smaller recreational output were these habitat differences: a smaller PRH, 81 percent as extensive as Yoredale's; a less varied PRH, 92 percent as varied; fewer town inhabitants, 63 percent as many; and fewer town inhabitants per cu of PRH, 78 percent as many.

In psychological language, these findings indicate that in 1963–64, *on the average*, Midwesterners *in comparison with Dalesmen* engaged in appreciably more behavior in the town's PRH, within settings where there was less recreational activity by Midwesterners; they

Table 9.17
Recreation
Behavior Output of Primary Habitat: Person-Hours (P-H)

	1954–55		1963–64	
	Midwest (1)	Yoredale (2)	Midwest (3)	Yoredale (4)
Output via all inhabitants				
(1) Total P-H			262,147	344,892
(2) Percent of GBP			13.9%	13.1%
(3) Mean P-H per cu			18,118	19,286
Output via town inhabitants				
(4) Total P-H	131,544	262,623	138,586	187,850
(5) Percent of TBP	14.1%	17.4%	12.3%	13.2%
(6) Mean P-H per cu	14,201	20,375	9,578	10,504
(7) Mean P-H per town inhabitant	184	202	167	143

did this within a town where there was appreciably less such activity, a smaller and less varied recreational habitat, with appreciably fewer town inhabitants to take advantage of the recreational opportunities and carry out the recreational duties, and fewer inhabitants in relation to the recreational opportunities and duties.

Changes. Midwest PRH produced more behavior in 1963–64 than in 1954–55, and Yoredale's produced less. Midwest's produced, via town inhabitants, 7042 more P-H of recreational behavior in 1963–64, amounting to 105 percent as much, to 67 percent as much per cu of PRH, and to 91 percent as much per inhabitant. Involved in Midwest's greater recreational output in 1963–64 were these habitat differences: a larger PRH, 156 percent as extensive as in 1954–55; a more varied PRH, 120 percent as varied; more town inhabitants, 116 percent as many; and fewer inhabitants per cu of PRH, 74 percent as many.

Yoredale produced less recreational behavior in 1963–64 than in 1954–55. It produced, via town inhabitants, 74,773 fewer P-H of recreational behavior, amounting to 71 percent as much to 52 percent as much per cu of PRH, and to 71 percent as much per inhabitant. Involved in Yoredale's smaller recreational output in 1963–64 were these habitat differences: a larger PRH, 139 percent as extensive as in 1954–55; a more varied PRH, 138 percent as varied; about the same number of town inhabitants, 101 percent as many; and fewer inhabitants per cu of PRH, 72 percent as many.

CLAIM-OPERATIONS GENERATED BY PRIMARY RECREATIONAL HABITAT

Salient findings, 1963–64. The total number of C-O generated by the towns' PRHs for members of sports' teams, game officials, cast members, and so forth, were approximately equivalent to those produced by 300 different recreational settings with 21 operatives each in Midwest and with 19 operatives each in Yoredale. Both towns PRHs were much more productive of responsible actions than expected on the basis of either their extent or their output of P-H. Midwest's PRH constituted 13.5 percent of its total habitat, produced 13.9 percent of its GBP, and generated 44.2 percent of its C-O; and Yoredale's PRH constituted 15.9 percent of its total habitat, produced 13.1 percent of its GBP, and generated 48.8 percent of its C-O. The mean yearly outputs per town inhabitant were 3.34 C-O per Midwesterner and 1.44 C-O per Dalesman, which were 153 and 148 percent, respectively, of the 1954–55 outputs. There were 44 percent of Midwest's and 33 percent of Yoredale's recreational C-O generated via town inhabitants.

C-O data are reported in Table 9.18.

Differences. Midwest's PRH produces more C-O than Yoredale's. In 1963–64 it produced, via town inhabitants, 883 more C-O than Yoredale's, amounting to 147 percent as many, to 181 percent as many per cu of PRH, and to 232 percent as many per inhabitant. Involved in Midwest's greater output of recreational C-O were these habitat differences: more PRH claims for operatives, 108 percent as many as Yoredale; fewer town inhabitants, 63 percent as many; and fewer town inhabitants per PRH claim, 58 percent as many.

Changes. Both towns' PRHs produced more C-O in 1963–64. Midwest produced, via town inhabitants, 1213 more C-O than in 1954–55, amounting to 178 percent as many, to 114 percent as many per cu of PRH, and to 153 percent as many per inhabitant. Involved in Midwest's greater output of recreational C-O in 1963–64 were these habitat differences: more PRH claims for operatives, 181 percent as many as in 1954–55; more town inhabitants, 116 percent as many; and fewer town inhabitants per PRH claim, 64 percent as many.

Yoredale's PRH produced, via town inhabitants, 630 more C-O in 1963–64, amounting to 150 percent as many to 108 percent as many per cu of PRH, and to 148 percent as many per inhabitant. Involved in Yoredale's greater output of recreational C-O in 1963–64 were these

Table 9.18

Recreation

Behavior Output of Primary Habitat: Claim-Operations (C-O)

	1954–55		1963–64	
	Midwest (1)	Yoredale (2)	Midwest (3)	Yoredale (4)
Output via all inhabitants				
(1) Total C-O	3,516	3,110	6,308	5,714
(2) Percent of Gross C-O	44.3%	48.2%	44.2%	48.8%
(3) Mean C-O per cu	379.6	241.3	436.0	319.5
Output via town inhabitants				
(4) Total C-O	1,562	1,262	2,775	1,892
(5) Percent of Town C-O	37.4%	41.3%	41.8%	45.0%
(6) Mean C-O per cu	168.6	97.9	192.0	105.8
(7) Mean C-O per town inhabitant	2.18	0.97	3.34	1.44

habitat differences: more PRH claims for operatives, 239 percent as many as in 1954–55; about the same number of town inhabitants, 101 percent as many; and fewer inhabitants per claim, 42 percent as many.

Religion

PERSON-HOURS OF BEHAVIOR GENERATED BY RELIGIOUS HABITAT

Salient findings, 1963–64. Those parts of the towns' habitats that have some religious attributes — the territorial range of Religion — produced 11 percent of Midwest's and of Yoredale's GBP, and the primary religious habitats of the towns (PR1H) produced, respectively, 2.9 and 2.7 percent of their GBP. The mean weekly PR1H outputs per town inhabitant were 37 minutes per Midwesterner and 31 minutes per Dalesman, which were 68 and 105 percent, respectively, of the 1954–55 outputs. About half of the PR1H outputs of both towns — 49 percent of Midwest's and 48 percent of Yoredale's — were generated via town inhabitants.

P-H data are reported in Table 9.19.

Differences. Midwest's PR1H produces less behavior than Yoredale's. In 1963–64 it produced, via town inhabitants, 8192 fewer P-H of religious behavior than Yoredale's, amounting to 77 percent as much to 40 percent as much per cu of PR1H, and to 121 percent as much per inhabitant. Involved in Midwest's smaller religious output were these habitat differences: a larger PR1H, 194 percent as extensive as Yoredale's; a less varied PR1H, 93 percent as varied; fewer town inhabitants, 63 percent as many, and fewer town inhabitants per cu of PR1H, 33 percent as many.

In psychological language, these findings indicate that in 1963–64, *on the average,* Midwesterners *in comparison with Dalesmen* engaged in more behavior in the town's PR1H, within settings where there was less religious activity by Midwesterners; they did this, within

Table 9.19
Religion
Behavior Output of Primary Habitat: Person-Hours (P-H)

	1954–55		1963–64	
	Midwest (1)	Yoredale (2)	Midwest (3)	Yoredale (4)
Output via all inhabitants				
(1) Total P-H			54,801	72,180
(2) Percent of GBP			2.9%	2.7%
(3) Mean P-H per cu			6,025	15,252
Output via town inhabitants				
(4) Total P-H	34,194	33,174	26,839	35,031
(5) Percent of TBP	3.7%	2.2%	2.4%	2.5%
(6) Mean P-H per cu	7,256	6,974	2,951	7,402
(7) Mean P-H per town inhabitant	47.8	25.5	32.3	26.7

a town where there was appreciably less such activity, a larger but less varied religious habitat, appreciably fewer town inhabitants to take advantage of the religious opportunities and carry out the religious duties, and many fewer town inhabitants in relation to the religious opportunities and duties.

Changes. Midwest's PR1H produced less behavior in 1963–64 than in 1954–55; Yoredale's produced more. Midwest's produced, via town inhabitants, 7355 fewer P-H of religious behavior in 1963–64, amounting to 78 percent as much, to 41 percent as much per cu of PR1H, and to 68 percent as much per inhabitant. Involved in Midwest's smaller religious output in 1963–64 were these habitat differences: a larger PR1H, 194 percent as extensive as in 1954–55; an equally varied PR1H, 100 percent as varied, more town inhabitants, 116 percent as many; and fewer inhabitants per cu of PR1H, 60 percent as many.

Yoredale produced more religious behavior in 1963–64 than in 1954–55. It produced, via town inhabitants, 1857 more P-H of religious behavior, amounting to 106 percent as much, to 106 percent as much per cu of PR1H, and to 105 percent as much per inhabitant. Involved in Yoredale's greater religious output in 1963–64 were these habitat differences: a smaller PR1H, 98 percent as extensive as in 1954–55; a more varied PR1H, 125 percent as varied; about the same number of town inhabitants, 101 percent as many, and more inhabitants per cu of PR1H, 103 percent as many.

CLAIM-OPERATIONS GENERATED BY PRIMARY RELIGIOUS HABITAT

Salient findings, 1963–64. The total number of C-O generated by the towns' PR1Hs for preachers, choir members, ushers, teachers, and so forth, are approximately equivalent to those produced by 200 different religious settings with 8.6 operatives each in Midwest and with 5.3 operatives each in Yoredale. Both towns' PR1Hs were more productive of responsible actions than expected on the basis of either their extent or their output of P-H. Midwest's PR1H constituted 8.5 percent of its total habitat, produced 2.9 percent of its GBP, and generated 12.1 percent of its C-O; and Yoredale's PR1H constituted 4.2 percent of its total habitat, produced 2.7 percent of its GBP, and generated 9.0 percent of its C-O. The mean yearly outputs per town inhabitant were 1.05 C-O per Midwesterner and 0.54 C-O per Dalesman, which were 91 and 93 percent, respectively, of the 1954–55 outputs. There were 50 percent of Midwest's and 67 percent of Yoredale's religious C-O generated via town inhabitants.

C-O data are reported in Table 9.20.

Differences. Midwest's PR1H produces more C-O than Yoredale's. In 1963–64 it produced, via town inhabitants, 164 more C-O than Yoredale's, amounting to 123 percent as many, to 64 percent as many per cu of PR1H, and to 194 percent as many per inhabitant. Involved in Midwest's greater output of religious C-O were these habitat differences: more PR1H claims for operatives, 167 percent as many as

Table 9.20
Religion
Behavior Output of Primary Habitat: Claim-Operations (C-O)

	1954–55		1963–64	
	Midwest (1)	Yoredale (2)	Midwest (3)	Yoredale (4)
Output via all inhabitants				
(1) Total C-O	1,262	912	1,724	1,053
(2) Percent of Gross C-O	15.9%	14.1%	12.1%	9.0%
(3) Mean C-O per cu	267.8	191.7	189.6	222.5%
Output via town inhabitants				
(4) Total C-O	825	761	871	707
(5) Percent of Town C-O	19.8%	24.9%	13.1%	16.8%
(6) Mean C-O per cu	175.0	160.0	95.8	149.4
(7) Mean C-O per town inhabitant	1.15	0.58	1.05	0.54

Yoredale; fewer town inhabitants, 63 percent as many; and fewer town inhabitants per PR1H claim, 38 percent as many.

Changes. Midwest's PR1H produced more C-O in 1963–64 than in 1954–55, and Yoredale's produced less. Midwest's produced, via town inhabitants, 46 more C-O in 1963–64, amounting to 106 percent as many, to 55 percent as many per cu of PR1H, and to 91 percent as many per inhabitant. Involved in Midwest's larger output of religious C-O in 1963–64 were these habitat differences: more PR1H claims for operatives, 126 percent as many as in 1954–55; more town inhabitants, 116 percent as many; and fewer town inhabitants per PR1H claim, 92 percent as many.

Yoredale's PR1H produced less C-O in 1963–64. It produced, via town inhabitants, 54 fewer C-O in 1963–64, amounting to 93 percent as many, to 93 percent as many per cu of PR1H, and to 93 percent as many per inhabitant. Involved in Yoredale's output of religious C-O in 1963–64 were these habitat differences: more PR1H claims for operatives, 113 percent as many as in 1954–55, about the same number of town inhabitants, 101 percent as many; and fewer inhabitants per claim, 89 percent as many.

Social Contact

PERSON-HOURS OF BEHAVIOR GENERATED BY
SOCIAL CONTACT HABITATS

Salient findings, 1963–64. Those parts of the towns' habitats that have some social attributes—the territorial range of Social Contact—produced 100 percent of Midwest's and of Yoredale's GBP, and the primary social habitats of the towns (PSH) produced, respectively, 67.6 and 63.1 percent of their GBP. The mean weekly PSH outputs per town inhabitant were 16 hours, 33 minutes per Midwesterner and 11 hours, 12 minutes per Dalesman, which were 104 and 102 percent,

Table 9.21
Social Contact
Behavior Output of Primary Habitat: Person-Hours (P-H)

	1954–55		1963–64	
	Midwest (1)	Yoredale (2)	Midwest (3)	Yoredale (4)
Output via all inhabitants				
(1) Total P-H			1,271,494	1,657,829
(2) Percent of GBP			67.6%	63.1%
(3) Mean P-H per cu			18,739	23,006
Output via town inhabitants				
(4) Total P-H	583,363	742,221	706,402	762,886
(5) Percent of TBP	62.7%	49.3%	62.8%	53.5%
(6) Mean P-H per cu	10,780	16,194	10,411	10,587
(7) Mean P-H per town inhabitant	815.9	570.9	851.1	582.3

respectively, of the 1954–55 outputs. About half the PSH output of both towns — 55 percent of Midwest's and 46 percent of Yoredale's — were generated via town inhabitants.

P-H data are reported in Table 9.21.

Differences. Midwest's PSH produces less behavior than Yoredale's. In 1963–64 it produced, via town inhabitants, 56,484 fewer P-H of social behavior than Yoredale's, amounting to 93 percent as much, to 98 percent as much per cu of PSH, but to 146 percent as much per inhabitant. Involved in Midwest's smaller social behavior output were these habitat differences: a smaller PSH, 94 percent as extensive as Yoredale's; a less varied PSH, 84 percent as varied; fewer town inhabitants, 63 percent as many; and fewer town inhabitants per cu of PSH, 67 percent as many.

In psychological language, these findings indicate that in 1963–64, *on the average,* Midwesterners *in comparison with Dalesmen* engaged in much more behavior in the town's PSH, within settings where there was slightly less social activity by Midwesterners; they did this within a town where there was less such activity, a smaller and less varied social habitat, appreciably fewer town inhabitants to take advantage of the social opportunities and carry out the social duties, and appreciably fewer inhabitants in relation to the social opportunities and duties.

Changes. Both towns' PSHs produced more behavior in 1963–64. Midwest's produced, via town inhabitants, 123,039 more P-H of social behavior than in 1954–55, amounting to 121 percent as much, to 97 percent as much per cu of PSH, and to 104 percent as much per inhabitant. Involved in Midwest's greater social behavior output in 1963–64 were these habitat differences: a larger PSH, 125 percent as extensive as in 1954–55; a more varied PSH, 111 percent as varied; more town inhabitants, 116 percent as many; and fewer inhabitants per cu of PSH, 92 percent as many.

Yoredale's PSH produced, via town inhabitants, 20,665 more P-H of social behavior in 1963–64 than in 1954–55, amounting to 103 percent as much to 65 percent as much per cu of PSH, and to 102 percent as much per inhabitant. Involved in Yoredale's greater social output in 1963–64 were these habitat differences: a larger PSH, 157 percent as extensive as in 1954–55; a more varied PSH, 154 percent as varied; about the same number of town inhabitants, 101 percent as many; and fewer inhabitants per cu of PSH, 64 percent as many.

CLAIM-OPERATIONS GENERATED BY PRIMARY SOCIAL HABITAT

Salient findings, 1963–64. The total number of C-O generated by the towns' PSHs for club officers, party organizers, and so forth, were approximately equivalent to those produced by 500 different social settings with 27 operatives each in Midwest and with 22 operatives each in Yoredale. Both towns' PSHs were more productive of responsible actions than expected on the basis of either their extent or their output of P-H. Midwest's PSH constituted 63.2 percent of its total habitat, produced 67.6 percent of its GBP, and generated 94 percent of its C-O; and Yoredale's PSH constituted 63.9 percent of its total habitat, produced 63.1 percent of its GBP, and generated 93.9 percent of its C-O. The mean yearly outputs per town inhabitant were 7.43 C-O per Midwesterner and 2.91 C-O per Dalesman, which were 137 and 139 percent, respectively, of the 1954–55 outputs. Less than half of the social C-O of both towns — 46 percent of Midwest's and 35 percent of Yoredales — were generated via town inhabitants.

C-O data are reported in Table 9.22.

Differences. Midwest's PSH produces more C-O than Yoredale's. In 1963–64 it produced via town inhabitants, 2350 more C-O than Yoredale's, amounting to 162 percent as many, to 171 percent as many per cu of PSH, and to 255 percent as many per inhabitant. Involved in Midwest's greater output of social C-O were these habitat differences: more PSH claims for operatives, 135 percent as many as Yoredale;

Table 9.22
Social Contact
Behavior Output of Primary Habitat: Claim-Operations (C-O)

	1954–55		1963–64	
	Midwest (1)	Yoredale (2)	Midwest (3)	Yoredale (4)
Output via all inhabitants				
(1) Total C-O	7,507	5,929	13,413	11,001
(2) Percent of Gross C-O	94.6%	91.8%	94.0%	93.9%
(3) Mean C–O per cu	138.7	129.4	197.7	152.7
Output via town inhabitants				
(4) Total C-O	3,884	2,718	6,167	3,817
(5) Percent of Town C-O	93.1%	89.0%	92.8%	90.8%
(6) Mean C-O per cu	71.8	59.3	90.9	53.0
(7) Mean C-O per town inhabitant	5.43	2.09	7.43	2.91

fewer town inhabitants, 63 percent as many; and fewer town inhabitants per PSH claim, 47 percent as many.

Changes. Both towns' PSHs produced more C-O in 1963–64 than in 1954–55. Midwest's produced, via town inhabitants; 2283 more C-O in 1963–64, amounting to 159 percent as many, to 127 percent as many per cu of PSH, and to 137 percent as many per inhabitant. Involved in Midwest's greater output of social C-O in 1963–64 were these habitat differences: more PSH claims for operatives, 193 percent as many as in 1954–55; more town inhabitants, 116 percent as many; and fewer town inhabitants per PSH claim, 60 percent as many.

Yoredale's PSH produced, via town inhabitants, 1099 more C-O in 1963–64, amounting to 140 percent as many, to 89 percent as many per cu of PSH, and to 139 percent as many per inhabitant. Involved in Yoredale's greater output of social C-O in 1963–64 were these habitat differences: more PSH claims for operatives, 198 percent as many as in 1954–55; about the same number of town inhabitants, 101 percent as many; and fewer inhabitants per claim, 51 percent as many.

Summary: Behavior Outputs of Primary Action-Pattern Habitats

In the sections above, we have separately presented detailed information on the behavior outputs of each of the 11 action pattern habitats. Next we present graphic overviews of the behavior outputs of these differential habitats of Midwest and Yoredale in 1963–64, and overviews of changes in their outputs between 1954–55 and 1963–64, as these are measured on two dimensions of habitat output: number of person-hours of behavior (P-H) and number of claim-operations (C-O) occurring in these habitats. These summary data are presented in Figures 9.1 and 9.2. Each graph has two parts: Part A shows a pair of curves representing mean output (in P-H or C-O) per town inhabitant in Midwest and Yoredale across the 11 action pattern habitats, arranged in order of increasing output in Midwest; Part B shows, with another pair of curves, data on changes between the survey years in output of the action pattern habitats of the two towns, as the ratio of the appropriate 1963–64 value to the corresponding 1954–55 value in each town.

Although we have chosen to present these data in the form of continuous line curves, there is no continuity across the 11 action pattern habitats; the action patterns are discrete attributes of the towns' habitats and the curves, therefore, should be understood as diagrams representing the behavior outputs in these discrete habitats and not as graphs showing unitary functional relationships. This mode of presentation reveals the differences and changes in output more clearly than do bar graphs or other representations that we have tried. The reader should note that the order of the action patterns on the abscissa, and the scales used on the ordinate, are not the same in both graphs.

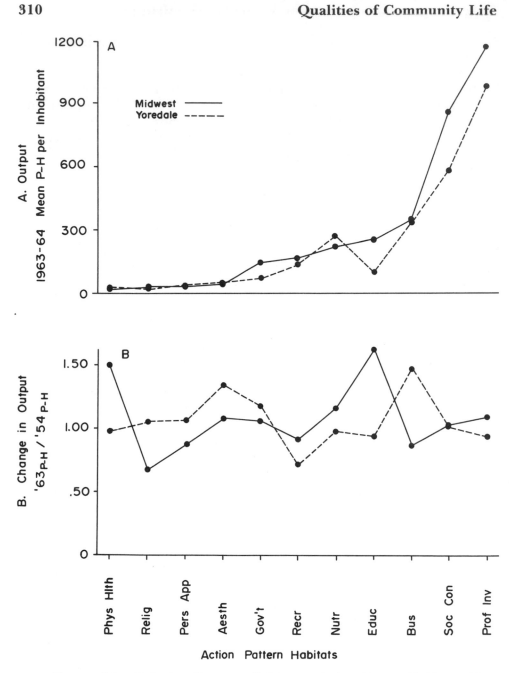

FIGURE 9.1. Behavior Outputs of Primary Action Pattern Habitats: Mean Person-Hours per Town Inhabitant. A: output, 1963–64; B: change in output, $'63_{P\text{-}H}/'54_{P\text{-}H}$.

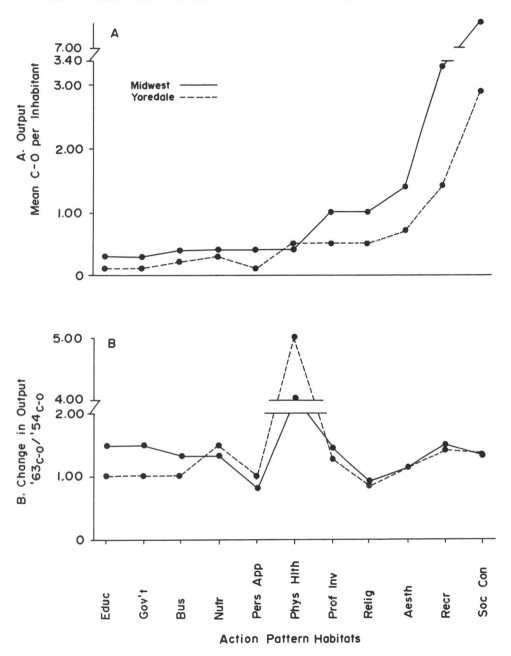

FIGURE 9.2. Behavior Outputs of Primary Action Pattern Habitats: Mean Claim-Operations per Town Inhabitant. A: output, 1963–64; B: change in output, $'63_{c\text{-}o}/'54_{c\text{-}o}$.

PERSON-HOURS

Mean P-H per town inhabitant. The output per town inhabitant of the 11 primary action pattern habitats in 1963–64 showed similar patterns in the two towns (Figure 9.1A). Physical Health, Religion, Personal Appearance, and Aesthetics had relatively small outputs, and Professional Involvement, Social Contact, and Business had relatively large outputs. Professional Involvement, the largest producer in both towns, exceeded Physical Health, the smallest producer in both towns, by a factor of 49 in Midwest and 37 in Yoredale.

Midwest's overall 25 percent superiority to Yoredale in P-H per town inhabitant was concentrated in the primary habitats for Education, Government, and Social Contact, especially the first two; its output was lower than Yoredale's in the primary habitats for Aesthetics, Personal Appearance, Nutrition, and Physical Health. Relative to Yoredale, Midwest's yield per town inhabitant of educational and governmental behavior was large and its yield of nutritional and health behavior was small.

Changes. There was little similarity between the towns in change between the survey years (Figure 9.1B). In Midwest, mean P-H per town inhabitant increased greatly in the primary action pattern habitats for Education and Physical Health and decreased in the primary habitats for Religion, Personal Appearance, Business, and Recreation.

In Yoredale, the biggest increases occurred in the primary habitats for Business, Aesthetics, and Government, and three others (Personal Appearance, Religion, and Social Contact) increased at slower rates. The other primary action pattern habitats, like the town's total habitat, showed small decreases in output of P-H per town inhabitant; Recreation decreased most (YD'63/YD'54 times 100 equals 71 percent). In view of the big increase in the extent of Yoredale's primary habitat for Education, the reduced output per town inhabitant (94 percent) is especially interesting. Yoredale's educational habitat was inhabited by nonresidents more extensively in 1963–64 than in 1954–55.

CLAIM-OPERATIONS

Mean C-O per town inhabitant. The pattern of C-O output across primary action pattern habitats is similar in the towns. In 1963–64 Social Contact was most highly productive of C-O in both towns; Recreation ranked second, but it produced less than half as many C-O per town inhabitant. Aesthetics ranked a poor third. All the other primary action pattern habitats of both towns produced 1 or fewer C-O per town inhabitant.

Midwest's overall superiority to Yoredale on this dimension (MW/YD times 100 equals 250 percent) was exceeded in two of the primary action pattern habitats: Personal Appearance and Social Contact. In addition, Midwest was also markedly superior to Yoredale on all the other primary action pattern habitats except Physical Health, in which Midwest's output was only 80 percent of Yoredale's.

Changes. Data on changes between the survey years in production of C-O by the primary action pattern habitats are presented in Figure 9.2B. There is general agreement between the towns in the direction and degree of change in output of C-O by 8 of the action pattern habitats. The mean output per town habitat increases between the survey years within the primary habitats for Education, Business, Nutrition, Professional Involvement, Aesthetics, Recreation, and Social Contact, with Nutrition and Recreation increasing most; the outputs of the towns' primary habitats for Religion decrease. Discrepant changes occur in the case of Physical Health (output increases in Yoredale and decreases in Midwest), Government (output increases much more in Yoredale), and Personal Appearance (output decreases much more in Yoredale).

BEHAVIOR OUTPUTS OF
BEHAVIOR-MECHANISM HABITATS

We next present data on the outputs of those parts of the towns where the behavior mechanisms Affective Behavior, Gross Motor Activity, Manipulation, and Talking occur.

Affective Behavior

PERSON-HOURS OF BEHAVIOR GENERATED BY AFFECTIVE HABITAT

Salient findings, 1963–64. Those parts of the towns' habitats that have some affective attributes—the territorial range of Affective Behavior—produced 53 percent of Midwest's and 46 percent of Yoredale's GBP, and the primary affective habitats of the towns (PAfH) produced, respectively, 14.1 and 5.9 percent of their GBP. The mean weekly PAfH outputs per town inhabitant were 2 hours, 47 minutes per Midwesterner and 1 hour, 5 minutes per Dalesman, which were 78 and 41 percent, respectively, of the 1954–55 outputs. Less than half the PAfH outputs of both towns—45 percent of Midwest's and 48 percent of Yoredale's—were generated via town inhabitants.

P-H data are reported in Table 9.23.

Differences. Midwest's PAfH produces more behavior than Yoredale's. In 1963–64 it produced, via town inhabitants, 46,009 more P-H of affective behavior than Yoredale's, amounting to 162 percent as much, to 104 percent as much per cu of PAfH, and to 255 percent as much per inhabitant. Involved in Midwest's greater affective output were these habitat differences: a larger PAfH, 156 percent as extensive as Yoredale's; a more varied PAfH, 141 percent as varied; fewer town inhabitants, 63 percent as many; and fewer town inhabitants per cu of PAfH, 40 percent as many.

In psychological language, these findings indicate that in 1963–64, *on the average,* Midwesterners *in comparison with Dalesmen* engaged in much more behavior in the town's PAfH, within settings

Table 9.23
Affective Behavior
Behavior Output of Primary Habitat: Person-Hours (P-H)

	1954–55		1963–64	
	Midwest (1)	Yoredale (2)	Midwest (3)	Yoredale (4)
Output via all inhabitants				
(1) Total P-H			265,241	155,736
(2) Percent of GBP			14.1%	5.9%
(3) Mean P-H per cu			18,387	16,841
Output via town inhabitants				
(4) Total P-H	131,977	179,214	120,236	74,227
(5) Percent of TBP	14.2%	11.9%	10.7%	5.2%
(6) Mean P-H per cu	12,938	21,572	8,335	8,027
(7) Mean P-H per town inhabitant	184.6	137.9	144.9	56.7

where there was slightly more affective activity by Midwesterners; they did this within a town where there was much more such activity, a much larger and more varied affective habitat appreciably fewer town inhabitants to take advantage of the affective behavior opportunities and carry out the affective duties, and many fewer town inhabitants in relation to the affective behavior opportunities and duties.

Changes. Both towns' PAfHs produced less behavior in 1963–64. Midwest's produced, via town inhabitants, 11,741 fewer P-H of behavior than in 1954–55, amounting to 91 percent as much, to 64 percent as much per cu of PAfH, and to 78 percent as much per inhabitant. Involved in Midwest's smaller affective output in 1963–64 were these habitat differences: a larger PAfH, 141 percent as extensive as in 1954–55; a more varied PAfH, 122 percent as varied; more town inhabitants, 116 percent as many; and fewer inhabitants per cu of PAfH, 82 percent as many.

Yoredale's produced, via town inhabitants, 104,989 fewer P-H of Affective Behavior in 1963–64, amounting to 41 percent as much, to 37 percent as much per cu of PAfH, and to 41 percent as much per inhabitant. Involved in Yoredale's smaller affective output in 1963–64 were these habitat differences: a larger PAfH, 111 percent as extensive as in 1954–55; a more varied PAfH, 115 percent as varied; about the same number of town inhabitants, 101 percent as many; and fewer inhabitants per cu of PAfH, 91 percent as many.

CLAIM-OPERATIONS GENERATED BY PRIMARY
AFFECTIVE BEHAVIOR HABITAT

Salient findings, 1963–64. The total number of C-O generated by the towns' PAfHs for cheerleaders, play casts, brides, ministers, and so forth, was approximately equivalent to those produced by 100 different affective behavior settings with 71 operatives each in Midwest and with

Table 9.24
Affective Behavior
Behavior Output of Primary Habitat: Claim-Operations (C-O)

	1954–55		1963–64	
	Midwest (1)	Yoredale (2)	Midwest (3)	Yoredale (4)
Output via all inhabitants				
(1) Total C-O	4,250	3,548	7,072	5,713
(2) Percent of Gross C-O	53.5%	55.0%	49.6%	48.8%
(3) Mean C-O per cu	416.6	427.1	490.2	617.8
Output via town inhabitants				
(4) Total C-O	1,814	1,401	2,588	1,638
(5) Percent of Town C-O	43.5%	45.8%	38.9%	39.0%
(6) Mean C-O per cu	177.8	168.6	179.4	177.1
(7) Mean C-O per town inhabitant	2.54	1.08	3.12	1.25

57 operatives each in Yoredale. Both towns' PAfHs were more productive of responsible actions than expected on the basis of either their extent or their output of P-H. Midwest's PAfH constituted 13.4 percent of its total habitat, produced 14.1 percent of its GBP, and generated 49.6 percent of its C-O; and Yoredale's PAfH constituted 8.2 percent of its total habitat, produced 5.9 percent of its GBP, and generated 48.8 percent of its C-O. The mean yearly outputs per town inhabitant were 3.12 C-O per Midwesterner and 1.25 C-O per Dalesman, which were 123 and 116 percent, respectively, of the 1954–55 outputs. There were 37 percent of Midwest's and 29 percent of Yoredale's affective behavior C-O generated via town inhabitants.

C O data are reported in Table 9.24.

Differences. Midwest's PAfH produces more C-O than Yoredale's. In 1963–64 it produced, via town inhabitants, 950 more C-O than Yoredale's, amounting to 158 percent as many, to 101 percent as many per cu of PAfH, and to 250 percent as many per inhabitant. Involved in Midwest's greater output of C-O were these habitat differences: more PAfH claims for operatives, 144 percent as many as Yoredale; fewer town inhabitants, 63 percent as many; and fewer town inhabitants per PAfH claim, 44 percent as many.

Changes. Both towns' PAfHs produced more C-O in 1963–64. Midwest's produced, via town inhabitants, 774 more C-O than in 1954–55, amounting to 143 percent as many, to 101 percent as many per cu of PAfH, and to 123 percent as many per inhabitant. Involved in Midwest's increased output of affective C-O in 1963–64 were these habitat differences: more PAfH claims for operatives, 177 percent as many as in 1954–55; more town inhabitants, 116 percent as many; and fewer town inhabitants per PAfH claim, 65 percent as many.

Yoredale's PAfH produced, via town inhabitants, 237 more C-O in 1963–64, amounting to 117 percent as many, to 105 percent as many per cu of PAfH and to 116 percent as many per inhabitant. Involved in

Yoredale's increased output of affective C-O in 1963–64 are these habitat differences: more PAfH claims for operatives, 193 percent as many as in 1954–55; about the same number of town inhabitants, 101 percent as many; and fewer inhabitants per claim, 52 percent as many.

Gross Motor Activity

PERSON-HOURS OF BEHAVIOR GENERATED BY GROSS MOTOR HABITAT

Salient findings, 1963–64. Those parts of the towns' habitats that have some gross motor attributes — the territorial range of Gross Motor Activity — produced 70 percent of Midwest's and 84 percent of Yoredale's gross behavior product (GBP), and the primary gross motor habitats of the towns (PGMH) produced respectively, 28.9 and 24.4 percent of their GBP. The mean weekly PGMH outputs per town inhabitant were 7 hours, 39 minutes per Midwesterner and 9 hours, 16 minutes per Dalesman, which were 67 and 82 percent, respectively, of the 1954–55 outputs. More than half the primary gross motor outputs of both towns — 61 percent of Midwest's and 54 percent of Yoredale's — are generated via town inhabitants.

P-H data are reported in Table 9.25.

Differences. Midwest's PGMH produces less behavior than Yoredale's. In 1963–64 it produced, via town inhabitants, 300,796 fewer P-H of gross motor behavior than Yoredale's, amounting to 52 percent as much, to 57 percent as much per cu of PGMH, and to 83 percent as much per inhabitant. Involved in Midwest's deficient gross motor output were these habitat differences: a smaller PGMH, 92 percent as extensive as Yoredale's; a less varied PGMH, 81 percent as varied; fewer town inhabitants, 63 percent as many; and fewer town inhabitants per cu of PGMH, 69 percent as many.

Table 9.25
Gross Motor Activity
Behavior Output of Primary Habitat: Person-Hours (P-H)

	1954–55		1963–64	
	Midwest (1)	Yoredale (2)	Midwest (3)	Yoredale (4)
Output via all inhabitants				
(1) Total P-H			543,710	1,165,423
(2) Percent of GBP			28.9%	44.4%
(3) Mean P-H per cu			18,288	36,193
Output via town inhabitants				
(4) Total P-H	425,261	767,057	330,440	631,236
(5) Percent of TBP	45.7%	50.9%	29.4%	44.3%
(6) Mean P-H per cu	12,313	22,849	11,115	19,603
(7) Mean P-H per town inhabitant	594.8	590.0	398.1	481.9

In psychological language, these findings indicate that in 1963–64, *on the average,* Midwesterners *in comparison with Dalesmen* engaged in less behavior in the town's PGMH, within settings where there was much less gross motor activity by Midwesterners; they did this within a town where there was much less such activity, a smaller and less varied gross motor habitat, appreciably fewer town inhabitants to take advantage of the gross motor opportunities and carry out the gross motor duties, fewer town inhabitants in relation to the gross motor opportunities and duties.

Changes. Both towns' PGMHs produced less behavior in 1963–64. Midwest's produced, via town inhabitants, 94,821 fewer P-H of gross motor behavior than in 1954–55, amounting to 78 percent as much, to 90 percent as much per cu of PGMH, and to 67 percent as much per inhabitant. Involved in Midwest's smaller gross motor output in 1963–64 were these habitat differences: a smaller PGMH, 86 percent as extensive as in 1954–55; a less varied PGMH, 98 percent as varied; more town inhabitants, 116 percent as many; and more inhabitants per cu of PGMH, 135 percent as many.

Yoredale's produced, via town inhabitants, 135,821 fewer P-H of gross motor behavior in 1963–64, amounting to 82 percent as much to 86 percent as much per cu of PGMH, and to 82 percent as much per inhabitant. Involved in Yoredale's smaller gross motor output in 1963–64 were these habitat differences: a smaller PGMH, 96 percent as extensive as in 1954–55; a more varied PGMH, 115 percent as varied; about the same number of town inhabitants, 101 percent as many; and more inhabitants per cu of PGMH, 105 percent as many.

CLAIM-OPERATIONS GENERATED BY PRIMARY GROSS MOTOR HABITAT

Salient findings, 1963–64. The total number of C-O generated by the towns' PGMHs for football players, walkers, baseball players, carpenters, and so forth, was approximately equivalent to those produced by 100 different gross motor settings with 47 operatives each in Midwest and with 55 operatives each in Yoredale. Both towns' PGMHs were more productive of responsible actions than expected on the basis of either their extent or their output of P-H. Midwest's PGMH constituted 27.7 percent of its total habitat, produced 28.9 percent of its GBP, and generated 33.0 percent of its C-O; and Yoredale's PGMH constituted 28.5 percent of its total habitat, produced 44.4 percent of its GBP, and generated 47.3 percent of its C-O. The mean yearly outputs per town inhabitant were 2.32 C-O per Midwesterner and 1.11 C-O per Dalesman, which were 139 percent of the 1954–55 outputs of each town. There were 41 percent of Midwest's and 26 percent of Yoredale's gross motor activity C-O generated via town inhabitants.

C-O data are reported in Table 9.26.

Differences. Midwest's PGMH produces more C-O than Yoredale's. In 1963–64 it produced, via town inhabitants, 471 more C-O, amounting to 132 percent as many, to 143 percent as many per cu of

Table 9.26
Gross Motor Activity
Behavior Output of Primary Habitat: Claim-Operations (C-O)

	1954–55		1963–64	
	Midwest (1)	Yoredale (2)	Midwest (3)	Yoredale (4)
Output via all inhabitants				
(1) Total C-O	2,810	2,720	4,715	5,538
(2) Percent of Gross C-O	35.4%	42.1%	33.0%	47.3%
(3) Mean C-O per cu	81.4	81.0	158.6	172.0
Output via town inhabitants				
(4) Total C-O	1,197	1,043	1,930	1,459
(5) Percent of Town C-O	28.7%	34.1%	29.0%	34.7%
(6) Mean *C-O* per cu	34.7	31.1	64.9	45.3
(7) Mean *C-O* per town inhabitant	1.67	0.80	2.32	1.11

PGMH, and to 209 percent as many per inhabitant. Involved in Midwest's greater output of gross motor C-O were these habitat differences: more PGMH claims for operatives, 144 percent as many as Yoredale; fewer town inhabitants, 63 percent as many; and fewer town inhabitants per PGMH claim, 85 percent as many.

Changes. Both towns' PGMHs produced more C-O in 1963–64. Midwest's produced, via town inhabitants, 733 more C-O than in 1954–55, amounting to 161 percent as many, to 187 percent as many per cu of PGMH, and to 139 percent as many per inhabitant. Involved in Midwest's increased output of gross motor C-O in 1963–64 were these habitat differences: more PGMH claims for operatives, 171 percent as many as in 1954–55; more town inhabitants, 116 percent as many; and fewer town inhabitants per PGMH claim, 68 percent as many.

Yoredale's PGMH produced, via town inhabitants, 416 more C-O in 1963–64, amounting to 140 percent as many, to 146 percent as many per cu of PGMH, and to 139 percent as many per inhabitant. Involved in Yoredale's increased output of gross motor C-O in 1963–64 are these habitat differences: more PGMH claims for operatives, 206 percent as many as in 1954–55; about the same number of town inhabitants, 101 percent as many; and fewer inhabitants per claim, 49 percent as many.

Manipulation

PERSON-HOURS OF BEHAVIOR GENERATED BY MANIPULATION HABITAT

Salient findings, 1963–64. Those parts of the towns' habitats that have some manipulation attributes—the territorial range of Manipulation—produced 86 percent of Midwest's and 76 percent of Yoredale's GBP, and the primary manipulation habitats of the towns (PMH) produced respectively, 33.5 and 29.2 percent of their GBP. The mean weekly PMH outputs per town inhabitant were 10 hours, 2 minutes per

Table 9.27
Manipulation
Behavior Output of Primary Habitat: Person-Hours (P-H)

	1954–55		1963–64	
	Midwest (1)	Yoredale (2)	Midwest (3)	Yoredale (4)
Output via all inhabitants				
(1) Total P-H			630,136	766,868
(2) Percent of GBP			33.5%	29.2%
(3) Mean P-H per cu			19,835	22,950
Output via town inhabitants				
(4) Total P-H	375,532	500,883	433,757	434,844
(5) Percent of TBP	40.4%	33.2%	38.5%	30.5%
(6) Mean P-H per cu	11,137	14,567	13,654	13,014
(7) Mean P-H per town inhabitant	525.2	385.3	522.6	331.9

Midwesterner and 6 hours, 23 minutes per Dalesman, which were 99 and 86 percent, respectively, of the 1954–55 outputs. More than half the primary manipulation outputs of both towns—69 percent of Midwest's and 57 percent of Yoredale's—were generated via town inhabitants.

P-H data are reported in Table 9.27.

Differences. Midwest's PMH produces less behavior than Yoredale's. In 1963–64 it produced, via town inhabitants, 1087 fewer P-H of manipulation behavior than Yoredale's, amounting to 99.7 percent as much, to 105 percent as much per cu of PMH, and to 157 percent as much per inhabitant. Involved in Midwest's deficient manipulation output were these habitat differences: a smaller PMH, 95 percent as extensive as Yoredale's; a less varied PMH, 83 percent as varied; fewer town inhabitants, 63 percent as many; and fewer town inhabitants per cu of PMH, 66 percent as many.

In psychological language, these findings indicate that in 1963–64, *on the average,* Midwesterners *in comparison with Dalesmen* engaged in more behavior in the town's PMH, within settings where there was somewhat more manipulation activity by Midwesterners; they did this within a town where there was slightly less such activity, a somewhat smaller but less varied manipulation habitat, appreciably fewer town inhabitants to take advantage of the manipulation opportunities and carry out the manipulation duties, and fewer town inhabitants in relation to the manipulation opportunities and duties.

Changes. Midwest's PMH produced more behavior in 1963–64, and Yoredale's produced less. Midwest's produced, via town inhabitants, 58,225 more P-H of manipulation behavior than in 1954–55, amounting to 115 percent as much, to 123 percent as much per cu of PMH, and to 99 percent as much per inhabitant. Involved in Midwest's increased manipulation output in 1963–64 were these habitat differences: a smaller PMH, 94 percent as extensive as in 1954–55; a more varied PMH, 105 percent as varied; more town inhabitants, 116 percent as many; and more inhabitants per cu of PMH, 123 percent as many.

Yoredale produced less manipulation behavior in 1963–64 than in 1954–55. It produced via town inhabitants, 66,039 fewer P-H of manipulation behavior in 1963–64, amounting to 86.8 percent as much, to 89 percent as much per cu of PMH, and to 86 percent as much per inhabitant. Involved in Yoredale's reduced manipulation output in 1963–64 were these habitat differences: a smaller PMH, 97 percent as extensive as in 1954–55; a more varied PMH, 122 percent as varied; about the same number of inhabitants, 101 percent as many; and more inhabitants per cu of PMH, 104 percent as many.

CLAIM-OPERATIONS GENERATED BY PRIMARY MANIPULATION HABITAT

Salient findings, 1963–64. The total number of C-O generated by the towns' PMHs for typists, sewing teachers, music directors, shoe repairers, and so forth, was approximately equivalent to those produced by 100 different manipulation settings with 41 operatives each in Midwest and with 30 operatives each in Yoredale. The PMHs of both towns were slightly less productive of responsible actions than expected on the basis of either their extent or their P-H output. Midwest's PMH constituted 29.6 percent of its total habitat, produced 33.5 percent of its GBP, and generated 28.4 percent of its C-O; and Yoredale's PMH constituted 29.6 percent of its total habitat, produced 29.2 percent of its GBP, and generated 26 percent of its C-O. The mean yearly outputs per town inhabitant were 1.79 C-O per Midwesterner and 0.76 C-O per Dalesman, which were 161 and 125 percent, respectively, of the 1954–55 outputs. There were 34 percent of Midwest's and 33 percent of Yoredale's manipulation C-O generated via town inhabitants.

C-O data are reported in Table 9.28.

Differences. Midwest's PMH produces more C-O than Yoredale's. In 1963–64 it produced, via town inhabitants, 496 more C-O than Yoredale's, amounting to 150 percent as many, to 158 percent as many per cu of PMH, and to 236 percent as many per inhabitant. Involved in Midwest's greater output of C-O were these habitat differences: more PMH claims for operatives, 132 percent as many as Yoredale; fewer town inhabitants, 63 percent as many; and fewer town inhabitants per PMH claim, 48 percent as many.

Changes. Both towns' PMHs produced more C-O in 1963–64. Midwest produced, via town inhabitants, 697 more C-O than in 1954–55, amounting to 188 percent as many, to 200 percent as many per cu of PMH, and to 161 percent as many per inhabitant. Involved in Midwest's increased output of manipulation C-O in 1963–64 were these habitat differences: more PMH claims for operatives, 223 percent as many as Yoredale; more town inhabitants, 116 percent as many; and fewer town inhabitants per PMH claim, 52 percent as many.

Yoredale's PMH produced, via town inhabitants, 196 more C-O

Table 9.28
Manipulation
Behavior Output of Primary Habitat: Claim-Operations (C-O)

	1954–55		1963–64	
	Midwest (1)	Yoredale (2)	Midwest (3)	Yoredale (4)
Output via all inhabitants				
(1) Total C-O	2,092	1,552	4,055	3,042
(2) Percent of Gross C-O	26.4%	24.0%	28.4%	26.0%
(3) Mean C-O per cu	62.0	45.1	127.6	91.0
Output via town inhabitants				
(4) Total C-O	792	797	1,489	993
(5) Percent of Town C-O	19.0%	26.1%	22.4%	23.6%
(6) Mean C-O per cu	23.5	23.2	46.9	29.7
(7) Mean C-O per town inhabitant	1.11	0.61	1.79	0.76

in 1963–64, amounting to 124 percent as many, to 128 percent as many per cu of PMH, and to 125 percent as many per inhabitant. Involved in Yoredale's increased output of manipulation C-O in 1963–64 were these habitat differences: more PMH claims for operatives, 171 percent as many as in 1954–55; about the same number of town inhabitants, 101 percent as many; and fewer inhabitants per claim, 59 percent as many.

Behavior Mechanism Talking

PERSON-HOURS OF BEHAVIOR GENERATED BY TALKING HABITATS

Salient findings, 1963–64. Those parts of the towns' habitats that have some talking attributes—the territorial range of Talking—produced 95 percent of Midwest's and 97 percent of Yoredale's gross behavior product (GBP), and the primary talking habitats of the towns (PTH) produced respectively, 14 and 16 percent of their GBP. The mean weekly PTH outputs per town inhabitant were 2 hours, 58 minutes per Midwesterner and 2 hours, 53 minutes per Dalesman, which were 103 and 74 percent, respectively, of the 1954–55 outputs. Less than half the primary talking outputs of both towns—49 percent of Midwest's and 47 percent of Yoredale's—were generated via town inhabitants.

P-H data are reported in Table 9.29.

Differences. Midwest's PTH produces less behavior than Yoredale's. In 1963–64 it produced, via town inhabitants, 68,618 fewer P-H of talking behavior than Yoredale's, amounting to 65 percent as much, to 86 percent as much per cu of PTH, and to 103 percent as much per inhabitant. Involved in Midwest's deficient talking output were these habitat differences: a smaller PTH, 76 percent as extensive as Yoredale's; a less varied PTH, 98 percent as varied; fewer town inhabitants, 63 percent as many; and fewer town inhabitants per cu of PTH, 82 percent as many.

Table 9.29
Talking
Behavior Output of Primary Habitat: Person-Hours (P-H)

	1954–55		1963–64	
	Midwest (1)	Yoredale (2)	Midwest (3)	Yoredale (4)
Output via all inhabitants				
(1) Total P-H			263,220	420,744
(2) Percent of GBP			14.0%	16.0%
(3) Mean P-H per cu			20,168	24,492
Output via town inhabitants				
(4) Total P-H	177,493	265,293	128,253	196,869
(5) Percent of TBP	19.1%	17.6%	11.4%	13.8%
(6) Mean P-H per cu	10,853	18,674	9,827	11,460
(7) Mean P-H per town inhabitant	248.2	204.1	154.5	150.3

In psychological language, these findings indicate that in 1963–64, *on the average,* Midwesterners *in comparison with Dalesmen* engaged in slightly more behavior in the town's primary talking habitat, within settings where there was less talking activity by Midwesterners; they did this within a town where there was appreciably less such activity, a smaller but slightly less varied talking habitat appreciably fewer town inhabitants to take advantage of the talking opportunities and carry out the talking duties and fewer town inhabitants in relation to the talking opportunities and duties.

Changes. Both towns' PTHs produced less behavior in 1963–64. Midwest produced, via town inhabitants, 49,240 fewer P-H of talking behavior than in 1954–55, amounting to 72 percent as much, to 90 percent as much per cu of PTH and to 62 percent as much per inhabitant. Involved in Midwest's reduced talking output in 1963–64 were these habitat differences: a smaller PTH, 80 percent as extensive as in 1954–55; a less varied PTH, 88 percent as varied; more town inhabitants, 116 percent as many; and more inhabitants per cu of PTH, 145 percent as many.

Yoredale produced via town inhabitants, 68,424 fewer P-H of talking behavior than in 1954–55, amounting to 74 percent as much, to 61 percent as much per cu of PTH, and to 74 percent as much per inhabitant. Involved in Yoredale's reduced talking output in 1963–64 were these habitat differences: a larger PTH, 121 percent as extensive as in 1954–55; a more varied PTH, 120 percent as varied; about the same number of town inhabitants, 101 percent as many; and fewer inhabitants per cu of PTH, 83 percent as many.

CLAIM-OPERATIONS GENERATED BY PRIMARY TALKING HABITAT

Salient findings, 1963–64. The total number of C-O generated by the towns' PTHs for the choir members, lecturers, preachers, and so forth, was approximately equivalent to those produced by 100 different talking settings with 61 operatives each in Midwest and 40 operatives each in Yoredale. The PTHs of both towns were more productive of responsible actions than expected on the basis of either their extent or their output of P-H. Midwest's PTH constituted 12.2 percent of its total habitat, produced 14 percent of its GBP, and generated 42.8 percent of its C-O; and Yoredale's PTH constituted 15.2 percent of its total habitat, produced 16 percent of its GBP, and generated 34.6 percent of its C-O. The mean yearly outputs per town inhabitant were 2.90 C-O per Midwesterner and 1.26 C-O per Dalesman, which were 95 and 108 percent, respectively, of the 1954–55 outputs. There were 39 percent of Midwest's and 41 percent of Yoredale's talking C-O generated via town inhabitants.

C-O data are reported in Table 9.30.

Differences. Midwest's PTH produces more than Yoredale's. In 1963–64 it produced, via town inhabitants, 751 more C-O than Yoredale's, amounting to 145 percent as many, to 191 percent as many per cu of PTH, and to 230 percent as many per inhabitant. Involved in Midwest's greater output of talking C-O were these habitat differences: more PTH claims for operatives, 130 percent as many as Yoredale; fewer town inhabitants, 63 percent as many; and fewer town inhabitants per PTH claim, 49 percent as many.

Changes. Both towns' PTHs produced more C-O in 1963–64. Midwest produced, via town inhabitants, 223 more C-O than in 1954–55, amounting to 110 percent as many, to 138 percent as many per cu of PTH, and to 95 percent as many per inhabitant. Involved in Midwest's increased output of talking C-Os in 1963–64 were these habitat differences: more PTH claims for operatives, 145 percent as many as in 1954–55; more town inhabitants, 116 percent as many; and fewer town inhabitants per PTH claim, 79 percent as many.

Table 9.30
Talking
Behavior Output of Primary Habitat: Claim-Operations (C-O)

	1954–55		1963–64	
	Midwest (1)	Yoredale (2)	Midwest (3)	Yoredale (4)
Output via all inhabitants				
(1) Total C-O	4,445	3,441	6,100	4,048
(2) Percent of Gross C-O	56.0%	53.3%	42.8%	34.6%
(3) Mean C-O per cu	271.8	242.2	467.4	235.6
Output via town inhabitants				
(4) Total C-O	2,181	1,520	2,404	1,653
(5) Percent of Town C-O	52.3%	49.7%	36.2%	39.3%
(6) Mean C-O per cu	133.4	107.0	184.2	96.2
(7) Mean C-O per town inhabitant	3.05	1.17	2.90	1.26

Yoredale's PTH produced, via town inhabitants, 133 more C-O in 1963–64, amounting to 109 percent as many, to 90 percent as many per cu of PTH, and to 108 percent as many per inhabitant. Involved in Yoredale's increased output of talking C-O in 1963–64 were these habitat differences: more PTH claims for operatives, 159 percent as many as in 1954–55; about the same number of town inhabitants, 101 percent as many; and fewer inhabitants per claim, 63 percent as many.

Summary: Behavior Outputs of Primary Behavior Mechanism Habitats

Graphic summaries of behavior output across primary behavior mechanism habitats are presented in Figures 9.3 and 9.4. The graphs and formats are similar to those summarizing the outputs of the primary action pattern habitats; the reader may find it helpful to review the explanatory comments given there.

PERSON-HOURS

Mean P-H per town inhabitant. Behavior outputs of the 4 primary behavior mechanism habitats of Midwest and Yoredale in 1963–64, as measured by mean P-H per town inhabitant, are shown in Figure 9.3A in order of increasing output in Midwest. Common to the two towns were relatively small outputs of the primary habitats for Affective Behavior and Talking, and relatively large outputs of the primary Gross Motor habitats.

Midwest's overall 25 percent superiority to Yoredale in P-H per town inhabitant did not occur evenly across these habitats; it was concentrated in the habitats for Affective Behavior and Manipulation. The output of Midwest's primary Gross Motor habitat was smaller than Yoredale's—83 percent as great. Relative to Yoredale, Midwest was affective, manipulative, and sedentary; the towns were almost exactly equal in their output of spoken words.

Changes. Changes between the survey years in output per town inhabitant (Figure 9.3B) were smaller for all primary behavior mechanism habitats of both towns. The greatest reduction was in Yoredale's Affective Behavior output; the decrement was over 50 percent.

CLAIM-OPERATIONS

Mean C-O per town inhabitant. Relative output of C-O per town inhabitant is similar in both towns (Figure 9.4A), the only difference being that Affective Behavior is the most productive in Midwest but is second in rank to Talking by a very small margin in Yoredale. Midwest's 150 percent overall superiority to Yoredale in productivity of C-O occurs quite evenly across the 4 primary behavior mechanism habitats.

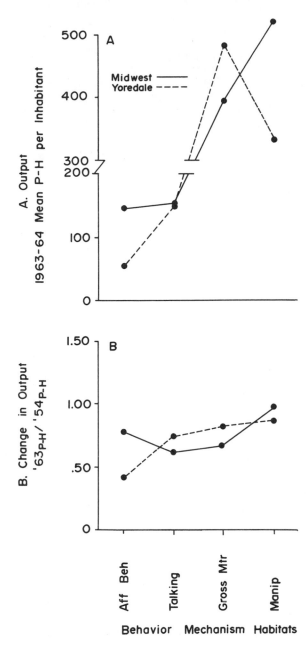

FIGURE 9.3. Behavior Outputs of Primary Behavior Mechanism Habitats: Mean Person-Hours per Town Inhabitant. A: output, 1963–64; B: change in output, $'63_{P-H}/'54_{P-H}$.

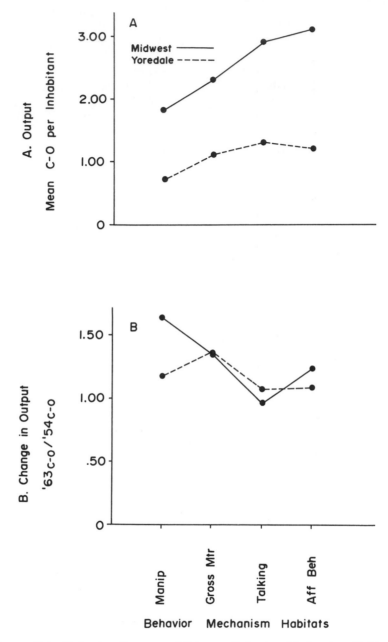

FIGURE 9.4. Behavior Outputs of Primary Behavior Mechanism Habitats: Mean Claim-Operation per Town Inhabitant. A: output, 1963–64; B: change in output, $'63_{c\text{-}o}/'54_{c\text{-}o}$.

Changes. The towns follow, with one exception, a common pattern of change (Figure 9.4B). In both towns the production of C-O increased most in the primary habitat for Gross Motor behavior, least in the primary habitat for Talking, and at an intermediate level in the Affective Behavior habitat. The exception was Midwest's primary habitat for Manipulation; it far exceeded all other habitats in either town, with a 164 percent increase in production of C-O between the survey years.

CHAPTER 10

Behavior Output of the Towns' Differential Habitats II

Authority System, Autonomy, Attendance and Beneficence Habitats

W e continue in this chapter with the behavior generated by the towns' differential habitats. The habitats are identified and described in Chapter 6, and the output measures and format of the presentation are described in Chapter 9. The action pattern Aesthetics (in Chapter 9) provides a key to the tabular location of these data and identifies the corresponding habitat and psychological statements regarding person-hours of output.

BEHAVIOR OUTPUT OF AUTHORITY SYSTEM HABITATS

Church Authority System

PERSON-HOURS OF BEHAVIOR GENERATED BY CHURCH HABITAT

Salient findings, 1963–64. The church habitats of the towns produced 3.7 percent of Midwest's and 1.6 percent of Yoredale's gross

Table 10.1
Church Authority System
Output of Person-Hours (P-H)

	1954–55		1963–64	
	Midwest (1)	Yoredale (2)	Midwest (3)	Yoredale (4)
Output via all inhabitants				
(1) Total P-H			69,753	43,299
(2) Percent of GBP			3.7%	1.6%
(3) Mean P-H per cu			5,708	6,858
Output via town inhabitants				
(4) Total P-H	43,760	34,028	33,173	34,156
(5) Percent of TBP	4.7%	2.3%	2.9%	2.4%
(6) Mean P-H per cu	6,880	5,978	2,715	5,410
(7) Mean P-H per town inhabitant	61.2	26.2	40.0	26.1

behavior product (GBP). The mean weekly church outputs per town inhabitant were 46 minutes per Midwesterner and 30 minutes per Dalesman, which were 65 and 99.6 percent, respectively, of the 1954–55 outputs. About 47 percent of Midwest's and 79 percent of Yoredale's outputs were generated via town inhabitants.

P-H data are reported in Table 10.1.

Differences. Midwest's church habitat produced less behavior than Yoredale's in 1963–64. It produced, via town inhabitants, 983 fewer P-H than Yoredale's, amounting to 97 percent as much, to 50 percent as much per cu of church habitat, and to 153 percent as much per inhabitant. Involved in Midwest's smaller church output via town inhabitants were these habitat differences: a larger church habitat, 194 percent as extensive as Yoredale's; a more varied church habitat, 111 percent as varied; fewer town inhabitants, 63 percent as many; and fewer town inhabitants per cu of church habitat, 33 percent as many.

In psychological language, these findings indicate that in 1963–64, *on the average,* Midwesterners *in comparison with Dalesmen* engaged in much more behavior in the town's church habitat, within settings where there was much less church activity by Midwesterners; they did this within a town where there was slightly less church behavior, a much larger and appreciably more varied church habitat appreciably fewer town inhabitants to take advantage of the church opportunities and carry out the church duties, and many fewer inhabitants in relation to the church opportunities and duties.

Changes. Midwest's church habitat produced less behavior in 1963–64 than in 1954–55. It produced via town inhabitants, 10,587 fewer P-H in 1963–64, amounting to 76 percent as much, to 39 percent as much per cu of church habitat, and to 65 percent as much per inhabitant. Involved in Midwest's smaller church output in 1963–64 were these habitat differences: a larger church habitat, 191 percent as extensive as in 1954–55; a more varied church habitat, 115 percent as varied; more town inhabitants, 116 percent as many, and fewer inhabitants per cu of church habitat, 61 percent as many.

Yoredale produced slightly more church behavior in 1963–64 than in 1954–55. It produced, via town inhabitants, 128 more P-H in 1963–64, amounting to 100 percent as much, to 90 percent as much per cu of church habitat, and to 100 percent as much per inhabitant. Involved in Yoredale's greater church output in 1963–64 were these habitat differences: a larger church habitat, 110 percent as extensive as in 1954–55; a more varied church habitat, 155 percent as varied; about the same number of town inhabitants, 101 percent as many; and fewer inhabitants per cu of church habitat, 92 percent as many.

CLAIM-OPERATIONS GENERATED BY PRIMARY CHURCH HABITAT

Salient findings, 1963–64. The total number of C-O generated by the towns' church habitats for preachers, ushers, teachers, group leaders, and so forth, was approximately equivalent to those produced by 100 different church settings with 26 operatives each in Midwest and with 12 operatives each in Yoredale. The church habitats of both towns were more productive of responsible actions than expected on the basis of either their extent or their output of P-H. Midwest's church habitat constituted 11.4 percent of its total habitat, produced 3.7 percent of its GBP, and generated 18.1 percent of its C-O; and Yoredale's church habitat constituted 5.6 percent of its total habitat, produced 1.6 percent of its GBP, and generated 10.3 percent of its C-O. The mean yearly outputs per town inhabitant were 1.55 C-O per Midwesterner and 0.63 C-O per Dalesman, which were 90 and 102 percent, respectively, of the 1954–55 outputs. Approximately half of Midwest's and two-thirds of Yoredale's church C-O were generated via town inhabitants.

C-O data are reported in Table 10.2.

Differences. Midwest's church habitat produces more C-O than Yoredale's. In 1963–64 it produced, via town inhabitants, 470 more C-O than Yoredale's, amounting to 157 percent as many, to 81 percent as many per cu of church habitat, and to 246 percent as many per inhabitant. Involved in Midwest's greater output of church C-O were these habitat differences: 202 percent as many claims as Yoredale; fewer

Table 10.2
Church Authority System
Output of Claim-Operations (C-O)

| | 1954–55 | | 1963–64 | |
	Midwest (1)	Yoredale (2)	Midwest (3)	Yoredale (4)
Output via all inhabitants				
(1) Total C-O	1,834	981	2,581	1,212
(2) Percent of Gross C-O	23.1%	15.2%	18.1%	10.3%
(3) Mean C-O per cu	288.3	172.3	211.2	192.0
Output via town inhabitants				
(4) Total C-O	1,239	812	1,289	819
(5) Percent of Town C-O	29.7%	26.6%	19.4%	19.5%
(6) Mean C-O per cu	194.8	142.7	105.5	129.7
(7) Mean C-O per town inhabitant	1.73	0.62	1.55	0.63

town inhabitants, 63 percent as many; and fewer town inhabitants per habitat-claim for operatives, 31 percent as many.

Changes. Both towns' church habitats produced more C-O in 1963–64 than in 1954–55. Midwest's produced, via town inhabitants, 50 more C-O in 1963–64, amounting to 104 percent as many, to 54 percent as many per cu of church habitat, and to 90 percent as many per inhabitant. Involved in Midwest's greater output of church C-O in 1963–64 were these habitat differences: more habitat-claims for operatives, 148 percent as many as in 1954–55; more town inhabitants, 116 percent as many; and fewer inhabitants per habitat-claim, 78 percent as many.

Yoredale's church habitat produced via town inhabitants, 7 more C-O in 1963–64, amounting to 101 percent as many, to 91 percent as many per cu of church habitat, and to 102 percent as many per inhabitant. Involved in Yoredale's slightly greater output of church-controlled C-O in 1963–64 were these habitat differences: more habitat-claims for operatives, 131 percent as many as in 1954–55; the same number of town inhabitants, 101 percent as many; and fewer inhabitants per habitat-claim, 71 percent as many.

Government Agency Authority System

PERSON-HOURS OF BEHAVIOR GENERATED BY
GOVERNMENT AGENCY HABITAT

Salient findings, 1963–64. The government agency habitats of the towns produced, respectively, 16.4 of Midwest's and 27.5 percent of Yoredale's GBP. The mean weekly outputs per town inhabitant were 4 hours, 20 minutes per Midwesterner and 6 hours, 24 minutes per Dalesman, which were 99 and 99.6 percent, respectively, of the 1954–55 outputs. Approximately two-thirds of the government agency outputs of both towns were generated via town inhabitants.

P-H data are reported in Table 10.3.

Table 10.3
Government Agency Authority System
Output of Person-Hours (P-H)

	1954–55		1963–64	
	Midwest (1)	Yoredale (2)	Midwest (3)	Yoredale (4)
Output via all inhabitants				
(1) Total P-H			308,075	723,517
(2) Percent of GBP			16.4%	27.5%
(3) Mean P-H per cu			17,628	58,571
Output via town inhabitants				
(4) Total P-H	162,406	438,717	186,896	439,386
(5) Percent of TBP	17.5%	29.1%	16.6%	30.8%
(6) Mean P-H per cu	9,610	33,517	10,694	35,570
(7) Mean P-H per town inhabitant	227.1	337.5	225.2	335.4

Differences. Midwest's government agency habitat produces less behavior than Yoredale's. In 1963–64 it produced, via town inhabitats, 252,489 fewer P-H than Yoredale's, amounting to 42 percent as much, to 30 percent as much per cu of government agency habitat, and to 67 percent as much per inhabitant. Involved in Midwest's smaller output were these habitat differences: a larger government agency habitat, 141 percent as extensive as Yoredale's; a more varied habitat, 127 percent as varied, fewer town inhabitants, 63 percent as many, and fewer town inhabitants per cu of government agency habitat, 45 percent as many.

In psychological language, these findings indicate that in 1963–64, *on the average,* Midwesterners *in comparison with Dalesmen* engaged in appreciably less behavior in the town's government agency habitat, within settings where there was much less activity by Midwesterners; they did this within a town where there was much less such activity, a much larger but more varied government agency habitat, fewer town inhabitants to take advantage of the opportunities in government agency settings and carry out the duties, and many fewer inhabitants in relation to the opportunities and duties.

Changes. The government agencies of both towns produced more behavior in 1963–64 than in 1954–55. Midwest's produced, via town inhabitants, 24,491 more P-H in 1963–64, amounting to 115 percent as much, to 111 percent as much per cu of government agency habitat, and 99 percent as much per inhabitant. Involved in Midwest's greater output in 1963–64 were these habitat differences: a larger government agency habitat, 103 percent as extensive as in 1954–55; a more varied habitat, 111 percent as varied; more town inhabitants, 116 percent as many; and more inhabitants per cu of government agency habitat, 112 percent as many.

Yoredale produced, via town inhabitants, 669 more P-H in 1963–64, amounting to 100 percent as much, to 106 percent as much per cu of government agency habitat, and to 99 percent as much per inhabitant. Involved in Yoredale's greater output in 1963–64 were these habitat differences: a smaller government agency habitat, 95 percent as extensive as in 1954–55; a more varied habitat, 117 percent as varied; about the same number of town inhabitants, 101 percent as many, and more inhabitants per cu of government agency habitat, 106 percent as many.

CLAIM-OPERATIONS GENERATED BY GOVERNMENT AGENCY HABITAT

Salient findings, 1963–64. The total number of C-O generated by the towns' government agency habitats for judges, clerks, police constables, council members, and so forth, were approximately equivalent to those produced by 100 different government agency settings with 13 operatives each in Midwest and with 8 operatives each in Yoredale. The government agency habitats of both towns were less productive of responsible actions than expected on the basis of either their extent or their output of P-H. Midwest's government agency habitat constituted

Table 10.4
Government Agency Authority System
Output of Claim-Operations (C-O)

	1954–55		1963–64	
	Midwest (1)	Yoredale (2)	Midwest (3)	Yoredale (4)
Output via all inhabitants				
(1) Total C-O	945	570	1,306	824
(2) Percent of Gross C-O	11.9%	8.8%	9.2%	7.0%
(3) Mean C-O per cu	55.9	43.5	74.7	66.7
Output via town inhabitants				
(4) Total C-O	366	141	453	353
(5) Percent of Town C-O	8.8%	4.6%	6.8%	8.4%
(6) Mean C-O per cu	21.7	10.8	25.9	28.6
(7) Mean C-O per town inhabitant	0.51	0.11	0.55	0.27

16.3 percent of its total habitat, produced 16.4 percent of its GBP, and generated 9.2 percent of its C-O; and Yoredale's government agency habitat constituted 10.9 percent of its total habitat, produced 27.5 percent of its GBP, and generated 7.0 percent of its C-O. The mean yearly outputs per town inhabitant were 0.55 C-O per Midwesterner and 0.27 C-O per Dalesman, which were 108 and 245 percent, respectively, of the 1954–55 outputs. There were 35 percent of Midwest's and 43 percent of Yoredale's government agency C-O generated via town inhabitants.

C-O data are reported in Table 10.4.

Differences. Midwest's government agency habitat produces more C-O than Yoredale's. In 1963–64 it produced, via town inhabitants, 100 more C-O than Yoredale's, amounting to 128 percent as many, to 90 percent as many per cu of government agency habitat, and to 204 percent as many per inhabitant. Involved in Midwest's greater output of government agency C-O were these habitat differences: more habitat-claims for operatives, 178 percent as many as Yoredale; fewer town inhabitants, 63 percent as many; and fewer town inhabitants per habitat-claim, 35 percent as many.

Changes. Both towns' government agency authority systems produced more C-O in 1963–64 than in 1954–55. Midwest's produced, via town inhabitants: 87 more C-O in 1963–64, amounting to 124 percent as many, to 119 percent as many per cu of government agency habitat, and to 108 percent as many per inhabitant. Involved in Midwest's greater output of government agency C-O in 1963–64 were these habitat differences: more habitat-claims for operatives, 140 percent as many as in 1954–55; more town inhabitants, 116 percent as many; and fewer inhabitants per habitat-claim, 83 percent as many.

Yoredale's government agency habitat produced, via town inhabitants, 212 more C-O in 1963–64, amounting to 250 percent as many, to 265 percent as many per cu of government agency habitat, and to 245 percent as many per inhabitant. Involved in Yoredale's greater output

in 1963–64 were these habitat differences: more habitat-claims for operatives, 181 percent as many as in 1954–55; about the same number of
town inhabitants, 101 percent as many; and fewer inhabitants per habitat-claim, 56 percent as many.

Private Enterprise Authority System

PERSON-HOURS OF BEHAVIOR GENERATED BY
PRIVATE ENTERPRISE HABITAT

Salient findings, 1963–64. The private enterprise habitats of the
towns produced, respectively, 61 and 58 percent of Midwest's and
Yoredale's GBP. The mean weekly outputs per town inhabitant were 12
hours, 19 minutes per Midwesterner and 10 hours per Dalesman, which
were 96 and 93 percent, respectively, of the 1954–55 outputs. Town
inhabitants generated 72 percent of Midwest's and 62 percent of Yoredale's private enterprise outputs.

P-H data are reported in Table 10.5.

Differences. Midwest's private enterprise habitat produces less
behavior than Yoredale's. In 1963–64 it produced, via town inhabitants,
156,563 fewer P-H than Yoredale's, amounting to 77 percent as much,
to 106 percent as much per cu of private enterprise habitat, and to 122
percent as much per inhabitant. Involved in Midwest's smaller private
enterprise output were these habitat differences: a smaller private enterprise habitat, 74 percent as extensive as Yoredale's; an almost equally
varied habitat, 99 percent as varied; fewer town inhabitants, 63 percent
as many, and fewer town inhabitants per cu of private enterprise habitat, 86 percent as many.

In psychological language, these findings indicate that in
1963–64, *on the average,* Midwesterners *in comparison with Dalesmen*
engaged in more behavior in the town's private enterprise habitat,

Table 10.5
Private Enterprise Authority System
Output of Person-Hours (P-H)

	1954–55		1963–64	
	Midwest (1)	Yoredale (2)	Midwest (3)	Yoredale (4)
Output via all inhabitants				
(1) Total P-H			734,183	1,101,843
(2) Percent of GBP			39.0%	42.0%
(3) Mean P-H per cu			18,073	19,782
Output via town inhabitants				
(4) Total P-H	476,717	730,189	531,555	688,118
(5) Percent of TBP	51.3%	48.5%	47.2%	48.2%
(6) Mean P-H per cu	10,846	13,590	13,085	12,354
(7) Mean P-H per town inhabitant	666.7	561.7	640.4	525.3

within settings where there was more private enterprise activity by Midwesterners; they did this within a town where there was appreciably less such activity, an appreciably smaller but equally varied private enterprise habitat, appreciably fewer town inhabitants to take advantage of the private enterprise opportunities and carry out the private enterprise duties, and fewer town inhabitants in relation to the private enterprise opportunities and duties.

Changes. Midwest's private enterprise habitat produced more behavior in 1963–64 than in 1954–55, and Yoredale's produced less. Midwest's produced, via town inhabitants, 54,838 more P-H in 1963–64, amounting to 111 percent as much, to 121 percent as much per cu of private enterprise habitat, and 96 percent as much per inhabitant. Involved in Midwest's greater private enterprise output in 1963–64 were these habitat differences: a smaller private enterprise habitat, 96 percent as extensive as in 1954–55; a more varied habitat, 108 percent as varied; more town inhabitants, 116 percent as many; and more inhabitants per cu of private enterprise habitat, 124 percent as many.

Yoredale's private enterprises produced less behavior in 1963–64 than in 1954–55. They produced, via town inhabitants, 42,091 fewer P-H in 1963–64, amounting to 94 percent as much, to 91 percent as much per cu of private enterprise habitat, and to 93 percent as much per inhabitant. Involved in Yoredale's smaller private enterprise output in 1963–64 were these habitat differences: a larger private enterprise habitat, 104 percent as extensive as in 1954–55; a less varied habitat, 97 percent as varied; about the same number of town inhabitants, 101 percent as many; and fewer inhabitants per cu of private enterprise habitat, 97 percent as many.

CLAIM-OPERATIONS GENERATED BY PRIVATE ENTERPRISE HABITAT

Salient findings, 1963–64. The total number of C-O generated by the towns' private enterprise habitats for managers, secretaries, mechanics, salesmen, and so forth, were approximately equivalent to those produced by 100 different private enterprise settings with 6.9 operatives each in Midwest and with 8.3 operatives each in Yoredale. The private enterprises of both towns were less productive of responsible actions than expected on the basis of either their extent or their output of P-H. Midwest's private enterprises constituted 38 percent of its total habitat, produced 39 percent of its GBP, and generated 4.9 percent of its C-O; and Yoredale's private enterprise habitat constituted 49 percent of its total habitat, produced 42 percent of its GBP, and generated 7.1 percent of its C-O. The mean yearly outputs per town inhabitant were 0.53 C-O per Midwesterner and 0.34 C-O per Dalesman, which were 115 and 103 percent, respectively, of the 1954–55 outputs. There were 63 percent of Midwest's and 53 percent of Yoredale's private enterprise C-O generated via town inhabitants.

C-O data are reported in Table 10.6.

Differences. Midwest's private enterprises produce fewer C-O than

Table 10.6
Private Enterprise Authority System
Output of Claim-Operations (C-O)

	1954–55		1963–64	
	Midwest (1)	Yoredale (2)	Midwest (3)	Yoredale (4)
Output via all inhabitants				
(1) Total C-O	421	816	694	836
(2) Percent of Gross C-O	5.3%	12.6%	4.9%	7.1%
(3) Mean C-O per cu	9.6	15.2	17.1	15.0
Output via town inhabitants				
(4) Total C-O	332	428	439	443
(5) Percent of Town C-O	7.9%	14.0%	6.6%	10.3%
(6) Mean C-O per cu	7.6	8.0	10.8	7.9
(7) Mean C-O per town inhabitant	0.46	0.33	0.53	0.34

Yoredale's. In 1963–64 they produced, via town inhabitants, 4 fewer C-O than Yoredale's, amounting to 99 percent as many, to 137 percent as many per cu of private enterprise habitat, and to 156 percent as many per inhabitant. Involved in Midwest's smaller output of private enterprise C-O were these habitat differences: fewer habitat-claims for operatives, 70 percent as many as Yoredale; fewer town inhabitants, 63 percent as many; and fewer town inhabitants per habitat-claim, 91 percent as many.

Changes. Both towns' private enterprises produced more C-O in 1963–64 than in 1954–55. Midwest's produced via town inhabitants, 107 more C-O in 1963–64, amounting to 132 percent as many, to 142 percent as many per cu of private enterprise habitat, and to 115 percent as many per inhabitant. Involved in Midwest's greater output of private enterprise C-O in 1963–64 were these habitat differences: more habitat-claims for operatives, 144 percent as many as in 1954–55; more town inhabitants, 116 percent as many; and fewer inhabitants per habitat-claim, 80 percent as many.

Yoredale's private enterprises produced, via town inhabitants, 15 more C-O in 1963–64, amounting to 103 percent as many, to 99 percent as many per cu of private enterprise habitat, and to 103 percent as many per inhabitant. Involved in Yoredale's greater output of private enterprise C-O in 1963–64 were these habitat differences: fewer habitat claims for operatives, 94 percent as many as in 1954–55; the same number of town inhabitants, 101 percent as many; and more inhabitants per habitat-claim, 107 percent as many.

School Authority System

PERSON-HOURS OF BEHAVIOR GENERATED BY SCHOOL HABITAT

Salient findings, 1963–64. The school habitats of the towns produced, respectively, 34.6 and 24.6 percent of Midwest's and Yoredale's

Table 10.7
School Authority System
Output of Person-Hours (P-H)

	1954-55		1963-64	
	Midwest (1)	Yoredale (2)	Midwest (3)	Yoredale (4)
Output via all inhabitants				
(1) Total P-H			650,124	646,684
(2) Percent of GBP			34.6%	24.6%
(3) Mean P-H per cu			26,237	22,142
Output via town inhabitants				
(4) Total P-H	205,081	192,367	310,516	209,059
(5) Percent of TBP	22.0%	12.8%	27.6%	14.7%
(6) Mean P-H per cu	12,704	25,642	12,531	7,158
(7) Mean P-H per town inhabitant	286.8	148.0	374.1	159.6

GBP. The mean weekly school habitat outputs per town inhabitant were 4 hours, 33 minutes per Midwesterner and 3 hours, 6 minutes per Dalesman, which were 130 and 108 percent, respectively, of the 1954–55 outputs. About half of Midwest's and one-third of Yoredale's school outputs were generated via town inhabitants.

P-H data are reported in Table 10.7.

Differences. Midwest's school habitat produces more behavior than Yoredale's. In 1963–64 it produced, via town inhabitants, 101,457 more P-H than Yoredale's, amounting to 148 percent as much, to 175 percent as much per cu of school habitat, and to 234 percent as much per inhabitant. Involved in Midwest's greater school output were these habitat differences: a smaller school habitat, 85 percent as extensive as Yoredale's; a less varied school habitat, 78 percent as varied; fewer town inhabitants, 63 percent as many; and fewer town inhabitants per centiurb of school habitat, 75 percent as many.

In psychological language, these findings indicate that in 1963–64, *on the average,* Midwesterners *in comparison with Dalesmen* engage in much more behavior in the town's school habitat, within settings where there was much more school activity by Midwesterners; they did this within a town where there was much more such activity, a smaller and appreciably less varied school habitat, appreciably fewer town inhabitants to take advantage of the school opportunities and carry out the school duties, and appreciably fewer inhabitants in relation to the school opportunities and duties.

Changes. Both towns' school habitats produced more behavior in 1963–64 than in 1954–55. Midwest's produced, via town inhabitants, 105,435 more P-H in 1963–64, amounting to 151 percent as much, to 99 percent as much per cu of school habitat, and to 130 percent as much per inhabitant. Involved in Midwest's greater school output in 1963–64 were these habitat differences: a larger school habitat, 154 percent as extensive as in 1954–55; a more varied school habitat, 124 percent as varied; more town inhabitants, 116 percent as many; and fewer inhabitants per cu of school habitat, 75 percent as many.

Yoredale produced, via town inhabitants, 16,692 more P-H in 1963–64, amounting to 109 percent as much, to 27.9 percent as much per cu of school habitat, and to 108 percent as much per inhabitant. Involved in Yoredale's greater output in 1963–64 were these habitat differences: a larger school habitat, 389 percent as extensive as in 1954–55; a more varied school habitat, 362 percent as varied; about the same number of town inhabitants, 101 percent as many; and fewer inhabitants per cu of school habitat, 26 percent as many.

CLAIM-OPERATIONS GENERATED BY SCHOOL HABITAT

Salient findings, 1963–64. The total number of C-O generated by the towns' school habitats for teachers, coaches, team members, administrators, and so forth, were approximately equivalent to those produced by 300 different school settings with 18 operatives each in Midwest and with 14.3 operatives each in Yoredale. The school habitats of both towns were more productive of responsible actions than expected on the basis of either their extent or their output of P-H. Midwest's school habitat constituted 23.1 percent of its total habitat, produced 34.6 percent of its GBP, and generated 37.3 percent of its C-O; and Yoredale's school habitat constituted 25.9 percent of its total habitat, produced 24.6 percent of its GBP, and generated 36.7 percent of its C-O. The mean yearly outputs per town inhabitant were 2.59 C-O per Midwesterner and 0.93 C-O per Dalesman, which were 159 and 258 percent, respectively, of the 1954–55 outputs. There were 40 percent of Midwest's and 28 percent of Yoredale's school C-O generated via town inhabitants.

C-O data are reported in Table 10.8.

Differences. Midwest's school habitat produces more C-O than Yoredale's. In 1963–64 it produced, via town inhabitants, 926 more C-O than Yoredale's, amounting to 176 percent as many, to 207 percent as

Table 10.8
School Authority System
Output of Claim-Operations (C-O)

	1954-55		1963-64	
	Midwest (1)	Yoredale (2)	Midwest (3)	Yoredale (4)
Output via all inhabitants				
(1) Total C-O	2,944	646	5,316	4,298
(2) Percent of Gross C-O	37.1%	10.0%	37.3%	36.7%
(3) Mean C-O per cu	182.4	86.1	214.5	147.2
Output via town inhabitants				
(4) Total C-O	1,162	473	2,149	1,223
(5) Percent of Town C-O	27.8%	15.5%	32.3%	29.1%
(6) Mean C-O per cu	72.0	63.0	86.7	41.9
(7) Mean C-O per town inhabitant	1.63	0.36	2.59	0.93

many per cu of school habitat, and to 278 percent as many per inhabitant. Involved in Midwest's greater output of school C-O were these habitat differences: more habitat-claims' for operatives, 123 percent as many as Yoredale, fewer town inhabitants, 63 percent as many; and fewer town inhabitants per habitat-claim, 51 percent as many.

Changes. Both towns' school authority systems produced more C-O in 1963–64 than in 1954–55. Midwest produced, via town inhabitants, 987 more C-O in 1963–64, amounting to 185 percent as many, to 120 percent as many per cu of school habitat, and to 159 percent as many per inhabitant. Involved in Midwest's greater output of school C-O in 1963–64 are these habitat differences: more habitat-claims for operatives, 196 percent as many as in 1954–55; more town inhabitants, 116 percent as many; and fewer inhabitants per habitat-claim, 60 percent as many.

Yoredale's school habitat produced, via town inhabitants, 750 more C-O in 1963–64, amounting to 258 percent as many, to 66 percent as many per cu of school habitat, and to 258 percent as many per inhabitant. Involved in Yoredale's greater output of school C-O in 1963–64 were these habitat differences: more habitat-claims for operatives, 628 percent as many as in 1954–55; about the same number of town inhabitants, 101 percent as many; and fewer inhabitants per habitat-claim, 16 percent as many.

Yoredale's increased output of C-O from its school habitat reflects the expansion of the School authority system associated with the establishment of the County Modern School between the survey years. As we have mentioned in other contexts, nonresidents of the towns often occupy positions of responsibility in the towns' behavior settings. This is again evident in these data, which show Yoredale's total school C-O increasing more than 6 times between the survey years, but school C-O by town inhabitants increasing only 2.58 times.

Voluntary Association Authority System

PERSON-HOURS OF BEHAVIOR GENERATED BY
VOLUNTARY ASSOCIATION HABITAT

Salient findings, 1963–64. The voluntary association habitats of the towns produced, respectively, 6.3 percent of Midwest's and 4.2 percent of Yoredale's GBP. The mean weekly voluntary association outputs per town inhabitant were 55 minutes per Midwesterner and 49 minutes per Dalesman, which were 129 and 49 percent, respectively, of the 1954–55 outputs. About half the voluntary association outputs of both towns — 53 percent of Midwest's and 54 percent of Yoredale's — were generated via town inhabitants.

P-H data are reported in Table 10.9.

Differences. Midwest's voluntary association habitat produces more behavior than Yoredale's. In 1963–64 it produced, via town inhabitants,

Table 10.9
Voluntary Association Authority System
Output of Person-Hours (P-H)

	1954-55		1963-64	
	Midwest (1)	Yoredale (2)	Midwest (3)	Yoredale (4)
Output via all inhabitants				
(1) Total P-H			118,595	110,472
(2) Percent of GBP			6.3%	4.2%
(3) Mean P-H per cu			9,666	11,934
Output via town inhabitants				
(4) Total P-H	41,896	111,438	62,994	55,395
(5) Percent of TBP	4.5%	7.4%	5.6%	3.9%
(6) Mean P-H per cu	6,468	11,178	5,134	5,984
(7) Mean P-H per town inhabitant	58.6	85.7	75.9	42.3

7599 more P-H than Yoredale's, amounting to 114 percent as much, to 86 percent as much per cu of voluntary association habitat, and to 180 percent as much per inhabitant. Involved in Midwest's greater output were these habitat differences: a larger voluntary association habitat, 132 percent as extensive as Yoredale's; a less varied voluntary association habitat, 81 percent as varied; fewer town inhabitants, 63 percent as many; and fewer town inhabitants per cu of habitat controlled by voluntary associations, 48 percent as many.

In psychological language these findings indicate that in 1963–64, *on the average,* Midwesterners in comparison with Dalesmen engaged in much more behavior in the town's voluntary association habitat, within settings where there was appreciably less voluntary association activity by Midwesterners; they did this within a town where there was much more such activity, an appreciably larger but less varied voluntary association habitat, appreciably fewer town inhabitants to take advantage of the voluntary association opportunities and carry out the duties, and many fewer inhabitants in relation to the opportunities and duties provided by the voluntary associations.

Changes. Midwest's Voluntary Associations produced more behavior in 1963–64 than in 1954–55, and Yoredale's produced less. Midwest's produced, via town inhabitants, 21,098 more P-H in 1963–64, amounting to 150 percent as much, to 79 percent as much per cu of habitat controlled by voluntary associations, but to 129 percent as much per inhabitant. Involved in Midwest's greater output in 1963–64 were these habitat differences: a larger voluntary association habitat, 189 percent as extensive as in 1954–55; a more varied voluntary association habitat, 126 percent as varied; more town inhabitants, 116 percent as many; and more habitats per cu of habitat controlled by voluntary associations, 110 percent as many.

Yoredale's Voluntary Associations produced less behavior in 1963–64 than in 1954–55. They produced, via town inhabitants, 56,043 fewer P-H in 1963–64, amounting to 50 percent as much, to 53 percent as much per cu of habitat controlled by voluntary associations, and to 49 percent as much per inhabitant. Involved in Yoredale's smaller output in 1963–64 were these habitat differences: a smaller voluntary association habitat, 93 percent as extensive as in 1954–55; a more varied voluntary association habitat, 107 percent as varied; about the same number of town inhabitants, 101 percent as many; and more inhabitants per cu of habitat controlled by voluntary associations, 108 percent as many.

CLAIM-OPERATIONS GENERATED BY VOLUNTARY ASSOCIATION HABITAT

Salient findings, 1963–64. The total number of C-O generated by the towns' voluntary association habitats for chairmen, scoutmasters, officers, hosts, team members, and so forth, were approximately equivalent to those produced by 100 different voluntary association settings with 43 operatives each in Midwest and with 45 operatives each in Yoredale. The voluntary associations of both towns were more productive of responsible actions than expected on the basis of either their extent or their output of P-H. Midwest's habitat controlled by voluntary associations constituted 11.4 percent of its total habitat, produced 6.3 percent of its GBP, and generated 30.5 percent of its C-O; and Yoredale's voluntary association habitat constituted 8.2 percent of its total habitat, produced 4.2 percent of its GBP, and generated 38.7 percent of its C-O. The mean yearly outputs per town inhabitant were 2.79 C-O per Midwesterner and 1.04 C-O per Dalesman, which were 186 and 113 percent, respectively, of the 1954–55 outputs. There were 53 percent of Midwest's and 30 percent of Yoredale's voluntary association C-O generated via town inhabitants.

C-O data are reported in Table 10.10.

Differences. Midwest's voluntary associations produce more C-O than Yoredale's. In 1963–64 they produced, via town inhabitants, 948 more C-O than Yoredale, amounting to 169 percent as many, to 128 percent as many per cu of voluntary association habitat, and to 268 per-

Table 10.10
Voluntary Association Authority System
Output of Claim-Operations (C-O)

	1954-55		1963-64	
	Midwest (1)	Yoredale (2)	Midwest (3)	Yoredale (4)
Output via all inhabitants				
(1) Total C-O	1,792	3,440	4,352	4,534
(2) Percent of Gross C-O	22.6%	53.3%	30.5%	38.7%
(3) Mean C-O per cu	276.6	345.0	354.7	489.8
Output via town inhabitants				
(4) Total C-O	1,074	1,201	2,312	1,364
(5) Percent of Town C-O	25.7%	39.3%	34.8%	32.5%
(6) Mean C-O per cu	165.8	120.5	188.4	147.3
(7) Mean C-O per town inhabitant	1.50	0.92	2.79	1.04

cent as many per inhabitant. Involved in Midwest's greater output of voluntary association C-O were these habitat differences: more habitat-claims for operatives, 127 percent as many as Yoredale; fewer town inhabitants, 63 percent as many; and fewer town inhabitants per habitat-claim, 49.6 percent as many.

Changes. Both towns' voluntary associations produced more C-O in 1963–64 than in 1954–55. Midwest's produced, via town inhabitants, 1238 more C-O in 1963–64, amounting to 215 percent as many, to 114 percent as many per cu of habitat controlled by voluntary associations, and to 186 percent as many per inhabitant. Involved in Midwest's greater output of voluntary association C-O in 1963–64 were these habitat differences: more habitat-claims for operatives, 256 percent as many as in 1954–55; more town inhabitants, 116 percent as many; and fewer inhabitants per habitat-claim, 45 percent as many.

Yoredale's voluntary associations produced via town inhabitants, 163 C-O in 1963–64, amounting to 113 percent as many, to 122 percent as many per cu of habitat controlled by voluntary associations, and to 113 percent as many per inhabitant. Involved in Yoredale's greater output of voluntary association C-O in 1963–64 were these habitat differences: more habitat-claims for operatives, 128 percent as many as in 1954–55; about the same number of town inhabitants, 101 percent as many; and fewer inhabitants per habitat-claim, 78.7 percent as many.

Summary: Behavior Output of Authority System Habitats

Next we present and discuss graphic summaries of the data on behavior outputs of the Authority System habitats of Midwest and Yoredale in 1963–64, and changes since 1954–55. The explanatory comments about the graphic presentations given earlier in the summary of Action Pattern data apply to the present section as well. The reader is reminded, however, that unlike Action Patterns and Behavior Mechanisms, the differential Authority System habitats are mutually exclusive—a particular behavior setting falls into one and only one of the Authority System habitats.

PERSON-HOURS

Mean P-H per town inhabitant. Common to the two towns are low levels of output from the Church and Voluntary Association habitats and very high outputs from the Private Enterprise habitat (Figure 10.1A). The outputs differ greatly—the Private Enterprise habitats produce 16 and 20 times as many P-H per inhabitant in Midwest and Yoredale, respectively, as do the Church authority system habitats.

Midwest's 25 percent overall superiority to Yoredale in P-H per town inhabitant is exceeded by its Church, Voluntary Association, and School habitats, whereas its Government Agency habitat produces only 67 percent as much as Yoredale's.

Changes. The habitats of both towns controlled by Government Agencies and Private Enterprises maintained a mean P-H output per

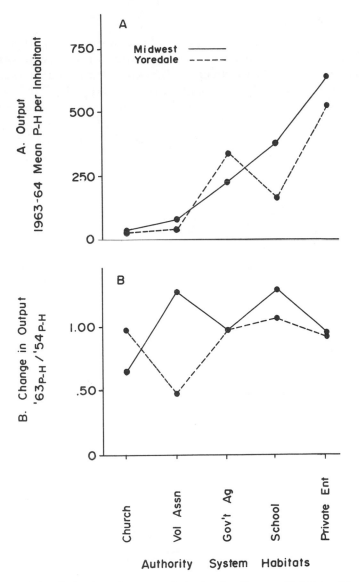

FIGURE 10.1. Behavior Outputs of Authority System Habitats: Mean Person-Hours per Town Inhabitant. A: output, 1963–64; B: change in output, $'63_{P-H}/'54_{P-H}$.

town inhabitant essentially unchanged over the decade, and the outputs of Yoredale's Church and School habitats were also stable (Figure 10.1B). The great changes occurred in Yoredale's Voluntary Associations, where output was less than half as great in 1963–64 as in 1954–55, in Midwest's Voluntary Association and School habitats, where output increased substantially, and in Midwest's Church habitat, where output was 65 percent as great as in 1954–55. Midwest's overall increase of 4 percent in P-H per town inhabitant was concentrated in its School and Voluntary Association habitats. Yoredale's overall decrement of 6 percent was concentrated in its Voluntary Association habitat.

CLAIM-OPERATIONS

Mean C-O per town inhabitant. There was a marked similarity in 1963–64 between the towns on this measure of behavior output — the outputs of the 5 habitats occured in the same rank order from Government Agencies and Private Enterprises, with the lowest outputs, through Churches and Schools to Voluntary Associations, the highest producer of C-O in both Midwest and Yoredale in 1963–64 (Figure 10.2A). The most productive habitat exceeded the least productive by factors of 5 in Midwest and 4 in Yoredale. Midwest's overall 150 percent

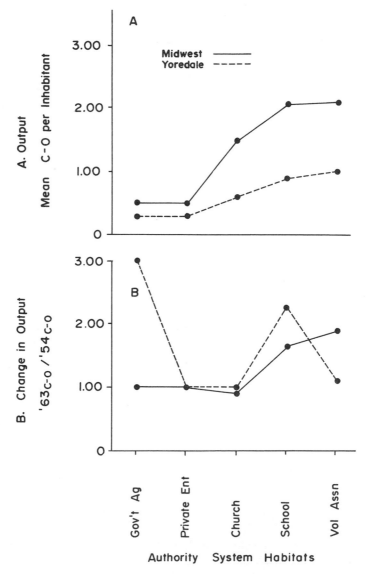

FIGURE 10.2. Behavior Outputs of Authority System Habitats: Mean Claim-Operation per Town Inhabitant. A: output, 1963–64; B: change in output, $'63_{C-O}/'54_{C-O}$.

superiority to Yoredale in C-O output was reflected fairly evenly across the authority system habitats.

Changes. Changes between the survey years were not uniform across the authority system habitats of either town (Figure 10.2B). Midwest's overall 38 percent increment in C-O output per town inhabitant occurred almost entirely in its School and Voluntary Association habitats; and Yoredale's 39 percent increment occurred almost entirely in its Government Agency and School habitats.

BEHAVIOR OUTPUT OF AUTONOMY HABITATS

High Local Autonomy

PERSON-HOURS OF BEHAVIOR GENERATED BY
LOCALLY CONTROLLED HABITAT

Salient findings, 1963–64. The locally controlled habitats of Midwest and Yoredale produced, respectively, 37 and 21 percent of their GBP. Mean weekly outputs were 12 hours per Midwesterner and 5 hours 40 minutes per Dalesman, which were 95 and 100 percent, respectively, of the 1954–55 outputs. Town inhabitants generated 74 percent of the output of Midwest's and 70 percent of the output of Yoredale's locally controlled habitats. P-H data are reported in Table 10.11.

Differences. Midwest's locally controlled habitat produces more behavior than Yoredale's. In 1963–64 it produced, via town inhabitants, 132,206 more P-H than Yoredale's, amounting to 134 percent as much, to 100 percent as much per cu of local habitat, and to 212 percent as much per inhabitant. Involved in Midwest's larger output were these habitat differences: a larger locally controlled habitat, 134 percent as extensive as Yoredale's, and a more varied one, 174 percent as varied;

Table 10.11
High Local Autonomy
Output of Person-Hours (P-H)

	1954-55		1963-64	
	Midwest (1)	Yoredale (2)	Midwest (3)	Yoredale (4)
Output via all inhabitants				
(1) Total P-H			695,904	549,900
(2) Percent of GBP			37.0%	20.9%
(3) Mean P-H per cu			14,867	15,786
Output via town inhabitants				
(4) Total P-H	469,273	381,960	517,790	385,584
(5) Percent of TBP	50.5%	25.3%	46.0%	27.0%
(6) Mean P-H per cu	11,031	10,418	11,062	11,069
(7) Mean P-H per town inhabitant	656.3	293.8	623.8	294.3

fewer town inhabitants, 63 percent as many; and fewer town inhabitants per cu of locally controlled habitat, 47 percent as many.

In psychological language, these findings indicate that in 1963–64, *on the average,* Midwesterners *in comparison with Dalesmen* engaged in much more behavior in the town's locally controlled habitat, within settings where there was the same amount of activity per cu by town inhabitants; they did this within a town which had appreciably more activity in the locally controlled habitat, which was appreciably larger and much more varied, with appreciably fewer town inhabitants to engage in the locally controlled opportunities and duties, and with many fewer inhabitants in relation to these opportunities and duties.

Changes. The locally controlled habitats of both towns produced more behavior in 1963–64 than in 1954–55. Midwest's produced, via town inhabitants, 48,507 more P-H in 1963–64, amounting to 110 percent as much, to 100 percent as much per cu, and to 95 percent as much per inhabitant. Involved in Midwest's greater output in 1963–64 were these habitat differences: a larger locally controlled habitat, 110 percent as extensive as in 1954–55, and a more varied one, 122 percent as varied; more town inhabitants, 116 percent as many; and more inhabitants per cu of local habitat, 105 percent as many.

Yoredale's locally controlled habitat produced, via town inhabitants, 3624 more P-H in 1963–64, amounting to 100 percent as much, to 106 percent as much per cu, and to 100 percent as much per inhabitant. Involved in Yoredale's greater output in 1963–64 were these habitat differences: a smaller locally controlled habitat, 95 percent as extensive as in 1954–55, and a less varied one, 96 percent as varied; about the same number of town inhabitants, 101 percent as many; and more inhabitants per cu of local habitat, 106 percent as many.

CLAIM-OPERATIONS GENERATED BY LOCALLY CONTROLLED HABITAT

Salient findings, 1963–64. The total C-O generated by locally controlled habitats for solicitors, mechanics, bowlers, women's club officers, and so forth were approximately equivalent to those produced by 300 different locally controlled settings with 18 operatives each in Midwest and with 6 operatives each in Yoredale. Midwest's habitat with high local autonomy was about as productive of responsible actions and Yoredale's was less productive than expected on the basis of either their extent or their output of P-H. Midwest's locally controlled habitat constituted 43.6 percent of its total habitat, produced 37 percent of its GBP, and generated 38.4 percent of its C-O; Yoredale's constituted 30.9 percent of its total habitat, produced 20.9 percent of its GBP, and generated 15.4 percent of its C-O. The mean yearly outputs per town inhabitant were 3.98 C-O per Midwesterner and 1.03 C-O per Dalesman, which were 128 and 96 percent, respectively, of the 1954–55 outputs. Town inhabitants generated 60 percent (MW) and 75 percent (YD) of the C-O produced by settings with high local autonomy.

C-O data are reported in Table 10.12.

Table 10.12
High Local Autonomy
Output of Claim-Operations (C-O)

	1954-55		1963-64	
	Midwest (1)	Yoredale (2)	Midwest (3)	Yoredale (4)
Output via all inhabitants				
(1) Total C-O	3,345	1,828	5,476	1,807
(2) Percent of Gross C-O	42.1%	28.3%	38.4%	15.4%
(3) Mean C-O per cu	78.6	49.9	117.0	51.9
Output via town inhabitants				
(4) Total C-O	2,214	1,386	3,300	1,354
(5) Percent of Town C-O	53.0%	45.4%	49.7%	32.2%
(6) Mean C-O per cu	52.0	37.8	70.5	38.9
(7) Mean C-O per town inhabitant	3.10	1.07	3.98	1.03

Differences. Midwest's locally controlled habitat produces more C-O than Yoredale's. In 1963–64 it produced, via town inhabitants, 1946 more C-O than Yoredale's, amounting to 244 percent as many, to 181 percent as many per cu, and to 386 percent as many per inhabitant. Involved in Midwest's greater output of local C-O were these habitat differences: more habitat-claims for operatives, 311 percent as many as Yoredale's; fewer town inhabitants, 63 percent as many; and fewer town inhabitants per habitat-claim, 20 percent as many.

Changes. Midwest's locally controlled habitat produced more C-O in 1963–64 than in 1954–55, and Yoredale's produced fewer. Midwest's produced, via town inhabitants, 1086 more C-O in 1963–64, amounting to 149 percent as many, to 136 percent as many per cu, and to 128 percent as many per inhabitant. Involved in Midwest's greater output of C-O in 1963–64 were these habitat differences: more habitat-claims for operatives, 168 percent as many as in 1954–55; more town inhabitants, 116 percent as many; but fewer inhabitants per habitat-claim, 69 percent as many.

Yoredale's locally controlled habitat produced, via town inhabitants, 32 fewer C-O in 1963–64, amounting to 98 percent as many, to 103 percent as many per cu, and to 96 percent as many per inhabitant. Involved in Yoredale's smaller output of C-O in 1963–64 were these habitat differences: fewer local habitat-claims for operatives, 92 percent as many as in 1954–55; about the same number of town inhabitants, 101 percent as many; and more inhabitants per habitat-claim, 109 percent as many.

Medium Local Autonomy

PERSON-HOURS OF BEHAVIOR GENERATED BY
REGIONALLY CONTROLLED HABITAT

Salient findings, 1963–64. The regionally controlled habitats of Midwest and Yoredale produced, respectively, 56 and 48 percent of

Table 10.13
Medium Local Autonomy
Output of Person-Hours (P-H)

| | 1954-55 | | 1963-64 | |
	Midwest (1)	Yoredale (2)	Midwest (3)	Yoredale (4)
Output via all inhabitants				
(1) Total P-H			1,057,037	1,261,936
(2) Percent of GBP			56.2%	48.0%
(3) Mean P-H per cu			20,300	29,864
Output via town inhabitants				
(4) Total P-H	398,968	589,016	558,570	733,381
(5) Percent of TBP	42.9%	39.1%	49.6%	51.4%
(6) Mean P-H per cu	10,062	17,464	10,727	17,356
(7) Mean P-H per town inhabitant	558.0	453.1	673.0	559.8

their GBP. The mean weekly outputs were 12 hours 54 minutes per Midwesterner and 10 hours 48 minutes per Dalesman, which were 121 and 123 percent, respectively, of the 1954–55 outputs. Town inhabitants generated 53 percent of the output of Midwest's and 58 percent of the output of Yoredale's regionally controlled habitats.

P-H data are reported in Table 10.13.

Differences. Midwest's regionally controlled habitat produces less behavior than Yoredale's. In 1963–64 it produced, via town inhabitants, 174,811 fewer P-H than Yoredale's, amounting to 76 percent as much, to 62 percent as much per cu, and to 120 percent as much per inhabitant. Involved in Midwest's smaller output were these habitat differences: a larger regionally controlled habitat, 123 percent as extensive as Yoredale's; a less varied one, 94 percent as varied; fewer town inhabitants, 63 percent as many; and fewer town inhabitants per cu of regional habitat, 51 percent as many.

In psychological language, these findings indicate that in 1963–64, *on the average,* Midwesterners *in comparison with Dalesmen* engaged in appreciably more behavior in the town's regionally controlled habitat within settings where there was appreciably less activity per cu by Midwesterners; they did this within a town in which there was appreciably less activity in the regionally controlled habitat, which was larger but less varied, with appreciably fewer town inhabitants to take advantage of the opportunities and carry out the duties, and many fewer inhabitants in relation to the regional opportunities and duties.

Changes. The regionally controlled habitats of both towns produced more behavior in 1963–64 than in 1954–55. Midwest's produced, via town inhabitants, 159,602 more P-H in 1963–64, amounting to 140 percent as much, to 107 percent as much per cu, and to 121 percent as much per inhabitant. Involved in Midwest's increased output in 1963–64 were these habitat differences: a larger regionally controlled habitat, 131 percent as extensive as in 1954–55; a more varied habitat, 124 percent as varied; more town inhabitants, 116 percent as many; and fewer inhabitants per cu of regional habitat, 88 percent as many.

Yoredale's produced, via town inhabitants, 144,365 more P-H, amounting to 124 percent as much, to 99 percent as much per cu, and to 123 percent as much per inhabitant. Involved in Yoredale's increased output in 1963–64 were these habitat differences: a larger regionally controlled habitat, 125 percent as extensive as in 1954–55; a more varied one, 134 percent as varied; about the same number of town inhabitants, 101 percent as many; and fewer inhabitants per cu of regionally controlled habitat, 80 percent as many.

CLAIM-OPERATIONS GENERATED BY REGIONALLY CONTROLLED HABITAT

Salient findings, 1963–64. The total C-O generated by regionally controlled habitats for county engineers, secretaries, council members, health officers, and so forth were approximately equivalent to those produced by 100 different regionally controlled settings with 80 operatives each in Midwest and with 58 operatives each in Yoredale. The habitats of both towns with medium local autonomy were slightly more productive of responsible actions than expected on the basis of either their extent or their output of P-H. Midwest's regionally controlled habitat constituted 48.5 percent of its total habitat, produced 56.2 percent of its GBP, and generated 56.4 percent of its C-O; and Yoredale's regionally controlled habitat constituted 37.4 percent of its total habitat, produced 48 percent of its GBP, and generated 49.4 percent of its C-O. The mean yearly outputs per town inhabitant were 3.76 C-O per Midwesterner and 1.44 C-O per Dalesman, which were 149 and 147 percent, respectively, of the 1954–55 outputs. Town inhabitants produced 39 percent (MW) and 33 percent (YD) of the C-O generated by settings with medium local autonomy.

C-O data are reported in Table 10.14.

Differences. Midwest's regionally controlled habitat produces more C-O than Yoredale's. In 1963–64 it produced, via town inhabitants,

Table 10.14
Medium Local Autonomy
Output of Claim-Operations (C-O)

	1954-55		1963-64	
	Midwest (1)	Yoredale (2)	Midwest (3)	Yoredale (4)
Output via all inhabitants				
(1) Total C-O	4,038	3,007	8,046	5,782
(2) Percent of Gross C-O	50.9%	46.6%	56.4%	49.4%
(3) Mean C-O per cu	101.8	89.2	154.5	136.8
Output via town inhabitants				
(4) Total C-O	1,802	1,272	3,125	1,887
(5) Percent of Town C-O	43.2%	41.6%	47.0%	44.9%
(6) Mean C-O per cu	45.4	37.7	60.0	44.7
(7) Mean C-O per town inhabitant	2.52	0.98	3.76	1.44

1238 more C-O than Yoredale's, amounting to 166 percent as many, to 134 percent as many per cu, and to 261 percent as many per inhabitant. Involved in Midwest's greater output of C-O were these habitat differences: more regional claims for operatives, 133 percent as many as Yoredale; fewer town inhabitants, 63 percent as many; and fewer town inhabitants per claim, 47 percent as many.

Changes. The regionally controlled habitats of both towns produced more C-O in 1963–64 than in 1954–55. Midwest's produced, via town inhabitants, 1323 more C-O in 1963–64, amounting to 173 percent as many, to 132 percent as many per cu, and to 149 percent as many per inhabitant. Involved in Midwest's increased output of regional C-O in 1963–64 were these habitat differences: more habitat-claims for operatives, 221 percent as many as in 1954–55; more town inhabitants, 116 percent as many; and fewer town inhabitants per habitat-claim, 52 percent as many.

Yoredale's regionally controlled habitat produced, via town inhabitants, 615 more C-O in 1963–64, amounting to 148% as many, 118 percent as many per cu, and to 147 percent as many per inhabitant. Involved in Yoredale's increased output of C-O in 1963–64 were these habitat differences: more habitat-claims for operatives, 200 percent as many as in 1954–55; about the same number of town inhabitants, 101 percent as many; and fewer inhabitants per habitat-claim, 50 percent as many.

Low Local Autonomy

PERSON-HOURS OF BEHAVIOR GENERATED BY
DISTANTLY CONTROLLED HABITAT

Salient findings, 1963–64. The habitats of the towns controlled from a distance produced, respectively, 7 and 31 percent of their GBP. The mean weekly outputs were 1 hour 6 minutes per Midwesterner and 4 hours 30 minutes per Dalesman, which were 68 and 57 percent, respectively, of the 1954–55 outputs. Town inhabitants produced 38 percent of the outputs of both Midwest's and Yoredale's habitat with low local autonomy.

P-H data are reported in Table 10.15.

Differences. Midwest's distantly controlled habitat produces less behavior than does Yoredale's. In 1963–64 it produced, via town inhabitants, 258,374 fewer P-H than Yoredale's, amounting to 16 percent as much, to 67 percent as much per cu, and to 25 percent as much per inhabitant. Involved in Midwest's smaller output were these habitat differences: a smaller habitat controlled from a distance, 24 percent as extensive as Yoredale's; a less varied one, 27 percent as varied; fewer town inhabitants, 63 percent as many; but more town inhabitants per cu of distantly controlled habitat, 266 percent as many.

In psychological terms, these findings indicate that in 1963–64, *on the average,* Midwesterners *in comparison with Dalesmen* engaged in

Table 10.15
Low Local Autonomy
Output of Person-Hours (P-H)

	1954-55		1963-64	
	Midwest (1)	Yoredale (2)	Midwest (3)	Yoredale (4)
Output via all inhabitants				
(1) Total P-H			127,791	813,980
(2) Percent of GBP			6.8%	31.0%
(3) Mean P-H per cu			15,057	22,776
Output via town inhabitants				
(4) Total P-H	61,621	535,763	48,775	307,149
(5) Percent of Town TBP	6.6%	35.5%	4.3%	21.5%
(6) Mean P-H per cu	8,065	27,345	5,747	8,594
(7) Mean P-H per town inhabitant	86.2	412.1	58.8	234.5

much less behavior in the town's habitat with low local autonomy, within settings where there was appreciably less activity per cu by town inhabitants; they did this within a town with much less activity in settings controlled from a distance, a much smaller and much less varied distantly controlled habitat, appreciably fewer town inhabitants to take advantage of the opportunities and carry out the duties that were controlled from a distance, and many more inhabitants in relation to these opportunities and duties.

Changes. The distantly controlled habitats of both towns produced less behavior in 1963–64 than in 1954–55. Midwest's produced, via town inhabitants, 12,846 fewer P-H in 1963–64, amounting to 79 percent as much, to 60 percent as much per cu, and to 68 percent as much per inhabitant. Involved in Midwest's reduced output in 1963–64 were these habitat differences: a larger habitat with low local autonomy, 112 percent as extensive as in 1954–55; a more varied one, 103 percent as varied; more town inhabitants, 116 percent as many; and more inhabitants per cu of distantly controlled habitat, 104 percent as many.

Yoredale's distantly controlled habitat produced, via town inhabitants, 228,614 fewer P-H, amounting to 57 percent as much, to 31 percent as much per cu, and to 57 percent as much per inhabitant. Involved in Yoredale's reduced output in 1963–64 were these habitat differences: a larger habitat with low local autonomy, 182 percent as extensive; a more varied habitat, 185 percent as varied; and about the same number of town inhabitants, 101 percent as many; but fewer inhabitants per cu of distantly controlled habitat, 55 percent as many.

CLAIM-OPERATIONS GENERATED BY DISTANTLY CONTROLLED HABITAT

Salient findings, 1963–64. The total C-O generated by the towns' distantly controlled habitats for soil conservation specialists, police sergeants, district judges, and so forth were approximately equivalent to those produced by 100 different settings controlled from a distance with

7 operatives each in Midwest and with 41 operatives each in Yoredale. Midwest's distantly controlled habitat was less and Yoredale's was slightly more productive of responsible actions than expected on the basis of either their extent or their output of P-H. Midwest's distantly controlled habitat constituted 7.9 percent of its total habitat, produced 6.8 percent of its GBP, and generated 5.1 percent of its C-O; and Yoredale's constituted 31.7 percent of its total habitat, produced 31.0 percent of its GBP, and generated 35.1 percent of its C-O. The mean yearly outputs per town inhabitant were 0.26 C-O per Midwesterner and 0.73 C-O per Dalesman, which were 118 and 235 percent, respectively, of the 1954–55 outputs. There were 30 percent of Midwest's and 23 percent of Yoredale's C-O in settings controlled from a distance that were generated via town inhabitants.

C-O data are reported in Table 10.16.

Differences. Midwest's distantly controlled habitat produces fewer C-O than does Yoredale's. In 1963–64 it produced, via town inhabitants, 744 fewer C-O than Yoredale's, amounting to 23 percent as many, to 95 percent as many per cu, and to 36 percent as many per inhabitant. Involved in Midwest's smaller output of distant C-O were these habitat differences: fewer habitat-claims for operatives, 22 percent as many as Yoredale's; fewer town inhabitants, 63 percent as many; and more town inhabitants per habitat-claim, 291 percent as many.

Changes. The habitats of both towns that were controlled from a distance produced more C-O in 1963–64 than in 1954–55. Midwest's produced, via town inhabitants, 60 more C-O in 1963-64, amounting to 138 percent as many, to 125 percent as many per cu, and to 118 percent as many per inhabitant. Involved in Midwest's increased output of distant C-O in 1963–64 were these habitat differences: more habitat-claims for operatives, 142 percent as many as in 1954–55; more town inhabitants, 116 percent as many; but fewer town inhabitants per habitat-claim, 82 percent as many.

Yoredale's distantly controlled habitat produced, via town inhabi-

Table 10.16
Low Local Autonomy
Output of Claim-Operations (C-O)

	1954-55		1963-64	
	Midwest (1)	Yoredale (2)	Midwest (3)	Yoredale (4)
Output via all inhabitants				
(1) Total C-O	553	1,618	727	4,115
(2) Percent of Gross C-O	7.0%	25.1%	5.1%	35.1%
(3) Mean C-O per cu	72.4	82.6	85.7	115.1
Output via town inhabitants				
(4) Total C-O	157	397	217	961
(5) Percent of Town C-O	3.8%	13.0%	3.3%	22.9%
(6) Mean C-O per cu	20.5	20.3	25.6	26.9
(7) Mean C-O per town inhabitant	0.22	0.31	0.26	0.73

tants, 564 more C-O in 1963–64, amounting to 242 percent as many, to 133 percent as many per cu, and to 235 percent as many per inhabitant. Involved in Yoredale's increased output of distant C-O in 1963–64 were these habitat differences: more habitat-claims for operatives, 388 percent as many as in 1954–55; about the same number of town inhabitants, 101 percent as many; but with fewer inhabitants per habitat-claim, 26 percent as many.

Summary: Behavior Output of Autonomy Habitats

We turn now to graphic summaries of the behavior outputs of the towns' autonomy habitats in 1963–64 and changes since 1954–55. We follow here the format established in previous summary sections.

PERSON-HOURS

Mean P-H per town inhabitant. There is a general similarity between the curves; the regionally controlled habitats of both towns are most productive, followed, in order, by the locally and distantly controlled habitats (Figure 10.3A). But the differences between Midwest and Yoredale in output per town inhabitant are more impressive than is the similarity. Midwest's habitat controlled from a distance produced only 25 percent as many mean P-H per inhabitant as did Yoredale's, but its locally controlled habitat generated 212 percent as many. In Chapter 6 we report similar relations between the towns in extent of autonomy habitats. More of Midwest's habitat and behavior output is self-determined, and less is directed from centers far distant from the town.

Changes. The change curves are remarkably similar (Figure 10.3B). The regionally controlled habitats of both towns increased substantially in output per town inhabitant between 1954–55 and 1963–64, the outputs of the distantly controlled habitats declined, and the locally controlled habitats changed little in output.

CLAIM-OPERATIONS

Mean C-O per town inhabitant. The pattern of the C-O curves resembles that of the P-H curves with two exceptions: most differences between the towns are greater, and the output of Midwest's locally controlled habitat is greater than that of its regionally controlled habitat (Figure 10.4A). Midwest's locally controlled habitat produced 386 percent as many mean C-O per town inhabitant as did Yoredale's, and its distantly controlled habitat produced 25 percent as many. Many more of the responsibilities of Midwesterners are locally planned and programed, and many fewer follow directives from a distance.

Changes. Outstanding here is the great increase in output of C-O by Yoredale's distantly controlled habitat; Dalesmen engaged in more than twice as many such C-O in 1963–64 as in 1954–55 (Figure 10.4B). Changes in the C-O outputs of other autonomy habitats were relatively minor.

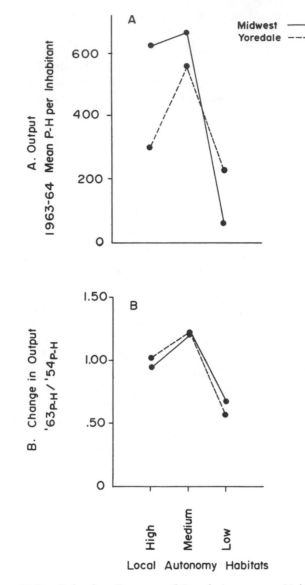

FIGURE 10.3.   Behavior Outputs of Local Autonomy Habitats: Mean Person-Hours per Town Inhabitant. A: output, 1963–64; B: change in output, $'63_{P-H}/'54_{P-H}$.

BEHAVIOR OUTPUT OF ATTENDANCE HABITATS

In the interest of brevity, the output data for these habitats are presented in graphic summary form, as was done with the habitat data. The attendance habitats are identified in Chapter 6.

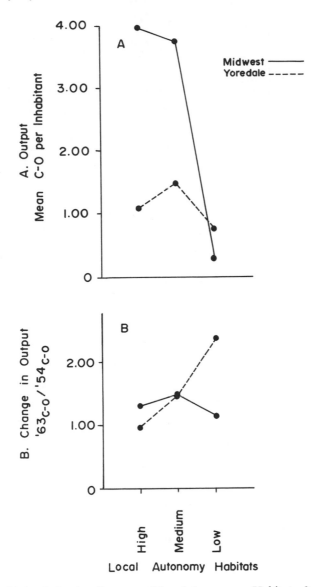

FIGURE 10.4. Behavior Outputs of Local Autonomy Habitats: Mean Claim-Operations per Town Inhabitant. A: output, 1963–64; B: change in output, $'63_{C-O}/'54_{C-O}$.

Child Attendance Habitats

PERSON-HOURS

Mean P-H per town inhabitant. Habitats neutral to child attendance produced far more P-H in 1963–64 than any of the other child attendance habitats—over 600 hours per town inhabitant in each town (Fig-

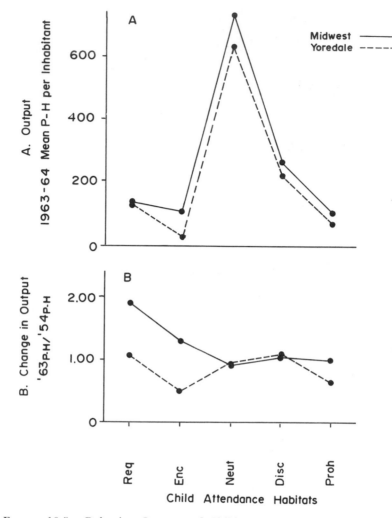

FIGURE 10.5.   Behavior Outputs of Child Attendance Habitats: Mean Person-Hours per Town Inhabitant. A: output, 1963–64; B: change in output, $'63_{P\text{-}H}/'54_{P\text{-}H}$.

ure 10.5A). Habitats neutral to children were followed in both towns by habitats which discourage child attendance, with about one-third as much output, and those which require children to attend, with approximately one-sixth the output of the neutral habitats. The greatest difference between the towns occurred in the habitats which encourage child attendance; these produced 4 times as many P-H per town inhabitant in Midwest as in Yoredale.

Changes. The changes between the survey years vary greatly across the child attendance habitats, and the towns have little in common (Figure 10.5B). In Midwest, output of the habitats which require and encourage child attendance increased at the expense of the others, which about maintained their 1954–55 rates; in Yoredale the habitats which encourage and prohibit child attendance decreased in output, and the others about maintained their earlier rates. In 1963–64 the more child-centered habitats of Midwest, those on the positive side of neutral (child attendance required and encouraged), contributed more to the mean P-H output of Midwesterners than they did in 1954–55; the sources of Yoredale's output did not change in this respect.

CLAIM-OPERATIONS

Mean C-O per town inhabitant. In both towns in 1963–64 the largest output was from the habitats neutral to child attendance (Figure 10.6A). This is the only similarity between the towns. Midwest's overall 150 percent superiority to Yoredale in C-O per town inhabitant was reflected fairly closely in the outputs of the habitats which discourage and prohibit child attendance, but Midwest's superiority was much greater than this in those habitats which encourage and are neutral to child attendance. Unexpectedly, the towns are almost equal in C-O output from their habitats which require child attendance.

Changes. The rates of change between the survey years in the C-O outputs of the habitats neutral and negative to child attendance were similar to the rates for the towns as wholes, with increments of approximately one-third. But output increased much more than this in the habitats which require child attendance, by 200 percent in Midwest and 133 percent in Yoredale. The towns changed in opposite directions in output from the habitats which encourage child attendance: Midwest's increased substantially more than the town as a whole, while Yoredale's decreased markedly between the survey years.

Adolescent Attendance Habitats

PERSON-HOURS

Mean P-H per town inhabitant. In 1963–64 the largest output in both towns occurred in the habitats neutral to adolescent attendance (Figure 10.7A). Beyond this, the curves for the two towns have only superficial similarity. Midwest's 25 percent overall superiority to Yoredale in output of P-H per town inhabitant was far exceeded by the habitats positive to adolescent attendance; by contrast, Midwest's output from the habitats which discourage or prohibit adolescent participation was about the same as Yoredale's or much less.

Changes. The towns have little in common with respect to changes between the survey years in mean P-H per town inhabitant. The outputs of Midwest's habitats positive to adolescent attendance increased much more than the 4 percent overall increase for the town, and the output of the habitat most negative to adolescent attendance decreased markedly. The more adolescent-centered habitats of Midwest contributed more to

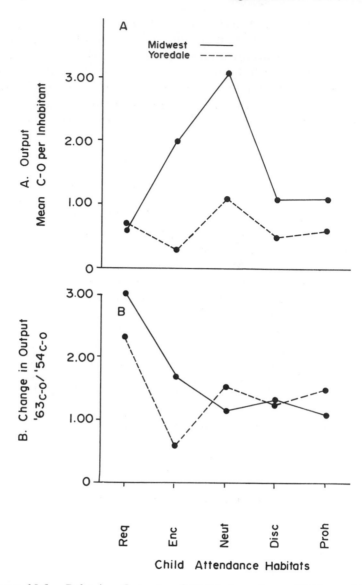

FIGURE 10.6.   Behavior Outputs of Child Attendance Habitats: Mean Claim-Operations per Town Inhabitant. A: output, 1963–64; B: change in output, $'63_{c-o}/'54_{c-o}$.

P-H output in 1963–64 than in 1954–55. This shift did not occur in Yoredale.

CLAIM-OPERATIONS

Mean C-O per town inhabitant. In 1963–64 the habitats of both towns most coercive to adolescent attendance — those which prohibit and require their attendance — were low in output of C-O (Figure 10.8A). Otherwise the towns differed widely. Midwest's 150 percent overall

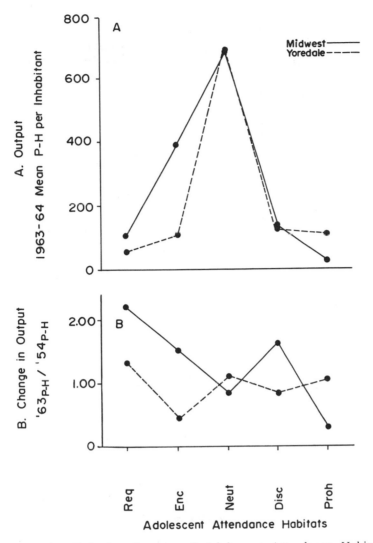

FIGURE 10.7. Behavior Outputs of Adolescent Attendance Habitats: Mean Person-Hours per Town Inhabitant. A: output, 1963–64; B: change in output, $'63_{\text{P-H}}/'54_{\text{P-H}}$.

superiority to Yoredale in mean C-O per town inhabitant occurred chiefly in its neutral habitat and in the one which mildly pressures adolescent attendance. In the habitats which apply strongest pressure on adolescent attendance, Midwest's superiority was reduced to 25 percent (attendance required) and 33 percent (attendance prohibited).

Changes. The patterns of change in the outputs of C-O in both towns are remarkably similar to those for outputs of P-H. Midwest's output shifted toward greater contributions from its habitats positive to adolescents, whereas Yoredale's did not change.

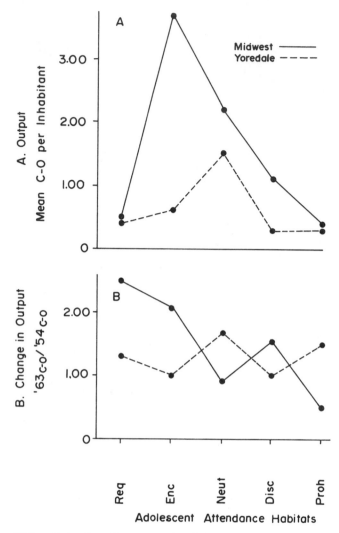

Figure 10.8.   Behavior Outputs of Adolescent Attendance Habitats: Mean
Claim-Operations per Town Inhabitant. A: output, 1963–64; B: change in output,
$'63_{c-o}/'54_{c-o}$.

BEHAVIOR OUTPUT OF BENEFICENCE HABITATS

As with the attendance habitats, the data for these habitats are
presented in graphic summary form. The differential beneficence habitats are identified in Chapter 6.

Child Beneficence Habitats

PERSON-HOURS

Mean P-H per town inhabitant. As expected because of its greater
extent, the habitat not concerned with children as a special group had

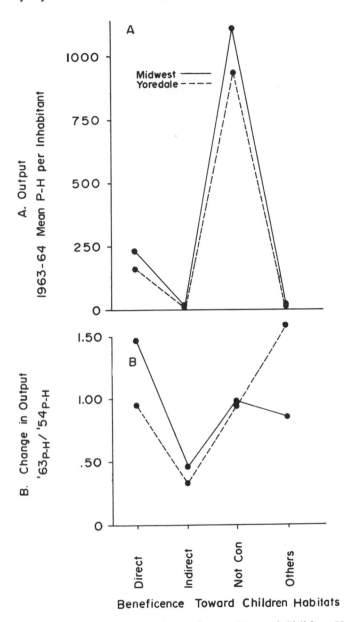

FIGURE 10.9. Behavior Outputs of Beneficence Toward Children Habitats: Mean Person-Hours per Town Inhabitant. A: output, 1963–64; B: change in output, '63$_{P-H}$/'54$_{P-H}$.

by far the greatest output in both towns in 1963–64 (Figure 10.9A). In second rank, but far below, was the habitat which benefits children directly. The other two child beneficence habitats had extremely small outputs in both towns. Across all but one of the child beneficence habitats, differences—uniformly in favor of Midwest—were in accordance with Midwest's 25 percent overall superiority; but in the habitat where

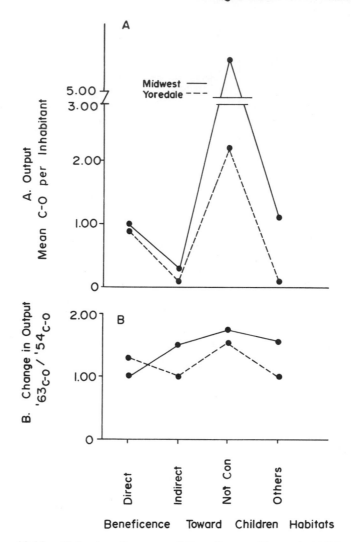

FIGURE 10.10.   Behavior Outputs of Beneficence Toward Children Habitats: Mean Claim-Operations per Town Inhabitant. A: output, 1963–64; B: change in output, $'63_{\text{c-o}}/'54_{\text{c-o}}$.

children benefit others, though the values were small, the mean P-H output per town inhabitant in Midwest was almost 14 times greater than the output in Yoredale.

Changes. In both towns the output of the habitat which benefits children indirectly dropped sharply from 1954–55 to 1963–64, and the output of the habitats not concerned with children remained essentially unchanged. Output from the habitat designed especially for the benefit of children increased substantially in Midwest but decreased slightly in Yoredale, whereas the reverse relation occurred in the habitat where children benefit members of other age groups—Yoredale's output increased substantially between the survey years, and Midwest's output declined.

CLAIM-OPERATIONS

Mean C-O per town inhabitant. Output data for C-O in 1963–64 closely resemble the pattern reported above for P-H (Figure 10.10A). Again, the greatest difference between the towns occurred in the habitat where children benefit other age groups; Midwest outproduced Yoredale in mean C-O per town inhabitant by a factor of 11.

Changes. In both towns the biggest increases in output of C-O per town inhabitant occurred in the habitats not concerned with children. The change ratios were greater than for the towns' total habitats (Figure 10.10B). The outputs of Midwest's habitat which benefits children indirectly and of its habitat where children benefit members of other age groups also increased more than did the town as a whole; only the habitat which benefits children directly lagged behind in Midwest. There were no laggard child beneficence habitats in Yoredale, but the increments over the decade were smaller than in Midwest. In addition to the habitat not concerned with children, only the habitat which benefits children directly had greater C-O output in 1963–64 than in 1954–55.

Adolescent Beneficence Habitats

PERSON-HOURS

Mean P-H per town inhabitant. In both towns in 1963–64 output was heavily concentrated in the habitat neutral to adolescents; in second rank, but much smaller in output, was the habitat which benefits adolescents directly (Figure 10.11A). In both towns the other two beneficence habitats had very small outputs. However, Midwest's superiority to Yoredale in output from the habitat where adolescents benefit members of other age groups was impressive — Midwest's output exceeded Yoredale's by a factor of almost 13.

Changes. Two similarities between the towns are apparent: habitats not concerned with adolescents remained essentially unchanged in output over the decade, and the P-H outputs of habitats where adolescents benefit members of other age groups were substantially reduced. Midwest had a marked increase in the output from its habitat which benefits adolescents directly and a decrease from its habitat which benefits adolescents indirectly. The output of these habitats did not change appreciably in Yoredale.

CLAIM-OPERATIONS

Mean C-O per town inhabitant. The output patterns are similar to those for P-H (Figure 10.12A). Differences across the adolescent beneficence habitats do not vary widely from the overall difference between the towns — Midwest's C-O output, 150 percent greater than Yore-

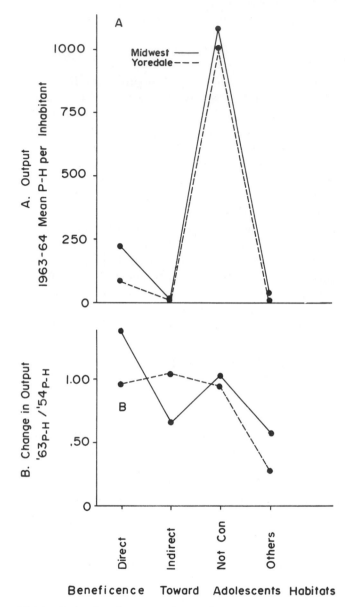

FIGURE 10.11. Behavior Outputs of Beneficence Toward Adolescents Habitats: Mean Person-Hours per Town Inhabitant. A: output, 1963–64; B: change in output, '63$_{P-H}$/'54$_{P-H}$.

dale's—except in the habitat where adolescents benefit members of other age groups, where Midwest's output is more than 8 times as large as Yoredale's—a finding consistent with trends established in the previously reported output measures.

Changes. In Midwest the habitats which benefit adolescents directly and indirectly gained in output of C-O somewhat more than did

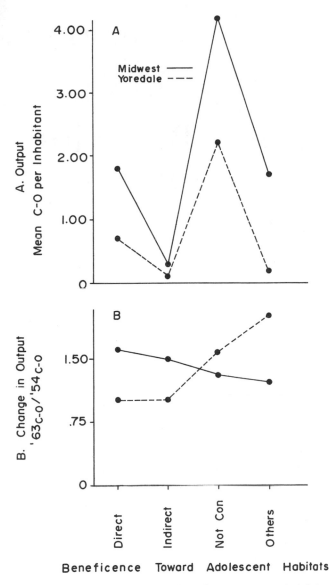

FIGURE 10.12. Behavior Outputs of Beneficence Toward Adolescents Habitats: Mean Claim-Operations per Town Inhabitant. A: output, 1963–64, B: change in output, $'63_{c\text{-}o}/'54_{c\text{-}o}$.

the town as a whole; but in Yoredale these habitats remained constant in output of C-O between the survey years (Figure 10.12B). Almost the opposite occurred in the other two adolescent beneficence habitats: in Midwest habitats neutral to adolescents and habitats where adolescents serve other age groups increased in output of C-O, but at rates below that for the town as a whole (138 percent); in Yoredale these two habitats both increased in productivity substantially more than the town as a whole did.

CHAPTER 11

Extent and Behavior Output of Subgroup Habitats

⫷∽⫷∽⫷∽⫷∽⫷∽⫷∽⫷∽⫷∽⫷∽⫷∽⫷∽⫷∽⫷∽⫷∽⫷∽⫷∽⫷∽⫷∽

T hus far we have dealt with measures of the extent, variety, and behavior output of the towns' total habitats and of their differential program habitats—those parts of their habitats with designated program attributes (aesthetic habitat, gross motor habitat, habitat with high local autonomy, and so forth). We turn here to the towns' differential subgroup habitats—those parts of their habitats with designated subgroups of their inhabitants as human components (infant habitat, female habitat, social class II habitat, and so forth). We report measures of extent and behavior output.

Populations of the Subgroups

The inhabitant subgroups (SG) with which we have dealt are identified in Table 11.1, where the number of *town* residents in each SG are reported. The population data for 1963–64 are represented in Figure 11.1, where it will be noted that Yoredale's greater total population—58 percent greater—was not distributed uniformly across all SGs. The greatest discrepancies were within the social classes where Yoredale had a greater excess of class III and a smaller excess of classes I and II than expected on the basis of the town's total population. Within the age SGs, Yoredale had a greater excess of infants than expected and no excess of younger school children.

366

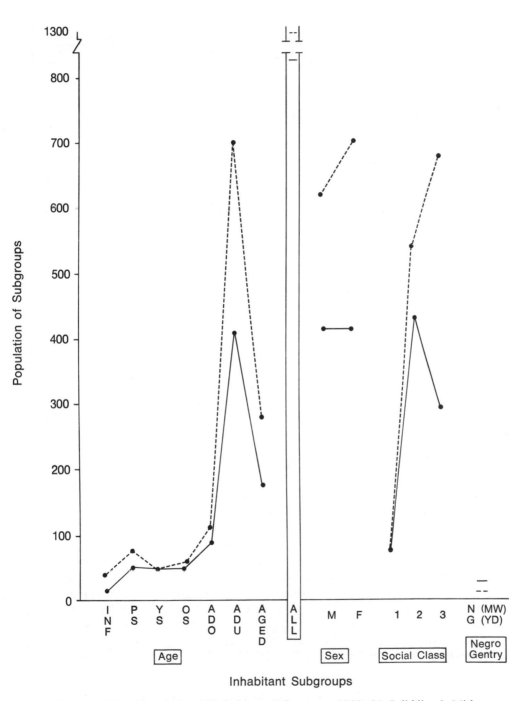

FIGURE 11.1. Population of Inhabitant Subgroups, 1963–64. Solid line is Midwest; dashed line is Yoredale.

Table 11.1

Number of Town Residents in Inhabitant Subgroups

		1954–55		1963–64	
		MW (1)	YD (2)	MW (3)	YD (4)
	Subgroup				
(1)	Infant (under 2)[a]	24	41	13	40
(2)	Preschool (2-5:11)	50	81	53	76
(3)	Younger School (6-8:11)	28	72	46	46
(4)	Older School (9-11:11)	26	51	47	58
(5)	Total Child (under 12)	128	245	159	220
(6)	Adolescent (12-17:11)	50	107	84	114
(7)	Adult (18-64:11)	375	770	411	689
(8)	Aged (65 and over)	162	178	176	287
(9)	Total Town	715	1300	830	1310
(10)	Male	346	612	415	621
(11)	Female	369	688	415	689
(12)	Social Class I[b]	84	78	73	85
(13)	Social Class II	307	283	438	543
(14)	Social Class III	295	931	293	674
(15)	Negro	29		26	
(16)	Gentry		8		8

[a] Age ranges in years: months.
[b] Social classes I, II, III correspond fairly well to Warner's Upper Middle, Lower Middle, and Upper Lower Classes, and Gentry to his Upper Upper Class (Warner et al., 1949).

Extent of Subgroup Habitats

TERRITORIAL RANGE OF SUBGROUPS

   The territorial range (TR) of the SG—the extent in centiurbs of settings with claims for SG members[1] at any penetration level—is reported in Table 11.2 and Figure 11.2A. The figure reveals dramatically the expansion to adulthood and the contraction in old age of the habitats over which the age SGs range. In 1963–64 (a) infants were behavior setting components of about half of each town's habitat; (b) TR increased with each older age group until adulthood; (c) adults were components of all the habitats of both towns; (d) TR was reduced for the aged to about that of adolescents in Midwest and of older school children in Yoredale; (e) more of the towns' public habitats generated behavior via males than via females; (f) members of the social class II SG were components of more of the towns' habitats than were the other social classes, and members of social class I were the least widely dis-

   [1] In identifying the territorial range of a subgroup, no distinction is made between town residents and out-of-town residents; for example, the TR of the infant SG consists of the behavior settings inhabited by one or more infants (either town or out-of-town residents) during the survey year. OR and LR are established on the same basis.

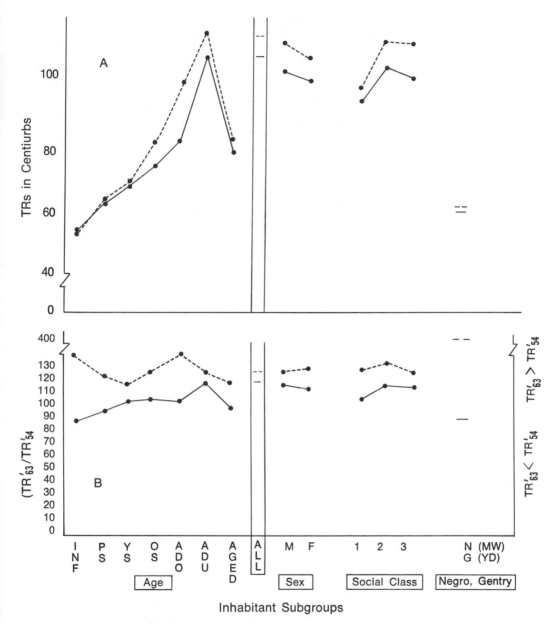

FIGURE 11.2 A: TR of the towns' inhabitant subgroups in centiurbs, 1963–64; B: change in Territorial Range, TR in 1963–64 as percentage of TR in 1954–55 (TR′63/TR′54) 100. Solid line is Midwest; dashed line is Yoredale.

tributed; and finally (*g*) the Negroes of Midwest and the gentry of Yoredale had similar TRs, just over 50 percent of the towns' habitats.

The figure shows that the TR of the various SGs within each town differs much more than the TR of the same SGs between the two towns. The maximum within-town differences are between the infant

Table 11.2
Territorial Range of Inhabitant Subgroups

	Subgroup	1954–55 MW (1) Centiurbs	YD (2)	1963–64 MW (3) Centiurbs	YD (4)
(1)	Infant	61.6	38.9	53.6	53.0
(2)	Preschool	65.0	52.7	61.4	63.9
(3)	Younger School	66.1	59.1	67.4	68.5
(4)	Older School	69.7	63.2	72.6	81.4
(5)	Total Child	72.4	64.3	80.0	83.7
(6)	Adolescent	78.8	69.1	81.3	96.7
(7)	Adult	89.7	89.9	107.0	113.0
(8)	Aged	78.6	69.2	77.7	80.1
(9)	Total Town	89.8	90.0	107.4	113.0
(10)	Male	87.2	87.2	102.3	111.0
(11)	Female	86.9	82.4	99.4	106.0
(12)	Social Class I	87.2	75.3	92.9	97.3
(13)	Social Class II	89.4	85.0	104.0	112.3
(14)	Social Class III	87.6	86.9	101.0	111.3
(15)	Negro	65.8		59.5	
(16)	Gentry		15.1		60.4

and adult SGs; in 1963–64 the differences in TR amounted to 53.4 cu in Midwest and 60 cu in Yoredale. The maximum between-town difference is between the adolescent SGs of the towns; in 1963–64 the TR of Yoredale's adolescents was 15.4 cu greater than that of Midwest's adolescents.

Differences. Because adults are components of the towns' entire habitats, the TRs of the adult habitats of Midwest and Yoredale have the same size relation as the towns' total habitats; in 1963–64, therefore, the TR of Midwest adults was 95 percent as extensive as that of Yoredale adults. Inspection of Figure 11.2A shows that the TR of most of the other SGs does not deviate greatly from this relation. The most deviant are infants and adolescents; the TR of Midwest's infants is 101 percent of the TR of Yoredale's infants, and Midwest's adolescent SG has 84 percent of the TR of Yoredales's adolescent SG.

Changes. From the change data in Figure 11.2B, we learn that the TR of most of Midwest's SGs declined or did not change, and the TR of all of Yoredale's SGs increased between 1954–55 and 1963–64. Midwest's infant, preschool, aged, and Negro SGs inhabited fewer centiurbs of its habitat in 1963–64 than in 1954–55; the TR of its younger school, older school, and adolescent SGs changed little; only the TR of the adult SG increased as much as the town's total habitat. The situation was quite different in Yoredale; the TR of all Yoredale SGs increased between 1954–55 and 1963–64, and the TR of 9 of them increased more, in percentage, than did the town's total habitat. Adolescents had the greatest rate of TR increment (excepting the very small Gentry SG);

their TR in 1963–64 was 140 percent as great as in 1954–55. One source of this increase was the great expansion of Yoredale's primary Education habitat, largely because of the new secondary modern school. This single new authority system added 19.8 cu of settings with adolescent components and accounted for more than two-thirds of the 27.6 cu increase in their TR (T11.2; R6; C4-2). In addition, Yoredale's primary Business habitat, most of which includes adolescents as components, increased 6.9 cu (T5.7; R4; C4-2). The reverse of some of these changes occurred in Midwest; its primary Business habitat, for example, decreased in extent 4.8 cu (T5.7; R4; C1-3).

OPERATIONAL RANGE OF SUBGROUPS

The operational range (OR) of a SG is the extent of a town's behavior settings with habitat-claims for SG operatives. It is a measure of the amount of habitat within which SG members have responsibilities for ongoing programs of activity. The finding that the 1963–64 OR of Yoredale's adolescent SG was 32.4 cu (T11.3; R6; C4) means that behavior settings with one or more adolescent operatives (inhabitants of penetration zones 4, 5, or 6) comprised 32.4 cu (28.7 percent) of the town; it indicates that adolescents engaged in responsible actions in somewhat over one-quarter of Yoredale's habitat.

Figure 11.3A reveals that in 1963–64 (*a*) infants were operatives in less than .025 cu of habitat in each town; (*b*) OR increased with each older age group to adulthood, where it encompassed 102 cu (95 per-

Table 11.3

Operational Range of Inhabitant Subgroups

		1954–55		1963–64	
		MW (1)	YD (2)	MW (3)	YD (4)
	Subgroup	Centiurbs		Centiurbs	
(1)	Infant	0.28	0.17	0.24	0.11
(2)	Preschool	1.08	0.43	0.84	0.59
(3)	Younger School	2.10	1.23	4.0	0.84
(4)	Older School	4.43	3.61	10.0	3.55
(5)	Total Child	5.18	3.72	10.6	3.82
(6)	Adolescent	25.8	24.0	33.3	32.4
(7)	Adult	84.2	86.5	102.0	109.5
(8)	Aged	22.5	8.54	29.2	18.3
(9)	Total Town	89.1	87.2	107.3	111.0
(10)	Male	71.6	75.9	85.8	93.3
(11)	Female	62.1	59.6	75.6	81.8
(12)	Social Class I	31.3	16.9	38.6	31.5
(13)	Social Class II	66.1	63.4	90.6	97.3
(14)	Social Class III	50.6	62.0	59.2	70.9
(15)	Negro	5.8		6.9	
(16)	Gentry		0.82		1.79

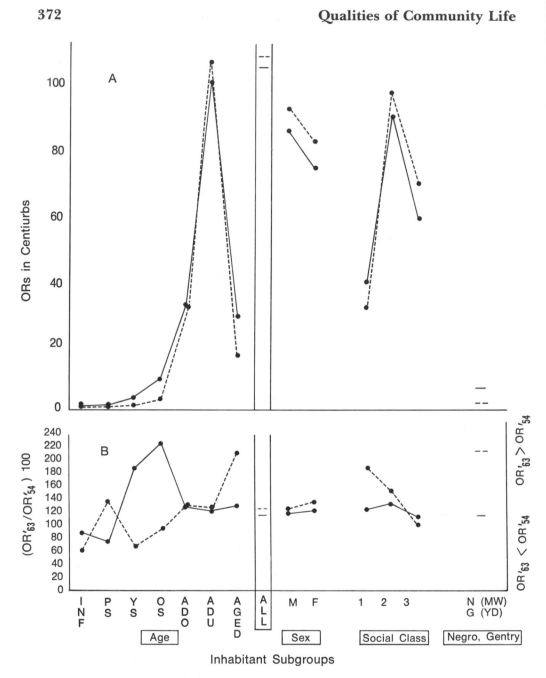

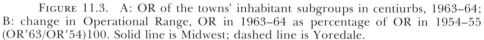

FIGURE 11.3. A: OR of the towns' inhabitant subgroups in centiurbs, 1963–64; B: change in Operational Range, OR in 1963–64 as percentage of OR in 1954–55 (OR'63/OR'54)100. Solid line is Midwest; dashed line is Yoredale.

cent) of Midwest's habitat and 109 cu (97 percent) of Yoredale's habitat; (c) OR receded in extent for the aged subgroup to less than that of adolescents in both towns; (d) more of the towns' public habitats installed males than installed females as operatives; (e) more of the towns' habitats produced claim-operations via social class II than via the other social classes, and members of social class I were less widely distributed as behavior setting operatives than members of class III; and finally (*f*) the ORs of the Negroes of Midwest and of the gentry of Yoredale were less than those of the older school children of the towns.

Differences. In contrast to Midwest's TR deficits relative to Yoredale on all SG habitats except the infant habitat, Midwest had OR surpluses on the infant, preschool, younger school, older school, aged, and class I SG habitats.

Changes. The change data, Figure 11.3B, show great differences in the amount and direction of change in the OR of the SGs of both towns. The ORs of Midwest's infant and preschool SGs diminished between the survey years, whereas those of its younger school and older school SGs increased and at much greater rates than the town's total habitat. The ORs of Yoredale's infant and younger school SGs decreased, whereas those of its aged and social class I SGs increased at greater rates than the town's total habitat. Few similarities are discernible in the changes in the OR of the towns' SGs, and we can find no general explanation of the differences.

LEADERSHIP RANGE OF SUBGROUPS

The leadership range (LR) of a SG is a measure of the amount of habitat within which SG members are very important and responsible persons; it is the extent of a town's behavior settings with habitat-claims for SG members within penetration zones 5 or 6.

The LR data are not reported in centiurbs of habitat, but in terms of number of behavior settings within which members of each inhabitant SG were joint or single leaders. They are not therefore comparable with the TR and OR data; but they are equivalent for Midwest and Yoredale. Data are presented only for age SG in 1963–64 (Table 11.4).

Differences. Midwest's behavior settings in 1963–64 produced leaders at a younger age (older school SG) than Yoredale's (adolescent SG), and at all ages Midwest's BSs produced leaders of more settings than Yoredale's BSs. The towns differed most in the leadership range of adolescents; Midwest's adolescents exceeded Yoredale's adolescents in the number of behavior settings where they were joint or single leaders by a factor of 4.4 (T11.4; R5; C1/2), and in number of settings where they were single leaders by a factor of 8.0 (T11.4; R5; C3/4). About twice as many of Midwest's as of Yoredale's behavior settings generated joint and single leaders from among the aged. We conclude that for all age SGs beyond the younger school group, there were leadership positions in more and greater percentages of Midwest's than of Yoredale's behavior settings, and that the differences were greatest at the youngest and oldest ages.

TERRITORIAL, OPERATIONAL, AND LEADERSHIP RANGES

Differences between Midwest and Yoredale in the ranges of the inhabitant SGs change in a systematic and important way across the ter-

Table 11.4
Leadership Range of Inhabitant Subgroups, 1963-64

		Penetration 5 or 6		Penetration 6	
		MW (1)	YD (2)	MW (3)	YD (4)
	Subgroup	Number of Behavior Settings			
(1)	Infant	0	0	0	0
(2)	Preschool	0	0	0	0
(3)	Younger School	0	0	0	0
(4)	Older School	2	0	0	0
(5)	Adolescent	61	14	16	2
(6)	Adult	805	702	435	466
(7)	Aged	123	56	61	34

ritorial, operational, and leadership ranges. Basic to this change is the fact that Midwest's SGs have a smaller habitat over which to range than do Yoredale's (95 percent as extensive); and also the TR of all but one of the 12 comparable inhabitant SGs and of 6 of the 7 age SGs, is *smaller* in Midwest than in Yoredale. However, the OR of 7 of the 12 SGs, and of 6 of the 7 age SGs, is *larger* in Midwest than in Yoredale, and the LR of all the age subgroups is greater in Midwest than in Yoredale. Members of Yoredale's SGs are more widely *present* across the town than are members of Midwest's SGs, but members of Midwest's SGs are more widely *operationally important* than are members of Yoredale's SGs.

Behavior Output of Subgroup Habitats

PERSON-HOURS OF BEHAVIOR GENERATED BY SUBGROUPS WITHIN THEIR TERRITORIAL RANGE

The person-hours of behavior (P-H) generated by a SG within its TR is a measure of the total amount of participation by SG members in the town's public habitat at all levels of penetration (from onlookers to leaders). Basic data are reported for town residents in Table 11.5. Output per town inhabitant in 1963–64 is represented in Figure 11.4A, which shows that in both towns (*a*) mean output per inhabitant differed greatly across the SGs, the least productive SG yielding less than one-fifth the behavior of the most productive SG; (*b*) output increased with age in both towns from the preschool and infant SGs (about 1 hour of behavior a day); (*c*) it reached a peak with the adolescents of Midwest (6 hours, 10 minutes per day) and with the younger school SG of Yoredale (4 hours, 48 minutes per day); (*d*) output was reduced in the aged to a few minutes more than an hour a day; (*e*) it was greater per male than per female inhabitant, (*f*) it differed greatly among social classes; (*g*) the output of the Negroes in Midwest fell between that of the preschool and younger school SGs; and (*h*) the output of the gentry in Yoredale was the lowest of all SGs (less than half an hour a day).

Differences. Midwest's 25 percent superiority to Yoredale in mean P-H output per town inhabitant does not occur uniformly across the

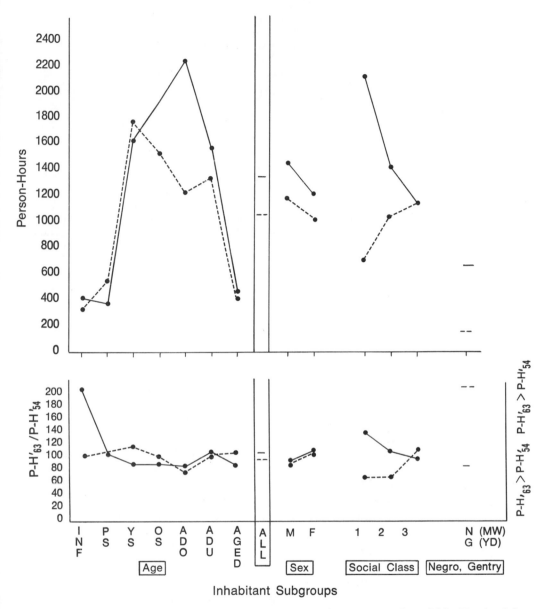

FIGURE 11.4. A: Mean behavior output per subgroup member within Territorial Range, 1963–64; B: change in P-H per subgroup member, P-H in 1963–64 as percentage of P-H in 1954–55 (P-H′63/P-H′54)100. Solid line is Midwest; dashed line is Yoredale.

inhabitant SGs (Figure 11.4A). Members of Midwest's social class I were almost 3 times as busy in the town's public habitats in 1963 as Class I Dalesmen; their habitancy of public behavior settings as spectators, clients, members, functionaries, joint and single leaders in meetings, classes, stores, offices, games, shops, programs, weddings, amounted to 5 hours, 45 minutes a day for seven days a week, on the average, whereas members of Yoredale's social class I were present in the public

Table 11.5
Person-Hours of Behavior Produced via Inhabitant Subgroups
Within Their Territorial Range

	Subgroup	1954–55 MW (1)	1954–55 YD (2)	1963–64 MW (3)	1963–64 YD (4)
(1)	Infant	4,924	13,276	5,397	13,143
(2)	Preschool	19,307	40,677	21,017	39,948
(3)	Younger School	50,129	108,990	74,089	81,575
(4)	Older School	55,504	78,323	90,442	88,968
(5)	Total Child	131,817	250,080	187,575	223,736
(6)	Adolescent	133,877	173,361	189,381	138,837
(7)	Adult	572,930	1,000,058	655,683	924,831
(8)	Aged	89,971	69,956	82,923	117,766
(9)	Total Town	929,861	1,506,739	1,125,134	1,426,115
(10)	Male	521,951	841,787	602,913	729,959
(11)	Female	409,409	659,896	499,281	692,772
(12)	Social Class I	128,153	83,689	153,816	60,975
(13)	Social Class II	415,312	446,283	620,223	570,420
(14)	Social Class III	361,691	947,655	338,013	776,456
(15)	Negro	23,460		17,339	
(16)	Gentry		621		1,269

settings of Yoredale for 1 hour, 57 minutes a day for seven days a week. Midwest's adolescents were still busier than its class I inhabitants; they inhabited the town's public regions for 6 hours, 31 minutes per day. Yoredale adolescents were also busier than its class I inhabitants, but they were not nearly so busy in the town's public habitat as Midwest adolescents; their mean habitation of Yoredale's public regions amounted to 3 hours 19 minutes a day. Members of the preschool and younger school SGs spent less time outside their homes in Midwest than in Yoredale. The preschool SG inhabited Midwest's public settings for a mean duration of 1 hour 5 minutes a day and inhabited Yoredale's public settings for 1 hour 28 minutes; younger school children inhabited public settings in Midwest for 4 hours 24 minutes per day, and they inhabited Yoredale's public settings for 4 hours 48 minutes a day.

Changes. Changes in the behavior outputs of inhabitant SGs are represented in Figure 11.4B. For all Midwest inhabitants, mean P-H per inhabitant in 1963–64 was 104 percent of the 1954–55 output (T7.2; R6; C3/1); only two of Midwest's inhabitant SGs (with the '63/'54 percentage in parentheses) had greater increments: infants (202) and social class I (138). Six of Midwest's inhabitant SGs declined in output per member between the survey years: Negro (82), adolescent (84), aged (85), younger school (90), older school (90), and males (96). For all Yoredale's inhabitants, mean P-H per inhabitant in 1963–64 was 94 percent of the output in 1954–55 (T7.2; R6; C4/2); four of Yoredale's inhabitant subgroups had a greater decrement than this: social class I

(67), social class II (67), adolescent (75), and male (85). Five Yoredale SGs increased in output per member: gentry (204), younger school (117), social class III (113), preschool (105), and female (105). We have been able to discover conditions connected with some of the more extreme changes.

The genotype locus of the great increase in output via the infant subgroup in Midwest is Day Care Homes and Nurseries, and in particular the addition of the behavior setting Day Care for Children of Working Mothers. This setting alone generated half of Midwest's P-H of infant behavior in 1963–64. In 1954–55 the few working mothers of infants arranged for the care of the child in a number of ways that did not involve public settings: exchanging child care with another mother during alternate working periods, having a baby-sitter in the home, leaving the infant with older children. By 1963–64 a licensed home for the day care of children had been established (since 1963–64 a number of such behavior settings have appeared in Midwest). This genotype did not occur in Yoredale in 1963–64 (and it has not occurred since); informal, nonpublic arrangements are still used in Yoredale.

The decrement in output of Midwest's adolescent subgroup occurred mainly in Business, Recreation, and Religious habitats. The mean output of all Midwest inhabitants declined in these habitats, and these are habitats where adolescents are important components. The question arises as to where adolescents spend the hours in 1963–64 which in 1954–55 they spent in Midwest's public habitat. The answer is that most of the 423 (14 percent) fewer hours per member are probably spent out of the town in recreational settings (moving pictures and dances have almost disappeared from the town). The greater mobility outward from the town by Midwesterners in general is undoubtedly involved in this.

The situation is both similar and different in Yoredale with respect to the main sources of the decline in adolescent output. It is similar in that a major locus of the decrement—170 P-H per adolescent—is in the town's primary Recreational habitat; Yoredale adolescents, like their Midwest compatriots, traveled more to out-of-town Recreational habitats in 1963–64 than in 1954–55. But it is different in that another major locus of the decrement in Yoredale—54 P-H per inhabitant—was in Yoredale's primary Educational habitat. In 1954–55, 26 percent of Yoredale's adolescents went out of town for their schooling; in 1963–64, 42 percent did. As a result, Yoredale's Educational habitat in 1963–64 generated fewer P-H of behavior per town adolescent than it did in 1954–55.

We could find no differential habitats where the decrements in the outputs of Midwest's social classes I and II chiefly occurred; the decline is general across most of the primary action pattern habitats.

The decline of 84 P-H per aged Midwest inhabitant was concentrated within the primary Business habitat. The availability of social security in 1963–64 increased the frequency of retirement at 65, so fewer aged persons were actively engaged in business. All the evidence suggests that no other specialized Midwest habitat received substantial amounts of the relinquished business hours of the aged; they apparently were staying at home in Midwest.

PERSON-HOURS OF BEHAVIOR GENERATED BY SUBGROUPS WITHIN
THEIR OPERATIONAL RANGE

The presence of members of an inhabitant SG within settings where some of its members are operatives—within its OR—has special psychological significance, especially for children and the aged, for at these times they see their peers belonging to an important class of persons: VIPs who chair meetings, entertain audiences, operate businesses. Within the OR of a SG, the members are people of significance. Basic data are reported in Table 11.6; mean P-H per member is presented in Figure 11.5. The figure shows that Midwest's general superiority to Yoredale in mean P-H per town inhabitant is fairly uniformly distributed across the OR of all inhabitant SGs except the social class SGs. Midwest's social class I generates much more behavior per member within settings where their peers are operatives than does Yoredale's social class I, and Midwest's social class III generates less behavior than does Yoredale's social class III.

PERSON-HOURS OF BEHAVIOR GENERATED BY INHABITANT SUBGROUPS
WITHIN THEIR LEADERSHIP RANGE

The behavior of an inhabitant SG within settings where its members are leaders—within its LR—has very special significance; it is a

Table 11.6
Person-Hours of Behavior Produced via Inhabitant
Subgroups Within their Operational Range

		1954–55		1963–64	
		MW (1)	YD (2)	MW (3)	YD (4)
	Subgroup				
(1)	Infant	155	11	35	3
(2)	Preschool	792	920	361	349
(3)	Younger School	1,918	2,592	2,675	861
(4)	Older School	4,821	6,931	8,093	6,851
(5)	Total Child	9,941	15,926	13,927	18,055
(6)	Adolescent	53,098	94,233	70,462	69,586
(7)	Adult	569,749	991,830	650,051	922,590
(8)	Aged	65,205	18,296	52,801	57,304
(9)	Total Town	928,834	1,495,505	1,125,113	1,422,485
(10)	Male	472,741	800,626	517,029	695,938
(11)	Female	350,900	454,778	433,803	522,067
(12)	Social Class I	89,072	35,596	93,593	29,219
(13)	Social Class II	356,612	349,696	601,894	497,523
(14)	Social Class III	296,132	782,907	257,263	647,126
(15)	Negro	10,033		5,665	
(16)	Gentry		26		55

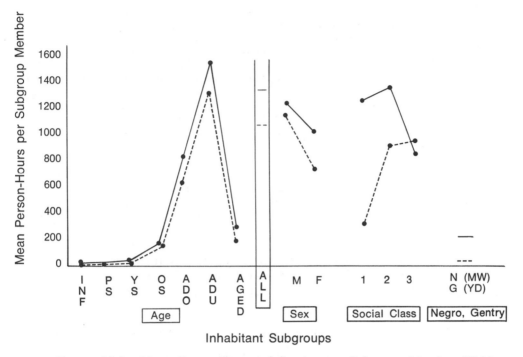

FIGURE 11.5. Mean Person-Hours of Output per Subgroup Member Within Operational Range, 1963–64. Solid line is Midwest; dashed line is Yoredale.

measure of the amount of time they are able to see their peers as belonging to the most important and powerful class of the town's inhabitants. The data (Table 11.7) show that Midwest's SGs that produce leaders generate more behavior within settings where some of their members are leaders than do Yoredale's SGs. For example, Midwest and Yoredale adolescents, respectively, spend 40.3 and 26.3 mean P-H per year in behavior settings where adolescents are joint or single leaders—that is, Midwest exceeds Yoredale by a factor of 1.5. In settings where an adolescent is the sole leader, Midwest exceeds Yoredale in P-H by a factor of 3.6. The aged of Midwest exceed the aged of Yoredale in behavior output by a factor of 1.6 in settings where they are joint or single leaders and by a factor of 1.9 in settings where they are sole leaders.

CLAIM-OPERATIONS GENERATED BY INHABITANT SUBGROUPS WITHIN THEIR OPERATIONAL RANGE

Data involving C-O are limited to the two large SGs, children (under 12 years of age) and others (adolescents, adults, and aged) for the single survey year 1963–64. The data show that Midwest is twice as demanding as Yoredale of difficult and important actions by its children, and that its demands on later age groups as a single class are greater than Yoredale's by a factor of 2.6 (T11.8; R3; C3/4). The mean number of important, difficult, and responsible positions in public habi-

Table 11.7
Mean Person-Hours of Behavior Produced per Subgroup
Member Within Leadership Range
1963–64

		Penetration Zone 5 or 6		Penetration Zone 6	
		MW	YD	MW	YD
		Mean Person-Hours per Member			
		(1)	(2)	(3)	(4)
(1)	Infant, Preschool, and Younger School	0	0	0	0
(2)	Older School	2.6	0	0	0
(3)	Adolescent	40.3	26.3	3.6	1.0
(4)	Adult	1,340	1,036	844	793
(5)	Aged	194	121	160	84

tats filled by children is smaller than the mean number filled by the other inhabitants of both towns, and the difference in this respect between children and others is larger in Midwest than in Yoredale (T11.8; R3; C1 to 4).

OUTPUT IN TERRITORIAL, OPERATIONAL, AND LEADERSHIP RANGES

In line with Midwest's increasingly greater superiority to Yoredale in range of habitancy from TR, through Or, to LR, and in line with Midwest's superior behavior output per inhabitant and its still greater output superiority in this respect in zones of deeper penetration, we now find that Midwest's superiority to Yoredale in behavior output holds for more inhabitant SGs. This finding means that members of most of Midwest's inhabitant SGs spend more time than their Yoredale counterparts in settings where their peers are also present (TR), and that their superiority to Yoredale in this respect is still greater in settings where their peers are operatives (OR) and leaders (LR). For example, the old people of Midwest, on the average, spend 115 percent as many P-H as the old people of Yoredale in settings where there are other old people, they spend 160 percent as many hours as Dalesmen

Table 11.8
Number of Inhabitants and Mean Number of Claim-Operations
of Town Children (under 12 years) and of Town
Adolescents, Adults, and Aged, 1963–64

		Town Children		Town Adolescents, Adults, and Aged	
		MW (1)	YD (2)	MW (3)	YD (4)
(1)	Inhabitants	159	220	671	1,090
(2)	Claim-Operations	782	537	5,859	3,665
(3)	Mean C-O per Inhabitant (R2/R1)	4.9	2.4	8.7	3.3

in settings where old people are operatives, and they spend 190 percent as many hours as Dalesmen in settings where old people are single leaders.

Habitat-Inhabitant Bias

In 1963–64, the mean yearly output per town inhabitant was 1356 hours for Midwesterners and 1089 hours for Dalesmen (T8.2; R6; C3,4). These constitute the best estimates available of the behavior output expected of any inhabitant, and of the mean output of any group. For SGs that produce less than these amounts of behavior, there are negative biases between SG members and habitats; there are either member biases against the habitats or habitat biases against the members. For SG habitats that produce more than these expected outputs there are positive biases between SG members and habitats. The deviation of the observed mean output of a SG from the expected output is a measure of the habitat-inhabitant bias.

In Table 11.9 the observed mean outputs of the SGs are expressed as percentages of the expected outputs. The SGs of each town are ordered in the table from the one with greatest negative habitat-inhabitant bias to the one with greatest positive habitat-inhabitant bias. We find, for example, that the mean output of Midwest's preschool SG is 29 percent of the mean output of Midwesterners in general; this is a measure of the negative habitat-inhabitant bias between Midwest's habitat and members of its preschool SG. Midwest's adolescent SG, on the other hand, yields 166 percent as much behavior per member as Midwesterners in general; there is a positive bias between Midwest and its adolescents.

Table 11.9
Bias Between the Towns' Habitats and
Their Inhabitant Subgroups, 1963–64

	Midwest Subgroups	Bias	Yoredale Subgroups	Bias
	Preschool	29	Gentry	15
	Infant	31	Infant	30
Negative	Aged	35	Aged	38
Bias	Negro	49	Preschool	48
	Social Class III	85	Social Class I	66
	Female	89	Female	92
			Social Class II	96
	All Inhabitants	100	All Inhabitants	100
	Social Class II	104	Social Class III	106
	Male	107	Male	108
Positive	Adult	118	Adolescent	112
Bias	Younger School	119	Adult	123
	Older School	142	Older School	141
	Social Class I	155	Younger School	163
	Adolescent	166		

The deviation measures may be interpreted as the reduction in a town's behavior output from the loss of a single, average SG member, stated as a percentage of the reduction due to the loss of a single, average town inhabitant. Loss of a preschool inhabitant would attenuate Midwest's behavior output less than the loss of any other SG inhabitant, and 29 percent as much as the loss of an average inhabitant; loss of an adolescent inhabitant would cost Midwest in behavior output more than the loss of any other SG inhabitant, and two-thirds more than the loss of an average inhabitant. As measured by their contributions to Midwest's total behavior output, infants are more expendable than adolescents. In these terms, Yoredale's most expendable inhabitants are its gentry, and its least expendable inhabitants are its younger school SG; loss of a younger school child would cost Yoredale in behavior output almost 11 times as much as the loss of a member of the gentry.

The deviation measures may also be interpreted as the relative exposure of SG members to influences within the public habitats of the towns. In these terms, the infants of both towns are confronted with the stimuli, the opportunities, the restraints, and the demands of the extra-home environment for about one-third the mean number of hours per person as unselected town inhabitants, and for almost one-fifth as many hours as the most exposed SGs, adolescents (MW) and younger school (YD).

AMOUNT OF BIAS

Habitat-inhabitant bias varies across the SGs from 29 (preschool) to 166 (adolescent) in Midwest and from 15 (gentry) to 163 (younger school) in Yoredale. Across the age SGs only, the range is from 29 to 166 in Midwest and from 30 to 163 in Yoredale. In terms of mean contribution to the towns' gross behavior products, the most productive age is superior to the least productive by factors of 5.7 (MW) and 5.4 (YD).

Differences. In both towns there are negative biases for preschool, infant, aged, and female inhabitants, and positive biases for male, adult, younger school, older school, and adolescent inhabitants; Midwest is negative and Yoredale positive to social class III, and Midwest is positive and Yoredale negative to social classes I and II.

The towns differ most in their biases for social class I (Midwest's is positive, Yoredale's negative; the difference in bias measures is 89), for adolescents (Midwest's is more positive than Yoredale's; the difference in bias measures is 54), for younger school children (Yoredale's is more positive than Midwest's; the difference in bias measures is 44), and for social class III (Yoredale's is positive, Midwest's negative; the difference in bias measures is 21). Relative to Yoredale's habitat-subgroup biases, Midwest's are positive instead of negative to social class I, more positive to adolescents, less positive to younger school children, and negative instead of positive to social class III.

We have discovered the basis of some of these differences. Midwest's greater negative bias for the preschool SG is located almost entirely in behavior settings of the School authority system; these settings reject all preschool children as pupils, whereas Yoredale's schools claim preschool children at five years of age. The situation is reversed for the adolescent SGs. Behavior settings under the aegis of Midwest's School authority system actively and successfully claim almost all the town's adolescents, whereas Yoredale actively ejects 27 percent of the town's adolescents during most daytime hours (it transports 25 percent of them to a government grammar school twelve miles distant), and another 15 percent actively reject the town's school settings for distant government and private schools.[2] In fact, the elimination process (ejection and permitted withdrawal) begins in Yoredale before adolescence; in 1963–64 two younger school children (4 percent) and eight older school children (13 percent) attended day schools outside Yoredale.

But Yoredale is not altogether more negative to adolescents than Midwest. Yoredale's Private Enterprise authority system has a greater positive bias for adolescents than does Midwest's; 17 percent of Yoredale adolescents are employed full-time within the town, and many continue as permanent inhabitants (as craftsmen, shop assistants, clerks, housewives, and so forth). And Midwest is not altogether more positive than Yoredale to adolescents; the elimination process occurs there, too, but at a later age. Most Midwest adolescents are full-time inhabitants of the town through all the adolescent years, but almost all leave immediately thereafter, for further schooling (technical school or college), employment, or military service; a few return later to become permanent inhabitants.

Some of the circumstances of Midwest's positive bias and of Yoredale's negative bias for social class I are revealed by data reported in Chapter 12. There we find that Midwest's positive bias occurs in these differential habitats (with deviation percentages in parentheses): Government (184), Religion (154), Personal Appearance (136), Business (132), Aesthetics (113), and Social Contact (107). And we find that Yoredale's negative bias for social class I occurs in differential habitats for Education (42), Personal Appearance (59), Manipulation (72), Nutrition (74), Gross Motor Activity (81), Social Contact (92), and Professional Involvement (96).

It is clear that Midwesterners of social class I are especially attracted to or pressured into settings where there are programs with prominent governmental, religious, personal adornment, and business qualities; it is these settings that generate the surplus behavior of class I Midwesterners which more than compensate for their output deficits in other differential habitats. Class I Dalesmen especially avoid or are im-

---

[2] These arrangements were changed in 1971. Some Midwest adolescents were ejected for several half-days per week to a distant technical school. Yoredale's Secondary Modern School had become a Comprehensive School; therefore more of Yoredale's adolescents attended school in town than did in 1963–64; however, some Yoredale adolescents continued to be ejected to sixth-form or technical schools, and about the same number as formerly attended private schools.

peded from entering settings with educational, personal adornment, manipulation, and gross motor attributes; it is these settings that generate the behavior deficits of class I Dalesmen which are not fully compensated by their output surpluses in other differential habitats. An important part of the deficit of class I Dalesmen is due to the habitat-inhabitant bias we have discussed between Yoredale's School authority system and adolescents; almost all class I adolescents are among the 42 percent that are ejected by or reject Yoredale's school settings.

CHAPTER 12

Biases Between Differential Habitats and Inhabitant Subgroups

I̶n this chapter we report the biases between 23 differential habitats and 12 inhabitant subgroups for 1963–64, as determined by the procedures explicated for the towns' entire habitats in Chapter 11. We elucidate the application of the procedures to the differential habitats by means of the data for the older school (OS) subgroup and the primary Health habitat (PHH) of Midwest.

Data previously reported show that Midwest's whole habitat is biased in favor of OS as habitat components. Midwest's mean output via all town inhabitants (the expected output for OS) is 1356 P-H, whereas its mean output via OS is 1924 P-H, 142 percent of the expected output; the deviation of this percentage from 100 is a measure of the bias between Midwest's whole habitat and the OS subgroup. We know that the mean output of Midwest's PHH via all town inhabitants is 23.8 P-H (T9.13; R7; C3); to improve our estimate of the output to be expected via OS, we assume that Midwest's positive bias for OS holds generally, within PHH and all other differential habitats; we therefore expect the mean output of PHH via OS to be 1.42 times 23.8, which equals 33.8 P-H per OS. Actually, the output is 127.5 P-H, 378 percent of the expected output (Table 12.7)—a measure of *positive bias* between Midwest's PHH and its OS subgroup. These values are reported in each differential habitat table.

As an example, the data for one differential habitat, the primary Aesthetic habitat (PAH), are discussed in the text accompanying Table 12.1. Only the tabular data are presented for all the other differential habitats. This chapter, therefore, is largely a compendium of tabular data; selective summaries and interpretations of some of them are in Chapter 14.

The data of Table 12.1 show that in both towns there is a negative bias between the PAH and infant, preschool, male, social class III, and adult SGs, and a positive bias between the PAH and social class I, social class II, female, aged, younger school, adolescent, and older school SGs. The towns differ most in the biases between their PAH and (*a*) adults, where Midwest's bias is more negative than Yoredale's and the difference in bias measures is 44; (*b*) social class I, where Midwest's bias is less positive than Yoredale's and the difference in bias measures is 95; (*c*) younger and (*d*) older school children, where Midwest's biases are more positive than Yoredale's and the difference in bias measures is 72 in each case. Relative to Yoredale's PAH-SG biases, Midwest's are much more negative to adults, much less positive to social class I, and much more positive to younger and older school-age children.

Table 12.1
Bias Between Primary Aesthetic Habitat
and Inhabitant Subgroups, 1963–64

	Midwest		Yoredale	
	Inhabitant Subgroups	Bias	Inhabitant Subgroups	Bias
Negative Bias	Infant	32	Infant	28
	Adult	46	Gentry	66
	Social Class III	60	Social Class III	69
	Males	84	Males	83
	Preschool	86	Adult	90
			Preschool	94
	All Inhabitants	100	All Inhabitants	100
Positive Bias	Social Class II	112	Younger School	111
	Social Class I	113	Aged	116
	Females	118	Females	121
	Aged	141	Older School	122
	Negro	167	Social Class II	135
	Younger School	183	Adolescent	164
	Adolescent	186	Social Class I	208
	Older School	194		

Table 12.2
Bias Between Primary Business Habitat
and Inhabitant Subgroups, 1963–64

	Midwest		Yoredale	
	Inhabitant Subgroups	Bias	Inhabitant Subgroups	Bias
Negative Bias	Younger School	19	Younger School	16
	Older School	21	Older School	18
	Adolescent	37	Preschool	56
	Preschool	59	Social Class III	77
	Infant	71	Infant	80
	Social Class III	83	Males	86
	Aged	86	Adolescent	95
	Females	87		
	Negro	89		
	All Inhabitants	100	All Inhabitants	100
Positive Bias	Social Class II	102	Social Class I	109
	Males	103	Females	115
	Social Class I	132	Aged	117
	Adult	143	Adult	118
			Social Class II	130
			Gentry	136

Table 12.3
Bias Between Primary Education Habitat
and Inhabitant Subgroups, 1963–64

	Midwest		Yoredale	
	Inhabitant Subgroups	Bias	Inhabitant Subgroups	Bias
Negative Bias	Infant	1	Infant	1
	Aged	9	Aged	4
	Adult	23	Gentry	7
	Preschool	76	Adult	16
	Males	90	Social Class I	42
	Social Class I	91	Males	88
	Social Class III	92		
	All Inhabitants	100	All Inhabitants	100
Positive Bias	Social Class II	106	Social Class II	104
	Females	112	Social Class III	105
	Negro	114	Female	108
	Adolescent	251	Adolescent	213
	Older School	269	Preschool	290
	Younger School	278	Younger School	469
			Older School	534

Table 12.4
Bias Between Primary Government Habitat
and Inhabitant Subgroups, 1963–64

	Midwest		Yoredale	
	Inhabitant Subgroups	Bias	Inhabitant Subgroups	Bias
Negative Bias	Younger School	4	Younger School	2
	Older School	5	Older School	2
	Adolescent	11	Preschool	4
	Preschool	13	Adolescent	5
	Infant	32	Infant	23
	Social Class III	87	Aged	38
	Social Class II	89	Females	43
			Gentry	61
			Social Class II	96
			Social Class III	96
	All Inhabitants	100	All Inhabitants	100
Positive Bias	Females	101	Adults	147
	Males	111	Males	152
	Adult	146	Social Class I	171
	Negro	176		
	Aged	179		
	Social Class I	184		

Table 12.5
Bias Between Primary Nutrition Habitat
and Inhabitant Subgroups, 1963–64

	Midwest		Yoredale	
	Inhabitant Subgroups	Bias	Inhabitant Subgroups	Bias
Negative Bias	Older School	38	Younger School	32
	Younger School	53	Older School	36
	Adolescent	54	Preschool	63
	Preschool	63	Social Class I	74
	Infant	75	Infant	82
	Aged	80	Adolescent	87
	Negro	86	Males	91
	Social Class I	90	Gentry	92
	Males	91	Social Class III	94
	Social Class II	99	Aged	100
	All Inhabitants	100	All Inhabitants	100
Positive Bias	Social Class III	105	Females	110
	Females	114	Adult	111
	Adult	134	Social Class II	112

Table 12.6
Bias Between Primary Personal Appearance Habitat
and Inhabitant Subgroups, 1963–64

	Midwest		Yoredale	
	Inhabitant Subgroups	Bias	Inhabitant Subgroups	Bias
Negative Bias	Negro	16	Younger School	16
	Older School	28	Older School	27
	Adolescent	28	Preschool	35
	Younger School	31	Males	52
	Males	44	Infant	57
	Social Class II	81	Social Class I	59
	Infant	86	Social Class III	76
	All Inhabitants	100	All Inhabitants	100
Positive Bias	Preschool	104	Adult	113
	Social Class III	117	Adolescent	123
	Adult	129	Social Class II	142
	Social Class I	136	Aged	143
	Females	174	Females	153
	Aged	179	Gentry	287

Table 12.7
Bias Between Primary Physical Health Habitat
and Inhabitant Subgroups, 1963–64

	Midwest		Yoredale	
	Inhabitant Subgroups	Bias	Inhabitant Subgroups	Bias
Negative Bias	Preschool	6	Aged	63
	Infant	13	Infant	80
	Aged	14	Adolescent	81
	Adult	21	Social Class III	84
	Social Class I	80	Adult	89
	Males	92	Males	90
	All Inhabitants	100	All Inhabitants	100
Positive Bias	Negro	102	Females	112
	Social Class III	106	Social Class II	113
	Social Class II	107	Preschool	114
	Females	119	Younger School	179
	Younger School	207	Social Class I	189
	Adolescent	254	Older School	199
	Older School	378	Gentry	281

Table 12.8
Bias Between Primary Professional Involvement Habitat
and Inhabitant Subgroups, 1963–64

	Midwest			Yoredale	
	Inhabitant Subgroups	**Bias**		**Inhabitant Subgroups**	**Bias**
Negative Bias	Adolescent	88		Adolescent	85
	Aged	90		Aged	92
	Negro	93		Older School	95
	Preschool	96		Social Class I	96
	Social Class I	98		Females	99
	Social Class II	98		Social Class II	99
	Females	99		Males	100
	Older School	100		Social Class III	100
	All Inhabitants	100		All Inhabitants	100
Positive Bias	Infant	101		Adult	102
	Males	101		Gentry	103
	Younger School	103		Preschool	105
	Adult	105		Infant	107
	Social Class III	105		Younger School	107

Table 12.9
Bias Between Primary Recreation Habitat
and Inhabitant Subgroups, 1963–64

	Midwest			Yoredale	
	Inhabitant Subgroups	**Bias**		**Inhabitant Subgroups**	**Bias**
Negative Bias	Social Class I	73		Infant	21
	Preschool	76		Gentry	33
	Adult	78		Preschool	73
	Females	85		Adult	81
	Social Class II	85		Females	81
	Infant	88		Adolescent	91
				Social Class III	99
	All Inhabitants	100		All Inhabitants	100
Positive Bias	Aged	106		Social Class II	101
	Younger School	112		Younger School	104
	Males	112		Social Class I	117
	Negro	115		Males	119
	Social Class III	132		Older School	127
	Adolescent	145		Aged	171
	Older School	147			

Table 12.10
Bias Between Primary Religion Habitat
and Inhabitant Subgroups, 1963–64

	Midwest		Yoredale	
	Inhabitant Subgroups	Bias	Inhabitant Subgroups	Bias
Negative Bias	Infant	28	Gentry	41
	Adolescent	54	Infant	42
	Social Class III	60	Younger School	58
	Males	69	Males	76
	Adult	78	Social Class III	76
	Older School	95	Adult	80
	Social Class II	99	Preschool	82
	All Inhabitants	100	All Inhabitants	100
Positive Bias	Younger School	111	Social Class II	119
	Females	134	Females	130
	Social Class I	154	Aged	157
	Negro	239	Older School	169
	Preschool	303	Adolescent	200
	Aged	308	Social Class I	260

Table 12.11
Bias Between Primary Social Contact Habitat
and Inhabitant Subgroups, 1963–64

	Midwest		Yoredale	
	Inhabitant Subgroups	Bias	Inhabitant Subgroups	Bias
Negative Bias	Aged	69	Infant	46
	Negro	86	Adult	88
	Adult	87	Gentry	88
	Preschool	91	Males	89
	Males	94	Social Class III	91
	Social Class III	96	Social Class I	92
			Aged	96
	All Inhabitants	100	All Inhabitants	100
Positive Bias	Social Class II	101	Preschool	102
	Females	107	Females	111
	Social Class I	107	Social Class II	115
	Infant	119	Adolescent	124
	Adolescent	124	Younger School	131
	Older School	138	Older School	160
	Younger School	140		

Table 12.12
Bias Between Primary Affective Behavior Habitat
and Inhabitant Subgroups, 1963–64

	Midwest		Yoredale	
	Inhabitant Subgroups	Bias	Inhabitant Subgroups	Bias
Negative Bias	Aged	35	Infant	59
	Adult	49	Adult	64
	Social Class I	83	Gentry	67
	Males	98	Social Class III	96
	Social Class III	99	Aged	99
			Males	99
	All Inhabitants	100	All Inhabitants	100
Positive Bias	Social Class II	103	Females	104
	Females	104	Social Class II	106
	Negro	134	Social Class I	150
	Adolescent	160	Adolescent	156
	Younger School	229	Preschool	195
	Older School	245	Younger School	251
	Preschool	266	Older School	258
	Infant	389		

Table 12.13
Bias Between Primary Gross Motor Habitat
and Inhabitant Subgroups, 1963–64

	Midwest		Yoredale	
	Inhabitant Subgroups	Bias	Inhabitant Subgroups	Bias
Negative Bias	Aged	60	Social Class II	74
	Social Class I	70	Older School	79
	Younger School	72	Social Class I	81
	Females	74	Females	94
	Preschool	84	Aged	97
	Adolescent	97	Adult	99
	All Inhabitants	100	All Inhabitants	100
Positive Bias	Social Class III	103	Adolescent	103
	Older School	104	Males	106
	Social Class II	106	Younger School	110
	Adult	108	Gentry	113
	Males	112	Social Class III	119
	Negro	137	Preschool	139
	Infant	172	Infant	197

Table 12.14
Bias Between Primary Manipulation Habitat
and Inhabitant Subgroups, 1963–64

	Midwest		Yoredale	
	Inhabitant Subgroups	Bias	Inhabitant Subgroups	Bias
Negative Bias	Younger School	32	Younger School	42
	Preschool	41	Preschool	54
	Older School	55	Older School	54
	Infant	59	Infant	63
	Adolescent	71	Social Class I	72
	Aged	78	Gentry	75
	Females	82	Aged	77
	Social Class I	92	Females	86
	Social Class III	97	Social Class II	100
	All Inhabitants	100	All Inhabitants	100
Positive Bias	Social Class II	102	Social Class III	104
	Males	110	Adolescent	108
	Negro	122	Males	114
	Adult	129	Adult	116

Table 12.15
Bias Between Primary Talking Habitat
and Inhabitant Subgroups, 1963–64

	Midwest		Yoredale	
	Inhabitant Subgroups	Bias	Inhabitant Subgroups	Bias
Negative Bias	Infant	42	Gentry	36
	Preschool	52	Adolescent	75
	Aged	64	Adult	76
	Adult	68	Infant	96
	Social Class I	76	Social Class III	96
	Males	86	Males	99
	Social Class II	91		
	All Inhabitants	100	All Inhabitants	100
Positive Bias	Females	119	Females	101
	Social Class III	120	Social Class II	105
	Negro	138	Social Class I	113
	Adolescent	159	Preschool	137
	Younger School	182	Younger School	145
	Older School	193	Aged	155
			Older School	160

Table 12.16
Bias Between Church Authority System Habitat
and Inhabitant Subgroups, 1963–64

	Midwest		Yoredale	
	Inhabitant Subgroups	Bias	Inhabitant Subgroups	Bias
Negative Bias	Adolescent	56	Infant	58
	Social Class III	60	Social Class III	68
	Male	66	Younger School	70
	Infant	70	Male	76
	Adult	76	Adult	94
	Older School	98		
	All Inhabitants	100	All Inhabitants	100
Positive Bias	Social Class II	101	Gentry	103
	Younger School	102	Preschool	104
	Female	142	Older School	104
	Social Class I	156	Adolescent	118
	Negro	222	Social Class II	126
	Preschool	284	Female	132
	Aged	357	Aged	164
			Social Class I	301

Table 12.17
Bias Between Government Agency Authority System Habitat
and Inhabitant Subgroups, 1963–64

	Midwest		Yoredale	
	Inhabitant Subgroups	Bias	Inhabitant Subgroups	Bias
Negative Bias	Adolescent	39	Older School	37
	Older School	48	Social Class II	62
	Younger School	51	Adolescent	66
	Social Class I	86	Younger School	89
	Infant	96	Female	98
	Female	97		
	Social Class II	98		
	All Inhabitants	100	All Inhabitants	100
Positive Bias	Male	105	Social Class I	101
	Social Class III	110	Male	102
	Adult	118	Adult	107
	Negro	153	Aged	113
	Preschool	171	Social Class III	124
	Aged	186	Gentry	125
			Preschool	150
			Infant	265

Table 12.18
Bias Between Private Enterprise Authority System Habitat
and Inhabitant Subgroups, 1963–64

	Midwest		Yoredale	
	Inhabitant Subgroups	Bias	Inhabitant Subgroups	Bias
Negative Bias	Younger School	20	Younger School	10
	Older School	23	Older School	14
	Adolescent	39	Preschool	28
	Negro	73	Infant	34
	Preschool	92	Adolescent	74
	Social Class II	94	Social Class III .	82
	Male	97	Female	97
	Female	99		
	All Inhabitants	100	All Inhabitants	100
Positive Bias	Aged	101	Male	103
	Social Class I	106	Aged	104
	Social Class III	108	Social Class I	108
	Adult	137	Gentry	113
	Infant	150	Adult	122
			Social Class II	124

Table 12.19
Bias Between School Authority System Habitat
and Inhabitant Subgroups, 1963–64

	Midwest		Yoredale	
	Inhabitant Subgroups	Bias	Inhabitant Subgroups	Bias
Negative Bias	Aged	5	Aged	1
	Preschool	13	Infant	6
	Infant	18	Adult	20
	Adult	31	Social Class I	27
	Social Class III	91	Gentry	37
	Social Class I	92	Male	86
	Male	94		
	All Inhabitants	100	All Inhabitants	100
Positive Bias	Negro	104	Social Class II	101
	Female	109	Social Class III	109
	Social Class II	110	Female	112
	Adolescent	245	Adolescent	229
	Older School	261	Preschool	258
	Younger School	271	Younger School	444
			Older School	516

Table 12.20
Bias Between Voluntary Association Authority System Habitat
and Inhabitant Subgroups, 1963–64

	Midwest			Yoredale	
	Inhabitant Subgroups	Bias		Inhabitant Subgroups	Bias
Negative Bias	Social Class III	64		Younger School	21
	Younger School	77		Preschool	29
	Adult	83		Infant	37
	Female	99		Adult	82
				Social Class II	91
				Female	97
				Older School	98
	All Inhabitants	100		All Inhabitants	100
Positive Bias	Male	102		Social Class III	108
	Adolescent	108		Male	111
	Social Class I	109		Social Class I	148
	Negro	109		Gentry	173
	Social II	119		Adolescent	188
	Older School	123		Aged	258
	Infant	141			
	Aged	155			
	Preschool	315			

Table 12.21
Bias Between High Local Autonomy Habitat
and Inhabitant Subgroups, 1963–64

	Midwest			Yoredale	
	Inhabitant Subgroups	Bias		Inhabitant Subgroups	Bias
Negative Bias	Younger School	38		Younger School	19
	Older School	40		Older School	23
	Adolescent	56		Infant	47
	Negro	73		Preschool	49
	Social Class II	94		Social Class I	70
	Social Class III	98		Social Class III	76
	Female	100		Male	84
	All Inhabitants	100		All Inhabitants	100
Positive Bias	Male	105		Adolescent	111
	Aged	120		Adult	113
	Social Class I	120		Female	119
	Adult	123		Gentry	129
	Preschool	152		Social Class II	135
	Infant	156		Aged	144

Table 12.22
Bias Between Medium Local Autonomy Habitat
and Inhabitant Subgroups, 1963–64

	Midwest		Yoredale	
	Inhabitant Subgroups	Bias	Inhabitant Subgroups	Bias
Negative Bias	Infant	48	Adolescent	72
	Preschool	57	Social Class II	84
	Adult	74	Adult	91
	Aged	78	Female	92
	Social Class I	83	Aged	93
	Male	95		
	Female	99		
	All Inhabitants	100	All Inhabitants	100
	Social Class III	103	Gentry	101
	Social Class II	104	Male	108
	Negro	120	Social Class III	110
Positive Bias	Adolescent	148	Social Class I	119
	Older School	162	Older School	136
	Younger School	165	Infant	141
			Preschool	148
			Younger School	170

Table 12.23
Bias Between Low Local Autonomy Habitat
and Inhabitant Subgroups, 1963–64

	Midwest		Yoredale	
	Inhabitant Subgroups	Bias	Inhabitant Subgroups	Bias
Negative Bias	Younger School	16	Gentry	15
	Older School	23	Social Class I	39
	Adolescent	28	Younger School	48
	Preschool	56	Aged	62
	Infant	75	Infant	70
	Social Class III	86	Preschool	85
	Social Class I	87	Social Class II	89
	All Inhabitants	100	All Inhabitants	100
	Female	101	Male	101
	Male	104	Female	101
Positive Bias	Social Class II	122	Adolescent	104
	Aged	123	Older School	109
	Adult	143	Adult	111
	Negro	172	Social Class III	131

PART **IV**

 

*We end this report of our explo-
ration of the ecological psychology of Midwest and Yoredale with a reconsideration of some of the methodological, substantive, and theoretical discoveries and
developments that have issued from the research. This is not a precis of the numerous results presented in detail in the preceding chapters. It is selective, dealing with issues we believe to be worthy of special note; it is synthetical, combin-
ing disparate data into more integrated perspectives of the whole towns, or parts of
them; and it is evaluative, offering our judgments on some of the larger significances of the methods and findings. These issues and their treatment are representative of others which readers may wish to examine in similar ways, selecting, in-
tegrating, and summarizing the pertinent dispersed data.*

Perspectives of Midwest and Yoredale

CHAPTER 13

Focused Views of the Towns

ಌಌಌಌಌಌಌಌಌಌಌಌಌಌಌಌಌಌಌಌಌಌಌಌಌ

We turn our attention to some particular features of the towns which the research revealed and to some research methods the study engendered.

SOME PARTICULAR FEATURES OF THE TOWNS

Value of a Man and Power of the People

Midwesterners have greater power over the town habitat than Dalesmen do in two ways: they hold more positions of power as behavior setting operatives, and as behavior setting members they control more settings, including the operatives. These different bases of power have some paradoxical consequences.

VALUE OF A MAN

The loss of an average Midwesterner without replacement or compensatory adjustment reduced the operating efficiency of the town in 1963–64 by a factor of .00056 (T8.4; R6/1; C3); that is, the town lost 8 of the 14,249 essential claim-operations that were implemented by its operatives. This, in percentage terms, .056, is the Pied Piper Index. The loss of an average Yoredale inhabitant reduced the operating efficiency of Yoredale by a factor of .00027 (T8.4; R6/1; C4); its Pied Piper Index is .027. On the average, therefore, Midwesterners were more valuable than Dalesmen as operatives of the towns' habitats by a factor of 2.07.

This is not a psychological finding; it is no more psychological than the fact that a building with fewer supporting beams per ton of weight places greater average burdens upon its beams than one with more supporting beams per ton of weight. But according to the theory we have presented and assessed in Chapters 7 and 8 this difference in the towns' Pied Piper Indexes has these important psychological resultants: Relative to Dalesmen, Midwesterners on the average are more important people, have greater responsibilities, have lower standards of adequate performance, value concrete accomplishments more and general personal qualities less, are more insecure, are more versatile, and work harder. These are the psychological costs and benefits of being more valuable as habitat components.

The Pied Piper data can be interpreted in terms of the expendability and redundancy of the towns' inhabitants as habitat operatives. In these terms Midwesterners are less expendable than Dalesmen, with the psychological consequences indicated, and Dalesmen are more redundant than Midwesterners. Redundancy has psychological consequences too. The leadership data are especially relevant here. Undoubtedly, approximately the same proportions of the towns' inhabitants are able to do the difficult things that habitat-claims for leaders entail. However, twice the percentage of Midwesterners are leaders; there are therefore more redundant leaders in Yoredale than in Midwest. In fact, from the data on leadership and population (T8.6; T3.4), we find that 275 Yoredale inhabitants who were not leaders in 1963–64 would be leaders if its habitat were similar to Midwest's with respect to human components and claims for leaders. Thus many more able Dalesmen experience the psychological consequences of being expendable, of not being important, of not having responsibilities in the operation and maintenance of the town. Furthermore, experience would doubtless teach the towns' potential but unclaimed leaders that future leadership opportunities were less bright in Yoredale than in Midwest (assuming they were in a position to compare the towns). For example, 60 percent of Yoredale's 1963–64 leaders, compared with 40 percent of Midwest's, were still in power three years later (T8.7; R2; C1,2). The consequences of the greater redundancy of Yoredale's able inhabitants are in general the converse of those listed above for Midwesterners. A more general resultant is that the cultivation of leisure is a more common pursuit in Yoredale, and it may be one source of Yoredale's more outstanding Aesthetic, Gross Motor, and Nutrition operations. More Dalesmen than Midwesterners have the time for flower gardening, countryside rambles, and long evenings at the pub. The Coronation Club, where many able Dalesmen spend much time, has no counterpart in Midwest.

POWER OF THE PEOPLE

Midwesterners are not only more frequently than Dalesmen in powerful, responsible positions as operatives where they carry out the programs of the town's behavior settings; they also have control of more of the town's habitat as behavior setting members, including the programs the operatives implement. In Midwest in 1963–64, there were 4290 claims for operatives in behavior settings whose programs were *locally determined* (T6.6; R8; C3). The average Midwesterner filled these positions 1 or more times per year in 4 settings (T10.12; R7; C3); this was half of the total number of responsible positions he filled. In Yoredale there were 1378 locally controlled positions of responsibility (T6.6; R8; C4), and a Dalesman filled them in 1 setting per year, on the average (T10.12; R7; C4); this was one-third of the total number of such positions he filled. Midwesterners had direct control of 4 times as many of the settings where their peers filled responsible positions as Dalesmen did.

Dalesmen are not only less frequently than Midwesterners in responsible positions as operatives, they also have direct control of less of the town's habitat. There were 2295 positions of responsibility in Yoredale in 1963–64 whose programs were *determined from a distance* — outside the town and surrounding region (T6.10; R8; C4). Dalesmen filled these positions in a mean of 0.7 settings in a year (T10.16; R7; C4), amounting to 23 percent of the total mean number of responsible positions they filled. There were 500 remotely controlled positions of responsibility in Midwest (T6.10; R8; C3), and Midwesterners filled them in a mean of 0.3 settings (T10.16; R7; C3), amounting to 3.3 percent of the total responsible positions they filled in a year. Remote authorities had control of twice as many of the settings where Dalesmen filled responsible positions.

POWER OF OPERATIVES VS. POWER OF MEMBERS

Having power over one's habitat, whether as operatives of behavior settings or as members of behavior settings with control of the operatives, promotes interest and activity, whereas powerlessness of either kind breeds detachment and passivity. To the degree that Dalesmen are more powerless than Midwesterners, they are more apathetic toward those aspects of the town's habitat they disapprove of. This is doubtless one factor behind the fewer person-hours of occupancy and fewer claim-operations per town inhabitant in Yoredale than in Midwest. Yoredale leaders frequently remark on the failure of Dalesmen to participate in correcting the shortcomings of the town about which they complain.

In addition to this general resultant of the two kinds of power difference, there are some other and paradoxical consequences. As operatives of more behavior settings, Midwesterners have immediate power over more of the town's habitat than Dalesmen do; and as members of more behavior settings with high local autonomy, they have indirect but ultimate power over more of the habitat. However, the greater ultimate power of Midwesterners diminishes the strength of the local base from which they wield their greater immediate power. The converse is true for Yoredale; how it occurs there may be indicated by a concrete instance.

The behavior setting Trafficways has low local autonomy in Yoredale; it is under the control of a distant authority—the County Council, with headquarters in County Hall, 18 miles distant. The power of Dalesmen over Trafficways is limited in three ways: (*a*) as operatives they are agents of the distant authority and have limited immediate power to make and implement decisions regarding the streets themselves or to influence the authority's decisions; (*b*) the small power of Dalesmen as operatives in turn limits the power of other Dalesmen to influence Trafficways by directly pressuring the local operatives; (*c*) the ultimate power of Dalesmen via the County Council is attenuated by distance and by their small representation upon it. These conditions render all Dalesmen, both Trafficway operatives and users, more helpless and more apathetic about the town's streets than are Midwesterners, for whom all these power conditions are reversed.

However, the very conditions that weaken the power of Dalesmen over the town's streets strengthen the local base of the operatives' limited power; their powerlessness enhances their security. On the contrary, the greater immediate power and influence of Midwest Trafficways operatives attract from their fellow townsmen both greater direct and indirect pressure—the latter via the local authority, the City Council, which the townsmen ultimately completely control—to alter inadequate street programs and policies, and in extreme cases to vacate the position of operative. The very conditions that strengthen the power of Midwesterners over the town's streets weaken the local base of the operatives' greater power; their powerfulness reduces their security.

These differences hold for many behavior settings of Midwest and Yoredale. The greater but more fragile power of Midwesterners is an important factor in its greater habitat erosion and accretion. More Midwesterners than Dalesmen have the power to make habitat changes (to initiate, to discard, to alter settings), but their greater insecurity more often retires them and rescinds the changes they have begun. This is one manifestation of a greater tension within Midwest between the operatives who at any moment are in charge of the habitat and the other inhabitants who oversee the operatives.

In both towns there is continuing conflict between those who wish to enhance the value of persons and the power of the people, at the cost of tension, hard work, low standards, and insecurity, and those who wish to decrease tension and effort, and increase standards and security—to increase efficiency—at the cost of the value of persons and the power of the people.

County Seat and Market Town

Visitors to Midwest on a typical day in 1963–64 found that Business settings, where exchanging goods, services, or privileges for money is prominent, were only a little more numerous than Government settings, where law-making, law-execution, or law-interpretation is prominent: they found that such Business settings as Banks, Grocery Stores,

Garages, Laundries, and Barber Shops were only 112 percent as numerous as Government settings such as County Clerk's Office, Farmers Home Administration Office, Welfare Office, City Council Meetings, and County Planning Board Meetings (T5.7; R2; C3/T5.19; R2; C3). And they did not find the town much different in these respects if they prolonged their visit for the entire year; in fact, over this period Business settings were 91 percent as numerous as Government settings (T5.7; R1; C3/T5.19; R1; C3). There were fewer habitat-claims for Business operatives (salesmen, clerks, proprietors, and so forth) than for Government operatives (chairmen, secretaries, office managers, and so forth) — 96 percent as many (T5.7; R8; C3/T5.19; R8; C3). The variety of Business settings was 110 percent as great as the variety of Government settings (T5.7; R11; C3/T5.19; R11; C3).

Visitors to Yoredale in 1963–64 found the situation there quite different. There were 55 Business settings and 13 Government settings on a typical day — 423 percent as many Business settings (T5.7; R2; C4/T5.19; R2; C4) — and over a year Business settings were 222 percent as numerous (T5.7; R1; C4/T5.19; R1; C4). There were many more habitat-claims for Business operatives than for Government operatives in Yoredale, 212 percent as many (T5.7; R8; C4/T5.19; R8; C4), and the variety of Business settings was 170 percent as great as the variety of Government settings (T5.7; R11; C4/T5.19; R11; C4).

Visitors to the two towns found that Business settings produced a greater proportion of the gross behavior output of both towns than did Government settings, but the Business excess was much greater in Yoredale than in Midwest. The percentages of the towns' gross behavior outputs produced by Business settings were greater than those produced by Government settings by a factor of 1.9 in Midwest (T9.3; R2; C3/T9.7; R2; C3) and 5.6 in Yoredale (T9.3; R2; C4/T9.7; R2; C4).

On the basis of the towns' Government and Business habitats and behavior output, Government is far behind Business in Yoredale and almost on a par in Midwest. Relative to Yoredale, therefore, Midwest is indeed a government center, a County Seat; and relative to Midwest, Yoredale is a business center, a Market Town.

Melting Pot and Enlightened Colonial
Systems of Child-Rearing

Insofar as the towns' public habitats are involved in child-rearing, Midwest and Yoredale have basically different systems. Evidence that the towns' public habitats are involved in the rearing of children is shown by the time children spend in public settings; for example, of the approximately 5110 waking hours per year (14 hours per day) of the older school subgroup (9 through 11 years), about 38 percent is spent in public settings by Midwest children and about 30 percent by Yoredale children (T11.1; R4; C3,4; T11.5; R4; C3,4). We have characterized the Midwest and Yoredale child-rearing systems as the Melting Pot System and the Enlightened Colonial System, for reasons that will be apparent from data we shall recapitulate for two wide age groups, children (under 12 years) and adolescents (12 to 17:11 years). But first we shall describe the systems.

According to the Midwest system, children are best prepared for adulthood by participating in a wide variety of the town's settings. Midwesterners think it is of particular benefit to children to undertake tasks that are important and difficult for them before they can discharge the tasks with complete adequacy. Primary educational settings are important in Midwest education, but they are thought to be most effective if children participate along with adults in other community settings too. This is one reason why "doing your part" is especially valued, even if "your part" cannot be carried out with great effectiveness. This responsible participation involves sharing of power with adults. These views are exactly in line with the dynamics of Midwest behavior settings which, being shorthanded, seek personnel to carry out important functions, even if this is done with considerably less than perfection.

According to the Yoredale system, children are best prepared for adulthood by removing them from the general, public settings and placing them in specially arranged and reserved children's settings under the direction of experts who, over a period of time, are able to prepare the children for entrance into the life of the community. In the Yoredale system, children are not welcomed into some community settings because they do not have requisite skills and attitudes to take their places smoothly. This viewpoint is, again, congruent with the dynamics of Yoredale's behavior settings which, with a relatively large pool of potential operatives, can enlist fully competent inhabitants, leaving others, including children, aside until they can pass the entrance requirements.

In terms of the Colonial System metaphor, Yoredale children are the underdeveloped people of the town, and Yoredale adults are the responsible bearers of a higher culture. As underdeveloped people, children are permitted to take part in few of the privileges and responsibilities the town reserves for adults, because children lack the necessary skills to participate successfully in them, and they lack the values to appreciate adult privileges and opportunities. However, the underdeveloped people of Yoredale (the children) are carefully placed in segregated reservations (Scout Troops, Schools, Sunday Schools) under benevolent administrators (masters), where as subordinate and relatively powerless candidates they are prepared for the good life of adulthood. According to Yoredale values, differences between people of various classes, cultures, educational levels, vocations, and ages should be respected and even encouraged; but mobility toward the circles of the elect should be accomplished outside these circles, and admissibility to them should be demonstrated before admittance is allowed. This is called *realism* (a good word) in Yoredale, and its opposite is termed *egalitarianism* (a bad word).

Midwest children are also in the position of an underdeveloped minority; but this minority, according to the Midwest system, becomes acculturated by processes which occur during interaction with the superior majority within integrated settings. Segregation even for the alleged purpose of achieving eventual equality and mutual acceptance is generally believed in Midwest to be not only wrong but ineffective. When a solicitous "foreigner" seated behind a family at a church service offered to remove the fussing infant and care for him outside, the mother responded, "When do you think he will *learn* to behave in church if you take him out?!" Egalitarianism is a central value in Midwest, and it is also looked on as a method for reducing differences—for teaching children appropriate behavior in church worship services.

These different child-rearing systems are by no means fully implemented in Midwest and Yoredale. However, their imperfectly realized, multiple, and often compensating and reinforcing trends bring very different and strong influences to bear upon children. Furthermore, the theories that support the systems are not univocally approved within the towns, and there is considerable tension within each town between those who approve and those who disapprove of each system in its pure form. Finally, there is evidence of change; Yoredale's new comprehensive school involves some elements of the Melting Pot System. Nevertheless, it is not possible to divorce the children from the towns' overall habitat-behavior systems, and so long as inhabitants have the functional differences as habitat components that we have discovered, it seems inevitable that the Melting Pot and Enlightened Colonial Systems will remain.

CHILDREN AND ADOLESCENTS IN THE MELTING POT AND ON THE RESERVATIONS

The general differences between the towns in habitat extent, habitat-claims, habitat variety, and human components hold, too, for their children and adolescents. Both age groups are in shorter supply in Midwest than in Yoredale. Midwest's 159 children and 84 adolescents, and Yoredale's 220 children and 114 adolescents, have similar numbers and kinds of public settings to inhabit—that is, the children and adolescents of both towns have approximately equivalent habitat resources for satisfying their similar needs via consummatory activities; they have about equal opportunities to ride bicycles, skip rope, take music lessons, view parades, play hopscotch, go to parties, and so on. We expect therefore that on the basis of their needs and opportunities the children and adolescents of Midwest and Yoredale will have similar territorial ranges. But within Midwest there are 10,220 difficult and important positions (habitat-claims) to be filled in the process of maintaining and operating the town's habitat, compared with 7764 within Yoredale. There are twice as many public responsibilities per Midwesterner as per Dalesman, and more than twice as many per inhabitant if the towns' surrounding districts and regions are included. Midwest has a smaller pool of human components than Yoredale from which to implement its greater number of habitat-claims for operatives.

The significance of this difference for the children and adolescents of the towns may be indicated by considering the consequences of a preposterous governmental policy. If both towns had decreed at the beginning of the survey year 1963–64 that only members of the most able age group (the adults) were sufficiently competent and responsible to be operatives, and that therefore the adults of the towns had in addition to their previous responsibilities the duty of implementing the claim-operations formerly implemented by the towns' children, adolescents, and aged, the average Midwest adult would have had to implement claim-operations in a total of 16.1 settings in 1963–64 (T8.4; R3; C3/T11.1; R7; C1), and the average Yoredale adult would have had to implement claim-operations in 6.1 settings (T8.4; R3; C4/T11.1; R7; C2). Since many behavior settings recur on a number of days in a year (mean 60.4 in Midwest and 86.0 in Yoredale), with many of the same inhabitants as operatives on each recurrence (71 percent of them in Midwest — 10,220 H-C/14,249 C-O — and 67 percent of them in Yoredale — 7764 H-C/11,704 C-O), this means that Midwest adults would, counting their regular and additional duties, have had to fill a responsible position in 689 behavior setting occurrences and each Yoredale adult would have had to fill a responsible position in 351 behavior setting occurrences. On a six-day-week work schedule, this amounts for Midwestern adults to responsible tasks at the rate of 2 a day, with an additional responsibility every fourth day (being an insurance salesman and a school bus driver every day, say, and a volunteer fireman every fourth day); for each Yoredale adult it amounts to 1 responsibility every day and an additional duty once a week. Obviously the adults of the towns would have to carry heavy responsibilities under this policy, Midwesterners many more than Dalesmen. The behavior-generating system of Yoredale could probably be maintained and operated by its adults alone, but it is clear that the habitat-claims of Midwest are far beyond the capacity of its adult inhabitants.

It is the latter fact that is the basis of the Melting Pot System for Midwest's children and adolescents: *the Midwest system requires the responsible participation of other than its most able class of human components.* Midwest's program-in-operation asserts that nonadults are able to perform difficult and important functions, and that they have a significant and valued place within the towns; in this respect they are not expendable. If a Pied Piper piped Midwest's children and adolescents from the town, there would not only be personal grief; many settings that serve the general population would cease, and programs of others would be severely curtailed for want of operatives. Among them are City Band Concert and Ice Cream Social, Chaco Garage and Service Station, Saddle Club Organization Meeting, Berry Firework Stand, Mother-Daughter Banquet, Capital City Paper Route, Old Settlers Amateur Talent Show, Midwest Weekly Newspaper. The child-rearing theory that undergirds the Melting Pot System asserts that this kind of integration within the zones of power and responsibility of regular, unsegregated settings is good for children and adolescents as well as for the town.

Within Yoredale, the significance of nonadults is more equivocal; but in any event, they are much less essential to the operation and maintenance of the town at its current functional level. This is the basis of the Enlightened Colonial System for Yoredale's children and adolescents: *the Yoredale system is not dependent upon nonadults to carry out important and difficult tasks.* Its program-in-operation asserts that nonadults are not important to maintenance and operation of the town as a human habitat; in this respect they are expendable. In some ways the town benefits by segregating children and adolescents from the community; for example, Yoredale's adult Dramatic Society plays are better theater than adolescent plays would be, and they are better than Midwest's High School Junior Class and Senior Class plays (the only plays regularly produced in Midwest). A Pied Piper in Yoredale would produce tremendous sadness, but would not seriously diminish the town as a human habitat. The child-rearing theory that undergirds the Enlightened Colonial System asserts that separation within child-centered reservations controlled by experts benefits the children and adolescents as well as the town.

RESPONSIBILITY AND FUNCTIONAL IMPORTANCE OF
CHILDREN AND ADOLESCENTS, 1963–64

One kind of evidence that the children and adolescents of the towns do, in fact, live and behave in accordance with the Melting Pot and Enlightened Colonial Systems is provided by differences in their functional importance and power as indicated by their participation in four categories of behavior setting penetration zones. We describe these categories, here, for children (they hold for adolescents too): (*a*) zones 1 to 6 (zones of occupancy), where children inhabit any penetration zone; these settings make up the Territorial Range of children; (*b*) zones 4, 5, and 6 (the zones of functionaries, multiple leaders, and single leaders), where inhabitants have clear responsibility and power over some parts of settings; these settings constitute the Operational Range of the child subgroup; (*c*) zones 5 and 6 (the zones of shared leadership), where the leaders en masse have responsibility and power over the entire programs of settings; these settings constitute the Leadership Range of children; and (*d*) zone 6 (the zone of single leader), where one person has responsibility and power over the entire programs of settings.

Expected differences between the two systems in these respects are: approximately equal child participation in behavior setting category (*a*) under the two systems, and more child participation in behavior setting categories *b, c, d* under the Melting Pot than under the Enlightened Colonial System.

Table 13.1

Children in Four Behavior Setting Penetration Categories

Behavior Setting Penetration Categories	Behavior Output Measures							
	Range		Mean Person-Hours per Child		Mean Claim-Operations per Child		Pied Piper Index	
	MW (1)	YD (2)	MW (3)	YD (4)	MW (5)	YD (6)	MW (7)	YD (8)
(1) Territorial Range	80 cu	84 cu	1180	1017	4.9	2.4	0.034	0.020
(2) Operational Range	11 cu	4 cu	88	82				
(3) Shared or Single Leadership Range	2 BS	0 BS	2.6	0				
(4) Single Leadership Range	0 BS	0 BS	0	0				

Expendability of children. The data for the towns' children are reported in Table 13.1 for the four behavior setting penetration categories via four behavior output measures: range of children, mean person-hours per town child, mean claim-operations per town child, and mean Pied Piper Index per town child. The penetration categories are ordered in the table, top to bottom, from the one that encompasses all penetration levels (TR) to the one with highest power (LR); the output categories are ordered, left to right, from the least precise measure of participation (range) to the most precise measures (claim-operations and Pied Piper Index.)

Perhaps the most revealing data of the table are those which show that whereas Midwest and Yoredale children are dispersed over extents of the towns' public habitats differing by .5 percent, and inhabit them for amounts of time differing by 16 percent (T13.1; R1; C2/1, 3/4), Midwest children become operatives on a per capita basis in twice as much habitat as Yoredale children (T13.1; R2; C5/6). This means, for example, that Midwest children play in City Band Concerts, assist in Household Auction Sales, collect tickets at the Parent-Teacher Association Carnival, run a lawn mower at the City Park Volunteer Work Group, carry the Capital City Paper Route, recite at the Mother-Daughter Banquet, act as secretary of the Jolly Juniors 4-H Club Meetings, and so forth, twice as often as Yoredale children, although they are actually present in some capacity in fewer settings.

The Pied Piper Index shows that the functional importance of children in maintaining and implementing the programs of the towns' habitats is greater in Midwest than in Yoredale by a factor of 1.7. The loss *without replacement* of a single average Midwest child leaves .034 percent of the town's total claim-operations without implementation; the loss of one Yoredale child leaves .020 percent of the town's claim-operations without implementation.

Midwest children are more important and more powerful—they are, truly, less expendable than Yoredale children; this is the kernel of the difference in the towns' public child-rearing systems.

Expendability of adolescents. We have no evidence that the adolescent period of life is a more difficult one for the adolescents of Yoredale than for those of Midwest, but the difficulties are different in the two towns in important respects, and as a group the natives called adolescents present more problems for the responsible bearers of Yoredale's higher culture, the adults, than for the older inhabitants of Midwest. Detailed data such as we have presented for children are not required to establish the fact that Yoredale's adolescents live under the Enlightened Colonial System, and that this is a source of many problems within Yoredale's behavior-generating machine.

Yoredale, as is true of every colonial system, faces the problem of determining when the natives are sufficiently acculturated to be admitted into the responsibilities and satisfactions of the good life. In 1963–64, Yoredale sorted 17 percent of its adolescents back into the life of the community on at least an apprenticeship basis, and it distributed the remainder between a number of acculturizing reservations. For some, the fifteenth birthday (the school-leaving age) was the divide between childhood and the lower orders of adulthood; 17 percent of the town's adolescents were 15 to 18 years of age and working full-time in its shops, bakeries, garages, construction firms, and neighboring farms as assistants; 3 percent were similarly employed in other towns. The journey into full adulthood was downhill all the way for these adolescents.

For others, the line was drawn at an indefinite age beyond the fifteenth birthday; during these years, 38 percent of Yoredale's adolescents attended the Secondary Modern School located in the town, waiting to be discharged into the outer zones of adulthood. For still others, matriculation to the lower adult zones was at an indefinite age between the sixteenth and twentieth birthdays; 42 percent of the town's adolescents were 15 to 20 years of age and attending schools outside the town; 27 percent were attending the state grammar school 12 miles distant from the town, 15 percent were attending private schools or government technical schools in various other towns.

The Enlightened Colonial System was, indeed, in full operation for the adolescents of Yoredale. Its assignments were of greatest personal significance to the individuals involved; many present privileges and opportunities were determined thereby, and the direction of their future lives was at stake. The assignments also presented the school authority system with tremendous difficulties requiring a great evaluation apparatus.

In contrast, Midwest's Melting Pot System functioned relatively serenely with respect to the town's adolescents as a group. In 1963–64 all of the town's adolescents attended the town's high school, and participated to the maximum of their abilities and desires in many of the town's behavior settings. No adolescents worked full-time. This is not to say that the adolescent period was less severe for Midwesterners personally, but their personal problems were not aggravated by arbitrary assignments to diverse child acculturation reservations. The problem of matriculating to adulthood was postponed for almost the entire adolescent group to 18 years of age. At this time, decisions were spread among many behavior settings within and outside the town, and the decisions usually involved negotiations between individual 18-year-olds and particular employers, colleges, technical schools, or government offices. Only one authority assigned some 18-year-olds, the Selective Service Office (military draft). The official school-leaving age of 16 years was not a sorting time in Midwest; almost all adolescents completed four years of high school. We judge that the reason for this resides in the Melting Pot System under which Midwest adolescents lived.

Not only does the Enlightened Colonial System confuse the lives of Yoredale's adolescents, it confuses the data we have assembled. The behavior output data for Midwest adolescents measure with about equal adequacy both the amount of behavior the town's habitat generates via the adolescent inhabitants and the amount of behavior the adolescents transact in the course of their lives. But the behavior output data for Yoredale adolescents by no means measure adequately the amount of behavior the adolescent inhabitants transact in the course of their lives; because the Enlightened Colonial System operates in Yoredale to eject 45 percent of the town's adolescents from the town for the greater parts of most days. A comparison of the towns' behavior outputs via their adolescent inhabitants involves almost all the behavior of Midwest's adolescents, but it involves almost all the behavior of only 55 percent of Yoredale's adolescents—55 percent that are by no means randomly selected. The treatment of adolescents by Midwest and Yoredale confirms most impressively the difference in their child-rearing systems, but it destroys any possibility of comparing the total living conditions and behavior of adolescents by means of the data at hand.

FREEDOM OF MOVEMENT FOR CHILDREN

Freedom to move about a habitat, to enter and leave behavior settings, is widely valued; it is an indication of power. Prohibited and coerced movements are widely deplored; they signify weakness. Differences in freedom to move provide another test of the proposition that the children and adolescents of Midwest and Yoredale live and behave in accordance with the Melting Pot and Enlightened Colonial Systems. We expect greater areas of free movement and greater output of free behavior, and smaller areas of coerced movement and smaller output of coerced behavior, in Midwest than in Yoredale.

The relevant data consist of the extent of two categories of behavior settings and the participation of children within them. The categories differ with respect to attendance vector attributes which we describe, here, for children. The first category consists of behavior settings with attendance vectors that encourage, are neutral to, or discourage the attendance of children. These settings constitute regions of relatively free movement for children; large parts of them impose no restrictions or coercions, and where restrictions and coercions are imposed they are not absolute, and can be breached by determined children. Within these regions the needs of children are dominant in determining the settings they inhabit. The second category consists of behavior settings with attendance vectors that require or prohibit the attendance of children. These settings constitute reserved areas of the towns. The required settings are reserved for children (under the control of older persons), and the prohibited settings are reserved for older persons, free from intruding children. Within these regions, behavior setting forces are dominant in determining settings inhabited by children.

The data for the towns' children in 1963–64 are reported in Table 13.2. They bear out expectations on the basis of the Melting Pot and Enlightened Colonial System. The reserved areas were more exten-

Table 13.2
Freedom of Movement for Children
1963–64

		Habitat Extent		Output per Town Child	
		MW (1)	YD (2)	MW (3)	YD (4)
(1)	Regions of free movement; behavior settings that encourage, are neutral to, or discourage attendance	83.7 cu	76.9 cu	645 P-H	452 P-H
(2)	of children.	78.1%	68.0%	52.9%	44.5%
(3)	Regions of coerced movement; behavior settings that require or pro-	23.7 cu	36.0 cu	575 P-H	564 P-H
(4)	hibit the attendance of children.	22.0%	31.9%	47.0%	55.0%

sive in Yoredale than in Midwest; they constituted almost one-third of Yoredale's habitat and just over one-fifth of Midwest's (T13.2; R4; C1,2). The converse holds for regions where children are free to come and go (T13.2; R2; C1,2). Midwest children spend about one and three-quarter hours a day, on the average, in the regions of free movement, whereas Yoredale children spend approximately one and one-quarter hours in them (T13.2; R1; C3,4). Midwestern children have 109 percent as much area of free movement as Yoredale children, and they spend 143 percent as much time in these areas.

CHILDREN AS BENEFACTORS AND BENEFICIARIES

The child-rearing systems of the towns are elucidated by the beneficence attributes of behavior settings. Settings can be sorted with respect to the classes of inhabitants who implement their programs as operatives and with respect to the classes who participate in their programs as users (members, customers, and spectators). The relation between operatives and users within behavior settings is universally one of more power vs. less power; and for the present analyses, behavior settings have been selected where operatives, in addition to being more powerful, are benefactors of the users, who are beneficiaries. Yoredale's Church of England Juniors Sunday School Class is an example; its program is implemented by adult and adolescent operatives (the teacher and her assistants), and its raison d'etre is to benefit the child members; the teacher and her assistants are operatives and benefactors, the children are users and beneficiaries.

We have selected two categories of behavior settings for analysis. In one category children are operatives and benefactors, and the older age groups are users and beneficiaries; in the other category the older age groups are operatives and benefactors, and the children are users and beneficiaries. Examples of the first category are Elementary Lower School Operetta in Midwest, and Methodist Sunday Afternoon Anniversary Program in Yoredale; in these settings, children as performers (program operatives) benefit (entertain, exhilarate, refresh) adolescents, adults, and aged persons as members of the audiences. Examples of the second category: Anita Kelly, Piano Lessons in Midwest, and County Primary School Playground in Yoredale; here, adults as teachers and custodians (program operatives) benefit (educate, entertain) children as pupils. Only a minority of the habitats of both towns have these particular operative-beneficence properties; about 80 percent of the habitats of both towns benefit all age groups equally.

We expect that in Midwest's Melting Pot System the first category of behavior settings, where children are powerful benefactors, will be more extensive and more productive than Yoredale's Enlightened Colonial System; and that the second category, where children are passive beneficiaries, will be more extensive and productive in Yoredale.

The data for the town's children are reported in Table 13.3. The expectations for the first category are strongly supported. On the average, Midwest children spend 21 hours per year and Yoredale children spend 1.5 hours per year in behavior settings where they—that is, members of their age group—benefit members of other age groups (T13.3; R1; C3,4). Behavior settings where these arrangements are built into the program constitute about 1 in 50 of the settings at hand for Midwesterners, which exceeds such arrangements in Yoredale by a factor of 10 (T13.3; R2; C1,2). Furthermore, the benefactions of Midwest children have greater impact than those of Yoredale children. Midwest adolescents are beneficiaries of children for 3374 person-hours, amounting to 2.0 percent of their total behavior output, whereas Yoredale adolescents are beneficiaries for 172 person-hours, 1.5 percent of their total output; Midwest adults are beneficiaries of children for 4777 person-hours, 0.7 percent of their total behavior output, whereas Yoredale adults are beneficiaries for 919 person-hours, 0.1 percent of

Table 13.3
Children as Benefactors and Beneficiaries
1963–64

		Habitat Extent		Output per Town Child	
		MW (1)	YD (2)	MW (3)	YD (4)
(1)	Regions where children are benefactors; behavior settings where children are operatives of programs that benefit other age groups as members, spectators,	2.2 cu	0.2 cu	21.0 P-H	1.5 P-H
(2)	etc.	2.1%	0.2%	1.7%	0.15%
(3)	Regions where children are beneficiaries; behavior settings where other age groups are operatives of programs that benefit children	17.0 cu	20.1 cu	828.3 P-H	638.4 P-H
(4)	as members, spectators, etc.	15.9%	17.8%	67.8%	62.7%

their total output; and Midwest aged are beneficiaries for 218 person-hours, 0.3 percent of their total behavior output, whereas Yoredale aged are beneficiaries for 144 person-hours, 0.1 percent of their total output.

It is clear that Midwest's Melting Pot System of child-rearing installs children in positions of relative power and worthiness in more of its habitat than does Yoredale's Enlightened Colonial System, and that the adolescents, adults, and aged of Midwest transact more behavior as beneficiaries (customers, spectators, guests) of children than the adolescents, adults, and aged of Yoredale.

The expectations for the second category of behavior settings, where children are recipients of the benefactions of others, are less clearly supported by the data. Settings where these relations are parts of the programs are more extensive in Yoredale than Midwest, as expected (T13.3; R3,4; C1,2), but output per child is greater in Midwest, contrary to expectations (T13.3; R3,4; C3,4). Midwest's children appear to have the best of the two systems: more of the satisfactions of both benefactors and beneficiaries.

Sunset Acres for Retirement

Persons seeking a place to retire may wish to consider Sunset Acres' two sites, Midwest and Yoredale. That many do is indicated by the fact that in 1963–64 approximately one-fifth of the populations of both towns were 65 years or older, whereas they constitute only 10 percent of the population of the United States and 13 percent of the entire population of England.

Whatever an older person's predilections may be, he will find strong pressures toward the patterns of elderly living that pervade the town he chooses. This pattern is a consequence of relatively enduring habitat conditions by which the newcomer as well as seasoned inhabitants are constrained. So the elderly person should ask himself which of the towns' features are more congenial and less uncongenial to him, and which are most crucial. Table 13.4 is a prospectus of some of the living conditions Midwest and Yoredale provide old people; they show that there are choices: between more (YD) and fewer (MW) people on the streets, in the stores, attending meetings; between more (YD) and less (MW) behavior in progress in the town and in its settings; between engaging in more (MW) and less (YD) activity in the public areas of the town; between having more (MW) and less (YD) social status; and between having more (MW) and fewer (YD) burdens of responsibility and leadership.

In general, if one fancies in old age the life of a bystander, onlooker, and consumer, one should choose Yoredale rather than Midwest; but if one wishes a life of more responsible participation in the maintenance and operation of the town as a human habitat, Midwest rather than Yoredale should be the choice. It is obvious from the pros-

Table 13.4
Prospectus: Qualities of Community Life for Old People
in Midwest and Yoredale, 1963–64

People

	MW	YD
Total inhabitants	830	1310
Aged inhabitants (no.)	176	287
Aged (% of total)	21%	22%

Old people have more potential associates in Yoredale than in Midwest; Yoredale has 480 (58 percent) more inhabitants than Midwest, and among these there are 111 (63 percent) more elderly inhabitants.

Extent and Variety of Habitat

	MW	YD
Total town (cu)	107	113
Territorial Range of aged (cu)	78	80
Territorial Range of aged (% of total)	72%	71%
Variety (no. of genotypes)	198	213

There are more, and more varied, settings at hand for the elderly of Yoredale than of Midwest. However, elderly inhabitants range over only about seven-tenths of the towns, so Yoredale's 6 percent potential advantage in public times and places for setting goals and accepting responsibilities shrinks to a 2.5 percent actual advantage. Yoredale's habitat is 8 percent more varied than Midwest's.

Areas of Power and Responsibility for the Aged

	MW	YD
Operational Range of aged (cu)	29	18
Operational Range of aged (% of total town)	27%	16%
Operational Range of aged (% of TR)	37%	20%

Midwest provides opportunities for its aged to exercise power and responsibility in 11 (61 percent) more cu of habitat than Yoredale does, amounting to 11 more percent of the towns' total habitats and to 17 more percent of the TR of the aged. Retirees who conform to the present pattern of the towns' aged engage in difficult, important, and responsible actions in more of Midwest's than of Yoredale's public habitat.

Areas of Leadership for the Aged

	MW	YD
Leadership Range of aged, behavior settings (no.)	61	34
Leadership Range of aged (% of total town)	7%	4%

At the highest levels of responsibility, that of joint or single leader, the aged of Midwest are relatively still more widely powerful and important than those of Yoredale. The aged of Midwest lead 27 (80 percent) more settings than do the aged of Yoredale.

Table 13.4 (*Continued*)
Behavior

	MW	YD
All Inhabitants		
Mean P-H per cu of habitat	17,517	23,272
All Town Inhabitants		
Mean P-H per inhabitant	1,356	1,089
Aged Inhabitants		
Mean P-H per inhabitant	471	410
Mean P-H within Operational Range	300	200
Mean P-H within Leadership Range	160	84

The aged of Yoredale live in a busier town than those of Midwest; Dalesmen inhabit behavior settings where 33 percent more behavior occurs (by both townsmen, visitors, and commuters). However, the townsmen with whom elderly Midwesterners live are busier than those with whom elderly Dalesmen live; the former spend 25 percent more time in the town's public habitat than the latter. The towns' aged themselves differ similarly, though in less degree. Retirees who behave as the present elderly of the towns do can expect, on the average, to spend 15 percent more time in Midwest's than in Yoredale's public regions, 55 minutes a day rather than 47 minutes. And those who retire to Midwest rather than Yoredale can expect to spend 50 percent more time in settings where aged persons have positions of responsibility, 25 hours a month rather than 17 hours; and they can expect to spend 90 percent more time in settings where old people are leaders, 13 hours a month rather than 7 hours.

pectus (Table 13.4) that particular differences are not great; nevertheless, all-in-all, life as an elderly vacationer encounters more encouragement and less resistance in Yoredale, and life as an elderly mover, shaker, and community operator encounters more encouragement and less resistance in Midwest.

The lives of the elderly are not only different in Midwest and Yoredale, they differ in both towns from the lives of inhabitants in general. For example, 13.2 percent of the behavior of all Dalesmen occurs in the town's primary Recreation habitat (PRH); if Yoredale's aged inhabitants conformed to the standards of the generality of Yoredale inhabitants, a yearly mean of 54.4 person-hours of their behavior would occur there. In fact, however, 93.2 person-hours of aged behavior occur in Yoredale's PRH. So there is a positive bias between Yoredale's elderly inhabitants and its PRH, which produces 171 percent as much of the behavior of Yoredale's old people as of unselected Dalesmen. This is a measure of Yoredale's PRH-Aged bias. An oldster who abhors being set aside from the town's general population in this respect — 71 percent more of his public behavior devoted to play — should eschew Yoredale; he would find Midwest's 106 percent recreational bias more congenial.

The biases between differential habitats and the elderly of the towns are reported in Table 13.5, where the order, top to bottom, is from the differential habitat that is most positive to the aged to the one that is most negative.

Table 13.5
Bias Between Differential Habitats
and Aged Inhabitants of the Towns, 1963–64

	Midwest		Yoredale	
	Differential Habitat	Bias[a]	Differential Habitat	Bias[a]
Positive Bias	Church	357	Voluntary Assn.	258
	Religion	308	Recreation	171
	Govt. Agency	186	Church	164
	Personal Appearance	179	Religion	157
	Government	179	Talking	155
	Voluntary Assn.	155	High Autonomy	144
	Aesthetics	141	Personal Appearance	143
	Low Autonomy	123	Business	117
	High Autonomy	120	Aesthetics	116
	Recreation	106	Govt. Agency	113
	Private Enterprise	101	Private Enterprise	104
Negative Bias	Professional Involvement	90	Nutrition	100
	Business	86	Affective Behavior	99
	Nutrition	80	Gross Motor	97
	Manipulation	78	Social Contact	96
	Medium Autonomy	78	Medium Autonomy	93
	Social Contact	69	Professional Involvement	92
	Talking	64	Manipulation	77
	Gross Motor	60	Phys. Health	63
	Affective	35	Low Autonomy	62
	Phys. Health	14	Government	38
	Education	9	Education	4
	School	5	School	1

$^a \left(\dfrac{\text{Mean obtained person-hours per aged town inhabitant}}{\text{Mean expected person-hours per aged town inhabitant}} \right) 100$

Both towns sort the behavior of their aged inhabitants quite differently from the behavior of their inhabitants in general. Habitat-aged bias varies in Midwest from the positive bias of 357 for the Church habitat to the negative bias of 5 for the School habitat; it varies in Yoredale from the positive bias of 258 for the Voluntary Association habitat to the negative bias of 1 for the School habitat.

In both towns there are large positive biases (150 or more) between old people and Church, Religion, and Voluntary Association habitats, and lesser positive biases (115–149) between old people and Aesthetic and High Local Autonomy habitats. There are large negative biases (65 or less) in both towns between aged inhabitants and School, Education, and Health habitats, and lesser negative biases (80–66) between old people and Manipulation and Medium Autonomy habitats. The towns are similar in exhibiting almost no bias toward the aged in connection with Private Enterprises.

But there are differences. Midwest's biases are positive and Yoredale's negative between the aged and Government and Low Autonomy habitats; Midwest's biases are negative and Yoredale's positive between old people and Business and Talking habitats. Midwest's positive biases are greater than Yoredale's between the aged and Government Agency habitats, and its negative biases are greater between aged inhabitants and Gross Motor and Affective habitats. Yoredale's positive biases are greater than Midwest's between the aged and Voluntary Association and Recreation habitats.

Popular Places

The most popular places are common to the towns. Elementary School Basic Classes, Grocery Stores, Restaurants (including pubs in Yoredale and organization dinners in Midwest), and Trafficways are the most popular classes of behavior settings in both towns. Each of these genotypes is the locus of more than 5 percent of each town's total behavior output via town inhabitants, and together they produce 30 percent of Midwest's and 38 percent of Yoredale's output. These findings are revealed by the data of Tables 13.6 and 13.7; where the

Table 13.6
Midwest's Most Popular Places

The behavior setting genotypes where Midwesterners spend the greatest amount of time; percent of total behavior output of town inhabitants in stated genotypes; 1963-64

Genotype Number	Genotype	Percent of Total Output
58.	Elem. School Basic Classes	8.73
162.	Restaurants & Organization Dinners	8.09
203.	Trafficways	7.76
83.	Grocery Stores	5.90
54.	Drugstores	2.69
177.	Service Stations	2.52
81.	Govt. Business & Records Offices.	2.43
15.	Banks	2.35
84.	Hallways	2.33
22.	Bowling Games, Ten Pins	2.12
20.	Billiard Parlors & Taverns	1.89
9.	Attorneys Offices	1.82
78.	Garages	1.76
140.	Phys. Ed. Classes	1.52
134.	Parks & Playgrounds	1.46
208.	Variety Stores	1.38
110.	Libraries	1.37
35.	Clothiers & Dry Goods Stores	1.26
18.	Basketball Games	1.25
24.	Building, Construction, & Repair Services	1.25
125.	Music Classes, Vocal	1.20
19.	Beauty Shops	1.16
146.	Post Offices	1.16
194.	Taverns	1.16
161.	Relig. Worship Servs.	1.12

Table 13.7
Yoredale's Most Popular Places

The behavior setting genotypes where Dalesmen spend the greatest amount of time; percent of total behavior output of town inhabitants in stated genotypes; 1963–64

Genotype Number	Genotype	Percent of Total Output
219.	Trafficways	21.33
170.	Pubs & Dining Rooms	5.89
106.	Grocery Stores	5.40
80.	Elem. School Basic Classes	5.35
181.	Restaurants	3.61
100.	Garages	3.38
33.	Butcher Shops	2.37
48.	Clothiers & Dry Goods Stores	2.35
15.	Bakeries	2.28
150.	Nursing Homes	1.99
53.	Confectioners & Stationers Shops	1.93
180.	Relig. Worship Servs.	1.83
16.	Banks, Commercial	1.76
129.	Markets, Public	1.73
171.	Railway Freight Stations	1.73
31.	Building, Construction, & Repair Services	1.71
51.	Commercial Co. Offices	1.41
22.	Beauty Shops (Ladies Hairdressers)	1.18
164.	Post Offices, Sorting	1.18
108.	Hardware (Ironmonger) Stores	1.10
155.	Parks & Playgrounds	1.07
138.	Milk Collection & Processing Plants	1.00

behavior setting genotypes that produce 1 percent or more of the public behavior of the towns' inhabitants are reported.

An outstanding difference between the towns is the greater amount of behavior within Yoredale's Trafficways; over one-fifth of the public behavior of Dalesmen occurs in the town's streets and sidewalks. Contributing to this are: (*a*) the great amount of walking in Yoredale, which derives from the smaller distances within the town and the lesser convenience of automobiles; (*b*) the small stores and offices, that interfere with conversation within them when shopping and doing business; and (*c*) the overflow from the market into the streets on Market Day. The streets and sidewalks are much more of an esplanade for social interaction in Yoredale than in Midwest.

The towns agree that Banks, Garages, Parks and Playgrounds, Clothiers and Dry Goods Stores, Building, Construction, and Repair Services, Beauty Shops, Post Offices, and Religious Worship Services are important magnets for behavior.

The remaining popular genotypes, 13 in Midwest and 10 in Yoredale, are not common to the towns. Very popular genotypes that are distinctive to Midwest (producing 2 percent of the public behavior of town inhabitants) are Drugstores, Service Stations, Government Offices, Hallways, and Bowling Games (Ten Pins); similarly popular, distinctive Yoredale genotypes are Butcher Shops and Bakeries.

Town and Country

Midwest is more of a townsman's town than Yoredale; Yoredale is more of a countryman's town than Midwest. Midwesterners in comparison with Dalesmen manage more of their town's habitat without outside directives, and they produce more of its behavior without outside assistance: 44 percent of Midwest's and 31 percent of Yoredale's habitats are locally autonomous (T6.6; R5; C3,4) — the plans and programs of these proportions of their habitats are determined within the towns or the surrounding school (MW) or rural (YD) districts — and 60 percent of Midwest's and 54 percent of Yoredale's gross behavior outputs are generated via townsmen. Both towns favor townsmen as inhabitants of their public habitat, but Midwest favors them more than Yoredale (T8.2; R4; C3,4). These findings mean that Midwest is somewhat more self-sufficient than Yoredale; it is less dependent than Yoredale for its continuance as a human habitat at its current level upon alien controls and out-of-town inhabitants.

The differences between the towns in their inclinations toward town and country inhabitants are by no means homogeneous across their differential habitats. We present data for behavior outputs in Table 13.8, where we find, for example, that 77 percent of the behavior output of Midwest's primary Nutritional habitat is generated via town inhabitants, whereas this is true of 56 percent of the output of Yoredale's primary Nutritional habitat. The habitats are ordered in the table, top to bottom, from those that favor townsmen as human components to those that favor countrymen and other foreigners as human components. In Midwest the habitats most favorable to townsmen are those where Nutrition, High Local Autonomy, Business, and Private Enterprise are prominent; and those most favorable to countrymen and others from out of town are habitats where Low Local Autonomy, Physical Health, Affective Behavior and Talking are prominent. For Yoredale, the habitats most favorable to townsmen are Churches, High local autonomy, Government, and Private Enterprise, whereas those most favorable to countrymen and out-of-town inhabitants are Schools, Education, Low Local Autonomy, and Physical Health. The habitats of both towns with High Local Autonomy, and those under the aegis of Private Enterprises, favor townsmen, whereas the primary Health habitats of the towns favor countrymen.

The greatest difference between the towns is in the inclinations of their Church authority systems. Midwest's Churches favor countrymen slightly; 53 percent of the output of Midwest's Church authority system is produced by countrymen (47 percent by townsmen); whereas 21 percent of the output of Yoredale's Churches is produced by countrymen (79 percent by townsmen). Midwest is a Church center for countrymen;

Table 13.8
Behavior Output by Townsmen
Percents of the Total Behavior Output of Differential Habitats
Generated via Town Inhabitants; 1963–64

Midwest   Yoredale

Habitat	Percent of Total Output	Habitat	Percent of Total Output
Nutrition	77	Church	79
High Local Autonomy	74	High Local Autonomy	70
Business	73	Government	68
Private Enterprise	72	Private Enterprise	62
Manipulation	69	Govt. Agency	61
Personal Appearance	68	Business	59
Professional Involvement	62	Medium Local Autonomy	58
Gross Motor	61	Manipulation	57
Govt. Agency	61	Aesthetics	56
Total Habitat	60	Nutrition	56
Government	56	Professional Involvement	56
Aesthetics	54	Recreation	54
Social Contact	54	Gross Motor	54
Medium Local Autonomy	53	Total Habitat	54
Voluntary Assn.	53	Voluntary Assn.	54
Recreation	53	Personal Appearance	54
Religion	49	Religion	48
Education	48	Affective Behavior	48
School	48	Talking	47
Church	47	Social Contact	46
Talking	46	Phys. Health	43
Affective Behavior	45	Low Local Autonomy	38
Phys. Health	44	Education	35
Low Local Autonomy	38	School	32

there are no rural or village churches to serve the country areas as there are in the regions around Yoredale. In view of these data, it is surprising to find that the primary Religious habitats of both towns are almost equally inclined toward town and country inhabitants—namely, 49 percent (MW) and 48 percent (YD) of their behavior outputs are generated by town inhabitants. The reason for this disharmony lies largely in the towns' Schools, which in both towns favor country inhabitants, and more so in Yoredale than in Midwest. Midwest's schools prohibit the occurrence of religious settings in the habitats they control, whereas Yoredale's schools require them—namely, Morning Assembly and Religious Instruction.

Something Old, Something New, Something Gained

Habitat conservation (maintaining something that is old) habitat innovation (producing something new), and habitat growth (something gained) are complexly interrelated in Midwest and Yoredale.

HABITAT CONSERVATION

Less of Midwest's than of Yoredale's 1954–55 habitat was conserved during the decade to become the core of its 1963–64 habitat; 65 percent (58 cu) of Midwest's and 75 percent (67 cu) of Yoredale's 1954–55 habitats were stable, continuing habitat components in 1963–64. The lesser conservation in Midwest did not occur across all authority systems of the towns.

1954–55 habitat conserved to 1963–64

	Midwest		Yoredale	
	%	cu	%	cu
Churches	61	3.9	64	3.7
Govt. Agencies	84	14.1	84	11.0
Private Enterprises	52	22.8	79	42.4
Schools	84	13.6	76	5.7
Voluntary Assns.	58	3.8	49	4.9

We find that there was not less, but more, conservation of those parts of Midwest's habitat under the aegis of Schools and Voluntary Associations; we furthermore find that equal percentages of the Government Agency habitats of the towns were conserved. In fact, the lesser overall conservation of Midwest's habitat occurred largely within its Private Enterprises in behavior settings operated by private citizens in the process of earning a living. Private Enterprises — attorneys' and solicitors' offices, delivery and collection routes, grocery stores, restaurants, hotels, pubs and dining rooms — was the largest authority system of both towns, the *least* extensively conserved of Midwest's authority systems but one of the two *most* extensively conserved of Yoredale's. The Private Enterprise habitat was a region of impermanence in Midwest and a bastion of conservation in Yoredale. The bastions of conservation in Midwest were its Schools and Government Agencies, with stability as great as in any of Yoredale's authority systems. The region of greatest impermanence in the towns occurred in Yoredale's Voluntary Associations — with their card parties, dinners and banquets, cultural meetings, business meetings, solicitations of funds, dart games and so forth — where less than half the 1954–55 habitat survived to 1963–64.

HABITAT INNOVATION

More of Midwest's than of Yoredale's 1963–64 habitat was acquired after 1954–55, replacing lost settings and adding new ones; 45 percent (48 cu) of Midwest's and 39 percent (44 cu) of Yoredale's 1963–64 habitats were post-1955 innovations. This was true for all but one of the towns' authority systems.

1963–64 habitats acquired after 1954–55

	Midwest		Yoredale	
	%	cu	%	cu
Churches	66	8.0	46	2.9
Govt. Agencies	20	3.5	9	1.1
Private Enterprises	47	19.2	20	11.1
Schools	36	8.9	80	23.5
Voluntary Assns.	66	8.1	54	5.0

Schools were the only authority system more innovative in Yoredale, where they were by far the most salient locus of innovation because of the establishment of the new district school. The greatest contributors to Midwest's overall greater habitat innovation were its Churches and its Voluntary Associations. In both towns the least innovative authority system was Government Agencies; however, they were not as slow to change in Midwest as in Yoredale.

Increment (+) and decrement (−) in
habitat extent after 1954–55

	Midwest		Yoredale	
	%	cu	%	cu
Churches	+91	+5.8	+10	+0.6
Govt. Agencies	+4	+0.6	−5	−0.7
Private Enterprises	−7	−3.0	+4	+2.0
Schools	+54	+8.7	+289	+21.7
Voluntary Assns.	+89	+5.8	−7	−0.7

HABITAT GROWTH

Habitat conservation and innovation combined to produce the changes that occurred in the extent of the towns' habitats. We have seen that Midwest's lesser habitat conservation and greater habitat innovation produced less habitat expansion (19 percent) than did Yoredale's greater habitat conservation and lesser habitat innovation (25 percent). The different rates of conservation and innovation across the authority systems of the towns produced different amounts of habitat change.

Yoredale's greater habitat growth was due to the tremendous expansion of its Schools, where conservation was average and innovation outstanding. Omitting Schools, Yoredale's remaining habitat increased by 2 percent over the decade, whereas Midwest's remaining habitat increased by 11 percent. Yoredale's greatest rate of growth, aside from its Schools, occurred in its Churches, where conservation was relatively low and innovation relatively high. Habitat decrements occurred in Yoredale's Government Agencies, where conservation was high and innovation low, and in Voluntary Associations, where conservation was low and innovation high. Midwest's greatest rates of growth occurred in connection with its Churches and its Voluntary Associations, which were among the least conserving and most innovative of its authority systems; its only habitat decrement occurred in its Private Enterprises, where conservation was smallest and innovation about average.

We may summarize as follows: Compared with Yoredale, Midwest during the decade retained less of its old, 1954–55 habitat (especially fewer old Private Enterprises) and added more that was new to its 1963–64 habitat. Its habitat had a smaller net gain over the decade, but one that was more general and less concentrated in a single authority system; many combinations of conservation and innovation .produced its habitat gains and losses.

METHODOLOGICAL SPINOFF

The fundamental units of the research are behavior settings.[1] We have emphasized that behavior settings are such commonly perceived phenomena that they frequently enter into the ordinary communications of laymen—but that our approach to Midwest and Yoredale nevertheless differs sharply from a commonsense, layman's approach. It does so because our descriptions and measurements of the towns are solely in terms of behavior settings, whereas commonsense makes use of many descriptive units; and because the central concepts and operations by which we have described and measured behavior settings—and in terms of them, the towns—do not occur in everyday experience. Habitat-claims, centiurbs, common genotypes, action patterns, claim-operations are not only uncommon terms, they refer to uncommon ideas and involve unusual identification and measurement procedures. For these reasons, the descriptions and analyses of the habitats and behavior outputs of Midwest and Yoredale reported here do not occur in common experience.

Of some interest in this connection is the general finding that Midwest and Yoredale are in most respects less different in terms of behavior settings than in terms of the common experience of laymen. No Dalesman viewing Midwest from the air, from its trafficways, or from the courthouse square would mistake it for Yoredale, and vice versa. The differences are impressive: stone vs. wood construction, an unsystematic vs. a grid layout of streets, gray-brown vs. white and light-colored buildings, many pedestrians vs. few pedestrians, abutting vs. spatially separated structures. On the other hand, we have found many small differences between Yoredale and Midwest in terms of behavior settings and their attributes: 17.9 vs. 14.5 cu of primary Recreational habitat; 48.7 vs. 46.7 person-hours of Aesthetic behavior per town inhabitant.

[1] Research not mentioned before in which behavior settings have a prominent place found in Barker, 1960, 1963a, 1963b, 1965; Barker & Barker, 1961a, 1961b; Barker, Barker, & Ragle, 1967; Botts, 1970; Gump, 1968a, 1968b, 1971a, 1971b; LeCompte, 1972; Olen, 1971; Ragle, Johnson, & Barker, 1967; Wicker, 1968, 1969a, 1969b, 1971, 1972; Willems, 1967, 1972; Willems & Raush, 1968; Wright, 1970a, 1970b.

This disparity in differences between the towns as seen by laymen and as measured in terms of behavior settings reminds one of the differences between a Kansas coon hound and a Yorkshire terrier, as they appear to laymen and to physiologists and anatomists. Some of the organs, tissues, cells, and physiological processes of coon hounds and terriers are very similar, and are undoubtedly much less easily discriminated by experts than the total hound and terrier gestalts are discriminated by laymen. Physiological records and anatomical atlases of the Kansas coon hound and the Yorkshire terrier would reveal little of their appearances as seen by laymen. This is expected, of course, in view of the different levels of phenomena with which scientists and laymen deal. And a similar discrepancy between our descriptions and laymen's descriptions of Midwest and Yoredale is to be expected, and for the same reason. The test of the adequacy of any description is its bearing upon important issues. Laymen's descriptions of dogs are more useful guides than those of scientists when choosing a house pet; but scientists' descriptions are more valuable when treating their diseases.

The same is true of descriptions of Midwest and Yoredale in laymen's terms and in terms of behavior settings. The test for behavior settings is: Do they make it possible to deal more adequately with phenomena of importance—for example, to understand the greater busyness of Midwesterners? Methods that have been developed in the course of the research have been identified in Chapter 2; we shall comment upon those that appear to us to be of special significance.

Urbs and Centiurbs as Measures of Habitat Extent

The problem of measuring the size of the habitat of human molar actions has been a perplexing one. Perhaps because of its ease of measurement and the fact that actions often have spatial parameters, available physical space has been widely reported, with the implication that it is coordinate with habitat size. But the size of the habitat of molar actions refers to an environmental variable that is positively related to molar behavior possibilities, and amount of physical space and behavior possibilities are not so related. The molar behavior opportunities of a lone traveler imprisoned by a desert of vast spatial extent are surely not much greater than those of a prisoner in solitary confinement in a 6- by 9-foot cell. It is true that the habitat of molar action always has a geographical locus and a physical milieu, and it always has temporal extent. How the temporal and milieu attributes combine to form the habitat is a problem to be solved by theories and concepts based upon and verified by empirical observation and experiment. The way they are combined in the centiurb measure of habitat extent is based upon a particular theory of molar action. This theory and the operations by means of which weights are assigned to the temporal and milieu attributes require evaluation, as well as empirical validation.

At the present time we have no independent measure of habitat extent against which to validate the centiurb measures. However, the data of the study do provide some unsystematic, fragmentary evidence. For example, between the survey years the county educational authorities took steps to increase opportunities for educational behavior within Yoredale, and they believe their manipulation of the environment—their establishment of a new school—did in fact accomplish this. And according to the centiurb measure, the increase was 9.6 cu, amounting to over 3 times the extent of the previous primary Educational habitat. As another example, certain inhabitants of Midwest became dissatisfied with the available habitat resources for religious behavior and took steps to extend the town's primary Religious habitat; one group created an additional Church authority system, other inhabitants took steps to extend the habitats of the existing churches. Following these environmental manipulations, there was general agreement that opportunities to engage in Religious behavior increased in Midwest; and according to the centiurb measure, they increased 4.4 cu and were 194 percent as great in 1963–64 as they were in 1954–55. Many other instances of these kinds of independent validation of the centiurb measure of habitat extent could be cited.

A more general source of evidence of the adequacy of the centiurb measure is found in the correctness of predictions on the basis of behavior setting theory. According to the theory, certain differences in the behavior outputs of the towns can be predicted from differences in the extents of their habitats and the numbers of their inhabitants. The theory was originally stated and verified in terms of the independent variable, mean number of inhabitants per behavior setting; in the present study, we have substituted mean number of inhabitants per centiurb of habitat for the original independent variable, and the theory is again verified. It appears that measurement of habitat extent in centiurbs is at least as true a measure, within the terms of the theory, as measurement by behavior settings; and, we have noted, centiurbs have other advantages that make them preferable to behavior settings.

Common and Distinctive Genotypes

We regard the procedures for measuring the degree of commonality and distinctiveness of the town's habitats to be among the most promising methodological developments of the research. These procedures are based upon those developed earlier for classifying the behavior setting of the towns into genotypes (Barker, 1968, pp. 80–89); they are applied here to behavior setting genotypes rather than settings, and they have been extended to take into account the different degrees of commonality that occur across cultures. We spent much time and effort in developing the degree-of-commonality categories—in the hope, especially, that the genotypes with zero commonality, the unique genotypes of each town, would reveal fundamental habitat differences. We saw this as analogous to the processes by which a chemist isolates the unique from the common elements of compounds. Such unique elements are sometimes keys to the understanding of important differences in the actions of compounds—for example, as therapeutic agents. However, we have not been able to find in the unique genotypes of the towns any keys to an understanding of fundamental habitat differences. Others may be more successful.

Habitat-Claims for Human Components

In earlier work we identified the different zones of penetration occupied by human components of behavior settings (Barker, 1968, pp. 49–52). During the course of the present comparative research it became clear that behavior settings have identifiable structures within their penetration zones into which human components with prescribed properties (skills, information, strength, and so forth) must be fitted if the standing pattern of the setting, its program, is to occur. These structures are homologous with fixtures within an engine (clips, brackets, sockets, housings, slots) that are made for the accommodation of prescribed, functional parts (fuses, motors, electric cells, bearings, pulleys). We have called these behavior setting loci *habitat-claims*, to emphasize their dynamic nature—for, unlike engines, behavior settings have mechanisms for obtaining the requisite human components; habitat-claims are not passive structures. For example, the behavior setting Elliots Taxi searches (solicits, advertises) for a person with a chauffeur's license (the prescribed human component) to act (implement the taxi) as driver (habitat-claim operative); Elliots Taxi also initiates processes to secure (solicits, advertises for) persons with enough money (the prescribed human components) to ride (implement) the taxi as a fare (habitat-claim for customer). Without both, Elliots Taxi could not function and in time would disappear.

HABITAT VIABILITY

Studies of habitat change in terms of behavior settings cannot be satisfied with measures of net change in habitat extent, because it is obvious that in any appreciable period of time some habitat parts expand, others retract, and still others remain constant over time. Behavior settings are identifiable (tagged by unique names) and are more or less permanent; one can determine, therefore, for a period between specific times if a setting persists, ceases, or is initiated during the period. For example, the *Midwest Weekly* reported in the January 17, 1963, issue:

> Biggest news in the county seat this week was the purchase of the Denton Drug Store by Mr. and Mrs. "Chick" Ellson. The Ellsons now have the only drug store in Midwest.
> Mr. Denton closed his store at 6:00 p.m. January 14, 1963. This in

itself was a history-making event, for this store, as Mr. Denton had not closed his store that early for many years.

And we learn from the *Burlington Times* that on August 28, 1964:

> A meeting in the Town Hall, Yoredale, was addressed by Capt. R. H. M. Marriott, agent to the Castleton Conservative and Unionist Association. It was decided to form a branch, and the following temporary committee was elected: Chairman, Mr. S. Graves; vice-chairman, Miss F. Welsh; joint secretaries, Miss D. Dover and Miss R. Whittington; treasurer, Mr. L. Simpson; committee members, Mr. W. Simpson and Miss K. Lowes.

At first it appeared to us that identifying behavior settings that continue, cease, and are initiated during a period of time would be a simple matter. But when we came to make the census of 1954–55 behavior settings still existing in 1963–64, we were confronted with the kinds of problems we have already described in Chapter 2. Here then is another instance of a new idea and method (behavior settings and their identification) revealing new problems (simultaneous expansion, retraction, and continuity of habitat) that require new ideas and methods (accretion and erosion and their measurement).

CHAPTER 14

Panoramic Views of the Towns

$\sim\sim\sim\sim\sim\sim\sim\sim\sim\sim\sim\sim\sim\sim\sim\sim\sim\sim\sim\sim\sim$

$\mathbf{W}$e end this report of our study of the ecological psychology of Midwest and Yoredale with two comprehensive comparisons of the towns: the first, Outstanding Qualities, weights habitat and behavior almost equally; the second, Great American-English Behavior Generating Machine, emphasizes the behavior output of the towns.

OUTSTANDING QUALITIES

In previous chapters we have reported many particular measures of the habitats and behavior outputs of Midwest and Yoredale. We now present an integration of a number of habitat and output measures by means of two indexes: Relative Habitat Salience Index and Relative Habitat Productivity Index. Like composite photographs, these indexes obscure much detail, but they reveal important general similarities and differences between the towns, and important constancies and changes in the decade between the survey years.

Integration Procedures

RELATIVE HABITAT SALIENCE INDEX

This is an index of the general standing of Midwest's habitat relative to Yoredale's habitat, based on four habitat dimensions: Territorial

Range (TR), Extent of Primary Habitat (PH), Habitat-Claims for Operatives (H-C), and Variety of Habitat (V). A habitat dimension is assigned a rating of +1, *superior,* if it is greater in Midwest than in Yoredale but not proportionately greater than the total habitat of Midwest relative to the total habitat of Yoredale on the dimension; or a rating of +2, *unexpectedly superior,* if it is both greater in Midwest than in Yoredale and proportionately greater than the total habitat of Midwest relative to the total habitat of Yoredale. Similarly, habitats that are smaller in Midwest than in Yoredale are assigned index ratings of −1, *inferior,* and −2, *unexpectedly inferior.* Habitat measures that are equal in the two towns are rated 0.

In addition to the salience of Midwest relative to Yoredale in 1963–64, we have computed the relative salience of each town in 1963–64 relative to 1954–55 by procedures parallel in all respects to those for Midwest relative to Yoredale.

RELATIVE HABITAT PRODUCTIVITY INDEX

This index is a measure of the general standing with respect to behavior output of Midwest's habitat relative to Yoredale's habitat. It is constructed on the same principles as the habitat salience index but in terms of two instead of four dimensions: mean Person-Hours (P-H) per town inhabitant, and mean Claim-Operations (C-O) per town inhabitant.

In addition to the productivity of Midwest relative to Yoredale in 1963–64, we have computed the relative productivity of each town in 1963–64 relative to 1954–55.

RELATIVE STANDING OF THE TOWNS' HABITATS

We identify four categories of differential habitat on the basis of the salience and productivity indexes as follows: (*a*) Habitats that are *substantially more outstanding* in one town than the other have relative salience and productivity indexes of the same sign (both are positive or both are negative), and summed index values that are equal to half or more of the maximum possible value. This identifies differential habitats that are greater in one town than the other on many dimensions of both salience and productivity. (*b*) Habitats that are *more outstanding* in one town than the other have relative salience and productivity indcxcs of the same sign, with summed values less than half the maximum possible value. This identifies habitats that are greater in one town than the other in terms of both salience and productivity, but less so and/or on fewer dimensions than the habitats of the first category. Categories *a* and *b* can be conveniently described by terms frequently used by farmers in the vicinity of Midwest. For them a *big operation* is a farm that covers many acres, involves much and varied equipment, and produces much grain and/or livestock. We shall occasionally use the terms *much bigger operation* and *bigger operation* in the place, respectively, of *substantially more outstanding* and *more outstanding.* (*c*) Habitats of *equal standing* in the towns have relative salience and productivity indexes that are both zero. (*d*) Habitats with *discrepant standings* have relative salience and productivity indexes that differ in sign; they are more salient but less productive, or vice versa, in one town than the other.

PRESENTATION AND INTERPRETATION OF THE INDEXES

Important features of the indexes can be construed by referring to Table 14.1, where the data for action pattern habitats of Midwest and Yoredale are reported. The values are the ratings assigned the indicated dimensions and habitats on the basis of data reported in Chapters 5 and 8. For example, we see (R3, C1) that dimension TR contributes -2 to the relative salience of the action pattern habitat Government—that is, the TR of Government in Midwest is inferior to its TR in Yoredale, and unexpectedly so on the basis of the TR of Midwest's total habitat relative to the TR of Yoredale's total habitat. The sums of the cell values in the rows across the columns constitute the salience index for the indicated habitats; thus we find (R3, C5) that the salience index for Government is $+3$: Government has greater salience in Midwest than in Yoredale.

It should be noted that rating $+1$ indicates that a differential habitat (D) is greater in Midwest than in Yoredale on a stated dimension (d), thus $MW_{Dd}/YD_{Dd} > 1.0$; whereas rating $+2$ indicates that in addition to being greater than 1.0, this ratio is also greater than the MW/YD ratio for the towns' total habitats (T) on the same dimension: $MW_{Dd}/YD_{Dd} > MW_{Td}/YD_{Td}$. When the last relation occurs the MW_{Dd}/YD_{Dd} ratio is unexpectedly great, since the only basis available for predicting the relative dimensions of the towns' differential habitats is the relative dimensions of their total habitats. It is in this sense that the $+2$ and -2 ratings are unexpected and therefore deserving of greater weight in calculating the relative salience and productivity indexes.

The relative habitat salience and productivity indexes are measures of habitat *differences;* they directly add up the weighted superiorities ($+2$ or $+1$) and the inferiorities (-2 or -1) of Midwest's habitat relative to Yoredale's habitat across the habitat dimensions. In the familiar "wins and losses" accounting of contests, the salience index totes up Midwest's wins and losses compared with Yoredale's, providing the basis for statements analogous to "team A has a higher standing than team B; it is ahead on three events out of four." We have dealt with differences in the standing of Midwest relative to Yoredale rather than with the towns' standings because the differences simplify tabular presentation and reveal more economically the overall features of the towns' habitats with which we are concerned. One who wishes to know the standings of the towns rather than the differences in their standings can determine the former from the tables by summing the plus and minus cell values separately and assigning the sum of the pluses to Midwest (its superiorities) and the sum of the minuses to Yoredale (its superiorities). For example, in the case of Government, the sum of Midwest's superiorities is 5 and the sum of Yoredale's is 2; the Midwest-Yoredale difference is $+3$, as indicated in the table. And one who wishes to know the "scores" and some of the bases and conditions of the towns' standings with respect to "wins and losses" will find them in Chapters 5, 6, 9, and 10.

The indexes always state Midwest's habitat relative to Yoredale's habitat and a town's 1963–64 habitat relative to its 1954–55 habitat. For example, when we say that the salience index is −5, we mean that Midwest's habitat is less salient, as defined, than Yoredale's. A Midwest inferiority is, conversely, a Yoredale superiority, and it is frequently so identified in the discussion.

Habitat productivity in the tables and in the discussion always refers to mean output per *town inhabitant*—that is, to how much a differential habitat engages the behavior of a town's resident inhabitants (Midwesterners and Dalesmen). Thus, the perspectives we present are of Midwest and Midwesterners and of Yoredale and Dalesmen; they do not include out-of-town inhabitants (visitors and commuters).

The order of the differential habitats in the tables is, top to bottom, from those that are substantially more outstanding in Midwest than Yoredale through those that are equal or discrepant by the two indexes to those that are substantially more outstanding in Yoredale than in Midwest.

The definitions and table formats are similar for the change data; the order in the tables is from those differential habitats that were more outstanding in 1963–64 than in 1954–55 to those more outstanding in the earlier year.

Action Patterns

RELATIVE STANDING OF MIDWEST AND YOREDALE

According to the arithmetic of wins and losses that determines the overall standings of the towns' action patterns, Midwest leads Yoredale in Religion, Education, and Government; and Yoredale leads Midwest in Physical Health, Nutrition, and Aesthetics (Table 14.1). The towns differ most in the relative standings of their differential habitats for Religion and Physical Health.

Religion is a much bigger operation in Midwest than in Yoredale; important sites of its superiority are Religion Classes (chiefly Sunday School Classes), Religion Study Groups (mainly women's society meetings), and Business Meetings (of Church organizations). Physical Health is substantially more outstanding in Yoredale than in Midwest; important loci of its superiority are Chemists' Shops, Health Department Offices, Nurses' Offices and Services, and Physicians' Offices. The towns differ only a little less in the relative standings of their habitats for Education and Government and for Nutrition and Aesthetics. Important sites of Midwest's bigger Education operation are Elementary School Basic Classes and Religion Classes, and important loci of its more outstanding Government habitat are Government Offices. The greater salience and productivity of Nutrition in Yoredale resides to an impor-

Table 14.1
Action Pattern Habitats
Relative Salience and Productivity Indexes
Midwest vs. Yoredale, 1963–64

		Salience Dimensions[a]					Productivity Dimensions[c]		
		TR	PH	H-C	V	RHSI$_{MW,YD}$[b]	P-H	C-O	RHPI$_{MW,YD}$[d]
		(1)	(2)	(3)	(4)	(5)	(6)	(7)	(8)
(1)	Religion	+2	+2	+2	−1	+5	+1	+1	+2
(2)	Education	+2	+2	+1	−2	+3	+2	+2	+4
(3)	Government	−2	+2	+2	+1	+3	+2	+2	+4
(4)	Personal Appearance	−2	−2	+2	+2	0	−2	+2	0
(5)	Social Contact	−1	−2	+2	−2	−3	+1	+2	+3
(6)	Professional In- volvement	−2	−2	−2	+2	−4	+1	+1	+2
(7)	Recreation	−2	−2	+1	−2	−5	+1	+1	+2
(8)	Business	−2	−2	−2	−2	−8	+1	+1	+2
(9)	Aesthetics	−2	−2	+2	+1	−1	−2	+1	−1
(10)	Nutrition	−2	−2	+1	−2	−5	−2	+1	−1
(11)	Physical Health	+1	−2	−2	−2	−5	−2	−2	−4

[a] Habitat dimensions on which salience index is based. TR: Territorial range, cu; PH: Extent of primary habitat, cu; H-C: Habitat-claims for operatives, no.; V: Variety, no. genotypes.
[b] RHSI$_{MW,YD}$: Relative habitat salience index, Midwest relative to Yoredale.
[c] Behavior outputs on which productivity index is based. P-H: Mean person-hours per town inhabitant; C-O: Mean claim-operations per town inhabitant.
[d] RHPI$_{MW,YD}$: Relative habitat productivity index, Midwest relative to Yoredale.

tant degree in Grocery Stores, Meat Markets, Milk Delivery Services, and Pubs and Dining Rooms; important loci of Yoredale's bigger Aesthetic operations are Art Classes, Antique Shops, Photographic Shops, and Wallpapering and Painting Services.

The remaining action patterns are either of equal standing in the towns (Personal Appearance) or of smaller salience and greater productivity in Midwest than in Yoredale (Social Contact, Professional Involvement, Recreation, Business).

CHANGES

The period between the surveys was a time of flowering for most of Midwest's action pattern resources and outputs; 7 action patterns were substantially more outstanding, and only 1 was less outstanding, in 1963–64 than in 1954–55 (Table 14.2). Bigger operations in 1963–64 were (with important sites of their increments in parentheses): Education (Religion, Physical Education, and Music Classes); Physical Health (Physical Education Classes, Optometrists' Offices); Aesthetics (Music Classes and Competitions); Professional Involvement (Day Care Homes and Nurseries, Restaurants); Social Contact (many genotypes); Government (Business Meetings, Machinery Repair Shops); and Nutrition (Water Supply Plants, Taverns, Restaurants). These action patterns in-

Table 14.2
Action Pattern Habitats
Relative Salience and Productivity Indexes
Midwest, '63 vs. 54

		Salience Dimensions					Productivity Dimensions		
		TR	PH	H-C	V	RHSI$_{MW63,54}$	P-H	C-O	RHIP$_{MW63,54}$
		(1)	(2)	(3)	(4)	(5)	(6)	(7)	(8)
(1)	Education	+2	+2	+1	+2	+7	+2	+2	+4
(2)	Phys. Health	+2	+2	+1	+2	+7	+2	+2	+4
(3)	Aesthetics	+2	+2	+1	+2	+7	+2	+1	+3
(4)	Professional Involvement	+1	+1	+1	+2	+5	+2	+2	+4
(5)	Social Contact	+1	+2	+2	+1	+6	+1	+1	+2
(6)	Government	+1	+1	+1	+1	+4	+2	+2	+4
(7)	Nutrition	+2	−2	+1	+2	+3	+2	+1	+3
(8)	Recreation	+2	+2	+1	+2	+7	−2	+2	0
(9)	Pers. Appearance	+2	+2	+1	+1	+6	−2	−2	−4
(10)	Religion	+2	+2	+1	−1	+4	−2	−2	−4
(11)	Business	+1	−2	+1	−2	−2	−2	+1	−1

Note: See notes, Table 14.1.

filtrated Midwest's habitat at greater rates than the habitat as a whole increased during the decade.

Business was a smaller operation in Midwest in 1963–64 than in 1954–55, due in important respects to the decline of Animal Feed Stores, Farm Implement Agencies, and Grocery Stores. The remaining 3 action patterns—Recreation, Personal Appearance, and Religion—gained in salience but declined or did not change in productivity during the decade.

As with Midwest, the decade under consideration was a time of enrichment of Yoredale's habitat by many action patterns; 6 were substantially more outstanding, and none less outstanding, in 1963–64 than in 1954–55 (Table 14.3). Bigger operations in 1963–64 were: Social Contact (many genotypes); Aesthetics (Craft and Art Classes); Physical Health (First Aid and Physical Education Classes); Nutrition (Cooking Classes, Egg Packing Plants, Bakeries, Grocery Stores); Business (Commercial Company Offices, Commission Agents, Insurance Offices); and Government (Business Meetings, Post Offices, Physicians' Offices, School Administrators Offices). There were 4 action patterns which gained in salience but declined or did not change in productivity—Recreation, Education, Professional Involvement, and Religion—and one, Personal Appearance, which declined in salience and increased in productivity.

There are striking similarities in the changes that occurred in the towns' action pattern habitats. Of those that were much bigger operations in 1963–64 than in 1954–55 (7 in Midwest and 6 in Yoredale), 5

Table 14.3
Action Pattern Habitats
Relative Salience and Productivity Indexes
Yoredale, '63 vs. '54

		Salience Dimensions					Productivity Dimensions		
		TR	PH	H-C	V	RHSI$_{YD63,54}$	P-H	C-O	RHPI$_{YD63,54}$
		(1)	(2)	(3)	(4)	(5)	(6)	(7)	(8)
(1)	Social Contact	+2	+2	+2	+2	+8	+2	+1	+3
(2)	Aesthetics	+2	+2	+1	+2	+7	+2	+1	+3
(3)	Phys. Health	+2	+2	+2	+2	+8	−1	+2	+1
(4)	Nutrition	+1	+1	+1	+2	+5	−1	+2	+1
(5)	Business	+1	+2	+1	+1	+5	+2	−1	+1
(6)	Government	+2	+1	+1	+1	+5	+2	−1	+1
(7)	Recreation	+1	+2	+2	+2	+7	−2	+2	0
(8)	Education	+2	+2	+1	+2	+7	−1	−1	−2
(9)	Professional Involvement	+2	+1	+1	+1	+5	−1	+1	0
(10)	Religion	+2	−2	+1	+1	+2	+2	−2	0
(11)	Pers. Appearance	+2	+1	−2	−2	−1	+2	0	+2

Note: See notes, Table 14.1.

were common to the two towns: Physical Health, Aesthetics, Social Contact, Government, and Nutrition. And of the action patterns that increased in salience but not in productivity (3 in Midwest and 4 in Yoredale), 2 were common to the towns: Recreation and Religion.

But there are striking differences, too, the most extreme being Business, Personal Appearance, and Education. Over the decade, Business became less outstanding in Midwest and more outstanding in Yoredale, Personal Appearance became more salient and less productive in Midwest, and vice versa in Yoredale; and Education became more outstanding in Midwest, whereas it increased in salience and decreased in productivity in Yoredale.

We find it impressive that towns so far separated as Midwest and Yoredale exhibit similar changes in 7 of the 11 action pattern habitats, and sharp differences in only 3 of them. We speculate that the similarities are manifestations of very general, cross-national culture changes, and that the differences reflect more limited, local conditions. On the whole, the decade 1954–55 to 1963–64 was one of greater and more harmonious expansion of Midwest's than of Yoredale's action pattern habitats: more of Midwest's than of Yoredale's action patterns were much bigger operations in 1963–64 than in 1954–55 (7 vs. 6, respectively); the extents of Midwest's increments were greater than those of Yoredale's (mean 9 vs. 8, respectively); and 3 of Midwest's and 5 of Yoredale's action patterns changed discrepantly in salience and productivity.

The greater harmony in Midwest may be due to its greater local autonomy. The imposition of the new school upon Yoredale by the county education authority appears to have been one important source of the town's less harmonious development; although located in Yoredale, it is almost completely separated from the community except for the adolescent residents who attend.

Behavior Mechanisms

RELATIVE STANDING OF MIDWEST AND YOREDALE

Midwest leads Yoredale in Affective Behavior, and Yoredale leads Midwest in Gross Motor Activity; the towns' standings with respect to Talking and Manipulation are discrepant (Table 14.4).

Important sites of Midwest's affective superiority are Basketball Games, Judges' Chambers, and Day Care Homes and Nurseries. It is important to note, however, that the territorial range of Affective Behavior is smaller in Midwest than in Yoredale, and smaller than expected (T14.4; R1; C1). This means that there is less emotional expressiveness in Midwest than in Yoredale, *except* in its greater number of more heavily inhabited settings where emotional expression is explicitly programed, such as Basketball Games, with their special "cheering sections" with "cheerleaders" (habitat-claim for operatives). Gross Motor Activity is a much bigger operation in Yoredale than in Midwest; important loci of Yoredale's superiority are Trafficways (streets and sidewalks are for feet in Yoredale, for wheels in Midwest), Milk Bottling Services (with heavy milk churns to lift), Hotels (with dining rooms above the ground floor, and much lugging of equipment up and down narrow stairs), and Machinery Repair Shops.

CHANGES

The period between the surveys was a decade of little change in the relative standings of the towns' behavior mechanisms (Tables 14.5;

Table 14.4
Behavior Mechanism Habitats
Relative Salience and Productivity Indexes
Midwest vs. Yoredale, 1963–64

		Salience Dimensions					Productivity Dimensions		
		TR	PH	H-C	V	$RHSI_{MW,YD}$	P-H	C-O	$RHPI_{MW,YD}$
		(1)	(2)	(3)	(4)	(5)	(6)	(7)	(8)
(1)	Affective Behavior	−2	+2	+2	+2	+4	+2	+2	+4
(2)	Manipulation	−2	−1	+2	−2	−3	+2	+1	+3
(3)	Talking	−2	−2	+1	−1	−4	+1	+1	+2
(4)	Gross Motor	−2	−2	−2	−2	−8	−2	+1	−1

Note: See notes, Table 14.1.

Table 14.5
Behavior Mechanism Habitats
Relative Salience and Productivity Indexes
Midwest '63 vs. '54

		Salience Dimensions					Productivity Dimensions		
		TR	PH	H-C	V	$RHSI_{MW63,54}$	P-H	C-O	$RHPI_{MW63,54}$
		(1)	(2)	(3)	(4)	(5)	(6)	(7)	(8)
(1)	Affective Behavior	+2	+2	+1	+2	+7	−2	+1	−1
(2)	Manipulation	+1	−2	+2	+1	+2	−2	+2	0
(3)	Gross Motor	+1	−2	+1	−2	−2	−2	+1	−1
(4)	Talking	+2	−2	+1	−2	−1	−2	−2	−4

Note: See notes, Table 14.1.

Table 14.6
Behavior Mechanism Habitats
Relative Salience and Productivity Indexes
Yoredale, '63 vs. '54

		Salience Dimensions					Productivity Dimensions		
		TR	PH	H-C	V	$RHSI_{YD63,54}$	P-H	C-O	$RHPI_{YD63,54}$
		(1)	(2)	(3)	(4)	(5)	(6)	(7)	(8)
(1)	Affective Behavior	+2	+1	+2	+1	+6	−2	+1	−1
(2)	Talking	+2	+1	+1	+1	+5	−2	+1	−1
(3)	Gross Motor	+1	−2	+2	+1	+2	−2	+1	−1
(4)	Manipulation	+2	−2	+1	+1	+2	−2	+1	−1

Note: See notes, Table 14.1.

14.6). Gross Motor Activity and Talking became less outstanding in Midwest; all others changed discrepantly in both towns.

Authority Systems

RELATIVE STANDING OF MIDWEST AND YOREDALE

Midwest leads in Church and Voluntary Association authority systems; Yoredale does not lead in any authority system. (Table 14.7). Important sites of the superiority of Midwest's Churches are Vocal Music Classes (choir practices), Plays and Programs (Sunday School, Christmas, and Promotion Programs), Religious Fellowship Meetings (youth meetings), and Business Meetings (of church organizations). Important loci of the higher standing of Midwest's Voluntary Associations are Baseball Games, Bowling Games, Golf Games, Dinners and Banquets, Card Parties, Lodge Meetings, and Scout Meetings. Government Agencies have greater salience and smaller productivity in Midwest,

Table 14.7
Authority System Habitats
Relative Salience and Productivity Indexes
Midwest vs. Yoredale, 1963–64

		Salience Dimensions[a]				Productivity Dimensions		
		Extent	H-C	V	RHSI$_{MW,YD}$	P-H	C-O	RHPI$_{MW,YD}$
		(1)	(2)	(3)	(4)	(5)	(6)	(7)
(1)	Churches	+2	+2	+2	+6	+2	+1	+3
(2)	Voluntary Assns.	+2	+1	−2	+1	+2	+2	+4
(3)	Govt. Agencies	+2	+2	+2	+6	−2	+1	−1
(4)	Schools	−2	+1	−2	−3	+2	+2	+4
(5)	Priv. Enterprises	−2	−2	−1	−5	+1	+1	+2

[a] Authority system habitats have only three salience dimensions; there is no dimension corresponding to the primary habitat dimensions of action patterns and behavior mechanisms.
Note: See notes. Table 14.1.

and Schools and Private Enterprises have smaller salience and greater productivity in Midwest.

CHANGES

The period between the survey years was a decade of the Schools in both Midwest and Yoredale; those parts of their habitats under the aegis of the Schools increased at greater rates than the towns' total habitats. Schools were substantially more outstanding in both towns in 1963–64 than in 1954–55 (Table 14.8; 14.9). There is one other similarity in authority system changes; Churches gained in salience and regressed in productivity in both towns. The other authority systems changed differently in the towns, and Voluntary Associations were most

Table 14.8
Authority System Habitats
Relative Salience and Productivity Indexes
Midwest, '63 vs. '54

		Salience Dimensions[a]				Productivity Dimensions		
		Extent	H-C	V	RHSI$_{MW63,54}$	P-H	C-O	RHPI$_{MW63,54}$
		(1)	(2)	(3)	(4)	(5)	(6)	(7)
(1)	Schools	+2	+2	+2	+6	+2	+2	+4
(2)	Voluntary Assns.	+2	+2	+2	+6	+2	+2	+4
(3)	Churches	+2	+1	+1	+4	−2	−2	−4
(4)	Govt. Agencies	+1	+1	+1	+3	−2	−1	−3
(5)	Priv. Enterprises	−2	+1	+1	0	−2	−1	−3

[a] See footnote *a*, Table 14.7.
Note: See notes, Table 14.1.

Table 14.9
Authority System Habitats
Relative Salience and Productivity Indexes
Yoredale, '63 vs. '54

		Salience Dimensions[a]				Productivity Dimensions		
		Extent	H-C	V	$RHSI_{YD63,54}$	P-H	C-O	$RHPI_{YD63,54}$
		(1)	(2)	(3)	(4)	(5)	(6)	(7)
(1)	Schools	+2	+2	+2	+6	+2	+2	+4
(2)	Churches	+1	+1	+2	+4	−1	0	−1
(3)	Govt. Agencies	−2	+1	+1	0	−1	+2	+1
(4)	Voluntary Assns.	−2	+1	+1	0	−2	+1	−1
(5)	Priv. Enterprises	+1	−2	−2	−3	−1	0	−1

[a] See footnote a, Table 14.7.
Note: See notes, Table 14.1.

divergent; in Midwest they were much bigger operations in 1963–64 than in 1954–55, whereas they changed very little in Yoredale.

Autonomy

RELATIVE STANDING OF MIDWEST AND YOREDALE

The story of autonomy is short and simple: Midwest is more of a local town than Yoredale (Table 14.10). Habitats of High and Medium Local Autonomy were substantially more outstanding in Midwest than in Yoredale, and habitats of Low Local Autonomy were substantially more outstanding in Yoredale. Important behavior setting genotypes that were locally organized, programed, and financed in Midwest, and organized, programed, and financed at a distance from Yoredale, were Elementary School Basic Classes, Fire Stations, Hotels, Libraries, Nursing Homes, and Trafficways.

Table 14.10
Autonomy Habitats
Relative Salience and Productivity Indexes
Midwest vs. Yoredale, 1963–64

		Salience Dimensions[a]				Productivity Dimensions		
		Extent	H-C	V	$RHSI_{MW,YD}$	P-H	C-O	$RHPI_{MW,YD}$
		(1)	(2)	(3)	(4)	(5)	(6)	(7)
(1)	High local autonomy	+2	+2	+2	+6	+2	+2	+4
(2)	Medium local autonomy	+2	+2	−1	+3	+1	+2	+3
(3)	Low local autonomy	−2	−2	−2	−6	−2	−2	−4

[a] Local autonomy habitats have only three salience dimensions; there is no dimension corresponding to the primary habitat dimensions of action patterns and behavior mechanisms.
Note: See notes, Table 14.1.

Table 14.11
Autonomy Habitats
Relative Salience and Productivity Indexes
Midwest, '63 vs. '54

		Salience Dimensions[a]				Productivity Dimensions		
		Extent	H-C	V	$RHSI_{MW63,54}$	P-H	C-O	$RHPI_{MW63,54}$
		(1)	(2)	(3)	(4)	(5)	(6)	(7)
(1)	Medium Local Autonomy	+2	+2	+2	+6	+2	+2	+4
(2)	High Local Autonomy	+1	+1	+2	+4	−2	+1	−1
(3)	Low Local Autonomy	+1	+1	+1	+3	−2	+2	0

[a] See footnote *a*, Table 14.10.
Note: See notes, Table 14.1.

Table 14.12
Autonomy Habitats
Relative Salience and Productivity Indexes
Yoredale, '63 vs. '54

		Salience Dimensions[a]				Productivity Dimensions		
		Extent	H-C	V	$RHSI_{YD63,54}$	P-H	C-O	$RHPI_{YD63,54}$
		(1)	(2)	(3)	(4)	(5)	(6)	(7)
(1)	Medium local autonomy	+1	+2	+2	+5	+2	+2	+4
(2)	Low local autonomy	+2	+2	+2	+6	−2	+2	0
(3)	High local autonomy	−2	−2	−2	−6	+2	−2	0

[a] See footnote *a*, Table 14.11.
Note: See notes, Table 14.1.

CHANGES

In the decade between the surveys, Medium Local Autonomy flourished; in both towns habitats controlled at regional levels were substantially more outstanding in 1963–64 than in 1954–55 (Tables 14.11; 14.12). During this period, distantly controlled habitats increased in salience in both towns, but not in productivity. On the other hand, the towns changed quite differently in locally controlled habitats, which increased in salience and decreased in productivity in Midwest and did not change in Yoredale.

Report Cards

We now offer summaries of the most pervasive similarities and differences between the towns and years in terms of the analogy of wins and losses. These are in the form of end-of-season reports on the relative standings of Midwest and Yoredale in 1963–64, and end-of-decade reports on the relative standings of each town in 1963–64 and 1954–55. In these reports, an *event* is a differential habitat (an action pattern, a behavior mechanism, an authority system, a local autonomy category); a *win* is a more outstanding differential habitat in a stated town or year; a *tie* is a differential habitat with equal salience and productivity standings in the towns or years; a *draw* is a differential habitat with discrepant salience and productivity standings in the towns or years; a *winning margin* is the sum of the salience and productivity indexes of a winning habitat; this is reported in the parenthesis following each winning event. These are the standings of the towns as determined by town inhabitants; the contributions of visitors and commuters to the towns' outputs are not included.

END-OF-SEASON REPORT 1963–64: MIDWEST VS. YOREDALE

Ties: Personal Appearance (1 tie)

Draws: Social Contact, Professional Involvement, Recreation, Business, Manipulation, Talking, Government Agencies, Schools, Private Enterprises (9 draws)

Wins: Midwest   Yoredale

Midwest	Yoredale
High Local Autonomy (12)	Low Local Autonomy (12)
Churches (11)	Physical Health (9)
Affective Behavior (8)	Gross Motor Activity (9)
Religion (7)	Nutrition (6)
Education (7)	Aesthetics (2)
Government (7)	
Medium Local Autonomy (7)	
Voluntary Associations (6)	

	MW	YD
Number of wins	8	5
Sum of winning margins	64	38
Mean of winning margins	8.0	7.6

END-OF-DECADE REPORT, MIDWEST: 1963–64 VS. 1954–55

Ties: No ties

Draws: Recreation, Personal Appearance, Religion, Affective Behavior, Manipulation, Churches, Government Agencies, Private Enterprises, High local autonomy, Low local autonomy (10 draws)

Wins: 1963–64   1954–55

1963–64	1954–55
Schools (12)	Talking (5)
Voluntary Associations (12)	Gross Motor Activity (3)
Medium Local Autonomy (12)	Business (3)
Education (11)	
Physical Health (11)	
Aesthetics (10)	
Professional Involvement (9)	
Social Contact (8)	
Government (8)	
Nutrition (6)	

	1963–64	1954–55
Number of wins	10	3
Sum of winning margins	99	11
Mean of winning margins	9.9	3.7

END-OF-DECADE REPORT, YOREDALE: 1963–64 VS. 1954–55

Ties: No ties

Draws: Recreation, Education, Professional Involvement, Religion, Personal Appearance, Affective Behavior, Talking, Gross Motor Activity, Manipulation, Churches, Government Agencies, Voluntary Associations, Low local autonomy, High local autonomy (14 draws)

Wins: 1963–64   1954–55

Schools (12)   Private Enterprises (5)
Social Contact (11)
Aesthetics (10)
Physical Health (9)
Medium Local Autonomy (9)
Nutrition (6)
Business (6)
Government (6)

	1963–64	1954–55
Number of wins	8	1
Sum of winning margins	69	5
Mean of winning margins	8.5	5

THE GREAT AMERICAN-ENGLISH BEHAVIOR GENERATING MACHINE

Important differences between the Models MW and YD, 1963–64 (Figure 14.1) may be briefly summarized: Model MW operates with 63 percent as many human components as Model YD, but its almost equal habitat capacity and its greater array of habitat-claims for operatives produced in a year 79 percent as many person-hours, 158 percent as many claim-operations, and 168 percent as many leader-acts as Model YD. The packaging is different, too. Model MW puts more behavior into each town inhabitant than Model YD: 125 percent as many person-hours, 250 percent as many claim-operations, 260 percent as many leader-acts. No data are yet available on component wastage and operating inefficiency through breakage, overheating, and sedimentation; but one interested in producing human components that are actively and strenuously involved in public activities without regard for possible side effects will find model MW better than Model YD.

Not only do the Midwest and Yoredale models of the Great American–English Behavior Generating Machine produce different amounts of behavior packaged in units of different dimensions, the qualities possessed by the behavior in the packages differ also. We find for example that the lives of Dalesmen (the packages) contain 9.3 hours

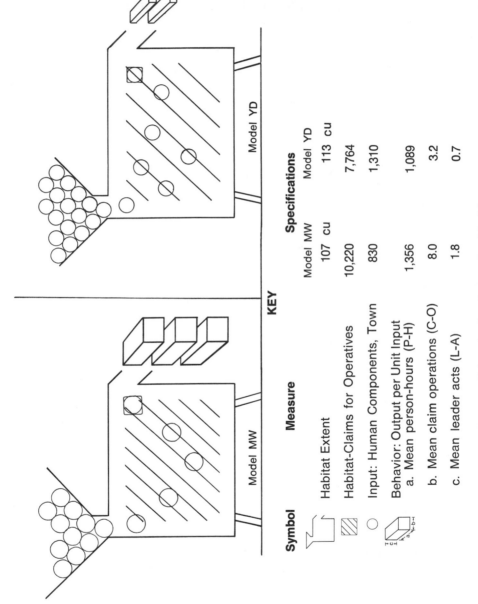

KEY

Symbol	Measure	Specifications	
		Model MW	Model YD
	Habitat Extent	107 cu	113 cu
	Habitat-Claims for Operatives	10,220	7,764
	Input: Human Components, Town	830	1,310
	Behavior: Output per Unit Input		
	a. Mean person-hours (P-H)	1,356	1,089
	b. Mean claim operations (C-O)	8.0	3.2
	c. Mean leader acts (L-A)	1.8	0.7

Model MW   Model YD

FIGURE 14.1. Great American-English Behavior Generating Machine.

of large muscle activity per week, on the average (Gross Motor Activity; walking, lifting, carrying, and so forth), whereas the lives of Midwesterners contain 7.7 hours of such behavior (T9.25; R7; C3,4); and we discover that the lives of Dalesmen contain 3.1 hours of school behavior per week (School Authority System; attending school classes, school games, school committees, and so forth), whereas the lives of Midwesterners contain 7.2 hours of such behavior (T10.7; R7; C3,4). In these respects Yoredale behavior differs from Midwest behavior: living is more muscular in Yoredale by a factor of 1.2, and it is more school-connected in Midwest by a factor of 2.3. The qualities in which Midwest's behavior surpasses Yoredale's are listed in Table 14.13, together with the ratios of Midwest's superiority (MW measure/YD measure).

Midwest's behavior packages greatly exceed Yoredale's in Beneficent Child and Adolescent qualities; each is over 13 times more abundant in Midwest's than in Yoredale's behavior product. These occur because Midwesterners behave on the average about one hour a month, and Dalesmen about one hour a year, in behavior settings whose programs are implemented largely by children; and Midwesterners behave for approximately one hour every ten days, whereas Dalesmen behave for approximately one hour every five months, in settings whose pro-

Table 14.13
Qualities of Behavior Produced by the
Great American–English Behavior Generating Machine
I: Qualities Produced in Greater Abundance by Model MW

Quality	Ratio of MW's Superiority ($MW_{meas.}/YD_{meas.}$)
Beneficent Child	14.50
Beneficent Adolescent	13.40
Affective Behavior	2.56
Leader Act	2.53[a]
Claim-Operation	2.50[a]
Education	2.36
School	2.34
Government	2.17
High Local Autonomy	2.12
Voluntary Association	1.80
Manipulation	1.57
Church	1.54
Social Contact	1.46
Private Enterprise	1.22
Religion	1.22
Medium Local Autonomy	1.20
Professional Involvement	1.18
Recreation	1.17
Business	1.06
Talking	1.03

[a] The measure in these cases is mean number of acts or operations per town inhabitant; all other measures in T14.13 and 14.14 are mean person-hours per town inhabitant.

Table 14.14
Qualities of Behavior Produced by the
Great American-English Behavior Generating Machine
II: Qualities Produced in Greater Abundance by Model YD

Quality	Ratio of YD's Superiority (YD/MW)
Low local Autonomy	3.99
Government Agency	1.49
Physical Health	1.28
Nutrition	1.27
Gross Motor Activity	1.21
Personal Appearance	1.12
Aesthetics	1.04

grams are implemented largely by adolescents. These findings mean that Midwesterners live for about one hour a week in public settings whose atmospheres are determined largely by adolescents or children exercising the power of operatives of concerts, games, plays, food sales, work days, and so forth whereas Dalesmen live for about three hours a year in such settings. The tone of public life in some Midwest settings is regularly set by its youth. Although Yoredale receives great infusions of young vibrations on very limited, special occasions (Sports Day, Speech Day, Tournament of Song), the general tone of Yoredale's public life is innocent of youthful qualities on a regular basis (Barker and Gump, 1964).

There are other qualities that are more than twice as abundant in Midwest as in Yoredale; more than twice as much of the living that occurs in Midwest is strongly colored by the responsibilities of Leadership and Claim-Operations, and by Affective, Education, School, Government, and High Local Autonomy qualities.

Yoredale surpasses Midwest in the behavior qualities listed in Table 14.14. Yoredale's greatest superiority to Midwest is in the quality related to Low Local Autonomy, which colors almost 4 times as much of the living of Dalesmen as of Midwesterners. In addition, Government Agency, Health, Nutrition, and Gross Motor qualities are more abundant in Yoredale, by factors of 1.5 to 1.2.

The behavior produced by the MW model of the Great American-English Behavior Generating Machine has 20 of the 27 qualities we have studied in greater abundance than the behavior produced by the YD model. This is not out of line with the greater total output of model MW, amounting in terms of person-hours per town inhabitant to 125 percent of the output of model YD. However, MW's general superiority does not occur uniformly with respect to the various qualities of behavior; the 11 qualities of Table 14.13 with ratios over 1.25 have still greater relative abundance in the output of model MW than is expected on the basis of its greater total output than model YD (Leader Acts and Claim-Operations are not included in these counts, as they are not measured in terms of person-hours). The remaining 14 qualities have less relative abundance than expected in the output of model MW.

UNFINISHED BUSINESS

We end this research effort and this report of its methods and findings with an intense awareness of uncompleted tasks: Many of the data we present are not analyzed and marshaled to bear on significant issues. What is the significance of Midwest and Yoredale for American and English life? Do they represent America and England at the behavior setting level? What are the origins of the towns' habitat differences? Why does Midwest, with 830 inhabitants, have 51 more Voluntary Association settings that demand attention and attendance than Yoredale, with 1310 inhabitants?

The list could be continued. But readers who have followed us thus far may know more about Midwest and Yoredale in terms of behavior settings than they wish to know. So we stop with the hope that others may be able to work profitably the data tailings we leave behind, to use the ideas and techniques in other studies and especially in investigating the generality of our findings for America and England, to take next steps in discovering what lies behind immediate habitat-behavior relationships, and more generally to bring the environment of human, molar action into studies of differences and changes in communities and institutions.

Catalogue of Midwest Behavior Setting Genotypes, 1954–55 and 1963–64; Behavior Settings, 1963–64

$\mathbf{A}$ll behavior setting genotypes occurring in Midwest in either survey year are listed by identification number and name, and each genotype is described by a precis of the programs of its different penetration zones from 1 to 6 (see Chapter 2). Genotypes unique to one of the survey years are identified with a special symbol placed adjacent to the identification number: ° unique to 1963–64, did not occur in 1954–55; * unique to 1954–55, did not occur in 1963–64.

Following each genotype description we report *for 1963–64 only* the habitat extent in centiurbs (cu) and the behavior settings belonging to the genotype, listed by number and name. Each behavior setting name begins with the identification of the particular authority system under which it operates: *Chamber of Commerce* Halloween Celebration Parade; *Church of England* Garden Fete; *Midwest City* Library.

Words indicating age groups vary in their meaning; for example,

Junior is used differently in Midwest and Yoredale; therefore the age range of the target inhabitants is indicated where appropriate: Peewee League Team (*8–11*) Baseball Practice; County Primary School Upper Junior (*9–11*) Academic Class; High School Junior (*16*) Car Wash. Persons and places in the behavior setting identification are coded.

The catalogue of Midwest's behavior setting genotypes for 1954–55 and 1963–64 constitutes a comprehensive description of the scope of the town's habitat in this decade, and the behavior setting lists for 1963–64 provide concrete documentation of its constituents in the last survey year.

1. Abstract and Title Company Offices. Abstracter (6) manages office and assistant (4) carries out office routines; both search files and records in County Clerks and Register of Deeds office for information about land titles, prepare summary statement (abstract) of the successive conveyances and other facts upon which a client's title to a piece of land rests, sell title insurance; land buyers and sellers (3) ask for title records, bring land identification, pay for services, discuss issues; 0.51 cu.
   1. Pintner Abstract and Title Company
2. Agricultural Advisers Offices. County agent (5) manages office, advises farmers, prepares material and programs, collects, analyzes, and evaluates agricultural data, plans 4-H program; home economics agent (5) manages office, prepares material and lectures on home and family life, distributes literature, advises leaders and homemakers; secretary (4) carries out office routines; interested citizens and members of farm organizations (3) consult, obtain material and literature; 0.43 cu.
   1. County Agricultural Extension Office
*3. Agricultural Economics Classes. County Agricultural Agent (6) is in charge of arrangement for meeting, introduces farm management specialist; specialist (4) teaches regarding economic principles of profitable farm management to class of farmers; farmers (3) listen, discuss, ask questions.
4. Agronomy Classes. County agricultural agent (6) is in charge of arrangements, introduces agronomy specialist; specialist (4) teaches regarding soil fertility, crops, etc.; farmers (3) or 4-H members (3) listen, discuss, ask questions; 0.10 cu.
   1. Agricultural Extension Agronomy Short Course
   2. Agricultural Extension 4-H Crop Judging School
°5. Animal Feed Mills. Manager (6) manages operation, operates mill, sells fertilizer, etc.; employees (4) fill fuel tank, load trucks, engage in office routines; farmer members (3) bring grain to be ground, weigh in, buy products, pay for service and materials; 0.61 cu.
   1. Midwest County Cooperative Feed Mill
6. Animal Feed Stores. Feed store proprietor (5) manages store,

buys and sells feed and feed additives, loads feed into trucks and cars; insurance agent (5) sells insurance, arranges for adjustor, engages in office routines; customers (3) buy and pay for feed, buy insurance or make claims; 0.54 cu.

    1. Hopkins Feed Store and Insurance Agency

7. Animal Husbandry Classes. County agricultural agent (6) is in charge of arrangements, introduces livestock specialist; specialist (4) teaches regarding livestock; farmers or 4-H members (3) listen, ask questions, discuss; 0.20 cu.

    1. Agricultural Extension Dairy Short Course
    2. Agricultural Extension 4-H Meat Judging Training School
    3. Agricultural Extension Livestock School
    4. Agricultural Extension Swine Producers School

8. Athletic Equipment Rooms. Coaches (6 or 5), both local and visiting prepare for physical education and sports, give out equipment, consult with individuals; athletes (3) get equipment for sports; 0.28 cu.

    1. High School Coaches Room, Men
    2. High School Coaches Room, Women

9. Attorneys Offices. Lawyers (6 or 5) initiate legal actions, prepare legal defense in civil and criminal cases, give legal advice, draw up contracts, prepare wills, prepare federal and state income tax returns, manage office; secretary (4) carries out office routines; clients (3) seek and pay for advice and service; 1.70 cu.

    1. Fowke Attorney Office
    2. French and French Attorneys and Abstract and Title Company
    3. Wiley Attorney Office
    4. Wolf Attorney Office

10. Auction Sales, Household Furnishings and General Merchandise. Sellers (5) determine what is to be sold, arrange for display articles to be sold; auctioneer (5) determines order of sale, calls for bids, sells to highest bidder; clerks (4) record bidder and accept payment; customers (3) bid, pay clerk, remove purchased articles, converse; 0.10 cu.

    1. Household Auction Sales
    2. Midwest Implement Company Auction Sale

°11. Auditing and Investigating Company Offices. Proprietor (6) consults with investigative staff in office and by phone, consults with clients via telephone, manages office; employees (4) get directions; clients (3) seek information; 0.46 cu.

    1. Bonded Audit Service Business Office, Blandson

°12. Automobile Washing Services. Teacher and student in charge (5) direct activities and help; other students (4) wash, sweep, polish, get cars from customers, deliver washed cars, accept payment; customers (3) arrange for and pay for having car washed; 0.10 cu.

    1. High School Junior (16) Car Wash
    2. High School Senior (17) Car Wash

13. Award Ceremonies. Master of ceremonies (6) organizes meeting, presents awards to the qualified persons with appropriate remarks; awardees (4) accept awards; audience (2) applaud; 0.15 cu.
    1. Boy Bowlers (11–13) Awards and Refreshments
    2. High School Award Assembly
    3. Masonic Lodge Public Presentation of 50 Year Award

14. Bakery Services, to Order. Baker (6) prepares and bakes food on order, accepts pay; customers (3) order, pick up, and pay for food; 0.10 cu.
    1. Mrs. Lyon Home Bakery

15. Banks. President (6) manages all operations, makes loans, gives financial advice, provides credit information; vice-president (4) makes loans, sells insurance; cashier (4) cashes checks, receives deposits, provides access to safe deposit, keeps records; clerks (4) engage in office routines; bank examiners (4) come at intervals to examine the routines, the assets and liabilities of the bank in relation to legal standards; customers (3) deposit and withdraw money, arrange for or pay back loans, seek advice, use safe deposit boxes, and converse; 0.43 cu.
    1. Midwest State Bank

16. Barbershops. Barber (6) cuts hair, sells products for grooming, manages shop; customers (3) wait for service, converse, have hair cut, pay barber; 0.77 cu.
    1. Keith Barbershop
    2. Riffle Barbershop

17. Baseball Games. Coach (6) or coaches (5) arrange game or practice and instruct players; players (4) play the game according to rules for baseball or softball; umpire (4) calls "strikes, balls, safe, out"; audience (2) cheer team, comment on play; 0.85 cu.
    1. Elementary Upper School (12–13) Baseball Game out of town.
    2. Girls Team Baseball (Softball) Game
    3. Girls Team Baseball (Softball) Game out of town
    4. Girls Team Baseball (Softball) Practice
    5. Little League Team (12–14) Baseball Practice
    6. Little League Team (12–14) Baseball Tournament out of town
    7. Little and Peewee League Teams (8–14) Baseball Game
    8. Little and Peewee League Teams (8–14) Baseball Game out of town
    9. Peewee League Team (8–11) Baseball Practice
    10. Peewee League Team (8–11) Baseball Tournament
    11. PONY League Team (15–17) Baseball Game
    12. PONY League Team (15–17) Baseball Game out of town

13. PONY League Team (15–17) Baseball Practice
14. Midwest Town Team Baseball (Softball) Game
15. Midwest Town Team Baseball (Softball) Game out of town
16. Midwest Town Team Baseball (Softball) Practice

18. Basketball Games. Coach (6) or coaches (5) arrange games, instruct players; referees (4) judge plays; players (4) play according to standard basketball rules; cheerleaders (4) lead cheers; salesmen (4) sell popcorn, soft drinks; band (4) plays music in intervals; audience (2) watch, cheer, applaud, eat; 0.79 cu.

1. Elementary Upper School (11–13) Basketball Game
2. Elementary Upper School (11–13) Basketball Game out of town
3. Elementary Upper School (11–13) Basketball Practice
4. Elementary Upper School (11–13) Basketball Tournament
5. High School Boys Basketball Game
6. High School Boys Basketball Game out of town including Tournament at Patton
7. High School Boys Basketball Practice
8. High School Freshman (14) Boys Basketball Tournament out of town
9. High School Freshman (14) and Sophomore (15) Girls Basketball Game
10. High School Freshman (14) and Sophomore (15) Girls Basketball Game out of town
11. High School Girls Basketball Practice
12. High School Girls and Freshman (14) Boys Basketball Game
13. High School Girls and Freshman (14) Boys Basketball Game out of town
14. Midwest Town Team Basketball Game

19. Beauty Shops. Operator-manager (6) cuts, washes, sets, styles, colors, combs hair of customer, carries out management routines; assistant (4) answers phone, assists operator; customers (3) receive operator's services, converse, read, pay for services; 0.60 cu.

1. Burgess Beauty Shop

20. Billiard Parlors and Taverns. Proprietor (6) manages business, serves drinks, gives out equipment for billiards, converses; assistant (4) helps manager; customers (3) order and pay for drinks, drink beer, converse, play cards or billiards; 0.71 cu.

1. Hookers Tavern and Pool Hall

*21. Book Exchange Services. PTA committee members (5) receive used school books, arrange, price, sell; students (3) bring in books, pay for needed books.

°22. Bowling Games. Proprietors (5) manage business, team managers (5) arrange games, keep scores; bowlers (4) bowl according to rules, watch, eat, converse; audience (2) watch, eat, converse; 2.02 cu.

1. Garland Lanes Saturday Junior (13–17) Girls League Bowling Game
2. Garland Lanes Saturday Junior (13–16) Girls Summer League Bowling Game
3. Garland Lanes Thursday Junior (10–17) Mixed Summer League Bowling Game
4. Garland Lanes Sunday Boys (10–17) League Bowling Game
5. Garland Lanes Saturday Bantam (7–14) Boys League Bowling Game
6. Garland Lanes Saturday Bantam (7–14) Boys Summer League Bowling Game
7. Garland Lanes Wednesday Father and Son Summer League Bowling Game
8. Garland Lanes Bowling Exhibitions
9. Garland Lanes Friday Mixed Couples Early League Bowling Game
10. Garland Lanes Friday Mixed Couples Late League Bowling Game
11. Garland Lanes Friday Mixed Couples Summer League Bowling Game
12. Garland Lanes Monday Men's League Bowling Game
13. Garland Lanes Monday Men's Scratch League Bowling Game
14. Garland Lanes Open Bowling and Tournament
15. Garland Lanes Sunday Mixed Couples League #1 Bowling Game
16. Garland Lanes Sunday Mixed Couples League #2 Bowling Game
17. Garland Lanes Sunday Mixed Couples Summer League Bowling Game
18. Garland Lanes Thursday Women's Early League Bowling Game
19. Garland Lanes Thursday Women's Late League Bowling Game
20. Garland Lanes Thursday Women's Summer League Bowling Game
21. Garland Lanes Tuesday Women's League Bowling Game
22. Garland Lanes Tuesday Women's Summer League Bowling Game
23. Garland Lanes Wednesday Little Four Summer League Bowling Game
24. Garland Lanes Wednesday Men's League Bowling Game
25. Garland Lanes Wednesday Men's Scratch Summer League Bowling Game

*23. Box Socials. Committee chairmen (5) plan, arrange, decorate; auctioneer (4) auctions decorated boxes each containing two suppers; entertainers (4) play instruments, sing; female customers (3) bring boxes, male customers (3) bid on boxes for food and partner; all (3) eat, converse, listen, applaud.

24. Building, Construction, and Repair Services. Operators (6) manage construction, engage in carpenter work, painting, wall-papering, cement work; helpers (4) do similar work under direction; employers (3) arrange for and pay for work, inspect work; onlookers (1) watch work being done; 2.00 cu.
    1. Betley General Construction Company
    2. Beyet and Sons General Construction Company
    3. Kerr, H. General Construction Service
    4. Kerr, S. General Construction Service
    5. Nading General Construction Service
    6. Saxe General Construction Company

25. Bus Stops. Driver (6) sells tickets, loads and unloads luggage; customers (3) get on or off bus; 0.43 cu.
    1. High School Bus Stop
    2. Lewistown-Capital City Bus Stop

26. Card Parties. Host (6) greets members, provides place, equipment, refreshments; members (3) or customers (3) play cards, converse, eat; 0.46 cu.
    1. American Legion Auxiliary Card Party for March of Dimes
    2. Duplicate Bridge at Parent-Teacher Association Carnival
    3. Married Couples Bridge Club
    4. Women's Supper Bridge Club I
    5. Women's Bridge Club II
    6. Women's Bridge Club III
    7. Women's Bridge Club IV
    8. Women's Bridge Club V

°27. Carnivals. Chairmen (5) of different concessions (games of skill and chance, sales of goods, competitions, exhibits, movie) organize effort, provide objects, act as salesmen, barkers, ticket sellers; helpers (4) assist in all activities; customers (3) buy, watch, eat, play, converse; 0.05 cu.
    1. Parent-Teacher Association Carnival

28. Cemeteries, including Graveside Services. Minister (5) and mortician (5) arrange and perform burial services according to ritual; casket bearers (4) assist; caretaker (4) mows grass, maintains cemetery; chairman of cemetery board (5) sells lots, oversees caretaker; gravediggers (4) dig graves; mourners (3) attend service; visitors (2) visit cemetery, bring flowers; 0.45 cu.
    1. Midwest Cemetery including Graveside Services

29. Charivaris. Ringleaders (5) collect friends of newlyweds, provide wheelbarrow, call on newlyweds; groom (5) wheels bride around Courthouse square; bride and groom (5) act as hosts to friends at their own home; onlookers (2) cheer, laugh, eat, converse; 0.05 cu.
    1. Charivari for Hanson, Grail, Bolling, Peece

30. Chiropractors Offices. Chiropractor (6) carries out office routines, consultations, manipulation of patient's vertebral column according to chiropractic theory and practice; patient (3) seeks advice, is treated, pays for services; 0.25 cu.
   1. Dr. Harbough Office
*31. Circuses. Owner-operators (5) arrange place and time, supervise setting up, publicity, sell tickets, supervise performances, act as M. C.; performers (4) do tricks, magic, show trained animals, sell lemonade, cotton candy, and popcorn; customers (3) buy tickets, watch, applaud, converse, buy, eat, and drink.
32. Civil Engineers Offices. Engineer (6) manages office, consults with county commissioners, county employees, rural residents, and state highway officials regarding roads and bridges and sanitation problems in the county; secretary (4) carries out office routines; county officials (3) and citizens (3) consult, converse, get maps; 0.43 cu.
   1. County Engineers Office
33. Classrooms, Free Time. Teacher (6) keeps order; pupils (3) converse, study, play quiet games; 2.53 cu.
   1. Elementary School Eighth Grade (13) Classroom Freetime, Cole
   2. Elementary School Eighth Grade (13) Classroom Freetime, Holmes
   3. Elementary School Seventh Grade (12) Classroom Freetime
   4. Elementary School Sixth Grade (11) Classroom Freetime
   5. Elementary School Fifth Grade (10) Classroom Freetime
   6. Elementary School Fourth Grade (9) Classroom Freetime
   7. Elementary School Third and Fourth Grade (8–9) Classroom Freetime
   8. Elementary School Third Grade (8) Classroom Freetime
   9. Elementary School Second Grade (7) Classroom Freetime
   10. Elementary School First and Second Grade (6–7) Classroom Freetime
   11. Elementary School First Grade (6) Classroom Freetime
   12. High School Commercial Classroom Freetime
   13. High School English Classroom Freetime
   14. High School Home Economics Classroom Freetime
   15. High School Social Science Classroom Freetime
°34. Cleaners, Dry Cleaning Plants. Owner-manager (6) manages business, cleans and presses clothes, waits on customers, accepts payment, sells insurance; helpers (4) assist manager in dry cleaning; customers (3) bring clothes to be cleaned, pick up clean clothes, pay for service; 0.51 cu.
   1. Ellsons Cleaning Plant and Route and Insurance Agency
35. Clothiers and Dry Goods Stores. Joint managers (5) manage business, serve customers, stock shelves; clerks (4) assist managers; customers (3) select, buy, and pay for merchandise; 0.57 cu.

1. Cabell Department Store, Clothing
36. Club Officers Training Classes. Members of agricultural extension advisory council (5) and home economics agent (5) arrange program and teach officers of home economics units their respective responsibilities; officers of home economics units (3) learn, discuss; 0.05 cu.

    1. Agricultural Extension Home Demonstration Unit Officers Training School

37. Commercial Classes. Commerce teacher (6) teaches typing, shorthand, business machine use, bookkeeping, office routines; students (3) learn, practice, and demonstrate office skills and routines; 0.27 cu.

    1. High School Commercial Classes

38. Commercial Company Offices. Proprietors (5) manage office; secretary (4) and bookkeeper (4) engage in office routines; customers (3) come to select and order windows and doors; 0.43 cu.

    1. Eggleston and Dean Window and Door Office

39. Cooking Classes. Leader (6) teaches theory and practice of cooking; assistants (4) help leader; members of 4-H club (3) cook under supervision, eat products; 0.15 cu.

    1. Agricultural Extension 4-H Cooking Class I
    2. Agricultural Extension 4-H Cooking Class II
    3. Agricultural Extension 4-H Cooking Class III

°40. Court Sessions, County. Judge (6) opens court, hears charges and witnesses, gives and records judgments in cases involving misdemeanors (including traffic violations), juvenile offenders, matters of probate; sheriff (4) or state traffic officer (4) or individuals (4) bring charges; counsel (4) or accused (4) or witnesses (4) offer evidence; accused may be acquitted, fined, or imprisoned; spectators (2) listen; 0.25 cu.

    1. County Court Session, including Probate Court and Juvenile Court

41. Court Sessions, District. Judge of the District Court, a professional (6), listens to presentation of case, rules on admissibility of evidence, instructs jury, settles disputes between opposing attorneys, sentences defendant in criminal cases, determines liability in civil cases; Clerk of the Court (4) swears in witnesses; bailiff (4) opens court, keeps order; court reporter (4) records proceedings; attorneys (4) present client's case; witnesses (4) give evidence; defendant (4) gives evidence; plaintiff (4) gives evidence; jury (4) (if present) listens, deliberates, gives verdict; spectators (2) listen; 0.08 cu.

    1. District Court Session

*42. Court Sessions, Justice of the Peace. Elected Justice of the Peace (6) presides over city court, listens to evidence in cases involving misdemeanors (including traffic violations), gives and records judgment; sheriff (4), town marshall (4), or individuals (4) bring charges; counsel (4) or accused (4) or witnesses (4) offer evidence; accused (4) may be fined, imprisoned in county jail for limited time; spectators (2) listen.

*43. Cream Collection Stations. Proprietor (6) provides refrigerated collection point for cream, records cream brought in, delivers to wholesaler; farmers (3) bring in cream to sell, wholesaler (3) buys cream.

°44. Custodial Work Groups. Person in charge (6 or 5) manages cleaning, gardening, meal or coffee break; volunteer workers (4) scrub, sweep, polish, rake, make minor repairs; others (2) watch, join in recreational eating; 0.26 cu.
  1. Baptist Church Volunteer Work Group
  2. City Park Volunteers Clean-Up
  3. Methodist Church Volunteer Work Group
  4. Presbyterian Church Volunteer Work Group

*45. Dairy Barns. Owner (6) supervises dairy processes; helpers (4) milk, clean barn, feed, drive cows.

46. Dances. Committee of students and teachers in charge (5) arrange for decorating, music, food, plan program; master of ceremonies (5) carries out program; operator of record player (4) or musicians (4) provide music; refreshment servers (4), decorators (4), ticket-takers (4) carry out specified routines; members and customers (3) dance, play games, converse, eat; audience (2) watch; 0.20 cu.
  1. Elementary School Eighth Grade (13) Graduation Party and Dance
  2. Halloween Dance
  3. High School Dance
  4. High School Dance after Football Game

47. Day Care Homes and Nurseries. Person in charge (6) cares for young children left in her care, may give them food, put them to bed, entertain, comfort; children (3) are cared for; parents (3) leave and call for children; 0.77 cu.
  1. Baptist Church Nursery during Church Service
  2. Day Care for Children of Working Mothers
  3. Methodist Church Nursery during Church Service and Vacation Church School
  4. Parent-Teacher Association Child Care during Meetings and Carnival
  5. Presbyterian Church Nursery during Church and Vacation Church School

48. Delivery and Collection Routes. Deliverers (6) take papers, etc., to homes and leave them, come at regular intervals to collect for goods and service; customers (3) pay for goods and services; 1.36 cu.
  1. Capital City Paper Route
  2. Grit Weekly Paper Route
  3. Manor Bakery Route
  4. The City Paper Route

5. Tip Top Milk Route
6. University City Journal World Paper Route

49. Dentists Offices and Services. Dentist (6) examines patients, using x-rays and mouth mirrors, explores, cleans, fills, extracts, and replaces teeth, using power and hand instruments, manages office; assistant (4) assists dentist, makes appointments, records treatments, accepts payment, develops x-rays, conducts office routines; patients (3) wait, are treated, pay, converse; 0.40 cu.
    1. Dr. Sterne Dental Service Office
    2. High School and Elementary School (6–17) Dental Inspection

50. Dinners and Banquets. Organizers (5) plan, buy, cook, serve meal, and clean up after meal; helpers (4) help with above or in some cases all bring ready-cooked food and place it for diners to serve themselves; members (3) or customers (3) eat and converse; 0.66 cu.
    1. African Masonic Lodge St. John's Day Dinner
    2. Baptist Church Basket Dinner
    3. Civic Club Dinner for Butledge Family
    4. Daylight Circle Luncheon
    5. Eastern Star Lodge Dinner
    6. Eastern Star Lodge Past Matrons Dinner
    7. Homemakers Club Dinner for Simson Family (Rural Club III)
    8. Methodist Church Family Night Supper
    9. Northeast Kansas Social Welfare Association Dinner
    10. Presbyterian Church Dinner for Butledge Family
    11. Presbyterian Church Dinner for Presbytery Quarterly Meeting
    12. Rebekah and Odd Fellows Lodges Family Dinners
    13. Rebekah Lodge Dinner for Bereaved Families

51. Dinners with Business Meetings. President of organization (6) arranges for dinner, presides at meeting; cooks (4), waitresses (4) prepare and serve dinner; secretary (4), treasurer (4), committee chairman (4) do prescribed work; invited speakers (4) make speeches; members (3) eat, converse, engage in business meeting activity, listen; 0.87 cu.
    1. Alpha Delta Kappa Educational Sorority Zeta Chapter Meeting
    2. American Legion World War I Barracks and Auxiliary Regular Meeting and Dinner
    3. Bapist Church Breakfast Meeting with Business for Ministers and Revivalists
    4. Chamber of Commerce Regular Luncheon Meeting with Business
    5. Elementary School Principals County Association Dinner Meeting with Business

    6. Farm Bureau County Membership Committee Luncheon Meeting with Business

    7. Farm Bureau District Dinner Meeting with Business

    8. Home Economists County Association Dinner Meeting with Business

    9. Hospital Board Dinner Meeting with Business

   10. Independent Grocers Association Distributors Dinner Meeting with Business

   11. Ministers County Association Luncheon Meeting with Business and Program

   12. Morca Company Cattle Feeders Dinner Meeting with Business

   13. Patrons Mutual Insurance Company Dinner Meeting with Business

   14. Secondary School (High School) Principals County Association Meeting with Dinner

   15. Secondary School (High School) Principals and Wives County Association Dinner Meeting with Business

   16. Soil Conservation District Annual County Luncheon Meeting with Business

   17. Tomco Seed Company Dinner Meeting with Business

52. Dinners with Dances. Chairmen of committees (5) arrange and manage dinner, program, dance; master of ceremonies (5) introduces speakers (4) and entertainers (4) for program; cooks (4) prepare and waitresses (4) serve food; guests (3) eat, dance, converse, listen; 0.05 cu.

    1. High School Junior Senior (16–17) Banquet and Dance

53. Dinners with Recreational and Cultural Programs. Chairmen (5) arrange for dinner, program, decorations; cooks (4), waitresses (4), decorators (4) prepare and serve dinner, decorate; master of ceremonies (5) presides; speakers (4) and/or entertainers (4) present after-dinner program; members (3) listen, eat, converse, applaud; 0.80 cu.

    1. Bowling Association, Women, Banquet and Program

    2. Bowling Congress, Men, Banquet and Program

    3. Boy Scouts Annual Cub Banquet and Program

    4. Farm Bureau Annual County Dinner and Program

    5. Rural Club III Thanksgiving Dinner and Program

    6. Masonic Lodge District Dinner

    7. Methodist Church Mother-Daughter Banquet and Program

    8. Midwest High School Alumni Dinner and Program for Seniors

    9. Northeast Kansas Officials Dinner and Program

   10. Republican County Committee Meet-Your-Candidate Dinner and Program

   11. Rotary Club Dinner and Program for Boy Scout Drive

      12. Rotary Club Dinner and Program for High School Foot-
           ball Team
      13. Rotary Club Dinner and Program for High School Seniors
      14. Rotary Club Dinner and Program for Rotary Anns
      15. Rotary Club Dinner and Program for Rotary Anns at Old
           Frontier Museum
      16. Rotary Club Dinner and Program with Vernon

54. Drugstores. Pharmacist (5) mixes and dispenses drugs according to prescription issued by physician, manages drug and general variety store; manager (5) manages cosmetic, jewelry departments and fountain; sales persons (4) sell and serve customers at counters or fountain, wash dishes, mix drinks; customers (3) select, buy, pay for merchandise, eat food, converse; 0.61 cu.
      1. Ellson Drugstore

55. Educational Methods Classes. Leaders (6) or co-leaders (5) teach methods and values of teaching to individuals who will teach; members (3) learn, listen, ask questions, discuss; 0.15 cu.
      1. Agricultural Extension 4-H Food Leaders Training Class
      2. Presbyterian Church Sunday School Teachers Teaching
         Methods Training Meeting
      3. School Teachers County Institute

56. Elections, Polling Places. Election board chairman (5) sees that voting and ballot counting is conducted according to law, makes up final tally for county clerk, seals pouch; bailiff (5) sets up booths, tables, supplies ballots, and canisters; election clerks (4) check off voters, hand out ballots, place ballots in appropriate canisters; counting board (4) counts ballots; watchers (4) watch procedures to detect any deviancy; voters (3) identify themselves, mark ballots, cast ballots; 0.20 cu.
      1. County School Unification Election North Midwest Polling
         Place
      2. County School Unification Election South Midwest Polling
         Place
      3. State Primary Election North Midwest Polling Place
      4. State Primary Election South Midwest Polling Place

57. Elections, Public Posting of Returns. County clerk (5) and election board chairmen (5) record votes as they come in; secretaries (4) place results on records and on blackboard for spectators to see; spectators (2) stand before blackboard, read how election is going, converse; 0.05 cu.
      1. Election Returns at Courthouse

58. Elementary School Basic Classes. Teacher (6) teaches reading, grammar, arithmetic, writing, elementary health, social studies, science, and engages in classroom routines; pupils (3) listen, write, recite, read, figure; 2.99 cu.
      1. Elementary School Eighth Grade (13) Academic Subjects
      2. Elementary School Seventh and Eighth Grade (12–13)
         Academic Subjects

    3. Elementary School Seventh Grade (12) Academic Subjects
    4. Elementary School Sixth Grade (11) Academic Subjects
    5. Elementary School Fifth Grade (10) Academic Subjects, Pearson
    6. Elementary School Fifth Grade (10) Academic Subjects, Hannah
    7. Elementary School Fourth Grade (9) Academic Subjects
    8. Elementary School Third and Fourth Grade (8–9) Academic Subjects
    9. Elementary School Third Grade (8) Academic Subjects
    10. Elementary School Second Grade (7) Academic Subjects
    11. Elementary School First and Second Grade (6–7) Academic Subjects
    12. Elementary School First Grade (6) Academic Subjects
    13. Elementary Lower School (6–9) Remedial Reading Class

59. English Classes. Teacher (6) teaches English literature, composition, speech, grammar, and engages in routine classroom management; high school students (3) study, recite, listen; 0.28 cu.
    1. High School English Classes
    2. High School English Classes Trip to Newspaper Editing and Production Conference at the University

°60. Examinations, Boy Scout. Examining Board (5) questions boy scouts regarding requirements for specific badges, makes judgment regarding competence of scout and informs him of decision; scout (4) answers questions, demonstrates knowledge; 0.05 cu.
    1. Boy Scout Board of Review

°61. Examinations, Standardized. School principal (6) gives test according to specific directions accompanying test; students (3) take examination, follow directions; 0.25 cu.
    1. High School Seniors (17) Kansas High School Comprehensive Tests
    2. High School Seniors (17) U.S. Air Force Qualifying Examination
    3. High School Juniors (16) National Merit Scholarship Qualifying Achievement Tests
    4. High School Sophomores (15) California Test of Mental Maturity
    5. High School Freshmen (14) Aptitude Test

62. Excavating Contracting Services. Owner-managers (6) direct earthmoving and engage in management routines; employees (4) operate and repair equipment; customers (3) arrange for and pay for earthmoving services; onlookers (1) watch activity; 0.51 cu.
    1. Higley Excavating Company
    2. Pechter Excavating Company
    3. Wallace Excavating Company

63. Excursions and Sightseeing Trips. Persons in charge (5) supervise

loading and unloading, keep order, keep track of young people; driver (5) drives bus; members (3) gather, wait for bus, enter bus, go on the trip, may sing and converse on the bus, eat, watch, walk; 0.76 cu.

1. Agricultural Extension Home Demonstration Unit, The Night Owls, Trip to Theater in Capital City
2. Elementary School Basketball Team (11–13) Trip to Game at the University
3. Elementary School Eighth Grade (13) Trip to Art Museum at The University
4. Elementary School Eighth Grade (13) Trip to State City
5. Elementary School Fifth Grade (10) Trip to Capital City
6. Elementary School Seventh Grade (12) Trip to County Soil Conservation Areas
7. Elementary School (6–9) Trip to Circus
8. High School Basketball Team Trip to Game at State College
9. High School Latin Club Trip to Theater in State City
10. High School Senior Class (17) Trip to Chicago
11. High School Shop Classes Trip to State City Industries
12. Methodist and Presbyterian Youth (13–17) Trip to Bible Display at Burris University
13. Presbyterian Youth (12–17) Trip to the University Vesper Service
14. Presbyterian Youth (14–17) Trip to Eakins for Halloween Party
15. Retarded Children's Outing to Capital City

°64. Factory Assembly Shops. Owner-managers (5) manage business, make general plans; foreman (5) directs workers on the floor in assembling aluminum parts; workers (4) assemble glass and aluminum into doors and windows, load and unload trucks; 0.51 cu.

1. Eggleston and Dean Window and Door Factory

65. Farm Implement Agencies. Owner-manager (6) manages business, sells parts, sells machinery, attends to office routines, directs repair; repairman (4) works on farm machinery; salesmen (4) sells parts, tools; customers (3) buy, bring in machinery for repair, pay; loafers (1) sit around and talk; 0.86 cu.

1. Lesters Farm Center
2. Midwest Implement and Hardware Company

*66. Farm Practices Classes. Teacher (6) teaches farm practices, using books, lectures, demonstrations; class members (3) listen, study, watch, discuss.

67. Fashion Shows. Teachers (5 or 6) in charge help exhibitors dress, arrange order; master of ceremonies (5) announces exhibitors, describes costumes; models (4) walk across stage to exhibit clothing; servers (4) serve refreshments; audience (2) watch, applaud, eat, converse; 0.10 cu.

      1. Agricultural Extension Best Dress Workshop on TV
      2. High School Home Economics Fashion Show and Tea for Mothers

68. Fire Alarms and Fire Fighting. Fire chief (6) directs activity, drives truck, helps with chemicals or hose; firemen (4) help extinguish fire; homeowner (3) calls firemen; onlookers (1) watch activity; 0.11 cu.
      1. Midwest Volunteer Firemen Fight Fires in town
      2. Midwest Volunteer Firemen Fight Fires out of town

69. Fire Drills. Principal (6) rings alarm bell, times and evaluates speed and efficiency of evacuation of building, records result; teachers (4) take charge of evacuating classes; pupils (3) conform to directions of rules and of teachers to leave the building quickly, return in prescribed order; 0.11 cu.
      1. Elementary Lower School (6–9) Fire Drill
      2. High School and Elementary Upper School (10–17) Fire Drill

70. Fire Stations. City engineer (5) and fire chief (5) use building for repair and maintenance of trucks, storage of chemicals; employee (4) and firemen (4) work on trucks under direction; farmers (3) come to purchase water and fill tanks from city hydrant in times of drought; 0.40 cu.
      1. City Garage and Fire Station
      2. City Firemen Regular Meeting

71. Fireworks Sales Stands. Manager (6) or family members (5) manage the enterprise, sell fireworks; helpers (4) assist in selling; customers (3) buy fireworks; onlookers (1) watch, converse; 0.13 cu.
      1. Berrys Fireworks Sales Stand
      2. Burris Fireworks Sales Stand

72. Floor Laying Services. Co-owners (5) manage business and do work of laying floor covering, building and finishing cabinets and installing them; helper (4) sometimes assists; customers (3) arrange for work, pay for work; 0.13 cu.
      1. Chase Floor Laying and Cabinet Making Service

73. Food and Rummage Sales. Committee members (5) arrange for use of space with building owner, solicit donations, arrange and price goods, sell; helpers (4) assist in all phases; customers (3) buy food or other objects; 0.35 cu.
      1. Agricultural Extension 4-H Food Sale
      2. Civic Club Rummage Sale
      3. High School Junior Class (16) Food Sale
      4. High School Pep Club Food Sale
      5. High School Senior Class (17) Food Sale
      6. High School Sophomore Class (15) Food Sale
      7. Rural Club I Food Sale

74. Football Games, American Football. Coaches (5) in charge in-

struct players; players (4) play ball according to rules; umpires (4) determine legality of plays, keep time; band (4) plays instruments, marches; concession stand workers (4) prepare and sell food; water boys (4) take water on to field; cheerleaders (4) lead organized cheering; announcer (4) tells audience of players involved in game, introduces band for its performance; Boy Scouts (4) have flag ceremony before band plays the national anthem; audience (2) watch, cheer, eat, applaud, converse; 0.29 cu.

1. High School A Team Football Game
2. High School A Team Football Game out of town
3. High School B Team Football Game
4. High School B Team Football Game out of town
5. High School Football Practice

75. Funeral Directors Services, including Funerals. Mortician-owner (6) embalms body, arranges for and directs all preparations for funeral and burial, takes care of management routines; assistants (4) help mortician, usher at service, arrange flowers; minister or priest (4) conducts service; pianist (4) plays; singers (4) sing; pallbearers (4) carry casket; customer (3) selects casket, makes plans with mortician; mourners (2) come to view body, attend funeral service; 0.16 cu.

1. Sherwin Funeral Home

76. Funeral Services, Church. Minister in charge at the church (6) conducts service according to ritual, accompanies casket out of the church; mortician and assistants (4) arrange and remove flowers, place casket, move casket from front to back of church, usher mourners, hand out order-of-service folders; singers (4) sing; organist (4) plays; pallbearers (4) carry casket out; mourners (3) sit, listen, sign order-of-service folders, view the deceased as they leave, wait outside until hearse drives away; 0.16 cu.

1. African Methodist Episcopal Church Funeral Service
2. Methodist Church Funeral Service
3. Presbyterian Church Funeral Service

77. Furniture Stores. Owner-manager (6) manages business, waits on customers, gives information regarding products; employees (4) keep books, wait on customers, service appliances; customers (3) look at merchandise, select, buy, pay for merchandise; 0.54 cu.

1. Sherwins Furniture Store

78. Garages. Owner-manager (6) manages garage, repairs cars, services cars; mechanic (4) repairs cars; attendant (4) puts in gas, oil, washes windshields; assistant (4) carries out office routines; customers (3) have cars serviced or repaired, pay; 1.21 cu.

1. Chacos Garage and Service Station
2. Eggleston Garage and Service Station

79. Gift Showers. Hostesses (5) provide decorations and refresh-

ments, invite guests, plan and introduce games; honoree (4) opens gifts, expresses thanks; assistants (4) record gifts, serve refreshments; guests (3) bring gifts, converse, play games, eat; 0.16 cu.

    1. Baby Showers
    2. Bridal Showers
    3. Gray Ladies Shower for Ellersons

°80. Golf Games. Executive committee (5) arranges tournament play, plans for upkeep of course; workmen (4) mow the course; volunteers (4) mow or do other upkeep work; members (3) and guests (3) play on the course; audience (2) watch play, converse; 0.39 cu.

    1. Golf Club Invitational Golf Tournament
    2. Golf Club Open Golf Play
    3. Golf Club Scotch Doubles Golf Tournament

81. Government Offices: Business and Records. Elected or appointed government official (6) manages office, is responsible for records and accounts, answers questions, confers with county commissioners or other boards, works as required by law; clerks (4) carry out office routines; customers (3) pay fees, obtain information; 3.33 cu.

    1. County Clerks Office
    2. County Register of Deeds Office
    3. County Treasurers Office
    4. District Court Clerks Office
    5. U.S. Agricultural Stabilization and Conservation Office
    6. U.S. Army Corps of Engineers Office
    7. U.S. Farmers Home Administration Office
    8. U.S. Selective Service Office
    9. U.S. Social Security Consultant Office

82. Graduation and Promotion Ceremonies. Master of ceremonies (6) arranges program to honor and compliment graduates, speaks, introduces other speakers; speakers (4) speak; official (4) gives out diplomas; musicians (4) play or sing; graduates (4) receive diplomas, audience (2) listen, applaud, congratulate; 0.20 cu.

    1. Elementary School Eighth (13) Grade Graduation Exercises
    2. High School Senior Class (17) Graduation Exercises
    3. Methodist Church Rally and Promotion Ceremony
    4. Presbyterian Church Rally and Promotion Ceremony

83. Grocery Stores. Manager (6) manages business, prices goods, prepares advertising, takes inventories; cashier (4) totals charges, takes money; butcher (4) cuts meat, serves customers, stocks meat case, weighs meat; stock clerk and carry-out boy (4) stock shelves, mark price on merchandise, carry out sacks to customer's car; salesmen, wholesale (4), interview manager; customers (3) select goods from shelves and cases, pay for merchandise; 1.33 cu.

1. Reids Grocery Store
2. Thomas Fruit Market
3. Weylens Grocery Store

84. Hallways. Principal or teacher (5) keeps order; janitor (4) keeps halls clean; employees (3), students (3), visitors (2) walk, converse; 1.67 cu.
    1. County Courthouse Annex Halls
    2. County Courthouse Halls
    3. Elementary Lower School (6–9) Halls
    4. High School and Elementary Upper School (10–17) Halls

85. Hardware Stores. Owner-manager (6) manages business, sells merchandise, repairs appliances; assistants (4) work with manager; customers (3) inspect and buy goods, pay for service, onlookers (1) watch TV, converse; 1.03 cu.
    1. Blanchard Hardware Store
    2. Western Auto Store

°86. Hayrack Rides. Host-driver (6) drives tractor, host at farm visited; committee members (4) arrange picnic, provide food; members (3) and guests (2) ride, sing, eat; 0.05 cu.
    1. Methodist and Presbyterian Youth (13–17) Hayrack Ride

87. Hikes and Camps. Scout leader (6) directs total camp activities; patrol leaders (4) direct small group activities; scouts (3) make camp, hike, cook, engage in programmed scout activities; 0.24 cu.
    1. Boy Scout Explorer Overnight Camping Trip
    2. Boy Scout Explorer Camping Trip to Grand Lake
    3. Boy Scout Troop Hike and Cookout
    4. Boy Scout Camp at Camp Jayhawk

88. Home Economics Classes. Home economist (6) in charge teaches skills and theory of homemaking, including cooking, sewing, family life; specialist (4) in one field may lecture; high school students (3), or 4-H members (3), or home economics units lesson leaders (3) learn, listen, practice; 0.42 cu.
    1. Agricultural Extension 4-H Demonstration and Judging School
    2. Agricultural Extension Home Demonstration Units Leaders Training Class
    3. High School Home Economics Classes
    4. High School Home Economics Class Trip to Cooking School at University City
    5. High School Home Economics Class Trip to Hospitality Day at State University

89. Home Economics Competitions. 4-H advisers (5) set up program and act as masters of ceremonies; judges (4) evaluate entries; contestants (4) exhibit clothing or other 4-H project work; 4-H leaders (4) help set up club members' exhibit; committee (4) sells

sandwiches and beverages; members (3) see exhibits, learn points
important for judging, eat; 0.10 cu.
　　1. Agricultural Extension 4-H Annual Style Revue
　　2. Agricultural Extension 4-H Project Judging Competition
°90. Horseshoe Pitching Contests. Game organizers and referees (5)
set up order of play, provide horseshoes, keep score, award
prize; players (4) play regulation horseshoe pitching game; spectators (2) watch; 0.05 cu.
　　1. Old Settlers Reunion Horseshoe Pitching Contest
*91. Horse Shows. Organizers (5) make arrangements; M. C. (5) with
public address system directs show; judges (4) judge entries; participants (4) ride, jump horses according to program; ticket
takers (4), food sellers (4) perform tasks; customers (3) watch,
applaud, converse, pay, eat.
　92. Hotels. Proprietor (6) or proprietors (5) manage business, greet,
register, and conduct guests to rooms, clean rooms; employees
(4) help with work; guests (3) stay in rooms, pay bills; 0.94 cu.
　　1. Eggleston Rooming House
　　2. Kayes Rooming House
　　3. Midwest Hotel
　93. Ice Cream Socials. President or hostess (6) in charge of arrangements greets members; helpers (4) serve, clean up; members (3)
eat, converse; 0.10 cu.
　　1. Agricultural Extension Home Demonstration Midwest
　　　Unit, Ice Cream Social
　　2. Methodist Church Ice Cream Social
*94. Ice Depots. Proprietor (6) provides refrigerated, automated ice
vending machine; wholesaler (4) stocks machine; customers (3)
operate vending apparatus, carry away ice.
*95. Initiations. H. S. senior class members (5), supervised by H. S.
principal (5) require freshman class members (4) to dress ridicu-
lously, parade, give program for school; students (3) and others
(2) watch, laugh, applaud.
　96. Installation and Induction Ceremonies. President of organization
and installing officer (5) arrange program, preside over ritual;
persons installed (4) participate in ritual; other performers (4)
take prescribed parts in ritual; refreshment committee (4) serves
refreshments; members (3) watch, applaud; 0.15 cu.
　　1. Eastern Star Installation of Officers at Lodge Meeting
　　2. High School National Honor Society Induction Ceremony
　　3. High School Thespian Installation and Induction Cere-
　　　mony
　97. Insurance Offices and Sales Routes. Insurance agent (6) manages
office, sells insurance, records claims, arranges for claim adjuster;
secretary (4) engages in office routines; adjuster (4) gets and gives
information; customers (3) buy insurance, make claims; 0.78 cu.

       1. Deed Farm Bureau Insurance Office
       2. Hardy Insurance Office

98. Ironing Services. Ironer (6) prepares clothes for ironing, irons, folds, charges for service; customers (3) bring and call for clothes, pay for service; 0.72 cu.
       1. Garner Ironing Service
       2. Hanchett Ironing Service
       3. Holman Ironing Service
       4. Kramer Ironing Service
       5. McKean Ironing Service

99. Jails. Sheriff (6) has responsibility for security and management of jail, places offenders in jail, releases offenders, admits visitors; sheriff's wife (4) prepares meals, sees to laundry, takes care of jail during sheriff's or deputy's absence; deputy sheriff (4) may act as sheriff; offenders (3) are confined to cells; 1.25 cu.
       1. Midwest County Jail and Sheriffs Residence

100. Jewelry Stores. Owner-operator (6) manages business, waits on customers, examines and repairs watches and clocks; clerk (4) waits on customers, wraps packages; customers (3) examine and purchase merchandise, bring in watches for repair, pay for service and goods; 0.47 cu.
       1. Ruttleys Jewelry and Watch Repair Shop

101. Judges Chambers. Judge (6) directs work of court reporter, clerk of the court, bailiff or deputy; confers with attorneys and their clients, often seeking out-of-court settlement, advising, admonishing; court reporter (4), clerk of the court (4), bailiff (4) carry out the judge's directives; attorneys (3) and their clients (3) consult with judge; 0.54 cu.
       1. County Probate Judges Office
       2. District Court Judges Chambers

°102. Kennels. Owner-managers (5) feed, breed, care for, show, and sell dogs; assistants (4) help care for dogs; customers (3) look at, buy, and pay for dogs; 0.65 cu.
       1. Crawfords Kennels
       2. Graysons Kennels

°103. Kindergarten Classes. Teacher (6) engages in classroom routines, teaches, supervises activities; pupils (3) play, draw, construct, sing individually and in groups; 0.13 cu.
       1. Kindergarten Classes (5)

°104. Knitting Classes and Services. Teacher-knitter (6) teaches knitting, knits herself, sells knitted garments; customer-pupil (3) learn knitting, pay for lessons or garments; 0.15 cu.
       1. Knitting Class, Mrs. Layman
       2. Layman Knitting Service

°105. Land Condemnation Hearings. Commission members (5) hear complaints regarding fair pay for condemned land; complainants

(4) make complaints orally to commission meeting for judgment; 0.05 cu.

　　1. State Land Condemnation Hearings

106. Landscaping and Floriculture Classes. County agents (5) in charge of arrangements introduce specialists; specialists (4) teach landscaping and floriculture; interested persons (3) attend as class members; 0.05 cu.

　　1. Agricultural Extension Landscaping and Flower School

107. Latin Classes. Latin teacher (6) teaches Latin language and literature, engages in classroom routines; high school students (3) study, recite; 0.25 cu.

　　1. High School Latin Classes
　　2. High School Latin Classes Trip to Convention at State College

°108. Laundries, Self-Service. Owner (6) services machines, collects money from machines weekly; cleaner (4) cleans premises daily; customers (3) wash and dry own clothes, sit in chairs and converse while waiting for machines to complete cycles; 1.25 cu.

　　1. Coin-Operated Laundry

109. Laundry Services. Owner-operator (6) manages laundry, washes, irons, receives payment; assistant (4) irons; both converse with customers; customers (3) bring clothing to be washed and ironed, pick up clean clothes, rent machines to wash own clothes, pay operator, converse; 0.50 cu.

　　1. Proctor Laundry and Ironing Service

110. Libraries. Librarian (6) checks out, checks in, orders, catalogues books, assists in finding information for patron, engages in managerial functions; assistants (4) act as librarian, reshelve books, clean, beautify surroundings; patrons (3) read, study, select, and check out books, return books; 0.53 cu.

　　1. High School and Elementary Upper School (12–17) Library and Study Hall
　　2. Midwest City Library
　　3. Midwest City Library Volunteer Work Group

111. Locker and Shower Rooms. Physical education teachers in charge (6) set and enforce standards of conduct; students (3) dress for athletic events and physical education, take showers, put on school clothes, converse; 0.32 cu.

　　1. High School Boys Locker and Shower Room
　　2. High School Girls Locker and Shower Room

112. Lodge Meetings. Chief officer (6) conducts meeting; secretary (4), treasurer (4), lodge officers (4), committee chairmen (4) take their assigned responsibilities, engage in ritual activities and business meetings; members (3) attend, listen, vote, participate in ritual, eat, socialize; 0.46 cu.

　　1. African Masonic Lodge Meeting

2. Eastern Star Lodge Meeting
3. International Order of Odd Fellows Lodge Meeting
4. Masonic Annual District Lodge Meeting
5. Masonic Lodge Meeting
6. Rebekah and International Order of Odd Fellows Joint Installation
7. Rebekah Lodge Meeting

*113. Lotteries. Organizers (5) bring lottery drum to appointed place with names in it, turn drum in public, choose drawer; drawer (4) draws slip for prize; audience (1) watches, winner comes to claim prize.

114. Lumberyards. Owner-manager (6) manages business, attends customers, loads truck; assistant (4) helps manager; customer (3) looks at merchandise, selects, buys; 0.98 cu.
1. Graham Lumberyard
2. Midwest Lumberyard

115. Machinery Repair Shops. Foreman (6) manages shop, may or may not engage in actual repair work; mechanics (4) repair and maintain machines, weld, grease, oil, adjust, service the buses, trucks, road equipment belonging to the county, state, or school district; bus drivers and road crews (3) store equipment, converse while waiting for workday to begin; 0.91 cu.
1. County Garage and Machine Shop
2. School Garage
3. State Garage and Machine Shop
4. State Inspection of County School Buses

116. Mathematics Classes. Teacher (6) teaches mathematical subjects of algebra, geometry, calculus, etc., engages in classroom routines; high school students (3) study, recite, converse; 0.23 cu.
1. High School Mathematics Classes

117. Meetings, Business. President or chairman (6) presides at meeting and conducts it in general accordance with Roberts' Rules of Order; secretary (4), treasurer (4), committee chairmen (4) engage in prescribed work; members (3) participate in meeting according to prescribed rules; 5.63 cu.
1. Agricultural Extension Agricultural Advisory County Committee Meeting
2. Agricultural Extension Artificial Breeders Association Board Meeting
3. Agricultural Extension County Executive Board Meeting
4. Agricultural Extension Dairy Herd Improvement Association Directors Meeting
5. Agricultural Extension 4-H County Advisory Committee Meeting
6. Agricultural Extension 4-H County Council Meeting
7. Agricultural Extension Home Economics Advisory Committee Meeting

8. Agricultural Extension Livestock Association County Board Meeting
9. Agricultural Extension Purebred Beef Association Directors Meeting
10. Agricultural Extension Township Electors Meeting
11. Baptist Church Kaw Valley Association Annual Delegates Meeting
12. Baptist Church Kaw Valley Association Executive Board Meeting
13. Baptist Church Officers Meeting
14. Baptist Church Sunday School Teachers and Officers Committee Meeting
15. Baseball Association Committee Meeting
16. Bowling Association Women's Executive Committee Meeting
17. Bowling Congress Men's Executive Meeting
18. Cancer Society County Executive Committee Meeting
19. Cemetery Board Meeting
20. Chamber of Commerce Executive Committee Meeting
21. City Council and Planning Commission Meeting
22. City Council Meeting
23. City Library Board Meeting
24. City Planning Commission Meeting
25. County Commissioners Meeting
26. County Planning Board Meeting
27. County School Planning Board for School Unification Meeting
28. County Social Welfare Board Meeting
29. Democratic County Club Meeting
30. Elementary School District 29 Annual Electors Meeting
31. Elementary School Faculty Meeting
32. Elementary School (12–13) Student Council Meeting
33. Farm Bureau County Board Meeting
34. Farm Bureau County Policy Meeting
35. Farm Bureau Northeast District Delegates Meeting
36. Golf Club Executive Committee Meeting
37. Golf Club Meeting
38. High School and Elementary School Board Meeting
39. High School District 105 Annual Electors Meeting
40. High School Drama Club Business Meeting
41. High School Drama Club Executive Meeting
42. High School Faculty Meeting
43. High School Freshman (14) Class Meeting
44. High School Girls Pep Club Meeting
45. High School Home Economics Club Meeting
46. High School Junior (16) Class Meeting
47. High School Latin Club Meeting

48. High School Senior (17) Class Meeting
49. High School Sophomore (15) Class Meeting
50. High School Student Council Meeting
51. High School Student Council Trip to Attend Conference at University City High School
52. Investment Club Meeting
53. Kindergarten Parents Association Meeting
54. Lake Club Executive Meeting with Annual Meeting
55. Mental Health County Association Board Meeting
56. Mental Health County Association Organizing Meet ing
57. Methodist Church Commission for Membership and Evangelism Meeting
58. Methodist Church Commission on Missions Meeting
59. Methodist Church Commission on Stewardship and Finance Meeting
60. Methodist Church Fourth Quarterly Conference Delegates Meeting
61. Methodist Church Official Board Meeting
62. Methodist Church Trustees Meeting
63. Methodist Church Vacation Church School Executive Meeting
64. Methodist Church Wesleyan Service Guild District Delegates Business Meeting
65. Methodist Church Woman's Society of Christian Service Executive Meeting
66. Northeast Kansas County Clerks Association Meeting
67. Northeast Kansas County Clerks of District Courts Association Meeting
68. Northeast Kansas County Engineers Association Meeting
69. Northeast Kansas County Officials Meeting
70. Northeast Kansas County Probate Judges Association Meeting
71. Northeast Kansas County Register of Deeds Association Meeting
72. Northeast Kansas County Sheriffs and County Attorneys Meeting
73. Northeast Kansas County Treasurers Association Meeting
74. Northeast Kansas County Welfare Directors Association Meeting
75. Northeast Kansas Social Welfare Association Annual Meeting
76. Parent-Teacher Association Executive Meeting
77. Patton Reservoir Area Association Committee Meeting
78. Presbyterian Church Committee on Christian Education Meeting

79. Presbyterian Church Committee on Church Building Improvement Meeting
80. Presbyterian Church Committee on Evangelism Meeting
81. Presbyterian Church Committee on Stewardship and Mission Meeting
82. Presbyterian Church Deacons Meeting
83. Presbyterian Church Junior High (12–13) Fellowship Executive Meeting
84. Presbyterian Church Members Meeting
85. Presbyterian Church Quarterly Presbytery Delegates Meeting
86. Presbyterian Church Session Meeting
87. Presbyterian Church Sunday School Teachers Membership Meeting
88. Presbyterian Church Trustees Meeting
89. Presbyterian Church Vacation Church School Executive Meeting
90. Presbyterian Church Women's Organization Executive Meeting
91. Presbyterian Church Youth Budget Committee Meeting
92. Republican County Committee Meeting
93. Retarded Children's Association Meeting
94. Saddle Club Organizing Meeting
95. School Boards County Association Meeting
96. School Coaches Association County Meeting
97. School Custodians County Association Meeting and Dinner
98. School Music Supervisors County Meeting
99. School Teachers County Association Meeting
100. Soil Conservation District Board of Supervisors Meeting
101. U.S. Agricultural Stabilization and Conservation County Committee Meeting
102. U.S. Agricultural Stabilization and Conservation County Delegates Convention
103. U.S. Farmers Home Administration County Committee Meeting

118. Meetings, Cultural. President (5) conducts business meeting; secretary (4), treasurer (4), committee chairmen (4) participate appropriately in business meeting; program chairman (5) arranges program, introduces program; hostess (5) has charge of social hour and refreshments; performers (4) present program; members (3) participate in business meeting, listen, applaud, eat, socialize; 1.09 cu.

1. Agricultural Extension Home Demonstration Unit Meeting, Circle Ten Unit
2. Agricultural Extension Home Demonstration Unit Meeting, Jolly Janes Unit

3. Agricultural Extension Home Demonstration Unit Meeting, Midwest Unit
4. Agricultural Extension Home Demonstration Unit Meeting, Night Owls Unit
5. Agricultural Extension 4-H Club Meeting, Jolly Juniors
6. American Legion Women's Auxiliary Meeting
7. High School Drama Club Meeting
8. High School Science Club Meeting
9. Parent-Teacher Association Meeting
10. Parent-Teacher Association and Drama Club Joint Meeting
11. Parent-Teacher Association Meeting with Program by Beginning and Intermediate Band
12. Republican Women's Club County Meeting
13. Rotary Club Meeting (with Dinner)
14. Rural Club I Meeting
15. Rural Club II Meeting
16. Rural Club III Meeting
17. School Teachers County Association Centennial Meeting
18. Women's Club I Meeting
19. Women's Club I and Women's Club II Joint Meeting
20. Women's Club II Meeting

119. Meetings, Discussion. Chairman (6) presides, may introduce speaker (4); hostess or servers (4) serve refreshments; members (3) discuss topic under consideration, eat, converse; 0.61 cu.

1. Agricultural Extension Wheat Information Meeting
2. American Legion and Auxiliary Annual Meeting with District Representatives
3. Civic Club Meeting
4. Civil Defense County Informational Meeting
5. Farmers Home Administration District Meeting
6. Foster Parents Group Discussion Meeting
7. Parents-Without-Partners Discussion Group Meeting
8. Parent-Teacher Association Open Meeting for All Electors with School Unification Committee
9. Patton Reservoir Area Association County Informational Meeting
10. Patton Reservoir Area Association Public Meeting
11. Presbyterian and Methodist Churches Youth Leaders Discussion Meeting
12. U.S. Engineers Meeting with County Commissioners and Citizens of Otis

120. Meetings, Social. President or chairman (5) presides; treasurer (4), secretary (4), other officers (4) take prescribed responsibilities; recreational chairman (5) organizes card and other games, provides food; others assist (4) in amusing program or games; members (3) engage in meeting behavior, play games, eat, converse; 0.16 cu.

      1. American Legion Post Meeting
      2. Eastern Star Men's Night
      3. Eastern Star Past Matrons Club Meeting

121. Memorial Services. Commander (6) of American Legion directs march of squad (4) to center of cemetery; gun bearers (4) fire salute; chaplain (4) offers a prayer; flag bearer (4) carries flag; bugler (4) plays taps; audience (2) watch quietly; 0.05 cu.
      1. American Legion Memorial Day Service

°122. Motor Vehicle Operators Classes and Examinations. Driver Education teacher (6) teaches technique and theory of safe driving, drives with students in practice, engages in classroom routines, examines students; state traffic officer (6) administers driving test to applicants for license; clerk (4) administers eye test and written examination; students (3) study, drive dual-control car, take examination on theory and practice; applicants for license (3) take written examination and driving test with oral questions; 0.18 cu.
      1. High School Driver Education Class
      2. State Motor Vehicle Operators License Examination

123. Moving Picture Shows. Projectionist-owner (6) projects film; ticket seller (4) sells tickets; usher (4) takes tickets, pops and sells popcorn, soft drinks; customers (3) watch picture, eat popcorn, drink pop; 0.11 cu.
      1. Chamber of Commerce Halloween Celebration Movie
      2. Midwest Theater

124. Music Classes, Instrumental. Music teacher (6) teaches skills and theory of instrumental music, engages in classroom routines; students (3) study and practice; 0.94 cu.
      1. Anita Kelly Piano Lessons
      2. Elementary Upper School (10–12) Beginners Band Class
      3. Elementary Upper School (10–13) Intermediate Band Class
      4. Ewart Kelley Music Lessons
      5. High School and Elementary Upper School (12–17) Concert Band Class
      6. High School and Elementary Upper School (10–17) Marching Band Class
      7. Odessa Jefferson Piano Lessons

125. Music Classes, Vocal. Teacher (6) or choir master (6) teaches technique and theory of singing, may engage in classroom routines; accompanist (4) plays organ or piano; pupils (3) or choir members (3) learn about singing, practice; 1.13 cu.
      1. Baptist Church Choir Practice
      2. Elementary School Seventh and Eighth Grade (12–13) Music Classes
      3. Elementary School Fifth and Sixth Grade (10–11) Music Classes

    4. Elementary School First to Fourth Grades (6–9) Music Classes

    5. High School Chorus Class

    6. Methodist Church Junior Choir (8–13) Practice

    7. Methodist Church Senior Choir Practice

    8. Presbyterian Church Boys Choir (9–13) Practice

    9. Presbyterian Church Girls Choir (9–11) Practice

    10. Presbyterian Church Senior Choir Practice

126. Music Competitions. Master of ceremonies (6) arranges order of appearance of music groups; judges (4) evaluate quality of playing, offer critique; director (4), performers (4) play instruments or sing singly or as a group; audience (2) listen; 0.10 cu.

    1. High School County Honors Band Tryouts

    2. High School District Music Festival at State University, Band and Chorus

°127. Newspaper Reporters Beats. Reporter (6) seeks news; interviewees (4) answer questions, volunteer information; 0.09 cu.

    1. Judith Gabbart, Reporter

128. Newspaper and Printing Plants. Proprietor (6) manages business, runs printing presses, writes and corrects copy, plans layout; employees (4) run job press and linotype, address and mail papers, get news; customers (3) subscribe to paper, arrange for printing and advertising, bring in news and announcements; 0.51 cu.

    1. Midwest Weekly Newspaper

129. Nursing Homes. Owner-operator (6) manages enterprise, cares for patients, gives medication, baths, etc.; employees (4) cook, serve meals, care for patients; patients (3) receive care, live housebound lives; 0.68 cu.

    1. Dexter Nursing Home

°130. Optometrists Services. Professional optometrists (5) test eyesight of all pupils; older students (4) assist in making records, bring children for testing; pupils (3) obey directions, respond to tests of visual acuity; 0.05 cu.

    1. High School and Elementary School (6–17) Visual Acuity Tests

°131. Painting Classes. Teacher (6) teaches theory and technique of oil painting, accepts pay; students (3) listen, learn, paint, pay; 0.08 cu.

    1. Painting Class, Mrs. Till

132. Parades. Band leader (6) or a committee (5) plans route and leads parade over designated route; judges (4) evaluate costumes and decorations, give prizes; paraders (4) play instruments, walk or ride in parade, behaving appropriately to costume; spectators (2) watch, applaud, converse; 0.36 cu.

    1. Chamber of Commerce Halloween Celebration Parade

   2. Chamber of Commerce Santa on the Square
   3. High School Band at Apple Blossom Parade, Rivertown
   4. High School Band Drill and Pep Drill on Football Field
   5. High School Band at State University Band Day
   6. High School Homecoming Pep Parade and Rally
   7. Old Settlers Reunion Pet Parade
°133. Parking Lots. School principal (4), teachers (4), custodians (4) correct deviations from rules governing parking positions and individual behavior in lot; users (2) park cars; 0.58 cu.
   1. High School Parking Lot
 134. Parks and Playgrounds. Principal (6), principal and teachers, or committee members (5) are responsible for proper behavior of users and for upkeep of property; school custodians or city employees (4) keep areas tidy; schoolchildren, citizens, and lake club members (3) use facilities and equipment for games, picnics, fishing (in case of lake); visitors (2) also use playgrounds and parks; 1.28 cu.
   1. City Park
   2. Elementary Lower School (6–9) Playground
   3. Elementary Upper School (10–13) Playground
   4. Midwest Lake
 135. Parties. Committee members (5) or host and hostess (5) plan and decorate, supervise games and entertainment, provide refreshments; servers (4) may assist; members (3) play games, eat food, converse; 0.91 cu.
   1. Baptist Youth (13–17) Party at Berry Home
   2. Elementary School Seventh and Eighth Grade (12–13) Evening Party
   3. Elementary School Sixth Grade (11) Schooltime Party
   4. Elementary School Fifth Grade (10) Schooltime Party
   5. Elementary School Fourth Grade (9) Schooltime Party
   6. Elementary School Third and Fourth Grade (8–9) Schooltime Party
   7. Elementary School Third Grade (8) Schooltime Party
   8. Elementary School Second Grade (7) Schooltime Party
   9. Elementary School First and Second Grade (6–7) Schooltime party
   10. Elementary School First Grade (6) Schooltime Party
   11. High School Home Economics Club Christmas Party
   12. High School Mixed Chorus Party and Christmas Caroling
   13. Methodist Church Youth Fellowship Halloween Party at Buchtels
   14. Presbyterian Church Going Away Party for Bonds
   15. Presbyterian Church Older Women's Sunday School Class Christmas Party
   16. Retarded Activities Center Christmas Party
 136. Parties, Stag. American Legion officers (5) plan party, cook

dinner, set up tables, make guests welcome; members (3) eat, play games, converse; 0.05 cu.

    1. American Legion Stag Party with Dinner

°137. Pastors Studies. Pastor (6) consults with individuals and groups, studies, takes care of correspondence; secretary (4) carries out office routines; church members (3) consult minister; 0.33 cu.

    1. Presbyterian Church Pastors Study

138. Photographic Studios. Photographer (5) takes pictures; school official or proprietor of business (5) arranges for photographer, makes appointments, takes the pay; customers (3) have pictures taken, bring children for pictures; 0.25 cu.

    1. High School and Elementary School Temporary Photographic Studio

    2. High School Senior Class (17) Trip to Capital City for Pictures

    3. Grail Plumbing Shop Temporary Photographic Studio

    4. Western Auto Store Temporary Photographic Studio

    5. Weylens Grocery Temporary Photographic Studio

139. Physical and Biological Science Classes. Science teacher (6) teaches and directs laboratory work in biology, chemistry, physics, engages in classroom routines; students (3) study, recite, take examinations, do laboratory work; 0.35 cu.

    1. High School Health Class

    2. High School Science Classes, Biology, Chemistry, Physics

140. Physical Education Classes. Physical education teacher (6) directs calisthenics and games, engages in classroom routines; pupils (3) exercise, play games; 1.78 cu.

    1. Elementary School Seventh and Eighth Grade (12–13) Physical Education Class

    2. Elementary School Sixth Grade (11) Physical Education Class

    3. Elementary School Fifth Grade (10) Physical Education Class

    4. Elementary School Fourth Grade (9) Physical Education Class

    5. Elementary School Third and Fourth Grade (8–9) Physical Education Class

    6. Elementary School Third Grade (8) Physical Education Class

    7. Elementary School Second Grade (7) Physical Education Class

    8. Elementary School First and Second Grade (6–7) Physical Education Class

    9. Elementary School First Grade (6) Physical Education Class

    10. High School Boys Physical Education Class

    11. High School Girls Physical Education Class

*141. Physicians' Offices and Services. Physician (6) sees patients, uses instruments, diagnoses, prescribes, administers treatment and medication, advises; nurse (4) or assistants (4) make appointments, assist physician, keep records, direct flow of patients; patients (3) wait, converse, request treatment and advice, are examined, listen to doctor or nurse, receive prescriptions.

142. Piano Recital. Teacher (6) acts as master of ceremonies; pupils (4) play the piano; audience (2) listen, applaud; 0.10 cu.
    1. Piano Recital, Odessa Jefferson Pupils
    2. Piano Recital, Anita Kelly Pupils

143. Picnics. Organizer (6) or organizers (5) make arrangements, bring food, direct cooking, plan transportation; helpers (4) assist organizers; members (3) eat, play, converse; 0.40 cu.
    1. Baptist Church Picnic at Prentice Home
    2. Elementary School Sixth Grade (11) Hike and Picnic
    3. Farm Bureau Board Picnic
    4. Golf Club Scotch Doubles Tournament Picnic
    5. Ministers County Association Picnic
    6. Presbyterian Church Junior Choir (9–11) Hike and Picnic
    7. Presbyterian Church Junior Department (9–11) Picnic
    8. School Custodians County Association Picnic

144. Plays and Programs. Director (6) or directors (5) plan, direct rehearsals, produce plays or programs including skits, speeches, vocal or instrumental numbers; performers (4) act, sing, dance, speak, play instruments; stage crew (4) arranges stage, shifts scenery; audience (2) watch, listen, applaud; 1.45 cu.
    1. African Methodist Episcopal Church Homecoming, Afternoon Program
    2. African Methodist Episcopal Church Sunday School Christmas Program
    3. Agricultural Extension Home Economics County Advisory Committee President's Tea
    4. Agricultural Extension Home Economics County Crafts Day
    5. Baptist Church Vacation Church School Evening Program
    6. Elementary Lower School (6–9) Assembly
    7. Elementary School (6–13) Christmas Program
    8. Elementary School (6–13) Christmas Program Practice
    9. Elementary Upper School (10–13) Assembly
    10. High School and Elementary School Assemblies
    11. High School Christmas Program
    12. High School Christmas Program Practice
    13. High School County Home Economics Day
    14. High School Drama Club Family Night Show
    15. High School Drama Club Variety Show
    16. High School Drama Club Variety Show Practice
    17. High School Junior Class (16) Play

18. High School Junior Class (16) Play Practice
19. High School Senior Class Night Program of Skits and Music
20. High School Senior Class (17) Play
21. High School Senior Class (17) Play Practice
22. Methodist Church Sunday School Christmas Program
23. Methodist Church Vacation Church School Evening Program
24. Old Settlers Reunion Amateur Talent Show
25. Old Settlers Reunion Professional Show
26. Presbyterian Church Junior Department (9–11) Demonstration for Parents
27. Presbyterian Church Sunday School Christmas Program
28. Presbyterian Church Vacation Church School Evening Program

145. Plumbing, Heating, and Electrical Service and Appliance Companies. Plumber-electrician (6) or partners (5) make installations in new and old houses, sell and repair appliances, manage business; assistants (4) help plumber-electrician; customers (3) arrange for work, examine appliances, pay for service and materials; 0.79 cu.
    1. Grail Plumbing, Heating, and Electrical Company
    2. Trench Brothers Plumbing, Heating and Electrical Company

146. Post Offices. Postmistress (6) manages post office according to regulations; postal clerks (4) sell stamps and money orders, sort in-mail, place in boxes, sort and cancel out-mail, place in sacks; rural mail carriers (4) sort route mail, get stamps; contract carrier (4) brings and takes mail bags; custodian (4) cleans premises; customers (3) buy stamps and money orders, mail packages, get mail from boxes and packages from employees; 0.61 cu.
    1. United States Post Office

147. Programs of Band Music. Director-teacher (6) conducts band, determines program; players (4) play instruments, march; audience (2) listen, applaud; 0.27 cu.
    1. City Band Concert and Ice Cream Social
    2. City Summer Band Practice
    3. High School Band Concert at Patton Dam Dedication
    4. High School County Band Festival at Patton
    5. High School County Band Festival Rehearsal at Patton

148. Programs of Choral Music. Director-teacher (6) or teachers (5) plan, rehearse, and conduct program; members (4) sing, play instruments; audience (2) listen, applaud; 0.30 cu.
    1. Elementary Lower School (6–9) Operetta
    2. High School County Vocal Music Festival
    3. High School County Vocal Music Festival Rehearsal
    4. High School Spring Music Concert, Chorus and Band
    5. Presbyterian Church Boys (9–13) Choir Trip to Sing at Fairview Home

6. Presbyterian Church Junior (9–11) Choir Trip to Sing at Fairview Home

149. Psychological Research Offices. Directors (5) manage office, plan work; secretaries (4) engage in office routines; research associates, students (4) code, write, compute; visitors (2) seek information, attend conferences; 0.43 cu.

1. The University Midwest Field Station Research Office

°150. Psychological Service Offices. School psychologist (5) manages office, interviews clients, tests children; speech therapist (5) writes reports, prepares for teaching; secretary (4) types reports, engages in office routines; clients (3) talk, take tests; 0.31 cu.

1. County School Psychologist and Speech Therapy Office

°151. Public Speaking and Drama Competitions. Play director (6) or 4-H leaders (5) organize contestants, direct activity; judge (4) evaluates performance, gives criticism and rating; contestants (4) perform in play or make speech; audience (2) listen, applaud; 0.10 cu.

1. Agricultural Extension 4-H Illustrated Talk Contest
2. High School County Play Festival at Nelson

152. Public Lavatories and Toilets. This genotype was omitted from all analyses.

153. Real Estate Agents Offices. Licensed real estate broker (6) lists farms and homes for sale, shows property to customers, closes sale; customers (3) consult with broker, sign papers, pay; 0.48 cu.

1. Haines Real Estate Office
2. Royce Real Estate
3. Town Real Estate

154. Receptions. Hostesses (5) make arrangements, greet guests; honorees (4) receive congratulations, converse with friends; assistants (4) register guests, serve refreshments; guests (3) bring gifts, converse, eat; 0.10 cu.

1. Golden Wedding Anniversary Reception
2. Registration of Old Residents at Old Settlers Celebration

155. Refreshment Stands. Scout Leaders (5) take charge of arrangement; scouts (4) sell pop, retrieve bottles, accept pay; customers (3) buy and drink pop, converse, pay; 0.05 cu.

1. Boy Scouts Explorer Pop Stand During Old Settlers

156. Refuse Hauling Services. Truck owner (6) collects trash from homes and businesses, collects pay for service; customers (3) arrange and pay for service; 0.34 cu.

1. Kerry Trash Wagon
2. Norris Trash Wagon

157. Religion Classes. Teacher (6) or teachers (5) conduct short worship service, teach about church history, doctrine, the Bible, lead discussion; class members (3) listen, study, discuss, pray, contribute money; 3.26 cu.

1. African Methodist Episcopal Church Sunday School Class
2. Baptist Church Adult Sunday School Class

3. Baptist Church Young Adult Sunday School Class
4. Baptist Church Intermediate Boys Sunday School Class (12–17)
5. Baptist Church Intermediate Girls Sunday School Class (12–17)
6. Baptist Church Junior Boys Sunday School Class (9–11)
7. Baptist Church Junior Girls Sunday School Class (9–11)
8. Baptist Church Primary Boys Sunday School Class (6–8)
9. Baptist Church Primary Girls Sunday School Class (6–8)
10. Baptist Church Beginners Sunday School Class (4–5)
11. Baptist Church Vacation Church School Intermediate Class (12–17)
12. Baptist Church Vacation Church School Junior Class (9–11)
13. Bapitist Church Vacation Church School Primary Class (6–8)
14. Baptist Church Vacation Church School Beginners Class (4–5)
15. Methodist Church Membership Class (9–11)
16. Methodist Church Men's Sunday School Class
17. Methodist Church Women's Sunday School Class
18. Methodist Church Rev. Sanborne's Adult Sunday School Class
19. Methodist Church Young Married Sunday School Class
20. Methodist Church High School (14–17) Sunday School Class
21. Methodist Church Seventh and Eighth Grade (12–13) Sunday School Class
22. Methodist Church Junior Department (9–11) Sunday School Classes
23. Methodist Church Primary Department (6–8) Sunday School Classes
24. Methodist Church Kindergarten (4–5) Class
25. Methodist Church Nursery (1–3) Sunday School Class
26. Methodist Church Vacation Church School Junior (9–11) Class
27. Methodist Church Vacation Church School Primary (6–8) Class
28. Methodist Church Vacation Church School Kindergarten (4–5) Class
29. Presbyterian Church Older Women's Sunday School Class
30. Presbyterian Church Adult Sunday School Class
31. Presbyterian Church Crossroads Sunday School Class
32. Presbyterian Church High School (15–17) Sunday School Class
33. Presbyterian Church Ninth Grade (14) Sunday School Class

34. Presbyterian Church Seventh and Eighth Grade (12–13) Sunday School Class
35. Presbyterian Church Junior Sunday School Department (9–11) Classes
36. Presbyterian Church Primary Sunday School Department (6–8) Classes
37. Presbyterian Church Kindergarten (5) Sunday School Class
38. Presbyterian Church Nursery (3–5) Sunday School Class
39. Presbyterian Church Vacation Church School Junior High (12–13) Class
40. Presbyterian Church Vacation Church School Junior (9–11) Class
41. Presbyterian Church Vacation Church School Primary (6–8) Class
42. Presbyterian Church Vacation Church School Kindergarten (4–5) Class

158. Religion Study Groups. Chairman (5) conducts business meeting; program leader (5) presents lesson, leads discussion; assistants (4) may present parts of lesson, play the piano, or serve refreshments; members (3) listen, discuss, eat; 1.50 cu.
    1. Baptist Church Adult Study Group
    2. Baptist Church Brotherhood Meeting
    3. Baptist Church Intermediate (12–17) Study Group
    4. Baptist Church Junior (9–11) Study Group
    5. Baptist Church Demonstration Meeting, re Training Union
    6. Baptist Church Training Union Adult Group
    7. Baptist Church Training Union Intermediate (12–17) Group
    8. Baptist Church Training Union Junior (9–11) Group
    9. Baptist Church Training Union Primary (6–8) Group
    10. Baptist Church Women's Missionary Union Meetings including Special Mission Prayer Meetings
    11. Methodist Church Study Group
    12. Methodist Church Town and Country Seminar Study Group
    13. Methodist Church Woman's Society of Christian Service Regular Meeting
    14. Methodist Church Woman's Society of Christian Service Study Group
    15. Presbyterian Church All Church Meeting on the "Mission of the Church"
    16. Presbyterian Church Family Night and Meeting on Ethiopia
    17. Presbyterian Church Family Night and Meeting on Stewardship

18. Presbyterian Church Family Night Study of Southeast Asia
19. Presbyterian Church Joint Monthly Meeting of Church Officers
20. Presbyterian Church Study Session for New Elders, Trustees, and Deacons
21. Presbyterian Church Women's Organization Meeting
22. Presbyterian Church Women's Organization Retreat
23. Presbyterian Church Women's Martha Circle Study Group
24. Presbyterian Church Women's Ruth Circle Study Group
25. Presbyterian Church Women's Sarah Circle Study Group

159. Religious Fellowship Meetings. Adult sponsor (5) and youth leader (5) or president (5) and program chairman (5) arrange meeting, preside; program participants (4) speak, pray, lead discussion; accompanist (4) plays piano; refreshment committee (4) provides and serves refreshments; members (3) discuss, sing, pray, eat; 0.56 cu.

    1. Baptist Church Girls (9–17) Auxiliary Meeting
    2. Baptist Church Royal Ambassadors Meeting, Boys (9–17)
    3. Methodist Church Junior High (12–13) Youth Fellowship Meeting
    4. Methodist Church Youth (12–17) Fellowship Meeting
    5. Methodist-Presbyterian Churches Junior High (12–13) Fellowship Meeting
    6. Methodist-Presbyterian Churches Senior High (14–17) Fellowship Meeting
    7. Methodist Church Wesleyan Service Guild Fellowship Meeting
    8. Presbyterian Church Junior High (12–13) Fellowship Meeting
    9. Presbyterian Church Senior High (14–17) Fellowship Meeting
    10. Presbyterian Church Youth (12–17) Fellowship Meeting at Sterne Farm

160. Religious Prayer and Meditation Services. Minister (6) or co-leaders (5) plan meeting, preside, speak, read, pray; assistants (4) play piano, take assigned parts; members (3) listen, sing, pray; 0.39 cu.

    1. African Methodist Episcopal Church Prayer Meeting
    2. Baptist Church Midweek Prayer meeting
    3. Baptist Church Women's Prayer Meeting
    4. Church Union World Day of Prayer Worship Service
    5. Methodist Church Prayer Group Meeting
    6. Methodist Church Week of Prayer and Self Denial Meeting

161. Religious Worship Services. Minister (6) or Sunday school superintendent (6) prays, speaks, reads scripture; minister (6) performs rituals, e.g., baptism; organist (4) or pianist (4) plays in-

strument; choir director (4) directs choir; choir members (4) sing; ushers (4) seat congregation, take up collection; candle-lighters (4) light and extinguish candles; members (3) and visitors (2) listen, sing, pray; 1.55 cu.

1. African Methodist Episcopal Church Fall Rally Service and Dinner
2. African Methodist Episcopal Church Homecoming Morning Worship Service
3. African Methodist Episcopal Church Worship Service, Regular
4. Baptist Church Revival and Regular Worship Service
5. Baptist Church Sunday School Opening Exercises
6. Baptist Church Training Union Opening Exercises
7. Baptist Church Vacation Church School Opening Exercises
8. Baptist Church Worship Service at Dexter Nursing Home
9. Baptist Church Worship Service at out-of-town Nursing Homes
10. Church Union Thanksgiving Worship Service
11. Church Union Worship Services During Holy Week
12. High School Baccalaureate Worship Service
13. Independent Baptist Church Gospel Worship Service
14. Methodist Church Easter Sunrise Worship Service and Breakfast
15. Methodist Church Four Nights for God Worship Service
16. Methodist Church Joash Worship Service
17. Methodist Church Juniors (9–11) Worship Service at Fairview Home
18. Methodist Church Sunday School Closing Exercises
19. Methodist Church Vacation Church School (6–11) Closing Exercises
20. Methodist Church Worship Service, Regular
21. Presbyterian Church Adult Sunday School Opening Exercises and Convocation
22. Presbyterian Church Easter Sunrise Worship Service and Breakfast
23. Presbyterian Church Worship Service, Regular
24. Presbyterian Church Youth Sunday Worship Service

162. Restaurants and Organization Dinners for the public. Cafe proprietor (6) or proprietors (5), school lunchroom manager (5) and principal (5), organization chairman (5) plan, order food, establish prices, may aid in cooking and serving food; assistants (4) cook and serve food, clean up; customers (3) eat, pay for food, converse; 2.98 cu.

1. African Methodist Episcopal Church Homecoming Public Dinner
2. Chets Drive-In

3. Elementary Lower School (6–9) Lunchroom
4. Gwyne Cafe
5. High School and Elementary Upper School (10–17) Lunchroom
6. High School Junior (16) Public Chili Supper
7. Highway Lunchroom
8. International Order of Odd Fellows Lunchroom at Old Settlers Reunion
9. Methodist Church Annual Public Dinner and Bazaar
10. Methodist Church Wesleyan Service Guild Halloween Public Supper
11. Pearl Cafe
12. Presbyterian Church Annual Public Dinner and Bazaar
13. Rebekah and Odd Fellows Lodges Lunch Farm Auction Sales
14. Rebekah and Odd Fellows Lodges Public Dinner
15. Wayside Restaurant

°163. Retarded Childrens Classes. Director (6) organizes program of activities for retarded children, secures volunteer teachers, teaches; assistants (4) teach and care for children, prepare and serve snacks; members (3) learn, play, eat; 0.08 cu.
  1. Retarded Children's Activities Center
°164. Roller Skating Parties. Adults (6) or (5) plan and conduct excursion to rink; may have assistants (4) drive cars or buses; members (3) skate, eat, converse; 0.16 cu.
  1. Baptist Youth (13–17) Trip to Roller Skating Rink
  2. Boy Scouts Roller Skating Party
  3. Elementary School Seventh and Eighth Grade (12–13) Trip to Roller Skating Rink
*165. Rug Weaving Services. Weaver (6) sets up loom and weaves; helper (4) assists; customers (3) choose, pay for rugs.
 166. Sales Promotion and Patron Attracting Openings. Proprietor (6) or proprietors (5) invite the public to inspect new or remodeled premises, greet guests, show guests around premises, offer refreshments, give souvenirs; assistants (4) assist proprietors; guests (2) inspect premises, eat, accept gift; 0.46 cu.
  1. Blanchards Hardware Open House
  2. Bowling Alley Open House
  3. Bryants Service Station Open House
  4. Chets Drive-In Open House
  5. Darrows Service Station Open House
  6. Midwest City Library Open House
  7. Midwest County Co-op Feed Mill Grand Opening
  8. Retarded Children's Center Open House
  9. Western Auto Open House
°167. Sales Promotion Parties. Hostess (5) invites guests, prepares and serves refreshments; saleswoman (5) shows wares, directs games,

takes orders; helpers (4) assist in serving guests; customers (3) inspect and order wares, eat, play games, converse; 0.05 cu.

    1. Sales Parties (Stanley, Tupperware, Jewelry)

168. Sales Routes: Cosmetics, Household Supplies, Magazines. Salesman-agents (5) plan route, sell, take orders, deliver goods; or sales organizers (5) plan sales route and campaign, give out order blanks, etc.; salesmen (4) sell, take orders, deliver goods, report to organizer; customers (3) inspect, order, pay; 0.63 cu.

    1. Avon Cosmetics Sales Routes
    2. Elementary School (12–13) Candy Sales Route for Trophy Case
    3. Fuller Brush Sales Route Household Supplies
    4. High School Drama Club (15–17) Christmas Card Sale
    5. High School Junior and Senior (16–17) Magazine Sales Route for Class Funds
    6. High School Seniors (17) Candy Sales Route for Class Trip
    7. High School Seniors (17) Magazine Sales Route for Class Trip

°169. Savings Stamp Sales Stands. Teacher (6) organizes and directs; pupil-salesmen (4) sell U.S. savings stamps; teacher and pupil customers (3) buy U.S. savings stamps; 0.06 cu.

    1. Elementary Upper School (10–13) U.S. Savings Stamp Sale Stand

170. School Administrators Offices. Principal (6) manages office routines, confers with school board members, faculty, students, parents, sales people, administers and deals with curricular, disciplinary, business problems of school; secretary (4) attends to office routines; board members (3), faculty (3), students (3), sales people (3), parents (2) talk with, are admonished by, or sell supplies to principal; 0.99 cu.

    1. County Superintendent of Schools Office
    2. Elementary Upper and Lower School Principals Office
    3. High School Principals Office

*171. School Custodians' Room. Head custodian (6) stores equipment, rests in off hours; helpers (4) assist; students (3) come for assistance.

172. School Enrollment Periods. Principal (5) and teacher (5) interview pupils and parents, enroll pupils in appropriate classes; clerks (4) issue books, accept book rental fee; pupils (3), parents (3) fill out information forms, pay book rental fee, discuss program; 0.15 cu.

    1. Elementary Lower School (6–9) Enrollment Day
    2. Elementary Lower School (5–6) Pre-enrollment Day
    3. High School and Elementary Upper School (10–17) Enrollment Day

173. School Offices. Principals (5) manage offices; secretaries (4) carry out office routines; student assistants (4) assist secretary; teachers

(3) may use equipment; pupils (3) run errands, get supplies; 0.59 cu.
   1. Elementary Upper School Office
   2. High School and Elementary Upper School Main Office

°174. School Rallies. Principal or teacher (5) on hand if control is necessary; head cheerleader (5) acts as master of ceremonies, calls for cheers, directs cheerleaders; cheerleaders (4) yell, do acrobatics, lead cheering; athletic team members (4) introduced; students (3) cheer in concert, applaud; 0.28 cu.
   1. Elementary School (10–13) Pep Rally
   2. High School Cheerleader Practice
   3. High School Cheerleaders Trip to Clinic at University City High School
   4. High School Cheerleader Tryouts
   5. High School Pep Club Pep Rally

175. Scout Meetings. Scout leaders (5) or den mothers (6) plan and direct activities, demonstrate skills; patrol or den leaders (4) assist leaders, take roll, raise flag; members (3) engage in games, handicraft, study, discussion, ceremony; 0.48 cu.
   1. Boy Scout Cub (7–11) Den I Meeting
   2. Boy Scout Cub (7–11) Den II Meeting
   3. Boy Scout Cub (7–11) Den III Meeting
   4. Boy Scout Cub (11) Den Meeting, Webelos
   5. Boy Scout Cub (7–11) Pack Meeting
   6. Boy Scout Explorer Post Meeting
   7. Boy Scout Troop Meeting

*176. Seed Corn Storage and Sales Routes. Salesman (6) stores seed and samples of hybrid corn, may deliver corn; customers (3) come for corn, take and pay for it.

177. Service Stations. Manager (6) manages business, fills tanks of cars and trucks with gasoline, checks oil, water, and tires, washes windshields, changes oil, greases cars, sells accessories; assistants (4) service cars as prescribed; customers (3) buy gasoline, oil, accessories, pay for servicing; 2.80 cu.
   1. Bethels Service Station
   2. Bryants Service Station
   3. Hamiltons Service Station
   4. Skelly Service Station

178. Sewing and Dressmaking Classes. Teacher-leader (6) teaches theory and skills of sewing, demonstrates sewing techniques; members (3) sew by hand and machine, learn principles of sewing; 0.16 cu.
   1. Agricultural Extension 4-H Sewing Class I
   2. Agricultural Extension 4-H Sewing Class II and III
   3. Agricultural Extension Home Economics Best Dress Workshop

179. Sewing Club Meetings. Chairman (6) plans activities, distributes

work (piecing quilts, sewing rags for rugs, mending); committee (4) prepares and serves refreshments; members (3) sew, converse, eat; 0.16 cu.

    1. Gray Ladies Club Meeting

    2. Presbyterian Church Ladies Sewing Group Meeting

°180. Sewing Services. Seamstress (6) manages work, takes orders, fits garments, sews, charges for service; customers (3) arrange for work, are fitted, pay for service; 0.61 cu.

    1. Betsons Sewing Service

    2. Dewdney Sewing and Baking Service

181. Sheriffs Offices. Sheriff (6) manages office, keeps in radio contact with sheriff's cars, state police, and other law enforcement agencies, keeps records, directs deputy, responds to calls for assistance; deputy (4) takes duty when sheriff is out; visitors (2) come for information, to give information; 0.43 cu.

    1. County Sheriffs Office

*182. Shoe Repair Shops. Repairman-owner (6) manages business, repairs shoes, sells sundries; customers (3) bring in shoes, pick up repaired shoes, pay.

°183. Sign Painting Services. Sign painter (6) designs and paints signs; 0.15 cu.

    1. Sanborn Sign Painting Service

184. Social Science Classes. Social Science teacher (6) teaches history and government of United States and other countries, engages in classroom routines; students (3) study, write, discuss; 0.33 cu.

    1. High School Citizenship Class

    2. High School Social Science Class

185. Soil Conservation Service Offices. Soil conservationist (6) manages office, directs assistants (4) in conducting surveys of soil erosion and water conservation projects, plans management practices such as contour plowing, reforestation, prepares plans in cooperation with farmers for soil and water conservation on individual farms; secretary (4) engages in office routines; farmers (3) come in for consultation on problems relating to soil and water conservation, give necessary information for planning; 0.43 cu.

    1. U.S. Soil Conservation Office

186. Solicitation of Funds. Organizers (6) or (5) plan campaign, direct solicitors to designated areas of town, distribute information leaflets and receipt forms to solicitors; solicitors (4) solicit donations from individuals, accept money, give receipt; donors (3) give or refuse to give money; 0.52 cu.

    1. African Methodist Episcopal Church Fund Drive for Homecoming

    2. American Legion Auxiliary Poppy Fund Drive

    3. Baseball Association Fund Drive

    4. Cancer Association Fund Drive

      5. Children's Service League Fund Drive

      6. Heart Association Fund Drive

      7. High School Home Economics Club Fund Drive for Cerebral Palsy

      8. Methodist Church and Presbyterian Church Youth Collection for CROP

      9. Red Cross Fund Drive

      10. Rotary Club Fund Drive for Boy Scouts

187. Solicitation of Goods. Drivers (5) distribute solicitation leaflets over town, return to pick up goods in Salvation Army truck; donors (3) leave donated goods in accessible place with Salvation Army sign; 0.06 cu.

      1. Salvation Army Pick-Up

°188. Speech Therapy Services. Speech therapist (6) teaches children correct enunciation of words, demonstrates placement of tongue and lips, uses taped speech to assist teaching; pupil (3) practices correct speech, demonstrates progress; 0.17 cu.

      1. Elementary Lower School (6–9) Speech Therapy Service

      2. High School and Elementary Upper School (10–17) Speech Therapy Service

189. Spelling Bees. County superintendent (6) arranges contest, appoints judge; judge (4) pronounces words, indicates success or failure in correct spelling; contestants (4) representing county schools spell words; audience (2) listen; 0.05 cu.

      1. Spelling Bee County Finalists

190. Staff Lounges. Janitors (4) keep room clean; teachers (3) use room for coffee break, smoking, correcting papers, conversing; 0.21 cu.

      1. High School Faculty Lounge

191. Street Fairs. Chamber of Commerce committee (5) arranges for carnival, provides facilities; carnival manager (5) directs placement of concessions, deals with committee; concessionaires (4) set up own concession or ride, take tickets, act as barkers, give prizes; ticket sellers (4) sell tickets usable at any concession; food sellers (4) sell popcorn, cotton candy, hot dogs; customers (3) ride on equipment, try games of skill, buy and eat food, stroll about, converse; 0.10 cu.

      1. Bread Company Miniature Train Ride

      2. Old Settlers Reunion Midway

192. Swimming Excursions and Classes. Leaders (6) or (5) organize swimming group, arrange transportation, are responsible for group until return to point of departure; bus drivers (5) drive school bus; members (3) ride in bus, converse, go swimming for enjoyment and instruction; 0.22 cu.

      1. Agricultural Extension 4-H Swimming Party with Vernon 4-H

      2. Presbyterian Boys (9–13) Choir Swimming Party

3. Red Cross Early (8–10 a.m.) Swimming Class
4. Red Cross Late (10–12 a.m.) Swimming Class

193. Tank Truck Lines. Driver-agent (6) takes orders for bulk fuel oil and gasoline, fills tank at depot, delivers fuel oil to town customers, charges for oil and delivery; customers (3) order and pay for gasoline and oil; 0.34 cu.

    1. Standard Oil Tank Truck and Bulk Storage

194. Taverns. Owner-manager (6) manages business, serves beer, accepts pay, converses; assistant (4) helps in serving customers; customers (3) drink, converse, play pinball machine, play juke box, pay; 0.73 cu.

    1. Corner Tavern

°195. Teacher Conferences with Parents. Teacher (6) confers with parent or parents of each elementary school child at an appointed time, gives parent child's report card; parents (3) listen, ask questions, confer with teacher, receive child's report card; 0.10 cu.

    1. Elementary Lower School (6–9) Teachers Conferences with Parents
    2. Elementary Upper School (10–13) Teachers Conferences with Parents

°196. Telephone Automatic Exchange Buildings. Telephone service man (6) uses building as headquarters, services automatic equipment; customers (3) may leave payment for telephone service at the building; 0.30 cu.

    1. Telephone Building

°197. Telephone Booths. Telephone service man (6) services phone, takes money from box at regular intervals; customers (3) put coins in phone, dial, talk; 0.31 cu.

    1. Midwest Telephone Booths

*198. Telephone Exchanges. Manager (6) assigns schedule, keeps records; operators (4) operate switch board, give information, implement fire service calls; customers (3) call in, pay bills.

°199. Timber Sales and Tree Removal Services. Tree faller (6) fells large trees, determines desired direction for tree to fall, saws undercut in bole of tree, saws backcut, using wedges to tip tree, cuts felled tree into lengths, removes on truck; assistant (4) helps, drives and loads truck, using winch; customers (3) arrange for and pay for service. (The Dutch elm disease made felling of large trees an important service in Midwest in 1963–64.); 0.18 cu.

    1. Garner Tree Service

°200. Tool Sharpening Services. Owner-operator (6) sharpens saws and other tools, receives pay, keeps books; customers (3) bring tools to be sharpened, pay for service; 0.27 cu.

    1. Betsons Saw and Tool Sharpening Service

201. Track and Field Meets. Track coaches (5) are in charge of arrangements, schedule, and organization; officials (4) at each

event judge and record winners and their records; starters (4) start races; competitors (4) run, jump, throw; public address announcer (4) announces contests, winners; audience (2) watch, cheer, applaud; 0.38 cu.

1. Elementary Upper School (11–13) Track Meet out of town
2. Elementary Upper School and High School (11–17) Track Meet
3. Elementary Upper School and High School (11–17) Girls Track Meet out of town
4. High School Boys Track Meet
5. High School Boys Track Meet out of town
6. High School Girls Track Meet
7. High School Track Meet Practice

°202. Tractor Pulling Contests. Organizers (5) take entries, explain rules, announce winners, start contests, give awards; contestants (4) drive tractors; designated spectators (4) jump on sled to add weight; judges (4) on flatbed truck record number of men on sled when tractor can no longer move sled, measure number of feet pulled, judge winner in each class; audience (2) watch, applaud; 0.05 cu.

1. Old Settlers Reunion Tractor Pulling Contest

203. Trafficways. City employees (4) repair streets; city marshall (4), county sheriff (4), and state traffic officers (4) enforce traffic regulations; pedestrians (2) walk on streets and sidewalks; automobile drivers (2) drive on streets; children (2) play in streets; 1.25 cu.

1. Midwest Streets and Sidewalks

°204. Trips by Organizations to Visit the Sick. President (6) organizes trip; members (4) gather at one member's home and drive to nearby nursing home, where they visit all able to receive visitors, sew, or write letters for them, converse; 0.06 cu.

1. Gray Ladies Trips to Fairview Home for Social Visiting

205. TV and Radio Repair Shop. Owner-operator (6) repairs TV sets and radios, charges for service and parts, manages business; helper (4) assists; customers (3) bring in sets or phone for service, pay for service; 0.45 cu.

1. Tamara Radio and TV Repair Shop

*206. Upholstery Services. Proprietor-upholsterer (6) buys materials, estimates costs, upholsters furniture; customers (3) bring in furniture, consider samples, choose, pay.

*207. Used Car Sales Lots. Proprietor (6) buys and sells used cars; customers (3) try out cars, may buy; others (3) either sell or trade in old cars.

208. Variety Stores. Owner-operators (5) manage store, sell merchandise, interview wholesale salesmen, stock shelves; clerk (4) sells merchandise; customers (3) look, select, buy, converse; 0.57 cu.

1. Kane Variety Store

*209. Veterinary Services. Veterinarian-owner (6) manages business, sees animals, gives and prescribes medication and treatment, drives to outlying farms to provide service, accepts payment; assistant (4) answers phone, keeps records; customers (3) seek advice, service, bring animals in, phone for services, pay.

°210. Vocational Counseling Services. High school principal (6) organizes trip for seniors to Career Day in another high school; members (3) gather at high school bus stop, ride to neighboring town, learn about possible careers, ask questions, discuss; 0.05 cu.
    1. High School Senior Class (17) Trip to Attend Career Day at Vernon

°211. Volleyball Games. Coaches (5) arrange game and umpire; players (4) play volleyball according to rules; audience (2) watch, applaud; 0.10 cu.
    1. Elementary Upper School (11–13) Volleyball Game
    2. Elementary Upper School (11–13) Volleyball Game out of town

212. Wallpapering and Painting Services. Operator (6) papers and paints as arranged, charges for service; customer (3) arranges for and pays for service; 0.17 cu.
    1. Gibbon Wallpapering and Painting Service
    2. Kelby Wallpapering and Painting Service

°213. Water Supply Plants. City engineer (5) and assistant (5) check plant daily, add chemicals, take samples of water, make minor repairs; 0.30 cu.
    1. Midwest Water Filtration Plant

214. Weddings, Church. Minister (5) is in charge of marriage service; bride's parents (5) are in charge of reception; bride (4), groom (4), attendants (4), ushers (4), musicians (4), helpers at reception (4) fill designated roles in marriage ceremony; guests (2) watch, congratulate, eat refreshments, may bring gift; 0.10 cu.
    1. Methodist Church Weddings, Call-Hanson, Stopt-Blond, Bequith-Beyet
    2. Presbyterian Church Weddings, Biddle-Bolling, Cam-Rockner

215. Weddings, Civil. Probate judge (6) performs marriage; bride (4), groom (4), witnesses (4) carry out prescribed roles; guests (2) watch, offer good wishes; 0.05 cu.
    1. Civil Weddings

216. Weed Inspectors Offices. Weed supervisor (6) arranges with farmers to inspect for noxious weeds or to spray along county roads; assistant (4) helps supervisor; farmers (3) come for advice and to make request for spraying and chemicals; 0.24 cu.
    1. County Weed Supervisors Office

217. Welfare Offices. Welfare director (6) manages office, interviews clients, works with county commissioners and state welfare of-

ficers, makes reports, presides at staff conferences; welfare workers (4) interview clients, implement law; secretaries (4) engage in office routines; clients (3) come to see welfare workers, get information, assistance; 0.43 cu.

    1. County Welfare Office

°218. Welfare Workers Classes. Welfare director (5) organizes class, arranges for place, etc.; teacher (5) teaches class, engages in classroom routines; students listen, take notes, discuss; 0.05 cu.

    1. County Welfare In-Service Staff Training Meeting

219. Woodworking and Machine Shop Classes. Teacher (6) teaches skills and theory of working with wood, demonstrates proper use of tools, teaches reading and drawing of plans, engages in classroom routines; students (3) work with wood, engage in mechanical drawing, study; 0.21 cu.

    1. High School Boys Shop Classes

°220. X-Ray Laboratories. X-ray specialist (5) is in charge of taking x-rays; local chairman (5) organizes volunteer help; clerical workers (4) get information from clients, type cards, give directions; clients (3) have chest x-ray taken, respond to directions, give information; 0.05 cu.

    1. State Department of Public Health Mobile X-Ray Laboratory

Catalogue of Yoredale Behavior Setting Genotypes, 1954–55 and 1963–64; Behavior Settings, 1963–64

~~~~~~

The Yoredale catalogue is arranged indentically like Midwest's. For explanation refer to the introduction to Appendix A.

1. Accountants Offices. Chartered accountant (6) or accountants (5) manage office, keep and audit accounts for individuals and businesses, prepare income tax reports; junior staff (4) carry out office routines, work under direction of accountant; clients (3) bring accounts to be worked on, seek advice, pay for services; 0.94 cu.
    1. Kettlewell, Jay and Company Accountants Office
    2. Mordue and Howells Accountants Office
    3. Straker and Son Accountants Office
2. Agricultural Fair Offices. Fair secretary (6) keeps records of Fair, receives entries, makes arrangements, organizes volunteer staff; treasurer (4) keeps track of expenses and income, pays bills; vol-

unteer office staff (4) work under direction of secretary; exhibitors and others (3) seek information, give information; 0.05 cu.

    1. Agricultural and Horticultural Fair, Secretaries Tent

3. Agricultural Fairs. Fair officials (show secretary, assistants) (5) supervise arrangements, maintain schedule, check gate receipts, collect money from other officials, keep records; other officials (stewards, assistants) (4) take money from customers, direct parking, assist in rings; judges (4) examine or watch competitors, compare, decide winners; competitiors (4) ride and show animals, groom animals, wait; customers (3) pay, walk, stand, watch, examine and compare animals, applaud winners; onlookers (2) watch from distance, wander; 0.05 cu.

    1. Agricultural and Horticultural Fair, Main Arena

°4. Agronomy Classes. Teacher (6) teaches crop husbandry, takes roll, engages in classroom routine, supervises field trips to farms; Evening Institute director (4) picks up roll; members (3) (farmers) learn, listen, practice; 0.13 cu.

    1. Evening Institute Crop Husbandry Class, Mr. Ellis
    2. Evening Institute Crop Husbandry Class, Mr. Lavin

°5. Animal Husbandry Classes. Chairman (6) in charge of arrangements, getting speaker, providing place, publicity; speaker (4) lectures (with film or slides); members (3) listen, question, receive pamphlets; 0.05 cu.

    1. B. C. O. M. Talk on Winter Milk Production

6. Antique Shops. Proprietors (5) buy, sell, repair antiques; assistant (4) cleans, polishes, sells; customers (3) buy or commission repairs, pay; 0.44 cu.

    1. Harken and Son Antique Shop

°7. Art Classes, General. Qualified teacher (6) teaches theory and techniques of art using a variety of media: paint, clay, pencil, paper, etc., engages in classroom routines; pupils (3) learn and practice various modes of creative art; 0.29 cu.

    1. Secondary Modern School Art Classes, Mr. Gibbons
    2. Secondary Modern School Art Classes, Mr. Kale
    3. Secondary Modern School Art Classes, Mr. Stokes

°8. Athletic Equipment Rooms. Coaches (6 or 5), both local and visiting, prepare for physical education and sports, give out equipment, consult with individuals; atheletes (3) get equipment for sports; 0.37 cu.

    1. Secondary Modern School Boys Physical Training Office
    2. Secondary Modern School Girls Physical Training Office

9. Auction Sales, Household Furnishings and General Merchandise. Representative (6) or representatives (5) of company in charge of arrangements, supervise selling, write receipts; assistants (4) set up display, help direct proceedings, move objects to cars or vans. Customers (3) inspect merchandise, bid, pay and remove objects from premises; onlookers (2) inspect merchandise and watch proceedings; 0.10 cu.

    1. Farm Equipment Auction, Grieg

    2. Furniture Auction in Church Rooms

10. Auction Sales, Livestock. Auction mart manager (5) supervises sales personnel, arranges for sales, and is responsible for financial transactions; auctioneers (5) start sales, call for bids, identify buyers; clerks (4) record transactions for auctioneer; yard assistants (4) receive livestock for sale and escort animals to and from sale ring; sellers (3) bring animals for sale, approve or refuse sale; buyers (3) bid on, pay for and remove animals, watch proceedings, inspect animals, converse; onlookers (2) watch, inspect animals, converse; 0.14 cu.

    1. Livestock Sales, Auction Mart

11. Auction Sales, Real Estate. Agents from solicitor's office (5) make arrangements with clients for place, time, etc., preside over bidding, write receipts; customers (3) inspect property, bid; onlookers (2) watch and converse; 0.15 cu.

    1. Farm Real Estate Sales

    2. Real Estate Auction Sales at Church Rooms

    3. Real Estate Auction Sales at Karim Arms

12. Automobile Association Services. Automobile association man (6) responds to calls for assistance, patrols town and area, gives information; members (3) ask for help or information, pay dues; 0.38 cu.

    1. Automobile Association Representative Route

    2. Royal Automobile Club Representative Route

13. Award Ceremonies. Officials (6 or 5) preside over meeting, present other performers, i.e., speakers (4) give speeches; musical performers (4) sing, play; presenters of awards (4) give awards with appropriate remarks; awardees accept awards. Committee members or servers (4) serve tea or food; audience members (3) and onlookers (2) listen, applaud, eat, converse, watch; 0.10 cu.

    1. Express Dairy Dinner to Present Safety Awards

    2. Secondary Modern School Speech Day in Assembly Hall

14. Badminton Games. Chairman (6) or team chairmen (5) arrange for play and players, set times, arrange for place; committee members (4) serve tea; players (4) play inter-club matches according to rules; referees (4) judge play; members (3) practice badminton; 0.21 cu.

    1. Badminton Club League Game

    2. Badminton Club League Game out of town

    3. Badminton Club Unscheduled Game

15. Bakeries. Owners-managers (5) or manager (6) manage bakery, buy materials, supervise sale of baked goods and sundries; bakers (4) bake; assistants (4) help; sales women (4) sell baked goods; customers (3) order, buy and pay for bread, cake, pasteries, and limited numbers of other foodstuffs; 0.96 cu.

    1. Dungait Bakery and Shop

    2. Walton Bakery and Shop

16. Banks, Commercial. Bank manager (6) manages bank in accord with policy of the owning bank, sees customers to arrange credit-investment payment, or to give financial advice; undermanager (4) chief cashier (4) sees customers, arranges some credits, investments; clerks (4) cash checks, receive deposits, handle money, engage in office routines; customers seek credit, advice, arrange financial matters; 0.97 cu.
    1. Barclays Bank
    2. Midland Bank

17. Banks, Savings. Bank clerk (6) opens office once a week, accepts savings, keeps accounts, takes records to home bank; customers (3) make deposits and withdrawals; 0.25 cu.
    1. Yorkshire County Savings Bank
    2. Yorkshire Penny Bank

°18. Baptism Services. Clergyman (6) baptizes infant in accordance with prescribed ritual; infant (4) is baptized; parents (4) present child for baptism; godparents (4) participate in service as prescribed; family members (3) and invited friends (3) watch; 0.11 cu.
    1. Church of England Baptism
    2. Roman Catholic Church Baptism

19. Barbershops (Mens Hairdressers). Owner-barber (6) cuts hair, manages shop, accepts payment, supervises helpers, orders materials, sells other merchandise; assistants (4) cut hair, brush off customers, sell merchandise, accept payments; customers (3) wait for service, read, converse, purchase articles, have haircut, get shaved, pay; 0.56 cu.
    1. Eddie, Mens Hairdresser
    2. Herman, Mens Hairdresser

°20. Basket-Making Classes. Teacher (6) instructs in art and techniques of basket-making, provides materials, engages in classroom routines; pupils (3) listen, practice the skills of basket-making; 0.06 cu.
    1. Secondary Modern School Basket-Making Class

*21. Beauty Culture Classes. Hostess (5) arranges home, provides needed mirrors, chairs, etc.; teacher (5) instructs in methods of make-up and skin care; committee (4) serves tea; members (3) receive instructions, try out make-up, converse, drink tea.

22. Beauty Shops (Ladies Hairdressers). Operator-manager (6) cuts, washes, sets, styles, colors, combs hair of customer, carries out management routines; assistant (4) answers phone, assists operator; customers (3) receive operator's services, converse, read, pay for services; 1.42 cu.
    1. Blackett, Ladies Hairdresser
    2. Herta, Ladies Hairdresser
    3. Martindale, Ladies Hairdresser
    4. Wheldon, Ladies Hairdresser

*23. Beetle Drives. Chairman (6) makes arrangements, appoints committees; committee members (4) sell tickets, set up tables, provide dice, paper, pencils, and serve tea; M. C. (4) directs play, explains rules; customers (3) play, converse, laugh, buy and drink tea, receive prizes.

*24. Bicycle Runs. Chairman (6) decides on run and makes arrangements; helpers (4) set up markers; club members (3) meet at clubhouse for instructions and set off together on designated run, record distance and time.

°25. Billiards Games. Home team captain (5) starts and supervises play; visiting team captain (5) and players (4) watch and play in turn, drink from adjacent bar room, eat dry snacks, and converse. Onlookers (2) watch, converse, eat and drink; 0.15 cu.
    1. Billiards Team Match
    2. Billiards Team Match out of town

°26. Bingo Games. Chairman of organization (5) provides prizes, arranges room; emcee (5) sells tickets, calls numbers, gives prizes; helpers (4) assist emcee, sell raffle tickets; customers (3) buy tickets, play bingo, converse, eat; 0.06 cu.
    1. Roman Catholic Church Womens League Bingo Game

27. Blood Collection Laboratories. Doctor (6) supervises arrangements and staff; assistants (4) do blood tests, watch container, keep records, volunteers (4) escort donors from one area to another, prepare and serve tea and biscuits; donors (3) follow instructions, lie down to give blood and recuperate, drink tea and eat biscuits after; 0.05 cu.
    1. National Health Service Blood Collection Unit

28. Bonfires, Public. Interested parties (4) bring materials to build fire to the traditional place, light fire. Spectators (2) watch, converse, enjoy bonfire; 0.05 cu.
    1. Guy Fawkes Day Bonfire

°29. Bookbinding Classes. Teacher (6) teaches mentods and theory of bookbinding, engages in classroom routines; pupils (3) learn and practice bookbinding; 0.14 cu.
    1. Secondary Modern School Bookbinding Class
    2. Secondary Modern School Bookbinding Club

30. Bowling Games (Lawn Bowling). Home team captain (5) greets visitors, responds to vote of thanks, supervises laying out of equipment, instigates play. Visiting team captain (5) gives vote of thanks to home team and players (4) play, converse, keep score. Home players (4) also lay out and serve tea after play ends. Onlookers (2) watch, converse, have tea; 0.19 cu.
    1. Bowling Club Match and Open Play
    2. Bowling Club Match out of town

31. Building, Construction, and Repair Services. Operator (6) or operators (5) manage construction, engage in carpentry, masonry, painting and wallpapering work, supervise assistants, arrange

with customers re undertaking services; engage in performing these services. Assistants (4) engage in similar activities under supervision; customers (3) arrange for services, pay for services, inspect work, request advice; onlookers (1) kibitz on large jobs. 1.41 cu.

1. Dent and Company Builder and Undertaker
2. Garbutt Builder
3. Lowes Builder and Undertaker

32. Bus Stops. Drivers (6) drive buses, give information; conductors (4) take money, give information, converse; customers (3) walk, board bus, ask information, pay money, leave bus; 1.19 cu.

1. Bus Stop on Market Square
2. Bus to Bingo (Castleton)
3. Bus to Romanton Camp
4. Bus to Cinema, Romanton Camp
5. Bus to Grammar School
6. Secondary Modern School Bus Loading and Unloading

33. Butcher Shops. Butcher (6) or butchers (5) buy animals and specialty foods, cut up beef, lamb, hogs, direct making of sausage, meat pies, cooked meats, wait on customers, manage shop; apprentices (4) learn trade under supervisor; assistants (4) wait on customers, prepare cooked meat, sausage, pies, clean premises; customers (3) order meat, pay, converse; 1.65 cu.

1. Guy Butcher Shop
2. Kerret Butcher Shop
3. Sinclair Butcher Shop
4. Whittington Meat Van Route

34. Caravan and Trailer Parks. Manager (6) takes fee for trailers, keeps place tidy; customers (3) pay for use of park, live in trailers; 0.31 cu.

1. Caravan Park

35. Card Parties. Represenative (6) or representatives (5) make arrangements for time and place, greet members, organize games, direct play; assistants (4) help direct play, give prizes, take money, serve tea; customers (3) pay money, engage in playing according to rules (Whist), follow instructions, have tea; 0.26 cu.

1. Conservative Party Society Whist Drive
2. Football Club Whist Drive
3. Moorside Nursing Home Whist Drive
4. Over Sixtys Club Whist Drive
5. Roman Catholic Church Womens League Military Whist Drive

36. Carnivals. Representatives of organization (5) make arrangements for time and place, solicit donations of goods and services, supervise helpers; helpers (4) man stalls, sell objects, make and serve food, supervise competitions, sell tickets; performers (4) play, sing, or dance; customers (3) examine and buy articles,

engage in competitions, listen to and look at performers, buy and consume food and drink on premises, pay; 0.35 cu.

1. Boy Scouts Garden Fete at Moultons Residence
2. Church of England Garden Fete
3. County Primary School Bring and Buy Sale
4. Playing Fields Committee Fair (August Bank Holiday Fair)
5. Secondary Modern School Westerdale Day Main Assembly Room Events
6. Secondary Modern School Westerdale Day Rifle Galleries
7. Secondary Modern School Westerdale Day Croquet Concession

37. Carpenters (Joiners) Services. Carpenter (6) constructs or repairs parts of building made with wood; assistant (4) may help carpenter carry tools; apprentices (4) learn and practice carpentry; customer (3) arranges for work, pays for service and materials; 0.64 cu.

1. Ewen Joiner Services
2. Vivien Joiner Services

38. Cemeteries, Clergyman (5) and Undertaker (5) arrange and perform burial services according to ritual; casket bearers (4) assist; caretaker (4) mows grass, maintains cemetery; clerk of the parish council (5) sells lots, oversees caretaker; gravediggers (4) dig graves; visitors (2) visit cemetery, bring flowers; 1.24 cu.

1. Cemetery

39. Chess Games. Club chairman (6) or chairmen (5) and secretary (5) arrange for place for play and matches with other clubs; secretary (4) keeps records; players (4) play chess according to rules in matches; members (3) practice chess, study moves; 0.22 cu.

1. Chess Club Game out of town
2. Chess Club Meeting and Game
3. Secondary Modern School Chess Club Meeting

40. Chimney and Window Repair Services. Chimney sweep (6) cleans chimneys, repairs windows; customers (3) arrange for service inspect result and pay; 0.07 cu.

1. Dearlove Chimney Cleaning Service

°41. China Painting Classes. Teacher (6) teaches theory and technique of china painting, provides materials, engages in classroom routines; pupils (3) practice techniques, pay for materials and instruction; 0.14 cu.

1. Evening Institute Afternoon China Painting Class
2. Evening Institute Evening China Painting Class

°42. Chiropodists Services. Qualified chiropodist (6) treats patients' feet in accordance with his training using bathing, medication, instruments; patients (3) ask for services, advice, and pay; 0.13 cu.

1. Mr. Gibb Chiropodist Services
2. National Health Service Chiropody Clinic

°43. Circuses. Owner-operators (5) arrange place and time, supervise

setting up, publicity, sell tickets, supervise performances, act as
M. C.; performers (4) do tricks, magic, exploits, show trained
animals, sell orange squash; customers (3) buy tickets, watch,
applause, converse, buy and drink drinks; 0.05 cu.

    1. Tinker Brothers Circus

°44. Civic Education Booths. Representative from Civil Defense and
Road Safety (5) set up stall with displays and pamphlets, give information; stall visitors (3) look at displays, listen, ask questions;
0.05 cu.

    1. Agricultural and Horticultural Fair Civil Defense and Road
Safety Booth

45. Civil Engineering (Clerk of the Works) and Public Health Inspectors Offices. Clerk of the Works (6) manages office, consults with
other officials and area residents about water and sanitation
problems, makes and maintains drawings of water distribution
and sewer systems; 0.29 cu.

    1. District Clerk of the Works and Public Health Inspectors
Offices

46. Classrooms, Freetime. Teacher (6) supervises generally. Class
captains (4) observe and record misbehavior; prefect (4) inter-
venes in noisy situations and gives lines to write as punishment;
pupils (3) study, converse, play games; 2.64 cu.

    1. County Primary School Upper Juniors (9–11) Classroom
Freetime
    2. County Primary School Middle Juniors (8–10) Classroom
Freetime
    3. County Primary School Lower Juniors (7–8) Classroom
Freetime
    4. County Primary School Infants (5–7) Classroom Freetime
    5. Roman Catholic School (5–16) Classroom Freetime
    6. Secondary Modern School Form 4E (14–16) Classroom
Freetime
    7. Secondary Modern School Form 4S (14–16) Classroom
Freetime
    8. Secondary Modern School Form 4X (14–16) Classroom
Freetime
    9. Secondary Modern School Form 3E (13–14) Classroom
Freetime
    10. Secondary Modern School Form 3S (13–14) Classroom
Freetime
    11. Secondary Modern School Form 2E (12–13) Classroom
Freetime
    12. Secondary Modern School Form 2S (12–13) Classroom
Freetime
    13. Secondary Modern School Form 2X (12–13) Classroom
Freetime
    14. Secondary Modern School Form 1E (11–12) Classroom
Freetime

15. Secondary Modern School Form 1S (11–12) Classroom Freetime

47. Cleaners, Dry Cleaning Depots. Manager (6) takes in clothing, drapes, bedding, to be cleaned, returns clean items to customers, keeps records, charges fee, supervises assistant; assistant (4) helps manager with service to customers; driver (4) picks up soiled articles and returns cleaned articles to the Depot; customers (3) bring in items to be cleaned, pay, collect cleaned articles, converse; 0.45 cu.
   1. Cleaners Agency

48. Clothiers and Dry Goods Stores. Owner-manager (6) managers (5) manage business, order stock, stock shelves, serve customer, keep records; shop assistant (4) assists manager, stock shelves, serves customers, takes payment, makes alterations, measurements; customers (3) inspect, select and pay for merchandise, get fittings; 2.69 cu.
   1. Chamberlain Dress Shop
   2. Halbert Draper
   3. Harbough and Lawern General Draper
   4. Sadler and Jeffery Ladies Wear Shop
   5. Stathard Mens and Ladies Outfitter and Tailor
   6. Woodcock Tailor and Mens Outfitter

*49. Coach Agents Offices. Agent (6) arranges outings for group by coach; member-customers (3) confer with, contract, and pay agent, go on tour.

50. Coal Depots and Delivery. Manager (6) orders, stores, and sells coal, manages business; drivers (4) deliver coal, accept payment; customers (3) order coal, pay; 0.69 cu.
   1. Marwood Coal Delivery Route
   2. Welsh Coal Depot and Delivery

51. Commercial Company Offices. Manager (6) or managers (5) manage office; secretary (4) and bookkeeper (4) engage in office routines; customers (3) pay bills, order services or merchandise, get information; 1.90 cu.
   1. Auction Mart Office and National Farmers Insurance Company Office
   2. Express Dairy Office
   3. Gas Company Show Room and Office
   4. Jordison Cattle Feed Company Office
   5. Lowes Company Office

52. Commission Agents (Betting Offices). Commission agent (6) receives racing information, takes bets, pays winnings, keeps records, files reports; helper (4) assists agent; customers (3) place bets, collect winnings, study guides; 1.37 cu.
   1. Hoonan Commission Agent Office
   2. Matson Commission Agent Office
   3. Miller Betting Shop

53. Confectioners and Stationers Shops. Proprietor (6) or proprietors

(5) manage shop, sell sweets, cigarettes, stationery, sometimes magazines and papers; assistants (4) sell, stock shelves; customers (3) select, buy, pay; 1.11 cu.

    1. Broxman Confectioner and Stationer Shop
    2. Calvert Confectioner and Stationer Shop

54. Confessions, Roman Catholic Church. Priest (6) listens to confession according to ritual; members (3) confess sins, pray; 0.29 cu.

    1. Roman Catholic Church Confessions

°55. Cooking Classes. Teacher (6) teaches theory and practice of food shopping and cookery, demonstrates, supervises pupils; pupils (3) watch, listen, take notes, learn about cooking, practice cooking under supervision, eat; 0.44 cu.

    1. Evening Institute Cooking Classes
    2. Secondary Modern School Domestic Science Class, Mrs. Barnett
    3. Secondary Modern School Domestic Science Class, Miss Ridgeway
    4. Women's Institute Produce Guild Meeting

56. Court Sessions, Coroners Courts. Coroner (6) presides, hears evidence by calling witnesses, instructs jury, hears jury when jury is appropriate, pronounces verdict, dismisses court; witnesses (4) give evidence, answer questions; clerk (4) records proceedings; jury (4) receive instructions and evidence, decide issues, report verdict; reporter (2) observes, takes notes; onlookers (1) watch; 0.15 cu.

    1. Coroners Inquest Frier
    2. Coroners Inquest Jewitt
    3. Coroners Inquest Kilden

57. Court Sessions, Magistrates Courts. Magistrates (5) conduct court, listen to evidence or requests, confer, give sentence or decision; clerk of the court (4) advises magistrates as to law, records; police (4) present cases, give evidence, keep order; barristers (4) question witnesses, instruct clients; plaintiff and witnesses (4) are sworn in, answer questions; defendent (4) answers questions, is charged, and is sentenced or dismissed; licensee (4) presents request for license to sell alcoholic beverages or to extend time of license; spectators (2) listen, watch; 0.08 cu.

    1. Magistrates Court Sessions

58. Cricket Games. Referees (5) and team captains (5) supervise play according to plan and game rules; players (4) play, watch, question rulings of referees; scorekeepers (4) keep time, score, and records; spectators (2) watch and cheer. All have tea during rest period; 0.48 cu.

    1. Cricket Club Game
    2. Cricket Game out of town
    3. Schoolboy Simpkins Cup (under 13) Competition Cricket Match

      4. Schoolboy Simpkins Cup (under 13) Competition Cricket Match Out of Town

      5. Secondary Modern School Interschool Cricket Match

      6. Secondary Modern School Staff versus Students Cricket Match

      7. Secondary Modern School Cricket, Rounders, and Tennis Interschool Match

      8. Secondary Modern School Cricket, Rounders, and Tennis Interschool Match out of town

      9. Secondary Modern School Cricket, Rounders, and Tennis House Match

59. Crockery Shops. Proprietor (6) or proprietors (5) manage shop, sell china and pottery, household or decorative objects; assistants (4) sell, stock shelves; customers (3) select, buy, pay; 0.34 cu.

      1. Hill Crockery Shop

°60. Cross Country Running Competitions. Headmaster (5) arranges times, places, and presides over event with coach (e.g., shoots gun); coach (5) organizes event, presides over event, coaches team; team members (4) run, jump, engage in other track events; officials (4) measure, judge winners, record results; award presenter (4) presents awards to winners, makes short speech; spectators (3) follow, cheer, jump, watch, applaud; 0.15 cu.

      1. Secondary Modern School House Competition Cross Country Running

      2. Secondary Modern School Interschool Competition Cross Country Running

      3. Secondary Modern School Cross Country Running out of town

61. Custodial Work Groups. Show secretary (6) advises and instructs helpers with regard to places for exhibits, stalls, animal quarters; committee members (4) aid secretary, clean up and set up in main area; exhibitors (4) set up prior to show, clean up after show; helpers (3) aid committee members and exhibitors; 0.05 cu.

      1. Agricultural and Horticultural Fair Preparation Day by Show Stewards

62. Dairy Barns. Owner (6) supervises dairy processes; helpers (4) milk, clean barn, feed, drive cows; 0.72 cu.

      1. Mather Dairy

63. Dances. Person in charge (6) or committee in charge (5) arrange time, place, band, publicity, supervise proceedings, take money, keep order; helpers (4) make tea, help take money, keep order; musicians (4) play, sing; customers (3) dance, have tea, converse; onlookers (2) watch; 0.16 cu.

      1. Public Dance in Town Hall

      2. Women's Institute Teenage Dance

      3. Youth Club Dance at Scout Hall

64. Dancing Classes. Teacher (6) teaches principle of dancing, dem-

onstrates steps, engages in classroom routines, operates record player; pupils (3) watch, listen, dance according to instructions; 0.20 cu.

    1. Evening Institute Folk Dancing Class
    2. Evening Institute Scottish Dancing Class
    3. Secondary Modern School Dancing Instruction

65. Dart Games. Team captains (5) supervise pairing of players, initiate and oversee play; players (4) watch and play-in turn; onlookers (2) watch and converse. All drink during match and have sandwiches after; 0.30 cu. [Drinks and food are obtained by individuals from setting, Pub].

    1. Intertown League Darts Match
    2. Intertown League Darts Match out of town
    3. Local Teams Darts Match
    4. Local Teams Darts Match out of town

66. Delivery and Collection Routes. Deliverers (6) take papers, etc., to homes and leave them, come at regular intervals to collect for goods and service; customers (3) pay for goods and services; 1.14 cu.

    1. Broxman Paper Route
    2. Calvert Paper Route
    3. Gale Sunday Paper Route
    4. Jay Paper Route
    5. Lakeland Laundry Route
    6. Lily Laundry Route

67. Dentists Offices and Services. Dentist (6) examines patient with mirrors, probes, pulls teeth, fills some teeth, instructs patient, supervises office; assistant (4) helps dentist, makes appointments, keeps records, accepts money, conducts office routines; prefects and secretary (4) (in school dental inspections) supervise the coming and going of the pupils; patients (3) wait, receive treatment, listen, pay where appropriate; 0.60 cu.

    1. County Primary School Dental Inspection
    2. Hart and Dunning Dental Service Office
    3. National Health Service Dental Clinic at Area Health Office
    4. Roman Catholic School Dental Inspection
    5. Secondary Modern School Dental Inspection

68. Dinners and Banquets. Person in charge (6) establishes order of business; waitresses (4) wait tables, serve drink; toastmaster (4) offers toast; designated persons (4) give speech in response; members (3) eat, drink, converse, smoke; 0.11 cu.

    1. Hunters Club Dinner
    2. Masonic Lodge Dinner

*69. Dinners with Business Meetings. President of organization (6) arranges for dinner, presides at meeting; waitresses (4) serve dinner; secretary (4), treasurer (4), committee chairman (4) do prescribed work; invited speakers (4) make speeches; members (3) eat, converse, engage in business meeting activity, listen.

70. Dinners with Dances. Toastmaster (mistress) (6) or masters (5) preside over dinner, offer toasts; toast responders (4) respond to toasts; waitresses (4) serve food and drink; band (4) plays, sings; customers (3) eat, drink, converse, dance, smoke; 0.70 cu.
    1. Bowling Club Annual Dinner and Dance
    2. British Legion Dinner and Dance
    3. County Police Dinner and Dance
    4. Cricket Club Kingsley Dinner and Dance
    5. Cricket Club Gigglesby Dinner and Dance
    6. Dalesmans Club Dinner and Dance
    7. Dramatic Society Dinner and Dance
    8. Express Dairy Social Club Dinner and Dance
    9. Luncheon Club New Year Dinner and Dance
    10. Post Office Staff Dinner and Dance
    11. Secondary Modern School Cadet Club Dinner and Dance
    12. Tennis Club Yoredale Annual Dinner and Dance
    13. Tennis Club Kingsley Dinner and Dance
    14. Women's Institute Annual Dinner and Dance

71. Dinners with Recreational and Cultural Programs. Toastmaster (6) or masters (5) preside, call for toasts, signal for procedure; toast givers (4) offer toasts as signaled; designated persons (4) give speech in response; speakers (4) or entertainers (4) perform; waiters (4) serve food and drink; barmen and maids (4) serve drink only; members (3) drink, eat, converse, listen, applaud, smoke; 0.70 cu.
    1. Agricultural Discussion Group Annual Dinner
    2. Agricultural Discussion Group Upper Westerdale Dinner
    3. British Legion Annual Stag Dinner
    4. British Legion Bridgetown Annual Dinner
    5. District Council Annual Dinner
    6. Dramatic Society Committee Dinner
    7. Fire Service Annual Dinner
    8. National Farmers Union Churchdale Branch Dinner
    9. National Union of Agricultural Workers Castleton Branch Dinner
    10. National Union of Agricultural Workers Gatesby Branch Dinner
    11. Over Sixtys Club Annual Dinner
    12. Royal Observer Corps and Annual Dinner
    13. St. Johns Ambulance Association Dinner
    14. Westerdale Cricket League Annual Dinner

°72. Dog Shows. Show secretary (6) supervises entries and fee paying, directs proceedings by announcing classes, introducing judges, calling for judges' results, presenting winners; show stewards (4) assist the secretary in accepting entries, collecting fees, directing competitors, consulting with judges; competitors (4) fill out entry forms, pay fees, groom and exercise dog, put dog through required paces at direction of the secretary, retire from ring, accept prizes, converse; veterinarian (4) inspects dogs, signs certificates, instructs owners; spectators (3) watch and listen, applaud, converse; 0.05 cu.

    1. Agricultural and Horticultural Fair Dog Show

73. Drugstores (Chemists). Chemist proprietor (6) dispenses medicine according to physician's prescription, manages drug department and store selling cosmetics, proprietary medicines, special foods and equipment to do with health, may sell liquor and wine; assistants (4) sell merchandise, stock shelves; accountant (4) keeps and audits records, fills out tax and other forms; customers (3) select merchandise, bring prescriptions, pay; 1.01 cu.

    1. Stanger Chemist Shop
    2. Thorn Chemist Shop

°74. Educational Methods Classes. Leader (6) [clergyman] lectures to teachers [Sunday School] about teaching and values of teaching, shows new materials; teacher-members (3) listen, look, ask questions, discuss; 0.05 cu.

    1. Methodist Sunday School Teachers Training Meeting

°75. Egg Packing Plants. Owner-proprietor (6) manages business, orders supplies, arranges sales, supervises workers; workers (4) receive eggs, grade and package eggs; sellers (4) leave eggs; drivers (4) pick up packaged eggs for delivery to customers; 0.50 cu.

    1. Express Dairy Egg Packing Plant

*76. Elections, Party Headquarters. Party Committee (5) arranges for room to serve as headquarters for poll watchers and information gatherers at general election; participants (4) phone, drink tea, discuss.

77. Elections, Polling Places. Election official (6), officials (5) set up and arrange space, provide official register, ballots, etc., supervise voting; clerks (4) check voters with register, give ballots to voter accept marked ballots, place ballots in appropriate receptacle; voters (3) identify selves, mark ballots, give ballots to clerks; 0.15 cu.

    1. Polling Place County Council Election
    2. Polling Place Bridgetown County Council Election
    3. Polling Place District Council and Parish Council Election

78. Elections, Vote Counts. Election official (6) or officials (5) accept boxes of ballots, count vote with help, announce results; helpers (4) count votes under supervision, post results, give results to official; candidates (3) await results, converse quietly, congratulate winners; residents (2) wait outside, go inside when results are announced, congratulate winners; 0.05 cu.

    1. County Council Counting of Ballots

79. Electrical Appliance and Service Companies. Proprietor (6) or proprietors (5) manage business, do and supervise repairs, make estimates, sell and rent appliances; electricians (4) install and repair electrical equipment; assistants (4) sell, record sales, engage

in office routines; customers (3) select, buy, pay for goods and service; 1.26 cu.

1. Co-op Home Appliances Store
2. Electrical Exhibit and Sale Town Hall
3. Loymond Brothers Electric Appliances and Service
4. Pearce Brothers Electric Appliances and Service

80. Elementary School Basic Classes. Teacher (6) teaches reading, grammar, arithmetic, writing, elementary health, social studies, science, and engages in classroom routines, supervises student teachers; student teachers (4) teach same subjects as teacher under teacher's supervision; pupils (3) listen, write, recite, read, figure; 1.92 cu.

1. County Primary School Upper Juniors (9–11) Academic Class
2. County Primary School Middle Juniors (8–10) Academic Class
3. County Primary School Lower Juniors (7–9) Academic Class
4. County Primary School Infants (5–7) Academic Class
5. Roman Catholic Upper School (9–15) Academic Class
6. Roman Catholic Lower School (5–9) Academic Class
7. Secondary Modern School Senior Remove (13–15) Academic Class
8. Secondary Modern School 3rd and 4th Year Progress (13–15) Academic Class.
9. Secondary Modern School Junior Remove (11–13) Academic Class
10. Secondary Modern School Handwriting Academic Class

°81. English Classes. Teacher (6) teaches English literature, composition, speech, grammar, engages in classroom management; student teacher (4) teaches specific lessons in literature, composition, speech and grammar under supervision of teacher; pupils (4) (adult, adolescent, and child) listen, read, study, recite, write, converse; 0.99 cu.

1. Evening Institute English and Maths Classes
2. Secondary Modern School English and Maths Classes, Miss Byerly
3. Secondary Modern School English Class, Miss Curry
4. Secondary Modern School English Class, Mrs. Bent
5. Secondary Modern School English Class, Mr. Gibbons
6. Secondary Modern School English Class, Mr. Johnstone
7. Secondary Modern School English Class, Mr. Kale
8. Secondary Modern School English and Maths Classes, Mrs. Thomson

82. Estate Agents Offices. Chartered estate agent (6) manages office, supervises assistants, meets with clients and farmers; collects rents, pays bills; assistants (4) work under direction of land agent

as surveyors, draftsmen, bookkeepers; secretaries (4) engage in office routines; clients (3) arrange for work, get reports, pay for work; 0.42 cu.

    1. Heywood Estate Agent Office

83. Examinations, Standardized. Person in charge, invigilator (6) or invigilators (5) arrange seating, pass out examination, supervise examination, keep order, answer questions, collect examination papers; exam-takers (pupils, children, and adults) (3) file in quietly, take examination paper, think, read, write, figure, hand in paper when done; 0.52 cu.

    1. County Primary School Eleven-plus Examination
    2. Evening Institute English, Maths and German Examinations
    3. Evening Institute Shorthand Examination
    4. Evening Institute Typing Examination
    5. Roman Catholic School Eleven-plus Examination
    6. Secondary Modern School Eleven-plus Second Stage Examination
    7. Secondary Modern School First Year (11–12) Maths and and English Examinations
    8. Secondary Modern School Fourth Year (14–16) Examinations
    9. Secondary Modern School Half-Year Examination
    10. Secondary Modern School Technical College Entrance Examination

84. Excursions and Sightseeing Trips. Person (6) or persons (5) in charge supervise boarding of bus, checking payment or eligibility of the boarder, make decisions about stops, and when passengers are children, keep order and supervise children; driver (4) drives, points out places of interest and tells about them; passengers (3) ride, eat, converse, sing, look, listen, and pay; 1.39 cu.

    1. Camera Club Outing to Burnside
    2. Camera Club Outing to Westcoast
    3. Church of England Sunday School Trip to Whitby
    4. County Primary and Roman Catholic School Outing to London
    5. Evening Institute Crop Husbandry Class Outing to Farm
    6. Methodist Church Sunday School Outing to Blackpool
    7. Methodist Youth Club Trip to Squash Tournament at West Beck
    8. Methodist Youth Club Trip to College at Sheffield
    9. Methodist Youth Club Trip to Floralby
    10. Methodist Youth Club Visit to a Historic Church
    11. Moorside Nursing Home Mystery Tour
    12. Over Sixtys Club Trip to High Force
    13. Over Sixtys Club Trip to Northbank Pantomime
    14. Over Sixtys Club Trip to Raycliffe and Floralby

15. Over Sixtys Club Trip to Whitby
16. Over Sixtys Club Trip to Women's Institute Party in Dalebank
17. Roman Catholic Church Womens League Outing
18. Secondary Modern School Field Trip
19. Secondary Modern School Canterbury House Outing
20. Secondary Modern School Durham House Outing
21. Secondary Modern School Edinborough House Outing
22. Secondary Modern School Westminister House Outing
23. Secondary Modern School Trip to See Antony and Cleopatra
24. Secondary Modern School Boys (13) Trip to Renwich and Whitewall
25. Secondary Modern School Trip to Switzerland
26. Women's Institute Trip to Gigglesby
27. Women's Institute Trip to Westbourne.

85. Farm Implement Sales and Exhibits. Person in charge (6) arranges for and supervises exhibit, presides over exhibit, shows objects, pamphlets to prospective customers, tells about products, answers questions, supervises removing; helpers (4) arrange exhibit under supervisor, talk with prospective customers, carry or help move objects, take down exhibit; customers (3) examine objects and pamphlets, listen to description, pay, converse; onlookers (2) browse and look at objects and pamphlets; 0.18 cu.
    1. Agricultural and Horticultural Fair Farm Implement and Supply Trade Stalls
    2. Boots Farm Supplies

86. Farm Livestock Exhibits and Competitions. Stewards (5) supervise the sequence of events following schedule previously set up by committee, call for events, introduce judges, answer questions for competitors, assign stalls, and supervise order of entrance into ring; judges (4) examine animals, think, make decisions, announce decisions; competitors (4) groom beasts, maintain stalls, pay, follow schedule, lead or drive beasts into judging area, follow instructions, receive judgments and awards, lead or drive beasts back to stall; customers (3) examine beasts, watch and listen to judging in ring, applaud winners, converse; 0.05 cu.
    1. Agricultural and Horticultural Fair Exhibition and Judging of Cattle and Sheep

°87. Farm Practices Classes. Person (6) or persons (5) in charge preside over meeting; when person is teacher (6) he or, in case of meeting, an invited speaker (4) discusses theory and practice of good farming with demonstrations when the site permits; helpers (4) perform appropriate operations, e.g., clean stalls, gather eggs, curry sheep, under supervision; members (3) listen, watch, ask questions, discuss; 0.43 cu.
    1. Secondary Modern School Farming Club Daily Duties

2. Secondary Modern School Farming Club Work Session
3. Secondary Modern School Farming Club Meeting
4. Young Farmers Club All Sections (11–25) Meeting
5. Young Farmers Club Senior Girls and Juniors (11–25) Meeting

88. Fire Alarms and Fire Fighting. Fire chief (6) directs activity, supervises firemen, drives truck, helps with apparatus; person on duty at fire house (4) takes calls, calls fire chief and firemen; firemen (4) drive truck, use hose and apparatus to extinguish fire; homeowner (3) calls station; onlookers (1) watch; 0.07 cu.
1. County Fire Brigade Fire Fighting

°89. Fire Drills. Headmaster or deputy head (5) rings alarm; teachers (5) supervise evacuation of building and return to building; form captains and prefects (4) keep order, direct traffic, report misbehavior; pupils (3) conform to rules and orders from headmaster, deputy head, teachers, form captains and prefects, walk out and in quickly, quietly and in a prescribed sequence; 0.05 cu.
1. Secondary Modern School Fire Drill

90. Fire Stations. Fire chief (6) directs activities, manages office, teaches fire fighting with assistants, checks on maintenance of equipment, supervises assignments; second-officer (4) helps fire chief in above duties; office worker (4) maintains records, answers telephone, keeps data assignments up to date, reports to chief and second officer; inspectors (4) visit to inspect equipment and techniques, rate activities, report to authorities and the chief; firemen (3) practice new firefighting techniques, watch demonstrations, clean and maintain equipment, test trucks and equipment, converse; 0.09 cu.
1. County Fine Brigade Training Meeting

°91. First Aid Classes and Demonstrations. Teacher (6) or instructors (5) (qualified) teach theory and practice of first aid, demonstrate practices and basic knowledge or procedures; assistant (4) helps set up, takes roll, puts things away, helps demonstrate; pupils (3) watch, listen, take notes, examine specimens (e.g., microscopic slides) draw diagrams, answer questions, practice first aid; 0.23 cu.
1. British Railways First Aid Class
2. Methodist Youth Club Emergency First Aid Class
3. Secondary Modern School Red Cross Cadets Meeting
4. Secondary Modern School Red Cross Cadets Westerdale Day Demonstration

92. Fish and Chips Shops. Proprietor (6) or proprietors (5) manage business, may also cook; cooks (4) cook fish and chips on order, wrap, accept payment; customers (3) take fish and chips home or eat on premises, pay; 0.41 cu.
1. Miller Fish and Chips Shop and Restaurant

93. Food and Rummage (Jumble) Sales. Chairman (6) or committee members (5) arrange for space and time, solicit donations, organize articles and decide prices, sell, take money, keep record of

amounts; helpers (4) aid committee organize articles, sell, accept payment, may serve tea to all helpers; customers (3) inspect merchandise, select and pay; 0.40 cu.

1. Church of England Jumble Sale
2. Methodist Church Cake Sale
3. Methodist Church Harvest Festival Auction
4. Methodist Church Jumble Sale
5. Over Sixtys Club Bring and Buy Sale
6. Women's Institute Annual Sale
7. Women's Institute Jumble Sale
8. Women's Institute Sale of Goods Made by the Blind

°94. Football (Rugby) Games. Coaches (5) or teachers (5) supervise, following prescribed rules, instruct players; referees (5) keep time, rule regarding play; players (4) play according to Rugby rules, follow instructions from coach and referees; spectators (2) watch, cheer, applaud, boo, converse; 0.25 cu.

1. Secondary Modern School Interschool (11–15) Rugby Match
2. Secondary Modern School Interschool (Under 13) Rugby Match out of town
3. Secondary Modern School Interschool (13–15) Rugby Match out of town
4. Secondary Modern School Rugby, Hockey, and Netball Match out of town
5. Secondary Modern School Rugby and Netball House Match

95. Football (Soccer) Games. [Same as 94 except play it by soccer rules] 0.43 cu.

1. Football Club Game
2. Football Club Game out of town
3. Secondary Modern School Football House Match
4. Secondary Modern School Interschool Football Match
5. Secondary Modern School Interschool Football Match out of town
6. Secondary Modern School Interschool Football and Hockey Match out of town
7. Secondary Modern School Interschool Football, Hockey, and Netball Match
8. Secondary Modern School Interschool Football, Hockey, and Jr. Football Match out of town

96. Freight Truck Lines. Owner-operator (6) manages business, directs office routines, assigns loads to drivers, may drive some routes; clerk (4) engages in office routines, takes calls, keeps records; drivers (4) receive assignments, drive horseboxes and other heavy lorries as directed; customers (3) order and pay for service; 0.48 cu.

1. Haw Haulage Service

°97. French Classes. Teacher (6) (qualified) teaches French vocabulary, grammar, and literature, engages in classroom routines; pupils (3) listen, write, read, study, and speak French; 0.15 cu.

    1. Secondary Modern School French and English Classes, Mrs. Jay

°98. Fund Raising Socials. Sponsor (6) or sponsors (5) arrange place for tea or coffee social, invite others to help, invite guests; stallholders (4) sell donated food, objects or raffle tickets; servers (4) serve tea or coffee; speaker (4) may speak briefly about the cause; guests (3) eat, buy, pay, converse; 0.25 cu.

    1. Church of England Coffee Evening and Bring and Buy Sale for Childrens Fund

    2. Coffee Evening and Bring and Buy Sale for Handicapped Children at Mrs. Grails

    3. Dramatic Society Tea and Sale

    4. Liberal Party Society Coffee Evening and Bring and Buy Sale

    5. Women's Institute Coffee Morning and Bring and Buy Sale

99. Funeral Services. Clergyman in charge at the church (6) conducts service according to ritual, accompanies casket out of the church; undertaker and assistants (4) arrange and remove flowers, place casket, move casket from front to back of church, usher mourners, hand out order-of-service folders; singers (4) sing; organist (4) plays; bearers (4) carry casket out; mourners (3) sit, listen, sign order-of-service folders, view the deceased as they leave, wait outside until hearse drives away; 0.16 cu.

    1. Church of England Funeral Service

    2. Methodist Church Funeral Service

    3. Roman Catholic Church Funeral Service

100. Garages. Owner-manager (6) manages garage, sells, services and repairs automobiles, supervises helpers, directs office routines; foreman (4) supervises repairs by assistants, does repair work, instructs apprentices; mechanics (4) do repair work under supervision, service cars; apprentices (4) learn to service and repair automobiles and other motors, work under supervision, tend petrol pump; clerk (4) manages office, engages in office routine, orders supplies, keeps records, calls for someone to tend pump; clerk's assistant (4) helps with office routines, tends petrol pump; customers (3) bring automobiles for service, repairs, petrol, oil, buy and sell automobiles; 1.94 cu.

    1. Bradley Garage

    2. Hay Garage

    3. Hobson Garage

*101. Garden Allotments. Parish clerk (6) assigns allotments; members (3) care for garden, reap produce, chat.

*102. Gas Works. Manager (6) directs; helpers (4) run gas works as required.

°103. Geography Classes. Teacher (6) teaches geography using maps, charts, books, samples of rocks, globes, lectures, supervises drawing, graphing and tracing; student teacher (4) assists teacher, learns how to teach, engages in classroom routines; pupils (3) read, listen, write, draw, graph, use equipment all related to geography; 0.22 cu.

    1. Secondary Modern School Geography Class

°104. German Classes. Teacher (6) teaches German language written and spoken, engages in classroom routines; tea hostess (4) provides and serves tea; class members (3) study, practice German speech, writing, and songs; 0.07 cu.

    1. Evening Institute German Class

105. Government Offices: Records and Business. Official in charge (6) manages office, engages in office routines, keeps records, attends to and accepts fees from customers; customers (3) give and receive information, pay for services; 0.12 cu.

    1. County Register of Births, Deaths, and Marriages Yoredale District Mrs. Thornson

106. Grocery Stores. Owner-manager (6) manages business, orders and prices goods, supervises inventories, prepares advertising, may drive truck, waits on customers; undermanager (4), senior shop assistant (4), supervise shop assistants, serve customers, accept payment; shop assistants (4) take written and verbal order from customers, fill orders, total charges, accept payment, make change, stock shelves; drivers (4) take filled orders to customers or drive mobile shop to customers; customers (3) give orders (written or verbal) to shop assistant, wait for goods, pay, may select own goods in some shops; 5.28 cu.

    1. Broughs Grocery
    2. Co-op Grocery
    3. Garnett Fruiterer
    4. Hill, E. Grocery
    5. Hill, G. Grocery
    6. Lawern Grocery
    7. Lawern Estate Grocery
    8. Miller Fresh Fish and Grocery
    9. Nolting Grocery
    10. Stoker Fruiterer
    11. Thomilson Pavilion General Store

107. Hallways and Coatrooms. Teacher (6) or teachers (5) supervise, set rules, keep order; prefects (4) maintain order, help small children with wraps, give lines as punishment to misbehavors; employees (3), pupils (3) hang up coats, walk, converse; visitors (2) walk, converse; 1.82 cu.

    1. County Primary School Boys (8–10) Cloak Room
    2. County Primary School Girls (8–10) Cloak Room
    3. County Primary School Infants (5–7) Cloak Room
    4. County Primary School Upper Juniors (10–12) Cloak Room
    5. Roman Catholic School (5–16) Cloak Room

6. Secondary Modern School Cloak Room and Corridor

7. Thornborough Hall Hallways

108. Hardware (Ironmonger) Stores. Owner-manager (6) manages business, sells merchandise, accepts payment, supervises assistants; shop assistants (4) find merchandise for customers, total charges, accept payment; customers (3) inspect and select merchandise, pay; 0.93 cu.

1. Grail Ironmonger and Crockery Shop

2. Herman Ironmonger and Crockery Shop

109. Health Department Offices. Public health doctor (6) and assistant official (4) manage office, provide information for records, supervise recordkeeping and sending records to proper authorities, supervise health rounds of nurses; nurses (4) report to office, organize activities, evaluate activities, discuss need with doctor and official, inventory food supplies, order and arrange food supplies for distribution via clinic, respond to public; clerk (4) engages in office routines, keeps records, sends records, greets public; patients-clients (3) request information, appointments, services, forms, return forms to office, wait, converse, receive information; 0.41 cu.

1. National Health Service Area Health Office

*110. Hikes and Camps. Scout leader (6) directs total camp activities; patrol leaders (4) direct small group activities; scouts (3) make camp, hike, cook, engage in programmed scout activities.

°111. History Classes. Teacher (6) teaches facts and implication of local, English, or World History via lecture, books, maps, engages in classroom routines; student teacher (4) (when not in charge) engages in teaching and aids teacher in classroom routines; pupils (3) listen, study, recite, write, read, peruse and draw maps; 0.35 cu.

1. Secondary Modern School History Class, Mr. Howe

2. Secondary Modern School History and English Classes, Mr. Mackley

3. Secondary Modern School History and Local Studies Classes, Mr. Seymour

°112. Hockey Games. Teacher (6), teachers (5) organize game to get it started according to rules, keep time, supervise generally, instruct own group of players before and during game; referee (4) rules on legality of play, calls game's end; team or house captains (4) encourage team, instruct team, play hockey; players (4) play hockey, accept awards, congratulate winners; spectators (3) watch, cheer, applaud, take tea; 0.15 cu.

1. Secondary Modern School Interschool Hockey Match

2. Secondary Modern School Staff versus Student Hockey Match

3. Secondary Modern School Hockey and Netball House Match

113. Home Economics Classes. Leaders (5) call group to order, introduce special teacher; teachers (5) lecture and demonstrate with regard to various aspects of homemaking, ask and answer questions; members (3) listen, watch, practice cookery, make up and other appropriate behavior; 0.06 cu.
    1. Young Farmers Club Senior Girls (15–25) Meeting
114. Home Economics Competitions and Exhibits. Organizer (6) or organizers (5) supervise setting up and removal of exhibits, assist judges in following procedures, announce or arrange for announcement of winners and presentation of awards; exhibitors (4) register, arrange own exhibit, accompany exhibits, listen to results, applaud winners; judge (4) inspects exhibits, compares, decides, notes winner, gives winner's name to announcer or places marker indicating winner's position on exhibit itself; customers (3) pay at entry gate, look at exhibits, converse, compare, applaud announcement of winners; 0.20 cu.
    1. Agricultural and Horticultural Fair Handicraft and Homecraft Tent
    2. Over Sixtys Club Annual Show of Work, Competition, and Auction Sale
    3. Secondary Modern School Westerdale Day Needlework Exhibit
    4. Young Farmers Club Cooking Competition
°115. Horse Racing. Clerk of the course (6) calls for start, announces winners, officiates, makes decision about entries; handicappers (4) and disqualifiers (4) make decisions on the basis of prescribed rules about eligibility of horses; clerk of the scales (4) weighs in jockeys; timekeepers (4) time the individual horses around track; bookmakers (4) accept bets, keep records, pay bets; jockeys (4) ride horses according to rules; veterinarian (4) and doctor (4) present to deal with emergency; customers (3) pay, place bets, watch, listen, cheer, groan, receive payment for winner; 0.05 cu.
    1. Agricultural and Horticultural Fair Pony and Sulky Racing
116. Horticulture Classes. Teacher (6) demonstrates, lectures on principles and techniques of gardening, shows films, engages in classroom routines; class members (3) listen, watch, read, write; 0.06 cu.
    1. Evening Institute Gardening Class
117. Horticulture Competitions and Exhibits. Organizers (5) provide space, time, supervise placement and removal of exhibits, supervise judges, maintain schedule; stewards (4) help organize, instructing exhibitors, maintaining schedule; exhibitors (4) set up exhibit, stay with exhibit, remove exhibit; judges (4) examine exhibits, compare, decide, note, and mark winner by ribbon or card or by voice; customers (3) pay, work, examine, compare; 0.10 cu.
    1. Agricultural and Horticultural Fair Horticultural Tent

2. Westerdale and Stardale—Women's Institute Bulb Display, Competition, and Egg Collection

118. Hotels. Proprietor (6) or proprietors (5) manage hotel, order materials, supervise cleaning (or do cleaning themselves), cooking (or do cooking themselves in Bed and Breakfast places), washing up, keep records, accept payment; helpers (4) (domestic) aid in cooking, cleaning and washing up; customers (3) arrange for rooms, eat meals in private hotel only, pay; 2.32 cu. [Time in rooms not included in standing pattern.]
    1. Blue Goose Hotel (excluding Pub and Dining Room)
    2. Culver Hotel
    3. Eyles Rooms
    4. Green Dragon Hotel (excluding Pub and Dining Room)
    5. Hopp Rooms
    6. Jeffery Rooms
    7. Karim Arms Hotel (excluding Pub and Dining Room)

119. Household Furnishings Sales and Exhibits. Manager (6) arranges for place, brings samples of furniture and household appliances; customers (3) examine, buy or may order, pay for merchandise; 0.17 cu.
    1. Carpet Sale
    2. Culvers Furniture Exhibit and Sale
    3. Tinsleys Furniture Exhibit and Sale

120. Installation and Induction Ceremonies. Official (6) of organization arranges for speaker (5), symbols (e.g., badges, pins, certificates), presides over meeting; speakers (4) give appropriate talks; award presenter (4) hands out symbols to individuals, may make short speech; awardees (4) listen, receive awards; committee (4) prepare and serve tea; spectators (2) listen, look, applaud, have tea; 0.05 cu.
    1. Secondary Modern School Red Cross Cadets Enrolling Ceremony

121. Insurance Offices and Sales Routes. Insurance agent (6) sells insurance at own home or office and at customers' offices, keeps records, sends records to regional or company office, consults with customers; customers (3) ask and receive advice, pay, receive payment; 1.23 cu.
    1. Greenwell Insurance Agent Route
    2. King-Hope Insurance Agent Route
    3. Prudential Insurance Agent Route
    4. Refuge Insurance Agent Route
    5. Yorkshire Insurance Agent Route

122. Jewelry Stores. Owner-operator (6) manages business, waits on customers, examines and repairs watches and clocks; clerk (4) waits on customers, wraps packages; customers (3) examine and purchase merchandise, bring in watches for repair, pay for service and goods; 0.48 cu.
    1. Tarn Jewelry and Watch Repair Shop

°123. Kitchens, Institutional. Head cook (6) orders, prepares, and cooks food, directs assistants; assistants (4) prepare, cook, and serve food; 0.32 cu.
    1. Secondary Modern School Kitchen
*124. Knitting Services. Skilled knitter (6) knits on order garments; customers (3) select, order, try on, pay for knitted garment.
  125. Libraries. Librarian (6) checks out, checks in, shelves books, may order, and catalogue books, assists in finding information for patron, engages in managerial functions; assistants (4) (when applicable) act as librarian, reshelve books, clean, beautify surroundings; patrons (3) read, study, select, and check out books, return books; 0.59 cu.
    1. County Library in Thornboro Hall
    2. Secondary Modern School Library
°126. Locker and Shower Rooms. Teachers (5) maintain order, instruct on use of facilities, supervise activities; prefects (4) monitor ongoing activities, direct pupils; pupils (3) dress for athletic events or physical education, take showers, dress in school clothes, converse; 0.63 cu.
    1. Secondary Modern School Boys Changing Room and Shower
    2. Secondary Modern School Girls Changing Room and Shower
  127. Lodge Meetings. Chief officer (6) conducts meeting; secretary (4), treasurer (4), lodge officers (4), committee chairmen (4) take their assigned responsibilities, engage in ritual activities and business meetings; members (3) attend, listen, vote, participate in ritual, eat, socialize; 0.05 cu.
    1. Masonic Lodge Meeting
  128. Machinery Repair Shops. Foreman (6), manager (6), or owner (6) manages shop, repairs machinery with help, keeps some records, orders materials; mechanics (4) repair machinery under supervision, test equipment; customers (3) and road workers (3) pick up repaired machinery or stored equipment, converse, pay for private enterprise machine shop; 0.98 cu.
    1. County Highway Depot
    2. Thomilson Blacksmith
  129. Markets, Public. Stall holders (5) bring merchandise, arrange in stall or van, pay rental fee, demonstrate and sell merchandise; sales people (4) sell merchandise; parish representative (4) collects, rents, arranges placement of stalls, helps set up stall; customers (3) look, select, pay for merchandise, converse; 0.18 cu.
    1. Agricultural and Horticultural Fair Home Hardware Trade Stall
    2. Market Day
°130. Maths Classes. Teacher (6) lectures, demonstrates mathematical principles and practice in arithmetic, business math, algebra and geometry, some trigonometry, engage in classroom routines; stu-

dent teacher helps teacher, engages in classroom routines; pupils
(3) listen, watch read, write, study, practice mathematics; 0.82 cu.

1. Secondary Modern School Maths and English Classes, Mrs.
   Dent
2. Secondary Modern School Maths Class, Mr. Gibbons
3. Secondary Modern School Maths Class, Mr. Johnstone
4. Secondary Modern School Maths Class, Mr. Noble
5. Secondary Modern School Maths and English Classes, Mr.
   Rotherford
6. Secondary Modern School Maths Class, Mr. Seymour

131. Meetings, Business. President (6 or 5), chairman (6), co-chairmen
   (5) presides at meeting and conducts in general accordance with
   accepted rules of order; secretary (4), treasurer (4), committee
   chairmen (4) engage in prescribed work; members (3) participate
   in meeting according to prescribed rules; 2.84 cu.

   1. After-Care Committee Meeting
   2. Agricultural and Horticultural Society Annual and Execu-
      tive Committee Meeting
   3. Badminton Club Annual and Committee Meeting
   4. Bowling Club Annual General Meeting
   5. British Legion Annual Meeting
   6. British Legion Committee Meeting
   7. British Legion Western Group Meeting
   8. British Red Cross Yoredale-Aronbeck Division Meeting
   9. Chess Club Annual Meeting
   10. Church of England Annual Church and Vestry Meeting
   11. Church of England Interdeanery Mothers Union Meeting
   12. Church of England Parochial Council Meeting
   13. Conservative Party Society Committee Meeting
   14. County Primary School Canteen Committee Meeting
   15. County Primary School Managers Meeting
   16. Cricket Club Annual Meeting
   17. District Council Civil Defense Committee Meeting
   18. District Council Regular and Standing Committee Meeting
   19. District Council Public Relations Committee Meeting
   20. District Council Road Safety Committee Meeting
   21. Dramatic Society Annual Meeting
   22. Dramatic Society Committee Meeting
   23. Evening Institute Advisory Committee Meeting
   24. Fishing Association Annual Meeting
   25. Liberal Party Society Committee Meeting
   26. Lower Westerdale Savings Group Annual General and
       Committee Meeting
   27. Methodist Church Annual Trustees Meeting
   28. Methodist Church Lay Preachers Meeting
   29. Methodist Church Leaders Meeting (Local)

30. Methodist Church Westerdale Circuit Meeting
31. Methodist Church Youth Council Meeting
32. Parish Council Association Stardale and Westerdale Branch Meeting
33. Parish Council Meeting
34. Parish Council Town Meeting
35. Playing Fields Committee Meeting
36. Poors Land Charity Trustees Meeting
37. Roman Catholic Church Womens League Committee Meeting
38. Roman Catholic School Managers Meeting
39. Secondary Modern School Board of Governors Meeting
40. Secondary Modern School Canteen Committee Meeting
41. Secondary Modern School House Meeting, Canterbury
42. Secondary Modern School House Meeting, Durham
43. Secondary Modern School House Meeting, Edinborough
44. Secondary Modern School House Meeting, Westminster
45. Secondary Modern School Parent-Teachers Association Committee Meeting
46. Secondary Modern School Staff Meeting
47. Tennis Club Annual Meeting
48. Tournament of Song Committee Meeting
49. Tradesmens Association Meeting
50. Westerdale Cricket League Annual and Committee Meeting
51. Westerdale Darts League Meeting
52. Westerdale Football League Annual and Committee Meeting
53. Women's Institute Committee Meeting
54. Young Farmers Club Advisory Committee Meeting

132. Meetings, Cultural. President (6), chairman (6), or teachers (5) conduct business meeting or preside and introduce speakers; speakers (4) give talk, answer questions; Vote of thanks giver (4) thanks speaker; committee (4) serves tea (when appropriate); members (3) participate in business meeting; listen, watch, discuss, converse, applaud, eat; 0.95 cu.

1. Agricultural Discussion Group Joint Meeting with Upper Dale
2. Agricultural Discussion Group Meeting
3. Camera Club Meeting
4. Conservative Party Society Open Meeting
5. County Primary School Infants (5–7) Visitors Lecture
6. County Primary School Juniors (8–12) Visitors Lecture
7. Methodist Youth Club Canoe Building Lecture and Demonstration
8. Methodist Youth Club Good Driving Lecture

9. Over Sixtys Club Meeting
10. Roman Catholic Church Womens League Meeting
11. Roman Catholic School Visitors Lecture
12. Secondary Modern School Lecture on Road Safety
13. Secondary Modern School Parent-Teachers Association Meeting
14. Women's Institute Meeting
15. Women's Institute Dales Area Special Meeting with Guest Speaker
16. Womens Luncheon Club Regular and Annual Luncheon Meeting
17. Young Farmers Club Junior Boys and Girls (11–15) Meeting

133. Meetings, Discussion. President or chairman (6), co-chairmen (5) preside; treasurer (4), secretary (4), other officers take prescribed responsibilities; committee (4) makes and serves tea; members (3) discuss issues and topics under consideration, take tea, converse; 0.11 cu.
   1. Methodist Youth Club "Sunday Night at Eight" Meeting
   2. Westerdale Head Teachers Association Meeting

134. Meetings, Social. Chairman (6 or 5) or organizer (5) presides, organizes activities or presides over business meeting prior to social hours; treasurer (4), secretary (4), other officers take prescribed responsibilities; committee (4) makes and serves food and drink; members (3) listen, discuss, converse, engage in planned activities; 0.25 cu.
   1. Methodist Youth Club Car Treasure Hunt
   2. Methodist Youth Club Hike and Moonlight Ramble
   3. Secondary Modern School Old Pupils Reunion
   4. Youth Club Meeting

°135. Metalwork Classes. Teacher (6) teaches principles and techniques of working with metal including use of machinery, engages in classroom routines; class members (3) listen, learn, practice use of machines and making of metal objects; 0.28 cu.
   1. Evening Institute Metalwork Class
   2. Secondary Modern School Metalwork Class, Mr. Massingham

°136. Military Communications Exhibitions and Demonstrations. Officer in charge (6) supervises setting up of exhibit, presides over exhibit, instructs, supervises putting away; military corps members (4) set up equipment, demonstrate equipment and procedures to visitors, answer questions, put away equipment; visitors (3) look, listen, ask questions; onlookers (2) stop by, look briefly; 0.05 cu.
   1. Secondary Modern School Signal Corps Demonstration at Westerdale Day

137. Military Training Classes. Officer in charge (6) or teachers (5)

direct training activities, lecture, demonstrate, lead in drills; junior officers (4) lead own group according to instructions; members (3) follow instructions, study, read, listen, practice routines; 0.39 cu.

1. Royal Observer Corps Meeting
2. Secondary Modern School Cadet Club Drill and Band Practice
3. Secondary Modern School Cadet Club Rifle Practice
4. Secondary Modern School Cadet Club Training Meeting and Examination
5. Secondary Modern School Cadet Club Visit to AFC Camp in Scotland
6. Secondary Modern School Cadet Club Visit to HMS Ganges

138. Milk Collection and Processing Plants. Manager (6) directs operations to collect, cool, and ship milk to city plants, manages plant; truck drivers (4) bring in milk in cans or tank trucks, collect cans or tanks; workers (4) treat milk, reship milk; 0.61 cu.

1. Express Dairy Plant

139. Milk Bottling and Delivery Services. Manager (6) buys milk from producer, strains, cools, bottles, and delivers milk to customers' homes, manages business; assistants (4) help manager; customers (3) order and pay for milk; 1.22 cu.

1. Haw Milk Retailer
2. Lowdon Milk Retailer
3. Mather Milk Retailer

°140. Motor Vehicle Operators Classes. Teacher (6) teaches principles of good and defensive driving; class members (3) listen, learn principles of driving; 0.05 cu.

1. District Council Safe Driving Lecture

141. Moving Picture Shows. Projectionist (6) shows film, keeps order; committee (4) takes money (where applicable); members (3), customers (3) watch, listen, applaud, and in the case of customers, pay; 0.16 cu.

1. Secondary Modern School Film in Mr. Grouts Room
2. Secondary Modern School Film of Switzerland
3. Secondary Modern School Film Show at Westerdale Day

142. Music Classes, Instrumental. Music teacher (6) teaches skills and theory of instrumental music, engages in classroom routines; students (3) study and practice; 0.50 cu.

1. Evening Institute Small Orchestra Class
2. Music Lesson, Mr. Mackley
3. Secondary Modern School Recorder Group Practice, Mr. Mackley
4. Secondary Modern School String Group Practice, Mr. Nobel
5. Violin and Elocution Lessons, Mrs. Sipson

143. Music Classes, Vocal. Teacher (6) or choir master (6) teaches technique and theory of singing, may engage in classroom routines; accompanist (4) plays organ or piano; pupils (3) or choir members (3) learn about singing, practice; 1.39 cu.
    1. Church of England Choir Practice
    2. County Primary School Infants (5–7) Music and Movement Class
    3. County Primary School Lower Juniors and Infants (5–9) Music Class
    4. County Primary School Middle Juniors and Infants (5–10) Music Class
    5. County Primary School Upper Juniors (9–11) Music Class
    6. Junior Choral Group Practice
    7. Methodist Church Choir Practice
    8. Roman Catholic School Lower School (5–9) Music Class
    9. Roman Catholic School Upper and Lower School (5–15) Music Class
    10. Secondary Modern School Music Class, Mr. Mackley
    11. Secondary Modern School Music Class, Mr. Noble and Mr. Mackley
    12. Women's Institute Choic Practice
144. Music Competitions. President (5) or organizer (5) opens the competition, introduces notables; officials (5) (marshalls, treasurer, secretary) announce events, introduce special persons; adjudicators (5) listen, watch, make decisions, comment and explain decisions and describe good performance; accompanist (4) plays piano as needed; competitors (4) talk, sing, play according to specified plan; patron (4) gives short speech about the competition's history; audience (3) comes and goes, listens, watches, applauds, eats candy; 0.05 cu.
    1. Tournament of Song
145. Nature Study Classes. Teacher (6) directs interested students in study of local flowers and birds; class members (3) learn about local botany and bird life; 0.12 cu.
    1. Secondary Modern School Bird Watching Club Meeting
    2. Workers Education Association Wild Life in the Dales Class
146. Needlecraft Materials Shops. Proprietors (5) or proprietor (6) manage needlecraft shop, buy, display, and sell patterns and materials for embroidery and other fancy work; shop assistants (4) serve customers, help proprietor; customers (3) examine, select, buy and pay for merchandise; 0.65 cu.
    1. Lawern Needlework Shop
    2. Westerdale Wool Shop
147. Newspaper Reporters Beats. Reporter-photographer (6) interviews, takes pictures, writes; secretary (4) types, engages in office routines; residents (3) take news items to office, converse; 0.32 cu.
    1. Pickering Reporter and Photographer Beat

°148. Newspapers, School. Teachers (5) supervise generally, aid in decisionmaking in crisis; foremen (5) supervise and write actual newspaper, duplicate, collect items; reporter-members (4) prepare individual items, turn in to foreman, help with preparation and distribution; 0.07 cu.

    1. Secondary Modern School Farming Club Putting out News-sheet

149. Nurses Offices and Services. District nurse (6) inspects school children for cleanliness, parasites and disease, provides first aid as needed; secretary (4) or teachers (4) direct flow of children to nurses' station; children (3) submit to inspection, receive care as needed; 0.21 cu.

    1. Agricultural and Horticultural Fair Red Cross Centre
    2. County Primary School Nurses Inspection
    3. Roman Catholic School Nurses Inspection
    4. Secondary Modern School Nurses Inspection

150. Nursing Homes. Manager (5) manages enterprise, engages in office routines, keeps records, arranges for services, supplies, schedules; matron (5) and assistant matron (5) give services, e.g., medication, baths, books, etc., to residents; residents (3) receive services, care; 0.76 cu.

    1. Moorside Nursing Home

151. Opticians Offices and Services. Optician (6) uses instruments and charts to diagnose visual defects, prescribes and fits glasses, keeps records; patients (3) seek advice and services, pay when necessary; 0.11 cu.

    1. Martindale and Wessoc Opticians Yoredale Office

°152. Organ Concerts. Clergyman (6) directs service, introduces musicians, makes dedication speech, thanks musicians; musicians (4) play instruments; ushers (4) show people to seats; audience (3) listen, watch; 0.05 cu.

    1. Church of England Organ Concert

153. Parades. Parade organizer (6) or organizers (5) arrange for parade, review or march in parade; honorees (4) stand as parade marches past; paraders (4) play instruments, march, carry flags, banners; spectators (2) watch, listen, stand at attention at appropriate times; 0.10 cu.

    1. British Legion Remembrance Day Parade
    2. Secondary Modern School Cadets Club Beating the Retreat for Howells

154. Parking Lots. Organizer (6) or organizers (5) [in the case of school headmaster (5), deputy head (5) and teacher (5)] supervise parking, coming and going according to rules; helpers (4) aid in directing traffic, collect money, where appropriate; users (2) park cars, pay where appropriate; 0.63 cu.

    1. Agricultural and Horticultural Fair Car Park
    2. Secondary Modern School Parking Lot

155. Parks and Playgrounds. Teachers (6) responsible for proper behavior of users and upkeep of property; members (3) play games, jump rope, walk, converse; visitors (2) watch, may engage in games. Unsupervised park members (3) and visitors (2) walk, converse, scan landscape, play games; 1.48 cu.
    1. County Primary School Playground
    2. Daleview
    3. Playing Fields Near Daleview
    4. Roman Catholic School Playground

156. Parties. Organizer (6), organizers (5) arrange for party, supervise activities; entertainers (4) sing, dance, do magic, give recitations; servers (4) or committee (4) help supervise activities, fix and serve refreshments, help with games; members (3) eat, play games, watch, listen, converse; 1.05 cu.
    1. British Legion Childrens Christmas Party
    2. Church of England Sunday School Juniors (3–10) Party
    3. Church of England Sunday School Seniors (10–15) Party
    4. County Primary School Infants (5–7) Party
    5. County Primary School Lower Juniors (7–9) Party
    6. County Primary School Upper Juniors (9–12) Party
    7. Dramatic Society Play Cast Party
    8. Express Dairy Social Club Childrens Christmas Party
    9. Methodist Church New Year's Eve Party
    10. Methodist Church Sunday School Junior (3–10) Party
    11. Moorside Nursing Home Entertainment
    12. National Health Service Childrens Clinic Party
    13. Over Sixtys Club Annual Party
    14. Roman Catholic Church Womens League Annual Party
    15. Roman Catholic School Scholars (5–15) Christmas Party
    16. Secondary Modern School Juniors (11–13) Party
    17. Secondary Modern School Prefects Party
    18. Secondary Modern School Red Cross Cadets Christmas Party
    19. Secondary Modern School Seniors (13–16) Party
    20. Women's Institute Childrens Christmas Party
    21. Women's Institute Thirlby Club Party

157. Photographic Supply and Service Shops. Photographer-owner (6) manages shop, takes and processes pictures, sells and rents equipment; assistants (4) wait on customers, assist photographer; customers (3) order pictures, pose, select, examine and buy merchandise, pay, seek advice; 0.53 cu.
    1. Secondary Modern School Photograph Day
    2. Snaith Photograph Studio and Shop

158. Physical Education Classes. Physical education teacher (6) directs calisthenics, games, and dances, engages in classroom routines; pupils (3) exercise, play games, and dance; 1.68 cu.
    1. County Primary School Upper Juniors (8–11) Physical Education Class

2. County Primary School Middle Juniors (8–10) Physical Education Class
3. County Primary School Lower Juniors (7–9) Physical Education Class
4. County Primary School Infants (5–7) Physical Education Class
5. Evening Institute Keep Fit for Men Class
6. Roman Catholic School Upper School (9–15) Physical Education Class
7. Roman Catholic School Lower School (5–9) Physical Education Class
8. Secondary Modern School Senior Boys (13–16) Games Physical Education Class
9. Secondary Modern School Senior Girls (13–16) Games Physical Education Class
10. Secondary Modern School Junior Boys (11–13) Games Physical Education Class
11. Secondary Modern School Junior Girls (11–13) Games Physical Education Class
12. Secondary Modern School Gymnastics Club Physical Education Class
13. Secondary Modern School Girls Physical Education Class, Mrs. Dent
14. Secondary Modern School Boys (12) Physical Education Class, Mr. Gibbons
15. Secondary Modern School Boys Physical Education Class, Mr. Howe
16. Secondary Modern School Boys Physical Education Class, Mr. Massingham

159. Physicians Offices and Services. Physician (6) [in case of school and clinic physician (5) and nurses (5)] see patients, use instruments, diagnose, prescribe, administer treatment and medication, advise; nurse (4) or assistants (4) make appointments, assist physician, keep records, direct flow of patients; patients (3) wait, converse, request treatment and advice, are examined, listen to doctor or nurse, receive prescription; 1.08 cu.
    1. Buckland Physician Office
    2. County Primary School Doctors Inspection
    3. Hill Physician Office
    4. National Health Service Childrens Clinic
    5. Roman Catholic School Doctors Inspection
    6. Secondary Modern School Doctors Inspection

160. Plays and Programs. Director (6), organizer (6), or directors (5), organizers (5) plan, direct rehearsals, produce plays or programs including skits, speeches, musical events; performers (4) act, sing, dance, speak, play instruments; prompters (4) remind of lines; stage crew (4) and stage manager (4) set stage, shift scenery, provide props and sound effects, strike set; ticket takers (4) sell

tickets, take money, where appropriate; ushers (4) show audience members to seats, give playbills; audience (3) watch, listen, applaud; 0.64 cu.

1. Dramatic Society Play
2. Dramatic Society Play Readings
3. Dramatic Society Play Rehearsals
4. Evening Institute Open Night and Program
5. Methodist Church Sunday School Afternoon Anniversary Program
6. Methodist Church Sunday School Evening Anniversary Program
7. Roman Catholic School Christmas and Summer Program
8. Secondary Modern School Drama Club Meeting
9. Secondary Modern School Fourth Year Drama Group Rehearsal
10. Secondary Modern School Fourth Year Drama Group One-Act-Play
11. Secondary Modern School Historical Play, Mrs. Thornson

161. Plumbing Services. Master plumber (6) manages business, installs and repairs plumbing as requested, sells fixtures, teaches apprentices; apprentice (4) assists plumber, learns trade; customer (3) orders work done, pays; 0.72 cu.

1. Grail Plumbing Service
2. Hopper Plumbing Service

162. Police Stations. Police sergeant (6) in charge organizes police work mans stations and regular beats, makes reports and arrests; police constables (4) man beats or office as directed, deal with law breakers, give advice and help; arrested persons (4) taken to police station and charged; custodian (4) cleans; citizens (3) come for information, papers, report accidents and losses; 0.68 cu.

1. County Police Station, Cells, and Policemen on Beat in Yoredale.

163. Post Offices Stationers Shops. Manager (6) contracts with government to provide services, i.e., sale of stamps, money orders, weighing and mailing of packages, licenses for radio, TV, motor vehicles, issuing of national pensions, national health insurance stamps, acceptance and disbursal of money in postal savings, manages stationery and sundries shop; postal assistants (4) carry out these functions under direction of post master and according to regulations; customers (3) buy stamps, deposit or withdraw savings, mail packages, receive pension, pay for licenses, national insurance, get information, buy and pay for sundries; 0.47 cu.

1. Graves Post Office and Stationers Shop

164. Post Offices, Sorting. Deputy postmaster (6) in charge of sorting, dispatch, and receiving of mail, assigns routes to postmen (4) who get and deliver mail to homes and businesses; 0.82 cu.

1. H. M. Post Office Sorting and Delivery of Yoredale Mail

165. Printing Shops. Printer (6) prints on job press as ordered, receives pay, manages business; customers (3) order printing, pay; 0.40 cu.
    1. Pooley Printing Shop

166. Programs of Choral Music. Director, organizer (6), clergyman (6), teacher (6), or teachers (5) manage programs, direct course of program, lead musicians; musicians (4) sing and play instruments; ticket takers (4) take money and tickets; ushers (4) give programs, show persons to seats; audience (3) pays (where appropriate), takes programs, sits down, listens, watches, applauds; 0.35 cu.
    1. County Primary School Christmas Concert and Charity
    2. County Primary School Trip to Carol Service at Aronbeck
    3. Methodist Church Choir Sunday
    4. Methodist Church Concert
    5. Secondary Modern School Choir Performance at Westerdale Day
    6. Secondary Modern School Trip to Carol Service at Aronbeck
    7. Tournament of Song Winners Concert

°167. Psychological Research Offices. Directors (5) manage office, plan work; secretaries (4) engage in office routines; research associates, students (4) code, write, compute; visitors (2) seek information, attend conferences; 0.38 cu.
    1. Psychological Research Office

°168. Public Inquiries and Hearings. Government Official (6) conducts hearing according to prescribed rules and procedures; solicitors (4) represent appellant and appellee, present witnesses, data, ask questions, through prescribed procedures; witnesses (4) (including appellant and appellee) present testimony as called, answer questions, wait; 0.05 cu.
    1. Ministry of Housing and Local Government Public Inquiry

169. Public Toilets and Lavatories. This genotype was omitted from all analyses

170. Pubs and Dining Rooms. Owner-manager (6), publican (6), managers (5) plan, order food, drink and supplies, supervise staff, keep records; barman (4) and barmaid (4) draw beer, mix drinks; cooks (4) cook and serve food, clean; dishwashers (4) wash up [may be same as cook]; customers (3) eat, drink, play games, darts, dominoes, cards, pay; 2.67 cu.
    1. Blue Goose Pub and Dining Room
    2. Coronation Club
    3. Green Dragon Pub and Dining Room
    4. Karim Arms Pub and Dining Room
    5. King's Arm Pub

171. Railway Freight Stations. Station master (6) supervises operation of station and managing station, oversees all work, helps with

work itself when necessary; clerks (4) take messages, keep records, assign freight, contact drivers and railway personnel, serve customers, accept payment; signalman (4) signals engineers; driver (4) receives freight; porter (4) carries; customers (3) arrange for receiving and shipping freight, fill out forms, pay; 0.49 cu.

    1. British Railways Freight Office and Delivery

*172. Railway Maintenance Shops. Superindendent (6) directs repair of railway tracks; work crew members (4) repair tracks.

173. Receptions. Organizer (6) or organizers (5) make arrangements, supervise setting up and preparing food trays, greet members and guests; committee (4) arranges furniture, flowers, may decorate, prepare food and drink; honored guests (3) receive thanks, respond to vote of thanks, eat, converse; members (3) greet guests, eat, converse; 0.20 cu.

    1. Church of England Reception and Supper after Archdeacons Visit
    2. Church of England Reception and Supper after Confirmation
    3. Dramatic Society Reception after Play for Visiting Societies
    4. Methodist Church Reception and Supper after Concert

°174. Refreshment Stands. Organizer (6) or organizers (5) secure and prepare food (if necessary), supervise others in preparation and selling food, may keep records; assistants (4) help prepare and sell food, accept money, give change; customers (3) select, pay for and eat food; 0.26 cu.

    1. Secondary Modern School Westerdale Day Hot Dog Sale
    2. Secondary Modern School Westerdale Day Ice Cream Sale
    3. Secondary Modern School Tuck Shop

175. Refuse Disposal Services. Foreman (6) drives and directs R.D.C. refuse wagon on route around town, load refuse, take to tip; assistant (4) helps foreman; citizens (3) place refuse in cans and boxes as required; 0.33 cu.

    1. District Council Refuse Wagon

176. Religion Classes. Teacher (6) or teachers (5) conduct worship service, teach about church history, doctrine, the Bible, lead discussion; assistants (4) teach small groups, supervise children, take collection; pianist (4) accompanies singing; class members (3) listen, study, discuss, pray, sing, contribute money; 0.96 cu.

    1. Church of England Opening Exercise, Special Service, and Seniors (9–15) Class
    2. Church of England Juniors (5–9) Sunday School Class
    3. Church of England Infants (Under 5) Sunday School Class
    4. Methodist Church Juniors and Seniors (9–15) Morning Sunday School Class
    5. Methodist Church Primary (5–10) Afternoon Sunday School Class

    6. Roman Catholic School Upper School (9–15) Diocesean Examination

    7. Roman Catholic School Lower School (5–9) Diocesean Examination

    8. Secondary Modern School Religious Instruction, Mr. Noble

    9. Secondary Modern School Religious Instruction, Mr. Stokes

    10. Secondary Modern School Religious Instruction, Miss Byerley.

    11. Westerdale Crusade Childrens (5–16) Meeting

°177. Religion Study Groups. Leader (6) or leaders (5) direct discussion, introduce speakers, if any; speaker (4) talks on topic, may lead discussion; assistants (4) may serve tea; members (3) talk, listen, converse, may eat; 0.49 cu.

    1. Anglican-Methodist Meeting

    2. Church of England Confirmation Class

    3. Church of England Discussion Group at the Vicarage

    4. Methodist Church Group I Meeting

    5. Methodist Church Group II Meeting

    6. Methodist Church Group III Meeting

    7. Methodist Church Members in Training Meeting

    8. Methodist Church Society Meeting

    9. Methodist Church Womens-Work Meeting

178. Religious Fellowship Meetings. Chairman (6) directs meeting, introduces worship service leader, speakers; leader of worship service (4) prays, introduces song, reads from scripture or other source; accompanist (4) plays piano; speaker (4) gives talk; committee (4) serves tea; members (3) listen, sing, talk, eat; 0.11 cu.

    1. Methodist Church Bright Hour Meeting

    2. Methodist Church Missionary Society Film on Nigeria

179. Religious Prayer and Meditation Services. Clergyman (6) or committee (5) responsible for behavior, direct service, give lesson; accompanist (4) plays organ; assistants (4) read scripture, lead singing; members (3) pray, meditate, listen, sing; 0.72 cu.

    1. Church of England Open Church

    2. Roman Catholic Church Open Church

    3. United Womens World Day of Prayer Service

180. Religious Worship Services. Clergyman (6) or teacher (6) directs service, speaks, prays, reads scripture, follows ritual; assistant (4) may perform some of clergyman's duties, i.e., read scripture; accompanist (4) plays piano or organ or other instrument; choir director (4) leads choir; choir members (4) sing; door stewards (4) seat congregation, take up collection; congregation members (3) visitors (2) listen, sing, pray, speak jointly in service where appropriate; 1.54 cu.

    1. Church of England Archdeacons Special Service

2. Church of England Confirmation Service
3. Church of England Eucharist Service including Communion
4. Church of England Service of Nine Lessons and Carols
5. Church of England Worship (Matins and Evensong) Service
6. County Primary School Morning Assembly
7. Methodist Church Dales Rally
8. Methodist Church Gift Night Service
9. Methodist Church Sunday School Carol Service
10. Methodist Church Morning and Evening Worship Service
11. Moorside Nursing Home Church of England Religious Service
12. Moorside Nursing Home Congregational Religious Service
13. Roman Catholic Church Mass and Benediction
14. Roman Catholic School Church Service
15. Secondary Modern School Morning Assembly Service
16. United Service on Good Friday
17. Westerdale Crusade Meeting

181. Restaurants. Proprietor (6) or proprietors (5), school canteen manager (6) plan, order food, establish prices, supervise and may help in preparing, serving food; assistants (4) cook, serve food, wash up; customers (3) eat, pay, converse. [In the case of school: teachers (6) take turns supervising behavior of children.]; 2.37 cu.
    1. Agricultural and Horticultural Fair Refreshment Tents and Food Trade Stalls
    2. Auction Mart Restaurant
    3. Contessa Tea Room
    4. County Primary School Canteen
    5. Dungait Cafe
    6. Marat Milk Bar and Shop
    7. Secondary Modern School Dinner at Noon
    8. Vista Cafe

182. Sales Routes, Corsets. Saleswoman-fitter (6) goes to customer, takes measurement, orders, and fits garment to customer; customer (3) is fitted, orders, pays for garment; 0.07 cu.
    1. Roddham Corset Saleswoman Route

°183. Sales Routes, Cosmetics and Household Supplies. Salesman-agents (5) plan route, sell, take orders, deliver goods; or sales organizers (5) plan sales route and campaign, give out order blanks, etc.; salesmen (4) sell, take orders, deliver goods, report to organizer; customers (3) inspect, order, pay; 0.23 cu.
    1. Cleaneasy Brush Salesman Sales Route
    2. Gibbons Avon Products Representative Sales Route

184. Sales Routes, Fish. Fishmonger (6) or mongers (5) drive horse and wagon or van around town with fresh fish, scales for weighing,

stopping at customers' houses; customers (3) go out to van with containers, select, and pay for fish; 0.10 cu.

    1. Graves Traveling Fish Shop Route

°185. School Administrators Offices. Headmaster (6) or deputy head (6) administer school plant, plan schedules, interview teachers, pupils, employees, make reports, discipline pupils; secretary (4) announces visitors, gets directions; prefects (4) run errands; pupils (3) are advised, admonished, ask permission; teacher (3) discusses problems, visitors (2) converse; 0.64 cu.

    1. Secondary Modern School Deputy Headmasters Office
    2. Secondary Modern School Headmasters Office

°186. School Enrollment Periods. Person in charge (6) supervises activity, engages in registration procedure with would-be students, advises, keeps records, supervises teachers; teachers (4) meet with individual to discuss suitability of course; students (3) queue up, ask and answer questions, fill out forms; 0.05 cu.

    1. Evening Institute Enrollment Session

°187. School Homeroom Periods. Form teacher (6) takes roll, makes announcements, takes dinner money, keeps records; form members (3) answer, listen, pay; 0.87 cu.

    1. Secondary Modern School Form 4E (14–15) Registration
    2. Secondary Modern School Form 4S (14–15) Registration
    3. Secondary Modern School Form 4X (14–15) Registration
    4. Secondary Modern School Form 3E (13–14) Registration
    5. Secondary Modern School Form 3S (13–14) Registration
    6. Secondary Modern School Form 2E (12–13) Registration
    7. Secondary Modern School Form 2S (12–13) Registration
    8. Secondary Modern School Form 2X (12–13) Registration
    9. Secondary Modern School Form 1E (11–12) Registration
    10. Secondary Modern School Form 1S (11–12) Registration

188. School Enquiry (Truant Officer) Offices. School enquiry officer (6) keeps records re school attendance, plans visitations, phones to make appointments, gets information; 0.05 cu.

    1. School Enquiry Officer

°189. School Monitors (Prefects) Headquarters. Headmaster (6) supervises activities, assignments; prefects (4) get assignments from rota, make tea and coffee to serve in other settings, repair uniforms; teachers (3) stop by with requests or errands; other pupils (2) converse, ask questions; 0.29 cu.

    1. Secondary Modern School Prefects Room

°190. School Offices. School secretary (6) acts as receptionist, conducts office routines, receives and records dinner money, keeps attendance records; prefects (4) run errands; teachers (3) and pupils (3) come for information, bring money and attendance records to office; 0.35 cu.

    1. Secondary Modern School Secretarys Office

°191. Science Classes. Teacher (6) teaches principles of general science,

engages in classroom routine, supervises laboratory work; pupils (3) do and record experiments, listen, read, and write; 0.42 cu.
 1. Secondary Modern School Science Class, Miss Byerley
 2. Secondary Modern School Science Class, Miss Curry
 3. Secondary Modern School Science Class, Mr. Ellis

192. Scout Meetings. Scout leader (6) plans and directs activities according to rules and ritual, demonstrates specific skills, supervises practice of these skills; members (3) watch, listen, follow ritual, engage in handicrafts, games, work on badges under supervision; 0.08 cu.
 1. Cub Scouts Meeting

193. Sewage Disposal Plants. Manager (6) supervises the sewage disposal plant, makes reports; assistants (4) operate equipment, clean, maintain equipment and plant, 0.27 cu.
 1. District Council Sewage Plant

194. Sewing and Dressmaking Classes. Teacher-leader (6) teaches theory and skill of sewing, demonstrates sewing and needlework techniques; members (3) sew by hand and machine, learn principles of sewing and machine operation and care; 0.48 cu.
 1. County Primary School Girls Needlework, Miss Rutherford
 2. Evening Institute Dressmaking Class, Miss Ridgeway
 3. Evening Institute Dressmaking Class, Mrs. Bradley
 4. Secondary Modern School Needlework Class

195. Sewing Club Meetings. Leaders (5) plan and arrange activities, direct sewing, distribute work; committee (4) makes and serves tea; members (3) sew, converse, eat; 0.05 cu.
 1. Women's Institute Sewing Group Meeting

*196. Sewing Services. Seamstress (6) manages work, takes orders, fits garments, sews, charges for service; customers (3) arrange for work, are fitted, pay for service.

197. Shoe Stores. Owner-manager (6) or managers (5) manage business, fit and sell shoes and other footwear, make shoes, repair shoes or accept for repair, sell; shop assistants (4) help manager, stock shelves, fit shoes, sell, accept money, make change; customer (3) is fitted, selects footwear, brings shoes for repair, pays; 1.56 cu.
 1. Cuttinghams Shoe Repair and Sales Shop
 2. Eyles Shoe Repair and Sales Shop
 3. Grail Shoe Shop
 4. Notalls Shoe Repair and Sales Shop

°198. Shorthand Classes. Commercial teacher (6) teaches the principles and practice of shorthand, supervises practice, engages in classroom routines; class members (3) learn and practice shorthand; 0.15 cu.
 1. Evening Institute Shorthand Class, Mrs. Pickering
 2. Evening Institute Shorthand Class, Mrs. Burdon

*199. Slaughter House. Butcher (5) directs; helpers (4) slaughter and eviscerate cattle, sheep, pigs to sell in their stores, clean up afterwards.

*200. Social Science Classes. Chairman (6) introduces speaker; qualified teacher (6) or speaker (4) teaches social science, leads discussion, answers questions, may correct or grade papers; students (3) or members (3) listen, ask questions, respond.

201. Solicitations of Funds. Organizer (6) or organizers (5) plan campaign, direct collectors to designated areas of town, distribute information, pamphlets, receipt forms to collectors, collect all donations at end of campaign, keep records; collectors (4) seek donations from individuals, accept money, give receipt, turn in money to organizer; donors (3) give or refuse to give money, accept receipt; 0.65 cu.
    1. Agricultural and Horticultural Fair Oxfam Exhibition
    2. Barnardos Orphanages Fund Drive
    3. British and Foreign Bible Society Fund Drive
    4. British Legion Remembrance Day Fund Drive
    5. British Red Cross Fund Drive
    6. British Union for Abolition of Vivesection Fund Drive
    7. Church Army Fund Drive
    8. Moral Welfare Fund Drive
    9. Roman Catholic Church Fund Drive for Nursing Sisters
    10. Roman Catholic Church Fund Drive for Poor Clare Sisters
    11. Royal Society for Prevention of Cruelty to Animals Fund Drive
    12. St. Dunstans Home for the Blind Fund Drive
    13. Salvation Army Fund Drive

*202. Solicitation of Goods. President of organization (6) appoints committees (4) who canvass area for goods, deliver collected goods for charity; donors (3) bring in goods for charitable purposes.

203. Solicitors Offices. Solicitor (6) manages office, assigns work to other solicitors and to law clerks, consults with clients on matters of law, business, and taxation, draws up wills, arranges for rent, lease, or sale of property, draws up contracts, gets information for defense of clients; associate solicitors (4) and law clerks (4) do similar work under direction; secretaries (4) engage in office routines, act as receptionists; clients (3) come for advice and service in connection with legal problems; 0.80 cu.
    1. Dover Solicitor Office
    2. Nattras Solicitor and Register Office

204. Sports Days. Headmaster (6) or headmistress (6) organizes program, directs events, appoints helpers; starters (4) start races; judges (4) judge winners; marshall (4) announces events, winners; groundsmen (4) prepare field; scorekeepers (4) keep score; presenters (4) present shield or cup to winners; selected children (4)

compete in events, running, jumping, throwing; audience (2) watch, converse; 0.10 cu.

    1. County Primary School and Roman Catholic School (5–15) Sports Day

    2. Headteachers Association Dales Area Primary School Students (5–12) Sports Day

°205. Staff Lounges. Headmaster (5), deputy (5), teachers (5) prepare work, give instructions to prefects, converse, smoke, eat and drink; prefects (4), girls from domestic science (4) bring in tea, coffee, remove tea cart, get errand assignments; 0.66 cu.

    1. Secondary Modern School Staff Lounge

    2. Secondary Modern School Staff Room

°206. Stage Make-up Classes. Teacher (6) teaches theory and practice of stage make-up, demonstrates make-up; members (3) watch, listen, practice on one another the art of stage make-up; 0.06 cu.

    1. Stage Make-up Class

°207. Stamp Club Exhibitions. Teacher (6) supervises arrangement of display of stamps, discusses importance of each display with visitors; members (3) help put up exhibit, loiter, converse; visitors (2) look, listen, converse; 0.05 cu.

    1. Secondary Modern School Westerdale Day Stamp Exhibition

208. Stamp Club Meetings. Teachers (5) direct meeting, discuss stamps, arrange for purchase of special issues of stamps, supervise trading; members (3) listen, discuss, examine and compare stamps, trade stamps; 0.06 cu.

    1. Secondary Modern School Stamp Club Meeting

209. Street Fairs. Committee or operators of commercial carnival (5) plan stalls and events, supervise the day's events, keep records, may man stalls, rides; assistants (4) man stalls, may direct events, run rides, accept money; contestants (4) may follow prescribed rules for fancy dress competition or Miss Westerdale contest; judges (4) may judge contest winners; ride operators (4) may operate machines, take tickets; customers (3) purchase tickets, items, try games of chance or skill, watch, listen, eat, converse; 0.10 cu.

    1. Agricultural and Horticultural Fair Street Fair

    2. Street Fair, May and October

°210. Swimming Classes. Teacher (6) or teachers (5) arrange for transport, supervise children round trip, teach principles and practices of swimming, demonstrate swimming; driver (4) drives bus to and from; members (3) enter bus, ride, practice swimming, listen, return on bus; 0.34 cu.

    1. Evening Institute Swimming Class at Romanton

    2. Methodist Youth Club Swimming Class at Romanton

3. Secondary Modern School Boys Swimming Class at Romanton
4. Secondary Modern School Girls Swimming Class at Romanton
5. Youth Club Trips to Swimming Baths at Romanton
°211. Swimming Competitions. Teachers (5) supervise travel and competitions, give directions and ribbons to winners, keep records; team captians (5) assist in directing activities, keep records; competitors (4) swim according to rules for class; 0.05 cu.
1. Secondary Modern School House Swimming Competition at Romanton
212. Tax Assessment (Rating) and Collection Offices. Rating officer (6) supervises and manages office, keeps records, figures rates, sees residents; librarian (4) maintains records, looks up records; secretary (4) engages in office routines, answers phone, keeps records; resident-customers (3) seek advice, information, pay rates; 0.45 cu.
1. District Rating Office including Collection of Rents and Rates
213. Taxis. Owner-operator (6), operators (5) take calls, drive taxis, keep records; drivers (4) drive taxis, receive pay or record charge; customers (3) request service, are driven, pay for service; 0.79 cu.
1. Elliot Taxi
2. Simpson Taxi
°214. Technical Drawing Classes. Teacher (6) teaches principles and techniques of mechanical drawing using appropriate instruments, engages in classroom routines; pupils (3) draw under direction, practice use of instruments; 0.15 cu.
1. Secondary Modern School Technical Drawing Class, Mr. Grout
2. Secondary Modern School Technical Drawing Class, Mr. Stokes
215. Telephone Automatic Exchange Buildings. Telephone service area directors (6) and assistants (4) use building as headquarters, service automatic equipment; 0.27 cu.
1. Telephone Building
216. Telephone Booths (Kiosks). Telephone service man (4) maintains and repairs phone, removes money from box; customers (3) put money in box, dial, talk; 0.59 cu.
1. Telephone Kiosks
°217. Tennis Matches. Teachers (5) or team captains (5) call for game, supervise play, call the score, judge balls to be fair or foul; competitors (4) play according to rules and schedule; spectators (2) watch, converse; 0.22 cu.
1. Tennis Club Game and Match

2. Tennis Club Match out of town

3. Secondary Modern School Staff versus Students Tennis Match

°218. Track and Field Meets. Teachers-officials (5) supervise standard track and field events according to rules; time-distance keepers (4) use measuring devices for measuring times, distances of competition, disqualify competitors; starters (4) shoot gun for running competition starts; competitors (4) engage in activity according to rules; spectators (2) watch, cheer, converse, eat, walk from one event to another; 0.10 cu.

1. Dales Area Track and Field Meet (11–13)

2. Secondary Modern School Track and Field Event House Match

219. Trafficways. Employees (4) clean streets, supervise general traffic, direct school children, inspect and maintain drains, repair streets; pedestrians (2) loiter, walk on sidewalks, marketplace, converse; automobile drivers (2) drive and park cars according to rules; children and adolescents (2) walk on sidewalks, cross streets, wait for buses in prescribed places; 1.08 cu.

1. Trafficways

*220. Trips by Organizations to Visit the Sick. President (6) organizes trip; members (4) gather at one member's home and drive to nearby nursing home, where they visit all able to receive visitors, sew, or write letters for them, converse.

*221. TV and Radio Repair Shop. Owner-operator (6) repairs TV sets and radios, charges for service and parts, manages business; helper (4) assists; customers (3) bring in sets or phone for service, pay for service.

°222. Typing Classes. Teacher (6) teaches principles and practice of typewriting, engages in classroom routines; class members (3) practice typewriting, learning to reach standard; 0.10 cu.

1. Evening Institute Typing Class

°223. Upholstering Classes. Teacher (6) teaches principles and techniques of upholstering soft furniture, provides tools and equipment needed; class members (3) upholster under direction; 0.14 cu.

1. Secondary Modern School Soft Furnishings Class

2. Women's Institute Handicraft Guild Meeting

224. Veterinary Services. Veterinarians-owners (5) manage business, see animals, give and prescribe mediation and treatment, drive to outlying farms to provide service, accept payment; assistant (4) answers phone, keeps records; customers (3) seek advice, service, bring animals in, phone for service; pay; 0.44 cu.

1. Busfield Veterinary Surgeon Office

°225. Vocational Counseling Services. Headmaster (5) arranges for interviewers or speaker; interviewers (5) interview school leavers, request information, give advice and information regarding employment and training possibilities, or speaker (5) talks to group about training and employment possibilities; pupils (3) follow schedule, ask questions, listen, fill out forms; 0.25 cu.

    1. Secondary Modern School December Youth Employment Interview

    2. Secondary Modern School March Youth Employment Interview

    3. Secondary Modern School School-Leavers Youth Employment Interview

    4. Secondary Modern School Fourth-Year Students February Youth Employment Officer Talk

    5. Secondary Modern School Fourth-Year Students September Youth Employment Officer Talk

226. Wallpapering and Painting Supplies and Services. Owner-operator (6) or operators (5) manage business, supervise services, advise customers, charge and accept money, supervise apprentices, may do some or all wallpapering and painting; assistants (4) do wallpapering, painting, minor repairs under supervision; apprentices (4) learn the techniques of wallpapering and painting, practice techniques under supervision; customers (3) arrange for, pay for services, seek advice; 1.34 cu.

    1. Dent and Company Decorators Shop

    2. Hay Painting Services

    3. Jewitt Decorators Shop and Service

227. Weddings, Church. Clergyman (6) is in charge of marriage service, speaks, chants, follows prescribed ceremony, registers marriage; bride (4), groom (4), bride's parents (4), attendants (4), ushers (4), musicians (4) follow prescribed ceremony routines; government marriage registrar (4) may register marriage; guests (2) watch, offer good wishes; children (2) tie gate, clamor for money as enticement to open gate; 0.15 cu.

    1. Church of England Wedding

    2. Methodist Church Wedding

    3. Roman Catholic Church Wedding

228. Weddings, Civil. Registrar (6) performs marriage; bride (4), groom (4) answer questions, fill out forms; witnesses (4) sign forms; guests (2) watch, offer good wishes; 0.06 cu.

    1. Civil Wedding

°229. Window Cleaning Services. Owner-operator (6) arranges for work, cleans outside windows of offices and homes using ladder, brushes, cleaning equipment; customers (3) order service, pay; 0.13 cu.

    1. Jay Window Cleaning Service

230. Woodwork Classes. Teacher (6) teaches principles and practices of working with wood, instructs in use of machines, tools, and finishes, engages in classroom routines; class members (3) make

objects of wood, practice use of tools and machines; 0.27 cu.
1. Evening Institute Woodwork Class
2. Secondary Modern School Woodwork Class

231. X-Ray Laboratories. Head technician (6) arranges schedule and supplies, personnel, supervises coach; assistants (4) help in taking x-rays, preparing people for x-ray, keeping records; clients (3) give information, follow instructions, have x-ray taken; 0.05 cu.
1. National Health Service TB X-Ray Unit

Bibliography

BARKER, J. S. "Situations, Politics, and the Political." Unpublished paper.

BARKER, R. G. "Ecology and Motivation." In M. R. Jones (Ed.), *Nebraska Symposium on Motivation*. Lincoln: University of Nebraska Press, 1960.

BARKER, R. G. "On the Nature of the Environment." *Journal of Social Issues*, 1963a, *19* (4), 17–38. (Reprinted in E. P. Hollander and R. G. Hunt (Eds.), *Current Perspectives in Social Psychology*. New York: Oxford University Press, 1967.)

BARKER, R. G. (Ed.) *The Stream of Behavior*. New York: Appleton-Century-Crofts, 1963b.

BARKER, R. G. "Explorations in Ecological Psychology." *American Psychologist*, 1965, *20* (1), 1–14.

BARKER, R. G. *Ecological Psychology: Concepts and Methods for Studying the Environment of Human Behavior*. Stanford, Calif.: Stanford University Press, 1968.

BARKER, R. G., AND BARKER, L. S. "Behavior Units for the Comparative Study of Cultures." In B. Kaplan (Ed.), *Studying Personality Cross-Culturally*. New York: Harper and Row, 1961a.

BARKER, R. G., AND BARKER, L. S. "The Psychological Ecology of Old People in Midwest, Kansas and Yoredale, Yorkshire." *Journal of Gerontology*, 1961b, *16*, 144–149.

BARKER, R. G., AND BARKER, L. S. "Social Actions in the Behavior Streams of American and English Children." In R. G. Barker (ed.), *The Stream of Behavior*. New York: Appleton-Century-Crofts, 1963. Pp. 127–159.

BARKER, R. G., BARKER, L. S., AND RAGLE, D. D. M. "The Churches of Midwest, Kansas and Yoredale, Yorkshire: Their Contributions to the Environments of the Towns." In W. Gore and L. Hodapp (Eds.), *Change in the Small Community*. New York: Friendship Press, 1967. Pp. 155–189.

BARKER, R. G., AND GUMP, P. V. *Big School, Small School*. Stanford, Calif.: Stanford University Press, 1964.

541

BARKER, R. G., AND WRIGHT, H. F. *Midwest and Its Children.* New York: Harper and Row, 1955. (Reprinted by Archon Books, Hamden, Conn., 1971.)

BINDING, F. R. S. *Behavior-Setting Leadership in an American Community.* Doctoral dissertation, University of Kansas, Lawrence, 1969.

BOTTS, P. J. *An Exploratory Study of the Use of Still Photography as a Research Tool in Ecological Psychology.* Master's thesis, University of Kansas, Lawrence, 1970.

GUMP, P. V. "Intra-Setting Analysis: The Third Grade Classroom as a Special but Instructive Case." In E. P. Willems and H. L. Raush (Eds.), *Naturalistic Viewpoints in Psychological Research.* New York: Holt, Rinehart and Winston, 1968a.

GUMP, P. V. "Persons, Settings, and Larger Contexts." In B. Indik and K. Barrien (Eds.), *People, Groups and Organizations: An Effective Integration.* New York: Teachers College, Columbia University Press, 1968b.

GUMP, P. V. "Milieu, Environment, and Behavior." *Design and Environment,* Winter 1971a, *2* (4), 49ff.

GUMP, P. V. "The Behavior Setting: A Promising Unit for Environmental Designers." *Landscape Architecture,* January 1971b, *61* (2), 130–134.

HAWTHORNE, N. Passages from the English Note-Books of Nathaniel Hawthorne. (11th Ed.) Vol II. Boston and New York: Houghton, Mifflin, 1855. (Reprinted by The Riverside Press, Cambridge, Mass., 1887.)

LAING, R. D. *The Politics of Experience.* Baltimore: Penguin, 1967.

LECOMPTE, W. F. "The Taxonomy of a Treatment Environment." *Archives of Physical Medicine and Rehabilitation,* March 1972, *53,* 109–114.

LEWIN, K. *Field Theory in Social Science.* New York: Harper and Row, 1951.

MILLER, G. A., GALANTER, E., AND PRIBRAM, K. H. *Plans and the Structure of Behavior,* New York: Holt, Rinehart and Winston, 1960.

OLEN, D. R. *Environmental Offerings and Students' Behavior in All Boy, All Girl and Coeducational Catholic High Schools.* Master's thesis, University of Kansas, Lawrence, 1971.

PRIESTLEY, J. B. *English Journey.* New York and London: Harper and Row, 1934.

RAGLE, D. D. M., JOHNSON, A., AND BARKER, R. G. "Measuring Extension's Impact." *Journal of Cooperative Extension,* Fall 1967, *5* (3), 178–186.

TOLMAN, E. C. *Purposive Behavior in Animals and Man.* New York: Century, 1932.

TROLLOPE, F. *Domestic Manners of the Americans.* New York: Dodd, Mead Vol. I, 1832.

WARNER, W. L., MEEKER, M., AND EELLS, K. *Social Class in America.* Chicago: Science Research Associates, 1949.

WICKER, A. W. "Undermanning, Performances, and Students' Subjective Experiences in Behavior Settings of Large and Small High Schools." *Journal of Personality and Social Psychology,* 1968, *10* (3), 255–261.

WICKER, A. W. "Cognitive Complexity, School Size, and Participation in School Behavior Settings." *Journal of Educational Psychology,* 1969a, *60,* 200–203.

WICKER, A. W. "Size of Church Membership and Members' Support of Church Behavior Settings." *Journal of Personality and Social Psychology,* 1969b, *13,* 278–288.

WICKER, A. W. "Processes Which Mediate Behavior-Environment Congruence." *Behavioral Science,* May 1972, *17* (3), 265–277.

WICKER, A. W., AND MEHLER, A. "Assimilation of New Members in a Large and a Small Church." *Journal of Applied Psychology,* 1971, *55,* 151–156.

WILLEMS, E. P. "Sense of Obligation to High School Activities as Related to School Size and Marginality of Student." *Child Development,* December 1967, *38* (4), 1247–1260.

WILLEMS, E. P. "The Interface of the Hospital Environment and Patient Behavior." *Archives of Physical Medicine and Rehabilitation,* March 1972, *53,* 115–122.

WILLEMS, E. P., AND RAUSH, H. L. *Naturalistic Viewpoints in Psychological Research.* New York: Holt, Rinehart and Winston, 1968.

WRIGHT, H. F. "Children in Smalltown and Largetown, U.S.A." Department of Psychology, University of Kansas, Lawrence, 1970a.

WRIGHT, H. F. "Urban Space as Seen by the Child." Paper given at Seminar on the Child in the City, International Children's Centre, Paris, November 1970b.

Index

544

J

L

M

W

Y

Z